Getting Started in Federal Contracting

Other Works by Barry L. McVay

Proposals That Win Federal Contracts
The Federal Procurement Process
Federal Profit Policy
Small Business Set-Asides and Preference Programs
Providing Foreign Products to the Federal Government
Facilities Capital Cost of Money
The Defense Priorities and Allocations System
The Federal Protest Package (Ed.)
The History of Federal Procurement
Public Law 99-661: The Department of Defense 5% Minority
      Contracting Goal (with Vivina H. McVay)
Buying Surplus Property from the Federal Government
Federal Supply and Service Code Book (Ed.)
Federal Contracting Offices – ADP Equipment and Supplies (Ed.)
Federal Contracting Offices – Research and Development (Ed.)

GETTING STARTED IN FEDERAL CONTRACTING

A GUIDE THROUGH THE FEDERAL PROCUREMENT MAZE

Sixth Edition, Revised and Expanded

by

Barry L. McVay, CPCM

PANOPTIC ENTERPRISES

BURKE, VIRGINIA

To Vi, Bill and Maggie, and Michael

This publication is designed to provide accurate and authoritative information in regard to the subject matter covered. It is sold with the understanding that the publisher is not engaged in rendering legal, accounting, or other professional service. If legal advice or other expert assistance is required, the services of a competent professional person should be sought.

**Publisher's Cataloging-in-Publication
(Provided by Quality Books, Inc.)**

McVay, Barry L., author.
    Getting started in federal contracting : a guide
through the federal procurement maze / by Barry L.
McVay. -- Sixth edition, revised and expanded.
    pages cm
    Includes index.
    LCCN 2017904378
    ISBN 978-0-912481-27-2

    1. Public contracts--United States.   I. Title.

KF849.M39 2017   346.7302'3
                          QBI17-674

Published by: PANOPTIC ENTERPRISES
                  6055 Ridge Ford Drive
                  Burke, VA 22015-3653
                  (703) 451-5953
                  (800) 594-4766
                  panoptic@fedgovcontracts.com
                  http://www.FedGovContracts.com

CONTENTS

FIGURES

INTRODUCTION

There are approximately **650,000 contractors** receiving **17,000,000 contracts** worth approximately **$440 billion** from the government each year. These are all at near-record levels, and more contractors are competing for federal contracts every day.

How can this be? The government is notorious for engulfing everything it touches in red tape. Indeed, many government solicitations are sizeable and intimidating, and the government's contracting rules are even more sizeable and intimidating. Sometimes the solicitation process is slow. Complying with the contracting rules and regulations takes patience and an eye for detail, because the failure to dot an "*i*" or cross a "*t*" can cause the disqualification of an otherwise winning bid. Why would 650,000 contractors (most of which are small businesses) want to compete for government contracts?

Because, despite the complexity and flaws of the federal contracting process, it provides many overriding benefits, some of the more obvious being:

- The federal government purchases practically every supply and service. For many supplies and services, it is the largest customer in the world.

- Many government contracts are on the "cutting-edge" of technology, and contractors chosen to perform these contracts gain knowledge and skills that frequently can be translated into commercial products or services – far ahead of the competition.

- To insure fairness to all, the federal government's rules and procedures are public information – there is no hidden agenda.

- A contractor does not have to belong to the right country club to compete for government contracts – the government's mandate is to obtain "full and open competition."

- In written solicitations, the government explains how it will evaluate bids and decide the winner – government evaluators must follow these evaluation procedures.

- The government has many "preference" programs to encourage small business participation in the federal contracting process. As a result, more than 35% of all money spent on federal contracts goes either directly to small businesses or indirectly to small business subcontractors from large prime contractors. That is about **$175 billion** going to small businesses each year.

- Through various financing methods and other means, the government will give companies the opportunity to perform larger contracts than they normally perform for commercial customers. These contracts expand the contractor's business base and allow for quicker growth.

- If a bidder or contractor believes the government has acted improperly in some manner, it may seek remedies through administrative procedures established specifically to avoid the expense and delays in pursuing justice through the courts.

- The government pays its bills.

There are so many advantages to contracting with the government that most contractors put up with the headaches. And there is a reason for these headaches. The federal contracting process has evolved over 220 years in response to the ideals of equality and fairness embodied in our Constitution. To insure it treats everyone equally and fairly in contractual matters, the government has developed an extensive body of rules and regulations that attempt to address all conceivable situations that *might* occur during solicitation and contract performance. The magnitude of the rules and regulations is a direct result of our complex and diverse society (which is another product of these Constitutional ideals).

In writing ***Getting Started in Federal Contracting***, my intention is to share the knowledge I have gained during 40 years of federal contracting, from both the government and commercial sides, to help those confronting the "federal procurement maze" with the knowledge and *insight* needed to be effective, confident, and successful. One who merely knows the rules is at a competitive disadvantage to someone who knows the rules and *why they exist*. This is because the federal procurement maze is not random; it has its own order. A person who understands this "order" can **anticipate what the government will do next rather than react to what it does**. In this book, I tried to avoid simply listing the basic rules, because such a list can appear to be a haphazard collection of disorganized mandates and prohibitions. Instead, I attempted to present the basic rules within the context of the process along with an explanation of how they affect other parts of the process. I believe this is the best way to help someone become a viable competitor for federal contracts.

The times are changing, and federal contracting is changing with the times. Federal contracting is like a river, changing directions as outside forces act on it. During the 1990s, several agencies, especially the Department of Defense, experienced budget cuts, and all government agencies had to economize in every way possible. President Clinton trimmed 272,000 federal employees from the government's payroll, and many of those jobs belonged to contracting personnel. Therefore, there had to be many changes in contracting procedures as the government attempted to streamline the process so it took less time and required fewer people. The process began with the enactment of the **Federal Acquisition Streamlining Act** and continued with the enactment of the **Clinger-Cohen Act of 1996** (a combination of two laws which were originally known as the **Federal Acquisition Reform Act** and the **Information Technology Management Reform Act**). Subsequently, in the 2000s, in response to the 9/11 terrorist attack and the wars in Afghanistan and Iraq, Congress established the Department of Homeland Security and appropriated so much money that the reduced contracting workforce couldn't spend it fast enough. Many corners were cut, and much money was wasted. Furthermore, in response to the financial crisis of late 2008, the federal government bailed out entire industries with hundreds of billions of dollars, and the government frantically awarded contracts to obtain the skills needed to dispense the money and try to account for it all. Of course, all that spending increased the national debt to record levels that have caused Congress to become concerned. Consequently, the contracting river is changing course once again, with President Trump and Congress proposing to reduce budgets, establish more controls on spending, impose more oversight, and cut back (once again) on the number of contracting personnel.

The information in *Getting Started in Federal Contracting* was current when it was published. However, because federal acquisition procedures are so unsettled, readers should not consider this book to be definitive. Readers should check an up-to-date copy of the applicable federal acquisition regulations to find out whether the official rules have changed and how they have changed. But remember: where there is change, there is opportunity.

In addition, there are many websites referenced in *Getting Started in Federal Contracting* where readers can obtain more information or read source material. As with federal acquisition procedures, these are continually being changed as websites are reorganized and assigned new addresses (URLs). Therefore, if a referenced website does not work or is no longer in existence, use an Internet search engine to find the current website.

I want to mention three stylistic conventions:

1. It is impossible to "start at the beginning and finish at the end" because the "federal procurement maze" is so intertwined and interconnected. The government's contracting officer needs to know how he wants the contract to end so he can make appropriate choices from a multitude of options. During

the writing of this book, there were occasions when I found I could not describe an action taken early in the contracting process without referring to a concept described in a later chapter because the contracting officer's action depends on where the contracting officer "wants to go." Conversely, sometimes I could not describe an action taken late in the contracting process without referring to an earlier chapter to remind the reader "how we got here." Therefore, throughout the book you will see references to other chapters.

2. Women are playing a larger role in all aspects of federal contracting, on both the business and government sides. While I recognize and appreciate this, I find it awkward to refer to "he or she approves the contract" or "it is his or her decision." Also, I find "he/she" and "his/her" unsightly, and I think the alternation of genders is particularly confusing. Therefore, to simplify matters, I use the masculine gender throughout the book when referring to those who take part in the process. In no way is this intended to slight women – it is merely a reflection on the inadequacies of the English language.

3. The Federal Acquisition Regulation (FAR), the set of rules that govern the conduct of federal contracting (see Chapter 1), was originally prepared 30 years ago when contracts and documents of record were printed on paper and saved in file cabinets. Now, with the advent of electronic commerce and the Internet, most federal commerce is conducted electronically. In fact, the FAR states, "the federal government shall use electronic commerce whenever practicable or cost-effective" (see paragraph (a) of FAR 4.502, Policy [on electronic commerce in contracting]). However, the FAR still reflects its origins, using terms commonly associated with paper transactions, such as "copy," "document," "page," "printed," "sealed envelope," and "stamped." Therefore, the FAR goes on to state that these words "shall not be interpreted to restrict the use of electronic commerce." This means a requirement that a document be "signed" could be satisfied with an electronic signature affixed to an electronic document.

Since these terms are still used throughout the FAR, I use them in this book – that is what the rules say. Just remember that, most of the time, you will not be handling paper but interacting with an electronic equivalent.

Also, most of the forms displayed in this book are the official paper versions. Because so much government business is being conducted electronically, agencies are authorized to use "electronic equivalents" that provide or require the same information. In fact, some forms are only available in electronic form, such as the Optional Form 347 and the Standard Form 1449 (see Chapter 6). In these instances, I have filled out the electronic form and used it for illustrative purposes.

Good luck, and happy contracting!

Barry L. McVay, CPCM

CHAPTER 1

THE REGULATIONS

Most federal regulations are incomprehensible. The federal contracting regulations are no different; they are convoluted and full of loopholes, exceptions, duplications, and contradictions. However, it is *not* true that bureaucrats deep in the bowels of some large, nondescript building in Washington create these regulations to confuse the innocent and terrify the unwary. The regulation-writers do their work at the end of a long and involved process that leaves them little choice in what they write.

The Constitution of the United States gives the federal government the power to contract for the supplies and services it needs "provide for the common Defence and general Welfare of the United States" (Article I, Section 8). Section 9 goes on to state "no money shall be drawn from the Treasury, but in Consequence of Appropriations made by law . . ." This means the federal government can purchase only those supplies and services that Congress votes to fund.

Actually, this is a two-step process: Congress "authorizes" an agency to acquire the supplies and services needed to fulfill its mission, then Congress "appropriates" the funds needed to acquire those needed supplies and services. When Congress authorizes the acquisition of supplies and services, it often places restrictions or conditions on how the agency is to acquire those supplies and services. These restrictions and conditions are the source of many of the quirks and loopholes in the contracting regulations. Senator Smith may decide a defense authorization bill is the perfect vehicle for a new code of contracting ethics. If Congress approves the authorization bill containing the code of contracting ethics and the president signs it, someone must tell the government's contracting personnel about the new ethics requirements. So the regulation-writers get to work and prepare a regulation that accurately depicts the Congressionally-mandated code of contracting ethics.

Of course, Congress does more than pass authorization and appropriations bills. It continually enacts laws that affect commerce. Many of these laws change the way the government contracts. If Congress decides, for whatever reason, that the government should no longer buy products from Malta, the government's contracting personnel must be told how to comply with the law. This means the regulation-writers must write another regulation.

Frequently Congress passes a law but leaves its implementation to the president. Congress might pass a law saying "the President shall take appropriate action to encourage the growth of the American clothespin industry." To fulfill this Congressional mandate, the president might issue an **executive order** restricting all government purchases of clothespins to those produced by domestic clothespin manufacturers. Since the government contracting personnel need to know this, the regulation-writers must write another regulation.

Years of piling laws and executive orders one on top of another produces a contracting process that is confusing, complicated, inefficient, and messy. Within the past twenty years, Congress has enacted several laws to impose some order on the government's contracting processes — to simplify, or "streamline," the procedures and make them more like the "best practices" of the commercial world. In addition, the rapid development and use of the **Internet** has had a profound effect on the methods used by the government in the conduct of *all* its activities, including contracting. Consequently, this confluence of trends has produced many changes that affect *everyone* involved in federal contracting. It is useful to have a little background on how the federal acquisition process got to where it is today so we can make an "educated guess" on where it is going in the near future.

SOME HISTORY OF FEDERAL CONTRACTING

The federal acquisition process has evolved over 220 years into a highly regulated and rule-driven process motivated by public accountability. The first appropriations laws were merely orders to obtain specific supplies and services necessary to the operations of the government. It soon became apparent that just making funds available and ordering federal agents to obtain the supplies or services was not sufficient – there was no guarantee that the money would be spent wisely or prudently. Therefore, Congress has enacted countless laws that have affected the way our government obtains what it needs to accomplish its mission – over 4,000 of those laws are still on the books and constitute the rules under which the government contracts today.

The Beginnings

■ Congress passed the first law regulating federal contracting in 1792. It required the Treasury Department to make all purchases for the Army. This law centralized the contracting function for the Army and took the troops out of the contracting business.

■ In 1809, Congress decided to require that supplies and services be acquired through "open purchase or by previously advertising for proposals." In 1852, Congress passed a law requiring purchases to be advertised for 60 days before bid opening. Then, in 1860, Congress enacted a law requiring the advertisement of all purchases except in matters of "public exigency." This law eliminated much of the "insider dealings" and corruption that plagued government procurement before the Civil War.

■ In 1861, just before the Civil War, the **Civil Sundry Appropriations Act** was passed, and it was the foundation of the federal contracting system until 1947. The act required competitive bidding except under nine exceptions:

1. Public emergencies
2. Purchases from federal prison industries
3. Purchases for less than $500
4. Horses and mules
5. Medical supplies
6. Bunting
7. Dies and gauges
8. Classified supplies
9. When only a single supplier was available

■ In 1909, a General Supply Committee, made up of members of the various departments and agencies, created General Schedules for Supplies. These schedules were negotiated price lists that could be used by any purchasing agent of the government to obtain needed goods. These General Schedules for Supplies were the forerunners of the **Federal Supply Schedules** (see Chapter 13).

■ Many other laws followed, such as the **Budget and Accounting Act of 1921**, the **Air Corps Act of 1926**, the **Davis-Bacon Act**, the **Buy American Act of 1933**, the **Vinson-Trammel Act of 1934**, and the **Miller Act of 1936**. These all defined and refined the responsibilities, functions, and duties of the government's contracting personnel and its contractors. Most of these laws are still in effect.

Post World War II – Beginnings of the Modern System

Problems encountered during World War II showed Congress the federal contracting system had become an unworkable and unresponsive hodgepodge. To fix the problem, Congress passed the Armed Services Procurement Act of 1947 for the military services and the Federal Property and Administrative Services Act of 1949 for the "civilian" agencies (that is, the Departments of Agriculture, Commerce, Interior, Justice, Treasury, the Environmental Protection Agency, etc.). These two acts established the systems under which all the departments and agencies of the federal government contract. To implement the Armed Services Procurement Act, the regulation-writers wrote the **Armed Services Procurement**

Regulation (renamed the **Defense Acquisition Regulation** in 1978); to implement the Federal Property and Administrative Services Act, the regulation-writers wrote the **Federal Procurement Regulation**.

These two regulations started as relatively concise sets of rules and guidance. But through the years Congress passed many laws and presidents issued many executive orders. Some of the more notable laws enacted during this period were the **Small Business Act**, the **Truth in Negotiations Act**, the **Service Contract Act**, and the **Cost Accounting Standards Act**. The Defense Acquisition Regulation grew to approximately 3,000 pages, and the Federal Procurement Regulation grew to almost 1,200 pages. They had become hodgepodges again.

The Federal Acquisition Regulation

In 1979, Congress passed the **Office of Federal Procurement Policy Act Amendments**. One amendment required the **Office of Federal Procurement Policy** (the organization that oversees the government's contracting processes and procedures) to develop a uniform and simplified contracting system. Accordingly, the regulation-writers prepared the **Federal Acquisition Regulation** (FAR). On April 1, 1984, the Federal Acquisition Regulation (FAR) replaced the Defense Acquisition Regulation, the Federal Procurement Regulation, and the National Aeronautics and Space Administration Procurement Regulation (which was an outgrowth of the old Armed Services Procurement Regulation). Finally, there was one contracting regulation for the entire government (sort of – several agencies, such as the Central Intelligence Agency, the Tennessee Valley Authority, and the Postal Service have their own acquisition regulations for various reasons, but all are based on the same principles as the FAR).

Though the FAR is almost 1,900 pages, it is about one-third smaller than the old Defense Acquisition Regulation. It is better organized (its structure generally follows the contracting process), and it is easier to understand.

In 1985, the **Competition in Contracting Act** (CICA) went into effect. It required the government to seek "full and open competition" in all its purchases unless one of seven exceptions applies. See Chapter 3 for more on this significant law.

The Modern Era

The dissolution of the Soviet Union and the ending of the Cold War in 1989 significantly reduced the threat to the United States, so Congress and the president decided to use the resulting "peace dividend" to scale-back the government and reduce the budget deficit. One of the ways Congress and the president decided to reduce government spending was to cut the number of government employees. The hardest hit group of government employees was the acquisition workforce – since the government was buying fewer weapons and armaments, there was less need for those who bought such things. So, while the government workforce was reduced by about 20% over a decade, the acquisition workforce shrunk by approximately *one-half!* During that decade, the government did not hire any new acquisition employees. As a result, the government now has a bifurcated acquisition workforce: one part experienced but nearing retirement, the other part young and inexperienced. There is practically no one in that ten-year gap who will be able to take over and perform competently once the old folks leave.

Even though the government workforce was reduced, the demand for government services was *not* reduced. With fewer government employees to provide the services, the government found itself having to hire contractors to perform those services, particularly for information technology and professional and management support services. In fact, more than half of government contracts are now for services (which are more difficult to negotiate and administer than contracts for supplies), and the amount the government spent *doubled* during that decade. However, since the acquisition workforce had shrunk, there were not enough contracting personnel to handle the increased demand for contracts. Caught in this bind, Congress and Presidents Bush, Clinton, and Bush (with a great deal of encouragement from the contractor community) decided to simply the acquisition process: make the procedures more flexible and "commercial," shorten the time needed to conduct procurements, reduce administrative burdens, and give the acquisition workforce more discretion to make "businesslike" decisions. By doing this, Congress and the presidents believed the government could simultaneously deliver the services demanded by the electorate and reduce expenditures. (President Obama did not display much interest in federal acquisition; President Trump, a businessman, has expressed much more interest.)

■ The **Federal Acquisition Streamlining Act of 1994** (FASA) was a long-awaited first step in the simplification of the federal contracting process. Five of the most significant provisions in its 167 pages were:

1. Purchases under $2,500, called "micro-purchases," could be made by non-procurement officials without regard to the Buy American Act or socio-economic requirements (see Chapter 6) (the micro-purchase threshold has since been increased to $3,500 for civilian agencies and $5,000 for the Department of Defense).

2. Government contracting personnel were authorized to use "**simplified procedures**" for purchases up to **$100,000** (since increased to $150,000 – see Chapter 6).

3. Purchases between the micro-purchase threshold and $100,000 were reserved for **small businesses** (since increased to $150,000 – see Chapter 11).

4. The government was required to purchase **commercial items** whenever possible (see Chapter 4).

5. The Office of Federal Procurement Policy was assigned the task of developing the architecture for the **Federal Acquisition Computer Net-**

work (FACNET), an electronic commerce system in which interested contractors could review solicitations, submit offers, receive contracts, and collect payments by computer. This was one of the first manifestations of "electronic government," which has come to be called "**e-gov**."

■   Many in the executive branch and Congress thought more needed to be done to simplify the federal contracting process. So Congress passed, and the president signed, the **Fiscal Year 1996 Defense Authorization Act**. Included in the act were two additional pieces of reform legislation: the **Federal Acquisition Reform Act of 1996**, and the **Information Technology Management Reform Act of 1996**. These two laws were subsequently renamed as the "**Clinger-Cohen Act**" in honor of the two primary sponsors.

The Federal Acquisition Reform Act (FARA) restricted the "full and open competition" requirement of the Competition in Contracting Act to the extent needed to "efficiently fulfill the government's requirements." Part of the "efficient fulfillment" was contained in another provision which permitted agencies to use "simplified procedures" to purchase commercial items up to **$5,000,000** (since increased to $7,000,000 – see Chapter 6). In addition, suppliers of commercial items were exempted from the requirement to submit certified cost or pricing data (as required by the Truth in Negotiations Act), and from compliance with the cost accounting standards that resulted from the Cost Accounting Standards Act.

The Information Technology Management Reform Act (ITMRA) repealed the **Brooks Automatic Data Processing Act of 1965**, which had given the overall responsibility for federal computer and telecommunications acquisitions to the **General Services Administration** (GSA). With the repeal of the Brooks Act, GSA no longer had any oversight responsibility for federal computer and telecommunications acquisitions – agencies became responsible for their own acquisitions of computer and telecommunications equipment and services.

■   The rapid development of the Internet has had a profound affect on federal acquisition, one that is on-going. The **Debt Collection Improvement Act of 1996** mandated that all federal payments be made by electronic funds transfer, including "vendor payments." To comply with the Debt Collection Improvement Act, the Department of Defense (DOD) announced that a contractor must be registered in its **Central Contractor Registration** (CCR) database to be eligible for a contract award. This was necessary so DOD could collect and maintain the information needed to make electronic funds transfers. Registering in the CCR became a government-wide requirement in 2003.

■   The **Fiscal Year 1998 National Defense Authorization Act** repealed the provision of FASA that required agencies to possess a "full-FACNET [Federal Acquisition Computer Network] capability." This change was made in recognition that the Internet was becoming the method-of-choice for conducting electronic transactions. In 2001, **FedBizOpps** (short for "Federal Business Opportunities") (**https://www.fbo.gov**) was designated the single point of electronic public access to government-wide procurement opportunities over $25,000, replacing the paper *Commerce Business Daily* (CBD), which went out of business in 2002. Besides posting notices of upcoming acquisitions, federal agencies were permitted to post the solicitations electronically on **FedBizOpps**, reducing the number of paper solicitations that were mailed. In 2012, the government merged **CCR** and several other electronic acquisition-related systems into a unified "**System for Award Management**" (SAM) (**https://www.sam. gov**) that simplifies accessibility to these databases by requiring a single log-in and enable federal agencies to make more informed procurement, logistical, and payment decisions through the use of this unified database (see Chapter 5).

■ The **terrorist attacks of September 11, 2001**, the anthrax attacks of **October 2001,** the subsequent destruction of the Taliban government in **Afghanistan** and the tracking down of al Qaeda members, the **war in Iraq**, the increased emphasis on **homeland security**, and the need to respond quickly to natural disasters such as Hurricane Katrina and Tropical Storm Sandy have all accelerated the streamlining of contracting procedures and the increased use by the government of electronic means to acquire supplies and services and communicate information.

One result of this streamlining is the "Balkanization" of the federal acquisition regulatory system. The FAR, the uniform set of regulations governing federal procurement, has been fragmented as agencies are authorized by Congress to try different acquisition methods. For example, acquisitions that "support a contingency operation or facilitate the defense against or recovery from nuclear, biological, chemical, or radiological attack" have different monetary limits on the use for "micro-purchases" and "simplified acquisition procedures."

And the fragmentation is not limited to defense and homeland security – the Federal Aviation Administration (FAA) convinced Congress that its problems associated with the acquisition of air traffic computer systems were the result of the strict FAR rules and procedures, so Congress exempted the FAA from the FAR. The FAA established its own set of regulations (which bear a striking resemblance to the FAR), but did no better – the Government Accountability Office (GAO) investigated and reported to Congress that the FAA's problems were not with the acquisition regulations but with poor management. But the damage had been done: FAA still has its separate set of acquisition regulations, so periodically other departments and agencies line up at the Capitol asking to be permitted to draft their own acquisition rules, too.

■ The **Services Acquisition Reform Act of 2003** (SARA) established the position of **chief acquisition officer** (CAO). The CAO is responsible for overseeing the agency's acquisition activities and programs, and advises the head of the agency regarding the appropriate business strategy to achieve the agency's mission. In addition, SARA established an "acquisition workforce training fund" to train those who will replace the retiring members of the acquisition workforce.

■ The **Fiscal Year 2005 Defense Authorization Act** required that acquisition-related thresholds be adjusted for inflation every five years (with certain exceptions). These adjustments are the reason some of the thresholds are rather odd – $3,500, $700,000, $7,000,000, etc.

■ In response to the **economic collapse of 2008**, President Obama signed the **American Recovery and Reinvestment Act of 2009** (ARRA) soon after taking office. The act provided $787 billion in tax relief, loans, and spending "for job preservation and creation, infrastructure investment, energy efficiency and science, assistance to the unemployed, and state and local fiscal stabilization..." The provisions of this statute required a new set of acquisition regulations to ensure "an unprecedented level of transparency and accountability" to minimize waste, fraud, abuse, or mismanagement of these funds.

Those wishing to sell to the federal government must become computer literate and remain alert to changes in the federal marketplace – the procedures, the methods, what's being bought, and who's doing the buying. One of the best ways to keep abreast of changes in the acquisition world is to visit frequently my acquisition website at **http://www.FedGovContracts.com**.

THE FEDERAL ACQUISITION REGULATION (FAR)

Those interested in doing business with the federal government need to become familiar with the FAR because it is the "Bible" of federal contracting personnel and government contractors. Officially, it is Chapter 1 of Title 48 of the Code of Federal Regulations (CFR). It is available at **http://www.acquisition.gov/**, (select "Federal Acquisition Regulation (FAR)").

The FAR is not a static document. Congress keeps passing laws, presidents keep issuing executive orders, and the government continues undertaking different "pilot programs" to see which ones reduce expenses and help stretch tight agency budgets. To keep the FAR up-to-date, **Federal Acquisition Circulars** (FAC) are issued that consist of all the changes to the FAR. The FAR on the Acquisition Central website is updated to reflect the changes made by each FAC, and the FACs can be downloaded individually.

The FACs are sequential, with the first two digits identifying the FAR edition. When the 1984 edition was revised by FAC 84-60 (the *60th* revision in *six* years), the people responsible for maintaining the FAR decided to publish a 1990 edition. The FACs for the 1990 edition were identified as 90-1, 90-2, through 90-46. Another "clean" edition was published in 1997 and then a 2001 edition. The 2005 version of the FAR is currently in force, and its FACs are identified as 2005-01, 2005-02, and so on (up to 2005-95 as this is written).

SAMPLE FAR PAGE

Figure 1 is a sample FAR page. Note that this page was part of FAC 2005-06, which went into effect September 30, 2005. The vertical line in the margin shows where the changes are: FAC 2005-06 revised FAR 19.602-1. The vertical line makes it easy to locate the change. Comparing the FAC 2005-06 version of that page with the corresponding page that was in effect *before* September 30, 2005 (such as the FAC 2005-05 version of the FAR in the FAR Archive at **http://www.acquisition.gov/?q=far_archives**) shows that the cross-references addressing sureties were added.

FORMAT OF THE FAR

The FAR consists of 51 parts numbered 1 through 53 (parts 20 and 21 are "reserved" for future regulations). Each part is divided into subparts, each subpart is subdivided into sections, and many sections are subdivided still further into subsections. Let's use part 19 to illustrate. FAR part 19 is titled "Small Business Programs," and it has 13 subparts (including two subparts that are "reserved," and introductory sections 19.000, Scope of Part, and 19.001, Definitions):

19.1	Size Standards
19.2	Policies
19.3	Determination of Small Business Status for Small Business Programs
19.4	Cooperation with the Small Business Administration
19.5	Set-Asides for Small Business
19.6	Certificates of Competency and Determinations of Responsibility
19.7	The Small Business Subcontracting Program
19.8	Contracting with the Small Business Administration (The 8(a) Program)
19.9	Reserved
19.10	Reserved
19.11	Price Evaluation Adjustment for Small Disadvantaged Business Concerns
19.12	Small Disadvantaged Business Participation Program
19.13	Historically Underutilized Business Zone (HUBZone) Program
19.14	Service-Disabled Veteran-Owned Small Business Procurement Program
19.15	Women-Owned Small Business (WOSB) Program

FAC 2005–06 SEPTEMBER 30, 2005

Subpart 19.6—Certificates of Competency and Determinations of Responsibility

19.601 General.

(a) A Certificate of Competency (COC) is the certificate issued by the Small Business Administration (SBA) stating that the holder is responsible (with respect to all elements of responsibility, including, but not limited to, capability, competency, capacity, credit, integrity, perseverance, tenacity, and limitations on subcontracting) for the purpose of receiving and performing a specific Government contract.

(b) The COC program empowers the Small Business Administration (SBA) to certify to Government contracting officers as to all elements of responsibility of any small business concern to receive and perform a specific Government contract. The COC program does not extend to questions concerning regulatory requirements imposed and enforced by other Federal agencies.

(c) The COC program is applicable to all Government acquisitions. A contracting officer shall, upon determining an apparent successful small business offeror to be nonresponsible, refer that small business to the SBA for a possible COC, even if the next acceptable offer is also from a small business.

(d) When a solicitation requires a small business to adhere to the limitations on subcontracting, a contracting officer's finding that a small business cannot comply with the limitation shall be treated as an element of responsibility and shall be subject to the COC process. When a solicitation requires a small business to adhere to the definition of a nonmanufacturer, a contracting officer's determination that the small business does not comply shall be processed in accordance with Subpart 19.3.

(e) Contracting officers, including those located overseas, are required to comply with this subpart for U.S. small business concerns.

19.602 Procedures.

19.602-1 Referral.

(a) Upon determining and documenting that an apparent successful small business offeror lacks certain elements of responsibility (including, but not limited to, capability, competency, capacity, credit, integrity, perseverance, tenacity, and limitations on subcontracting, but for sureties see 28.101-3(f) and 28.203(c)), the contracting officer shall—

(1) Withhold contract award (see 19.602-3); and

(2) Refer the matter to the cognizant SBA Government Contracting Area Office (Area Office) serving the area in which the headquarters of the offeror is located, in accordance with agency procedures, except that referral is not necessary if the small business concern—

(i) Is determined to be unqualified and ineligible because it does not meet the standard in 9.104-1(g), provided, that the determination is approved by the chief of the contracting office; or

(ii) Is suspended or debarred under Executive Order 11246 or Subpart 9.4.

(b) If a partial set-aside is involved, the contracting officer shall refer to the SBA the entire quantity to which the concern may be entitled, if responsible.

(c) The referral shall include—

(1) A notice that a small business concern has been determined to be nonresponsible, specifying the elements of responsibility the contracting officer found lacking; and

(2) If applicable, a copy of the following:

(i) Solicitation.

(ii) Final offer submitted by the concern whose responsibility is at issue for the procurement.

(iii) Abstract of bids or the contracting officer's price negotiation memorandum.

(iv) Preaward survey.

(v) Technical data package (including drawings, specifications and statement of work).

(vi) Any other justification and documentation used to arrive at the nonresponsibility determination.

(d) For any single acquisition, the contracting officer shall make only one referral at a time regarding a determination of nonresponsibility.

(e) Contract award shall be withheld by the contracting officer for a period of 15 business days (or longer if agreed to by the SBA and the contracting officer) following receipt by the appropriate SBA Area Office of a referral that includes all required documentation.

19.602-2 Issuing or denying a Certificate of Competency (COC).

Within 15 business days (or a longer period agreed to by the SBA and the contracting agency) after receiving a notice that a small business concern lacks certain elements of responsibility, the SBA Area Office will take the following actions:

(a) Inform the small business concern of the contracting officer's determination and offer it an opportunity to apply to the SBA for a COC. (A concern wishing to apply for a COC should notify the SBA Area Office serving the geographical area in which the headquarters of the offeror is located.)

(b) Upon timely receipt of a complete and acceptable application, elect to visit the applicant's facility to review its responsibility.

(1) The COC review process is not limited to the areas of nonresponsibility cited by the contracting officer.

(2) The SBA may, at its discretion, independently evaluate the COC applicant for all elements of responsibility, but may presume responsibility exists as to elements other than those cited as deficient.

(c) Consider denying a COC for reasons of nonresponsibility not originally cited by the contracting officer.

Figure 1 - Sample Federal Acquisition Regulation Page

Subpart 19.6 has two sections:

19.601   General
19.602   Procedures

Section 19.602 has four subsections:

19.602-1 Referral
19.602-2 Issuing or Denying a Certificate of Competency (COC)
19.602-3 Resolving Differences Between the Agency and the Small Business Administration
19.602-4 Awarding the Contract

The numbers to the left of the decimal identify the part. The first number to the right of the decimal identifies the subpart. The second and third numbers to the right of the decimal identify the section. The number following the hyphen identifies the subsection. Any notations that are in parentheses and follow the section or subsection number represent paragraph and subparagraph numbers. FAR 19.602-1(a)(1) represents subparagraph 1 to paragraph (a) of FAR 19.602-1.

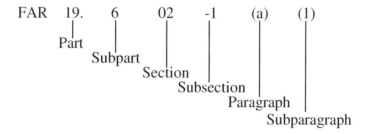

It may seem complicated, but the FAR numbering system is actually quite easy to use once one understands how it works.

AGENCY SUPPLEMENTS TO THE
FEDERAL ACQUISITION REGULATION

Though the FAR is the government's unified contracting regulation, each federal agency is subject to rules that do not apply to other agencies. Contracting personnel in the Department of Agriculture do not need to know how the Department of Energy contracts for the operation of nuclear research facilities. Similarly, contracting personnel in the Department of Energy do not need to know the unique rules that apply to Forest Service contracts for the construction of roads through timber stands.

To keep the FAR from being cluttered with these "agency specific" rules, Congress allows each agency to issue a FAR **supplement**. The rules and regulations included in an agency's supplement cannot contradict the provisions of the

FAR but merely elaborate and provide more detailed guidance. However, Congress can direct an agency to follow rules that do not comply with those in the FAR. For instance, Congress has directed the Department of Defense to restrict its purchases of certain types of supplies to United States and Canadian sources (see Chapter 12). These restrictions do not apply to the other government agencies, so they appear in the **Defense FAR Supplement** (DFARS), not the FAR.

Just as the FAR is Chapter 1 of Title 48 of the CFR, each agency supplement is assigned its own chapter. For example, the DFARS is Chapter 2 of Title 48, the **Health and Human Services Acquisition Regulation** (HHSAR) is Chapter 3, the **Agriculture Acquisition Regulation** (AGAR) is Chapter 4, and so on. The agency supplements parallel the FAR in format, arrangement, and numbering system. For example, FAR 15.304, Evaluation Factors and Significant Subfactors, addresses which factors and subfactors must be evaluated in source selections: price, quality of the supply or service, past performance, and the extent of subcontracting with small disadvantaged businesses (only required to be evaluated when the contract is expected to exceed $700,000 [or $1,500,000 for construction]). FAR 15.304 also requires that the relative importance of each factor and subfactor be clearly stated in the solicitation.

DOD has a slightly different requirement. In addition to the evaluation factors required by FAR 15.304, "the extent of participation of small businesses and historically black colleges or universities and minority institutions in the performance of the contract shall be addressed in source selection" when the contract is expected to exceed $700,000 (or $1,500,000 for construction of a public facility). This additional requirement is included in a corresponding DFARS 215.304, Evaluation Factors and Significant Subfactors. Note the section identification is the same except the DFARS number begins with the 48 CFR chapter number – 2 15.304. The **Department of Housing and Urban Development Acquisition Regulation** (HUDAR) is Chapter 24 of 48 CFR, and HUDAR *24*15.304, Evaluation Factors and Significant Subfactors, includes the department's supplemental instructions for conducting evaluations.

An agency that has acquisition-related material for which there is no FAR counterpart identifies the information by using chapter, part, subpart, section, or subsection numbers of 70 and up. For example, the National Aeronautics and Space Administration (NASA) FAR Supplement (NFS) is Chapter 18 of 48 CFR. NFS 1815.304, Evaluation Factors and Significant Subfactors, addresses how small business participation in contract performance is to be evaluated. However, NASA has an additional evaluation factor that can be used: "mission suitability." Since "mission suitability" is not addressed in FAR 15.304, NASA uses NFS 1815.304-70, NASA Evaluation Factors, to describe "mission suitability" and how to evaluate it.

To further illustrate how the numbering works, NASA has developed an "ombudsman program" on its own ("an ombudsman has been appointed to hear and facilitate the resolution of concerns from offerors, potential offerors, and contractors during the preaward and postaward phases of this acquisition"). The FAR does not require the appointment of an ombudsman, so NASA decided to publish

NFS subpart 1815.70, Ombudsman, which describes NASA's ombudsman program and procedures for seeking resolution of concerns from offerors and contractors.

Most agency FAR supplements are available at (1) **http://www.acquisition.gov/?q=Supplemental_Regulations**; (2) **http://farsite.hill.af.mil/**; and (3) the electronic CFR at **http://www.ecfr.gov** (select "Title 48").

Agency Acquisition Guidance

Several agencies have examined their acquisition FAR supplements and determined they were needlessly cluttered with a lot of internal operating procedures that are of no interest to contractors. Also, because the information was in the agency's supplement and the agency supplement is a chapter of Title 48 of the CFR, the internal procedures could not be changed without going through the regulatory process. Considering how quickly the acquisition process is changing, these agencies decided to remove the internal operating procedures from their FAR supplements and put them in a separate, non-regulatory document. For example, the Department of Defense has placed all its mandatory and non-mandatory internal procedures, non-mandatory guidance, and supplemental information in its "Procedures, Guidance, and Information" (PGI); the Department of Commerce has developed a "Commerce Acquisition Manual" (CAM); and the General Services Administration had developed a "General Services Administration Acquisition Manual" (GSAM). These documents are usually accessible from the same website as the agency's FAR supplement.

*   *   *   *   *

The FAR is all one needs when getting started. Once a contractor finds out which agencies buy its particular products and begins winning contracts, then it will want to look at those agencies' FAR supplements.

CHAPTER 2

THE CONTRACTING ACTIVITY, THE CONTRACTING OFFICER, AND KEY PLAYERS

The Constitution assigns the responsibility for executing the duties of the executive branch to the president. The president delegates the actual execution of those duties to the various federal departments and agencies, and the **head of the agency** (that is, the secretary, attorney general, administrator, or other chief official of an agency) has the authority to execute, administer, modify, and terminate contracts for his agency. However, the head of the agency has many more responsibilities and duties than the execution and administration of contracts, so he delegates his contracting authority to the agency's **chief acquisition officer** and **senior procurement executive**, who are the agency's senior acquisition policy makers. The actual day-to-day procurement is conducted at more than 3,200 "contracting activities" where over 200,000 federal employees work (including 40,000 "contracting officers"). The trick is to know which ones are the "key players" and to concentrate on them.

THE CONTRACTING ACTIVITY

Every federal agency has an assigned mission. Each year every agency analyzes its mission, assesses the resources it has to accomplish that mission, and decides what additional resources it needs to acquire. First, the agency will determine whether its own resources are sufficient to accomplish its mission. If not, the agency will ask other agencies whether they have excess resources they could spare, such as surplus equipment, unused facilities, or unique expertise. If no federal agency has the necessary resources, the agency will seek to acquire them in the commercial marketplace.

Because many of the resources each agency needs can be acquired only in the commercial marketplace, each agency has **contracting activities** that specialize in the acquisition process. There are two basic kinds of contracting activities:

- Those that purchase the products needed by other agency offices with funds provided by those offices. For example, the Department of Labor's Office of Procurement Services purchases most of the supplies and services required by the department's various offices, bureaus, and administrations.

- Those that project the agency's needs, determine the necessary resources to fulfill the projected needs, and acquire those resources. For example, the Army's Tank-Automotive and Armaments Command has its own budget and its own staff of scientists, logisticians, analysts, lawyers, and support personnel. With this budget and staff, it develops specifications and executes contracts for the production of tanks, personnel carriers, trucks, jeeps, construction equipment, artillery, small arms, and ammunition.

Overseeing all the agency's contracting activities is the **chief acquisition officer** (CAO), a non-career employee (that is, a political appointee, such as an assistant secretary) who oversees the agency's acquisition activities and programs, and advises the head of the agency regarding the appropriate business strategy to achieve the agency's mission. The reason the CAO is a political appointee is because Congress believes such a person has more access to, and influence with, the leadership of the agency than does a career employee.

The **senior procurement executive** (SPE) is responsible for the agency's day-to-day contracting operations. Usually, the SPE is a career employee, and he is responsible for the overall management of the agency's acquisition program, including the development and implementation of the agency's unique acquisition policies, regulations, and standards.

The **head of the contracting activity** (HCA) is responsible for the overall operation and management of a contracting activity. The HCA's primary duty is to coordinate the efforts of those in the contracting activity – the scientists, engineers, technicians, accountants, attorneys, and contracting personnel – so:

- The agency obtains the resources it needs on time;

- Those resources meet the agency's quality requirements; and

- The agency pays a reasonable price.

Within each contracting activity is a **contracting office**. This is where the actual contracting process takes place: drafting solicitations, evaluating bids, conducting negotiations, awarding contracts. This is where the **contracting officer** works.

THE CONTRACTING OFFICER

The **contracting officer** is the most important government official in the contracting process. He is the *only* person empowered to bind the government to a contract over $3,500 (see "micro-purchasers" later in this chapter for those authorized to make purchases up to $3,500). No one else can legally obligate the government to pay more than $3,500 for products: not the engineer who designed the item, not the program manager who needs the service, not the comptroller who has the money. Only a duly-appointed contracting officer can sign and administer contracts for the government.

The contracting officer is not the person who decides how many widgets the government needs; the supply and logistics personnel tell him how many to buy. He does not decide the color, the dimensions, or the packaging requirements. He is responsible for ensuring four things:

1. The solicitation accurately depicts the government's requirements (that is, it contains no "goldplating");

2. The solicitation complies with all applicable regulations;

3. The contracting process is conducted according to all applicable regulations; and

4. The contract satisfies the government's needs at a "**fair and reasonable**" price.

Because the contracting officer is the only person authorized to decide when a price is fair and reasonable, he is also the only person authorized to conduct negotiations. On complicated purchases, he may lead a negotiating team consisting of technical, legal, and other government personnel. While the contracting officer might consult legal counsel on some fine points of contract law or allow engineers to clarify the technical aspects of a proposal, he is the one who ultimately decides when to say "you've got a deal."

Once the contracting officer and the contractor execute the contract, only the contracting officer has the *legal* authority to interpret its terms and conditions. Though an engineer might have written the specification for the widget, he cannot tell the contractor what the specification requires. The contracting officer's opinions, interpretations, and decisions are the only ones the government must support.

The contracting officer can choose *not* to recognize the validity of directions given by other government personnel. When an engineer and a contracting officer have conflicting interpretations of a specification requirement, the government will *invariably* recognize the contracting officer's interpretation as binding (of course, whether the contracting officer prevails in a disagreement with an engineer is another matter). If a contractor relies on the engineer's interpretation and performs the contract accordingly, the contracting officer can order the work re-done at no increase in price – or even terminate the contract for default! Even interpretations by government lawyers are only advisory; the contracting officer always makes the final, binding decision (however, see Chapter 18 for an explanation of the "Disputes" clause).

A contracting officer's success depends on the suitability of the choices he makes. The FAR is written specifically for the contracting officer, and it gives him hundreds of options to consider. Though getting a fair and reasonable price is always a primary concern of the contracting officer, the interests of the government are not necessarily served by purchasing the products with the lowest prices. The contracting officer must recognize when to consider factors other than cost in a contract award. For instance, under certain circumstances the "correct" decision might be to pay a premium for expedited delivery of emergency supplies or to award a "sole source" contract to keep a firm's production line ready to manufacture ammunition for a military operation. Also, the contracting officer may decide to award a contract to other than the lowest price offeror or other than the highest technically-rated offeror – in other words, to the offeror providing the "**best value**" to the government, after cost and other factors are considered.

The FAR also provides the contracting officer with guidance on how to achieve the national, social, and economic goals established by Congress and the president, such as when to restrict competition to small businesses. The contracting officer must consider all these factors as he prepares each solicitation and contract.

To a contractor whose aim is to earn a profit, the actions and decisions of a contracting officer may seem nonsensical. But because the government's reason for existence is not to make a profit but to "provide for the common Defence and general Welfare," the actions of contracting officers cannot be judged by normal commercial standards.

Contracting Officer's Certificate of Appointment

Federal agencies select their 40,000 contracting officers based on experience, training, education, business acumen, judgment, character, reputation, and ethics. When an agency selects a person to be one of its contracting officers, it issues him a **Standard Form 1402, Contracting Officer's Certificate of Appointment** (see Figure 2), which is commonly called a "warrant." The warrant identifies that person as a duly-appointed contracting officer who has the power to take all actions authorized by the procurement regulations in the conduct of government business. The warrant also identifies any limitations placed on this authority by the appointing agency. For example, the contracting officer's warrant might state that his authority extends only to contracts that do not exceed $150,000.

Certificate of Appointment

Under authority vested in the undersigned and in conformance with Subpart 1.6 of the Federal Acquisition Regulation

Helen Wheles

is appointed

Contracting Officer

for the

United States of America

Subject to the limitations contained in the Federal Acquisition Regulation and to the following:

Supplies and Services Not to Exceed the Simplified Acquisition Threshold as Defined in Federal Acquisition Regulation 2.101

Unless sooner terminated, this appointment is effective as long as the appointee is assigned to:

_____

Procurement and Contracts Division
(Organization)

_____

Environmental Protection Agency
(Agency/Department)

_____

Head of the Contracting Activity
(Signature and Title)

05/17/2012
(Date)

EPA-543
(Number)

STANDARD FORM 1402 (10-83)
Prescribed by GSA - FAR (48 - CFR) 53.201-1

**Figure 2 - Contracting Officer's Certificate of Appointment
(Standard Form 1402)**

The warrant is an important document that tells contractors the named person is authorized by the government to represent it in contractual matters. If someone has concerns about a government official's authority to conduct negotiations or to provide interpretations of solicitation and contract provisions, he should ask to see that person's warrant. If that person does not have a contracting officer's warrant or has exceeded any of the limitations placed on his warrant, his directions and instructions **should be ignored**. *Contractors should follow only the directions and interpretations provided by a contracting officer operating within the limitations of his warrant.* A contractor that follows the directions of an unauthorized government official does so at its own risk because the contracting officer may not recognize the unauthorized directions as contractually binding!

Different Types of Contracting Officers

There are three types of contracting officers: the **procuring contracting officer** (PCO), the **administrative contracting officer** (ACO), and the **termination contracting officer** (TCO).

The PCO issues solicitations, conducts the negotiations, and signs the contracts. The ACO, used extensively by the Department of Defense and many civilian agencies, performs specific administrative functions after the PCO signs the contract. The TCO negotiates settlements of terminated contracts and makes sure all government inventory and property are protected. These contracting officers can be the same person or different people, depending on the size and complexity of the contract.

Because this book is concerned primarily with obtaining contracts, the PCO is the focus. The term "contracting officer," as used in this book, refers to the PCO unless otherwise stated. However, the following briefly describes the other two types of contracting officers and explains how they fit in the contracting process. See Chapter 18 for more on the functions performed by these two types of contracting officers.

Administrative Contracting Officer

As a rule, whenever the PCO awards a contract to a contractor outside the contracting activity's geographical area, he transfers the administration of the contract to the appropriate administrative contracting officer (ACO). There are two reasons for this transfer:

1. ACOs are stationed around the country and oversee the contracts awarded to businesses in their regions. Thus, they can keep a closer eye on the contractor's performance than can the PCO.

2. It frees the PCO to concentrate on issuing solicitations, conducting negotiations, and awarding contracts.

The ACO monitors contract performance, makes sure the contractor submits all required reports, accepts or rejects the contractor's supplies or services, and makes sure the contractor receives payment for accepted supplies or services.

The ACO performs only those administrative duties delegated to him by the PCO. Since the PCO works directly for the agency purchasing the product, the PCO has the final word on how the ACO administers the contract. For example, the PCO rarely allows the ACO to negotiate changes to the terms and conditions of a contract without his approval. Sometimes the PCO decides to retain *all* the administrative duties – there is no separate ACO.

However, since the ACO is in closer contact with the contractor, the PCO usually relies on him to oversee contract performance. The ACO acts as the eyes and ears of the PCO.

Termination Contracting Officer

Whenever a PCO terminates a contract for the convenience of the government or for default (see Chapter 18), he turns the contract settlement over to the termination contracting officer (TCO). The TCO orders the contractor to stop work, terminate all subcontracts, protect any government property and inventory in the contractor's possession, and submit a settlement proposal. He monitors the contractor's actions to make sure the government's interests are protected, and he alerts the PCO to any legal or contractual matters that may have a bearing on the termination.

Upon receiving the contractor's settlement proposal, the TCO and government auditors examine the contractor's accounts to verify the accuracy of the proposal. Frequently the TCO will disagree with some of the proposed charges, such as indirect costs or the value of retained inventory. If this happens, the TCO and the contractor have to negotiate a settlement agreement. Once the TCO and the contractor arrive at an agreement, the TCO can sign the agreement and bind the government. The TCO does not need the PCO's approval.

THE CONTRACT SPECIALIST

This book concentrates on the contracting officer, continually specifying that "the contracting officer does this" and "the contracting officer does that." These statements are technically correct because the contracting officer is responsible for the overall conduct of the procurement process and is the only one authorized to enter into contractual agreements. However, he is physically incapable of drafting all the solicitations, conducting all the negotiations, writing all the supporting documentation, and preparing all the contracts. Therefore, in most contracting offices, the contracting officer has **contract specialists** (sometimes called "contract assistants") who prepare the solicitations and negotiate most of the contracts.

Because the contract specialist is the one who verifies the accuracy of the specifications or requirements documents and drafts the solicitation, he knows more about the solicitation's contents and requirements than the contracting officer. For that reason, the contract specialist is ordinarily the point of contact for information about a solicitation. This does not mean the contracting officer is ignorant of what is going on. The contracting officer gives directions and reviews each contract specialist's work. Naturally, he supervises the inexperienced contract specialists more closely than the experienced ones. But even the hardened veterans consult the contracting officer when complications arise because the contracting officer is the one who signs his name on the contract.

If a businessman asks a contract specialist a question about a solicitation or contract, he can be *almost* certain the answer is the one authorized by the contracting officer. However, if the businessman wants to be *absolutely* certain, he will put the question to the contracting officer *in writing* and the contracting officer will send a signed response.

While businessmen always have the option of talking directly to the contracting officer, they should not expect the contracting officer to be their personal contact. The contracting officer will insist that they first try to resolve their questions and problems with the contract specialist. Usually the contract specialist will satisfy their concerns.

THE CONTRACTING OFFICER'S REPRESENTATIVE

Frequently, the contracting officer will appoint a **contracting officer's representative** (COR) (some contracting activities call this person the **contracting officer's technical representative** [COTR]). The contracting officer appoints a COR (or COTR) to give directions and make decisions on the performance of a contract for a highly technical product or service (for example, software development, research, construction). Frequently, when the contracting officer decides to appoint a COR for a contract, he will appoint the "acquisition planner" (see below).

The contracting officer makes the appointment in writing. The contracting officer's letter of appointment delineates the authority granted the COR and specifies the limits placed on that authority. This appointment letter is the COR's "warrant," and one should always ask to see it before following any directions.

Why would a contracting officer appoint a COR? Though the contracting officer is the only person authorized to direct changes to contracts, he is not an expert in research or construction or software development. He has to rely on the government's scientists and engineers to tell him which changes to make to the contract specifications or requirements. This takes time, and workers idly waiting for the contracting officer to modify the contract cost the government money.

The contracting officer avoids these delays by appointing a COR and authorizing him to make "no-cost" changes on-the-spot. When the COR directs such a change, the contractor makes the change promptly and the government keeps the project on schedule with minimal paperwork.

The following are typical situations in which the contracting officer might appoint a COR:

- To provide a government scientist with the necessary authorization to pursue promising alternatives in case a contractor's experiments under a government research contract produce unexpected results.

- To permit corrections of minor errors in blueprints so construction can continue without delay while the contracting officer formally modifies the contract.

- To provide a software developer technical advice and direction so the software meets the government's unique needs.

The key point to remember is that these contract changes can be made at no additional cost if they are made early. The COR *cannot* direct the contractor to make a change if the change will increase the contract price – only the contracting officer can obligate the government to such a commitment. Nevertheless, a COR can help the contracting officer speed up the contract change and keep additional costs to a minimum.

THE SMALL BUSINESS SPECIALIST

Each contracting activity has an **Office of Small and Disadvantaged Business Utilization** (OSDBU) (several departments and agencies call it an **Office of Small Business Programs**) staffed by at least one **small business specialist** (SBS). Some agencies call these people "small and disadvantaged business utilization specialists." They all do the same job.

The SBS is an advocate for small businesses. To help small businesses, he:

- Provides information on the supplies and services his contracting activity purchases;

- Actively seeks qualified firms capable of providing those supplies and services;

- Gives advice and counsel; and

- Strives to ensure his contracting activity meets its assigned contracting "goals."

Recognizing how important small businesses are to the American economy, Congress passed the Small Business Act in 1953. The act established the Small Business Administration (SBA) to help small businesses develop and become viable entities through guidance, low-interest loans, and other forms of assistance. One of the most direct ways the government can help small businesses is through federal contracts. So Congress directed the SBA to make sure the government awards a "fair portion" of its contracts to small businesses.

Every year, the SBA and each federal agency negotiate separate contract "goals" for small businesses, small disadvantaged businesses, small veteran-owned businesses, small service-disabled veteran-owned small businesses, and women-owned businesses. The agency then assigns each of its contracting activities portions of these goals. The SBS' primary task is to help his contracting activity meet its assigned goals. He is *not* an employee of the SBA, but a member of the head of the contracting activity's staff.

The SBS reviews each procurement over the **simplified acquisition threshold** (currently $150,000 – see Chapter 6) to see if it can be performed by a small business. If the SBS believes two or more small businesses can perform the work, he recommends to the contracting officer that the procurement be "set-aside" for small businesses (see Chapter 11). An alternative might be to convince the contracting officer to "offer" the procurement to the SBA for a disadvantaged firm in the 8(a) program (see Chapter 11).

The contracting officer makes the final decision on whom to solicit. However, if the small business specialist believes the solicitation method chosen by the contracting officer needlessly or unfairly hampers small business competition, he can appeal to the head of the contracting activity. If the contracting officer does not have a compelling reason for his decision, the contracting activity's need to meet its small business goals will usually prevail.

The OSDBU should be the first stop for all small businesses when contacting a contracting activity. Businesses that have never contracted with the contracting activity should make an appointment if possible; face-to-face meetings are more productive and informative than telephone calls or e-mail.

When meeting with a businessman, the SBS will provide information on the products his contracting activity purchases, such as:

- A general description of the required specifications
- Typical delivery or performance schedules
- Normal packaging requirements
- Usual quantities purchased
- How frequently the contracting activity purchases the supply or service
- Last price paid
- Last company to provide the supply or service
- Projected requirements

The SBS may not volunteer this information, so the businessman should be prepared to ask for it.

The businessman should describe his firm's capabilities, its business experience, and its current product line so the SBS has an idea of what the firm can do. If it appears the firm is capable of fulfilling some of the contracting activity's needs, the SBS can arrange a meeting with those who prepare the specifications and determine the government's needs (the "acquisition planners") so the businessman can get a better idea of what the contracting activity buys.

THE ACQUISITION PLANNERS

Each agency decides what resources it will need to accomplish its mission. These decisions are made by the people who prepare the specifications or requirements documents and forecast how much the agency will need. There is no single term for those who perform these functions. Some call them "users," but an engineer who drafts the specifications for a waste incinerator may never "use" it. Conversely, a soldier driving a tank may "use" it but not know its mechanical and electrical requirements. Some people, called "item managers," monitor inventory levels of the items assigned to them and decide when the inventory needs replenishment; however, they do not establish the specifications for those items. Some prepare documents for the "program manager" or "project manager." Therefore, I call all those who decide the designs of items, the types of services, and the quantities to buy "**acquisition planners**."

Many different government employees are acquisition planners. A contracting officer tries to determine what he and his staff will "require" to operate effectively during the upcoming year: office supplies, furniture, training. Another person consolidates all the requirements for office supplies, furniture, and training that were submitted by authorized personnel and decides how many of each to order. Others determine the kinds and quantities of weapons needed to counter the "threat" (however that might be defined: bombs for the Air Force; pesticides for the Department of Agriculture). Still others decide where to direct cancer research, how many automobiles in the government's fleet to replace, what kind of computer to acquire for the payroll office, how often to mop the floors in a federal office building, and so forth. Everything the government buys starts as someone's "requirement."

A businessman should try to identify the person in the contracting activity who determines the requirements for his firm's kind of supplies or services and make an appointment to meet that person (the SBS can probably help make the arrangements). The businessman should discuss his firm's products and capabilities, find out the specifications the contracting activity typically uses, and explain how his firm's products meet (or can be modified to meet) those specifications. A smart businessman tries to ascertain the needs of the acquisition planner and then explain how his firm's product will meet those needs.

The government *encourages* these exchanges because they help the acquisition planner find out what supplies, services, and technologies are available to fulfill his agency's needs. And, of course, the businessman's presentation may persuade the acquisition planner to take a closer look at his firm's solution. However, the acquisition planner person will not discuss current and upcoming solicitations because to do so would violate **procurement integrity** rules and subject both the acquisition planner and the businessman to severe penalties (see Chapter 17 for more on procurement integrity and ethics rules). Because of these penalties, some acquisition planners are reluctant to discuss *anything*. Nevertheless, most are willing to describe long-range requirements and listen to possible solutions because they are required to survey the market before drafting specifications and requirements.

The acquisition planner is a window on the procurement process through which a businessman can see and influence the future. The wise businessman will search out the acquisition planner.

MICRO-PURCHASERS

To reduce the cost of making small, routine purchases, the Federal Acquisition Streamlining Act allows contracting agencies to authorize *non-contracting* employees to purchase supplies and services their particular office needs as long as the purchases do not exceed **$3,500** (under most circumstances – see Chapter 6). These "**micro-purchases**" are intended to be simple and fast. The "micro-purchaser" is not required to prepare a requisition; he is not required to go through the contracting office; he is not required to obtain competitive quotations (see Chapter 6 for more on micro-purchases).

Micro-purchasers combine the duties and functions of "acquisition planners" (in that they decide what to buy and how many to buy) and "contracting officers" (in that they decide from whom to buy and whether the price is fair and reasonable). They must be appointed by their agencies in writing, though the agencies are not required to issue them a Standard Form 1402.

There are more than **300,000** micro-purchasers in the government, few of whom are contracting officers or contract specialists. Most have been issued "purchase cards" (another name for "credit cards" – see Chapter 6). Because there are so many micro-purchasers and their purchases are relatively small, it is difficult to market to them in a cost-effective manner. Probably the best way is to consider them to be just another consumer group and to try to catch their attention through advertisements in newspapers, magazines, radio, television, or other media. Being close to government offices (or providing quick delivery or service), having quality supplies or services at competitive prices, and having a reputation for cooperation and honesty should help garner business from micro-purchasers.

CHAPTER 3

THE COMPETITION IN CONTRACTING ACT

The law that most affects the way the government conducts business is the **Competition in Contracting Act of 1984** (CICA). Congress passed and the president signed the Competition in Contracting Act (CICA) in response to widely reported news stories of noncompetitive contract awards for $600 toilet seats and $7,000 coffeemakers.

Since CICA went into effect on April 1, 1985, the government has been required to obtain its products through **full and open competition** whenever possible. "Full and open competition" means *giving all responsible sources the opportunity to compete for the contract*. The "full and open competition" requirement applies to all contracts over the **simplified acquisition threshold** ($150,000 – see Chapter 6) except those awarded through procedures expressly authorized by statute. For instance, small business set-asides are considered fully and openly competitive though large businesses are not allowed to compete (see Chapter 11); orders placed against Federal Supply Schedule (FSS) contracts are considered to be awarded through full and open competition because the basic FSS contracts were awarded competitively (see Chapter 13); and architect-engineering contracts awarded under the procedures in FAR subpart 36.6, Architect-Engineer Services, are considered to be competitively awarded (see Chapter 14).

The **Clinger-Cohen Act of 1996** modified the full and open competition requirement to require that full and open competition be conducted "in a manner that is consistent with the need to efficiently fulfill the government's requirements." This modification is in the policy statement in paragraph (b) of FAR 6.101, Policy.

SEVEN EXCEPTIONS TO FULL AND OPEN COMPETITION

There are only seven exceptions to the full and open competition requirement:

■ **FAR 6.302-1, Only One Responsible Source and No Other Supplies or Services Will Satisfy Agency Requirements** – This exception applies when the government must obtain specific supplies or services from a "sole source." A sole source contractor is one that has unique supplies or capabilities; owns data rights, patent rights, or copyrights; has a secret process; or controls basic raw materials. This exception also applies to electric power, gas (natural or manufactured), water, and other utilities. In addition, this exception applies to "brand-name descriptions," which specify a particular product, or feature of a product, peculiar to one manufacturer (an example would be a requirement for Campbell's® tomato soup). However, the contracting officer *must* consider any proposal submitted in response to a solicitation that cites this exception.

There is one minor variation to this rule: the Department of Defense, Coast Guard, and National Aeronautics and Space Administration may cite this CICA exception to restrict competition when "only one *or a limited number* of sources" can satisfy their requirements.

■ **FAR 6.302-2, Unusual and Compelling Urgency** – The government may limit the number of sources it solicits when its need is so urgent it would suffer serious financial or other injury if it used full and open competition. For example, the government might use this exception to purchase emergency relief supplies without using formal solicitation procedures. However, a contracting activity's lack of adequate planning or fear of losing funds at the end of the fiscal year (September 30) are *not* sufficient reasons for restricting competition under this CICA exception (see paragraph (c) of FAR 6.301, Policy).

■ **FAR 6.302-3, Industrial Mobilization; or Engineering, Developmental, or Research Capability; or Expert Services** – The government need not obtain full and open competition when the contract is to:

(i) keep vital facilities or suppliers in business or make them available in a national emergency;

(ii) train a selected supplier in furnishing critical supplies or services; prevent the loss of a supplier's ability and employees' skills; or maintain active engineering, research, or development work;

(iii) create or maintain a domestic capability to produce critical items by limiting competition to those furnishing products manufactured in the United States or Canada;

(iv) continue manufacturing critical items when there would be a break in production;

(v) divide production requirements among two or more contractors to provide an adequate industrial mobilization base;

(vi) establish or maintain an essential engineering, research, or development capability of an educational or other nonprofit institution or a federally funded research and development center (such capabilities include theoretical analyses, exploratory studies, experiments in any field of science or technology, or engineering or developmental work calling for the practical application of investigative findings and theories of a scientific or technical nature);

(vii) acquire the services of an expert to use in any litigation or dispute involving the government in any trial, hearing, or proceeding before any court, administrative tribunal, or agency; or

(viii) acquire the services of a mediator or arbitrator to facilitate the resolution of issues in an alternative dispute resolution process (see Chapter 18 for more on alternative means of dispute resolution).

In other words, the government can restrict competition to firms and facilities that either (1) possess vital capabilities, or (2) agree to keep their production lines operational and make them available during national emergencies; or to an individual or firm that possesses expert knowledge that will be used during litigation or disputes.

- **FAR 6.302-4, International Agreement** – This exception applies when a treaty or international agreement between the United States and a foreign government (or an international organization) names the source or sources for specific supplies or services. Also, this exception applies when a foreign country is to reimburse the United States for acquiring the supplies or services of a particular firm.

- **FAR 6.302-5, Authorized or Required by Statute** – The government need not obtain competition when: (i) a statute authorizes or requires that the purchase be made through another government agency or from a specified source (for example, Federal Prison Industries [see Chapter 4], qualified nonprofit agencies for the blind or severely handicapped [see Chapter 4], awards under Section 8(a) of the Small Business Act [see Chapter 11], or government printing and binding); or (ii) the purchase is for a brand name commercial item for authorized resale (such as products intended for sale through military commissaries or similar facilities).

- **FAR 6.302-6, National Security** – If disclosure of the government's needs would compromise national security (that is, the purchase is "classified"), the government may limit the number of sources it solicits. However, just because a purchase is "confidential," "secret," or "top secret" does *not* mean the requirement for full and open competition is waived. FAR 6.302-6(c)(3) states that "agencies shall request offers from as many potential sources as is practicable under the circumstances."

■ **FAR 6.302-7, Public Interest** – The head of the agency (that is, the secretary or administrator of any federal department or agency) can forgo full and open competition for a particular purchase when he decides it would not be in the public interest. When the head of the agency invokes this exception, he must notify Congress at least 30 days before contract award.

For all other purchases over $150,000, contracting officers must obtain full and open competition.

ESTABLISHING OR MAINTAINING ALTERNATE SOURCES

CICA allows the head of an agency to exclude a particular source from competing (usually a contractor with such a competitive advantage over all others in the industry that it is effectively a "sole source") when the exclusion would:

1. Increase or maintain competition and probably result in reduced overall costs for the supplies or services;

2. Be in the interest of national defense by making a facility (or producer, manufacturer, or other supplier) available in case of national emergency or industrial mobilization;

3. Be in the interest of national defense by establishing or maintaining an essential engineering, research, or development capability of an educational or other nonprofit institution or a federally funded research and development center;

4. Ensure the continuous availability of a reliable source of the supplies or services;

5. Satisfy projected needs for the supplies or services based on a history of high demand; or

6. Satisfy a critical need for medical, safety, or emergency supplies.

The head of the agency will use one of the first three authorities when he wants to develop a second source for the supply or service. By preventing the "sole source" from competing for a relatively small "learning quantity," the head of the agency hopes the second source will learn how to manufacture the supplies or perform the services and be able to compete with the current "sole source" contractor for future contracts. (See FAR subpart 6.2, Full and Open Competition After Exclusion of Sources, for more on alternate sources.)

WRITTEN JUSTIFICATIONS

Whenever a contracting officer decides one of the exceptions to CICA's full and open competition requirement applies to a particular solicitation, he must write down the facts supporting his decision in a **justification** (with some exceptions). If the contract is expected to exceed $700,000, the contracting officer must obtain **approval** of his justification from a superior – the larger the purchase, the higher the level of the official who must approve the justification. This document is called a **justification and approval** (J&A).

Each J&A must explain, in detail, the reasons the contracting officer believes the purchase cannot be made using full and open competition. The justification must include, as appropriate:

- A demonstration that the proposed contractor's unique qualifications or the nature of the acquisition requires a noncompetitive purchase;

- A description of the efforts undertaken to insure the solicitation of bids or proposals from as many potential sources as practicable, including whether a synopsis will be published on **FedBizOpps** (see Chapter 5);

- The results of any market survey conducted by the government or the reasons one was not conducted;

- An explanation of the reasons competitive technical data packages, specifications, engineering descriptions, statements of work, or purchase descriptions are not available;

- A list of the sources that have expressed an interest in the acquisition; and

- The actions the agency may take to remove or overcome barriers to competition before making any further purchases of the supplies or services.

These J&As are available to the public and must be published on **FedBizOpps** and on the agency's website (except for "unusual and compelling urgency" J&As). The J&As must remain available to the public for at least 30 days. Before publishing a J&A on **FedBizOpps**, the contracting officer will screen the J&A and remove any contractor's proprietary data that may be included. Those who believe they are being wrongfully excluded from competition may challenge the justification under the protest procedures described in Chapter 16.

THE ADVOCATE FOR COMPETITION

CICA requires each contracting activity to employ an **advocate for competition** to ensure compliance with CICA. The advocate reviews the contracting activity's operations to make sure all appropriate actions are being taken to encourage competition and the acquisition of commercial items (see Chapter 4). For example, the advocate for competition might want to know whether major components of a sole source weapon system can be "broken out" and bought competitively, or why a commercial item cannot meet the government's needs as well as an item manufactured according to a government-unique specification. Also, the advocate challenges anything that unnecessarily restricts competition, like needlessly detailed specifications.

The advocate for competition has a staff that helps him review all proposed noncompetitive purchases over the simplified acquisition threshold ($150,000). He is one of the "higher authorities" who must approve the contracting officer's J&As for noncompetitive contracts between $700,000 and $13,500,000; he must concur in J&As for noncompetitive contracts over $13,500,000 before submission to higher authority for approval. He can use the contracting activity's specialists in engineering, technical operations, contract administration, financial management, supply management, and small business specialist (SBS) to help him carry out his mandate. Like the SBS, the advocate for competition is a member of the head of the contracting activity's staff.

Because it is the advocate's responsibility to ensure that everyone in the contracting activity complies with CICA, he wants to know when competition is needlessly restricted. If a businessman believes a solicitation contains unreasonable limitations or should not be solicited on a sole source basis, he should discuss his concerns with the contracting officer first. If the contracting officer cannot satisfy him, he may want to talk to the advocate for competition. Given the emphasis on competition, the advocate can be a powerful ally. (See FAR subpart 6.5 for more on advocates for competition.)

CHAPTER 4

DEFINING THE GOVERNMENT'S NEEDS

The heart of any government contract is its description of the supplies or services the government needs. A description that defines clearly what the government needs helps the contractor deliver what the government requires, ensures the government pays no more than a fair and reasonable price, and reduces the effort spent by both the contractor and the government on contract administration. Conversely, an unclear or ill-defined description can cause the contractor to guess at what the government wants, which usually produces increased costs and delayed performance when the contractor misdirects its efforts.

Until about 25 years ago, the government usually relied on its own **specifications** and **statements of work** (SOW) to describe what it wanted. While specifications and SOWs are costly for the government to prepare, and the products of specifications and SOWs are often expensive, the development of government-unique specifications and SOWs was appropriate and necessary when the government was the leader in technological advancement. However, with limited budgets extending well into the foreseeable future, the government is moving away from detailed specifications and SOWs toward the acquisition of commercial supplies and services (collectively called "commercial items"). In fact, many solicitations now incorporate **statements of objectives** (SOO), which identify the broad, basic top-level objectives of the acquisition and permit the offerors to propose their own solutions.

This trend recognizes four facts:

1. Much of the technological innovation is taking place in the commercial market and not in the Department of Defense or the National Aeronautics and Space Administration.

2. Many government specifications require obsolete technology because they take so long to prepare and approve.

3. Government-unique supplies and services are usually more expensive than commercial items.

4. The government no longer has staff that is capable of determining and articulating the government's needs.

Therefore, agencies are required, to the maximum extent possible, to state their needs (1) in terms of functions to be performed, performance required, or essential physical characteristics; and (2) in terms that permit the acquisition of commercial items.

This does not mean that government-unique specifications and SOWs have disappeared – there are still many government requirements that cannot be fulfilled by commercial products. But the government is finding that more and more of its needs *can* be fulfilled by commercial products and services, and that some of those commercial products and services have features and capabilities that *far exceed* those required by the government.

DEFINITION OF COMMERCIAL ITEMS

To qualify as a **commercial item**, an **item of supply** must have been sold, leased, or licensed to the general public, or *offered* for sale, lease, or license. An item that has evolved from an item sold, leased, or licensed to the general public but has not yet been offered to the general public qualifies, too. In addition, an item that has been sold, leased, or licensed to the general public but needs *minor modifications* to meet government requirements is considered commercial.

To qualify as a commercial item, a **service** must be either (1) for the installation, maintenance, or repair of a commercial item of supply (as defined above), *and* the source of such service must provide the service to the general public under similar terms and conditions; or (2) offered and sold competitively in substantial quantities in the commercial marketplace *and* the price is based on an established **catalog** or **market price** for specific tasks performed under standard commercial terms and conditions.

See FAR 2.101 for the detailed definition of "commercial item."

MARKET RESEARCH

FAR 2.101 defines "market research" as "collecting and analyzing information about capabilities within the market to satisfy agency needs." The purpose of market research is to determine the most suitable way to acquire, distribute, and support supplies and services. Before the government attempts to fulfill its needs through a contract with a commercial source, it must exhaust all other potential sources of the supplies or services. The following are the mandatory sources of supplies, in descending order of priority:

1. The agency's own inventories;

2. Other agencies' excess inventories (see FAR subpart 8.1, Excess Personal Property);

3. Federal Prison Industries, Inc. (see FAR subpart 8.6, Acquisition from Federal Prison Industries, Inc.) (**http://www.unicor.gov**);

4. Products that are on the "Procurement List" ("a list of supplies…and services that the Committee has determined are suitable for purchase by the government…") maintained by the Committee for Purchase from People Who Are Blind or Severely Disabled (see FAR subpart 8.7, Acquisition from Nonprofit Agencies Employing People Who Are Blind or Severely Disabled) (**http://www.abilityone.gov**); and

5. Stock programs operated by the General Services Administration (GSA) (such as furniture and office supplies), the Defense Logistics Agency (military-unique items and fuel), the Department of Veterans Affairs (medical supplies), and military inventory control points (spare parts for military equipment).

Agencies must acquire services that are on the "Procurement List" maintained by the Committee for Purchase from People Who Are Blind or Severely Disabled from "AbilityOne" participating nonprofit agencies.

Also, the following supplies and services must be acquired from or through specified sources:

- Public utility services (see FAR part 41, Acquisition of Utility Services)

- Printing and related supplies (see FAR subpart 8.8, Acquisition of Printing and Related Supplies)

- Leased motor vehicles (see FAR subpart 8.11, Leasing of Motor Vehicles)

- Strategic and critical materials (for example, metals and ores) from inventories exceeding Defense National Stockpile requirements (detailed information is available from the Defense Logistics Agency Strategic Materials, 8725 John J. Kingman Road, Suite 3229, Fort Belvoir, VA 22060-6223)

- Helium (see FAR subpart 8.5, Acquisition of Helium).

If an agency is unable to satisfy its requirements for supplies and services from these mandatory sources, it is *encouraged* to consider satisfying requirements from or through the following non-mandatory sources (in no order of priority):

- *For supplies*: Federal Supply Schedules (FSS), governmentwide acquisition contracts (GWACs), multi-agency contracts (MACs), and any other procurement instruments intended for use by multiple agencies, including blanket purchase agreements (BPAs) under FSS contracts (see Chapter 13).

- *For services*: In addition to the procurement instruments for supplies mentioned above, agencies are encouraged to consider Federal Prison Industries, Inc.

If the agency cannot fulfill its requirements for supplies or services through *any* of these sources, it may solicit commercial sources (including educational and nonprofit institutions) in the open market.

All of the government sources of supplies and services publish catalogs online. For example, GSA publishes catalogs and bulletins of property declared "excess" by federal agencies, as well as catalogs of the items in its stock program. Federal Prison Industries and the Committee for Purchase from People Who Are Blind or Severely Disabled publish catalogs of the supplies and services they (or their partners) can provide. Contractors awarded FSS contracts by GSA must submit their pricelists to **GSA** *Advantage!* (**https://www.gsaadvantage.gov**), and those FSS contracts are posted on the **GSA eLibrary (http://www.gsaelibrary. gsa.gov/)** (see Chapter 13). So it is relatively easy for a market researcher (usually the "acquisition planner" – see Chapter 2) to determine whether a particular supply or service is available from somewhere other than a commercial source.

If the market research indicates the needed supplies or services are not available from any of the mandatory or preferred sources, the market researcher may investigate the commercial marketplace to determine whether it has something suitable. Because the conduct of detailed market research entails some expense to the government, it is performed only before:

- Developing new requirements documents (such as specifications or SOWs);

- Soliciting offers expected to exceed the $150,000 simplified acquisition threshold (see Chapter 6); or

- Soliciting offers not expected to exceed the simplified acquisition threshold when adequate information is not available and the circumstances justify the cost.

However, even those making micro-purchases (generally, purchases that do not exceed $3,500 for civilian agencies or $5,000 for the Department of Defense – see Chapter 6) are required to consult readily-available information (such as advertisements or on-line commercial catalogs) to ensure the selected supply or service will meet the government's needs at a fair and reasonable price. The extent of the research will depend on such factors as urgency, estimated dollar value, complexity, and past experience.

Regardless of the magnitude of the research effort, market research attempts to determine the following:

- Whether the government's needs can be met by items available in the commercial marketplace, available in the commercial marketplace with modifications, or "**nondevelopmental items**" (that is, any previously developed item used *exclusively* by a federal agency, a state or local government, or a foreign government with which the United States has a mutual defense cooperation agreement – see FAR 2.101 for the full definition of "nondevelopmental item").

- Customary practices regarding customizing, modifying, or tailoring of commercial items to meet customer needs (and associated costs).

- Customary practices under which commercial sales are made (such as warranties, buyer financing, and discounts).

- Requirements of any laws and regulations unique to the item (such as Department of Defense restrictions on foreign sources of particular items – see Chapter 12).

- The availability of items that contain recovered materials and items that are energy efficient (see below).

- Distribution and support capabilities of potential suppliers.

- Size and status of potential sources (see Chapter 11).

The market researcher can use any or all of the following techniques when conducting his research:

- Contact knowledgeable individuals in government and industry regarding the markets capabilities.

- Review recent market research on the same or similar supplies or services.

- Publish "**requests for information**" (RFI) in technical, scientific, or business publications.

- Query government databases for information relevant to the acquisition.

- Participate in interactive, on-line communications among industry, acquisition personnel, and customers.

- Obtain source lists for similar supplies or services from other contracting activities, trade associations, or other sources.

- Review catalogs and other generally available product literature published or placed on-line by manufacturers, distributors, and dealers.

- Hold presolicitation conferences early in the acquisition process to obtain opinions and suggestions from potential sources.

If the market research establishes that a commercial supply or service can meet the government's needs, the acquisition planner must describe the need in sufficient detail for potential offerors to know which commercial supplies or services may be suitable. For purchases of commercial supplies or services expected to exceed the simplified acquisition threshold (generally, $150,000), the description must describe the supply or service *and* how the agency intends to use the supply or service in terms of the function to be performed (that is, what the government wants the item or contractor to do), the required performance (such as the minimum "miles per hour" a vehicle must attain), or essential physical characteristics (such as size or color). When the contracting officer receives the description of the government's needs and funds from the acquisition planner, and those needs can be satisfied by a commercial item, the contracting officer uses the procedures in FAR part 12, Acquisition of Commercial Items, to make the purchase (see Chapter 6).

If the market research does not identify any commercial supply or service that can meet the government's needs, the acquisition planner will select either an existing requirements document (such as a specification or an SOW), modify or combine existing requirements documents, or create a new requirements document, consistent with the following order of precedence:

- Documents mandated by law.

- Documents that describe the government's needs in terms of required performance or function (such as a "performance work statement" [PWS] or "statement of objectives" [SOO] – see below).

- Documents that describe the government's needs in detail (such as required dimensions, configuration, tolerances, chemical composition, components, procedures, processes, and similar characteristics).

- Standards, specifications, and related publications issued by the government for the non-repetitive acquisition of items.

See FAR part 10, Market Research, and FAR part 11, Describing Agency Needs, for more on the process.

Contract "Bundling"

"Bundling" is defined in FAR 2.101, Definitions, as "consolidating two or more requirements for supplies or services, previously provided or performed under separate smaller contracts, into a solicitation for a single contract that is likely to be unsuitable for award to a small business concern due to: (i) the diversity, size, or specialized nature of the elements of the performance specified; (ii) the aggregate dollar value of the anticipated award; (iii) the geographical dispersion of the contract performance sites; or (4) any combination of the factors described in paragraphs (i), (ii), and (iii) of this definition."

With a bundled contract, the government awards a contract for the operation of an entire organization (such as a military base), or a contract for several commercial activities that have been "bundled" together for administrative ease, and leaves it to the contractor to subcontract the individual activities as necessary (such as the laundry, cafeteria, motor pool). Where a small business might have had a chance of winning a contract for an individual activity, it has little or no chance of winning a bundled contract.

The bundle concept was favored by many in government because there are fewer administrative costs associated with the award of one large contract as opposed to dozens of small contracts. With a single large contractor operating an entire organization, it was easy for the government to point out a problem and tell the contractor to fix it. However, Congress was concerned that the bundle concept reduced contract opportunities for small businesses, so it passed the **Small Business Reauthorization Act of 1997** (Public Law 105-135), which requires agencies to conduct market research and justify "the measurably substantial benefits" that would be derived from the bundling. "Measurably substantial benefits" may include cost savings, quality improvements that will save time or improve or enhance performance or efficiency, reduction in acquisition cycle times, better terms and conditions, and any other benefits.

The agency may determine bundling to be necessary and justified if it would derive measurably substantial benefits equivalent to: (1) 10% of the estimated contract if its value is $94,000,000 or less; or (2) 5% of the estimated contract value or $9,400,000, whichever is greater, if its value exceeds $94,000,000.

In addition, the law allows small businesses to team on bundled contracts without losing their small business status (see Chapter 11).

Just because an agency may use the bundle concept to contract out an entire organization does not mean small businesses are eliminated from participation. Generally, the winning prime contractor subcontracts pieces of the operation to small businesses – perhaps the military base's laundry, cafeteria, and motor pool. In fact, dealing with a large prime contractor rather than directly with the government usually means less paperwork and administrative red tape for the small business subcontractor. However, a small business with a government contract enjoys all the rights of a government contractor, rights that a large prime contractor might not extend to its subcontractors. This is an on-going battle that will only get rougher as agency budgets get stretched to the limit and the aging federal workforce retires at an increasing rate.

SPECIFICATIONS

Ordinarily, a specification describes the technical and quality requirements for **supplies** that the government purchases regularly, although some specifications describe the requirements for commercial-type services. Government specifications are divided into two groups: federal specifications and military specifications. Federal specifications cover the "civilian-type" supplies or services that both civilian and military agencies use (such as brooms, paint, and filing cabinets). Military specifications describe supplies or services that are peculiar to the military and have no application or potential use by civilian agencies (such as bombs, cannons, and tanks).

Federal specifications are identified by a letter (or letters), followed by the first letter of the first word in the title, and a set of numbers. For example, the federal specification for Sulfuric Acid, Electrolyte (for Storage Batteries) is O-S-801; the federal specification for Setscrews: Hexagon Socket and Spline Socket, Headless is FF-S-200. Military specifications are identified in the same way as federal specifications except that the first group of letters is "MIL". For example, MIL-C-2202 is a military specification for Coveralls, Men's, Cotton, Sateen. Some military specifications are identified as "MIL-DTL-", which indicates the specification identifies the important details of the item.

Many specifications cover several different grades, types, or styles of a supply or service. In addition, most specifications provide the contracting officer with several options from which to choose: several methods of performing inspections, different types of packaging, optional testing procedures, and similar choices. When a specification gives the contracting officer options, the contracting officer must state in the solicitation (and resulting contract) the options that apply.

There are two indexes of government specifications: the **General Services Administration Index of Federal Specifications, Standards, and Commercial Item Descriptions** (GSA Index) (**http://www.gsa.gov/portal/content/100847**), and the Department of Defense **Acquisition Streamlining and Standardization Information System** (ASSIST) (**http://quicksearch.dla.mil/**).

With the emphasis on moving away from purchasing supplies and services that comply with detailed government specifications to purchasing commercial products, federal and military specifications are being converted to "**commercial item descriptions**" whenever possible.

Commercial Item Descriptions

A **commercial item description** (CID) is a simplified specification that describes the essential design, functional, or performance characteristics of commercially available products that will satisfy the government's needs. CIDs are technical documents that are easy for suppliers to use and that allow manufacturers to provide products to the government from their standard product line. CIDs are concise, descriptive documents that relay requirements to potential suppliers in simple language. They are not intended to be instructions on how to make a particular product.

CIDs are numbered sequentially from A-A-1, through A-A-99999 and are identified as either "Metric," "Inch-Pound," or "Not Measurement Sensitive." Each concisely describes the salient functional and performance characteristics of the product that ensure the required levels of quality and serviceability are attained. Design requirements, such as dimensions, materials, composition, and formulation are included in a CID only to the extent design control is necessary. When other than form, fit, and functional interchangeability are essential with respect to reparable items, design details may be specified to the extent necessary to ensure interchangeability of replacement parts.

CIDs are included in the GSA Index along with federal specifications. A CID is included as an attachment to the sample solicitation in Appendix B.

Purchase Descriptions

A purchase description is another simplified specification. It is used when the preparation of a specification would be impracticable or uneconomical, such as when the government purchases the supply or service infrequently and there is no commercial equivalent (if the supply or service is purchased *frequently* and there is no commercial equivalent, the government develops a specification). A purchase description must describe the essential physical and functional characteristics of the supply or service, including the following information when applicable:

- Common nomenclature;

- Kind of material (type, grade, alternatives);

- Electrical data;

- Dimensions, size, or capacity;

- Principles of operation;

- Restrictive environmental conditions;

- Intended use, including location within an assembly and the essential operating conditions;

- Equipment with which the item is to be used; and

- Other pertinent information that further describes the item, material, or service.

Purchase descriptions have no set formats, but normally they do not exceed a few pages.

Purchase descriptions do not specify a product or a particular feature that is peculiar to one manufacturer's product unless that feature is essential to the government's requirements and similar products lacking the feature will not meet the minimum requirements.

The minimum acceptable purchase description is a **brand name or equal**. For example, "Campbell's® tomato soup or equal" is the minimum purchase description that the government may use in defining its requirements for tomato soup. Each solicitation that specifies a "brand name or equal" must contain the following information, as applicable, in addition to the essential physical and functional characteristics of the supply:

- Complete common generic identification of the required item;

- Applicable model, make, or catalog number for each brand name product referenced, and the identity of the commercial catalog in which it appears;

- The name of the manufacturer, producer, or distributor of each brand name product referenced; and

- A general description of the salient physical, functional, or performance characteristics of the brand name item that an "equal" item must meet to be acceptable for award.

If a bidder offers the "brand name" product, its bid is evaluated normally. However, if a bidder offers an "equal" product (for example, "Heinz® tomato soup"), it must supply descriptive literature with its bid that will enable the government to determine the "equality" of the offered product. This descriptive literature might include specifications, illustrations, drawings, and other information. The government is not responsible for locating or securing any information that is not identified in the bid or is not reasonably available.

STATEMENTS OF WORK

Though the government acquires many commercial-type services described by specifications, most services the government acquires must be tailored to the particular characteristics of the problem or the location where the services are to be performed. The government provides this information to prospective contractors through a **statement of work** (SOW). After the government awards the contract, the SOW becomes part of the contract and the primary standard for measuring the contractor's performance.

Because the SOW defines the work to be performed under the contract and is written to address a particular situation, it is critical that the SOW writer (normally the acquisition planner – see Chapter 2) work closely with the contracting officer to insure consistency between the SOW and the solicitation.

Though there is no set format for SOWs, the following format is commonly used:

- **Section 1 – Scope**: Includes a brief statement of what is and is not covered, and sometimes includes necessary background information.

- **Section 2 – Applicable Documents**: Includes all specifications, standards, and other documents cited in the Section 3 of the SOW.

- **Section 3 – Requirements**: Identifies the specific work or tasks the contractor is to perform and what the result should be; includes the inspection and acceptance criteria and the respective duties of the contractor and the government.

Because SOWs are custom-tailored, they are not listed in the GSA Index or the ASSIST. However, because they are custom-tailored, many SOWs suffer from:

- *Over-specification*: The SOW writer specifies in detail all the actions the contractor is to perform rather than allowing the contractor to choose the method that best suits the situation and its capabilities; SOWs should describe **functions** or expected **performance**; or

- *Ambiguous phrases*: The SOW writer, unsure how to describe the government's needs, uses phrases that can have many different meanings, such as "skillfully fitted," "commercial practices," "highest quality," and "as directed by the contracting officer."

Prospective contractors should carefully review each SOW to make sure it clearly and concisely describes the tasks and the contractor's obligations.

Performance-Based Acquisition

Performance-based acquisition (PBA) is a method of contracting for services in which the agency describes its needs in terms of what it wants to achieve, not how to do it. The difference between a PBA and the traditional way of contracting is the difference between "I want the cattle to remain in this field" and "I want a barb-wire fence 4 and 1/2 feet high, supported by posts placed 10 feet apart and inserted 30 inches in the ground, to surround the field . . . " The first approach identifies what the desired outcome is (cattle remain in the field) and allows the offeror to propose a solution (perhaps an electric invisible fence), while the second dictates a solution that may not be the best or most effective.

As mentioned above, "documents that describe the government's needs in terms of required performance or function" are preferred over all other types of requirements documents except those "mandated by law." This preference reflects the increasing reliance of the government on the commercial sector to perform its work and provide solutions. The government has set a PBA goal of 40% of all eligible service contracts – not all service contracts are suitable for PBA: research and development, architect-engineering, construction, utilities, and medical services are not suited for PBAs.

PBAs have three characteristics:

1. They describe the requirements in terms of results required rather than the methods of performance of the work;

2. They use measurable performance standards (in terms of quality, timeliness, quantity, etc.) and quality assurance surveillance plans; and

3. They rely on financial incentives to encourage competitors to develop and institute innovative and cost-effective methods of performing the work.

While most PBAs describe the requirements with an SOW (called a "performance work statement" [PWS]) as is the case with most service contracts, **statements of objectives** (SOOs) are used with increasing frequency. The SOO is prepared by the acquisition planner and identifies the government's primary objectives in entering into a contract. Then each offeror uses that SOO to develop and propose a PWS that will meet those stated objectives. The winning approach is incorporated into the contract as the PWS (the SOO does not become part of the contract).

An effective SOO is one that is clear, concise, and provides potential offerors enough information and detail to structure a sound program that is executable and will satisfy the government. Though there is no standard format for an SOO, the SOO includes the following information:

- Purpose;
- Scope or mission;
- Period and place of performance;
- Background;
- Performance objectives (that is, required results); and
- Any operating constraints.

The increased use of the SOO is directly attributable to the emphasis on commercial solutions for government needs; a SOO gives offerors the maximum flexibility to propose an innovative approach.

In addition to the key performance requirements (generally no more than 4 or 5), an **acceptable quality level** (AQL) is specified for each – "Performance Standard: Bus arrives within two minutes of the scheduled arrival time at each stop on the route. AQL: Bus may be up to five minutes late at 5% of the stops."

Based on this information and any supplemental information and attachments, the offeror prepares a proposed PWS for the effort, and this proposed PWS will be evaluated against all other offers in accordance with the evaluation criteria in the solicitation's Section M, Evaluation Factors for Award (see the discussion of the "Uniform Contract Format" in Chapter 7, and "Evaluating Proposals" in Chapter 8). The offeror providing the "best value" to the government wins the contract.

Once the agency selects a contractor to perform the PBA, the agency monitors the contractor's performance closely to make sure the contractor is complying with the PWS it proposed:

■ Is the acquisition achieving its cost, schedule, and performance goals?

■ Is the contractor meeting or exceeding the contract's performance-based requirements?

■ How effective is the contractor's performance in meeting or contributing to the agency's program performance goals?

■ Are there problems or issues that can be addressed to mitigate contract risk?

This close surveillance is all the more important with a PBA contract because the offeror won the PBA contract based on the solution it proposed, and the PBA contract contains disincentives for work that does not meet the AQLs (and possibly incentives for exceeding the AQLs).

To help contracting professionals throughout the government understand and implement PBA, the Departments of Agriculture, Commerce, Defense, and the Treasury, and the General Services Administration have collaborated on the development of **"Seven Steps to Performance-Based Acquisition,"** which is available at **http://www.acquisition.gov/seven_steps/home.html**. It contains guidance, samples, policy documents, and other helpful information.

See FAR subpart 37.6, Performance-Based Contracting, for more information.

QUALIFICATION REQUIREMENTS

Occasionally, the quality of a product (a supply or service) is critical to the agency's mission but the testing necessary to determine the product's quality is expensive and time-consuming. The head of the agency can establish **qualification requirements** for these products, and require manufacturers to have their products examined and tested prior to contract award. These qualification requirements must specify all the requirements a manufacturer (or its products) must satisfy to become eligible for contract award.

There are **three** kinds of qualification requirements:

■ *Qualified bidders list (QBL)*: A list of bidders that have had their products examined and tested and that have satisfied all applicable qualification requirements;

- *Qualified manufacturers list (QML)*: A list of manufacturers that have had their products examined and tested and have satisfied all applicable qualification requirements; and

- *Qualified products list (QPL)*: A list of products that have been examined, tested, and found to satisfy all applicable qualification requirements.

Manufacturers and other potential sources that meet, or whose products meet, the qualification requirements are placed on the appropriate QBL, QML, or QPL and are eligible for future contract awards. However, an offeror that is *not* on the appropriate QBL, QML, or QPL *can* receive the contract if it demonstrates to the satisfaction of the contracting officer that the offeror (or its products) meets the qualification requirements or can meet them before contract award. Nevertheless, the contracting officer does not have to delay a contract award so an offeror can demonstrate its ability to meet the qualification requirements.

The government must notify the public of the qualification requirements through **FedBizOpps** (see Chapter 5), urging manufacturers and other potential sources to demonstrate their ability to meet the standards specified for qualification. Normally, the manufacturer bears the cost of the evaluation and testing, but the government may choose to bear the cost for a small business if the government determines that additional qualified sources or products are likely to produce enough savings from increased competition to amortize the qualification costs within a reasonable period.

Specifications requiring a qualified product are identified in the GSA Index and the ASSIST. **FAR 52.209-1, Qualification Requirements**, is required to be in all solicitations and contracts subject to qualification requirements.

FAR subpart 9.2, Qualification Requirements, has more information on the topic.

ACCEPTABLE MATERIAL

All supply contracts, except those for commercial items, include **FAR 52.211-5, Material Requirements**, which requires contractors to provide "supplies that are new, reconditioned, or remanufactured" that meet contract requirements, including performance, reliability, and life expectancy. The clause defines "new supplies" as:

- **Virgin material:** Previously unused raw material, including previously unused copper, aluminum, lead, zinc, iron, other metal or metal ore, or any undeveloped resource that is, or will be, a source of raw materials. However, agencies *may not require* virgin materials *unless* compelled by law or regulation or virgin material is vital for safety or for meeting performance requirements.

- **Recovered material:** Waste materials and by-products that have been recovered or diverted from solid waste, including postconsumer material.

- **Materials and byproducts generated from, and reused within, an original manufacturing process.**

However, offerors *may propose* providing **unused former government surplus property,** or supplies that are **used, reconditioned** ("restored to the original normal operating condition by readjustments and material replacement"), or **remanufactured** ("factory rebuilt to original specifications"). However, such material must be authorized by the contracting officer.

When acquiring commercial items, the contracting officer must consider the customary practices in the industry for the item being acquired. The contracting officer may include in the solicitation a requirement that offerors provide information on any unused former government surplus property or used, reconditioned, or remanufactured supplies the offeror intends to use under the contract, but the information must be limited to that normally provided in commercial practice.

See FAR Subpart 11.3, Acceptable Material, for more on the requirements.

SUSTAINABLE ACQUISITIONS

Agencies are required to advance "sustainable acquisition" by ensuring that 95% of new contract actions (including those for construction) contain requirements for products that are designated as energy-efficient, water-efficient, biobased, environmentally preferable, non-ozone depleting, or made with recovered materials (these are commonly referred to as "green" products). Contracts performed outside the United States and weapons systems are excepted from this requirement, and the head of the agency may exempt intelligence activities, law enforcement activities, and other activities in the interest of national security.

Energy-Efficient Products

When buying energy-consuming products, contracting officers must obtain products listed in the **ENERGY STAR®** program or **Federal Energy Management Program** (FEMP).

ENERGY STAR® is an Environmental Protection Agency (EPA) program that identifies energy-efficient products and practices, primarily consumer products. ENERGY STAR® products include computers, televisions, water heaters, refrigerators, clothes washers, dishwashers, windows/doors/skylights, air conditioners, lighting (compact fluorescent light bulbs [CFLs], bulbs, and fixtures), and insulation (seal and insulate). Information is available at **http://www.energystar. gov/**.

FEMP is a Department of Energy (DOE) program that identifies energy- and water-efficient products not covered by the ENERGY STAR® program – FEMP-designated products are primarily industrial products, such as chillers, commercial water heaters, exterior lighting, water cooled ice machines, and food service equipment. Information is available at **http://energy.gov/eere/femp/federal-energy-management-program**.

An agency is not required to procure an ENERGY STAR® or FEMP-designated product if none is reasonably available that meets the agency's functional requirement, or none is cost-effective over the life of the product when taking energy cost savings into account.

FAR 52.223-15, Energy Efficiency in Energy-Consuming Products, must be included in solicitations and contracts when energy-consuming products listed in the ENERGY STAR® program or FEMP will be delivered; acquired by the contractor for use in performing services at a federally-controlled facility; furnished by the contractor for use by the government; or specified in the design of a building or work, or incorporated during its construction, renovation, or maintenance.

For more on the acquisition of energy-efficient products, see FAR subpart 23.2, Energy and Water Efficiency and Renewable Energy.

Water-Efficient Products

Executive Order 13514, Federal Leadership in Environmental, Energy, and Economic Performance, established policy that the government use and manage water through water-efficient means by: (1) reducing potable water consumption intensity to include low-flow fixtures and efficient cooling towers; (2) reducing agency, industry, landscaping, and agricultural water consumption; and (3) storm water management.

For more on the acquisition of water-efficient products, see paragraph (b) of FAR 23.202, Policy.

Products Made with Recovered Materials and Biobased Products

These two types of products are grouped together in FAR subpart 23.4, Use of Recovered Materials and Biobased Products. "EPA-designated items" are products that are or can be made with recovered material ("waste materials and by-products recovered or diverted from solid waste..." [FAR 2.101, Definitions]). "U.S. Department of Agriculture (USDA)- designated items" are products that are or can be made with biobased materials ("a product determined by the U.S. Department of Agriculture to be a commercial or industrial product [other than food or feed] that is composed, in whole or in significant part, of biological products, including renewable domestic agricultural materials and forestry materials" – FAR 2.101).

If an item being acquired is on either of these lists, "agencies shall purchase these products to the maximum extent practicable without jeopardizing the intended use of the product while maintaining a satisfactory level of competition at a reasonable price." This applies if the price of the designated item exceeds $10,000, or the aggregate amount paid for designated items in the preceding fiscal year was $10,000 or more.

- **EPA-Designated Items:** EPA-designated items are grouped into eight categories: construction products (such as floor tiles and roofing materials), landscaping products (such as lawn and garden edging), nonpaper office products (such as presentation folders and toner cartridges), paper and paper products (such as sanitary tissue products and newsprint), park and recreation products (such as park benches and picnic tables), transportation products (such as traffic barriers and traffic cones), vehicular products (such as engine coolant and retread tires), and miscellaneous products (such as bike racks and industrial drums).

  EPA-designated items are those for which EPA has provided recommendations for post-consumer content and recovered materials content (at **https://www3.epa.gov/epawaste/conserve/tools/cpg/products/index.htm**).

  A company can request that its product(s) be added to the "CPG [Comprehensive Procurement Guideline] Product Supplier Directory" (**https://www3.epa.gov/epawaste/conserve/tools/cpg/supplier_support.htm**) by sending information on the product's recycled content, product category, and specific product type, and contact information for the company. Such a request must be sent by email to CPG Supplier Directory Support (**reddoor.marlene @epa.gov**), and a response should be provided within 15 business days.

- **Biobased Products:** USDA-designated products are in 97 biobased program product categories, and those are grouped into 14 functional areas, among them: minor construction (such as plastic lumber and wood stains); custodial services (such as air fresheners and glass cleaners); grounds maintenance (such as animal repellents and fertilizers)' personal care and toiletries (such as hair care and hand cleaners); food service/cafeteria (such as disposable cutlery and dishwashing products); office supplies (such as paper products and inks), and household supplies (such as bed linens and laundry detergent). The biobased product categories are available at **http://www.biopreferred. gov/BioPreferred/faces/catalog/Catalog.xhtml**.

  A company can request that its product(s) be added to the "BioPreferred Catalog" if it meets the minimum biobased content standard for the product category. The company must acquire a USDA eAuthentication account first (**https://www.eauth.usda.gov/MainPages/index.aspx**), then use the account to submit products for inclusion in the BioPreferred catalog.

  Detailed information on the biobased program is available at **http://www. biopreferred.gov/BioPreferred/**.

Environmentally Preferable Products

FAR subpart 23.7, Contracting for Environmentally Preferable Products and Services, specifically identifies two products:

■ **<u>Plastic ring carriers that are degradable</u>** must be acquired ("a device that contains at least one hole greater than $1\frac{3}{4}$ inches in diameter which is made, used, or designed for the purpose of packaging, transporting, or carrying multipackaged cans or bottles") (see 40 CFR part 238, Degradable Plastic Ring Carriers). See paragraph (b)(8) of FAR 23.703, Policy.

■ **<u>Electronic Products Environmental Assessment Tool (EPEAT)</u>:** Agencies must meet at least 95% of their annual acquisition of electronic products with EPEAT-registered electronic products unless there is no EPEAT standard for such products.

There are three general classes of EPEAT-registered products: imaging equipment (such as copiers and printers), computers and displays (such as desktop computers and tablet notebooks), and televisions.

EPEAT-registered personal computer products must meet one of the Institute of Electrical and Electronics Engineers (IEEE) 1680™ , Family of Standards for Environmental Assessment of Electronic Products: 1680.1™ – Standard for Environmental Assessment of Personal Computer Products, Including Notebook Personal Computers, Desktop Personal Computers, and Personal Computer Displays; 1680.2™ – Standard for the Environmental Assessment of Imaging Equipment; and 1680.3™ – Standard for the Environmental Assessment of Televisions (**http://grouper.ieee.org/groups/1680/**). The IEEE 1680™ family of standards meets EPA-issued guidance on environmentally preferable products and services.

Each of the standards specify several categories of environmental attributes that cover the full life-cycle of electronic products: from material selection, energy conservation, product longevity, through end-of-life management. Each of these categories include "required" and "optional" criteria. For example, each of the general classes of EPEAT-registered products address packaging. One of the packaging "required" criterion is "separable packing materials," and one of the packaging "optional" criterion is "provision of take-back program for packaging."

EPEAT-registered products come in three levels: "Bronze" products must meet all required IEEE 1680™ criteria; "Silver" products must meet all required criteria and 50% of the optional criteria; and "Gold" products must meet all required criteria and 75% of the optional criteria. The three EPEAT clauses (FAR 52.223-13, Acquisition of EPEAT®-Registered Imaging Equipment; FAR 52.223-14, Acquisition of EPEAT®-Registered Televisions; and FAR 52.223-16, Acquisition of EPEAT®-Registered Personal Computer Products) make EPEAT® Bronze registration the standard that contractors must meet. However, agencies are encouraged to acquire EPEAT® silver- or gold-registered products, and may require that EPEAT® silver- or gold-registered products be provided when there are sufficient EPEAT® silver- or gold-registered products available to meet agency needs.

Manufacturers seeking to have their product(s) listed in the EPEAT® registry must execute an EPEAT® Market Surveillance Entity (MSE) Registry License and Subscriber Agreement, then contract with an EPEAT® approved Product Registration Entity (PRE) for product verification. Additional information on the EPEAT® registry process is available at **http://www.epeat.net/resources/for-manufacturers/**.

Go to **http://www.epeat.net/** for more information on EPEAT-registered products.

Non-Ozone Depleting Substances and Minimizing Hydrofluorocarbon Use

FAR subpart 23.8, Ozone-Depleting Substances and Hydrofluorocarbons, requires the inclusion of four clauses when appropriate: FAR 52.223-11, Ozone-Depleting Substances, in solicitations and contracts for ozone-depleting substances or for supplies that may contain or be manufactured with ozone-depleting substances; FAR 52.223-12, Refrigeration Equipment and Air Conditioners, in solicitations and contracts for services when the contract includes the maintenance, repair, or disposal of any equipment or appliance using ozone-depleting substances as a refrigerant, such as air conditioners, including motor vehicles, refrigerators, chillers, or freezers; FAR 52.223-20, Aerosols, in solicitations and contracts for products that may contain hydrofluorocarbons as a propellant or a solvent, or that involve maintenance or repair of electronic or mechanical devices; and FAR 52.223-21, Foams, in solicitations and contracts for products that may contain hydrofluorocarbons or refrigerant blends containing hydrofluorocarbons as a foam blowing agent (such as building foam insulation or appliance foam insulation). Also, FAR subpart 23.8 identifies EPA's Significant New Alternatives Policy (SNAP) program as a source of safe alternatives to ozone-depleting substances and hydroflurocarbons. For more information, go to **https://www.epa.gov/snap**.

SINGLE PROCESS INITIATIVE

The Department of Defense is undertaking a **single process initiative** (SPI) in which offerors are encouraged to propose the substitution of the commercial manufacturing or management processes being used in their facilities for the military or federal specifications cited in the solicitation. The proposed SPI processes are reviewed and accepted by a Management Council, which includes representatives of the contractor and various military agencies (such as the Defense Contract Management Agency and the Defense Contract Audit Agency). In procurements of previously developed items, SPI processes that were previously accepted by a Management Council are considered valid replacements for military or federal specifications and standards unless the head of the contracting activity determines the SPI process is not acceptable for the specific acquisition.

See Defense FAR Supplement (DFARS) 211.273, Substitutions for Military or Federal Specifications and Standards, for more on the SPI.

CHAPTER 5

FINDING GOVERNMENT CONTRACT OPPORTUNITIES

Knowing where to look for government business is no simple matter. There is no centrally located information center a contractor can contact to find out which federal agencies are buying its kinds of supplies and services. The contractor must identify the appropriate contracting activities and contact them. There are over **3,200** federal contracting activities around the world; a person can waste much precious time seeking the right ones. But that person does not have to – *if he knows where and how to look!*

FEDERAL BUSINESS OPPORTUNITIES (FedBizOpps)

The **Federal Business Opportunities** website, or "FedBizOpps" (or "FBO") is the "governmentwide point-of-entry" (GPE) for notices of upcoming solicitations **over $25,000** and contract awards **over $25,000 likely to result in the award of any subcontracts**. Businesses seeking federal markets for their supplies and services can search and retrieve solicitations for the entire federal government. A contractor does not have to register to have access – all anyone needs to do is go to **https://www.fbo.gov**, insert key words that describe the product or service, and click "Search." (**NOTE:** FedBizOpps will be consolidated with other acquisition-related databases into the **System for Award Management** [SAM] in the near future. See below for an explanation of SAM and the existing databases that will be incorporated into it.)

Synopses of Upcoming Solicitations

A contracting officer may not issue a solicitation over $25,000 until **fifteen days after its synopsis appears in FedBizOpps** (except the contracting officer may establish a shorter period for solicitations of commercial items). There are several exceptions to the synopsis requirements: purchases of perishable subsistence; electric power, gas, water, or other utilities (but not telecommunications); classified purchases; purchases from other federal agencies; purchases of emergency supplies; orders against indefinite-delivery contracts (see Chapter 10); acquisitions for foreign governments under the terms of a treaty; etc. Nevertheless, these must be synopsized whenever possible.

Even when the contracting officer intends to contract on a sole source basis, he must synopsize the solicitation in FedBizOpps. Though this requirement is intended primarily to alert the public to subcontracting opportunities, an interested contractor may submit a capability statement, proposal, or quotation that the contracting officer *must consider*.

Contractors can search synopses of upcoming solicitations in several ways:

- By keywords.

- By agency (such as "Department of Agriculture"), or by a particular office in the agency (such as "Animal and Plant Health Inspection Service"), or by a particular location of the office ("Administrative Services Division, Contracting, Minneapolis, MN").

- By the date the notice was posted.

- By type of set-aside (see Chapter 11).

- By place of performance.

- By North American Industry Classification System (NAICS) code (go to **http://www.census.gov/eos/www/naics/** and Chapter 11).

- By classification code (Figure 3 lists the alphabetic service classification codes, and Figure 4 lists the two digit supply classification codes the government uses to identify the kind of supply or service being acquired – the missing letters and numbers in the alphabetic and numeric sequences are reserved for possible later use).

Clicking on any of the links in the search results brings up the listing page for the solicitation. On the listing page will be everything posted on FedBizOpps that is related to the solicitation – the synopsis, the solicitation, solicitation amendments, attachments, and similar documents (such as "Responses to Questions").

The synopsis should be the first document viewed, because it gives a basic description of what is being acquired through the solicitation and the points-of-contact (such as the name, telephone number, and e-mail address of the contract specialist).

If interested in a particular presolicitation notice or solicitation, a contractor can click on "Add Me to Interested Vendors" or "Watch This Opportunity" (the contractor will receive email notifications for the solicitation). To do this, the contractor must register and log-on.

A – Research and Development
B – Special Studies and Analyses – Not Research and Development
C – Architect and Engineering Services
D – Information Technology and Telecommunications
E – Purchase of Structures and Facilities
F – Natural Resources Management
G – Social Services (for example, recreation, social rehabilitation, geriatric, and funeral services)
H – Quality Control, Testing, and Inspection
J – Maintenance, Repair, and Rebuilding of Equipment
K – Modification of Equipment
L – Technical Representative Services (for example, services of technical specialists required to advise and assist in the installation, checking, operation, and maintenance of complex equipment)
M – Operation of Structures and Facilities
N – Installation of Equipment (code K is appropriate when the procurement also involves modification, alteration, or rebuilding of equipment)
P – Salvage Services (services required to salvage property of any kind)
Q – Medical Services
R – Professional, Administrative, and Management Support Services
S – Utilities and Housekeeping Services (for example, gas, electricity, water, and telephone; laundry and drycleaning; custodial janitorial services; insect and rodent control; storage; garbage and trash collection; food service; fueling; fire protection; grounds maintenance; guard services)
T – Photographic, Mapping, Printing, and Publication Services (for example, film processing; cataloging; charting; reproduction; technical writing; art; printing)
U – Education and Training Services
V – Transportation, Travel, and Relocation Services (for example, passenger transportation; air charter; port operations; stevedoring; vehicle hire; vessel towing; travel agent)
W – Lease or Rental of Equipment (for example, lease of ground handling equipment; lease of metalworking machinery)
X – Lease or Rental of Structures and Facilities
Y – Construction of Structures and Facilities (new construction and major additions to existing buildings or facilities)
Z – Maintenance, Repair, and Alteration of Real Property (painting, building maintenance, roads maintenance and repair)

Figure 3 – Service Classification Codes

10 – Weapons
11 – Nuclear Ordnance
12 – Fire Control Equipment
13 – Ammunition and Explosives
14 – Guided Missiles
15 – Aircraft and Airframe Structural Components
16 – Aircraft Components and Accessories
17 – Aircraft Launching, Landing, and Ground Handling Equipment
18 – Space Vehicles
19 – Ships, Small Craft, Pontoons, and Floating Docks
20 – Ship and Marine Equipment
22 – Railway Equipment
23 – Ground Effect Vehicles, Motor Vehicles, Trailers, and Cycles
24 – Tractors
25 – Vehicular Equipment Components
26 – Tires and Tubes
28 – Engines, Turbines, and Components
29 – Engine Accessories
30 – Mechanical Power Transmission Equipment
31 – Bearings
32 – Woodworking Machinery and Equipment
34 – Metalworking Machinery
35 – Service and Trade Equipment
36 – Special Industry Equipment
37 – Agricultural Machinery and Equipment
38 – Construction, Mining, Excavating, and Highway Maintenance Equipment
39 – Materials Handling Equipment
40 – Rope, Cable, Chain, and Fittings
41 – Refrigeration, Air Conditioning, and Air Circulating Equipment
42 – Fire Fighting, Rescue, and Safety Equipment; and Environmental Protection Equipment and Materials
43 – Pumps and Compressors
44 – Furnace, Steam Plant, and Drying Equipment; and Nuclear Reactors
45 – Plumbing, Heating, and Waste Disposal Equipment
46 – Water Purification and Sewage Treatment Equipment
47 – Pipe, Tubing, Hose, and Fittings
48 – Valves
49 – Maintenance and Repair Shop Equipment
51 – Hand Tools
52 – Measuring Tools
53 – Hardware and Abrasives
54 – Prefabricated Structures and Scaffolding

55 – Lumber, Millwork, Plywood, and Veneer
56 – Construction and Building Materials
58 – Communication, Detection, and Coherent Radiation Equipment
59 – Electrical and Electronic Equipment Components
60 – Fiber Optics Materials, Components, Assemblies, and Accessories
61 – Electric Wire, and Power and Distribution Equipment
62 – Lighting Fixtures and Lamps
63 – Alarm, Signal, and Security Detection Systems
65 – Medical, Dental, and Veterinary Equipment and Supplies
66 – Instruments and Laboratory Equipment
67 – Photographic Equipment
68 – Chemicals and Chemical Products
69 – Training Aids and Devices
70 – Automatic Data Processing Equipment (Including Firmware), Software, Supplies, and Support Equipment
71 – Furniture
72 – Household and Commercial Furnishings and Appliances
73 – Food Preparation and Serving Equipment
74 – Office Machines, Text Processing Systems, and Visible Record Equipment
75 – Office Supplies and Devices
76 – Books, Maps, and Other Publications
77 – Musical Instruments, Phonographs, and Home-Type Radios
78 – Recreational and Athletic Equipment
79 – Cleaning Equipment and Supplies
80 – Brushes, Paints, Sealers, and Adhesives
81 – Containers, Packaging, and Packing Supplies
83 – Textiles, Leather, Furs, Apparel and Shoe Findings, Tents, and Flags
84 – Clothing, Individual Equipment, and Insignia
85 – Toiletries
87 – Agricultural Supplies
88 – Live Animals
89 – Subsistence (Food)
91 – Fuels, Lubricants, Oils, and Waxes
93 – Nonmetallic Fabricated Materials
94 – Nonmetallic Crude Materials
95 – Metal Bars, Sheets, and Shapes
96 – Ores, Minerals, and Their Primary Products
99 – Miscellaneous

Figure 4 – Supply Classification Codes

The following is a typical synopsis:

Agency: Department of Health and Human Services
Office: Agency for Healthcare Research and Quality (AHRQ), 540 Gaither Road, Rockville, Maryland 20850
Solicitation Number: AHRQ-17-10004
Posted: February 28, 2017
Classification Code: D – Information Technology and Telecommunications
NAICS Code: 519130 – Internet Publishing and Broadcasting and Web Search Portals
Title: Electronic Dissemination and Library Support Services
Description: AHRQ intends to request proposals and negotiate on a full and open competitive basis for electronic information dissemination and library support services. This contract will provide on-site contractor staff for the AHRQ website and the Information Resources Center (IRC) to respond to the electronic information needs of AHRQ, including IRC research support and web services, and to provide experienced and qualified personnel to perform IRC and web-related administrative, technical, and information management support services. The proposed action is anticipated to be a one-year labor-hour contract, with options for two additional years. AHRQ anticipates the Request For Proposals (RFP) will be available on or about March 15, 2017, and that the closing date will be on or about April 16, 2017.

Points of Contact: Q. Zilch, Contract Specialist, 301-555-9876, **qzilch@ahrq.hhs.gov**; and J. Doe, Contracting Officer, 301-555-7654, **jdoe@ahrq.hhs.gov**.

What does all this mean? Let's go through the synopsis step by step:

1. The synopsis begins by identifying the Department of Health and Human Services "agency," and the Agency for Healthcare Research and Quality (AHRQ) as the "office."

2. The solicitation number is "AHRQ-17-10004."

3. It identifies February 28, 2017, as the date the synopsis was posted on FedBizOpps.

4. It identifies the classification code as "D," which means it is an "information technology and telecommunications" service, and the applicable NAICS code is 519130.

5. "Electronic Dissemination and Library Support Services" is what is to be acquired.

6. The body of the synopsis briefly describes the contract effort. It will be solicited on a full and open competition basis (see Chapter 3), and is expected to produce a labor-hour contract (see Chapter 9).

7. The synopsis gives the anticipated release date (March 15, 2017) and the anticipated closing date (April 16, 2017).

8. Q. Zilch, the contract specialist, and J. Doe, the contracting officer, are the "points of contact." Their respective telephone numbers and e-mail addresses are provided. Those with questions should contact Q. Zilch first.

There is a considerable amount of information in the few lines of the synopsis. Once a person learns how to read the abbreviations, the codes, and the notes, he can quickly scan a synopsis and decide whether to request a copy of the solicitation.

One can use the synopses in FedBizOpps to find out about future solicitations. For example, construction contractors watch the architect-engineer services classification synopses ("C") because architects design buildings that someone will have to construct. Many air conditioning contractors watch the information technology equipment classification synopses ("70") because an agency that buys a mainframe computer probably will require increased air conditioning capacity. These contractors will download the solicitation, study it, and then visit the acquisition planners to find out more about the "follow-on" contract – the one in which the contractor is truly interested.

There are several other specialized "notices" that come under the "Synopsis" heading:

■ **Streamlined synopses/solicitations** are authorized for commercial items (see FAR 12.603, Streamlined Solicitation for Commercial Items, and Chapter 4 for the definition of "commercial items"). In this method, the synopsis and the solicitation are posted on FedBizOpps at the same time, and no separate solicitation is issued. The combined synopsis/solicitation is in a simplified format that is appropriate for relatively simple solicitations that do not include lengthy addenda. Since the synopsis and the solicitation are published simultaneously, the 15 day wait between publication of the synopsis and issuance of the solicitation does not apply. In addition, because the streamlined solicitation is for commercial items, the solicitation does not have to allow offerors 30 days to respond as normally required for invitations for bids and requests for proposals (see Chapters 7 and 8); however, the contracting officer must establish a solicitation response time that will afford potential offerors a reasonable opportunity to respond. See Chapter 6 for more on the streamlined synopsis/solicitations for commercial items.

■ **Sources sought notices** are placed by agencies to survey the market and alert potential sources of upcoming solicitations. Firms with the capabilities described in a sources sought notice are invited to submit information describing their capabilities to the contracting officer. A sources sought synopsis does not describe an existing solicitation, merely an agency's interest.

■ A **broad agency announcement** (BAA) is a special procedure that agencies can use when acquiring (1) basic and applied research, and (2) development unrelated to any specific system or hardware. The BAA invites proposals for studies and experiments that will advance the state of the art or increase overall knowledge and understanding in the agency's particular area of research interest. The BAA has no detailed work statement; its purpose is to elicit different technical and scientific approaches. Proposals responding to the BAA are submitted to a peer or scientific review, and the agency negotiates contracts with those proposing the most innovative efforts. The BAA is an open invitation to submit proposals during an extended period, frequently a year.

Some people tell prospective contractors to forget the FedBizOpps and concentrate their efforts on marketing to the acquisition planners. They claim a contractor cannot win a contract if it first learns of the purchase through a FedBizOpps synopsis, that there is not enough time between the synopsis and the bid or proposal due date to put together a winning bid or proposal. This may be true for innovative research and development projects and complex systems or services, but the time between the publication of the synopsis and the bid opening is sufficient to respond to most solicitations for supplies and routine or commercial services. Also, FedBizOpps is the only source for streamlined synopses/solicitations and the other notices. That is why FedBizOpps has been designated the "governmentwide point-of-entry" (GPE).

Solicitation Documents

Solicitations synopsized in FedBizOpps (including specifications, technical data, solicitation amendments, and any other pertinent information) are required to be made available through FedBizOpps (except under a few circumstances, such as when disclosure would jeopardize national security, or the size of the file makes it impracticable to post the solicitation electronically). This saves postage and gives prospective bidders and offerors instantaneous access to the solicitation, thus providing extra time to prepare a bid or offer. If FedBizOpps is not used to make solicitations available because of national security or size of the file, the contracting officer may provide solicitation documents on CD-ROM disks, by e-mail, or in paper form.

Search Agents

FedBizOpps permits prospective bidders and offerors to create and save "search agents" to look for synopses or notices that contain certain key words or meet specified criteria, such as a particular agency/office/location, procurement classification code, NAICS code, set-aside type, or place of performance zip code. The prospective bidder or offeror can run the search agent whenever desired, or can set the frequency for enabling the search agent – for example, it can be scheduled to search once a week, once a month, every three days, every day. When a search agent finds a notice that contains the key words or meets the specified criteria and has been added since the last search, it sends an e-mail notice containing a link to the solicitation or notice.

The prospective bidder or offeror is not restricted to the creation of a single search agent but may create multiple search agents for different criteria – different NAICS codes, different places of performance, etc. It is up to the prospective bidder or offeror to decide how many search agents to employ.

Interested Vendors List

FedBizOpps permits contracting officers to allow prospective bidders and offerors to join and view a published list of vendors interested in a particular solicitation. This is useful for those who are interested in teaming on procurement opportunities. If the contracting officer enables this capability, those who are interested in a particular solicitation (and registered with FedBizOpps) may click on the "Add Me to Interested Vendors" button on the listing page for a solicitation. The contracting officer has the option of making the Interested Vendors List available to the public, and anyone (registered or not) can view the list of interested vendors by clicking on the "Interested Vendors List" link. If a link is not available, the contracting officer has decided *not* to make the list public. No one who identifies himself as an "interested vendor" is committed to submitting a bid or proposal in response to the solicitation.

Contract Awards

Contracting officers must synopsize in FedBizOpps most contract awards that **exceed $25,000 and are likely to result in the award of subcontracts**. Contracts for classified products, perishable subsistence, utilities only available from a single source, and a few other exceptions need not be synopsized. The following is a sample award synopsis:

> **Department of Commerce, National Institute of Standards and Technology, Acquisition Management Division, 100 Bureau Drive, Building 301, Room B130, Gaithersburg, Maryland 20899-1410**
>
> **Item:** Dry Vacuum Pump Systems (6 each)
> **Classification Code:** 43 – Pumps and Compressors
> **NAICS Code:** 333911 – Pump and Pumping Equipment Manufacturing
> **Solicitation Number:** SB1341-17-R-0310
> **Contract Award Date:** March 29, 2017
> **Contract Number:** SB1341-17-C-1090
> **Contract Award Amount:** $254,745.00
> **Contractor:** Jones Vacuum Company, 1 Main Street, Suite 101, Tewksbury, Massachusetts 01876
> **Contractor DUNS:** 012345678
> **Point of Contact:** Barbara Ayn, Contracting Officer; phone 301-555-3720; fax 301-555-3214; email: **barbara_ayn@central.unicor.gov**.

Though the primary purpose of synopsizing contract awards is to alert the public to subcontracting opportunities, a smart businessperson will also check the contract awards section to find out which companies are competitors.

SYSTEM FOR AWARD MANAGEMENT (SAM)

The **System for Award Management** (SAM) (**https://www.sam.gov**) is a consolidation of several acquisition-related databases. SAM will provide users one login for access to all the capabilities previously found in the old systems, will eliminate data overlap by sharing the data throughout the award lifecycle, and will have a standardized format across all webpages to make it easier to navigate and find information.

This consolidation is being conducted in phases – Phase I was completed in 2012 and merged the Central Contractor Registration (CCR), Online Representations and Certifications Application (ORCA), and the Excluded Parties List System (EPLS). Other databases to be consolidated in future phases will be the Electronic Subcontracting Reporting System (eSRS)/the Federal Funding Accountability and Transparency Act Subaward Reporting System (FSRS); Federal Business Opportunities (FedBizOpps or FBO – see above) ; Wage Determinations On-Line (WDOL); Federal Procurement Data System (FPDS); and the combination of Past Performance Information Retrieval System (PPIRS), Contractor Performance Assessment Reporting System (CPARS), and the Federal Awardee Performance and Integrity Information System (FAPIIS). Each of these databases will be explained in the appropriate chapter of this book.

Registration

The Debt Collection Improvement Act of 1996 requires each contractor doing business with the government to furnish its Taxpayer Identification Number (TIN), and requires that the government make all contract payments by electronic funds transfer (EFT) (with a few exceptions). To collect and maintain each contractor's TIN and EFT information, the **Central Contractor Registration** (CCR) was developed. CCR is now part of SAM.

The basic registration requires the registrant to provide such information as:

- Its Data Universal Numbering System (DUNS) number (for information on obtaining a DUNS number, call Dun and Bradstreet at 1-866-705-5711, or visit its Internet address at **http://fedgov.dnb.com/webform**). Some of the information provided to obtain the DUNS number will be used in SAM, such as the registrant's address.

- Its Marketing Point of Contact Identification Number (MPIN) (a self-created password that will be used to provide access to the other systems within SAM, and as a signature when providing the Internal Revenue Service [IRS] Taxpayer Identification Number [TIN]).

- Its TIN (or Social Security Number if the registrant is a sole-proprietor) (see FAR Subpart 4.9, Taxpayer Identification Number Information).

- Its Commercial and Government Entity (CAGE) code (if the registrant does not have a CAGE code, one will be assigned).

- Corporate status (sole proprietorship, partnership, corporation, etc.).

- Type of business (tribal government, manufacturer, etc.).

- Applicable socio-economic categories (such as veteran-owned business, women-owned business, etc.).

- The financial institution's American Bank Association Routing/Transit Identification Number.

- The financial institution's Automated Clearing House (ACH) contact information.

- Registrant's remittance information (point-of-contact, address).

- Executive compensation information (names of top five executive compensated employees' names and their total compensation).

- Six-digit NAICS codes for the registrant's products or services (search at **http://www.census.gov/eos/www/naics/**).

- Product and Service Codes (PSC) (go to **https://www.acquisition.gov/ sites/default/files/page_file_uploads/PSC Manual - Final - 9 August 2015_0.pdf**) (optional).

- Average receipts over the last three fiscal years.

- Average number of employees (this information is used to calculate the registrant's business size using the Small Business Administration's [SBA] official size standards for the industry identified by the NAICS code [see Chapter 11]).

In addition, registrants are required to make "representations" and "certifications" on a variety of topics (these representations and certifications were included in the Online Representations and Certifications Application [ORCA], which is now part of SAM). Some of the representations and certifications registrants must make are:

- Whether the registrant has other plants or facilities at different addresses.

- Whether the registrant is following the guidelines established by the Environmental Protection Agency (EPA) for recovered material (see Chapter 4).

- If any of the registrant's principals are debarred, suspended, proposed for debarment, or declared ineligible for the award of contracts by any federal agency (see Chapter 7).

- Whether the registrant has been terminated for default within the past three years (see Chapter 18).

- Whether any end products delivered to the government by the registrant are foreign (non-domestic) end products.

- Whether the registrant has filed all required Equal Employment Opportunity (EEO) compliance reports (see Chapter 15).

- Whether the registrant wants to bid on, or currently holds, any Department of Defense (DOD) contracts.

The representations and certifications made in SAM are incorporated into the contract by reference. For more on representations and certifications, see FAR subpart 4.12, Representations and Certifications.

Anyone can go to the SAM website, type in a company name, DUNS number, or CAGE code, and look at the registrant's information (the registrant's financial information is restricted to government officials with a need-to-know).

See FAR subpart 4.11, System for Award Management, for more information.

OTHER SOURCES OF PROCUREMENT INFORMATION

Bid Boards

Every contracting office must maintain a bid board in a public place on which it displays either notices of solicitations or copies of solicitations between $15,000 and $25,000 (except for oral solicitations [see Chapter 6]). Many contracting offices display all solicitations over $25,000 as well. The information must be posted no later than the date the solicitation is issued, and the information must remain posted for at least 10 days or until after quotations have been opened, whichever is later. A businessperson who is in the neighborhood should stop by the contracting office and look at the bid board to see if there are any interesting solicitations "on the street."

As an alternative to this public display requirement, a contracting office can post its requirements electronically in a place that is accessible by the general public. Contracting offices that use electronic systems for public posting must periodically publicize the methods for accessing the information.

Agencies' Forecasts

Most agencies post on their contracting websites their forecasts of upcoming acquisitions during the next quarter or the rest of the fiscal year. These forecasts normally provide the supply or service that will be acquired; when the solicitation is expected to be released (month or fiscal year quarter); dollar range of the acquisition ("between $500,000 and $1,000,000"); whether the solicitation will be set-aside for a particular type of business (see Chapter 11); and a point-of-contact for more information. While this information is not binding on the agency (after all, it is a forecast and circumstances can change), these forecasts are usually fairly reliable, and prospective contractors use this information to get prepared and organized for a competitive effort. These forecasts can be accessed from the website at **https://www.acquisition.gov/procurement-forecasts**.

The Federal Procurement Data System (FPDS)

The **Federal Procurement Data System** (FPDS) (**https://www.fpds.gov**) maintains computerized records of all contract actions over $3,500. Originally, this information was compiled at Congressional direction so congressmen and senators could see how the government was spending the money Congress appropriated. But Congress decided to make this information public. The FPDS is a good source of information on which departments and agencies buy which supplies and services.

When a contracting officer makes an award, he is required to electronically report to FPDS approximately 100 pieces of information on the contract, such as:

- Contract number
- Agency
- Date signed
- Amount
- Estimated completion date
- Name of contractor
- Address of contractor
- Type of contractor (small, veteran-owned, women-owned, etc. – see Chapter 11)
- DUNS number
- Product or service code
- Principal NAICS code
- Country of product origin
- Place of manufacture
- Extent of competition (full and open, set-aside, sole source, etc.)
- Number of offers received
- If not awarded to small business, reason

Anyone may register at **https://www.fpds.gov** and have access to approximately 50 reports that are generated in "real time" – depicting current information on the state of the government's acquisition programs (and those of 60 agencies). The following are a sample of the reports that are available:

- Awards to 8(a) Contractors by Agency
- Awards to HUBZone Small Businesses by Agency
- Competition Summary Report by Agency
- Contractor Search by Department
- Federal Contract Actions and Dollars by Agency
- Federal Procurement State Summary
- List of Awards with Veteran-Owned Contractors
- List of Agencies Awarding Work in State/County
- NAICS Summary
- Product or Service Search by Agency
- Small Business Goaling Report by Agency
- Socio-Economic Accomplishments by Agency
- Supplies and Equipment
- Top 100 Federal Contractors by Agency
- Top 25 NAICS by Agency
- Top 50 Contractors with Awards in the State
- Total Federal Snapshot Report for the Fiscal Year

While all the information is useful, those new to federal contracting should download reports that list or identify:

- The contracting activities that bought supplies or services similar to those produced by their firms;
- The contractors that received those contracts;
- The contract identification numbers; and
- The contract amounts.

With this information, the businessman will get off to a quick start. He will be able to contact each contracting activity's small business specialist (SBS) (see Chapter 2). He will know who his competitors are. With a contract identification number, he can request information about the contract (for example, quantity or unit price) or even a copy of the contract itself. The time spent on this detailed and targeted "market research" is time well spent.

For more on FPDS, see FAR subpart 4.6, Contract Reporting.

Service Contract Inventories

Each civilian agency is required by law to prepare an annual inventory of their service contracts that exceed $25,000. These **service contract inventories**, which are compiled from data in the FPDS (see above), contain much information that is beneficial to service contractors:

- A description of the services purchased (by "product or service code" [PSC] – see above).
- The contracting agency and the funding agency.
- The place of performance.
- The date signed.
- The extent competed (see Chapter 3).
- The type of contract (see Chapter 9).
- Description of the requirement acquired.
- The contractor's name.
- The dollar amount obligated for services.
- The contractor's DUNS number (see above).

Links to the agencies' service contract inventories are available at **https:// www.whitehouse.gov/omb/procurement-service-contract-inventories** (the Department of Defense's inventory is available at **http://www.acq.osd.mil/dpap/ cpic/cp/acquisition_of_services_policy.html**). As an alternative, go to the agency's website and search for "service contract inventory." See FAR subpart 4.17, Service Contract Inventory, for more information.

Acquisition Gateway

The "Acquisition Gateway" (**https://hallways.cap.gsa.gov/**) is a portal with various acquisition-related information that is intended to make contracting easier for contracting officers – "Our vision is to provide a workspace with accurate, useful, and unbiased advice." While intended for the federal contracting community, the Acquisition Gateway provides the public with access to a subset of what is available to federal government employees.

The Acquisition Gateway provides resources in 19 different "hallways." The hallways are:

- Administrative Support
- Card Services
- Cleaning Supplies & Chemicals
- Employee Relocation
- Facilities Maintenance Services
- Freight
- Human Capital
- Information Technology (IT) Hardware
- IT Security
- IT Services
- IT Software
- Motor Vehicles
- Professional Services
- Security & Protection
- Small Package Delivery
- Telecommunications
- Tools & Hardware
- Travel
- Workplace Environment

Within each hallway, users of the Acquisition Gateway can find:

- *Articles and News:* Each hallway contains articles that provide users with expertise and unbiased advice that they can use to research market trends, begin an acquisition, obtain specific information to help select the most appropriate contract vehicle, and more. Also, each hallway contains news that may interest those visiting the hallway.

- *The Solutions Finder:* This allows users to compare government contract solutions that are available to each agency for specific categories and subcategories of products and services.

- *Transactional Platforms:* Each hallway highlights applicable transactional platforms where government buyers can go to make purchases (transactional platforms require government credentials to use, but the public may view them for informational purposes).

Federal contracting professionals can use the Acquisition Gateway to:

- Build acquisition projects;
- Find historical prices paid for products/services;
- Seek advice from product/service category experts;
- Compare governmentwide contract vehicles and solutions (see Chapter 13);
- Search a Statement of Work (SOW) library as a reference for similar procurements (see Chapter 4);
- View active and closed Requests for Quotations (RFQs) for reference on similar procurements (see Chapter 6); and
- Connect with other federal government buyers via message boards.

Because some information can only be accessed by government contracting officials, there are two entrances to the Gateway: "federal government users" (full access) and "non-federal government & public users."

The Freedom of Information Act (FOIA)

Once a businessman determines which agencies are buying the kinds of supplies and services provided by his firm, learns the names of the current and previous contractors, and obtains the identification numbers of their contracts, he may want to look at copies of those contracts. The businessman might want to review these contracts to find out the prices previously paid by the government for the supplies or services, the quantities purchased, the specifications or statements of work used, the contracts' terms and conditions, and whether there are any special or unique provisions in the contracts. This information is *extremely useful* to anyone conducting market research.

Most contracting offices will provide copies of current and previous contracts upon request. However, some contracting offices refuse to provide these contracts because they fail to understand that *public contracts are public property*. That is one of the reasons Congress enacted the **Freedom of Information Act** (FOIA) in 1966, to provide the public the **right** to obtain **public information**.

The FOIA states that the public has a right to information about the activities of its government. The FOIA makes it the government's policy to conduct its activities openly and to provide the public with accurate and timely information concerning its activities, consistent with the legitimate public and private interests of the American people.

Any member of the public may send a request to a government agency for any record in its possession that is not exempted under the provisions of the FOIA. The request must identify a *specific* record that already exists; the government is under no obligation to create or compile records to satisfy an FOIA request. A "record" is a compilation of data made or received by an agency during the transaction of public business, and it can be in *any* form or format (including electronic, such as e-mail and database software). Contracts are considered "records."

The government may charge the requester a fee for search time and duplication costs. If, in his request, the requester offers to pay all charges related to the search and duplication of the records and the cost incurred is small (usually under $250), the government will normally forward the record with a bill for the cost. If the cost for the search and duplication is expected to be substantial (usually over $250), the government will request payment before sending the records. If the record is small and did not entail an extensive search, the government may furnish the record free of charge.

There are nine types of information that are exempt from release under the FOIA. Examples of such information are:

- Classified information;

- Investigative records compiled to enforce civil, criminal, or military law;

- Internal memoranda relating to the decision-making process of an agency;

- Personnel and medical files;

- Trade secrets; and

- Commercial or financial information received by the government in confidence concerning bids, proposals, or contracts (such information should be marked with the legend specified in paragraphs (e)(1) and (2) of **FAR 52.215-1, Instruction to Offerors – Competitive Acquisition** – see Chapter 8). This includes proposals submitted in response to a competitive solicitation.

Any record that comes under one of the nine exemptions *may* be withheld in whole or in part from the public; however, an agency *may* release a record that comes under one of these exemptions when no significant and legitimate government purpose is served by its withholding *unless* a statute specifically requires the withholding of the record.

Besides these nine exemptions, an agency can reject a FOIA request if:

- The requested information is not a record within the meaning of the FOIA (the government is not required to compile or collate information for the requester, but merely to release records).

- The record was not described in sufficient detail to enable the agency to locate it by conducting a reasonable search.

- The requester fails unreasonably to comply with procedural requirements, including the payment of fees.

- The agency determines it does not hold the requested record.

- The agency determines that the request is for a personnel record and should be handled under the Privacy Act (which governs the release of personal information).

This still leaves a lot of information that might interest a person preparing a response to a solicitation: old contracts, correspondence between the previous contractor and the government, bid abstracts, test reports, inspection records, and similar information. The FOIA is particularly useful in getting history on past contractual efforts and when preparing a dispute (see Chapter 18). Figure 5 is a sample request letter.

The government must respond to the requester within **20 working days** after receipt of the request. If the agency needs more time to search for or gather the information, it will acknowledge receipt of the request within the 20 working day period and attempt to fulfill the request within an additional 10 working days. If the request is denied, the agency's FOIA officer informs the requester in writing of the reasons for the denial. Any denial may be appealed to the agency's designated final authority. A requester may seek an order from a United States district court to compel release of the record if the agency's final authority denies the appeal. The burden of proof is on the government agency to justify its refusal to release the record.

FAR subpart 24.2, Freedom of Information Act, provides summary information on the FOIA. Each agency is responsible for instituting its own FOIA implementation instructions, and these instructions are contained in their respective FAR supplements. Also, a FOIA guide and other resources are available at the Department of Justice website at **http://www.justice.gov/oip**.

Date

Agency Head or FOIA Officer
Name of Agency or Agency Component
Address

Dear _____,

    Under the Freedom of Information Act, 5 U.S.C. 552, I am requesting access to, or copies of [identify the records as clearly and specifically as possible].

    If there are any fees for copying or searching for the records, please let me know before you fill my request. [Or "please supply the records without informing me of the cost if the fees do not exceed $_____, which I agree to pay."]

    If you deny all or any part of this request, please cite each specific exemption you think justifies your refusal to release the information and notify me of appeal procedures available under the law.

    If you have any questions about handling this request, you may telephone me at _____ (home phone) or _____ (work phone).

Sincerely,

Name
Address

Figure 5 – Freedom of Information Act Request Letter

CHAPTER 6

SIMPLIFIED ACQUISITIONS AND COMMERCIAL ITEMS

Whenever the government intends to make a major purchase, it usually goes through an elaborate procedure of soliciting bids or proposals (see Chapters 7 and 8). The contracting officer, engineers, lawyers, and other government experts evaluate these bids and proposals to determine which one is most advantageous to the government "price and other factors considered." The government performs these costly evaluations because the savings will likely exceed the money spent on the salaries of the evaluators and related administrative expenses.

Like a person shopping for a new house, the government puts forth this extra effort to make sure it gets what it needs at the best possible price. However, the government cannot spend the same amount of time and effort on **simplified acquisitions** (what used to be called "small purchases") or **commercial items** (see Chapter 4 for the definition of "commercial items"). After all, people do not shop all over town looking for the least expensive loaf of bread, nor do they ask for bids when purchasing a television.

REASONS FOR SIMPLIFIED PROCEDURES

The government uses the procedures authorized by FAR part 13, Simplified Acquisition Procedures, to make most of its purchases. The FAR defines a simplified acquisition as any purchase of **$150,000 or less**, and the vast majority of all government contract actions meet this definition. The $150,000 limit is called the **"simplified acquisition threshold."** In addition, the Clinger-Cohen Act authorizes simplified procedures for purchases of commercial items that do not exceed **$7,000,000** (the threshold is **$13,000,000** for acquisitions of commercial items that "facilitate defense against or recovery from nuclear, biological, chemical, or radiological attack") (see FAR subpart 13.5, Test Program for Certain Commercial Items).

FAR 13.003, Policy, requires agencies to "use simplified acquisition procedures to the maximum extent practicable for all purchases of supplies or services not exceeding the simplified acquisition threshold..." The primary reason the government authorizes these simplified procedures for relatively small purchases is to avoid most of the administrative expenses and time-consuming processes associated with the preparation and evaluation of formal solicitations. On a purchase of $150,000 or less, these expenses could exceed any savings that might be realized by using a formal solicitation.

The primary reasons simplified procedures are authorized for commercial items up to $7,000,000 are (1) to encourage the purchase of commercial items instead of unique government-designed items, and (2) to encourage companies in the commercial marketplace to offer their products to the government (many companies that produce commercial items are not familiar, or are incapable of complying, with the "intimidating and complex" government contracting procedures).

Simplified procedures also improve contract opportunities for small businesses. To aid small businesses, purchases **greater than $3,500** (or $5,000 for the Department of Defense) but **not greater than $150,000** are **reserved exclusively for small businesses** if two or more small businesses can submit competitive offers – that is, if two or more small businesses can:

1. Provide a supply or service that meets the government's specifications;

2. Meet the government's required delivery schedule; and

3. Provide the supply or service at a fair and reasonable price.

This is called the "**rule of two**" (see Chapter 11). Unless there are mitigating circumstances (as when a product is available only from a large company with an exclusive license), contracting officers purchase most supplies or services between $3,500 and $150,000 from small businesses (for purchases of commercial items between $150,000 and $7,000,000, see the "rule of two" in Chapter 11).

Just because a purchase is $150,000 or less (or $7,000,000 or less for commercial items) does not mean the contracting officer must use the FAR part 13 simplified procedures. He can solicit bids or proposals whenever appropriate and necessary. For example, the contracting officer would not use simplified procedures when making a "top secret" purchase because the restrictions placed on the classified information make simplified procedures inappropriate. The contracting officer might want to evaluate several commercial products before deciding which best meets the government's needs. The contracting officer might be able to obtain the supplies or services from other existing contract vehicles, such as from a Federal Supply Schedule (see Chapter 13) or an indefinite-delivery, indefinite-quantity (IDIQ) contract (see Chapter 10). There are other circumstances in which simplified procedures are not required for "small" purchases, but they are relatively few.

MICRO-PURCHASES

A substantial amount of government business takes place in orders that are $3,500 or less (some estimates are that more than *85%* of all federal purchases are $3,500 or less). Most of these "**micro-purchases**" are for normal, day-to-day purchases of consumable supplies and routine services. Before enactment of the Federal Acquisition Streamlining Act, purchases of $3,500 or less were required to be made by a contracting officer in the contracting office. These micro-purchases not only burdened the contracting office and required extra staff, but frequently months would go by between the preparation of the low-dollar requisition and delivery of the supply or performance of the service. (**NOTE:** For the Department of Defense, the micro-purchase threshold is **$5,000**.)

With enactment of the Federal Acquisition Streamlining Act, agencies may authorize employees who are *not* acquisition officials to make micro-purchases. If a government office needs an item that costs $3,500 or less (or $5,000 or less for the Department of Defense), and one of its employees is an authorized "micro-purchaser" (see Chapter 2), that employee can go to a supplier, purchase the item, take it back to the office and use it *immediately*. However, the micro-purchase limit for **most services is $2,500** (see Chapter 15), and the micro-purchase limit for **construction is $2,000**.

There are few restrictions on a micro-purchaser:

- He does *not* have to obtain the supply or service from a small business.

- He does *not* have to concern himself about whether the item of supply is a domestic or foreign product because the provisions of the **Buy American Act** do not apply (see Chapter 12).

- He needs to obtain **only one quotation**, and he can make the purchase if the quoted price is **reasonable**.

The only requirements placed on a micro-purchaser is that (1) the prices he pays must be reasonable (not necessarily the "lowest"), and (2) he must distribute the micro-purchases equitably among qualified suppliers.

The micro-purchaser can use one of several different methods to acquire the supply or service:

- The preferred choice is a **governmentwide commercial purchase card**, which is actually a credit card. Purchases made with a commercial purchase card can be over-the-counter or orally (normally by telephone) (see below).

- Another recommended method is the use of electronic purchasing techniques, such as posting the solicitation on **FedBizOpps (https://www.fbo.gov)** (see Chapter 5).

- **Third-party drafts** are used by several agencies to make purchases up to **$2,500** as a substitute for credit cards, imprest funds, and Standard Form 44s (see below). These drafts are almost the same as checks in that the government employee prepares the third-party draft for the amount of the purchase and the supplier deposits the draft in its bank account. These are addressed in FAR 13.305.

- Some agencies maintain **imprest funds**, which are cash funds of a fixed amount established by an advance of funds from an agency finance or disbursing officer to a duly appointed cashier for disbursement as needed from time to time in making payment in cash for relatively small amounts (less than $500).

- The **Standard Form 44**, Purchase Order-Invoice-Voucher (SF 44), is designed primarily for on-the-spot, over-the-counter purchases while an employee is away from a purchasing office or at an isolated activity. Essentially, the SF 44 is a blank form with space for the government employee to list the supplies or services he wants to purchase. If the employee pays cash, he signs the SF 44 and gives "copy 2" to the supplier as a record of the transaction. If the employee does not pay cash, he signs the SF 44 and gives "copy 1" to the supplier to use as an invoice. Either way, the supplier then provides the supplies or services over-the-counter to the employee or to the designated address.

  As with the third party draft and imprest funds, the SF 44 is being replaced by the governmentwide commercial purchase card.

The micro-purchase threshold is not always $3,500 (or $5,000 for the Department of Defense). For acquisitions made by institutes of higher education, nonprofit research organizations, independent research institutes, and the Department of Defense's science and technology reinvention laboratories, the micro-purchase threshold is **$10,000**. For acquisitions that are to be used to support a "contingency operation" (that is, a military operation against an enemy of the United States or an opposing military force) or "to facilitate defense against or recovery from nuclear, biological, chemical, or radiological attack," the micro-purchase threshold is **$20,000** for purchases inside the United States and **$30,000** for purchases outside the United States. Furthermore, in extraordinary circumstances, Congress can change the micro-purchase threshold – during the recovery from Hurricane Katrina in 2005, which devastated the Gulf Coast and flooded New Orleans, Congress increased the micro-purchase threshold in affected counties to **$250,000**.

See FAR subpart 13.2, Actions At or Below the Micro-Purchase Threshold, for more information.

Governmentwide Commercial Purchase Card

The **governmentwide commercial purchase card** is a credit card that is assigned to an authorized "cardholder" to purchase supplies and services – generally under the micro-purchase threshold ($3,500/$5,000) because they are not contracting officials (individual limits can be set as low as $100), though a purchase card may be used for larger orders placed under **blanket purchase agreements** (see below), **indefinite-delivery contracts** (see Chapter 10), and **Federal Supply Schedule** contracts (see Chapter 13). There are approximately **300,000** federal employees with commercial purchase cards, and they spend about **$18 billion** on **20 million transactions** a year.

While the whole point of the commercial purchase card is to reduce administrative expense (estimated to be $70 per transaction) and expedite the receipt of needed supplies or services by government offices (and permit cardholders to take advantage of sales and discounts), it opens up additional sources of supply – many companies and vendors that refuse to get involved in the government's "red tape" are familiar with credit cards. They will accept the card "over-the-counter," over the telephone, by fax, and electronically.

Before a federal employee can become a cardholder, he must receive training in the use of the card and have his "approving official" (usually his immediate supervisor) verify that he has a need for the card (the approving official will also determine the purchase limitations on the card). Then the federal employee submits an application through his agency's "program coordinator," who submits it to the purchase card company (the employee's personal credit rating has *nothing* to do with the approval of a commercial purchase card). Usually, the employee receives his card within 10 days.

The card is in the name of the cardholder, and he is responsible for ensuring that all purchases made with the card are *proper* and *required*. He must protect the card like any other credit card, and he must not *lend the card to anyone*. If the cardholder's approving official discovers any unauthorized purchases on the account statement, the government will **recoup the cost of the unauthorized purchase from the cardholder**.

Each commercial purchase card has a magnetic strip on the back. The strip contains the cardholder's purchase limit, the limit on purchases during a monthly billing period (most agencies place such a limit on their cardholders), any restrictions on the types of supplies or services the cardholder is authorized to purchase (the card can be "blocked" for unauthorized supplies or services – for example, a purchaser may be authorized to buy paper but not furniture), and the particular account from which the cardholder may draw. When handed the card, the vendor will verify that the purchase is authorized by contacting the purchase card company (just like it does with any credit card purchase). If the purchase is over the cardholder's purchase limit, the cardholder has exceeded his purchase limit for the billing period, the purchase is for blocked supplies or services, or there are insufficient funds in the account, the purchase will not be authorized.

Before a cardholder runs out and buys needed supplies or services from a commercial source, he must *check all other potential sources of the supplies or services first*, just like for any other purchase. As mentioned in Chapter 4, the cardholder must make sure the following sources cannot provide the needed supplies or services, in descending order of priority:

Supplies:

1. The agency's own inventories;

2. Other agencies' excess inventories;

3. Federal Prison Industries, Inc.;

4. Products available from the Committee for Purchase from People Who Are Blind or Severely Disabled;

5. Stock programs operated by the General Services Administration (GSA), the Defense Logistics Agency, the Department of Veterans Affairs, and military inventory control points;

6. Federal Supply Schedules, governmentwide acquisition contracts (GWACs), multi-agency contracts (MACs), and any other procurement instruments intended for use by multiple agencies; and finally

7. **Commercial sources**.

Services:

1. The "Procurement List" maintained by the Committee for Purchase from People Who Are Blind or Severely Disabled from "AbilityOne" participating nonprofit agencies.

2. Federal Supply Schedules, governmentwide acquisition contracts (GWACs), multi-agency contracts (MACs), and any other procurement instruments intended for use by multiple agencies; and Federal Prison Industries, Inc.; and finally

3. **Commercial sources**.

Most, if not all, of these sources accept the commercial purchase card.

Even when the cardholder gets down to commercial sources as the last available source, there are several restrictions on commercial purchase cards:

■ They must be used for government business *only*.

■ They must *not* be used for cash advances (cannot use "automatic teller machines" at banks).

■ Funds must be available (this means the cardholder cannot use the commercial purchase card to finance a purchase, such as by using the "float" between the time the supply or service is purchased and the time it is paid for).

■ The supply *must* be in stock (cannot purchase out-of-stock items for later delivery).

■ They must *not* be used to purchase:
  - Real property
  - Telecommunications services
  - Detective services
  - Personal travel expense (a mandatory GSA travel and subsistence card must be used)
  - Gas or oil for GSA vehicles (a GSA gasoline credit card must be used)

■ The cardholder *may* need to obtain a waiver, special authority, or approval before acquiring:
  - Paid advertising
  - Legal services
  - Architectural services
  - Engineering services
  - Temporary help
  - Advisory or assistance services (such as consultants or experts)
  - Telecommunications equipment

  The cardholder must refer to his agency's regulations or consult with his "approving official."

■ The cardholder is *required* to purchase "green" products unless the products do not meet the government's performance needs, are not reasonably available, or are only available at an unreasonable price (see "Sustainable Acquisitions" in Chapter 4).

Then, after the cardholder has made sure the purchase complies with all the rules and restrictions, he can select the vendor, select the supply or service, and make the purchase. *But it does not end there!* The cardholder must make sure he:

■ Does *not* split the purchase to get under his purchase limit (dividing a $6,000 purchase into two $3,000 purchases is **illegal** – such a purchase must be made by the contracting office and requires a requisition)

■ Does *not* pay any sales tax (the card has "Tax Exempt" printed on it)

■ Does *not* pay a higher price for using the card (meaning he must avoid any vendor that provides discounts for cash)

■ Rotates the purchases among qualified sources (he cannot keep returning to the same vendor)

■ Obtains any rebates

■ Provides necessary information to the agency's property control officials

■ Keeps the receipts so he can reconcile his purchases with his monthly **statement of account**.

If the supply or service is not satisfactory or not received, the cardholder must try to resolve the matter with the vendor. If the cardholder is unable to settle the matter with the vendor, he must dispute the charge through the issuing bank. Many agencies have a "**transaction dispute officer**" who works with all the parties to resolve the problem. The most common problems are:

■ Merchandise or service not received.
■ Merchandise returned but not credited.
■ Merchandise not as described.
■ Duplicate processing.
■ Different amount charged.
■ Inadequate description/unrecognized charge.
■ Unauthorized mail or phone order.

Commercial purchase cards are the preferred method for making and paying for micro-purchases; many agencies *require* use of the commercial purchase card when making purchases less than the micro-purchase threshold. As an experiment, some agencies are issuing cards to their contracting officers so they can make purchases between $3,500 ($5,000 for the Department of Defense) and $150,000 **without paperwork**.

See FAR 13.301, Governmentwide Commercial Purchase Card, for more information.

PURCHASES BELOW THE SIMPLIFIED ACQUISITION THRESHOLD

There are additional rules for purchases that exceed the micro-purchase threshold but do not exceed the simplified acquisition threshold (which is **$150,000**, except the threshold for supplies or services that support a contingency operation or facilitate defense against or recovery from nuclear, biological, chemical, or radiological attack is **$750,000** for purchases inside the United States, and **$1,500,000** for purchases outside the United States):

■ A contracting officer (not a micro-purchaser) must make the purchase (except for non-contracting personnel who are authorized to place orders against blanket purchase agreements [see below] or indefinite-quantity contracts [see Chapter 10]).

■ The contracting officer must obtain competitive quotations (usually at least three), unless the solicitation is posted on FedBizOpps (see Chapter 5).

■ The contracting officer must reserve the purchase exclusively for small businesses if he expects offers from two or more small businesses that are competitive with regard to price, quality, and delivery or performance.

■ The contracting officer must comply with the **Buy American Act** and only purchase American products unless they are unreasonably priced (or come under one of four other exceptions – see Chapter 12).

■ Purchases over **$25,000** *must* be synopsized on FedBizOpps (this is a significant restriction on the use of governmentwide commercial purchase cards for purchases over $25,000).

FAR part 13 authorizes the contracting officer to use several different simplified procedures to make purchases between the micro-purchase threshold and the simplified acquisition threshold: post the solicitation on FedBizOpps, conduct oral solicitations, issue requests for quotations (RFQ), or issue an order against a blanket purchase agreement (BPA).

Solicitations on FedBizOpps

Posting solicitations on FedBizOpps (**https://www.fbo.gov**) is the preferred method of soliciting and receiving quotations for purchases exceeding the micro-purchase threshold but not exceeding the simplified acquisition threshold. The contracting officer may place the solicitation on FedBizOpps and permit offerors to respond electronically with a "quotation." In the FedBizOpps solicitation, the contracting officer describes the supply or service as concisely as possible, such as by identifying the part numbers of replacement components. He specifies the quantity needed, any special requirements (such as packaging or marking requirements), the required delivery date, and the destination. The solicitation asks the offeror if any discounts apply (such as quantity discounts or discounts for prompt payment), whether the offeror is a small business (see Chapter 11), and for any other information the contracting officer might need to evaluate the quotation.

Potential offerors can review the solicitations on FedBizOpps and submit quotations through FedBizOpps. However, each FedBizOpps solicitation has a deadline for the transmittal of quotations – in general, quotations received after the deadline are not accepted or considered (although contracting officers *may* consider late quotations if it is in the best interest of the government). The contracting officer must provide sufficient "response time" for potential suppliers to respond to the solicitation, taking into account such factors as the complexity of the supply or service being solicited, its availability in the commercial marketplace, and the urgency of the government's need.

Once the deadline for transmitting quotations has passed, the contracting officer examines the quotations received. The contracting officer must determine that the low offeror is **responsible** before awarding it a "**purchase order**." He does this by:

- Checking the **Excluded Parties List System** (EPLS) in the System for Acquisition Management (SAM – **https://www.sam.gov** [see Chapter 5]) to see if the offeror is **debarred** or **suspended** from government business (see Chapter 7); and

- Deciding whether the offeror is capable of delivering the supplies or performing the services as required (see Chapter 7 for more on how the contracting officer determines a firm's responsibility).

If the small business is not listed as debarred or suspended, and the contracting officer believes the offeror submitting the lowest quotation is capable of performing as required, the contracting officer either (1) transmits a purchase order to the winning offeror electronically, or (2) executes a written purchase order by signing and sending to the supplier an **Optional Form 347, Order for Supplies or Services** (OF 347 – see Figure 6) or similar form (for example, the Department of Defense uses a **DD Form 1155**), or if the supplies or services are considered to be "commercial items", by signing and sending a **Standard Form 1449, Solicitation/Contract/Order for Commercial Items** (SF 1449 – see below and Appendix B).

[**NOTE ABOUT FORMS:** Most of the forms displayed in this book are the official paper versions. Because so much government business is being conducted electronically, agencies are authorized to use "electronic equivalents" that provide or require the same information – see FAR 52.253-1, Computer Generated Forms, which is required to be included in all solicitations and contracts. Some forms are available in electronic form only, such as the OF 347 and SF 1449.]

However, if the contracting officer does *not* believe the offeror submitting the lowest quotation is capable of performing as required, and the offeror is a small business (which the offeror must be if the acquisition is below the simplified acquisition threshold unless qualified small businesses are not available – see above), he must refer the matter to the Small Business Administration (SBA). After reviewing the matter, the SBA decides whether to issue a **certificate of competency** (COC) stating that the small business is responsible and eligible for award (see Chapter 7 for more on COCs). If the SBA issues a COC, the contracting officer *must* transmit or issue the purchase order to the small business.

If the contracting officer receives only one quotation, or the prices quoted are so far apart it appears no price competition exists, the contracting officer cannot rely on "market forces" to insure the lowest quoted price is fair and reasonable. Therefore, he will compare the single (or lowest) quoted price with those considered fair and reasonable on previous purchases, current price lists and catalogs, advertisements, or any other reasonable basis. If the contracting officer decides the price is fair and reasonable (and the offeror is responsible), he transmits or issues a purchase order to the offeror (now the "contractor").

Legal Effect of Purchase Orders

Because the contractor does not sign the order, the order is not a binding contractual agreement. Legally, the order is an offer **by the government** to pay the contractor the price it quoted if it performs according to the order's terms and conditions.

If the contractor, for whatever reason, cannot deliver the supplies or perform the services called for by the order, the contracting officer cannot penalize or default the contractor. The government recognizes that small contractors have limited inventories that might become depleted between the time of the quotation and receipt of the order. The same applies to services: a painting contractor might have landed a job painting apartments between the time it quoted a price for painting military barracks and when it received the purchase order. If the two painting jobs are scheduled for the same time, the painting contractor might not be able to do both.

If a contractor finds itself in this situation, all it has to do is notify the contracting officer that it is unable to perform the order. The contracting officer will rescind the order and issue an order to another contractor. This is another reason these are "simplified procedures" – there are no legal proceedings for "breach of contract." The contracting officer may cancel the order as long as he does so before the supplier begins work. Once the supplier begins work on the order, the government must honor it. If the government wishes to back out of the order, the contracting officer must terminate the order for the convenience of the government (see Chapter 18) and reimburse the supplier for the expenses it incurred in fulfilling the order.

Occasionally, the contracting officer may decide the purchase is so important that he will require the winning contractor to formally accept the purchase order in writing. When the contractor accepts the order in writing, the order becomes a **binding** contract and the contractor can no longer refuse to perform. The order also becomes binding on the government.

Oral Solicitations

The contracting officer will usually solicit the purchase **orally** if that is more efficient than soliciting through **FedBizOpps** (oral solicitations are authorized for commercial items between $150,000 and $7,000,000). He selects several *local* small business suppliers (usually at least three), calls them on the telephone, and solicits a quotation from each. Normally, the contracting officer will solicit the previous supplier and two others that were not solicited for the previous purchase, thus rotating the sources.

ORDER FOR SUPPLIES OR SERVICES			PAGE	OF	PAGES
IMPORTANT: Mark all packages and papers with contract and/or order numbers.			1		2

1. DATE OF ORDER	2. CONTRACT NO. *(If any)*	6. SHIP TO:		
01/23/2017		a. NAME OF CONSIGNEE		
3. ORDER NO.	4. REQUISITION/REFERENCE NO.	Document Production Division		
MEP-17-81N	SP-17-9361-007	b. STREET ADDRESS		
5. ISSUING OFFICE *(Address correspondence to)*		14th & C Streets, SW, C Wing, Room 312		
Treasury Procurement Div., Room 65, Wash, DC 20228		c. CITY	d. STATE	e. ZIP CODE
		Washington	DC	20228
7. TO:		f. SHIP VIA		

a. NAME OF CONTRACTOR	8. TYPE OF ORDER	
AAA Printing Equipment Company		
b. COMPANY NAME	[X] a. PURCHASE	[ ] b. DELIVERY – Except for billing instructions on the reverse, this delivery order is subject to instructions contained on this side only of this form and is issued subject to the terms and conditions of the above-numbered contract.
	REFERENCE YOUR: 1/19 Quote	
c. STREET ADDRESS	Please furnish the following on the terms and conditions specified on both sides of this order and on the attached sheet, if any, including delivery as indicated.	
3911 Freemont Avenue, Room 142		

d. CITY	e. STATE	f. ZIP CODE	10. REQUISITIONING OFFICE
Vienna	VA	22180	Document Production Division
9. ACCOUNTING AND APPROPRIATION DATA			
19475.0824571-675211500000 AP			

11. BUSINESS CLASSIFICATION *(Check appropriate box(es))*				12. F.O.B. POINT
[X] a. SMALL [ ] b. OTHER THAN SMALL [ ] c. DISADVANTAGED [ ] d. WOMEN-OWNED [ ] e. HUBZone				Destination
[ ] f. SERVICE-DISABLED VETERAN-OWNED [ ] g. WOMEN-OWNED SMALL BUSINESS (WOSB) ELIGIBLE UNDER THE WOSB PROGRAM [ ] h. EDWOSB				

13. PLACE OF		14. GOVERNMENT B/L NO.	15. DELIVER TO F.O.B. POINT ON OR BEFORE *(Date)*	16. DISCOUNT TERMS
a. INSPECTION	b. ACCEPTANCE			
Destination	Destination		03/09/2017	1%-20; Net-30

17. SCHEDULE *(See reverse for Rejections)*

ITEM NO. (a)	SUPPLIES OR SERVICES (b)	QUANTITY ORDERED (c)	UNIT (d)	UNIT PRICE (e)	AMOUNT (f)	QUANTITY ACCEPTED (g)
0001	Dunleevy Digital Printing Press, Model No. 8572Z2A	3	ea	$8,200.00	$24,600.00	

	18. SHIPPING POINT	19. GROSS SHIPPING WEIGHT	20. INVOICE NO.		17(h) TOT. ◁ *(Cont. pages)*
SEE BILLING INSTRUCTIONS ON REVERSE	21. MAIL INVOICE TO:				
	a. NAME Treasury Office of Financial Management				
	b. STREET ADDRESS *(or P.O. Box)* P.O. Box 11995				17(i)
	c. CITY Washington		d. STATE DC	e. ZIP CODE 20228	$ 24,600.00 ◁ GRAND TOTAL

22. UNITED STATES OF AMERICA BY *(Signature)* ▷	23. NAME *(Typed)* Nancy Bauman
	TITLE: CONTRACTING/ORDERING OFFICER

AUTHORIZED FOR LOCAL REPRODUCTION
PREVIOUS EDITION NOT USABLE

OPTIONAL FORM 347 (REV. 2/2012)
Prescribed by GSA/FAR 48 CFR 53.213(f)

Figure 6 - Order for Supplies or Services (Optional Form 347)

When soliciting over the telephone, the contracting officer will describe the supply or service, specify the quantity needed, explain any special requirements, specify the required delivery date and the destination, and ask if any discounts apply to the order. If the supplier can deliver the item or perform the service by the required date, it quotes a price.

If the contracting officer obtains competitive quotations, he relies on the competition to insure the lowest quoted price is fair and reasonable. However, if the contracting officer gets only one response from a small business or the prices quoted suggest one small business has a prohibitive advantage over the others, the contracting officer will determine whether the single (or lowest) quotation is fair and reasonable by checking the prices paid for previous purchases, catalog prices, and other available information. If the quoted price is *not* reasonable, the contracting officer may solicit large businesses.

Once the contracting officer determines the lowest (or only) quoted price is fair and reasonable and the supplier is responsible, he executes a purchase order by signing an OF 347 or similar form (or SF 1449 if the purchase order is for commercial items – see below) and sending it to the supplier. As with purchase orders placed through solicitations posted on FedBizOpps, a purchase order issued in response to an oral solicitation is an offer by the government to pay the supplier the price it quoted if it performs according to the order's terms and conditions. The purchase order is not binding on the supplier unless the supplier accepts it in writing.

Restrictions on Oral Solicitations

If the contracting officer expects the purchase to exceed $25,000, he must synopsize the purchase on FedBizOpps and give interested suppliers a chance to submit quotations. If two or more small businesses respond to the FedBizOpps synopsis with competitive quotations, the contracting officer does not need to obtain any additional quotations (orally or otherwise) – he can award a purchase order on an OF 347 (or SF 1449 if the purchase order is for commercial items) to the supplier quoting the lowest price. (**NOTE:** Purchases for construction over **$2,000** may *not* be solicited orally [see Chapter 14].)

Written Solicitations

Normally, contracting officers use **FedBizOpps** solicitations or orally solicit quotations for purchases between the micro-purchase threshold and the simplified acquisition threshold. Nevertheless, there are circumstances in which using a **FedBizOpps** solicitation or the telephone is impracticable, such as when the supply or service must comply with drawings or specifications, or there are many different kinds of items being procured under the same purchase order. In these situations, the contracting officer may decide to issue a written solicitation. If so, he prepares a **Standard Form 18, Request for Quotations** (SF 18) (see Figure 7) *unless* the purchase will be for a commercial item (see below, and Chapter 4 for the definition of "commercial item").

REQUEST FOR QUOTATION (THIS IS NOT AN ORDER)		THIS RFQ [X] IS	IS NOT A SMALL BUSINESS SET-ASIDE		PAGE OF	PAGES
					1	2

1. REQUEST NO. W81XWH-17-Q-0009	2. DATE ISSUED 04/29/2016	3. REQUISITION/PURCHASE REQUEST NO. W81XWH-4159-4483	4. CERT. FOR NAT. DEF. UNDER BDSA REG. 2 AND/OR DMS REG. 1 ▶	RATING DO-C9

5a. ISSUED BY	6. DELIVER BY (Date)
US Army Medical Research Acquisition Activity, Frederick, MD	09/29/2017

5b. FOR INFORMATION CALL (NO COLLECT CALLS)			7. DELIVERY	
NAME		TELEPHONE NUMBER	[X] FOB DESTINATION	OTHER (See Schedule)

	AREA CODE	NUMBER	9. DESTINATION
Jerome Spector	301	619-1161	a. NAME OF CONSIGNEE
8. TO:			TRICARE Management Activity

a. NAME	b. COMPANY	b. STREET ADDRESS 6111 Leesburg Pike
c. STREET ADDRESS		c. CITY Falls Church
d. CITY	e. STATE	f. ZIP CODE	d STATE VA	e. ZIP CODE 22041-3206

10. PLEASE FURNISH QUOTATIONS TO THE ISSUING OFFICE IN BLOCK 5a ON OR BEFORE CLOSE OF BUSINESS (Date) 05/26/2017	IMPORTANT: This is a request for information and quotations furnished are not offers. If you are unable to quote, please so indicate on this form and return it to the address in Block 5a. This request does not commit the Government to pay any costs incurred in the preparation of the submission of this quotation or to contract for supplies or service. Supplies are of domestic origin unless otherwise indicated by quoter. Any representations and/or certifications attached to this Request for Quotation must be completed by the quoter.

11. SCHEDULE (Include applicable Federal, State and local taxes)

ITEM NO. (a)	SUPPLIES/ SERVICES (b)	QUANTITY (c)	UNIT (d)	UNIT PRICE (e)	AMOUNT (f)
0001	Copy Editing of Textbook of Military Medicine in accordance with Statement of Work marked "Attachment No. 1"	1	lot		0.00

12. DISCOUNT FOR PROMPT PAYMENT ▶	a. 10 CALENDAR DAYS (%)	b. 20 CALENDAR DAYS (%)	c. 30 CALENDAR DAYS (%)	d. CALENDAR DAYS	
				NUMBER	PERCENTAGE

NOTE: Additional provisions and representations [ ] are [ ] are not attached.

13. NAME AND ADDRESS OF QUOTER	14. SIGNATURE OF PERSON AUTHORIZED TO SIGN QUOTATION	15. DATE OF QUOTATION
a. NAME OF QUOTER		
b. STREET ADDRESS	16. SIGNER	
c. COUNTY	a. NAME (Type or print)	b. TELEPHONE AREA CODE
d. CITY	e. STATE	f. ZIP CODE	c. TITLE (Type or print)	NUMBER

AUTHORIZED FOR LOCAL REPRODUCTION Previous edition not usable	STANDARD FORM 18 (REV. 6-95) Prescribed by GSA-FAR (48 CFR) 53.215-1(a)

Figure 7 - Request For Quotations (Standard Form 18)

When a supplier receives an RFQ on an SF 18, it examines any specifications or drawings that may be attached and reviews any terms and conditions required as a condition of business. If the supplier decides to submit a quotation, it enters the price in block 11 of the SF 18 (columns e and f), has its representative sign in block 14, and returns the form by the date specified in block 10.

As with oral solicitations, the contracting officer selects the lowest quotation, decides whether the supplier is responsible, prepares the purchase order on an OF 347 or similar form, sends it to the supplier, and synopsizes the award on FedBizOpps if it exceeds $25,000 and is expected to produce subcontracting opportunities.

Again, the supplier does not sign the purchase order because it is an offer by the government to pay the supplier the price it quoted. If the supplier cannot deliver the supplies or perform the services, it notifies the contracting officer, who rescinds the purchase order and issues a new one to another supplier. Of course, if the contracting officer requests the supplier to accept the purchase order in writing, it becomes binding on both the supplier and the government.

SOLICITATIONS FOR COMMERCIAL ITEMS

Whenever an acquisition is greater than the micro-purchase threshold but no greater than **$7,000,000,** *and* market research (see Chapter 4) indicates there are commercial items ("any item that is of a type customarily used by the general public") or nondevelopmental items ("any previously developed item of supply used exclusively for governmental purposes") that will fulfill the government's needs, *and* the contracting officer decides a written solicitation is necessary, **FAR part 12, Acquisition of Commercial Items**, applies to the acquisition *in conjunction* with the policies and procedures prescribed in FAR part 13 (see Chapter 4 and FAR 2.101 for definitions of "commercial items" and "nondevelopmental items").

If the purchase is expected to be between the micro-purchase threshold and $25,000, and commercial or nondevelopmental items are available, but a written solicitation is necessary, the contracting officer selects several small business suppliers (generally three) and sends each a **Standard Form 1449, Solicitation/Contract/Order for Commercial Items** (SF 1449 – see Appendix B). The contracting officer rotates suppliers as he would if he were conducting an oral solicitation. (**NOTE:** The SF 1449 is used whenever the government solicits for commercial items *regardless of dollar amount.* This means the SF 1449 is also used in solicitations for commercial items that are over $7,000,000, such as **invitations for bids** (see Chapter 7) and **requests for proposals** [see Chapter 8].)

However, if the contracting officer expects the purchase to exceed $25,000, he must synopsize the purchase on FedBizOpps at least 15 days before issuance of the solicitation (unless the contracting officer establishes a shorter period). If the contracting officer decides a written solicitation is necessary, he will usually send SF 1449s to several local small businesses because he cannot be sure those responding to the FedBizOpps synopsis will submit offers.

When a supplier downloads or receives an SF 1449, it examines the description in block 20 and any additional descriptions that may be attached, determines whether it meets the applicable size standard in block 10, and reviews any attached clauses or special terms and conditions. If the supplier decides to submit an offer, it enters any discount terms in block 12, types its name and address in block 17, enters the unit price in block 23 and the extended price in block 24 (unit price x quantity), has its representative sign in block 30, and returns the completed SF 1449 by the time and date specified in block 8 (the contracting officer can allow fewer than 30 days for the submittal of offers).

While most of the information necessary for completion of an offer is included on the form, the contracting officer may attach additional instructions or addenda. For example, the contracting officer may request offerors to submit existing product literature or allow offerors to propose more than one product that will meet the government's needs. He may attach to the solicitation a license that specifies which rights the government intends to acquire with commercial computer software or software documentation (such rights might include reproduction, modification, display, or release of the software or documentation). The contracting officer may include special terms and conditions which market research indicates are normal for the particular industry. The SF 1449 is intended to be a flexible document.

The SF 1449 normally has no more than four FAR provisions and clauses:

- **FAR 52.212-1, Instructions to Offerors – Commercial Items**

- **FAR 52.212-3, Offeror Representations and Certifications – Commercial Items**

- **FAR 52.212-4, Contract Terms and Conditions – Commercial Items**

- **FAR 52.212-5, Contract Terms and Conditions Required to Implement Statutes or Executive Orders – Commercial Items**

While that seems like a manageable number, each of these four actually consist of other FAR provisions and clauses; FAR 52.212-5 can require compliance with **more than 90 different FAR clauses!** Furthermore, the contracting officer can:

- Tailor FAR 52.212-1 and 52.212-4

- Include provisions and clauses for options

- Include provisions and clauses regarding the use of "recovered material"

- Include requirements for express warranty provisions

- Include **FAR 52.212-2, Evaluation – Commercial Items**, to specify evaluation factors that will be used to determine which offeror will receive the award (such as option prices, past performance [see Chapter 18], or quality of the supply or service).

So offerors should examine this "simple" document very carefully to make sure an important requirement or condition does not get overlooked.

Once the deadline for submittal of offers passes, the contracting officer usually selects the lowest offer, decides whether the offeror is responsible and, if responsible, signs the SF 1449 in block 31, thus creating a contract. (**NOTE:** Besides being a solicitation and award document, the SF 1449 may be used for documenting the receipt, inspection, and acceptance of commercial items.)

However, if the contracting officer specified in the SF 1449 any evaluation factors that would be used to determine the winner (that is, included FAR 52.212-2), the selected offeror might not necessarily be the one with the lowest price. If, for example, an offeror that always delivers quality supplies on time offers the supplies at $105 a unit, and another offeror that frequently delivers defective supplies and is chronically late offers the supplies at $100 a unit, the contracting officer would be justified awarding the contract to the first offeror at $105 *provided the SF 1449 (FAR 52.212-2) said past performance and quality would be evaluation factors*.

The contracting officer does *not* notify unsuccessful offerors that another offeror won unless specifically requested. When an unsuccessful offeror requests information on an award that was made considering price *and other factors*, the contracting officer must provide a brief explanation of the reasons for the award decision. Nevertheless, if the contract exceeds $25,000 and the contracting officer believes the contract will produce subcontracts, he must synopsize the award on FedBizOpps.

Unlike oral solicitations, an offer made on an SF 1449 becomes a contract when the contracting officer signs block 31 because the offeror's representative has already signed the SF 1449 in block 30. The "contractor" cannot walk away from the SF 1449 contract as with a purchase order. Failure of the contractor to comply with *any* contract term or condition (including those referenced in FAR 52.212-4 and 52.212-5) gives the contracting officer the right to terminate the contract "for cause" (a "termination for cause" is a simplified version of a "termination for default" – see Chapter 18). When an SF 1449 contract is terminated for cause:

- The government has no obligation to accept any more supplies or services from the contractor, even if the supplies or services are acceptable in all other respects;

- The government may acquire similar items from another source and charge the terminated contractor with any excess reprocurement costs (that is, the difference between the contract price for the terminated supplies or services and the price of the replacement supplies or services); and

- The government may charge the terminated contractor with any incidental or consequential damages incurred because of the termination (see paragraph (c) of FAR 12.403, Termination, and FAR 52.212-4(m)).

Termination for cause is *not* a good thing. However, if the contractor believes the contracting officer wrongly terminated the contract for cause (such as the contractor experienced an "excusable delay" as defined by FAR 52.212-4(f)), it has the right to appeal the contracting officer's decision under the **Contract Disputes Act** (see FAR subpart 33.2, Disputes and Appeals, and Chapter 18). If it is determined that the contracting officer improperly terminated the contract for cause, the termination will be converted to one for "the government's convenience" (the termination for the government's convenience provision of FAR 52.212-4 is a simplified version of the termination for convenience clauses that are found in all other contracts – see Chapter 18). Under a termination for convenience, the government will pay the contractor:

- The percentage of the contract price reflecting the percentage of the work performed prior to the termination; and

- Any charges the contractor can demonstrate directly resulted from the termination (see FAR 12.403(d) and FAR 52.212-4(l)).

All in all, a termination for convenience is much better for a contractor than a termination for cause.

See FAR part 12, Acquisitions of Commercial Items, for more information.

Streamlined Synopsis/Solicitations for Commercial Items

When the solicitation is simple and does not include lengthy addenda, the contracting officer may publish the solicitation in FedBizOpps along with its synopsis as an alternative to the SF 1449. This expedites acquisitions of commercial items between $25,000 and $7,000,000 by eliminating the 15-day wait between publication of the synopsis and the issuance of the solicitation. In addition, the contracting officer is not required to allow offerors 30 days to respond to the solicitation but can allow as few as 15 days.

The combined synopsis and solicitation must include the following:

- A synopsis of the acquisition (see Chapter 5).

- The statement:

   This is a combined synopsis/solicitation for commercial items prepared in accordance with the format in FAR subpart 12.6, as supplemented with additional information included in this notice. This announcement constitutes the only solicitation; proposals are being requested and a written solicitation will not be issued.

- The solicitation number.

- A statement that the solicitation document and incorporated provisions and clauses are those in effect through Federal Acquisition Circular ___ (see Chapter 1).

- A notice regarding any set-aside and the associated North American Industrial Classification System (NAICS) code and small business size standard (remember that all purchases between the micro-purchase threshold and $150,000 must be made from small businesses unless there is some extenuating circumstance, and purchases between $150,000 and $7,000,000 are subject to the "rule of two" – see Chapter 11).

- Items (with a description), quantities, and units of measure (including any options).

- Description of requirements for the items to be acquired.

- Date and place of delivery, and acceptance and FOB point.

- A statement that FAR 52.212-1, Instructions to Offerors – Commercial, applies and a statement regarding any addenda to the provision.

- A statement regarding the applicability of FAR 52.212-2, Evaluation – Commercial Items, and the specific evaluation criteria to be included in paragraph (a) of the provision (if FAR 52.212-2 is not used, a description of the evaluation procedures to be used).

- A statement advising offerors to include a completed copy of FAR 52.212-3, Offeror Representations and Certifications – Commercial Items, with its offer.

- A statement that FAR 52.212-4, Contract Terms and Conditions – Commercial Items, applies and a statement regarding any addenda to the clause.

- A statement that FAR 52.212-5, Contract Terms and Conditions Required to Implement Statutes or Executive Orders – Commercial Items, applies and a statement regarding which, if any, of the additional FAR clauses cited in the clause are applicable.

- A statement regarding any additional contract requirements or terms and conditions (such as contract financing arrangements or warranty requirements) that are determined by the contracting officer to be necessary and are consistent with customary commercial practices.

- The date, time, and place offers are due.

- The name and telephone number of the point of contact for information regarding the solicitation.

Offerors interested in responding must address each of the requirements included in the synopsis/solicitation (such as including commercial literature and a completed copy of FAR 52.212-3 with its offer) along with its price. There is no required format for offers in response to a synopsis/solicitation; the contracting officer will accept any offer that provides the required information and is signed by a person authorized to bind the offeror to a contract.

Once the deadline for offers has expired, the contracting officer follows the same procedures to evaluate the offers and award the contract as if he had used an SF 1449 to solicit offers for the commercial items. However, the contracting officer will fill in the appropriate information on an SF 1449, check block 29 ("Ref. _____ offer dated _____. Your offer on solicitation [block 5], including any additions or changes which are set forth herein, as accepted as to items: _____"), and sign it, creating a binding contract as if the offer had been made on a SF 1449. Then, if the contract exceeds $25,000, the contracting officer will synopsize it on FedBizOpps if he thinks it will produce subcontracting opportunities.

BLANKET PURCHASE AGREEMENTS

The **blanket purchase agreement** (BPA) is a contractual instrument frequently used by contracting officers to make repetitive purchases of $150,000 or less for the same or similar supplies or services ($7,000,000 or less for commercial items). It is nothing more than a "charge account" on which authorized government personnel may place orders with a supplier. The BPA is *not* a contract: no money is spent when the government issues a BPA to a supplier. The orders are the actual "contracts" that contain the money.

The primary reason contracting officers establish BPAs is to reduce administrative expenses for both the government and the supplier. With BPAs, the contracting officer does not issue a purchase order for each purchase. Instead, one of the government employees identified in the BPA as authorized to place orders obtains competitive quotations from suppliers with BPAs and places the order with the supplier quoting the lowest price. The government employee usually places the order electronically or over the telephone, although he can request that the BPA supplier accept the order in writing. The supplier furnishes the supplies or services on each order and then submits an invoice (at least monthly) for all the deliveries made during the billing period (however, some payment offices have systems that require an individual invoice for each delivery). Upon receipt of the invoice, the government makes a consolidated payment to the BPA supplier. With this procedure, the BPA cuts out much effort and eliminates the need to track individual invoices.

Contracting officers usually establish BPAs with several suppliers. Each BPA may cover individual items, specific commodity groups ("Federal Supply Classes 2530 and 2540"), or general classes of supplies or services ("hand tools" or "computer maintenance"). The BPA may be limited to specific supplies or services or it may encompass all the supplies or services the supplier can furnish. The BPA limits the size of each order to $150,000 ($7,000,000 for commercial items), and the BPA may also place a limit on the aggregate amount of each month's orders to keep the supplier from becoming overwhelmed by an unexpected flood of orders. However, this limitation does not apply to Federal Supply Schedule contracts (see Chapter 13 for more on Federal Supply Schedule contracts).

To establish BPAs, the contracting officer contacts the suppliers with which he frequently does business and asks each if it would like a BPA. If a supplier says "yes," the contracting officer and the supplier come to an agreement on discounts, the documentation for individual transactions, periodic billing procedures, government personnel authorized to place orders against the BPA, and other necessary details. By accepting a BPA, the supplier agrees to provide the covered supplies or services when the contracting officer or those authorized by the contracting officer place orders. (**NOTE:** Some agencies hold competitions for BPAs that cover information technology products and services, and they issue BPAs to the suppliers providing the "best value" to the government.)

A new supplier can ask the contracting officer to issue it a BPA the next time he issues BPAs for the supplier's particular types of supplies or services.

When soliciting competitive quotations from BPA suppliers, the authorized government employee rotates suppliers as with any other small purchase. Once the government employee has three or more quotations, he places the order against the BPA of the lowest supplier. The only exception is for orders of $3,500 or less – only one "fair and reasonable" quotation is needed, and the government employee must rotate his orders among the BPA suppliers. Usually, BPA orders are placed electronically or orally. However, a paper purchase document may be issued to insure the supplier and purchaser agree on the terms of the transaction. When a paper document is necessary, the order is issued on the SF 1449 if the supply or service is a commercial item or the OF 347 (or authorized equivalent) for non-commercial supplies or services.

The small business set-aside requirement applies to BPAs as well. If two or more BPA suppliers are small businesses that can perform the contract on time and at a reasonable price, the authorized government employee must solicit only small BPA suppliers if the order will exceed the micro-purchase threshold. The small business set-aside requirement does not apply to orders equal to or less than the micro-purchase threshold.

Restrictions on BPA Orders

If a BPA order will exceed $25,000, it must first be synopsized on FedBizOpps to give interested small business suppliers a chance to submit quotations. The contracting officer considers the quotations submitted in response to the FedBizOpps synopsis along with the quotations he obtained from local BPA suppliers and places an order with the supplier submitting the lowest quotation. When the contracting officer places the order, he must synopsize it in FedBizOpps if he believes it will produce subcontracting opportunities.

See FAR 13.303, Blanket Purchase Agreements (BPAs), for more information. See Chapter 13 for special procedures applicable to BPAs established under Federal Supply Schedule contracts.

ON-THE-SPOT PURCHASES

Sometimes, a government employee is away from the office and needs to purchase supplies or services. Since it is impossible for the employee to prepare and process a requisition to acquire the supplies or services, government employees other than a contracting officer can be authorized to make purchases of **$25,000 or less** with travel charge cards (credit cards restricted to travel, lodging, meals, and other travel-related expenses), governmentwide commercial purchase cards, and third-party drafts. However, when authorized employees make purchases between the micro-purchase threshold and $25,000, they must follow the procedures of FAR part 13: obtain competitive quotations, rotate sources, and purchase from small businesses if possible. Because of these requirements, credit cards and third-party drafts are not frequently used for such purchases.

FAST PAYMENT PROCEDURE

A **fast payment procedure** is available to those delivering *supplies* (not services) under purchase orders or BPAs that do not exceed $35,000. By speeding payment for small purchases, the fast payment procedure improves supplier cash-flow and relations with the government.

The fast payment procedure provides for payment for supplies immediately upon receipt of the supplier's invoice, even before the government inspects and accepts the supplies. Under the fast payment procedure, the supplier's invoice constitutes a representation that:

1. The supplies have been delivered to a post office, common carrier, or point of first receipt by the government;

2. The supplies are in the quantity and are of the quality specified in the purchase order or BPA order; and

3. The supplier agrees to replace, repair, or correct supplies that are not received at the destination, are damaged in transit, or do not conform to the purchase order or BPA requirements.

The supplier must prepay the transportation or postage, mark all outer shipping containers "**FAST PAY**," and submit invoices marked "**FAST PAY**" directly to the payment office. The supplies become the property of the government when the supplier delivers them to the post office or common carrier.

This procedure shortcuts the normal process in which the consignee inspects the supplies, accepts them, and then sends the completed invoice to the finance office for payment. Instead, the fast payment procedure allows the supplier to send the invoice directly to the finance office and receive payment while the shipment is making its way to the consignee. Of course, the government is willing to do this because the supplier has agreed to replace, repair, or correct defective or damaged items as a condition for using the fast payment procedure. This protects the government.

Suppliers should always ask to have fast payment procedures included in any purchase order for supplies that is less than $35,000. The contracting officer may include fast payment procedures in purchase orders or BPAs upon request, and most suppliers would prefer to have the money "in hand."

See FAR subpart 13.4, Fast Payment Procedures, for additional information.

REVERSE AUCTIONS

In recent years, federal agencies have been using **reverse auctions** as a tool to reduce the price they pay for certain types of items and services. Unlike a traditional ("forward") auction, in which multiple buyers bid against one another to push the price of an product up, in a reverse auction sellers compete against one another to provide the buyer the lowest price or highest-value offer.

Reverse auctions are best suited for high-volume, commodity-type commercial items or commodity-like services that do not need exact or lengthy specifications, are available off-the-shelf, and are appropriate for competition based on price alone. Agencies generally use reverse auctions to acquire commercial products and services that are less than the simplified acquisition threshold ($150,000), primarily for information technology products and the lease or rental of equipment. As a result, in keeping with the requirement that acquisitions expected to be between $3,500 ($5,000 for the Department of Defense) and $150,000 be reserved for small businesses, most winners are small businesses (see Chapter 6). However, reverse auctions are not restricted to purchases less than the simplified acquisition threshold, nor are they restricted to commercial products.

Reverse auctions are *not* addressed in the FAR, and this has produced extensive confusion about their use and conduct. Therefore, rather than figure out what regulations and procedures to employ, most agencies utilize commercial reverse auction providers to conduct their reverse auctions, the vast majority being conducted by the firm **FedBid** (**http://www.FedBid.com**), which was established specifically to conduct reverse auctions. However, the General Services Administration (GSA) and the Defense Logistics Agency (DLA) have established/manage their own reverse auction sites at **http://www.reverseauctions.gsa.gov** and **https://dla.procurexinc.com**, respectively. Regardless of the type of organization conducting the reverse auction ("auctioneer"), the contracting officer is responsible for following established contracting procedures.

When deciding whether to acquire a product or service through reverse auctions or use some other authorized procedure, the contracting officer must consider whether there is a domestic supplier base that is large enough to encourage competition, and whether the products or services can be acquired primarily on the basis of price (with limited ancillary considerations, such as accelerated delivery, past performance, warranty provisions, etc.) If the contracting officer decides to employ a reverse auction, he establishes the terms for the auction. He may decide to restrict reverse auction bids to those possessing Federal Supply Schedule contracts (see Chapter 13). He may decide to restrict reverse auction bids to a specific type of small business (such as only service-disabled veteran-owned small businesses or only women-owned small businesses [see Chapter 11]) – in fact, reverse auctions are subject to all the SBA's small business regulations, such as the "rule of two" (see Chapter 11) and "certificates of competency" (see Chapter 7). In addition, the contracting officer must decide how long the auction will be conducted (usually three or four days).

To take part in an auction, a bidder must register and agree to the terms and conditions set by the auctioneer, such as bidding procedures, whether the acquisition must be a brand name item, delivery terms, payment processing; etc. The auctioneer will verify that the bidder is registered in the SAM and not on the EPLS (see above). Once the bidder is approved to participate and an account is established, the auctioneer will notify the bidder of opportunities it might be able to fulfill (based on the North American Industry Classification System [NAICS] codes it entered during registration in the SAM). In addition, opportunities that are expected to exceed $25,000 are synopsized in FedBizOpps (see Chapter 5).

If the contracting officer decides to conduct a reverse auction on FedBid's system, he can choose to set a "**target price**," which may be based on a government cost estimate or market research. If a target price is in effect ("active") during the auction, a bidder must bid below that price. However, the target price is ***not*** made available to bidders, nor are the identities of the other bidders or their bid prices made available. The only information given a bidder participating in the auction is whether its bid status is "**LEAD**" or "**LAG**." A "LEAD" bid is one that is below the target price (if "active") and is the lowest overall. A "LAG" bid is one that is not a "LEAD" bid – a bidder that sees its bid status is "LAG" needs to rebid with a reduced price and hope it becomes the "LEAD" bid. A bid's status may change during the auction depending on what the other bidders bid. However, a "LEAD" bid at the end of the auction is not necessarily guaranteed to be the winning bid – the results of the auction are given to the contracting officer and he makes the final award decision – for example, the contracting officer might determine the low bidder is not responsible (see above), is not eligible to receive an award under the set-aside (see Chapter 11), has stipulated an unacceptable delivery schedule, has submitted a bid that is not fair and reasonable, etc. If none of the bids are acceptable, the government can cancel the reverse auction and either conduct another reverse auction (possibly with different specifications, terms and conditions, etc.) or engage in another solicitation process (such as issuing an RFQ [see above]).

Commercial reverse auction systems charge the government buyer a fee. FedBid adds 3% to the price of the bid selected by the government for award, the government pays the winning bidder its bid price plus the 3% fee, and the winning bidder pays FedBid the 3% fee. If the government buyer requires that bids utilize a Federal Supply Schedule contract, the bidder must be sure to add the 0.75% Industrial Funding Fee (IFF) to its bid price and forward that fee to GSA (see Chapter 13 – for GSA reverse auctions).

Government-operated reverse auction systems do not charge fees. However, if the reverse auction requires that bids utilize a Federal Supply Schedule contract, the bidder must be sure to add the 0.75% IFF to its bid price and forward that fee to GSA.

OTHER WAYS OF MAKING SIMPLIFIED ACQUISITIONS

In addition to purchase orders, BPAs, imprest funds, purchase cards, and third-party drafts, the government uses several other techniques to make purchases of $150,000 or less ($7,000,000 or less for commercial items). The two most significant are the "**indefinite-delivery contract**" and the "**Federal Supply Schedules.**" While these are not restricted to purchases of $150,000 or less ($7,000,000 or less for commercial items), many such orders are placed against them.

Indefinite-delivery contracts are addressed in Chapter 10 and Federal Supply Schedules are addressed in Chapter 13.

CHAPTER 7

INVITATIONS FOR BIDS

Whenever the government intends to make a purchase for a non-commercial supply or service that exceeds the simplified acquisition threshold (or commercial items that exceed $7,000,000), it uses a more formal type of solicitation. One of these is **sealed bidding**. Sealed bidding, covered in FAR part 14, is a very rigid procedure in which competitors submit bids, the government opens the bids in public, and the government awards the contract to the lowest *responsive* and *responsible* bidder. Under sealed bidding, a bidder's success or failure normally depends on the price it bids. The contracting officer is prohibited from conducting negotiations during sealed bidding. For this reason, it is not used much anymore. Sealed bidding is usually restricted to construction projects built to detailed blueprints, and it is used to award between 1% and 3% of all federal contract dollars. However, it was the solicitation method of choice for more than 120 years – from 1861 (with the passage of the **Civil Sundry Appropriations Act** [see Chapter 1]) until 1984 (with the passage of the **Competition in Contracting Act** [see Chapter 3]) – and it is the foundation upon which all other solicitation methods are based.

CRITERIA FOR USING SEALED BIDDING

Sealed bidding is the appropriate solicitation method when the government's requirements can be clearly, accurately, and completely described, and two or more bidders are expected to compete independently for the contract. Ordinarily, the contracting officer will use sealed bidding to purchase construction, commercial items over $7,000,000, supplies that are completely described by a product description or a technical data package, or readily-defined services that all trade practitioners perform in the same general manner (such as trash collection and grounds maintenance), and are not available through the Federal Supply Schedules (see Chapter 13). All contracts that are the result of the sealed bidding process must be **firm-fixed-price** unless the contracting officer decides "some flexibility is necessary and feasible" (FAR 14.104, Types of Contracts), in which case he may solicit a **fixed-price with economic price adjustment** contract (see Chapter 9 for more on these two types of contracts).

Sealed bidding is *not* appropriate if the contractor must design a product, if there is no reasonable estimate of the effort the contractor will have to put forth to complete the contract, if the government wants to consider alternate approaches to solving the problem, if the contracting officer intends to award the contract to the offeror providing the "best value" to the government, or if the supply or service must be obtained from a "sole source." The contracting officer uses sealed bidding when he is *reasonably* sure an award of a contract to the lowest bidder, *without discussions*, will provide the government with satisfactory supplies or services at a fair price. If the contracting officer is not reasonably sure this will occur, he uses some other method, such as negotiation procedures (see Chapter 8) or ordering against a multiple award schedule (see Chapter 13).

Paragraph (a) of FAR 6.401, Sealed Bidding and Competitive Proposals, requires contracting officers to solicit sealed bids if the following four conditions exist:

1. Time permits the solicitation, submission, and evaluation of sealed bids (besides the requirement that a synopsis be published in **FedBizOpps** at least 15 days prior to issuance of the solicitation, paragraph (a) of FAR 14.202-1, Bidding Time, requires the contracting officer to allow *at least 30 days* between the issuance of the solicitation and bid opening – but see below for the exception to this rule for streamlined commercial items synopses/solicitations);

2. The award will be based on price and other price-related factors;

3. It is not necessary to conduct discussions with the responding bidders about their bids; and

4. There is a reasonable expectation of receiving more than one sealed bid.

If any of these four conditions is absent, the contracting officer must forego sealed bidding and use another method instead.

THE INVITATION FOR BIDS

The solicitation document in sealed bidding is called an **Invitation For Bids** (IFB). The IFB is an invitation for interested parties to submit bids for the supplies or services needed by the government. The IFB is a set of terms and conditions under which the government will agree to contract. To be considered for an award, a bidder must agree to comply *in all material respects* with the stated terms and conditions of the IFB at the price bid. Such bids are considered **responsive** to the terms and conditions of the IFB and are the only ones the contracting officer may consider for award. The contracting officer may not consider any bids that are **nonresponsive** – those bids that propose alternate terms or contain restrictive conditions, *even if the proposed alternate terms or conditions are more advantageous to the government!* In this way the contracting officer safeguards the integrity of the sealed bidding process and makes sure all bids are comparable.

Every IFB contains a description of the supplies or services the government needs, the quantity required, the specifications or statement of work, the delivery schedule, quality assurance provisions, inspection and acceptance criteria, the deadline for submission of bids, and other necessary provisions. To make it easier for bidders to locate the information, the contracting officer uses one of four formats when preparing the IFB: the **Standard Form 1449** for commercial items (see Chapter 6 and Appendix B for a sample IFB), the **streamlined synopsis/solicitation for commercial items** (see Chapter 6), the **uniform contract format**, or the **simplified contract format**. The resulting contract retains the same appearance and arrangement as the IFB, regardless of the format chosen.

The Standard Form 1449

Since the Standard Form 1449, Solicitation/Contract/Order for Commercial Items, is required for the purchase of **all commercial items** when a paper solicitation or contract is being issued, IFBs for commercial items over $7,000,000 are in the same format as SF 1449s used to acquire commercial items under $7,000,000 through simplified procedures (see Chapter 6). The only difference is that the IFB includes FAR 52.212-2, Evaluation Factors, as an addendum. In FAR 52.212-2, the contracting officer must include only *price-related* factors since IFBs are awarded to the lowest bidder. He cannot state in the SF 1449 addendum that he will be considering such factors as accelerated delivery or quality of the item when making his decision, as he is permitted to do when making a small purchase. The following are some of the price-related factors he can use for evaluation purposes:

■ Differences in costs to the government that would be incurred if one bid was accepted rather than another. For example, if bids are on an f.o.b. origin basis (that is, the government will pay for transportation), transportation costs from the factory to the place of delivery will be added to each bid.

■ If the IFB calls for two or more different items, the contracting officer must consider the advantages or disadvantages to the government of awarding multiple contracts. For example, if the IFB asked for bids on knives and forks, the contracting officer might decide *not* to award a single contract to the overall low bidder if awarding one contract to the lowest bidder on knives and another contract to the lowest bidder on forks would produce the lowest aggregate cost to the government.

- Federal, state, and local taxes.

- The origin of the supplies and, if the supplies are foreign, the application of the Buy American Act or any other restriction on the purchase of foreign products (see Chapter 12).

IFBs issued on SF 1449s (or electronic replicas) must be synopsized in **FedBizOpps** at least 15 days before releasing the IFB. However, the contracting officer is not required to allow 30 days for bidders to submit bids as with IFBs in the uniform and simplified formats (see below), but can allow a shorter period for the submission of bids.

The Streamlined Synopsis/Solicitation for Commercial Items

As with solicitations for commercial items under $7,000,000 that are simple and do not include lengthy addenda (see Chapter 6), the contracting officer may use the streamlined synopsis/solicitation for commercial items over $7,000,000. The contracting officer may publish the IFB in **FedBizOpps** along with its synopsis as an alternative to the SF 1449, thereby eliminating the 15 day wait between publication of the synopsis and the issuance of the IFB. And, as is the case with IFBs on SF 1449s, the contracting officer can allow a period shorter than 30 days for the submission of bids.

Uniform Contract Format

The Uniform Contract Format (UCF) is still the most used format for solicitation documents and contracts. The UCF consists of thirteen sections, divided into four parts. All IFBs for non-commercial supplies and services must be in the UCF, except those in the simplified contract format (see below) and IFBs for construction (see Chapter 14), shipbuilding, ship overhaul or repair, subsistence, and supplies or services that require special contract forms.

Part I – The Schedule

The Schedule is the part of the IFB in which the contracting officer explains the government's requirements and specifications. Most of the Schedule is custom-tailored for each IFB.

- Section A, Solicitation/Contract Form, consists of **Standard Form 33, Solicitation, Offer, and Award**, or an electronic equivalent (see Figure 8). The SF 33 contains:

  - the solicitation number
  - the date the IFB was issued

SOLICITATION, OFFER AND AWARD	1. THIS CONTRACT IS A RATED ORDER UNDER DPAS (15 CFR 700)		RATING DO-C9	PAGE 1	OF	PAGES 16

2. CONTRACT NUMBER	3. SOLICITATION NUMBER	4. TYPE OF SOLICITATION	5. DATE ISSUED	6. REQUISITION/PURCHASE NUMBER
	SPM600-17-B-0987	[X] SEALED BID (IFB) [ ] NEGOTIATED (RFP)	01/30/2017	T0012/235-17-P

7. ISSUED BY   CODE [ ]   **8. ADDRESS OFFER TO** *(If other than item 7)*

Defense Supply Center Philadelphia, Subsistence
700 Robbins Avenue, Room 254, Philadelphia, PA 19111-5096

NOTE: In sealed bid solicitations "offer" and "offeror" mean "bid" and "bidder".

SOLICITATION

9. Sealed offers in original and   **2**   copies for furnishings the supplies or services in the Schedule will be received at the place specified in item 8, or if

hand carried, in the depository located in   **Room 254**   until **4:00 pm** local time **03/06/2017**

                                                                             (Hour)   (Date)

CAUTION - LATE Submissions, Modifications, and Withdrawals: See Section L, Provision No. 52.214-7 or 52.215-1. All offers are subject to all terms and conditions contained in this solicitation.

10. FOR INFORMATION CALL:	A. NAME Joseph Blow	B. TELEPHONE *(NO COLLECT CALLS)*			C. E-MAIL ADDRESS
		AREA CODE 215	NUMBER 5554321	EXTENSION 101	joseph.blow@dla.mil

11. TABLE OF CONTENTS

(X)	SEC.	DESCRIPTION	PAGE(S)	(X)	SEC.	DESCRIPTION	PAGE(S)
		PART I - THE SCHEDULE				PART II - CONTRACT CLAUSES	
X	A	SOLICITATION/CONTRACT-FORM	1	X	I	CONTRACT CLAUSES	6-9
X	B	SUPPLIES OR SERVICES AND PRICES/COSTS	2			PART III - LIST OF DOCUMENTS, EXHIBITS AND OTHER ATTACH.	
X	C	DESCRIPTION/SPECS./WORK STATEMENT	3	X	J	LIST OF ATTACHMENTS	9
X	D	PACKAGING AND MARKING	3			PART IV - REPRESENTATIONS AND INSTRUCTIONS	
X	E	INSPECTION AND ACCEPTANCE	3-4	X	K	REPRESENTATIONS, CERTIFICATIONS AND OTHER STATEMENTS OF OFFERORS	9-13
X	F	DELIVERIES OR PERFORMANCE	4-5				
X	G	CONTRACT ADMINISTRATION DATA	5-6	X	L	INSTRUCTIONS, CONDITIONS, AND NOTICES TO OFFERORS	13-16
X	H	SPECIAL CONTRACT REQUIREMENTS	6	X	M	EVALUATION FACTORS FOR AWARD	16

OFFER *(Must be fully completed by offeror)*

NOTE: Item 12 does not apply if the solicitation includes the provisions at 52.214-16, Minimum Bid Acceptance Period.

12. In compliance with the above, the undersigned agrees, if this offer is accepted within _____ calendar days *(60 calendar days unless a different*

period is inserted by the offeror) from the date for receipt of offers specified above, to furnish any or all items upon which prices are offered at the set opposite each item, delivered at the designated point(s), within the time specified in the schedule.

13. DISCOUNT FOR PROMPT PAYMENT *(See Section I, Clause No. 52.232-8)*	10 CALENDAR DAYS (%)	20 CALENDAR DAYS (%)	30 CALENDAR DAYS (%)		CALENDAR DAYS(%)

14. ACKNOWLEDGMENT OF AMENDMENTS *(The offeror acknowledges receipt of amendments to the SOLICITATION for offerors and related documents numbered and dated)*	AMENDMENT NO.	DATE	AMENDMENT NO.	DATE

15A. NAME AND ADDRESS OF OFFEROR	CODE		FACILITY		16. NAME AND THE TITLE OF PERSON AUTHORIZED TO SIGN OFFER *(Type or print)*

15B. TELEPHONE NUMBER			15C. CHECK IF REMITTANCE ADDRESS IS [ ] DIFFERENT FROM ABOVE - ENTER SUCH ADDRESS IN SCHEDULE.	17. SIGNATURE	18. OFFER DATE
AREA CODE	NUMBER	EXTENSION			

AWARD *(To be completed by Government)*

19. ACCEPTED AS TO ITEMS NUMBERED	20. AMOUNT	21. ACCOUNTING AND APPROPRIATION

22. AUTHORITY FOR USING OTHER THAN FULL OPEN COMPETITION: [ ] 10 U.S.C. 2304 (c) [ ] 41 U.S.C. 3304(a) ( )	23. SUBMIT INVOICES TO ADDRESS SHOWN IN *(4 copies unless otherwise specified)*	ITEM

24. ADMINISTERED BY *(If other than Item 7)*	25. PAYMENT WILL BE MADE BY CODE

26. NAME OF CONTRACTING OFFICER *(Type or print)*	27. UNITED STATES OF AMERICA *(Signature of Contracting Officer)*	28. AWARD DATE

IMPORTANT - Award will be made on this Form, or on Standard Form 26, or by other authorized official written notice.

AUTHORIZED FOR LOCAL REPRODUCTION
Previous edition is unusable

STANDARD FORM 33 (REV. 6/2014)
Prescribed by GSA - FAR (48 CFR) 53.214 (c)

Figure 8 - Solicitation, Offer, and Award (Standard Form 33)

- – the issuing contracting office
- – the person to call for more information (the "point of contact")
- – the time, date, and place where the bids will be opened (the **"bid opening date"** must be at least **30 days** after the IFB issuance to give bidders a reasonable amount of time to prepare and submit bids [except IFBs for commercial items may specify a shorter period]; if no time for the bid opening is specified, the bid opening is 4:30 pm, local time)
- – a table of contents
- – a place for the bidder to sign the bid
- – a place for the contracting officer to countersign if he chooses to accept the bid and form a binding contract

The form provides a place for the bidder to specify any discounts for prompt payment, and it states the acceptance period during which the bid is valid and can be accepted by the government. It also provides a place for the bidder to acknowledge solicitation amendments.

- ■ Section B, Supplies or Services and Prices/Costs, is where the bidder enters its bid price. It includes a brief description of the supplies or services being purchased, the quantities of those supplies or services, and any provisions for quantity variation (an agreement by the government to consider the contract complete if the contractor delivers a quantity within a specified percentage of the quantity being purchased; for example, 2% over or under the quantity required by the contract).

  If there is more than one supply or service being purchased under the IFB, each is set out separately and identified with its own **contract line item number** (CLIN). Technical and other data that the government intends to buy, such as a contractor-prepared test and demonstration report that provides and analyzes test results, will also be listed in Section B. The contracting officer can include any other information that helps identify the line item(s).

- ■ Section C, Description/Specifications/Work Statement, contains a more comprehensive description of the supplies or services. The description may reference specifications, standards, drawings, technical data packages, or any other product descriptions.

- ■ Section D, Packaging and Marking, provides the packaging, packing, and marking requirements. Packaging and marking specifications and standards may be referenced.

- ■ Section E, Inspection and Acceptance, specifies the inspection and acceptance requirements and the location(s) where the inspection and acceptance will take place. It specifies any sampling criteria, first article test requirements, special requirements for inspection or quality assurance programs, and other similar requirements as necessary.

■ <u>Section F, Deliveries or Performance</u>, specifies the delivery or performance schedule and also the place and method of delivery or performance.

■ <u>Section G, Contract Administration Data</u>, provides accounting and appropriation data and other instructions to the contract administration office. Also, it may identify the contracting officer's representative (COR) (see Chapter 2).

■ <u>Section H, Special Contract Requirements</u>, contains the customized provisions that apply to the IFB. Such provisions might include the terms for options, provisions for multiyear contracting (see Chapter 10), any applicable Service Contract Act wage determinations by the secretary of labor (see Chapter 16), economic price adjustment provisions (see Chapter 9), or any other provision that will govern the contract and does not fit into any of the other sections.

Part II – Contract Clauses

■ <u>Section I, Contract Clauses</u>, contains the clauses required by law or regulation. Normally, only those clauses in FAR part 52, Solicitation Provisions and Contract Clauses, and part 52 of the agency's FAR supplement are included in this section. The clauses in Section I are predetermined by the very characteristics of the proposed contract. For example, a $135,000 supply contract is required to have certain contract clauses and a $850,000 research and development contract is required to have different contract clauses. The contracting officer has little leeway when preparing this section.

   FAR subpart 52.3 contains matrices that list all the clauses in part 52, the different products the government purchases (supplies, research and development, services, construction, motor vehicle leasing, and others), and indicates whether each clause is required, required-when-applicable, optional, or not applicable to IFBs for that particular product. Bidders with doubts about whether a particular clause applies to an IFB should refer to FAR subpart 52.3 before contacting the contracting officer (see Figure 9).

Part III – List of Documents, Exhibits, and Other Attachments

■ <u>Section J, List of Documents, Exhibits, and Other Attachments</u>, is an inventory of all the documents that are too lengthy to be included in the IFB in full text. For example, a list of data to be bought under the contract might be identified as "Exhibit A." A federal specification that provides details of the item being purchased will be listed here if it is provided with the solicitation. When a bidder receives an IFB, it should check Section J to make sure all the attachments to the solicitation are included.

52.301 Solicitation provisions and contract clauses (Matrix).

KEY:

Type of Contract:

P or C	=	Provision or Clause
IBR	=	Is Incorporation by Reference Authorized? (See FAR 52.102)
UCF	=	Uniform Contract Format Section, when Applicable
FP SUP	=	Fixed-Price Supply
CR SUP	=	Cost-Reimbursement Supply
FP R&D	=	Fixed-Price Research & Development
CR R&D	=	Cost Reimbursement Research & Development
FP SVC	=	Fixed-Price Service
CR SVC	=	Cost Reimbursement Service
FP CON	=	Fixed-Price Construction
CR CON	=	Cost Reimbursement Construction
T&M LH	=	Time & Material/Labor Hours
LMV	=	Leasing of Motor Vehicles
COM SVC	=	Communication Services
DDR	=	Dismantling, Demolition, or Removal of Improvements
A&E	=	Architect-Engineering
FAC	=	Facilities
IND DEL	=	Indefinite Delivery
TRN	=	Transportation
SAP	=	Simplified Acquisition Procedures (excluding micro-purchase)
UTL SVC	=	Utility Services
CI	=	Commercial Items

Contract Purpose:

R	=	Required
A	=	Required when Applicable
O	=	Optional
I	=	Revision

PRINCIPLE TYPE AND/OR PURPOSE OF CONTRACT

PROVISION OR CLAUSE	PRESCRIBED IN	P OR C	IBR	UCF	FP SUP	CR SUP	FP R&D	CR R&D	FP SVC	CR SVC	FP CON	CR CON	T&M LH	LMV	COM SVC	DDR	A&E	FAC	IND DEL	TRN	SAP	UTL SVC	CI
52.202-1 Definitions.	2.201	C	Yes	I	R	R	A	R	R	R	R	R	R	R	R	R	R	R	R	R		R	
52.203-2 Certificate of Independent Price Determination.	3.103-1	P	No	K	A		A		A		A				A	A	A	A	A	A		A	
52.203-3 Gratuities.	3.202	C	Yes	I	A	A	A	A	A	A	A	A	A	A	A	A	A	A	A	A		A	
52.203-5 Covenant Against Contingent Fees.	3.404	C	Yes	I	R	R	R	R	R	R	R	R	R	R	R	R	R	R	R	R		R	
52.203-6 Restrictions on Subcontractor Sales to the Government.	3.503-2	C	Yes	I	R	R	R		R	R					R	R	R	R	R	R		R	
Alternate I																							R
52.203-7 Anti-Kickback Procedures.	3.502-3	C	Yes	I	R	R	R	R	R	R	R	R	R	R	R	R	R	R	R	R		R	
52.203-8 Cancellation, Rescission, and Recovery of Funds for Illegal or Improper Activity.	3.104-9(a)	C	Yes	I	A	A	A	A	A	A	A	A	A	A	A	A	A	A	A	A		A	
52.203-10 Price or Fee Adjustment for Illegal or Improper Activity.	3.104-9(b)	C	Yes	I	A	A	A	A	A	A	A	A	A	A	A	A	A	A	A	A		A	
52.203-11 Certification and Disclosure Regarding Payments to Influence Certain Federal Transactions.	3.808(a)	P	Yes	K	A	A	A	A	A	A	A	A	A	A	A	A	A	A	A	A		A	
52.203-12 Limitation on Payments to Influence Certain Federal Transactions.	3.808(b)	C	Yes	I	A	A	A	A	A	A	A	A	A	A	A	A	A	A	A	A		A	
52.203-13 Contractor Code of Business Ethics and Conduct.	3.1004(a)	C	Yes	I	A	A	A	A	A	A	A	A	A	A	A	A	A	A	A	A		A	

(FAC 2005–83)   52.3-3

Figure 9 - FAR subpart 52.3, Contract Clauses Matrix

Part IV – Representations and Instructions

This part of the IFB does not become a physical part of the resulting contract. However, the winning bidder's "reps and certs" are incorporated into the contract by reference (see FAR 52.204-19, Incorporation by Reference of Representations and Certifications) and retained by the contracting officer in case the validity of a particular representation or certification is challenged later. The contracting officer uses the representations and certifications to determine whether the bidder is eligible for award.

- Section K, Representations, Certifications, and Other Statements of Bidder, is where the bidder must make representations concerning its business and certify that it complies with all applicable laws and regulations. Because the bidder completed most of the "reps and certs" when it registered in the **System for Award Management** (SAM – see Chapter 5), the bidder does nothing to **FAR 52.204-8, Annual Representations and Certifications**, *unless* one of the 28 reps or certs is not accurate for the particular solicitation. When that is the case, the bidder identifies in paragraph (d) the changed rep or cert that applies to the solicitation. For example, the bidder must represent in **SAM** whether it intends or does not intend "to use one or more plants or facilities located at a different address from the address of the bidder as indicated in this bid" (FAR 52.214-14, Place of Performance – Sealed Bidding). If the bidder has only one facility, it would have checked "does not intend" in **SAM**. However, if the bidder intends to lease another facility to perform the contract should it win, the bidder would identify its **SAM** representation for FAR 52.214-14 as inaccurate for the solicitation, and notify the contracting officer that it "intends" to use a facility at a different address.

  While **SAM** takes care of the common reps and certs, there are some miscellaneous reps and certs that the bidder may be requested to complete, or some information that the bidder may be requested to provide. For example:

  - FAR 52.207-4, Economic Purchase Quantity – Supplies (if the quantity of supplies is not economically advantageous to the government, at what quantity would there be a significant price break?)

  - FAR 52.214-16, Minimum Bid Acceptance Period (what is the minimum bid acceptance period the bidder will allow?)

  - What will be the weights and dimensions of a shipment? (of particular importance if the government will be arranging for transportation)

  Bidders should make sure they *know* the meaning of all the reps and certs, both in **SAM** and in Section K. If a contracting officer discovers that a contractor is not complying with, or is violating the terms of, any of the certifications, he can terminate the contract for default and turn the matter over to the

Department of Justice for prosecution as a **willful misrepresentation, false statement**, or **fraud** (see Chapter 17 for prohibitions and penalties). Bidders that confront an unfamiliar certification or representation should first look it up in the FAR or agency FAR supplement. If the bidder still does not understand the rep or cert, it should contact the contracting officer for an explanation. The contracting officer will either explain it or put the bidder in touch with someone who can.

■   <u>Section L, Instructions and Conditions, and Notices to Bidders</u>, is where the contracting officer tells the bidder how to prepare and submit its bid. Section L also contains information on the various circumstances that may affect the bid, such as:

   –   The procedures the government will use to handle late bids;

   –   Whether electronic bids will be accepted (see later in this chapter);

   –   The addresses of offices that will provide copies of those specifications and drawings incorporated by reference;

   –   Any requirements for the submission of bid samples or descriptive literature with the bid (see below);

   –   Whether progress payments will be authorized (see Chapter 18); and

   –   Any other notices and instructions the contracting officer decides are appropriate and important to a complete understanding of the IFB.

■   <u>Section M, Evaluation Factors for Award</u>, explains exactly how the government will evaluate the bids and determine the low bidder. Just because a bidder submits the lowest bid does not mean its bid will produce the lowest overall cost to the government. Therefore, this section tells the bidder which factors will be used by the government in making this determination. For example, the following are some typical evaluation factors that may be added to (or subtracted from) the bid prices:

   –   Transportation costs on bids calling for f.o.b. origin delivery;

   –   Prices of options (see below);

   –   Savings from the waiver of first article testing requirements (see Chapter 18);

   –   Federal, state, and local taxes; and

   –   The fair market rental cost of government-furnished property in the possession of the bidder (see Chapter 18).

Depending on the supply or service being purchased, there are many other factors that can be evaluated to determine the bidder submitting the lowest evaluated price. However, the contracting officer is prohibited from evaluating bids using any factors other than those specified in Section M. If the contracting officer discovers he left out of the IFB an evaluation factor he will use to determine the overall lowest bidder, he must amend the IFB to add the evaluation factor to Section M.

Order of Precedence

The following clause is included in Section I of every IFB in the UCF:

FAR 52.214-29, ORDER OF PRECEDENCE – SEALED BIDDING. Any inconsistency in this solicitation or contract shall be resolved by giving precedence in the following order: (a) the Schedule (excluding the specifications) [Part I of the IFB except for Section C]; (b) representations and other instructions [Part IV of the IFB]; (c) contract clauses [Part II of the IFB]; (d) other documents, exhibits, and attachments [Part III of the IFB]; and (e) the specifications [Section C of the IFB].

This clause allows the bidder to proceed with the preparation of its bid without having to ask the contracting officer to resolve every discrepancy or inconsistency in the solicitation. There are almost always conflicts or contradictions within any moderately complex IFB, and this order of precedence eliminates the need for the contracting officer to amend the IFB whenever a conflict or contradiction between provisions is brought to his attention. The clause assigns the highest priority to those portions of the IFB written by the contracting officer and the lowest priority to the inflexible specifications (which, as mentioned in Chapter 4, can only be amended with the concurrence of all using agencies).

For example, if the IFB cites a specification that requires blue widgets and Section C of the IFB requires red widgets, the Order of Precedence clause establishes that the widgets must be red. Section C is part of the Schedule and, when the contracting officer prepared the IFB, he consciously decided to require the color red. Because of the Order of Precedence clause, the bidder can safely prepare a bid for red widgets without using valuable time asking the contracting officer which color he wants. The clause also protects the contract winner when it delivers red widgets instead of blue ones. Of course, the bidder is entitled to a clarification from the contracting officer should the bidder want one. (FAR 52.215-8, the "Order of Precedence" clause used in negotiated procurements, contains the same language as the sealed bidding clause.)

Simplified Contract Format

Contracting officers have the option of using the simplified contract format (SCF) for their IFBs. The SCF provides more flexibility in the preparation and organization of the IFB than does the UCF, but contracting officers must arrange the information in the following format to the maximum practical extent:

■ Solicitation/Contract Form consists of **Standard Form 1447, Solicitation/ Contract** (see Figure 10). It contains much the same information as the SF 33 in the UCF: the solicitation number, the date the IFB is issued, the contracting office, a place for the bidder and contracting officer to sign. However, the SF 1447 does not provide a block in which the contracting officer specifies the time and date of the bid opening (at least 30 days after IFB issuance, except that bids for commercial items may provide for a shorter period), the place where the bids will be opened, and the point of contact. The contracting officer has to type this information on the form, usually in block 9, Agency Use.

■ The Contract Schedule is on the SF 1447, too. The SF 1447 provides space for a description of the supplies or services being purchased (or data sufficient to identify the supply or service, such as a part number), the quantities being purchased, the bid price, the total amount for each line item, and prompt payment discounts. In addition, the contract schedule must include any of the following when applicable:

– Packaging and marking requirements;
– Inspection and acceptance, quality assurance, and reliability requirements;
– Place of delivery, delivery dates, period of performance, and f.o.b. point; and
– Other information as necessary (such as fund citations).

■ Clauses contains only those provisions and clauses required by the FAR and those considered by the contracting officer to be *absolutely necessary* to the purchase.

■ List of Documents and Attachments is included when necessary.

■ Representations and Instructions corresponds to Part IV of the UCF and is divided into three sections that correspond to Sections K, L, and M of the UCF:

– Representations and Certifications (many of the representations and certifications are completed annually by the offeror in the SAM [see above]);
– Instructions, Conditions, and Notices; and
– Evaluation Factors for Award.

SOLICITATION/CONTRACT BIDDER/OFFEROR TO COMPLETE BLOCKS 11, 13, 15, 21, 22, & 27			1. THIS CONTRACT IS A RATED ORDER UNDER DPAS (15 CFR 700)	RATING DO-A3	PAGE 1	OF 12

2. CONTRACT NO.	3. AWARD/EFFECTIVE DATE	4. SOLICITATION NUMBER HSCG85-17-B-6250	5. SOLICITATION TYPE ☐ SEALED BIDS (IFB) ☐ NEGOTIATED (RFP)	6. SOLICITATION ISSUE DATE 01/12/2017

7. ISSUED BY   CODE `HSCG85`

Commander, Maintenance & Logistics Command, Pacific
1300 Stedman Street, Room 303
Ketchikan, AK 99901

For information call Rose Budde at 907-555-6789

NO COLLECT CALLS

8. THIS ACQUISITION IS ☐ UNRESTRICTED OR ☐ SET ASIDE: 100 % FOR:

☒ SMALL BUSINESS

☐ HUBZONE SMALL BUSINESS

☐ SERVICE-DISABLED VETERAN-OWNED SMALL BUSINESS

☐ 8(A)

☐ WOMEN-OWNED SMALL BUSINESS (WOSB) ELIGIBLE UNDER THE WOSB PROGRAM

☐ EDWOSB

NAICS: 336611

SIZE STANDARD: 1,250 employees

9. (AGENCY USE)

Submit original and one copy of bid to 1300 Stedman St., Room 303, Ketchikan, AK no later than 11:00 am on Feb. 13, 2017

10. ITEMS TO BE PURCHASED *(BRIEF DESCRIPTION)*

☐ SUPPLIES   ☒ SERVICES   Drydock and Repair of CGC SPAR (WLB 206)

11. IF OFFER IS ACCEPTED BY THE GOVERNMENT WITHIN _____ CALENDAR DAYS (60 CALENDAR DAYS UNLESS OFFEROR INSERTS A DIFFERENT PERIOD) FROM THE DATE SET FORTH IN BLOCK 9 ABOVE, THE CONTRACTOR AGREES TO HOLD ITS OFFERED PRICES FIRM FOR THE ITEMS SOLICITED HEREIN AND TO ACCEPT ANY RESULTING CONTRACT SUBJECT TO THE TERMS AND CONDITIONS STATED HEREIN.

12. ADMINISTERED BY   CODE _____

13. CONTRACTOR OFFEROR   CODE _____   FACILITY CODE _____

14. PAYMENT WILL BE MADE BY   CODE _____

TELEPHONE NUMBER _____ DUNS NUMBER _____

☐ CHECK IF REMITTANCE IS DIFFERENT AND PUT SUCH ADDRESS IN OFFER

SUBMIT INVOICES TO ADDRESS SHOWN IN BLOCK:

15. PROMPT PAYMENT DISCOUNT

16. AUTHORITY FOR USING OTHER THAN FULL AND OPEN COMPETITION ☐ 10 U.S.C. 2304 ( ) ☐ 41 U.S.C. 253 ( )

17. ITEM NO.	18. SCHEDULE OF SUPPLIES/SERVICES	19. QUANTITY	20. UNIT	21. UNIT PRICE	22. AMOUNT
0001	Drydock and Repair of CGC SPAR (WLB 206) in accordance with Attachment 1	1	Lot		

23. ACCOUNTING AND APPROPRIATION DATA

24. TOTAL AWARD AMOUNT *(FOR GOVERNMENT USE ONLY)*

25. CONTRACTOR IS REQUIRED TO SIGN THIS DOCUMENT AND RETURN _____ COPIES TO ISSUING OFFICE. CONTRACTOR AGREES TO FURNISH AND DELIVER ALL ITEMS SET FORTH OR OTHERWISE IDENTIFIED ABOVE AND ON ANY CONTINUATION SHEETS SUBJECT TO THE TERMS AND CONDITIONS SPECIFIED HEREIN.

☐

26. AWARD OF CONTRACT: YOUR OFFER ON SOLICITATION NUMBER SHOWN IN BLOCK 4 INCLUDING ANY ADDITIONS OR CHANGES WHICH ARE SET FORTH HEREIN, IS ACCEPTED AS TO ITEMS:

☐

27. SIGNATURE OF OFFEROR/CONTRACTOR

28. UNITED STATES OF AMERICA *(SIGNATURE OF CONTRACTING OFFICER)*

NAME AND TITLE OF SIGNER *(TYPE OR PRINT)*   DATE SIGNED

NAME OF CONTRACTING OFFICER   DATE SIGNED

AUTHORIZED FOR LOCAL REPRODUCTION
PREVIOUS EDITION NOT USABLE

STANDARD FORM 1447 (REV. 2/2012)
Prescribed by GSA - FAR (48 CFR) 53.214(d)

Figure 10 - Solicitation/Contract (Standard Form 1447)

This portion of an IFB in the SCF does not become a physical part of the resulting contract but is kept in the contract file. However, as with the UCF, the representations and certifications are used by the contracting officer to determine whether the bidder is eligible for award, and the winning bidder's representations, certifications, and other statements are incorporated into the contract by reference.

REVIEWING THE IFB AND PREPARING TO BID

Once a prospective bidder obtains a copy of the IFB, it normally reviews the description of the item, the specifications or the statement of work, and decides whether to submit a bid. Most bidders, if they decide to submit a bid, call the point of contact identified on the face of the IFB (usually the contract specialist) to obtain the **price history** of the supply or service:

- What was the last price paid?
- What was the quantity purchased?
- When was the contract awarded?
- To whom was the contract awarded?

This is public information, and the point of contact should have it readily available. Many contracting officers put this information in the IFB itself.

If, during the review of the IFB, the bidder has questions, it must address those questions to the contracting officer (going through the point of contact). Contracting officers are prohibited from releasing any information that is not available to the public. A contracting officer can provide price history but not the amount of money on the requisition; he can explain the meaning of a particular FAR clause but not how the bidder should comply with that clause. There are strict rules concerning procurement integrity and disclosure of information – see Chapter 17 for more details.

If the bidder has a simple question, the contracting officer may answer it over the telephone. If the question is complex or involves technical considerations, the contracting officer will ask the bidder to put the question in writing (usually by email), and he will respond in writing. The contracting officer is the only one who can commit the government to an interpretation of the IFB. Any other person's interpretation is *not* binding on the government, and a bidder relies on that person's interpretation at its own risk. The contracting officer can even overrule the interpretation of the engineer who wrote the specifications or statement of work. The contracting officer must enforce what is in the solicitation, not what the engineer or anyone else intended.

Amending the IFB

When bidders' questions demonstrate the IFB is seriously flawed or misleading in some manner, the contracting officer will **amend** the IFB to clarify the questionable language or correct the deficiency. For example, if the intentions of the engineer who wrote the specifications are not reflected accurately in the solicitation, the contracting officer will direct the engineer to define and explain the requirements more clearly. Then the contracting officer will amend the solicitation to incorporate the clarified requirements. Also, the contracting officer may amend the IFB when the government's requirements change after the release of the IFB, such as for changes in quantities, specifications, or delivery schedule.

The contracting officer amends the IFB by issuing a **Standard Form 30, Amendment of Solicitation/Modification of Contract**, or electronic equivalent, to all the prospective bidders sent a copy of the IFB (see Appendix B for a sample amendment), or by publishing the amendment in **FedBizOpps**. If the amendment is relatively minor or issued well before the bid opening date, the contracting officer will *probably not* extend the bid opening date. However, if the amendment makes major changes to the IFB or is issued just before the bid opening date, the contracting officer *may* extend the bid opening date. (Those who obtain a copy of the IFB from **FedBizOpps** should routinely check back to see if any amendments have been posted. Contracting offices are unable to send SF 30s to those who download IFBs because they do not leave their mailing addresses.)

When the contracting officer issues an IFB amendment, a bidder must either (1) sign (actually or electronically) the SF 30 and return it with the bid, or (2) acknowledge the amendment in block 14 of the SF 33 in the UCF, or in its response to the streamlined synopsis/IFB (there is no place to acknowledge amendments on the SF 1447 in the SCF or the SF 1449 for commercial items). Either method shows the contracting officer that the bidder received the IFB amendment and intends to comply with all the terms and conditions of the IFB *as amended*. If the bidder does not acknowledge or sign each amendment, the contracting officer may disqualify its bid as "nonresponsive."

When a bidder fails to acknowledge an amendment, the contracting officer has no way of knowing whether the bid applies to the original requirements or to the amended requirements. Because one of the conditions for using IFBs is that the contracting officer cannot "conduct discussions with the responding bidders about their bids," he cannot contact the bidder and ask what the bidder meant. Therefore, all the contracting officer can do is disqualify the bid (the only exception is if the unacknowledged amendment is very minor, such as when it merely corrects a spelling error). So, a smart bidder *always* checks with the contracting officer *before* submitting its bid to find out if it has all the amendments.

A prospective bidder can initiate a request to amend an IFB. For example, a bidder might alert the contracting officer that the required delivery date for supplies is impossible to achieve because the lead-time for materials exceeds the delivery date. The contracting officer would then investigate to determine whether the "required" delivery date is firm or can be extended without injuring the government. If the contracting officer finds the delivery date can be extended, he will issue an SF 30 amending the IFB to reflect a revised delivery date (or publish the amendment in **FedBizOpps** if a streamlined synopsis/IFB was used). If the contracting officer finds the delivery date cannot be extended, he will notify the bidder of his decision and let the IFB delivery date stand. The decision is the contracting officer's.

Canceling the IFB

Occasionally, an IFB must be canceled because there is no longer a requirement for the supplies or services or the specifications are undergoing extensive revision. When this occurs, the contracting officer sends a "notice of cancellation" to all the prospective bidders furnished a copy of the IFB and publishes the notice in **FedBizOpps**. The notice will identify the IFB, briefly explain the reason for the cancellation, and assure the bidder that it will be given the opportunity to bid on any future requirements for the supplies or services involved. Any responses to the IFB that the contracting office has received will be returned unopened (if bids were received electronically, the data is purged from primary and backup data storage systems).

PRE-BID CONFERENCE

Sometimes the contracting officer will hold a **pre-bid conference** to brief prospective bidders on complicated specifications and requirements (streamlined synopses/IFBs should not be used if the items are complicated enough to require a pre-bid conference). The contracting officer usually holds these conferences between one and two weeks after issuing the IFB. There are two primary reasons for holding the conference then: (1) it gives the bidders time to look over the IFB and prepare questions; and (2) it gives the bidders time to prepare their bids based on the information obtained at the conference.

Normally, the IFB contains the notice of the pre-bid conference. The notice will specify the time and place of the conference, request that prospective bidders submit questions in writing so prepared answers can be distributed during the conference, and often ask that those interested in attending make reservations with the contracting officer. If, after release of the IFB, the contracting officer decides to hold a pre-bid conference, he will provide notice to all the prospective bidders sent the IFB and post it electronically on **FedBizOpps**.

Attendance at the pre-bid conference is optional, and prospective bidders are responsible for making all arrangements necessary to attend the conference.

In a typical pre-bid conference, the contracting officer will summarize the IFB's requirements, provide the prepared answers to those present and explain the reasons for those answers, and entertain questions from the attendees. Normally, the contracting officer will invite appropriate government technical and legal personnel to attend the conference, and he may ask them to answer specific questions. Sometimes the conference discussions identify a significant flaw in the IFB that must be corrected. However, remarks and explanations at the conference do *not* qualify or change the terms of the IFB or the specifications. Any changes to the IFB must be made through an amendment to the IFB.

At the end of the conference, the contracting officer prepares a complete record of the conference and provides a copy to all known prospective bidders, and usually posts a notice on **FedBizOpps** that the record is available for downloading.

BID OPENING

The bid opening is a public ceremony. Anyone may attend the bid opening. The bids, which the contracting office stores in a locked bid box or safe, are brought to the bid opening room just before the time designated for bid opening (block 8 of the SF 1449 for commercial items, block 9 of the SF 33 in the UCF, and usually block 9 of the SF 1447) by the **bid opening officer**, who is not normally the same person as the contracting officer (electronic bids are kept in a secured, restricted-access electronic bid box). The bid opening officer accepts hand-carried bids until the actual bid opening.

The bid opening officer announces to those present that the time set for the opening of bids has arrived. Once he announces the bid opening, he may no longer accept bids. The bid opening officer then opens all the bids (one at a time) and reads them aloud, including the following information:

- The name of the bidder;
- The prices bid for each line item;
- Discount terms;
- Other price-related information (such as prices for options); and
- Other pertinent information.

The bid opening officer records the bids on an **Abstract of Bids** form as he reads them, then certifies the record.

The bid opening officer must allow interested persons to examine the bids if it does not interfere with the bid opening. However, paragraph (c) of FAR 14.402-1, Unclassified Bids, states:

> "Original bids shall not be allowed to pass out of the hands of a government official unless a duplicate bid is not available for public inspection. The original

bid may be examined by the public only under the immediate supervision of a government official and under conditions that preclude possibility of a substitution, addition, deletion, or alteration in the bid."

The reason those attending the bid opening might want to examine the bids (particularly the low bid) is to see whether the bidder took any exceptions or placed any conditions on the bid that renders it "nonresponsive" (see below). If the low bid *does* contain a disqualifying exception or condition, then any bidder may file a **protest** challenging the award of a contract to the offending bidder. Chapter 17 describes protest procedures in detail.

After the bid opening officer opens and announces all the bids and allows the public to examine the bids, he forwards them and the bid abstract to the contracting officer for evaluation.

Late Bids

All bids (including electronic bids) must be received at the designated location by the time specified for bid opening, and the bidder is solely responsible for ensuring its bid arrives on time. The bid opening officer will not accept a bid even if it is only one minute late and the reason for the tardiness is understandable (as when a security guard directs the bidder's courier to a wrong building), *unless* the bid is received before award is made, and the contracting officer determines that accepting the late bid would not unduly delay the acquisition, and either:

1. If the bid was transmitted through an electronic commerce method authorized by the IFB, and it was received at the initial point of entry to the government infrastructure not later than 5:00 p.m. one working day prior to the date specified for receipt of bids; or

2. There is acceptable evidence to establish that the bid was received at the government installation designated for receipt of bids and was under the government's control prior to the time set for receipt of bids (paragraph (b)(1) of FAR 14.304, Submission, Modification, and Withdrawal of Bids).

EVALUATION OF BIDS

Of all the bids eligible for award (that is, those opened at the bid opening and the late bids that may be considered), the contracting officer must decide which one is most advantageous to the government. Just because a bid is the lowest does not mean its acceptance will cost the government the least. If the IFB states the government will pay to have the supplies shipped to Philadelphia ("f.o.b. origin") and the low bidder is in Los Angeles, the government might save money by accepting a higher bid from a company in Pittsburgh. If the IFB asks for bids on two different products and Bidder A is low on one product and Bidder B is low on the other, the contracting officer might decide it is more advantageous to award two separate contracts. The contracting officer has to take these **price-related factors** into consideration when deciding which bid is *really* the lowest. These factors are found in Section M of the UCF; FAR 52.212-2, Evaluation – Commercial Items, or in an addendum to the SF 1449; the streamlined synopsis/IFB; and the "evaluation factors for award" section of the SCF.

The contracting officer's evaluation does not end there. He must adjust the bid prices under certain circumstances to comply with congressional mandates. For example, when a bidder offers to furnish a foreign product to the government, the contracting officer may have to apply additional **evaluation factors** as required by the **Buy American Act** to give American-built products preference (see Chapter 12). Only then does the contracting officer know which bid to consider for award.

Mistakes in Bid

After bid opening, the contracting officer examines all the bids to see if any bidders made apparent mistakes. Some mistakes are obvious, such as when the unit price times the quantity does not equal the total amount bid. Also, the contracting officer looks for other, not so obvious, mistakes – when the low bid is much lower than all the other bids, the low bidder could have made a mistake. If the contracting officer detects an apparent mistake or suspects the possibility of a mistake, he will contact the bidder and ask it to verify its price (a bidder sometimes finds a mistake after bid opening and notifies the contracting officer of the mistake on its own). This is one of the very few times a contracting officer can discuss a bid with a bidder.

When the contracting officer asks a bidder to verify its bid price, the bidder has two choices: confirm its bid price or claim a mistake. If the bidder confirms its bid price, the contracting officer continues with the award process. However, if the bidder claims it made a mistake, the contracting officer will advise the bidder to make a written request to withdraw or modify its bid.

The request must be supported by statements (sworn if possible) about the alleged mistake and should include all the available evidence. Such evidence might consist of the bidder's copy of the bid, the original worksheets and other data it used in preparing the bid, subcontractor's quotations, published price lists, and any other evidence that establishes the existence of an error, explains how the mistake occurred, and shows what was the intended bid price.

Because all the other bidders' prices have been announced publicly at the bid opening, the government is very reluctant to allow a bidder to modify its bid under *any* circumstances. When a bidder alleges it made a mistake in preparing its bid and provides evidence, the government has four options:

1. If the low bidder presents clear and convincing evidence that it made a mistake and requests permission to withdraw its bid, the government may allow the bidder to do so. However, if the evidence clearly shows the bid price that was actually intended (as with an arithmetic error on a worksheet), and the bid would remain the lowest received even if corrected, the head of the agency may decide to correct the bid and not allow its withdrawal.

2. If the bidder presents clear and convincing evidence that it made a mistake, and the evidence clearly shows the bid price that was actually intended, the government may allow the bidder to correct its bid *if* the mistaken bid was the lowest received and it would remain the lowest even if corrected.

3. When the bidder submits a bid that was *not* low, and the bidder presents clear and convincing evidence that it made a mistake and the evidence clearly shows the intended bid price, but the corrected bid would *become the low bid*, the bidder will *not* be allowed to correct its mistaken bid *unless* the mistake and the actual intended bid price are ascertainable from the bid document itself (worksheets and other supporting documents are insufficient for this purpose). In other words, if the second low bidder can prove it made a mistake and that the correct bid would have been low, it will not be allowed to correct the bid unless the mistake was made on the IFB itself. If the bid document provides clear and convincing evidence of a mistake but does not clearly show what the intended bid price was, the government may let the bidder withdraw its bid.

4. When the evidence is not clear and convincing that the bidder made a mistake, the government will consider the bid as submitted.

The gathering of supporting documents and the writing of a presentation that is convincing to the contracting officer are not particularly pleasant or productive activities. Bidders can avoid this by double-checking their figures and all other entries on the bid document before submitting it.

See FAR 14.407, Mistakes in Bids, for additional information on mistake in bid procedures.

RESPONSIVENESS AND RESPONSIBILITY

Once the contracting officer calculates the projected total cost to the government of each bid and decides which is the "apparent" low bid, he must determine whether (1) the apparent low bid is **responsive** to the requirements contained in the IFB, and (2) the apparent low bidder is **responsible**.

Responsiveness

The FAR requires the contracting officer to consider only those bids that are responsive to the terms and conditions of the IFB. He must reject the apparent low bid as *nonresponsive* if it:

1. Fails to conform to the essential requirements of the IFB, as when the bidder:

   - fails to sign the bid;
   - fails to acknowledge all amendments; or
   - submits the bid by telegram, facsimile ("fax"), or electronic means when not expressly permitted by the IFB (see below);

2. Does not conform to the specifications contained or referenced in the IFB, as when the bid offers a different product or modifies the delivery schedule; or

3. Imposes conditions that would modify the requirements of the IFB or limit the bidder's liability to the government, such as when the bidder:

   - attempts to protect itself against future changes in conditions, such as increased costs;
   - qualifies its bid with a statement that the actual price is to be "the price in effect at time of delivery";
   - conditions or qualifies its bid by stipulating that its bid be considered only if the bidder receives (or does not receive) another contract; or
   - limits the rights of the government under any contract clause.

The purpose of the IFB is to treat all bidders equally. A bidder that tries to impose these or any other conditions on its bid is attempting to "tilt the playing field" and obtain an unfair advantage over its competitors. To accept such conditions would be prejudicial to the other bidders. That is why the contracting officer *must* declare such bids nonresponsive and not consider them for award.

Even though the bidder takes no exception to the terms and conditions of the IFB, the contracting officer cannot consider the bid unless the person who signed the bid is empowered to bind the bidder to the contract. The bid is an offer by the bidder that the contracting officer can accept by countersigning. If the person signing the bid for the bidder is not so empowered, there is no legal offer the contract officer can accept; there is no bid for the contracting officer to consider. Bidders should have someone sign the bid who is clearly authorized to do so, such as the president, vice president, or director of contracting. If an agent submits a bid on behalf of a bidder, the bid must be accompanied by documentation establishing the agent's authority to bind the bidder to a contract.

Electronic and Facsimile Bids

Electronic Bids. FAR 14.202-8, Electronic Bids, permits the contracting officer to authorize electronic bids. If the contracting officer decides to authorize electronic bids, he must specify in the IFB the electronic commerce method or methods that bidders may use (such as electronic mail ["email"]).

If an electronic bid is so unreadable that the contracting officer cannot determine whether it conforms to the essential requirements of the IFB, the contracting officer immediately notifies the bidder that its bid will be rejected unless it provides clear and convincing evidence: (1) of the content of the bid as originally submitted; and (2) that the unreadable condition of the bid was caused by government software or hardware error, malfunction, or other government mishandling.

Facsimile Bids. Paragraph (a) of FAR 14.202-7, Facsimile Bids, permits the contracting officer to authorize facsimile ("fax") bids. If the contracting officer decides to authorize fax bids, he will include **FAR 52.214-31, Facsimile Bids**, in Section L of the IFB if in the UCF or the Representations and Instructions section of the IFB if in the SCF. The contracting officer may notify bidders they are authorized to submit fax bids in an addendum to the SF 1449 or in the streamlined synopsis/IFB.

The contracting officer will *not* consider electronic or fax bids if he did not authorize their use – such bids are nonresponsive.

Firm Bid Rule

There is a concept called the "firm bid rule" which is contrary to normal commercial practice. The rule is that a bidder cannot withdraw its bid after the bid opening until its bid is either accepted, rejected, or the bid acceptance period expires. In commercial contracting, a bidder can withdraw its bid any time before the bid's acceptance. However, in government contracting, once the bid opening has taken place, no bid may be withdrawn during the "bid acceptance" period specified in block 9 of the SF 33 and block 11 of the SF 1447 (60 days unless the bidder inserts a longer period); some longer period specified by the contracting officer in **FAR 52.214-16, Minimum Bid Acceptance Period**; or 30 days if the bid is submitted on an SF 1449. Any bid that specifies a bid acceptance period shorter than the specified period is nonresponsive and cannot be considered for award.

The only exception to the firm bid rule is if a bidder proves it made a mistake in the preparation of its bid – see "Mistakes in Bid" above.

Before bid opening, a bidder may modify or withdraw its bid by providing written notice to the contracting officer.

Use of Bidder's Own Forms

A bidder can submit a bid even though it does not have a copy of the IFB. The bidder may use its own bid form, or it may submit a letter stating it accepts all the terms and conditions of the IFB and that an award based on its letter will produce a binding contract. Of course, the bidder's own form or letter may (1) contain wording that causes the bid to be nonresponsive, or (2) be legally deficient in a manner that prevents its use as a legally binding contract. However, if a bidder does not have a copy of an IFB and cannot download one from **FedBizOpps**, and time is running out, it can use its own bid form or letter as a last resort.

Cover Letters

A bidder should *not* attach a cover letter to its bid; the bid is sufficient. Many bidders send cover letters with language that casts doubt on the firmness of their bids, causing contracting officers to declare their bids nonresponsive. For example, language such as "we anxiously await the opportunity to discuss our bid with you," or "we look forward to negotiations," may suggest to the contracting officer that the bidder is qualifying its prices. Since the contracting officer is not allowed to discuss a bid or the bidder's intentions, he has little choice but to eliminate the bid from competition. Bidders should forget the cover letter and send the bid alone.

Bid Samples

IFBs sometime require bidders to provide a bid sample with their bids to disclose the characteristics of the products being offered and to determine the responsiveness of the bids. Contracting officers do not normally require bid samples unless there are certain product characteristics that cannot be described adequately in the specifications. For example, the contracting officer may require a bid sample when the IFB is for a product that must be suitable from the standpoint of balance, facility of use, feel, color, pattern, or other difficult to describe characteristics.

IFBs requiring bid samples must list all the characteristics that will be examined, and the contracting officer will reject a bid as nonresponsive if the sample fails to conform to any of those characteristics.

If the bid samples are not destroyed in testing, the contracting officer will return them to the bidders at their request and expense unless the solicitation states otherwise.

If the IFB does not require the submission of bid samples but a bidder submits a sample with the bid, the contracting officer will disregard the sample *unless* it is clear from the bid or accompanying papers that the bidder intends to qualify its bid, in which case the contracting officer will declare the bid nonresponsive.

Therefore, *bidders should not furnish bid samples unless specifically required by the IFB.*

See FAR 14.202-4 for the regulations governing bid samples.

Descriptive Literature

Descriptive literature is information (such as illustrations, drawings, and brochures) that a bidder furnishes as part of its bid to show a product's characteristics or construction or explains its operation. Contracting officers require bidders to furnish descriptive literature only when they need the information to determine whether the offered products meet the IFB's requirements and to establish exactly what each bidder proposes to furnish. An IFB may have a requirement for descriptive literature when highly technical or specialized equipment is being purchased, or where considerations such as design or style are important in determining acceptability of the product.

As with bid samples, bidders should not furnish descriptive literature unless specifically required by the IFB.

See FAR 14.202-5 for the regulations governing descriptive literature.

Responsibility

Once the contracting officer determines the apparent low bid is responsive, he must determine whether the bidder is **responsible**. FAR 9.104-1, General Standards, states:

> To be determined responsible, a prospective contractor must –
>
> (a) Have adequate financial resources to perform the contract, or the ability to obtain them . . . ;
>
> (b) Be able to comply with the required or proposed delivery or performance schedule, taking into consideration all existing commercial and governmental business commitments;
>
> (c) Have a satisfactory performance record . . . A prospective contractor shall not be determined responsible or nonresponsible solely on the basis of a lack of relevant performance history . . . ;
>
> (d) Have a satisfactory record of integrity and business ethics...;
>
> (e) Have the necessary organization, experience, accounting and operational controls, and technical skills, or the ability to obtain them...;
>
> (f) Have the necessary production, construction, and technical equipment and facilities, or the ability to obtain them...; and
>
> (g) Be otherwise qualified and eligible to receive an award under applicable laws and regulations...

System for Award Management Exclusions

When determining responsibility, the contracting officer first checks to see whether the bidder is in the **System for Award Management Exclusions**, which is part of the System for Acquisition Management (SAM) at **https://www.sam.gov** (see Chapter 5). It is compiled by the **General Services Administration** and includes the names of individuals and businesses forbidden by *any* federal agency from receiving government contracts; in effect, it is a *blacklist*. If the contracting officer finds the bidder on the list, he cannot award the contract to it, because any bidder appearing on the list is defined as nonresponsible. (**EDITOR'S NOTE:** This database was called the "Excluded Parties List System" [EPLS] before it became part of SAM.)

A contractor can be placed on the list as "debarred," "suspended," "proposed for debarment," or "ineligible."

Debarred. A contractor may be placed on the list as "debarred" from government contracting for up to **three years**, depending on the seriousness of the offense, if it is convicted of:

- Commission of fraud or a criminal offense in obtaining, attempting to obtain, or performing a federal contract or subcontract;

- Violating federal or state antitrust statutes relating to the submission of bids;

- Embezzlement;

- Theft;

- Forgery;

- Bribery;

- Falsification or destruction of records;

- Making false statements;

- Tax evasion;

- Violating federal criminal tax laws;

- Receiving stolen property;

- Intentionally affixing a label bearing a "Made in America" inscription when the product was not made in the United States; or

- Commission of any other offense that indicates a lack of business integrity or honesty (see Chapter 17 for more on procurement ethics and integrity).

In addition, a contractor can be placed on the list as debarred, *upon a preponderance of evidence* ("the fact at issue is more probably true than not"), for:

- Willful failure to perform according to the terms of one or more contracts;

- A history of failure to perform or of unsatisfactory performance;

- Violations of the Drug-Free Workplace Act of 1988 (a contractor can be debarred up to **five years** for this offense – see Chapter 18 and FAR subpart 23.5, Drug-Free Workplace);

- Intentionally affixing a label saying "Made in American" (or similar inscription) to a product not made in the United States;

- Commission of an unfair trade practice as defined in FAR 9.403, Definitions;

- Delinquent federal taxes exceeding $3,500;

- Failure to disclose significant overpayments on the contract within three years after final contract payment; or

- Employment of illegal aliens in violation of the Immigration and Nationality Act (a contractor is debarred for one year, and the debarment may be extended for continued violations).

A debarment of a contractor applies to all agencies of the government. The *only* exception is if the head of an agency states, in writing, that there are compelling reasons for continuing to do business with the contractor.

Proposed for Debarment. A contractor may be "proposed for debarment" when there are matters involving disputed facts. A conviction of an offense justifying debarment does not involve disputed facts – such a contractor may be debarred immediately. A contractor is proposed for debarment by an agency that claims there is a "preponderance of evidence" indicating the contractor willfully failed to perform contracts, had a history of failure to perform, had so many employees convicted of drug-related crimes that the contractor must have failed to make a good faith effort to provide a drug-free workplace, employed illegal aliens, or affixed "Made in America" labels to products not manufactured in the United States. Contractors proposed for debarment have 30 days to provide information and arguments against debarment, including any additional specific information that raises a "genuine dispute over the material facts."

Suspended. A contractor may be placed on the list as "suspended" from government contracting while it is under indictment for any of the offenses that can debar a contractor, or when there is "adequate evidence" (meaning there is "information sufficient to support the reasonable belief that a particular act or omission has occurred"). The suspension is temporary pending the completion of criminal investigations and any ensuing legal proceedings (no more than 12 months unless an assistant attorney general requests a six-month extension).

As with debarment, a suspension of a contractor applies to all agencies of the government except when the head of an agency states, in writing, that there are compelling reasons for continuing to do business with the contractor.

Ineligible. A contractor is placed on the list as "ineligible" to receive government contracts because of a law, executive order, or regulatory authority (other than the FAR or various agency supplements). For example, the secretary of labor can debar contractors that violate labor laws such as the Davis-Bacon Act (construction contracts – see Chapter 14), the Service Contract Act (service contracts – see Chapter 15), and the Equal Employment Opportunity executive order (see Chapter 15). The particular law, executive order, or regulation establishes the conditions under which the contractor is ineligible and the period of its ineligibility.

Restrictions on Subcontracting. FAR 52.209-6, Protecting the Government's Interests When Subcontracting with Contractors Debarred, Suspended, or Proposed for Debarment, prohibits contractors from entering into subcontracts exceeding $35,000 with parties that have been debarred, suspended, or proposed for debarment unless: (1) the subcontract is for a commercially available off-the-shelf item, or (2) there is a compelling reason. Contractors intending to enter into a subcontract with a party that has been debarred, suspended, or proposed for debarment must notify the contracting officer before entering into the subcontract.

Continuation of Current Contracts. An agency may continue contracts or subcontracts in existence at the time the contractor was debarred, suspended, or proposed for debarment unless the head of the agency decides otherwise. However, agencies are not permitted to: (1) place orders exceeding the guaranteed minimum under indefinite quantity contracts (see Chapter 10); (2) place orders under blanket purchase agreements (see Chapter 6), basic ordering agreements (see Chapter 10), or Federal Supply Schedule contracts (see Chapter 13); or (3) add new work, exercise options, or otherwise extend the duration of current contracts or orders.

Federal Awardee Performance and Integrity Information System (FAPIIS)

Whenever the contracting officer intends to award a contract exceeding the simplified acquisition threshold ($150,000), he must review the **Federal Awardee Performance and Integrity Information System** (FAPIIS) and use the information on the apparent low bidder in FAPIIS to assist in his responsibility determination. (**NOTE:** FAPIIS is a module of the **Past Performance Information Retrieval System** [https://www.ppirs.gov] [see Chapter 18]. Since all information in FAPIIS is publicly available except past performance evaluations, select either "FAPIIS Government" or "FAPIIS Public," as appropriate, once in PPIRS).

Integrity. If a contractor has federal contracts and grants that, when combined, total more than $10,000,000, the contractor must enter into FAPIIS whether it or any of its principals (such as an officer, director, owner, or partner) has been the subject of a federal or state proceeding within the last five years that resulted in any of the following:

1. A conviction in a criminal proceeding.

2. A finding of fault and liability that results in the payment of a monetary fine, penalty, reimbursement, restitution, or damages of $5,000 or more in a civil proceeding.

3. In an administrative proceeding, a finding of fault and liability that results in the payment of a monetary fine or penalty of $5,000 or more; or the payment of a reimbursement, restitution, or damages in excess of $100,000.

4. A disposition by consent or compromise with an acknowledgment of fault by the contractor if the proceeding *could* have led to any of the outcomes specified above.

The contractor is required to update this information semi-annually.

In addition, a contracting officer is required to report into FAPIIS any of the following actions:

1. He determines a contractor is nonresponsible;

2. He issues a final determination that a contractor has submitted defective cost or pricing data (see Chapter 8), or he makes a change to the final determination because of subsequent events (such as a court decision);

3. He issues a termination for default (see Chapter 18); or

4. He withdraws or converts a termination for default to a termination for convenience (see Chapter 18).

The contracting officer must consider all the information in FAPIIS when making his responsibility determination, and "use sound judgment in determining the weight and relevance of the information contained in FAPIIS and how it relates to the present acquisition" (paragraph (b) of FAR 9.104-6, Federal Awardee Performance and Integrity Information System). For example, the contracting officer would not consider information that may not be relevant to a determination of present responsibility, such as a debarment or suspension that has expired or been resolved, or information relating to contracts for completely different products or services.

Past Performance Information. Past performance information is relevant information regarding a contractor's actions under previously awarded contracts. It includes, for example, the contractor's record of:

1. Conforming to requirements and to standards of good workmanship;

2. Forecasting and controlling costs;

3. Adherence to schedules, including the administrative aspects of performance;

4. Reasonable and cooperative behavior and commitment to customer satisfaction;

5. Reporting into required databases (such as FAPIIS);

6. Integrity and business ethics; and

7. Business-like concern for the interest of the customer.

Annually, agencies evaluate the past performance on each contract that exceeds the simplified acquisition threshold, and prepare a final evaluation upon contract completion. Agencies submit all past performance evaluations electronically to the **Contractor Performance Assessment Reporting System** (CPARS) at **http://www.cpars.gov/** (see Chapter 18), and these evaluations are automatically transmitted to FAPIIS through PPIRS. (**NOTE:** CPARS is the system into which the past performance evaluations are entered, and PPIRS is the system that displays the information in FAPIIS.)

Capability to Perform the Contract

If the apparent low bidder is not in the SAM Exclusions database, the contracting officer must have in his possession, or must obtain, sufficient information to satisfy himself that the apparent low bidder meets the minimum financial capabilities necessary to perform the contract.

Every contracting activity has access to past performance data through FAPIIS. In addition, the contracting officer includes provisions in the "representations and certifications" portion of the IFB that require the bidder to provide much of the information needed by the contracting officer to make this determination. The contracting officer may require the bidder to provide financial data, current and past production records, personnel records, and lists of tools, equipment, and facilities. However, the contracting officer cannot reject the low bidder as nonresponsible solely because it lacks relevant experience unless contract performance requires unusual expertise and the contracting officer has identified the required expertise in the IFB.

In addition, the contracting officer can obtain information from other sources. He can contact others in the contracting activity, in other contracting activities, or in contract administration offices. The contracting officer can obtain information from financial institutions; suppliers, subcontractors, and customers of the bidder; business and trade associations; and better business bureaus. However, if the contracting officer decides this information is still not sufficient for him to determine the bidder's responsibility, he will request a **preaward survey**.

Preaward Survey

When the contracting officer is unable to determine a bidder's responsibility because he does not have enough information on the bidder's capabilities (including information from commercial sources), he requests that the appropriate contract administration office (usually the one physically closest to the bidder's facilities) or other designated organization conduct a **preaward survey**. He identifies those aspects of the bidder's capabilities he believes might be deficient or inadequate. These might involve the bidder's:

- Understanding of the specifications;

- Ability to meet the delivery schedule;

- Ability to manufacture the supply or provide the service;

- Access to adequate financial resources; and

- Past performance record.

The administrative contracting officer (ACO), or other official designated for this task, has **seven working days** to perform the preaward survey. Because the amount of time is so short, first the ACO decides whether he has enough information on hand to address the contracting officer's concerns. If the ACO has enough information or has recently conducted a preaward survey on the same bidder, he will conduct a "desk audit." Otherwise, he will send a **preaward survey team** (consisting of a **preaward survey monitor** and other government personnel as appropriate) to conduct an "on-site survey."

An on-site survey usually consists of an interview between the preaward survey team and the bidder's representatives and an investigation of the bidder's resources and operating procedures. The preaward monitor will ask bidder's management officials to go over the organizational structure of the company, the history of the company, and how they propose to perform the contract. How the bidder proposes to perform the contract is important because a major cause of poor performance and delinquent contracts is the contractor's misunderstanding or misinterpretation of the contract's requirements.

The preaward survey team discusses the IFB in detail to make sure the bidder's representatives understand all the technical documents (such as the specifications, drawings, technical data, and provisioning technical documentation), the testing and packaging requirements, the various rights reserved by the government, and other significant terms of the IFB. Depending on the concerns of the requesting contracting officer, the preaward survey team investigates the following:

- The bidder's **production** or **performance plan** is reviewed and compared with the bidder's resources to see whether the resources are adequate for the job and whether the planning and scheduling of work will insure timely contract performance.

- The bidder's **quality assurance procedures and organization** are evaluated to assess the qualifications of the quality assurance personnel, the adequacy of the inspection and test equipment, the physical arrangement of the plant, tool and gauge control, and whether the bidder has a documented or verifiable inspection system.

- The bidder's **financial position** is checked, using the latest balance sheet and profit and loss statement to determine rates and ratios, working capital as represented by current assets over current liabilities, and financial trends such as net worth, sales, and profit.

- The bidder's planned **method of financing** the contract is assessed and, if the bidder proposes to use sources of outside financing (other than any financing provided by the government), the availability of the outside financing will be verified. Since it is the government's policy that a contractor should exhaust all other sources of financing before utilizing government financing (see Chapter 18), the preaward monitor will verify that the company has exhausted those sources if it intends to seek government financing.

- The bidder's **past performance** on recent contracts is reviewed to determine whether its performance has been seriously deficient, the extent of any deficiencies, the reasons for the deficiencies, and any corrective actions planned or taken (this information is usually obtained from the FAPIIS database – see above).

After all this information has been gathered, analyzed, and reviewed, the preaward monitor prepares a report of his findings and recommendations and forwards it to the requesting contracting officer. With this information, the contracting officer can determine whether the apparent low bidder is responsible.

Because of the expense involved in the conduct of a preaward survey, FAR 9.106-1, Conditions for Preaward Surveys, states that the contracting officer should *not* request a preaward survey when the contract will be (1) less than the simplified acquisition threshold (currently $150,000), or (2) for commercial items, *unless* the circumstances justify the cost.

Rejecting Bids

If the contracting officer rejects the apparent low bid because the bidder is nonresponsible, and the bidder is a *large* business (see Chapter 11), the contracting officer takes the next lowest bid and goes through the same process to determine that bid's responsiveness and that bidder's responsibility. If the second low bidder is responsive and responsible, the contracting officer will sign its SF 33, SF 1447, or SF 1449 (or prepare an SF 1449 accepting the bidder's response to the streamlined synopsis/IFB) and form a contract. If the contracting officer rejects the second low bid and the second lowest bidder is also a large business, the contracting officer takes the third lowest bid and goes through the identical process. The contracting officer does this until he either:

■ Finds a responsive bid submitted by a responsible bidder at a fair and reasonable price;

■ Goes through all the bids without finding one that is responsive and submitted by a responsible bidder, in which case he cancels the solicitation, investigates the reasons there were no responsive bids submitted by responsible bidders, and either resolicits as an IFB or resolicits using negotiation procedures (see Chapter 8); or

■ Determines that all responsive bids are unreasonably priced, in which case he cancels the IFB and either resolicits as an IFB or resolicits using negotiation procedures.

However, if the contracting officer rejects an apparent low bid because the bidder is nonresponsible, and the bidder is a *small* business, the contracting officer must refer the matter to the **Small Business Administration** (SBA) for **certificate of competency** (COC) consideration.

Certificate of Competency

The SBA has the legal authority to certify the competency of any small business concern on any element of responsibility: capability, competency, capacity, integrity, perseverance, tenacity, and credit. Should the SBA issue a certificate of competency (COC) for a prospective contractor, the contracting officer must accept the certificate as conclusive proof that the small business is responsible and award the contract to it. (*The COC procedure does not apply to debarred or suspended small businesses, nor does it apply to a contracting officer's determination that a bid is nonresponsive.*)

When the contracting officer determines that a small business is nonresponsible, he furnishes the SBA the reasons for his determination along with a copy of the IFB, drawings, specifications, the abstract of bids, preaward survey findings, technical and financial information, and any other information that supports his determination. He then withholds award for fifteen working days to permit SBA to complete its review (or longer if agreed to by the SBA and the contracting officer).

The SBA informs the small business of the contracting officer's determination and gives the small business an opportunity to apply for a COC. If the small business applies for a COC, the SBA will send a team to investigate those areas cited by the contracting officer as the reason for his determination. The SBA team may ask for additional records and information, ask for a rebuttal of the contracting officer's determination, or ask any question that will help them come to a decision.

If the financial position of the small business is weak or if its management effort is inadequate, the SBA may employ assistance programs (such as small business loans or management counseling) to strengthen the small business' capability.

After completing the survey, the team reports its findings to the SBA Area Director. He decides whether the SBA will certify the prospective contractor's competency to perform the contract. If he determines that a COC is warranted, and the contract is $25,000,000 or less, he gives the contracting officer two options:

1. Accept the Area Director's decision; or

2. Ask the Area Director to suspend the case so that one or more of the following actions can be taken:

    −   Allow the SBA to forward a detailed rationale of the decision to the contracting officer for review;

    −   Allow the contracting officer to meet with the Area Director to attempt to resolve any issues;

    −   Allow the contracting officer to submit any information to the Area Director that he believes the SBA did not consider; or

    −   Allow the contracting agency to appeal to SBA Headquarters (however, there are no appeals permitted for contracts of $100,000 or less). If the contracting agency appeals to SBA Headquarters, the SBA Associate Administrator for Government Contracting, will make the final decision whether to issue a COC or not.

If the Area Director determines that a COC is warranted, and the contract exceeds $25,000,000, he refers the matter to SBA Headquarters for the COC decision.

If the SBA issues a COC, the bidder is considered responsible and the contracting officer awards the contract to the small business. If the SBA decides not to issue a COC, the contracting officer's nonresponsibility determination stands − the small business is not eligible to receive the award. The contracting officer goes on to the next apparent low bidder and repeats the entire responsiveness and responsibility determination process.

The contracting officer must give the SBA the opportunity to issue a COC *whenever* a small business is in line for the contract award but he determines it is nonresponsible. The contracting officer must do this even if the small business is the second, third, or fourth firm considered for award, and even if the SBA has already refused to issue COCs to other small businesses for the same IFB.

The SBA will not issue a **blanket** COC certifying the small business is qualified to perform *any* government contracts. Each COC addresses a specific solicitation. A small business may be able to perform a $250,000 contract for a particular supply but not a $2,500,000 contract. A small business might be able to perform a $250,000 contract for one type of service but not a $250,000 contract for another type. Each COC determination stands alone.

See FAR subpart 19.6, Certificates of Competency and Determinations of Responsibility, for more on COCs.

CANCELING IFBs AFTER BID OPENING

Occasionally, a contracting officer finds it necessary to cancel an IFB after the bids have been opened: for example, none of the bids are reasonable, the specifications are discovered to be defective, the agency no longer needs the supplies or services, or there was collusive bidding. Canceling IFBs after bid opening is a much more difficult problem than canceling before bid opening because the bids have been announced in public. Any cancellation at this stage tends to undermine the integrity of the IFB process in that it may appear the government is playing games to get a better deal. Therefore, the contracting officer may cancel an IFB after bid opening only when there are compelling reasons to do so and if the head of the agency provides written approval.

AWARDING THE CONTRACT

After the contracting officer determines the apparent low bidder, determines the bid is responsive, and determines the bidder is responsible (or receives a COC from the SBA), the contracting officer accepts the bid by signing block 27 of the SF 33, block 28 of the SF 1447, or block 31a of the SF 1449. The contracting officer's signature forms a binding contract between the government and the bidder.

Once the contracting officer signs the SF 33, SF 1447, or SF 1449 and forms a contract, he:

■ Sends a copy of the contract to the successful bidder;

■ Notifies unsuccessful bidders of the winning bidder and its bid price within three days of contract award by written or electronic means;

■ Places a synopsis of the contract award in **FedBizOpps** if subcontract opportunities exist (see Chapter 5);

■ Distributes copies of the contract to the appropriate contract administration office and payment office; and

■ Submits information on the contract action to the Federal Procurement Data System (see Chapter 5).

The contracting officer then moves on to other business.

TWO-STEP SEALED BIDDING

Two-step sealed bidding is a hybrid method of solicitation that combines sealed bidding with negotiation. It is designed to obtain the benefits of sealed bidding when inadequate specifications preclude the use of conventional sealed bidding. It is especially useful in acquisitions requiring technical proposals, particularly those for complex items.

In the first step of the process, each bidder must submit a technical proposal describing the supplies or services being offered along with an explanation of the bidder's proposed engineering approach, special manufacturing processes, and/or special testing techniques. In addition, the contracting officer may require bidders to describe their management approach, manufacturing plan, facilities, or other pertinent information. Step one does not solicit prices nor are prices discussed. If a bidder submits a price proposal during step one, the contracting officer will ignore it. Only technical negotiations are conducted, and only those bidders that submit technically acceptable proposals are allowed to participate in step two.

Step two is conducted using sealed bidding procedures. The contracting officer invites the bidders that submitted acceptable technical proposals during step one to submit bids on their proposals. Step two of two-step sealed bidding is not synopsized in **FedBizOpps**, although the names of bidders that submitted acceptable proposals in step one are listed in **FedBizOpps** for the benefit of prospective subcontractors.

Bidders may not submit bids on alternate technical proposals or modify their technical proposals. A bid opening is conducted as with any other sealed bidding purchase, and the contracting officer awards the contract to the lowest responsive, responsible bidder. The contract incorporates the lowest bidder's technical proposal as the statement of work.

The two-step sealed bidding procedure takes considerable time to conduct: the preparation and evaluation of the technical proposals in step one and the solicitation of bids in step two extend the process. To the busy contracting officer, the length of time and the amount of effort required to conduct the two-step sealed bid process are considerable detriments. However, contracting officers still use it, especially when the government has a good idea of its requirements but does not have specifications that are sufficiently detailed for conventional sealed bidding.

See FAR subpart 14.5 for additional information on two-step sealed bidding procedures.

OPTIONS

Many IFBs and resulting contracts contain "**option**" provisions. FAR 2.101, Definitions, defines an option as "a unilateral right in a contract by which, for a specified time, the government may elect to purchase additional supplies or services called for by the contract, or may elect to extend the term of the contract." In other words, an option is an offer by the contractor to sell additional supplies or services to the government upon the government's request during a stated period.

The contracting officer may include an option in an IFB when it is in the government's interest. An option is normally in the government's interest in the following circumstances:

■ A need for additional supplies or services is anticipated during the contract term;

■ There is a need for continuity of supply or service; or

■ Funds are not available for all the government's needs, but funds are likely to become available during the contract.

An option for increased quantities of supplies or services may be expressed in the solicitation and resulting contract as: (1) a percentage of a specific line item ("The government retains the option to increase the number of hose assemblies acquired under Line Item 0001 by up to 50% during the first six months of the contract"); (2) an increase in a specific line item ("the government has the option to acquire an additional 17 robotic systems as described in Line Item 0001 during the first year of the contract"); or (3) an additional line item identified as the option ("Line Item 0002, Option to extend for one year the services described in Line Item 0001"). An option for additional services may be expressed as an amended completion date or as additional time for performance (in days, weeks, or months).

The contracting officer is not to include an option in the contract if:

■ The contractor will incur undue risks (for example, the price or availability of necessary materials or labor is not reasonably foreseeable);

■ Market prices for the supplies or services involved are likely to change substantially; or

■ The option represents firm requirements for which funds are available *un-less* the basic quantity is a learning or testing quantity and competition for the option is impracticable once the initial contract is awarded.

Normally, IFBs allow an option quantity to be offered without limitation on price, and bidders may offer varying prices depending on the quantity actually ordered and when the option is ordered. For example, a bidder might bid $1,000 per unit if the option is exercised for a quantity of 1 to 10, and $950 per unit if the option is exercised for a quantity of 11 to 20; a bidder might bid $1,000 per unit if the option is exercised within the first three months of the option period, and $1,100 if the option is exercised after the first three months of the option period to the end of the option period.

The contracting officer must explain in Section M of the IFB how he will evaluate the option price when determining the winning bid. The contracting officer will evaluate the option's bid price when it is likely the government will exercise the option by "adding the total price for all options to the total price for the basic requirement" to produce a total evaluated price (**FAR 52.217-5, Evaluation of Options**), but will *not* evaluate the option's bid price when it is not in the government's interest to do so (such as when there is a reasonable certainty that funds will *not* be available to permit exercise of the option, in which case he will include **FAR 52.217-3, Evaluation Exclusive of Options**). If the contracting officer anticipates that the government may exercise the option at the time of award, the IFB will include **FAR 52.217-4, Evaluation of Options Exercised at Time of Contract Award**, which states that the price of the basic requirement will be added to that of any option exercised at contract award to determine the total evaluated price (and low bidder). However, the evaluation of the option does *not* obligate the government to exercise it – after all, it is an *option*.

After the contracting officer evaluates the bids (and options when appropriate), determines which is the low bid, and awards the contract to the low bidder (with the appropriate option clause in Section I: **FAR 52.217-6, Option for Increased Quantity**; **FAR 52.217-7, Option for Increased Quantity – Separately Priced Line Item**; **FAR 52.217-8, Option to Extend Services**; or **FAR 52.217-9, Option to Extend the Term of the Contract**), the contracting officer may exercise the option by providing written notice to the contractor within the time period specified in the clause. To exercise the option, the contracting officer must determine that:

■ Funds are available;

■ The requirement covered by the option fulfills an existing government need;

■ The exercise of the option is the most advantageous method of fulfilling the government's need, price and other factors considered (such as the government's need for continuity of operations and potential costs of disrupting operations; and the effect on small business);

■ The option was synopsized with the IFB and was evaluated as part of the initial competition;

■ The contractor is not listed in the System for Award Management Exclusions (see above);

■ The contractor's past performance evaluations on other contract actions have been considered (see Federal Awardee Performance and Integrity Information System [FAPIIS] above); and

■ The contractor's performance on this contract has been acceptable.

Finally, after considering all these factors, the contracting officer may *not* exercise the option unless:

■ A new solicitation has failed to produce a better price or a more advantageous offer than that offered by the option;

■ An informal analysis of prices or an examination of the market indicates that the option price is better than prices available in the market or that the option is the more advantageous offer; or

■ The time between the award of the contract containing the option and the exercise of the option is so short that it indicates the option price is the lowest price obtainable or the more advantageous offer.

Then, and only then, can the contracting officer exercise the option.

See FAR subpart 17.2, Options, for more information.

CHAPTER 8

REQUESTS FOR PROPOSALS

Ideally, sealed bidding is the way the government would like to conduct all its purchases. The entire process is in the open: bids are opened and announced in public, and the responsible bidder submitting the lowest responsive bid wins the contract. For many years, sealed bidding *was* the way the government made most of its purchases. However, sealed bidding is a rigid method of contracting. When the government uses sealed bidding, the government restricts itself to purchasing the exact supply or services specified in the IFB. The contracting officer is not allowed to consider alternate solutions to fulfilling the government's needs. In these times of rapidly changing technology, it is common for an item that represented the state-of- the-art one year ago to be superseded by an item that performs twice as well at one-third the cost. However, a bid offering to sell such an item to the government would be nonresponsive in sealed bidding. Furthermore, the complex services the government is buying are very difficult to acquire using "low bid" procedures.

Of course, there are very good reasons the government might want to purchase an "obsolete" supply or service, such as spare parts for an older piece of equipment. However, the government found, with increasing frequency, that its purchases lacked one of the four conditions for sealed bidding specified in paragraph (a) of FAR 6.401, Sealed Bidding and Competitive Proposals. The government wanted to consider alternate solutions, or it was willing to pay a premium for a superior supply or service, or it wanted to discuss how the company intended to perform the contract if it won the award. Whenever the government wanted to do any of those, it could not use sealed bidding.

CRITERIA FOR USING NEGOTIATION PROCEDURES

When a contracting officer cannot use simplified procedures or sealed bidding, he must use the **negotiation procedures** described in FAR part 15, Contracting by Negotiation. Generally, the contracting officer negotiates a contract when he needs flexibility in crafting a contract that satisfies the requirements of the government *and* the eventual contractor. For example, the government may need emergency supplies immediately following a disaster, and it might be willing to pay a premium price for expedited delivery. The government would not want to award a contract for cancer research to the lowest bidder without considering the contractor's expertise and technical approach. Also, there are situations in which sealed bidding serves no useful purpose, as when a contractor holds a patent on the required item and is the "sole source." So there is nothing inherently wrong with conducting negotiations. In fact, because of the limitations of sealed bidding, more than 95% of all the contracts that exceed the applicable simplified acquisition thresholds are negotiated.

Under negotiation procedures, the contracting officer can negotiate price, specific terms and conditions, technical requirements, delivery schedules, or any other part of the contract that is not mandated by law or regulation. The only constraints on the contracting officer during a negotiated purchase are that he (1) treat all competitors fairly and impartially, (2) comply with the regulations, (3) negotiate a contract that gives the winning contractor the greatest incentive to perform the contract on time at the lowest possible cost to the government, (4) make sure to purchase only the minimum essential requirements of the government (no "goldplating" or "nice-to-have" features, though the contracting officer can pay a higher price for a better supply or service if the solicitation specifically permits it), and (5) make sure the negotiated price is "fair and reasonable."

THE REQUEST FOR PROPOSALS DOCUMENT

If the acquisition is expected to exceed the simplified acquisition threshold ($150,000), and the contracting officer decides that one (or more) of the four conditions for sealed bidding is absent, he prepares a **Request For Proposals** (RFP). A company submitting a proposal in response to an RFP is called an **offeror** and its proposal is called an **offer**. Under certain circumstances, the contracting officer can sign the offer and form a binding contract as if it were an IFB. However, the contracting officer usually conducts negotiations with those offerors in the **competitive range** (that is, those whose proposals are being considered for award).

At first glance, the RFP looks identical to the IFB. Both can be in the uniform contract format (UCF) (see Chapter 7), both can use the SF 33, Solicitation, Offer, and Award (see Figure 9); and both can use the SF 1449, Solicitation/Contract/Order for Commercial Items (see Appendix B). The language in an RFP's "Order of Precedence" clause (FAR 52.215-8) is the same as that in an IFB's "Order of Precedence" clause (FAR 52.214-29). Both IFBs and RFPs are synopsized in **FedBizOpps** (see Chapter 5), and both are required to solicit full and open competition unless one of seven exceptions authorized by the Competition in Contracting Act exist (see Chapter 3). Both can contain "**option**" provisions that grant the government the unilateral right to order additional supplies or services during a specific period of time (see Chapter 7). The quickest way to differentiate between the two is to look at block 4 of the SF 33, or block 14 of the SF 1449 to see whether "Sealed Bid (IFB)" or "Negotiated (RFP)" is checked. Another way to tell is to check whether the cover page of the solicitation is an **Optional Form 308, Solicitation and Offer – Negotiated Acquisition** (the main difference between the OF 308 and the SF 33 is that the OF 308 does not have an "IFB" box to check, and it cannot be signed by the contracting officer and turned into a contract). But since contracting officers are not *required* to use *any* of these forms when preparing RFPs, even that is not a fool-proof method of differentiating the two types of solicitations.

There are differences buried in the solicitation document. Some solicitation provisions apply only to IFBs and others apply only to RFPs. An RFP may require offerors to submit technical proposals or to submit a cost proposal detailing all of the costs making up the proposed price. RFPs typically have evaluation criteria in Section M that are more detailed and comprehensive than those found in IFBs. The RFP might permit the contracting officer to award the contract to the offeror submitting the technical proposal that strikes the best balance between technical considerations and cost. The RFP can result in any type of fixed-price or cost-reimbursement contract (though RFPs on the SF 1449 *must* be for a firm-fixed-price, a fixed-price with economic price adjustment, a time-and-materials, or a labor-hour contract – see Chapter 9 for more on the different types of contracts).

The proposal preparation instructions and the evaluation factors are the two portions of an RFP that differ most from the corresponding portions of an IFB. Price is the only concern in sealed bidding – the contracting officer awards the contract to the lowest responsive, responsible bidder. However, with negotiation procedures, the contracting officer has to:

■ Identify which characteristics of the purchase are important to the government (such as price, delivery, technical excellence, quality, or management) and how important each is in relation to each other;

■ Decide how the government will evaluate proposals to determine how well each proposal meets the government's requirements;

■ Decide whether it is appropriate to provide additional credit for offers that propose technical solutions that exceed any mandatory minimums;

■ Decide which kinds of data to require offerors to submit with their proposals to facilitate the evaluation; and

■ Impart this information to prospective offerors clearly and completely.

This final point is important because the government *must* follow the evaluation scheme the contracting officer specifies in the evaluation factors section of the RFP. The government cannot decide to evaluate additional undisclosed factors, ignore any of the factors in the RFP, or change the relative importance of the factors without amending the RFP.

An RFP might require offerors to submit the following in a proposal to conduct a research study:

L.13 TECHNICAL PROPOSAL

The offeror shall submit a technical proposal that includes sufficient information to describe the research procedures and allow the merits of the proposed study to be assessed. The following information shall be included in the technical proposal, which shall not exceed twenty (20) single-spaced pages:

(a) An identification sheet containing the topic title, a synopsis of the proposed study, and the signature of the official who will be responsible for administering the contract.

(b) A detailed description of the proposed study to include a brief statement of the purpose, database, design, scope, and methodology of the study; the timetable (with milestones) for the study; and any other matters pertinent to the study, such as its relevance to national policy considerations.

(c) *Curricula vitae* and bibliography of the principal researcher(s).

(d) Offeror's experience performing similar studies.

(e) How the offeror intends to manage the effort. The offer should explain how it intends to: (1) ensure the meeting of contract schedules; (2) monitor the work of its principal researchers and any subcontractors or consultants; (3) ensure the work meets contractual quality requirements; and (4) control expenditures.

L.14 PAST PERFORMANCE DATA

The offeror's past contract performance is an evaluation factor in the award of this contract (see paragraph M.2 of this solicitation). Therefore, each offeror is invited to identify all federal government, state government, local government, and private research contracts it has performed within the previous three years that were similar to the research effort being solicited by this request for proposals (see Section C of this solicitation).

Offerors are requested to provide the following information on each similar previous contract:

(a) Contract number, or other contract identification;

(b) The contracting organization and its address;

(c) The contracting organization's point of contact for the contract and his or her telephone number;

(d) Contract performance period (including scheduled completion date and actual completion date);

(e) The identity of any researcher(s) who performed research on the previous contract and is proposed for this contract (including his or her role on the previous contract);

(f) Where the research was performed;

(g) A description of the research performed (offerors may provide a copy of the statement of work);

(h) A summary of the results of the research;

(i) The dollar amount of the contract;

(j) Problems encountered on the identified contracts and the offeror's corrective actions; and

(k) Any additional information or explanation the offeror believes will help the contracting officer assess its past performance record.

Offerors are advised that the contracting officer (or representatives of the contracting officer) will verify the information provided and may obtain past performance information from other sources.

L.15 COST BREAKDOWN

A separate and complete cost breakdown shall be submitted that will include, but not necessarily be limited to, the following:

(a) DIRECT LABOR

(i) Explain the basis for the proposed labor rates.

(ii) Indicate the number of hours per year on which the rates are computed and whether this includes time for vacation, sick leave, holidays, and other approved charges.

(iii) List the number of manhours or manmonths by category of employee (for example, clerical, technical assistant, professional researcher).

(b) OVERHEAD, GENERAL AND ADMINISTRATIVE EXPENSES, AND OTHER INDIRECT EXPENSES

(i) Explain the basis for the proposed rates.

(ii) List the last rates audited by a government auditor, and any provisional billing rates approved for forward pricing.

(c) OTHER DIRECT COSTS

Attach schedules explaining the reasons for these costs (for example, material, travel, etc.) and the methods used to compute these costs.

(d) SUBCONTRACTS

Show the proposed subcontractor's name, address, and telephone number, the nature of the effort, and the basis for the price (that is, verbal or written quotation).

The RFP also specifies the **evaluation factors** the government will use to determine which proposal best meets its requirements (in Section M in UCF RFPs). These evaluation factors clearly stipulate the criteria and qualifications the contracting officer will weigh when making his award decision.

The contracting officer might include the following evaluation factors in the RFP for the above research study. These make it clear the government is looking for the most qualified personnel performing the most innovative study at a "fair and reasonable" price.

M.2 EVALUATION FACTORS FOR AWARD

(a) TECHNICAL EVALUATION

(i) All offers received shall be subject to a technical evaluation by a duly selected panel of qualified government personnel to assist in the selection of the offeror(s) with whom negotiations may be conducted.

(ii) The following factors and subfactors shall be used in making the technical evaluation:

(A) *Problem Comprehension:* The extent to which the offeror demonstrates an understanding of:

(1) The study's objectives;

(2) The issues involved;

(3) Their relationships; and

(4) Their relevance to the subject of the study.

Subfactor (1) is approximately twice as important as subfactors (2), (3), and (4) combined.

(B) *Technical Approach:*

(1) The soundness and completeness of the proposed approach;

(2) The feasibility of the approach and the method(s) to be employed to accomplish it;

(3) The uniqueness of the ideas or concepts outlined in the technical proposal and their bearing on the subject;

(4) Familiarity with the issues involved in the proposed study;

(5) Evidence of capability and capacity to do the work proposed.

Subfactors (1), (2), and (5) are of approximately equal importance, and each is approximately three times as important as subfactors (3) and (4).

(C) *Specific Experience:*

(1) Background and experience of the offeror performing similar work;

(2) Background and experience of the principal investigator(s);

(3) Evidence that the offeror can meet the contracted research study objectives, tasks, and delivery requirements.

All subfactors are of approximately equal importance.

(D) *Organization and Management:* The extent to which the offeror demonstrates the capability and capacity for sound planning, organizing, staffing, controlling subcontractors, and producing the proposed study.

(iii) Factors B, C, and D are of approximately equal importance. Factor A will be weighed approximately twice as heavily as factors B, C, or D.

(b) PAST PERFORMANCE

(i) The offeror's record of past performance, if any, on previous research contracts within the previous three years will be evaluated in according to the following factors:

(A) Its record of conforming to contract requirements;

(B) Its record of forecasting and controlling costs;

(C) Its adherence to contract schedules (including the administrative aspects of performance);

(D) Its history of reasonable and cooperative behavior and commitment to customer satisfaction; and

(E) Its business-like concern for the interest of the customer.

(ii) Factors A, B, and C are of approximately equal importance, and each are approximately twice as important as factors D and E, which are of approximately equal importance.

(iii) Offerors that have not previously performed contracts that were similar to the research effort being solicited by this request for proposals will not be evaluated favorably or unfavorably.

(c) COST EVALUATION

The cost elements proposed for this effort will be evaluated for their reasonableness relative to the proposed effort to ensure maximum quality of performance with realistic cost.

(d) WEIGHTING OF EVALUATION FACTORS

The evaluation of the technical factors will constitute approximately one-half (1/2) of the overall evaluation, past performance will constitute approximately one-third (1/3) of the overall evaluation, and the cost of the proposed effort will constitute approximately one-sixth (1/6) of the overall evaluation. Award will be made to the offeror that submits the proposal judged as providing the best value to the government in accordance with the evaluation factors specified herein.

The nature of the supplies or services being purchased and the environment in which the purchase is being made have the largest influence on how the government will evaluate proposals. Some evaluations are conducted by a single acquisition planner who simply rates proposals as "acceptable" or "unacceptable," and the contracting officer awards the contract to the responsible offeror that submitted the lowest priced acceptable proposal (this type of evaluation is called "**lowest-price technically acceptable**" – see FAR 15.101-2). Other evaluations involve teams of evaluators assessing multi-volume proposals against multiple factors and subfactors to determine which proposal offers the "**best value**" to the government, with the results and recommendations forwarded to a source selection authority for the final award decision. No matter which evaluation method the government decides to use, it must be identified in the RFP.

EXCHANGES OF INFORMATION BETWEEN THE GOVERNMENT AND INDUSTRY

As mentioned in Chapter 7, the government uses negotiations when sealed bidding is not appropriate. One of the most common reasons the government foregoes sealed bids and uses negotiations is that it is unsure what supplies or services are available to meet its requirements. Another common reason is that the government will be awarding the contract based on considerations other than price, such as quality or speed of delivery. For these and other similar reasons, it is important that the government make clear to industry its needs and that industry make clear to the government what is available to meet those needs.

Exchanges of information about future purchases among the acquisition planners (see Chapter 2), the contracting officer, and potential contractors are *encouraged*. Paragraph (b) of FAR 15.201, Exchanges with Industry Before Receipt of Proposals, states that "the purpose of exchanging information is to improve the understanding of government requirements and industry capabilities, thereby allowing potential offerors to judge whether or how they can satisfy the government's requirements, and enhancing the government's ability to obtain quality supplies and services, including construction, at reasonable prices, and increase efficiency in proposal preparation, proposal evaluation, negotiation, and contract award." This exchange of information, if conducted early in the process, allows all participants to address and resolve such issues as:

- the appropriate contract type (see Chapter 9);

- terms and conditions;

- the feasibility of requirements (including performance requirements, statements of work, data requirements, and delivery or performance schedules);

- the suitability of proposal instructions and evaluation criteria; and

- the availability of documents (such as specifications or industrial standards).

There are many ways the government promotes this exchange of information. For example, it:

- attends industry or small business conferences;

- conducts public hearings;

- performs market research (see Chapter 4);

- meets with potential offerors (after the solicitation is released, all discussions must be channeled through the contracting officer);

- publishes presolicitation notices in **FedBizOpps** (see Chapter 5);

- issues draft RFPs;

- issues **Requests for Information** (RFI) when the government does not intend to award a contract but wants to obtain price, delivery, other market information, or capabilities for planning purposes; and

- conducts site visits.

However, this exchange of information must be conducted in compliance with the procurement integrity requirements and other standards of ethical conduct explained in Chapter 17.

In addition, the contracting activity can help potential offerors decide whether to pursue a particular contract by advising them if they have the potential to be viable competitors. When the contracting activity decides to do this, it will publish a presolicitation notice that provides a general description of the scope or purpose of the upcoming solicitation and invites potential offerors to submit information such as their qualifications, proposed concepts, past performance, and limited pricing information. The contracting activity evaluates all the responses and advises each respondent that either (1) it will be invited to submit a proposal when the RFP is released, or (2) it is unlikely to be a viable competitor (the contracting activity provides a general basis for that opinion). However, those told that they will probably not be competitive are allowed to submit a proposal in response to the RFP, just like any other competitor. See FAR 15.202, Advisory Multi-Step Process, for more on this procedure.

PREPARING RFPs

A contracting officer follows the same basic procedures when preparing and issuing an RFP that he follows when preparing an IFB. Once he decides that sealed bidding is inappropriate for the particular purchase and decides to use negotiation procedures, he:

- Synopsizes the RFP in **FedBizOpps** at least 15 days before issuing it (though the contracting officer may establish a shorter period of acquisitions of commercial items under FAR part 12);

- Prepares an RFP (usually in the uniform contract format [UCF] – see Chapter 7) that explains as completely as possible the needs and requirements of the government, including proposal preparation instructions and evaluation factors for award (but remember that acquisitions of commercial items under FAR part 12 procedures are in a simplified format);

- Posts the RFP on **FedBizOpps** after the synopsis period expires; and

- Holds a **pre-proposal conference** if necessary (which is essentially the same as the pre-bid conference described in Chapter 7).

The face page of the RFP (the SF 33, the OF 308, or the SF 1449 for commercial items) specifies the time and date of the deadline for submitting proposals – this is the RFP **closing date** (if no time is specified in the solicitation, the time for receipt is 4:30 pm, local time). The closing date must be at least **30 days** after issuance of the RFP if the acquisition is expected to exceed the simplified acquisition threshold – the same as for IFBs and their opening dates (though, like IFBs for commercial items, RFPs for commercial items may provide for a shorter period). As with IFBs, the contracting officer will not accept a late proposal unless: (1) government personnel mishandled the proposal at the government facility; or (2) if electronic offers were authorized, the electronic offer was received by the government not later than 5:00 pm **one *working* day** before the closing date. And there is an additional exception for RFPs: if the late proposal is the *only* proposal received, the contracting officer will accept it.

As with IFBs, the contracting officer issues amendments to the RFP if necessary and, depending on the magnitude of the amendment and how close its issuance is to the RFP's closing date, the contracting officer may decide to extend the closing date. In addition to the SF 30, Amendment of Solicitation/Modification of Contract (see Chapter 7), the contracting officer may issue RFP amendments on an **Optional Form 309, Amendment of Solicitation (Negotiated Procurements)**, which is a slightly simplified form in that it only has to address RFP amendments and not contract modifications.

EVALUATING PROPOSALS

Unlike IFBs, proposals are **not** opened in public on the closing date. Instead, the contracting officer and technical personnel review the proposals in private. If the RFP required offerors to submit technical proposals along with their price proposals, the contracting officer forwards a copy of all the technical proposals to the technical personnel for an evaluation conducted according to the evaluation factors specified in the RFP.

Normally, the contracting officer retains the pricing proposals because they could improperly influence the technical evaluators (although he may provide cost information to the technical evaluators under conditions established by his agency). If the RFP states that technical factors are three times more important than cost, but the technical evaluators know the price of the most technically innovative proposal is over the allotted budget, they might be tempted to bias their evaluations toward a marginal proposal that is within the budget. If the evaluation factors do not accurately reflect the government's needs, the proper way to correct the problem is to amend the RFP, not to slant the evaluations to obtain the desired result. This is why the contracting officer usually keeps the price proposals to himself (and his price analysts).

Unlike IFBs, an offeror can submit a proposal in response to an RFP that proposes alternate terms and conditions, and the contracting officer cannot disqualify the proposal as "nonresponsive." The offeror can propose a different delivery schedule, propose changes to the specifications or statement of work, or offer an alternate product. As long as the proposal conforms to the material terms and conditions of the RFP, the contracting officer can consider it.

If the proposal includes information (such as trade secrets) or proprietary data (such as financial statements) that the offeror does not want disclosed to the public or used by the government for any purpose other than evaluation, the offeror should mark the proposal title page with the following legend, as required by paragraph (e)(1) of FAR 52.215-1, Instructions to Offerors – Competitive Acquisition:

> This proposal includes data that shall not be disclosed outside the Government and shall not be duplicated, used or disclosed – in whole or in part – for any purpose other than to evaluate this proposal. If, however, a contract is awarded to this offeror as a result of – or in connection with – the submission of this data, the Government shall have the right to duplicate, use, or disclose the data to the extent provided in the resulting contract. This restriction does not limit the Government's right to use information contained in this data if it is obtained from another source without restriction. The data subject to this restriction are contained in sheets [*insert numbers or other identification of sheets*].

Also, paragraph (e)(2) of FAR 52.215-1 requires the offeror to mark each page (sheet) containing information or data it wants to restrict with the following legend:

> Use or disclosure of data contained on this sheet is subject to the restriction on the title page of this proposal.

Evaluating Technical Proposals

Typically, the technical evaluators prepare a **proposal evaluation matrix**, listing the evaluation factors down one side of the page and the names of the offerors along the top. Then the technical evaluators judge how well each proposal meets each evaluation factor (and subfactor). They may rate the technical proposals as acceptable or unacceptable, on a scale of 0 to 100, with adjectival descriptions (such as unacceptable, poor, acceptable, good, excellent, outstanding), colors (red, yellow, green), from best to worst, or using any other method that is clearly described in the RFP.

The following are some common reasons evaluators will downgrade a proposal:

- It indicates the offeror misinterpreted the specifications or statement of work;
- It proposes a plan that cannot be performed within the required delivery or performance schedule;
- It is too optimistic in estimating performance;
- It promises a solution without further explanation; or

■ It does not explain personnel requirements, how the offeror proposes to manage the effort, describe the equipment and facilities the offeror intends to use, or provide other essential information required by the RFP.

Once the technical evaluators have rated each proposal, they prepare a report for the contracting officer (or, for particularly significant acquisitions, a "**source selection authority**" – a senior official selected by the agency to weigh all the evaluations and select the winning contractor). The report contains an analysis of each proposal's technical and managerial merits, including:

■ An assessment of each offeror's ability to perform the contract as required;

■ A description of each proposal's strengths, weaknesses, and areas requiring further clarification;

■ The proposal evaluation matrix (or other ranking representation); and

■ A summary of the analysis.

Evaluating Past Performance

Past performance must be an evaluation factor in all competitively negotiated RFPs that exceed the simplified acquisition threshold ($150,000).

It is impossible for a contracting officer to compare the performance of two different contracts in an objective, mathematical manner. While evaluators can make an **objective** assessment of how well each technical proposal will satisfy the *exact same* requirements of the government, the contracting officer must use **subjective** criteria when evaluating past performance since no two offerors have performed the exact same contracts under the exact same circumstances. For example, which offeror should receive the higher numerical score?

■ Offeror A, which delivered a $1,000,000 contract for commercially available smartphones in 30 days and on time (the leadtime for commercial smartphones is 10 days), but was uncooperative when defective smartphones were returned for exchange and balked at providing a refund; or

■ Offeror B, which designed and installed a state-of-the-art $10,000,000 telecommunications system in an agency, but completed the work two weeks later than the twelve months called for in the contract (the agency admitted the twelve month performance period was "extremely tight")?

The evaluation of these offerors' past performance is a classic "apples and oranges" situation – though the contracting officer is not able to make a direct comparison between the two, he may be able to distinguish between a "rotten apple" and a "ripe orange."

When the contracting officer will be evaluating offerors' past performance, he will invite the offerors to identify similar contracts they have performed for federal, state, and local governments, and for private companies during the previous several years. In addition to the information provided by each offeror, the contracting officer will usually check past performance information compiled by the government for each contract over $150,000. This information is available to contracting officers electronically in the **Past Performance Information Retrieval System** (PPIRS) (**https://www.ppirs.gov/** – see Chapter 18). The PPIRS information is not retained for longer than three years after completion of contract performance.

Normally, the contracting officer will select the previous contracts that most closely resemble the effort being solicited and contact the administrative contracting officers (ACO – see Chapter 2) for the government contracts and the buyers for the private contracts. He will ask the ACO or buyer such questions as:

- Was the contract performed on time? If not, why not? Was the government responsible for any of the delay?

- Was the contract performed within budget? If not, why not?

- Was the work satisfactory? Did the contractor correct any unsatisfactory work promptly and willingly?

- Was the contract ever amended to relieve the contractor of contract requirements it could not meet? How much was the contract price reduced for the amendment?

- What kind of problems did the contractor have? Were they unusual problems? How did the contractor resolve the problems? Was the resolution satisfactory?

- Was the contractor reasonable? Cooperative? Did it display a business-like concern for the customer?

- If you had a choice, would you contract with this company again?

If the contracting officer obtains unfavorable past performance information on a contract, and this unfavorable information is the determining factor preventing the offeror from being placed in the competitive range (see below), he must give the offeror an opportunity to discuss the information and its performance under the contract if the offeror has not previously had an opportunity to comment (contractors are given an opportunity to comment on the past performance information entered into PPIRS). However, the contracting officer will *not* disclose to the offeror the name of the individual who provided the information.

When making his evaluation, the contracting officer will consider the number and severity of the offeror's problems, the effectiveness of its corrective actions, the offeror's overall work record, and the age and relevance of the contract (recent contracts are generally more representative of current performance than old contracts – that is why past performance information is not retained longer than three years after contract completion). Though the contracting officer does not, as a rule, assign each offeror's past performance a score, he uses the information when selecting the most advantageous proposal, and he prepares a written explanation of the rationale for his decision.

If an offeror does not have relevant past performance history (for example, it is a new company, or it has never before performed a contract as large as the one being solicited), the contracting officer must not give a favorable or unfavorable past performance evaluation (the evaluation must be "neutral").

Evaluating Price (or Cost) Proposals

While the technical evaluators perform their duties, the contracting officer evaluates the price proposals (with the help of his price analysts). He conducts either a **price analysis** or a **cost analysis** of each proposal. Normally, a contracting officer conducts a price analysis when the contract is for commercial items or will be awarded to the offeror proposing the lowest price, and a cost analysis when the contract will be awarded on a basis other than price (for example, to the offeror submitting the most technically innovative proposal with price being a secondary consideration, or to a "sole source").

Contracting officers must obtain only the minimum amount of information needed to establish the reasonableness of the offered prices. They use the following order of preference in determining the type of information needed for this purpose:

■ **No information** is to be requested if the price is based on adequate price competition. "Adequate price competition" is defined as being present when:

   – Two or more responsible offerors, competing independently, submit offers that are responsive to the government's requirement, and award will be made to the responsible offeror whose offer represents either the "greatest value" to the government or the lowest evaluated price; or

   – Only one offer is received from a responsible offeror *if* the market research conducted prior to the solicitation (see Chapter 4) indicated that two or more responsible offerors would compete independently and submit offers, *provided* the contracting officer can reasonably conclude that the offer was submitted with the expectation of competition; or

    – Price analysis (see below) clearly demonstrates the offered price is reasonable in comparison with current or recent prices for the same or similar items, adjusted to reflect changes in market conditions, economic conditions, quantities, or terms and conditions under contracts that resulted from adequate price competition..

■ **"Data other than certified cost or pricing data"** (see below for "certified cost or pricing data") is to be requested from offerors when adequate price competition is not expected or, for example, when the proposed item has evolved from a commercial item though technological advances but it is not yet available to the commercial marketplace (see Chapter 4). Typically, it includes pricing, sales, or cost information. Data other than certified cost or pricing data could include any of the following:

    – The catalog, price list, schedule, or other verifiable record that is regularly maintained by the manufacturer or vendor and is published or available for customer inspection.

    – Data substantiating that a claimed market price was established in the course of ordinary and usual trade.

    – Data on sales to the general public, such as quantities, the size of the market, and when the item was introduced into the market.

    – Information demonstrating that the proposed costs are consistent with the technical proposal.

    – Cost and technical information explaining the differences between the proposed item and the commercial item from which it evolved.

    – Rulings, reviews, or similar actions of a government body that set the price for the offered supply or service (such as a utility rate commission).

The contracting officer must first seek this information from within the government, then from sources other than the offeror (such as customers or industry associations), then from the offeror (but only if necessary). The contracting officer must limit his request to the minimum amount of information needed to determine the reasonableness of the price or to evaluate cost realism.

■ **Certified cost or pricing data** (see below). This detailed information is required only when the contracting officer will not be able to verify the reasonableness of proposed prices from other information, usually because the supply or service is not commercially available. The contracting officer may require cost or pricing data only when he will conduct a cost analysis.

Price Analysis

Price analysis is the process of examining and evaluating a proposed price without evaluating its separate cost elements and proposed profit. When conducting a price analysis to determine whether a proposed price is fair and reasonable, the contracting officer usually uses one of three price analysis methods:

■ Comparing the proposed price with the prices of other proposals received in response to the solicitation;

■ Comparing the proposed price to those of recent contracts, adjusting for differences between the current purchase and previous purchases (such as for inflation since the earlier purchases, different quantities, shorter or longer delivery schedules, changed specifications, and unusual packaging requirements); or

■ Comparing the proposed price with published market prices, price lists, advertisements, and similar current information.

If the contracting officer finds there are significant differences between the proposed price and the other data used in the price analysis, these differences *may* indicate vendor collusion, defective specifications, inadequate competition, mistakes, changes in market conditions, or other factors. The contracting officer will investigate further to determine whether the differences are justified.

If the offeror proposes a commercial item, the contracting officer may request that the offeror submit data other than certified cost or pricing data if he is unable to obtain data adequate for the performance of a price analysis from within the government or from sources other than the offeror.

Cost Analysis

Cost analysis is a more complicated process than price analysis. When conducting a cost analysis, the contracting officer evaluates the necessity and reasonableness of *all* the elements of cost proposed by the offeror, such as:

■ The types and cost of the materials;

■ The types of labor and corresponding number of hours;

■ Subcontracts;

■ Transportation costs;

■ Equipment to be purchased;

■ The various overhead rates applicable to the effort;

■ The general and administrative expenses rate;

- Profit or fee; and

- Any other costs that make up the proposed price.

The contracting officer is to conduct the cost analysis with data other than cost or pricing data whenever possible. However, when no other information is suitable for determining the reasonableness of proposed prices and the contract is expected to be greater than **$750,000**, he is required by law to obtain **certified cost or pricing data**.

Cost or Pricing Data. FAR 2.101, Definitions, defines "cost or pricing data" as:

> ". . . all facts that . . . prudent buyers and sellers would reasonably expect to affect price negotiations significantly . . . they are all the facts that can be reasonably expected to contribute to the soundness of estimates of future costs and to the validity of determinations of costs already incurred."

This definition encompasses such data as vendor quotations, union labor agreements, make-or-buy decisions, projections of business prospects and objectives, unit cost trends associated with labor efficiency, evaluations that led the offeror to select a particular vendor, changes in production methods, and any other data expected to have a significant effect on the proposed contract price. Compiling and furnishing cost or pricing data is expensive for offerors – that is why it is a last resort reserved for acquisitions over $750,000. Though a contracting officer *may* obtain certified cost or pricing data for acquisitions that are $750,000 or less, he must obtain the approval of the head of the contracting activity. In addition, contracting officers are *prohibited* from obtaining certified cost or pricing data for acquisitions that are less than the simplified acquisition threshold ($150,000) under *any* circumstances.

When the contracting officer decides he will need certified cost or pricing data to conduct a cost analysis, he will include a provision in the RFP requiring each offeror to submit cost or pricing data to support its cost proposal. The cost or pricing data is to be presented as instructed in **FAR Table 15-2, Instructions for Submitting Cost/Price Proposals When Certified Cost or Pricing Data Are Required**. The proposed price of each supply or service must be broken down into its constituent cost elements (see Figure 11), and each constituent cost element must be further broken down and explained (see Figure 12). Submitting certified cost or pricing data does *not* mean merely making books, records, and other documents available without identification. While the offeror does not have to submit copies of all the certified cost or pricing data with its proposal, it must clearly identify the data used in developing the proposed price (for example, the name of a vendor, the quotation number, and the quoted price). Furthermore, the offeror must make this data available to the contracting officer or authorized representative upon request for inspection.

**REFERENCE A – COST PROPOSAL FOR LINE ITEM 0001,
12 EACH A6 TEST VEHICLES**

COST ESTIMATE	PROPOSED CON-TRACT ESTIMATE - UNIT COST	PROPOSED CON-TRACT ESTIMATE - TOTAL COST	REFERENCE
Materials	$10,606.62	$127,279.44	–
Raw Materials	*5,610.89*	*67,330.68*	Exhibit 1
Subcontracted Items	*3,258.75*	*39,105.00*	Exhibit 2
Purchased Parts	*1,736.98*	*20,843.76*	Exhibit 3
Material Overhead (8.3%)	880.35	10,564.20	Exhibit 4
Manufacturing Labor	13,479.80	161,757.60	Exhibit 5
Manufacturing OH (179.3%)	24,169.28	290,031.36	Exhibit 6
Engineering Labor	11,437.50	137,250.00	Exhibit 7
Engineering OH (62.4%)	7,137.00	85,644.00	Exhibit 8
Subtotal	**$67,710.55**	**$812,526.60**	
General and Admin (10.2%)	6,906.48	82,877.76	Exhibit 9
Proposed Cost	**$74,617.03**	**$895,404.36**	
Profit (12.5%)	9,327.13	111,925.56	–
TOTAL PRICE	***$83,944.16***	***$1,007,329.92***	

Figure 11 – Sample Cost Breakdown

EXHIBIT 1 – RAW MATERIALS FOR 12 EACH A6 TEST VEHICLES

MATERIAL	SQ. FEET PER UNIT	COST PER SQ. FOOT	TOTAL COST PER UNIT	UNITS REQUIRED	TOTAL COST
Composite Sheet (DOD-K-9876, Grade IIB)	1389.66*	$4.12**	$5,725.40	12	$68,704.80
				Less 2% Discount***	-1,374.12
				TOTAL	***$67,330.68***
				Unit Cost	***$5,610.89***

* This estimate was developed from ABC Corp. technical data package R998A, dated July 31, 2008, and includes a 3% scrap factor. This scrap factor is based on experience in performing a contract for 28 each model B83 test vehicles which was completed on April 19, 2014. The B83 is the desert version of the A6.

** Cost is based on current purchase price from Acme Composite Co. which is delivering the same grade composite sheet to ABC Corp. under purchase order Z27-88624.

*** Quantity discount extended by Acme Composite Co. for orders of 10,000 square feet or more.

Figure 12 – Sample Cost Element Breakdown and Explanation

The contracting officer evaluates each element of proposed cost to judge its necessity to the contract effort, to detect whether the offeror has included allowances for contingencies in its proposed price, and to determine whether the offeror is allocating its indirect costs properly (that is, the offeror is not proposing that the government contract absorb more than its fair share of rent, utilities, employee benefits, and similar "indirect" expenses).

In addition, the contracting officer decides whether each element of cost is **allowable**. The government will pay only those costs that:

- Are **reasonable**;

- Are **allocable**, meaning the cost is either:

    – incurred specifically for the contract (such as material and labor costs, which are commonly called "direct costs");

    – benefits both the contract and other work and can be distributed to them in reasonable proportion (that is, indirect costs); or

    – is necessary to the overall operation of the business, though no direct relationship between the cost and the contract can be shown (such as headquarters expenses, legal fees, and depreciation, commonly called "general and administrative expenses");

- Comply with the **Cost Accounting Standards** (which only apply to large government contractors performing large non-commercial government contracts – see FAR part 30, Cost Accounting Standards Administration) or **generally accepted accounting principles and practices** appropriate to the particular circumstances of the contract;

- Comply with the **terms of the contract**; and

- Are not restricted by any **limitations in FAR subpart 31.2**, Contracts with Commercial Organizations (FAR subpart 31.3 covers contracts with educational institutions; FAR subpart 31.6 covers contracts with state, local, and federally recognized Indian tribal governments; and FAR subpart 31.7 covers contracts with nonprofit organizations).

FAR Subpart 31.2 lists 46 different costs that are commonly incurred by a contractor during the course of business and identifies those that are "allowable" and those that are "unallowable." This list has nothing to do with whether the **Internal Revenue Service** (IRS) considers a particular cost tax-deductible. For example, since the government does not allow advertising to influence its purchasing decision, it obtains no benefit from most advertising expenditures. Therefore, FAR 31.205-1, Public Relations and Advertising Costs, prohibits the government from paying most advertising costs incurred by the contractor (with some exceptions, such as "help wanted" ads). Offerors should not include such unallowable costs in their proposals, and contractors should not ask the government to reimburse such costs – see FAR 31.110, Indirect Cost Rate Certification and Penalties on Unallowable Costs, for more on penalties that can be assessed against contractors that include unallowable indirect costs in their proposals.

Audits. To assist the contracting officer with his cost analysis, an auditor is often sent to the contractor's facility to audit the contractor's proposal. The auditor uses the certified cost or pricing data submitted by the offeror in support of its proposal to:

■ Verify the offeror obtained competitive quotations for subcontracted items or services;

■ Assess proposed labor rates, overhead rates, and general and administrative expenses;

■ Verify that only allowable costs (those permitted by FAR subpart 31.2) are included in the proposal, that all unallowable costs have been excluded, and to identify those costs that are questionable; and

■ Substantiate any other proposed charges that have a significant bearing on the proposed price.

Upon completing the audit, the auditor submits his findings, evaluations, and recommendations to the contracting officer.

Oral Presentations

Oral presentations are being used with increasing frequency by agencies as one method to reduce the cost of proposals for both offerors and the government. The purpose of requesting oral presentations is to reduce the volume of written materials the offeror has to prepare for its proposal (and which government evaluators have to evaluate). In fact, paragraph (a) of FAR 15.102, Oral Presentations, states that oral presentations by offerors as requested by the government may augment *or substitute for* written proposals (prerecorded videotaped presentations are *not* considered oral presentations, although they may be included in offeror submissions).

The National Aeronautics and Space Administration (NASA) uses oral presentations as a proposal "road map," asking each offeror to explain the structure of its proposal so the NASA evaluators can find the information they need quickly. Other agencies use oral presentations as an opportunity to allow the offeror's key personnel to "audition" for roles such as lead researcher, requesting that they demonstrate their understanding of the contract requirements by providing "quick responses" to sample tasks. Some agencies allow the offeror to do all the talking, others use the presentation as a forum for clarifying points in the proposal. One contracting officer might use oral presentations to help him make his "competitive range" determination (see below), another might use oral presentations to help him select the winning offeror.

Information pertaining to an offeror's capability, past performance, work plans or approaches, staffing resources, transition plans, and sample tasks are particularly suited to oral presentations. However, cost information and highly technical information are *not* suited to oral presentations. In addition, the signed offer sheet and any exceptions to the government's terms and conditions must be submitted in writing.

When deciding what, if any, information to require each offeror to submit as part of its proposal through oral presentations, the contracting officer must consider:

- the government's ability to evaluate the information adequately;

- the need to incorporate any of the information into the resultant contract;

- the effect oral presentations will have on the conduct of the acquisition; and

- the effect (particularly cost) oral presentations will have on small businesses (the contracting officer may want to consider alternatives such as teleconferencing).

If the contracting officer decides that oral presentations are appropriate, he must include in the RFP:

- the types of information offerors are to present and the associated evaluation factors that will be used;

- the qualifications of the personnel who will be required to provide the oral presentation (such as the project manager);

- any requirements for written material or other media to supplement the oral presentations (including any limitations or prohibitions);

- the location, date, and time for the oral presentations;

- the amount of time permitted for each oral presentation; and

- the scope and content of exchanges that may occur between the government and the offeror's representatives, including whether negotiations (or "discussions") will be permitted (see below).

The contracting officer will try to have the same government evaluators attend *all* the oral presentations to make sure all evaluators share a common basis for comparison. The contracting officer will maintain a record of the oral presentations. The nature of the records documenting the oral presentations (such as videotape of the presentations, audio tape recording, written record, notes, or copies of the offerors' briefing slides) will be at the government's discretion. The contracting officer may provide the offeror a copy of the record that is placed in the file.

If the oral presentation includes material terms and conditions that the parties intend to include in the contract, those terms and conditions must be put in writing (merely referencing the oral statements is *not* permissible).

PRENEGOTIATION OBJECTIVES

The contracting officer uses the results of the technical evaluations and his price or cost analysis (supported by the audit results if the proposal was audited) to develop the government's **prenegotiation objective** *for each proposal under consideration*. The contracting officer's prenegotiation objective represents his estimate of a **fair and reasonable price** for the offeror to perform the proposed work. To develop the prenegotiation objective, the contracting officer considers the offeror's proposed technical approach, material costs, labor structure, labor rates, overhead rates, and similar factors. The eventual winner will be selected according to the evaluation factors in the RFP.

Establishing the Government's Profit or Fee Objective

The contracting officer completes the development of the government's prenegotiation objective when he adds a profit or fee objective to the recommended price. Paragraph (b) of FAR 15.404-4, Profit, requires each agency to use "*a structured approach for determining the profit or fee objective in those acquisitions that require cost analysis.*" Each agency is free to develop the structured approach that best meets its needs and complies with the FAR. In military purchases, the contracting officer uses a **DD Form 1547, Record of Weighted Guidelines Application**, to calculate the government's profit or fee objective (see Figure 13), the instructions for completion of which are in **Defense FAR Supplement (DFARS) 215.404-71, Weighted Guidelines Method**. Some civilian agencies use forms based on the DD Form 1547, other civilian agencies use methods that are substantially different. Some agencies don't provide any guidance at all, leaving it up to the contracting officer to decide how to determine the appropriate profit or fee objective. Each agency that has a structured approach for calculating an appropriate profit or fee objective describes it in its FAR supplement.

ESTABLISHING THE COMPETITIVE RANGE

Once the contracting officer receives the technical evaluation report, conducts the price analysis or cost analysis, and develops his prenegotiation objectives, he must decide which proposals are in the "**competitive range**" – that is, which proposals have a reasonable chance of being selected for award. The contracting officer does this for two reasons:

1. To reduce the number of negotiations he has to conduct; and

2. To eliminate those offerors with no realistic chance of winning so they do not spend additional time, effort, and money pointlessly pursuing the contract.

Many negotiated contracts are awarded to the responsible offeror that submits the lowest acceptable proposal. For purchases such as these, the contracting officer might decide to include in the competitive range the lowest three or four proposals. However, if the RFP states that the contract will be awarded based on technical excellence, he might decide to include in the competitive range the three or four most highly rated technical proposals. If six proposals are tightly clustered at the top of the evaluation, the contracting officer might decide to include all six proposals in the competitive range. The number of proposals the contracting officer includes in the competitive range is up to him – paragraph (c)(1) of FAR 15.306, Exchanges with Offerors After Receipt of Proposals, states the competitive range "must be comprised of all of the most highly rated proposals..." However, paragraph (c)(2) states that the contracting officer "may limit the number of proposals in the competitive range to the greatest number that will permit an efficient competition among the most highly rated proposals..." *provided* the solicitation contained a notice alerting offerors of this (see paragraph (f)(4) of FAR 52.215-1, Instructions to Offerors – Competitive Acquisition, below).

Before establishing the competitive range, the contracting officer must conduct "communications" with offerors whose past performance evaluations are the determining factor preventing them from being included in the competitive range. These communications must address adverse past performance information (see Chapter 18) to which the offeror has not had an opportunity to respond.

Before establishing the competitive range, the contracting officer must conduct "communications" with offerors whose past performance evaluations are the determining factor preventing them from being included in the competitive range. These communications must address adverse past performance information (see Chapter 18) to which the offeror has not had an opportunity to respond.

Also, the contracting officer *may* hold communications with offerors whose inclusion in the competitive range is uncertain. Such communications may be conducted to enhance the government's understanding of the offeror's proposal, allow reasonable interpretation of the proposal, or otherwise facilitate the proposal's evaluation. The communications may address perceived deficiencies, weaknesses, errors, omissions, or mistakes, but are *not* to permit the offeror to cure proposal deficiencies or material omissions, or to give the offeror the opportunity to revise its proposal.

RECORD OF WEIGHTED GUIDELINES APPLICATION						REPORT CONTROL SYMBOL DD-AT&L(Q)1751	
1. REPORT NO. 0012-17	2. BASIC PROCUREMENT INSTRUMENT IDENTIFICATION NO.				3. SPIIN	4. DATE OF ACTION	
	a. PURCHASING OFFICE W52H09	b. FY 17	c. TYPE PROC INST CODE R0987	d. PRISN		a. YEAR 2017	b. MONTH 03

5. CONTRACTING OFFICE CODE AH09			ITEM	COST CATEGORY	OBJECTIVE
6. NAME OF CONTRACTOR JKL Corporation			13.	MATERIAL	163,155.00
			14.	SUBCONTRACTS	266,221.00
7. DUNS NUMBER 98-765-4321	8. FEDERAL SUPPLY CODE 1520		15.	DIRECT LABOR	269,173.00
			16.	INDIRECT EXPENSES	334,885.00
9. DOD CLAIMANT PROGRAM DO-A1	10. CONTRACT TYPE CODE J		17.	OTHER DIRECT CHARGES	59,150.00
			18.	SUBTOTAL COSTS *(13 thru 17)*	1,092,584.00
11. TYPE EFFORT 1	12. USE CODE 2		19.	GENERAL AND ADMINISTRATIVE	107,073.00
			20.	TOTAL COSTS *(18 + 19)*	1,199,657.00

	WEIGHTED GUIDELINES PROFIT FACTORS				
ITEM	CONTRACTOR RISK FACTORS	ASSIGNED WEIGHTING	ASSIGNED VALUE	BASE *(Item 20)*	PROFIT OBJECTIVE
21.	TECHNICAL	30 %	5.00		
22.	MANAGEMENT/COST CONTROL	20 %	4.50		
23.	PERFORMANCE RISK (COMPOSITE)		4.40	1,199,657.00	48,074.00
24.	CONTRACT TYPE RISK		1.00	1,199,657.00	10,996.00

		COSTS FINANCED	LENGTH FACTOR	INTEREST RATE	
25.	WORKING CAPITAL	299,914.00	.4	2%	2,399.00

	CONTRACTOR FACILITIES CAPITAL EMPLOYED	ASSIGNED VALUE	AMOUNT EMPLOYED	
26.	LAND		88,099.00	
27.	BUILDINGS		220,247.00	
28.	EQUIPMENT	17.50	132,148.00	23,136.00

		ASSIGNED VALUE	BASE *(Item 20)*	
29.	COST EFFICIENCY FACTOR	2.00 %	1,199,657.00	23,993.00
30.		TOTAL PROFIT OBJECTIVE		108,598.00

	NEGOTIATED SUMMARY			
		PROPOSED	OBJECTIVE	NEGOTIATED
31.	TOTAL COSTS			
32.	FACILITIES CAPITAL COST OF MONEY *(DD Form 1861)*			
33.	PROFIT			
34.	TOTAL PRICE *(Line 31 + 32 + 33)*	0.00	0.00	0.00
35.	MARKUP RATE *(Line 32 + 33 divided by 31)*	%	%	%

	CONTRACTING OFFICER APPROVAL			
36. TYPED/PRINTED NAME OF CONTRACTING OFFICER *(Last, First, Middle Initial)*	37. SIGNATURE OF CONTRACTING OFFICER	38. TELEPHONE NO.	39. DATE SUBMITTED *(YYYYMMDD)*	

	OPTIONAL USE			
96.	97.	98.	99.	

DD FORM 1547, JUL 2002   PREVIOUS EDITION IS OBSOLETE.   Adobe Professional 8.0

Figure 13 - Record of Weighted Guidelines Application (DD Form 1547)

Once the contracting officer has conducted the necessary communications and determined which offerors to include in the competitive range, he notifies each offeror excluded from the competitive range, provides the reasons for his decision in general terms, and states he will not consider any revisions to the offeror's proposal.

Before establishing the competitive range, the contracting officer must conduct "communications" with offerors whose past performance evaluations are the determining factor preventing them from being included in the competitive range. These communications must address adverse past performance information (see Chapter 18) to which the offeror has not had an opportunity to respond.

Also, the contracting officer *may* hold communications with offerors whose inclusion in the competitive range is uncertain. Such communications may be conducted to enhance the government's understanding of the offeror's proposal, allow reasonable interpretation of the proposal, or otherwise facilitate the proposal's evaluation. The communications may address perceived deficiencies, weaknesses, errors, omissions, or mistakes, but are *not* to permit the offeror to cure proposal deficiencies or material omissions, or to give the offeror the opportunity to revise its proposal.

Once the contracting officer has conducted the necessary communications and determined which offerors to include in the competitive range, he notifies each offeror excluded from the competitive range, provides the reasons for his decision in general terms, and states he will not consider any revisions to the offeror's proposal.

When requested by an excluded offeror, the contracting officer will provide a **debriefing** as soon as practicable (though the contracting officer may refuse to debrief the excluded offeror until after contract award if it is not in the best interests of the government to conduct a debriefing at that time – see below).

CONDUCTING NEGOTIATIONS

Paragraph (f)(4) of FAR 52.215-1 states *"the government intends to evaluate proposals and award a contract without discussions with offerors . . ."* The contracting officer can do this by signing block 27 of the SF 33 or block 31a of the SF 1449, just as if it were a bid. While this gives the contracting officer the right to award the contract without talking to any of the offerors, he usually wants to contact each offeror in the competitive range individually to discuss the parts of the offeror's proposal that may be unclear or need further explanation.

The contracting officer and the offeror may discuss technical considerations, the terms and conditions, changes proposed by the offeror, the amount and types of labor, the labor rates, overhead rates, travel expenses, material costs, testing costs, type of contract, amount of profit or fee, past performance information, or practically anything else about the proposal. The contracting officer may reveal to all offerors in the competitive range the price or cost the government has determined is reasonable. However, the contracting officer is not required to discuss every area of a proposal that could be improved, and the contracting officer is prohibited from revealing the strengths or weaknesses of competing proposals. Nevertheless, the contracting officer can tell the offeror that the government considers its price to be too high.

During these negotiations (or "discussions"), the contracting officer might accept some changes proposed by the offeror and reject others. The offeror has to decide whether to accept the contracting officer's position or make a counteroffer. If the offeror makes a counteroffer, the contracting officer must decide whether to accept it, reject it, or make a counteroffer of his own. This may go back and forth several times with the parties getting a little closer to agreement after each exchange. However, just because the offeror and contracting officer reach an agreement on the price and the terms and conditions does not mean the offeror will receive the contract. The contracting officer may be negotiating with other offerors in the competitive range and will make his award decision based on which negotiated agreement is most advantageous to the government (as prescribed by the evaluation factors).

If the RFP stated that evaluation credit would be given for technical solutions exceeding any mandatory minimums, the contracting officer may negotiate with offerors for increased performance beyond any mandatory minimums. The contracting officer may suggest to offerors that have exceeded any mandatory minimums (in ways that are not integral to the design) that their proposals would be more competitive if the excesses were removed and the offered price decreased.

Proposal Revisions

During negotiations, the contracting officer may request or allow an offeror to submit a proposal revision to clarify and document understandings that have been reached (this is why there is no "mistake in proposals" procedure as there is with bids). During the course of lengthy negotiations, an offeror might be requested or allowed to make several proposal revisions.

After the contracting officer completes negotiations with all of the offerors in the competitive range, he gives each offeror an opportunity to submit a **final proposal revision** (what used to be called a "best and final offer"). He establishes a common cut-off date for receipt of the final proposal revisions, and will not accept final proposal revisions after that date.

There is one key exception to this rule. Besides the usual exceptions to the late proposal modification rule (that is, the proposal was mishandled by the government, or the proposal was sent by an electronic commerce method and received by the government by 5:00 pm the day before the deadline), FAR 52.215-1(c)(3)(ii)(B) states *"a late modification or revision of an otherwise successful proposal that makes its terms more favorable to the government will be considered at any time it is received and may be accepted.*" This means the contracting officer will not consider a late proposal modification unless it is submitted by the offeror that was going to receive the contract anyway, and the late modification *improves* the winning proposal's terms and conditions. Otherwise, the contracting officer will *ignore* the late proposal modification and award the contract based of the terms and conditions in effect on the final proposal revision deadline (that is, before the arrival of the late final proposal revision).

This provision also means the contracting officer will not consider late modifications from any offerors other than the one about to receive the contract. This prevents a second or third place offeror from submitting a late modification and leapfrogging into first place. Because of these restrictions, prudent offerors make sure their final proposal revisions get to the contracting officer on time.

Certificate of Current Cost or Pricing Data

If the contracting officer required cost or pricing data and the proposal is over $750,000, the offeror must submit a **Certificate of Current Cost or Pricing Data** with the submission of its final proposal revision (or at the end of negotiations if there is no competition). The text of the certification is as follows:

> This is to certify that, to the best of my knowledge and belief, the cost or pricing data (as defined in section 2.101 of the Federal Acquisition Regulation (FAR) and required under FAR subsection 15.403-4) submitted, either actually or by specific identification in writing, to the contracting officer or to the contracting officer's representative in support of _____(identification of the proposal) are accurate, complete, and current as of _____(the date the negotiations were concluded). This certification includes the cost or pricing data supporting any advance agreements and forward pricing rate agreements between the offeror and the government that are part of the proposal.
>
> Firm _____
> Signature _____
> Name _____
> Title _____
> Date of execution _____

Upon signing this, the offeror certifies that the cost or pricing data it provided to the government in support of its proposal are "accurate, complete, and current." This means the offeror updated the cost or pricing data as new or revised data became available and notified the contracting officer of the updates, thus allowing him to consider the new or revised data during negotiations. Some examples of new or revised data that the offeror must provide the contracting officer are lower quotations for raw materials received after the initial proposal was submitted, the acquisition of more-efficient machinery, new union contracts, and new overhead rates for an upcoming period issued by the company's headquarters.

If, after contract award, the government discovers the offeror had data that would have had a material effect on the negotiations (such as lower quotations for raw materials or revised overhead rates) but did not tell the contracting officer, the contracting officer may *unilaterally* reduce the contract price to that which would have been negotiated had the information been provided! (Cost or pricing data that were not complete, accurate, and current upon execution of the Certificate of Current Cost or Pricing Data are called "**defective cost or pricing data**.")

In addition, if the RFP requires offerors to submit cost or pricing data, each offeror must obtain certified cost or pricing data from its *proposed subcontractors* for any subcontract that (1) is not for a commercial item, *and* (2) will not be awarded based on lowest price, *and* (3)(i) will exceed $750,000 and constitute more than 10% of the proposed contract's price, or (ii) will be $13,500,000 or more (though the contracting officer *may* require the submission of subcontractor cost or pricing data below these thresholds if he believes it is needed for adequate pricing of the prime contract). When the offeror signs the certificate of current cost or pricing data, it certifies that any cost or pricing data that a prospective subcontractor submitted and the offeror used in preparing its proposal are accurate, complete, and current. If the offeror wins the contract, awards a subcontract to the subcontractor, and the government discovers the subcontractor's cost or pricing data were not accurate, complete, and current, the contracting officer may unilaterally reduce the price of the *prime* contract to that which would have been negotiated had the information been provided.

SELECTING THE WINNER AND AWARDING THE CONTRACT

Once the contracting officer receives the final proposal revisions, he gives all the technical proposal changes to the technical evaluators so they can revise their proposal evaluations as necessary. As with the original proposals, the contracting officer retains the final proposed prices (although, as mentioned earlier, he may provide the cost information to the technical evaluators under conditions established by the agency).

Upon receiving the technical evaluators' final ratings, the contracting officer decides which offeror is the "apparent" successful offeror according to the RFP's evaluation factors. Normally, the contracting officer will not reopen negotiations after final proposal revisions unless it is clearly in the government's interest, such as when the information is still not sufficient for the contracting officer to select a winner.

Having selected the apparent successful offeror, the contracting officer still must determine whether the apparent successful offeror is responsible. The procedures are the same as those described in Chapter 7 for determining the responsibility of low responsive bidders. The contracting officer can award the contract if he has enough information to determine the offeror's responsibility, or he can request a preaward survey if he needs more information.

If the contracting officer decides the offeror is not responsible and it is a small business, he must refer the matter to the Small Business Administration (SBA) so it can decide whether to issue a certificate of competency (COC) (see Chapter 7).

As previously mentioned, the contracting officer can accept the proposal as submitted without conducting negotiations by signing the SF 33 or SF 1449. This unilateral action institutes a contract.

If the contracting officer issued the RFP on an OF 308, Solicitation and Offer – Negotiated Acquisition (see earlier in this chapter), he cannot sign the OF 308 and form a binding contract. To form a binding contract, the contracting officer will usually prepare an **Optional Form 307, Contract Award**, check block 15 (*"the government hereby accepts your offer on the solicitation . . . as reflected in this award document"*), and sign in block 15A.

However, the negotiations and proposal revisions usually produce changes to the original proposal. To award a contract based on a modified proposal submitted under a SF 33, the contracting officer must prepare a **Standard Form 26, Award/Contract** (see Figure 14). The contracting officer will draft a "fresh" contractual document that incorporates all the negotiated agreements, check block 17 of the Standard Form 26 (*"contractor agrees to furnish and deliver all items or perform all the services set forth or otherwise identified above and on any continuation sheets"*), and require the successful offeror to sign in block 19b. After the offeror signs the SF 26 and returns it to the contracting officer, the contracting officer can sign in block 20b and create a contract. With the SF 1449, the contracting officer will draft a new contractual document, check block 28, require the successful offeror to sign in block 30a, and sign in block 31a. With the OF 307, the contracting officer will prepare a new contractual document, check block 14 (which has the same basic language as block 17 of the SF 26), require the successful offeror to sign in block 14B, and then sign in block 15A.

Contracting officers use the unilateral acceptance when the proposal and modifying letters are simple and easy to follow. They use the bilateral agreement when a fresh document containing all the negotiated agreements would be more easily understandable to all parties (including government contract administration offices, payment offices, and others involved during contract performance). Both methods are equally binding.

Award Notification

After the contracting officer has signed the award document (the SF 26, SF 33, OF 307, or SF 1449) and created a contract, he furnishes copies of the contract to the successful offeror, the administration office, and the payment office. Within

AWARD/CONTRACT	1. THIS CONTRACT IS A RATED ORDER UNDER DPAS (15 CFR 700) ▶	RATING DO-A7	PAGE 1	OF	PAGES 26

2. CONTRACT (Proc. Inst. Ident.) NO. N00421-17-C-7890	3. EFFECTIVE DATE 04/28/2017	4. REQUISITION/PURCHASE REQUEST/PROJECT NO. 1234.17-33007/093553

5. ISSUED BY CODE N00421	6. ADMINISTERED BY (If other than Item 5) CODE S2101A
Naval Air Systems Command Naval Air Warfare Center, Aircraft Division Building 441, 21983 Bundy Road, Unit 7 Patuxent River, MD 20670	DCMA Maryland 217 East Redwood Street, Suite 1800 Baltimore, MD 21202-3375

7. NAME AND ADDRESS OF CONTRACTOR (No., street, county, State and ZIP Code)	8. DELIVERY
Electrophonics, Inc. 1733 East Ninth Street Baltimore, MD 21203	☒ FOB ORIGIN ☐ OTHER (See below)
	9. DISCOUNT FOR PROMPT PAYMENT 1% - 20 days; Net - 30 days
	10. SUBMIT INVOICES (4 copies unless otherwise specified) TO THE ADDRESS SHOWN IN ▶ ITEM Block 12
CODE FACILITY CODE	

11. SHIP TO/MARK FOR CODE	12. PAYMENT WILL BE MADE BY CODE HQ0338
See Section F	DFAS Columbus Center P.O. Box 182264 Columbus, OH 43218-2264

13. AUTHORITY FOR USING OTHER THAN FULL AND OPEN COMPETITION: ☒ 10 U.S.C. 2304(c)(1) ☐ 41 U.S.C. 3304(a)( )	14. ACCOUNTING AND APPROPRIATION DATA 1710401.74 2N0605 1223 S574022

15A. ITEM NO.	15B. SUPPLIES/SERVICES	15C. QUANTITY	15D. UNIT	15E. UNIT PRICE	15F. AMOUNT
0001	Receiver/Transmitter, NSN 5810-01-529-8472				
0001AA	First Article Test	1	Lot	2,989.21	2,989.21
0001AB	Production Units	30	Each	5,138.12	154,143.60
0001AC	Option Units	30	Each	5,035.36	151,060.80
			15G. TOTAL AMOUNT OF CONTRACT ▶		$ 308,193.61

16. TABLE OF CONTENTS

(X)	SEC.	DESCRIPTION	PAGE(S)	(X)	SEC.	DESCRIPTION	PAGE(S)
		PART I - THE SCHEDULE				PART II - CONTRACT CLAUSES	
X	A	SOLICITATION/CONTRACT FORM	1	X	I	CONTRACT CLAUSES	4
X	B	SUPPLIES OR SERVICES AND PRICES/COSTS	1			PART III - LIST OF DOCUMENTS, EXHIBITS AND OTHER ATTACH.	
X	C	DESCRIPTION/SPECS./WORK STATEMENT	3	X	J	LIST OF ATTACHMENTS	1
X	D	PACKAGING AND MARKING	1			PART IV - REPRESENTATIONS AND INSTRUCTIONS	
X	E	INSPECTION AND ACCEPTANCE	5	X	K	REPRESENTATIONS, CERTIFICATIONS AND OTHER STATEMENTS OF OFFERORS	1
X	F	DELIVERIES OR PERFORMANCE	3				
X	G	CONTRACT ADMINISTRATION DATA	1		L	INSTRS., CONDS., AND NOTICES TO OFFERORS	
X	H	SPECIAL CONTRACT REQUIREMENTS	5		M	EVALUATION FACTORS FOR AWARD	

CONTRACTING OFFICER WILL COMPLETE ITEM 17 (SEALED-BID OR NEGOTIATED PROCUREMENT) OR 18 (SEALED-BID PROCUREMENT) AS APPLICABLE

17. ☒ CONTRACTOR'S NEGOTIATED AGREEMENT (Contractor is required to sign this document and return ___2___ copies to issuing office.) Contractor agrees to furnish and deliver all items or perform all the services set forth or otherwise identified above and on any continuation sheets for the consideration stated herein. The rights and obligations of the parties to this contract shall be subject to and governed by the following documents: (a) this award/contract, (b) the solicitation, if any, and (c) such provisions, representations, certifications, and specifications, as are attached or incorporated by reference herein. (Attachments are listed herein.)	18. ☐ SEALED-BID AWARD (Contractor is not required to sign this document.) Your bid on Solicitation Number _____ including the additions or changes made by you which additions or changes are set forth in full above, is hereby accepted as to the terms listed above and on any continuation sheets. This award consummates the contract which consists of the following documents: (a) the Government's solicitation and your bid, and (b) this award/contract. No further contractual document is necessary. (Block 18 should be checked only when awarding a sealed-bid contract.)
19A. NAME AND TITLE OF SIGNER (Type or Print) Brianna Jones Vice President, Finance	20A. NAME OF CONTRACTING OFFICER Peter Greene
19B. NAME OF CONTRACTOR BY _____ (Signature of person authorized to sign)	19C. DATE SIGNED 04/25/2016	20B. UNITED STATES OF AMERICA BY _____ (Signature of Contracting Officer)	20C. DATE SIGNED 04/28/2017

AUTHORIZED FOR LOCAL REPRODUCTION Previous edition is NOT usable	STANDARD FORM 26 (REV. 3/2013) Prescribed by GSA - FAR (48 CFR) 53.214(a)

Figure 14 - Award/Contract (Standard Form 26)

three days after contract award, the contracting officer also sends notices (by written or electronic means) to the unsuccessful offerors included in the competitive range, listing:

- the number of prospective contractors solicited;

- the number of proposals received;

- the name and address of the offeror receiving the award;

- the items, quantities, and unit prices; and

- in general terms, the reasons why the offeror's proposal was not accepted, unless the price readily reveals the reason.

If the RFP was set-aside for small businesses (see Chapter 11), or for HUBZone concerns (see Chapter 11), or for service-disabled veteran-owned small businesses (see Chapter 11), or for women-owned small businesses (see Chapter 11), the contracting officer must notify each unsuccessful offeror of the name and address of the apparent successful offeror before awarding the contract (paragraph (a)(2) of FAR 15.503, Notifications to Unsuccessful Offerors). This preaward notification gives unsuccessful offerors the opportunity to protest the small business size status, HUBZone status, small disadvantaged business (SDB) status, service-disabled veteran-owned small business (SDVOSB) status, or women-owned small business (WOSB) status of the apparent successful offeror (see FAR 19.302, Protesting a Small Business Representation or Rerepresentation; FAR 19.305, Reviews and Protests of SDB Status; FAR 19.306, Protesting a Firm's Status as a HUBZone Small Business Concern; FAR 19.307, Protesting a Firm's Status as a Service-Disabled Veteran-Owned Small Business Concern; FAR 19.308, Protesting a Firm's Status as an Economically Disadvantaged Women-Owned Small Business Concern or Women-Owned Small Business Concern Eligible Under the WOSB Program; and Chapter 16 for information on protesting an offeror's status).

The contracting officer prepares a synopsis of the award for publication in **FedBizOpps** if there are likely to be subcontracting opportunities. Also, he transmits electronically information on the solicitation method, the contract, and the winning contractor to the Federal Procurement Data System (see Chapter 5).

Debriefings

To help unsuccessful offerors improve future proposals and to assure them that the selection process was conducted fairly and according to the regulations, the government will **debrief** unsuccessful offerors upon request. During the debriefing, the contracting officer identifies for the unsuccessful offeror the strengths and weaknesses of its proposal.

Preaward Debriefings

When a contracting officer excludes an offeror from the competitive range because it has no reasonable chance of winning, he must notify the offeror of its exclusion. Within three days of receiving the notice, the excluded offeror may request a debriefing prior to award. Paragraph (b) of FAR 15.505, Preaward Debriefing of Offerors, requires the contracting officer to "make every effort to debrief the unsuccessful offeror as soon as practicable," but it also permits the contracting officer to postpone the debriefing until after contract award if "it is not in the best interests of the government to conduct a debriefing at that time." If denied a preaward debriefing, the contracting officer must provide the excluded offeror a *postaward* debriefing (see below).

The preaward debriefing must include the following:

- The agency's evaluation of the significant elements in the debriefed offeror's offer;

- A summary of the rationale for the debriefed offeror's exclusion; and

- Reasonable responses to relevant questions posed by the unsuccessful offeror as to whether the source selection procedures specified in the solicitation and applicable regulations were followed by the agency.

However, the contracting officer may not disclose the number or identity of other offerors, and he may not disclose information about the content, ranking, or evaluation of other offerors' proposals.

As an alternative, an offeror excluded from the competitive range may request (within three days of receiving contracting officer's notice) that it be provided a postaward debriefing. See FAR 15.505 for more on preaward debriefings.

Postaward Debriefings

FAR 15.506, Postaward Debriefing of Offerors, gives unsuccessful offerors the right to be debriefed when the contract is awarded on a basis other than lowest price. Any unsuccessful offeror that wants a postaward debriefing must submit its request to the contracting officer in writing within three days of receiving the award notification (offerors excluded from the competitive range that choose to receive a postaward debriefing must make such request within three days of receiving the contracting officer's notice – see above). The contracting officer must hold the debriefing within five days of receiving the request from the unsuccessful offeror if possible. Usually, the contracting officer holds the debriefing in his office.

Normally, the contracting officer invites government officials who are familiar with the rationale for the selection decision to the debriefing. As a minimum, the government officials provide:

- The agency's evaluation of the significant weaknesses or deficiencies in the debriefed offeror's proposal;

- The overall evaluated cost or price and technical rating of the winning proposal and the debriefed offeror's proposal;

- The past performance information on the debriefed offeror;

- The overall ranking of *all* offerors;

- A summary of the rationale for the award;

- The makes and models of commercial items that will be provided under the contract by the winning contractor; and

- Reasonable responses to relevant questions posed by the unsuccessful offeror about compliance with the source selection procedures described in the RFP, applicable regulations, and other requirements.

The government officials will *not* make point-by-point comparisons of the debriefed offeror's proposal with the successful proposal, nor will they disclose:

- Trade secrets;

- Privileged or confidential manufacturing processes and techniques;

- Privileged or confidential commercial and financial information such as cost breakdowns, indirect cost rates, profit, and similar information; or

- The names of individuals who provided information about the offeror's past performance.

A smart offeror makes it a practice to request a debriefing if its proposal is unsuccessful because of technical or managerial deficiencies. An unsuccessful offeror willing to accept **constructive criticism** can learn and understand more from a single debriefing than from writing a dozen unsuccessful proposals. Also, information obtained during the debriefing may provide grounds for filing a **protest** (see Chapter 17).

UNSOLICITED PROPOSALS

FAR 2.101, Definitions, defines an **unsolicited proposal** as "*a written proposal for a new or innovative idea that is submitted to an agency on the initiative* *of the offeror for the purpose of obtaining a contract with the government, and that is not in response to a request for proposals...or any other government-initiated solicitation or program.*" While the government prefers that new and innovative ideas be submitted through existing programs whenever possible (such as a Broad Agency Announcements [see Chapter 5], the Small Business Innovation Research program [see Chapter 11], or the Small Business Technology Transfer program [see Chapter 11]), the unsolicited proposal is a valuable means by which unique or innovative methods or approaches can be offered to government agencies to help them accomplish their missions.

Government agencies are required to provide information to potential offerors regarding their policies and procedures for unsolicited proposals. Agencies also encourage potential offerors to contact their technical and "requirements" personnel to gain an understanding of the agency's mission and needs before expending extensive effort preparing a detailed unsolicited proposal or submitting any proprietary information to the government.

An offeror has a reasonable chance of receiving a contract through an unsolicited proposal if the proposal can demonstrate the offeror is uniquely capable to solve a problem of, or render a service to, the agency. This unique capability might be the employment of highly qualified personnel, proprietary techniques, patents, or facilities.

The supply or service offered in the unsolicited proposal must be **unique and innovative**. An unsolicited proposal offering a special deal on a particular supply or service that the agency regularly purchases will be rejected because its intent is to circumvent the full and open competition requirement. The fact that the supply or service is unique and innovative is no guarantee the agency will give the offeror a contract, especially if the supply or service does not meet the agency's needs. Furthermore, if the substance of the unsolicited proposal is available to the government without restriction from another source, or if the unsolicited proposal closely resembles a pending competitive solicitation, the agency will not accept it.

The unsolicited proposal should be signed by a person authorized to represent and contractually obligate the offeror. While there is no established format for unsolicited proposals, each should contain at least the following information (see FAR 15.605, Content of Unsolicited Proposals):

- Name and address of the offeror and its type of organization (such as profit, nonprofit, educational, small business);

- Names and telephone numbers of the technical and business personnel who may be contacted;

- Identification of any proprietary data that the offeror is providing only for evaluation purposes;

- Names of other federal, state, or local agencies, or other parties that are receiving the proposal or are funding the proposed effort;

- An abstract of the proposed effort (approximately 200 words);

- A narrative that discusses the relevance of the proposed work to the agency, the objectives of the effort, the proposed approach, the nature of the anticipated results, and the manner in which the work will help to support the accomplishment of the agency's mission;

- The names and brief biographies of the key personnel who will be involved;

- A description of previous work and experience in the field;

- A brief description of the facilities the offeror will use;

- A description of any support the offeror requests of the agency (for example, facilities, equipment, materials, personnel);

- A proposed price or estimated cost, with appropriate supporting information and explanations;

- The type of contract preferred (such as firm-fixed-price or cost-plus-fixed-fee – see Chapter 9);

- Period of time for which the proposal is valid (the proposal acceptance period should be a minimum of six months);

- Proposed duration of the effort;

- Environmental impacts, if any;

- Security clearance status, if appropriate; and

- Any other information that may be pertinent, such as a financial statement or a descriptive brochure.

If an unsolicited proposal includes data that the offeror does not want disclosed for any purpose other than evaluation, and the offeror wants to restrict the proposal, the title page *must* be marked with the following legend from paragraph (a) of FAR 15.609, Limited Use of Data:

USE AND DISCLOSURE OF DATA

This proposal includes data that shall not be disclosed outside the Government and shall not be duplicated, used, or disclosed – in whole or in part – for any purpose other than to evaluate this proposal. However, if a contract is awarded to this offeror as a result of – or in connection with – the submission of these data, the Government shall have the right to duplicate, use, or disclose the data to the extent provided in the resulting contract. This restriction does not limit the Government's right to use information contained in these data if they are obtained from another source without restriction. The data subject to this restriction are contained in Sheets _____ [*insert numbers or other identification of sheets*].

In addition, each restricted page (sheet) must be marked with the following legend from FAR 15.609(b):

Use or disclosure of data contained on this sheet is subject to the restriction on the title page of this proposal.

Offerors should send their unsolicited proposals to the agency's **unsolicited proposal contact point**, who coordinates the receipt and handling of unsolicited proposals. Upon receipt, the contact point determines if the unsolicited proposal is in an area of interest to the agency, contains sufficient technical and cost information, and has scientific or technical merit. If the proposal meets these requirements, the contact point will promptly acknowledge and process the proposal. If the proposal does not meet these requirements, the contact point will notify the offeror. If the proposal does not contain sufficient information to permit a complete and thorough evaluation, the contact point will give the offeror an opportunity to submit the required data.

The contact point coordinates the evaluation of the unsolicited proposal among appropriately qualified agency personnel. The evaluation takes into account:

- Unique and innovative methods, approaches, or ideas that have originated with or are assembled by the offeror;

- Overall scientific, technical, or socioeconomic merits of the proposed effort;

- The potential contribution the proposed effort is expected to make to the agency's specific mission;

- The capabilities, related experience, facilities, techniques, or unique combinations of these that the offeror possesses and which are considered to be integral factors for achieving the scientific or technical objectives of the proposal;

- The qualifications, capabilities, and experience of the proposed principal investigator, team leader, or key personnel who are considered critical in achieving the objectives of the proposal; and

- The realism of the proposed cost.

If the proposal is favorably evaluated and the substance of the proposal is not otherwise available to the government, the proposal will form the basis for noncompetitive negotiations with the offeror and, if an agreement can be reached, a contract.

See FAR subpart 15.6, Unsolicited Proposals, for more information.

CHAPTER 9

THE DIFFERENT TYPES OF CONTRACTS

There are two basic kinds of contracts the government uses when purchasing supplies or services: the **fixed-price** contract and the **cost-reimbursement** contract. A fixed-price contract is one in which the government agrees to pay the contractor a fixed amount upon completion of the contract. A cost-reimbursement contract is one in which the government agrees to reimburse the contractor for the costs it incurs in performing the contract.

The most important difference between the two kinds of contracts is the amount of responsibility, or "risk," assumed by the contractor for the cost of performance. With a fixed-price contract, the contractor assumes the risk of contract performance and its performance determines whether it makes a profit. With a cost-reimbursement contract, the government reimburses the contractor for its expenses and assumes the risk of contract performance.

PREFERENCE FOR FIXED-PRICE CONTRACTS

The government prefers to use fixed-price contracts whenever possible. Because the contractor is responsible for contract performance, the government has little or no involvement between contract award and contract delivery. The government does not care whether the contractor discovers a way to perform the contract more cheaply than expected (thus earning more profit) or runs into difficulties and incurs higher expenses than expected (thus earning less profit or losing money). As long as the contractor delivers a product that meets the government's specifications or statement of work when contractually scheduled, the government is satisfied.

People encounter fixed-prices everyday – when buying groceries, when buying a car, when buying a house. The seller agrees to deliver a product in return for the buyer paying a fixed-price. Fixed-price contracts are not restricted to acquisitions made through simplified procedures or sealed bidding; most negotiations between the seller and buyer result in an agreement on a fixed-price that is not subject to later revision. Fixed-price contracts are particularly suited for supplies or services that are sold in the commercial marketplace or are described by reasonably definite specifications or statements of work. In fact, fixed-price contracts are *required* for commercial items.

Since most of the supplies or services the government purchases are either sold commercially or have reasonably definitive specifications or statements of work, most of its contractual actions are fixed-price. If fact, *all* purchases made through simplified procedures, *all* purchases made through sealed bidding, and *75%* of all purchases made through negotiation procedures are fixed-price.

CRITERIA FOR USING COST-REIMBURSEMENT CONTRACTS

Cost-reimbursement contracts are definitely the government's second choice. FAR 16.301-2, Application, prohibits contracting officers from using cost-reimbursement contracts unless the *"uncertainties involved in contract performance do not permit costs to be estimated with sufficient accuracy to use **any** type of fixed-price contract."* This is because a cost-reimbursement contract obligates the government to reimburse the contractor for its costs and, in most cases, to pay an additional "fee" in return for the contractor exerting its best efforts. Besides, under a cost-reimbursement contract, the contractor is entitled to the reimbursement of its costs no matter how successful (or unsuccessful) those efforts are!

Since the contractor has little incentive to control costs, the government must monitor the contractor's performance closely to make sure the contractor performs efficiently and effectively. This increased administrative burden is expensive for the government: the government must pay for the government personnel monitoring the contractor's performance *and* the costs the contractor incurs in reporting its progress and spending.

For example, the government will *not* enter into a cost-reimbursement contract unless the contractor has an accounting system that adequately segregates the costs attributable to the performance of the cost-reimbursement contract from the costs incurred in the performance of other contracts. That means the accounting system must conform to generally accepted accounting principles (or the Cost Accounting Standards if the contractor is a large business performing large non-commercial contracts – see Chapter 18), permit the tracking of the contract's direct costs, and apply indirect costs reasonably and consistently. Such an accounting system can be expensive for the contractor to set up, operate, and maintain.

However, there are circumstances in which the cost-reimbursement contract is a useful and necessary tool. Research and development contracts, which require contractor creativity and have relatively broad statements of work, are frequently cost-reimbursement. A contractor would be foolish to agree to produce a cancer cure for a fixed price – the uncertainty of performance would make any fixed price a wild guess. The contractor could lose a considerable amount of money searching for the elusive cure, even to the point of bankruptcy.

Similarly, the government would be foolish to seek a fixed price for a cancer cure because the offerors would undoubtedly add so many contingencies to their proposed prices that a fixed-price contract would be unaffordable. Even if the government and the contractor could agree on a fixed-price contract for a cancer cure, the contractor might become overly concerned with its budget, especially as its expenditures approached the fixed price. This could tempt the contractor to cut corners in its research and even falsify test results. Obviously, this is not what the government wants. For development of a cancer cure, a fixed-price contract would give the contractor the wrong motivation; a cost-reimbursement contract would free the contractor to do its research work without "distractions."

For these reasons, the contracting officer must carefully analyze each purchase to decide which contract type will give the contractor the greatest incentive to perform the contract on time and at a reasonable cost to the government. And bidders and offerors need to evaluate whether the contract type is appropriate for the supplies or services being purchased – that the contract type distributes the risk of performance equitably and the bidder or offeror is willing to assume its share of that risk. The right contract type can go a long way to making the contractual relationship a harmonious one.

THE MOST COMMON TYPES OF CONTRACTS

Because the government purchases a large variety and volume of products under many diverse circumstances, there are different types of fixed-price and cost- reimbursement contracts available to the contracting parties. The most commonly used types are:

- Firm-Fixed-Price (FFP)
- Fixed-Price with Economic Price Adjustment (FP/EPA)
- Fixed-Price with Award Fee (FPAF)
- Cost-Plus-Fixed-Fee (CPFF)
- Cost-Plus-Incentive-Fee (CPIF)
- Cost-Plus-Award-Fee (CPAF)
- Time-and-Materials (T&M)
- Labor-Hour

There are other types of fixed-price and cost-reimbursement contracts authorized in FAR part 16, Types of Contracts (and sometimes both fixed-price and cost-reimbursement pricing arrangement are used in the same contract). However, these other types of contracts are used in special situations or on multimillion dollar contracts. These eight contract types are used by the government for approximately **95%** of its contract dollars.

Generally, when both the contractor and the government can identify and predict the risks of contract performance, a firm-fixed-price (FFP) contract is preferred. As the risks of performance become more uncertain and significant, other types of fixed price contracts are used, such as the fixed-price with economic price adjustment (FP/EPA) contract. When the risks of performance are unknown or unpredictable, cost-reimbursement contracts are used to avoid having the contractor assume too much risk.

Because fixed-price contracts have relatively simple pricing arrangements, *all* purchase orders, *all* IFBs, *all* RFPs in the simplified contract format (SCF), and *all* RFPs for commercial items must result in either an FFP or an FP/EPA contract. Many non-commercial RFPs also result in FFP or FP/EPA contracts. The quickest way to tell which type of contract the government expects to award under an RFP in the uniform contract format (UCF) is to go to Section L and find **FAR 52.216-1, Type of Contract**. The entire provision consists of a single sentence:

> The government contemplates award of a _____ contract resulting from this solicitation.

The contracting officer inserts the type of contract he thinks is appropriate for the purchase. This provides guidance to offerors as they prepare their proposals. Offerors should *always* look for FAR 52.216-1 before responding to an RFP.

FIRM-FIXED-PRICE

The **firm-fixed-price** (FFP) contract is the type most used by the government. It is preferred to all other types of fixed-price contracts because the contractor agrees to deliver the supplies or perform the services for a price that does not change regardless of the contractor's cost experience. This type of contract places *all* the risk of performance on the contractor. The government pays the contractor the firm-fixed-price specified in the contract when the supplies are delivered or services are performed and accepted – no more and no less.

The following shows how the contractor's profit varies with its cost of performance:

Contract Price	$300,000	$300,000	$300,000
Final Cost of Performance	$270,000	$250,000	$320,000
PROFIT (or loss)	$30,000	$50,000	($20,000)

Because the contractor's performance determines whether it will make or lose money on an FFP contract, the FFP contract gives the contractor the most incentive to control costs and perform the contract according to the terms and conditions.

However, the FFP contract is not appropriate under all circumstances. It is appropriate only for (1) commercial supplies or services, and (2) supplies or services described by detailed specifications or statement of work if the contractor and government can establish a fair and reasonable price at the time of contract award. A fair and reasonable price can be established through competitive bids or proposals, cost or pricing data (see Chapter 8), data other than cost or pricing data (see Chapter 8), or by identifying the uncertainties of performance and estimating their possible effect on the contract price.

The FFP contract is particularly suitable when purchasing standard or modified commercial supplies, such as "off-the-shelf" items. The FFP contract is also suitable for standard services, such as trash pick-up or grounds maintenance. Usually, if the contracting officer believes he can obtain acceptable supplies or services from the lowest bidder, he will use an FFP contract.

All purchase orders must be FFP, most contracts awarded through sealed bidding are FFP, and many contracts awarded through negotiation techniques are FFP. FFP proposals do not need to be supported by cost or pricing data *if* the award will be based on price or data other than cost or pricing data is available that clearly demonstrates the reasonableness of the price.

See FAR 16.202, Firm-Fixed-Price Contracts, for the regulations governing FFP contracts.

FIXED-PRICE WITH ECONOMIC PRICE ADJUSTMENT

A variation of the FFP contract is the **fixed-price with economic price adjustment** (FP/EPA) contract. This type of contract is an FFP contract in which specific, potentially volatile cost elements are addressed separately from the rest of the contract. It allows the contract price to be adjusted upward or downward depending on the cost behavior of those volatile cost elements. In other words, the FP/EPA contract is FFP except for the portion that is "price at the time of delivery."

The FP/EPA is appropriate when the government and contractor can identify most *but not all* performance uncertainties for contracts with extended performance periods, typically longer than **six months**. Economic price adjustment provisions are usually restricted to fluctuations that are industry-wide and not under the control of the contractor (for example, changes to an industry-wide labor contract or raw material prices). The amount of increase allowable under most economic price adjustment provisions is limited to **10% of the unit price**, but there is *never* any limit on the downward adjustment.

Economic price adjustments are not made to supplies that have been delivered nor services that have been performed. Once the material has been bought or the labor has been expended, those costs are not affected by subsequent price fluctuations. Only *undelivered* supplies or *unperformed* services may be adjusted. However, the government will not make upward adjustments to the price of late supplies or services *if* the cost increase occurred *after* the contract delivery or performance date. It *will* make downward adjustments to the price of late supplies or services even if the cost decrease occurred after the contract delivery or performance date.

In addition, the government will not adjust the contract price to compensate the contractor for poor performance or lack of cost control.

The following is an example of how an FP/EPA contract works. Assume the government wanted to purchase widgets over a 12 month period. The price of a widget consists of gold, steel, labor, and profit. The price of a widget, if bought today, would be:

Steel	$800
Gold	$300
Labor	$700
Profit	$200
PRICE	$2,000

The contracting officer assessed the marketplace and determined that the current price of the steel in a widget is expected to be stable for the next 12 months at $800 a unit, and the widget industry's workforce is working under a union contract for the next three years (thus insuring the cost of labor will remain stable though the 12 month contract). However, the contracting officer also noted that the cost of gold has fluctuated between $100 and $500 a widget during the previous several months.

If the contracting officer were to disregard this fact and insist on an FFP contract, bidders would probably try to protect themselves in case the price of gold increased to $500. To eliminate the risk associated with the gold price fluctuations, a bidder would price the widget as follows:

Steel	$800
Gold	$500
Labor	$700
Profit	$200
PRICE	$2,200

If the bidder won the contract at $2,200 each, but the cost of the gold did not increase to $500, the government would be paying more than it should for the widget. Conversely, if the bidder submitted an FFP bid of $2,000 based on the current $300 cost of gold, and the cost of gold increased to $500, it would have to deliver the widgets at a loss or cut corners in the manufacturing process to save money, thus degrading the quality of the widgets. The potential risks of a 12 month FFP contract for widgets would be too great for both the government and the contractor.

A more equitable way of handling widget pricing might be to isolate the effect of the gold on the price of the widget, and provide for an "economic price adjustment" based on the actual cost of the gold to the contractor. The economic price adjustment provision would make the $300 the "baseline" – if the price of gold rises above $300, the contract price would increase correspondingly; if the price of gold falls below $300, the contract price would decrease correspondingly.

If the price of gold rises to $400 a unit, the price of the widget is adjusted as follows:

Steel	$800
Gold	$400
Labor	$700
Profit	$200
PRICE	$2,100

The contract price of the widget is increased by $100 to reflect the gold price rise from $300 to $400.

Note the steel, labor, and profit portions of the widget price remain unchanged. Because the contracting officer determined that steel and labor prices would be stable or predictable for the duration of the contract, the contracting officer did not make these portions of the widget cost subject to economic price adjustment. The contract will not be adjusted to reflect their actual final cost to the contractor. And, with an FP/EPA contract, profit is never increased or decreased because of an economic price adjustment. It would not be fair to the government to reward the contractor with additional profit merely because the contract price is adjusted upward, especially since the contractor had no control over the cost of the gold. Conversely, it would not be fair to the contractor to penalize it by reducing its profit merely because the contract is adjusted downward. By subjecting the price of gold to economic price adjustment, the government assumes the risk for the gold fluctuations, and the contractor is not rewarded or penalized for the fluctuations.

Should the price of gold drop to $175 a unit, the price of the widget would be reduced by $125:

Steel	$800
Gold	$175
Labor	$700
Profit	$200
PRICE	$1,875

In essence, this contract is a $1,700 FFP contract for steel, labor, and profit, with the gold element of the widget price allowed to float. However, since the FP/EPA contract limits increases to 10% of the original unit price, the government will pay no more than $2,200 ($2,000 + 10%) for a widget. The contractor assumes the risk of the cost of gold exceeding $500 a unit, because $500 is the point at which the widget unit price exceeds $2,200.

There are three general kinds of FP/EPA contracts:

1. ***Adjustments Based on Established Prices*** – The contracting officer will use either FAR 52.216-2, Economic Price Adjustment – Standard Supplies (for supplies that have an established catalog or market price), FAR 52.216-3, Economic Price Adjustment – Semistandard Supplies (for supplies that are *nearly* equivalent to standard supplies except they are slightly modified to meet the government's needs), or an agency-prescribed clause (if authorized);

2. ***Adjustments Based on Actual Costs of Labor or Material*** – The contracting officer will use either FAR 52.216-4, Economic Price Adjustment – Labor and Material (when one or more identifiable labor or material cost factors are subject to change), or an agency-prescribed clause (if authorized); and

3. ***Adjustments Based on Cost Indexes of Labor or Material*** – The contracting officer has to prepare a clause tailored to the specific circumstances and obtain agency approval if: (1) the contract involves an extended period of performance with significant costs to be incurred more than one year after performance begins; (2) the contract amount subject to adjustment is substantial; and (3) the economic variables for labor and materials are too unstable to permit a reasonable division of risk between the government and the contractor.

The contracting officer selects the appropriate kind of FP/EPA contract depending on the particular supply or service being purchased and the nature of the cost elements that will be subject to fluctuation.

Some IFBs and some RFPs result in FP/EPA contracts. FP/EPA proposals do not need to be supported by cost or pricing data *if* the award will be based on price or data other than cost or pricing data is available that clearly demonstrates the reasonableness of the price.

Though the FP/EPA contract is not used as extensively as about 30–35 years ago when inflation was in the double digits, the government still uses it for long-term contracts. And, if inflation heats up again, look for the FP/EPA contract to make a quick return.

See FAR 16.203, Fixed-Price Contracts with Economic Price Adjustment, for regulations governing FP/EPA contracts.

FIXED-PRICE WITH AWARD-FEE

With a **fixed-price with award-fee** (FPAF) contract, the government and the contractor negotiate a FFP contract (including a normal profit) which will be paid for satisfactory contract performance. However, the government sets aside an additional pool of money, some or all of which it may award to the contractor depending on the contractor's performance – the award-fee is like a "tip" given to a waiter or waitress in a restaurant. If the performance is excellent, then the **fee-determining official** gives the contractor a large reward; if the performance is satisfactory, the fee-determining official gives the contractor a small-to-moderate reward; if the performance is unsatisfactory, the fee-determining official gives the contractor no reward.

The FPAF contract is used when the government wants to motivate a contractor but the criteria for acceptance of the work is inherently *judgmental* – there is nothing to measure that would indicate compliance or noncompliance with the contract requirements. Typically, the FPAF contract involves services (such as cleaning, grounds maintenance, food services, security, training, or moving) which are normally acquired on a fixed-price basis but do not have objective acceptance criteria. For example, it is difficult to quantify the quality of food or employees in a contract for the operation of a cafeteria. However, it *is possible* to define the various criteria that constitute *superior* service: for the food, it might be freshness, variety, quantity, and proper temperature; for the employees, it might be demeanor, hygiene, quickness to clean tables and spills, and responsiveness to special requests. While one may not be able to define "good service," one recognizes "good service" when he receives it.

Each FPAF solicitation and contract identifies the cost, schedule, and/or technical performance criteria that will be evaluated to determine the amount of fee to award the contractor. These criteria are supported by an **award-fee plan**, which establishes the procedures for the conduct of the award-fee evaluations by the **award-fee board**, which evaluates the contractor's performance during the period and recommends to the fee-determining official an appropriate award-fee for the contractor. The fee-determining official makes the final decision on the amount of the award-fee.

For example, one criteria for security services might be "responsiveness to emergencies." The award-fee plan might state that this criterion constitutes 25% of the award-fee pool and lists the following performance standards:

Excellent – Always responds in less than 2 minutes (91% to 100% of the award-fee pool set aside for this criterion [25%])

Very Good – Usually takes less than 2 minutes to respond; occasionally takes more than 2 minutes to respond but never more than 3 minutes (76% - 90%)

Good – Consistently takes between 2 and 3 minutes to respond; occasionally takes more than 3 minutes to respond but never more than 4 minutes (51% - 75%)

Satisfactory – Consistently takes between 3 and 4 minutes to respond; occasionally takes more than 4 minutes to respond (no more than 50%)

Unsatisfactory – Consistently takes more than 4 minutes to respond (0%)

(The award-fee adjectival ratings and the amounts of the award-fee pool that are available for each rating are specified in Table 16-1 of FAR 16.401, General.)

Based on how quickly the contractor responds to emergencies, the award-fee board will recommend to the fee-determining official an award-fee amount appropriate for the contractor's performance. The fee-determining official either agrees with the award-fee board's recommendation or rejects the recommendation and sets a different award-fee amount. This amount will be taken from the 25% of the award-fee pool set-aside for "responsiveness to emergencies" and given to the contractor through a unilateral contract modification (see Chapter 18 for the different kinds of contract modifications). The decision of the fee-determination official is not subject to the "**Disputes**" clause and cannot be appealed (see Chapter 18 for an explanation of the Disputes clause). Because the award fee decision is final, the contract usually requires that the contractor's performance be evaluated periodically (usually every three to six months) so the contractor is aware of how the government is evaluating its work and it can make adjustments to earn a larger award-fee. Award-fee that is not earned during a period (that is, performance is less than "excellent") cannot be "rolled over" and available to be earned in the next period – that unearned fee is *gone*.

The FPAF contract is to be used *only* if the administrative costs of conducting the award fee evaluations are not expected to exceed the anticipated benefits. That means the government and the contractor must negotiate an award-fee pool that is sufficiently large to (1) provide a meaningful incentive to the contractor, and (2) justify the administrative burdens inherent in the conduct of an FPAF contract. The head of the contracting activity (HCA, see Chapter 2) must prepare a written statement that he has determined the use of this type of contract is in the best interest of the government.

There is no FAR clause for the FPAF contract – either the contracting officer must use a clause prescribed by the agency's acquisition regulations or he must prepare a clause and obtain agency approval. If the contracting officer has to prepare a FPAF contract clause, undoubtedly he will consider his expenditure of time and effort as an "administrative burden" that must be countered by additional "anticipated benefits."

See FAR 16.404, Fixed-Price Contracts with Award Fees, for the regulations governing FPAF contracts.

COST-PLUS-FIXED-FEE

The most commonly used type of cost-reimbursement contract is the **cost-plus-fixed-fee** (CPFF) contract. In a CPFF contract, the government agrees to reimburse the contractor for the costs it incurs during contract performance plus an additional fixed "fee." It's like paying a detective $5,000 plus expenses to track a philandering spouse: he maintains his surveillance (and thus incurs costs) until he has positive proof, spends a predetermined amount of money for expenses, or is told to stop the surveillance.

The following is an example of how the CPFF works, assuming an estimated cost of $300,000 and a fixed fee of $25,000, for a total cost-plus-fixed-fee of $325,000:

Actual Cost	$300,000	$350,000*	$250,000
Fixed Fee	$25,000	$25,000	$25,000
TOTAL PAYMENT	$325,000	$375,000	$275,000

* This would require the government to modify the contract to permit work beyond the original $300,000 estimated cost. A more detailed explanation is provided later in this section.

Unlike a contractor's profit under an FFP contract, the contractor's fee under a CPFF contract has no relationship to the money spent performing the contract. The fee is set when the contract is awarded and will not change irrespective of the actual costs incurred. This absence of an incentive for the contractor to control costs is the reason the CPFF is the government's *least preferred type of contract*. It is also the reason the government has to monitor the contractor's performance so closely – to ensure the contractor is being diligent and economical in its spending and is employing efficient techniques and processes.

The government uses the CPFF contract primarily in research and engineering contracts where neither the government nor the contractor has a good estimate of the amount of work required to perform the contract. Its use is appropriate when there are no definitive specifications or the scope of work is vague: "the optimization of nuclear weapons effects (NWE) capabilities in pulsed power diagnostics, modeling, and simulation; and X-ray source diagnostics, modeling, and simulation" is one such scope of work from a recent **FedBizOpps** synopsis. Most of the government's contracts for medical research are CPFF.

An offeror writing a proposal for a CPFF contract must fully explain what it plans to do. Since the government may not have a definitive idea of what is required to perform the contract, it typically wants the offeror to:

- Identify the problem;

- Demonstrate an understanding of the problem (or objective);

- Explain how the problem affects government operations;

- Explain its proposed approach to the problem;

- Provide the qualifications of its personnel;

- Justify the amount of labor it thinks will be needed to carry out the proposed approach;

- Justify the labor rates and related costs;

- Describe the cost and technical controls it has in place or intends to implement for the contract;

- Explain how it will ensure the quality of its subcontractors' work; and

- Submit a detailed explanation of fringe benefits, overhead rates, proposed subcontract costs, consultant fees, and any other expenses that would affect the cost of the contract.

This means the government will want each offeror to submit a technical proposal, a management proposal, and a cost proposal (consisting of certified cost or pricing data if the estimated cost and fixed fee is expected to exceed $750,000, or data other than cost or pricing data if the contract is not expected to exceed $750,000 [see Chapter 8]). The government feels it needs this information to make an informed contract award decision, especially since the government will be reimbursing the eventual contractor for the costs it incurs during contract performance.

Upon receiving the offeror's proposal for the CPFF effort, the contracting officer and the technical evaluators (along with auditors, lawyers, and such other government personnel as the contracting officer deems necessary) evaluate the soundness of the proposed approach:

- How well does the proposal address the government's problem?

- How innovative is the proposal?

- Are the personnel who will be performing the contract qualified?

- Is the number of proposed manhours reasonable?

- Are the types of labor proposed appropriate for the effort?

- Are the other proposed charges reasonable?

- Are there any proposed charges the government should *not* agree to reimburse?

- Does the cost proposal contain any unallowable costs?

Based on this evaluation, the contracting officer and the offeror negotiate the scope of work and an estimated cost to perform the contract. This estimated cost becomes a **ceiling** that the contractor (assuming the offeror wins the contract) may not exceed except at its own risk. The contracting officer is not obligated to reimburse the contractor for any costs it incurs over the estimated cost.

After the government and the offeror reach agreement on the estimated cost of the proposed contract, they negotiate the fixed fee. The amount of fee the government will agree to pay depends on the difficulty of the task, the qualifications of the personnel who will perform the contract, innovative approaches that the contractor will pursue, and similar factors. The maximum amount of fee allowed by law is **10% of the estimated cost**, except that the maximum fee for an experimental, developmental, or research contracts is **15%** of the estimated cost. The fixed fee is a set dollar amount and is not stated as a percentage because the government is prohibited by law from entering into a "cost-plus-a-percentage-of-cost" contract.

Once awarded the contract, the contractor performs the contract until it either completes the contract and delivers the end product (which might be a prototype or something as simple as a report of its findings) or reaches the contract ceiling (that is, the estimated cost). If the contractor completes the contract under the ceiling, it submits its incurred costs to the contracting officer and those costs are audited. The government auditor checks the incurred costs to determine whether they were appropriate and necessary to the conduct of the contract, then reports his findings and recommendations to the contracting officer. The contracting officer and the contractor negotiate the final contract cost and the contractor is paid that amount. In addition to the reimbursement of its costs, the contractor receives the fixed fee.

If the contractor incurs costs equaling the contract ceiling before completing the contract, the contracting officer has two choices: (1) end the contract, or (2) require the contractor to continue the contract effort.

If the contracting officer decides to end the contract, he will have the contractor submit its costs for audit as if it had completed the task. The contracting officer and the contractor negotiate the final contract cost and the contractor is reimbursed that amount. However, the contracting officer is not required to pay the contractor the entire fixed fee since the contractor failed to complete the contract and deliver the end product.

On the other hand, if the contracting officer decides to require the contractor to continue the contract effort until completion, he must obtain additional funds and place them in the contract. The contracting officer does this by increasing the contract's estimated cost. Then the contractor will be reimbursed for its additional expenses and, upon delivery of the end product and completion of the contract, will receive the full fixed fee. However, the contractor will receive no *additional* fee for the additional work; no matter how much work the contractor does to complete the task and deliver the end product, it will only receive the fixed fee originally negotiated. That is why it is called a "fixed fee."

There are two forms of CPFF contract. The form just described is the "completion" form. It is the most frequently used form of CPFF contract and is the form preferred by the government. In the completion form of CPFF contract, the scope of work describes a definite goal and specifies the delivery of an end product (such as a report) as a condition for payment of the entire fixed fee. If the contractor fails to deliver the end product before reaching the contract's ceiling, the contracting officer can require the contractor to continue the contract at cost, with no increase in fee, until it delivers the product.

However, the CPFF contract also can be written in the "term" form. The term form describes the scope of work in general terms and obligates the contractor to expend a specific number of labor hours during a stated period ("level of effort"). Under this form of CPFF contract, the contractor is reimbursed for the costs it incurred during contract performance, as with all cost-reimbursement contracts. However, it receives the fixed fee at the end of the contract period once it certifies it has expended the number of labor hours required by the contract and the government considers the performance satisfactory. The contractor receives its costs and the fixed fee regardless of the contract results. If the government wants the contractor to continue the contract effort, the contracting officer must conduct negotiations to establish a new estimated cost and fixed fee for the continuation. Because the contractor has practically no obligations under the term form of CPFF contract, paragraph (d)(3) of FAR 16.306, Cost-Plus-Fixed-Fee Contracts, states "*the completion form is preferred over the term form whenever the work, or specific milestones for the work, can be defined well enough to permit development of estimates within which the contractor can be expected to complete the work.*" One can understand why!

RFPs expected to result in CPFF contracts will contain FAR 52.216-8, Fixed Fee. All CPFF proposals over $750,000 must be supported by cost or pricing data, and all CPFF proposals under $750,000 must be supported by information other than cost or pricing data.

See FAR 16.306 for the regulations governing CPFF contracts.

COST-PLUS-INCENTIVE-FEE

As a project begins to mature and move from research and development to prototype fabrication and initial production, the government's contract goals become more focused. It begins to get a better idea of what the item should look like or what the contractor should be doing. Once the government is able to develop definite performance objectives that are *probably* achievable, but the probability is not high enough to warrant use of a fixed-price contract, the contracting officer may decide to use a **cost-plus-incentive-fee** (CPIF) contract (provided the HCA [see Chapter 2] determines the use of a CPIF contract is in the best interest of the government).

The CPIF contract introduces an incentive sharing formula into a cost-reimbursement contract. Under a CPIF contract, the government and contractor negotiate a **target cost**, a **target fee**, a **minimum and maximum fee**, and a **fee adjustment formula**. The fee adjustment formula provides, within the limits established by the minimum and maximum fees, for the payment of (1) a greater fee when the contractor completes the contract for less than the target cost, (2) a lesser fee when the contractor exceeds the target cost. This fee adjustment formula is a powerful incentive for the contractor to manage the contract effectively.

The best way to explain the CPIF contract is to use an example. Assume the contracting officer and the contractor negotiate a target cost of $1,000,000 for the production of a small quantity of experimental widgets for testing. The $1,000,000 target cost represents the government's and the contractor's reasonable estimate of the eventual cost to perform the contract.

Also assume that the contracting officer and the contractor negotiate a target fee of $80,000. The $80,000 is the fee the contractor will receive if it completes the contract *exactly* at the target cost of $1,000,000. So far, the CPIF contract is very similar to the CPFF contract: the government reimburses the contractor for the costs it incurs during performance of the contract and, if it completes the contract upon expenditure of the one millionth dollar, it also receives the $80,000 target fee.

However, the contractor needs an incentive to control costs. Therefore, the contracting officer and contractor also negotiate a fee adjustment formula that establishes how the government and contractor will share costs (if the contractor exceeds the target cost) and savings (if the contractor completes the contract under the target cost). This fee adjustment formula is frequently called a "**share ratio.**"

Assume that the contracting officer and contractor negotiate an **80/20** fee adjustment formula. This formula means that the contractor's fee will be reduced by 20 cents for every dollar it goes over the target cost, and the government will absorb the other 80 cents. For every dollar the contractor comes *under* the target cost, its fee will be *increased* by 20 cents and the government will keep the other 80 cents.

Fee adjustment formulas are normally in the **90/10** to **70/30** range, although the contracting officer might decide that a formula of 95/5 or higher is justified for highly risky ventures. However, if the venture is that risky, the contracting officer usually resorts to a CPFF contract because a CPFF contract's ratio is actually **100/0** – the government reimburses all the contractor's costs and the fee remains fixed (in comparison, the FFP contract has a **0/100** share ratio since the contractor keeps all savings but is also responsible for all losses).

Because the CPIF is a cost-reimbursement contract, by definition it is for a project in which the amount of effort needed to complete the contract is uncertain. So it makes sense to protect the contractor in case the task is much harder than expected. Therefore, the parties negotiate a **minimum fee** that the contractor will receive no matter how much it might exceed the target cost.

Similarly, to protect the government should the task be much easier than expected, the parties also negotiate a **maximum fee** that places a limit on the contractor's fee.

Continuing with the earlier example, assume the contracting officer and the contractor negotiated a $40,000 minimum fee and a $100,000 maximum fee. The contract terms would be:

Target Cost	$1,000,000
Target Fee	$80,000
Maximum Fee	$100,000
Minimum Fee	$40,000
Fee Adjustment Formula (gov't/contractor)	80/20

Should the contractor complete the contract after spending only $950,000, it would receive the following:

Cost	$950,000
Fee ($1,000,000 - $950,000 = $50,000; 20% of $50,000 = $10,000; $80,000 + $10,000 = $90,000)	$90,000
TOTAL PAYMENT	$1,040,000

Since the $90,000 fee is less than the $100,000 maximum fee, the contractor receives the full $90,000 fee.

If the contractor spends $1,100,000 to complete the contract, it would receive the following:

Cost	$1,100,000
Fee ($1,000,000 - $1,100,000 = -$100,000; 20% of -$100,000 = -$20,000; $80,000 - $20,000 = $60,000)	$60,000
TOTAL PAYMENT	$1,160,000

While the contractor is reimbursed for its expenses, its fee is reduced by 20% of the overrun (the amount in excess of the $1,000,000 target cost).

Now assume that the contractor spends $1,300,000 to complete the contract. It would receive the following:

Cost $1,300,000

Fee ($1,000,000 - $1,300,000 = -$300,000; 20% of -$300,000 =
    -$60,000; $80,000 - $60,000 = $20,000). However, the
    minimum fee is $40,000, so the contractor receives $40,000
    instead of $20,000. $40,000

TOTAL PAYMENT $1,340,000

Conversely, if the contractor completes the contract after spending only $500,000, it would receive reimbursement for its costs ($500,000) but only the $100,000 maximum fee.

Cost is not the only part of the contract that can be the subject of an incentive. Early deliveries can be rewarded with more fee, and late deliveries can be penalized with the payment of a smaller fee. Similarly, exceeding specific technical goals (such as power, speed, reliability, and similar characteristics) can be rewarded by additional fee. However, these types of incentive arrangements are harder to construct than are cost incentives and, therefore, are not as frequently included in contracts.

RFPs expected to result in CPIF contracts will contain FAR 52.216-10, Incentive Fee. All CPIF proposals over $750,000 must be supported by cost or pricing data, and all CPIF proposals under $750,000 must be supported by information other than cost or pricing data.

See FAR 16.405-1, Cost-Plus-Incentive-Fee Contracts, for the regulations governing CPIF contracts. See FAR 16.402, Application of Predetermined, Formula-Type Incentives, for guidance on objective performance incentives (cost, performance, and delivery).

COST-PLUS-AWARD-FEE

The **cost-plus-award-fee** (CPAF) contract is similar to the FPAF contract mentioned earlier in this chapter in that the fee determinating official "awards" some or all of the award fee to the contractor based on its quality of work, timeliness, ingenuity, cost effectiveness, or any other aspect of performance that the government wishes to motivate and reward. However, unlike a FPAF contract, a CPAF contract also has a small base fee that is not dependent on the contractor's performance. The existence of this base fee, which the contractor receives regardless of performance, recognizes that the CPAF contract is used instead of a FPAF when there are more uncertainties involved in the contract.

Typically, contracting officers use the CPAF contract for services that are more complex than those under FPAF contracts: management of facilities, gathering and analyzing of statistics, operation of computers, and engineering services are some examples. With these types of services, the scope of work can be clearly defined but the quality of performance must be determined by subjective evaluation rather than objective measurement.

At stated periods during the contract, the award-fee board (with supporting personnel) *subjectively* evaluates the contractor's performance against the cost, schedule, and/or technical performance criteria specified in the contract and the award-fee plan using the same process and adjectival rating table used for FPAF contracts (see above). Upon completion of this evaluation, the award-fee board recommends to the fee-determination official the amount of fee it considers appropriate based on the contractor's performance, and the fee-determining official decides the amount of fee to award the contractor. As with the FPAF contract, the decision by the fee-determining official on the amount of award fee is not subject to the "**Disputes**" clause and cannot be appealed (see Chapter 18 for an explanation of the Disputes clause). Because the decision on the award fee is final, the contract usually requires the award-fee board conducts these periodic evaluations every three to six months, just as with the FPAF contract. These frequent evaluations keep the contractor aware of how the government rates its performance so it can make adjustments to earn more award fee in the future. As with FPAF contracts, award-fee that is unearned during one evaluation period cannot be rolled over and made available to be earned in the next period.

The base fee portion of a CPAF contract is relatively small. For example, the Department of Defense and National Aeronautics and Space Administration limit the base fee to 3% of the estimated contract cost.

As an example, assume that the contractor and government have negotiated a CPAF contract for engineering services with the following provisions:

Estimated Cost	$1,000,000
Base Fee	$30,000
Award Fee	$70,000

If the contractor completes the contract at $950,000 and the quality of its work is satisfactory, the contracting officer would reimburse the contractor its $950,000 costs, pay it the $30,000 base fee, and the fee-determining official would award an award-fee that does not exceed 50% of the available award-fee pool. If the fee-determining official officer decides to award the contractor $25,000 additional fee for its satisfactory performance, the contractor will be paid a total of $1,005,000 ($950,000 + $30,000 + $25,000).

If the contractor completes the contract at $950,000 and the quality of its work was unsatisfactory, the fee-determining official cannot award any fee, so the contractor would be paid $980,000 ($950,000 + $30,000 + $0).

If the contractor completes the contract at $950,000 and the quality of its work was excellent, the fee-determining official might decide to award the contractor the entire $70,000 award-fee for a total of $1,050,000 ($950,000 + $30,000 + $70,000).

As is the case with FPAF contracts, there is no FAR clause for CPAF contracts, so the contracting officer must either use a clause prescribed by the agency's acquisition regulations or prepare a clause and obtain agency approval. All CPAF proposals over $750,000 must be supported by cost or pricing data, and all CPAF proposals under $750,000 must be supported by information other than cost or pricing data.

For the contracting officer to use a CPAF contract, the HCA (see Chapter 2) must prepare a written determination that the use of this type of contract is in the best interest of the government.

See FAR 16.405-2, Cost-Plus-Award-Fee Contracts, and paragraph (e) of FAR 16.401, General, for the regulations governing CPAF contracts.

TIME-AND-MATERIALS

The **time-and-materials** (T&M) contract is a hybrid that combines fixed-price and cost-reimbursement features. It provides for the payment of a fixed hourly labor rate for direct labor expended in performance of the contract and reimbursement for materials used by the contractor. The fixed hourly labor rate includes wages, overhead, general and administrative expenses, and profit. The contractor is reimbursed for the materials at cost, and the contractor may charge material handling costs if such costs can be separately identified by the contractor's accounting system.

The contracting officer will use a T&M contract when it is impossible to estimate the extent or cost of the work with any degree of certainty. Some examples of work that might be placed on a time and materials (T&M) contract are:

- Engineering and design services in connection with the production of supplies;

- The engineering, design, and manufacture of dies, jigs, fixtures, gauges, and special machine tools;

- Repair, maintenance, or overhaul work (for example, overhauling 50 diesel engines when the exact condition of each is not discernible until teardown and examination); and

- Work to be performed in emergency situations (for example, making emergency repairs to a ship that ran aground).

The common element in these examples is that it is impossible to estimate ahead of time the amount of work or the types and quantities of materials that will be needed until the contractor actually performs the work.

Because T&M contracts do not give the contractor any incentive to keep costs down, T&M contracts require continual government surveillance. Therefore, a T&M contract can be used only when the contracting officer certifies in writing that no other contract type is suitable.

In addition, each T&M contract contains a ceiling price that the contractor may not exceed. If the contractor is unable to complete the work within the ceiling price, the contracting officer must justify, in writing, why it is necessary to raise the ceiling price.

See FAR 16.601, Time-and-Materials Contracts, for the regulations governing T&M contracts.

LABOR-HOUR

A variation of the T&M contract is the **labor-hour** contract. This type of contract provides for reimbursement of the contractor's direct labor costs at a fixed hourly labor rate but no reimbursement of materials costs. The labor hour contract is appropriate when no materials will be needed during the performance of the contract or all the materials will be furnished by the government.

See FAR 16.602, Labor-Hour Contracts, for the regulations governing labor hour contracts.

CHAPTER 10

OTHER CONTRACTUAL INSTRUMENTS

Most of the government's fixed-price and cost-reimbursement contracts are straightforward: they state the supplies or services the contractor will provide, how many the contractor will provide, when the contractor will provide them, and where the contractor will provide them. If a contract requires the contractor to deliver 220 blue widgets to Camp Lejeune by March 15, the terms of the contract are clear. However, there are times when the government is not sure how many products it will need, when it will need them, where it will need them, or even *what* it will need. All the government knows is that it is going to need a quantity of something somewhere sometime.

When the government knows there will be needs to fulfill but not what those needs will be, the situation calls for a kind of contract that is more flexible than a conventional contract. The contractual instruments described in this chapter give the government the flexibility it needs to fulfill its needs whenever they develop without delay and with minimal administrative burden. Furthermore, each of these contractual instruments gives the government a different kind of flexibility. Though they are used only when the situation requires, they are not rare in government contracting.

INDEFINITE-DELIVERY CONTRACTS

The contracting officer will use an **indefinite-delivery** contract when the government does not know how much of a particular supply or service it will require during a specified period (usually one year) or does not know when it will need the product.

There are three types of indefinite-delivery contracts: the **definite-quantity** contract, the **requirements** contract, and the **indefinite-quantity** contract. Each is useful in eliminating repetitive solicitations for supplies and services that are needed periodically throughout the term of the contract. Orders against each of these contracts may be placed electronically, telephonically, by written order, or by any medium specified in the contract.

The following is a brief description of each type of indefinite-delivery contract, highlighting the important characteristics of each.

- The **definite-quantity** contract requires the contractor to provide a specific quantity of products to locations designated in the contract whenever the government needs them. The definite-quantity contract is particularly useful when the products are regularly available, and the government knows the exact quantity it will need during the term of the contract (usually one year), but it does not know exactly *when*. In effect, a definite-delivery contract allows the government to use the contractor as a storage depot.

  Definite-quantity contracts contain the clause **FAR 52.216-20, Definite Quantity**. See FAR 16.502, Definite-Quantity Contracts, for more on this kind of contract.

- A **requirements** contract makes the contractor the "sole source" for specific supplies or services during the term of the contract. The contract lists the government activities that *must* fulfill their needs for the specific products by placing orders with the contractor. However, the government is under no obligation to purchase any products if no needs ever materialize.

  The requirements contract contains the government's estimate of the total quantity it believes will be ordered during the contract term. This estimate is based on previous experience and current consumption rates. In addition, it usually includes a ceiling on the total quantity the government may order during the contract period. This ceiling limits the contractor's obligation to deliver should the government's needs far exceed the estimated total quantity stated in the contract. Also, the contract may place minimum and maximum restrictions on the size of the orders.

  There are two kinds of requirements contract: the **delivery-order contract**, which does not specify a firm quantity of supplies other than the total quantity ceiling, and the **task-order contract**, which does not specify a firm quantity of services other than the total quantity ceiling.

  The requirements contract is appropriate when the government is unable to determine the exact quantity it will need during the contract period, such as for spare parts. Requirements contracts may permit faster deliveries of supplies because contractors are usually willing to maintain limited stocks when the government will obtain all of its requirements for those particular supplies from the contractor.

Requirements contracts contain the clause **FAR 52.216-21, Requirements**. See FAR 16.503, Requirements Contracts, for this kind of contract.

■ An **indefinite-quantity** contract requires the contractor to provide a *minimum* quantity of supplies or services to the government during the contract period and to provide additional quantities *if ordered by the government*, up to a *maximum quantity*. However, once the government orders the minimum quantity, it is under no obligation to place any additional orders with the contractor no matter what its actual needs may be. (These are commonly referred to as "indefinite-delivery, in-definite-quantity," or "**IDIQ**" contracts.)

Once the government orders the minimum quantity, the indefinite-quantity contract becomes nothing more than another source for the supplies or services on the IDIQ. The government is free to purchase the product elsewhere if it can find a better price.

Like requirements contracts, if the IDIQ contract involves supplies, it is called a **delivery order contract**, and if it involves services, it is called a **task order contract**.

The government prefers to award multiple IDIQ contracts for the same supplies or services, and to give each IDIQ contractor a "**fair opportunity**" to be considered for each order exceeding $3,500 (after each IDIQ contract's minimum quantity has been fulfilled). However, in providing IDIQ contractors a "fair opportunity" to be considered for each order, the contracting officer does not have to comply with the competition requirements of FAR part 6, Competition Requirements (see Chapter 3). He may exercise broad discretion and use his business judgment to select the appropriate method of providing the fair opportunity, such as oral proposals or streamlined procedures. Nevertheless, each agency has a "**task order and delivery order ombudsman**" who is responsible for ensuring that all contractors are given a fair opportunity to be considered for each award and reviews complaints from contractors (the ombudsman may be the agency's competition advocate – see Chapter 3).

For task or delivery orders exceeding $5,500,000, the requirement to provide each contractor a fair opportunity to be considered is not be met unless all such contractors are provided notice and given a reasonable time to provide a proposal.

There are several exceptions to the fair opportunity requirement:

– The agency needs the supplies or services urgently, and providing a fair opportunity would result in unacceptable delays;

– Only one IDIQ contractor is capable of providing the supplies or services required;

– The order must be issued on a sole-source basis because it is a logical follow-on to an order already issued under the IDIQ contract (provided all the multiple IDIQ contractors were given a fair opportunity to be considered for the original order);

– It is necessary to place an order to satisfy a minimum quantity guarantee;

– For orders exceeding the simplified acquisition threshold ($150,000), a statute expressly authorizes or requires that the purchase be made from a specified source; and

– Contracting officers may set aside orders for small businesses (see Chapter 11 for more on set-asides).

As with the requirements contract, the IDIQ contract lists the government activities authorized to place orders under the contract. The contract may include minimum and maximum limitations on individual orders, and it may place a maximum limitation on the quantity that can be ordered each month.

An IDIQ contract is appropriate when the government cannot determine the exact quantity it will need during the contract period but does not want to commit itself to more than the minimum quantity.

One particular kind of IDIQ contract is called a **governmentwide acquisition contract**, or "GWAC." A GWAC is for information technology supplies or services, and it is established by one agency for use by all other government agencies. Five agencies have been authorized to establish GWACs: the Department of Commerce, the Environmental Protection Agency (EPA), the General Services Administration (GSA), the National Aeronautics and Space Administration (NASA), and the National Institutes of Health (NIH). For more on GWACs, see Chapter 13.

In addition, **Federal Supply Schedule** (FSS) contracts are IDIQ contracts, although they have their own rules. For more on FSS contracts, see Chapter 13.

IDIQ contracts contain the clause **FAR 52.216-22, Indefinite Quantity**. See FAR 16.504, Indefinite-Quantity Contracts, for more on this kind of contract.

There are two features of indefinite-delivery contracts that make them particularly attractive to contracting officers: (1) orders are not synopsized in **FedBizOpps** (see Chapter 5), so there are no corresponding delays; and (2) orders cannot be protested except: (a) on the grounds that the order increases the scope, period, or maximum value of the contract; or (b) the order exceeds $10,000,000, in which case the protest must be filed with the Government Accountability Office (GAO) (see Chapter 17 for more on protests). This means the contracting officer can place an order quickly, and his decision cannot be challenged by disgruntled contractors (except under these particular circumstances). These two features have made indefinite-delivery contracts (including Federal Supply Schedules and GWACs) increasingly popular throughout the government.

BASIC ORDERING AGREEMENT

Technically, a **basic ordering agreement** (BOA) is not a contract but an agreement between a contractor and the government to include certain clauses in contracts they enter into during the term of the agreement. The BOA includes a general description of the products that are covered, but it does not obligate the government to order any products. In addition, the BOA specifies the method for calculating the prices of products that the government orders; any type of fixed-price or cost-reimbursement method that is appropriate can be used.

The BOA is an instrument that allows the government to expedite the purchase of products when the specific products, quantities, and prices are not known at the time the agreement is reached. The government enters into a BOA when it knows from experience or future plans that it will need a substantial number of products from the contractor during the term of the agreement but does not know the exact products, quantities, or their prices. For example, a BOA would be useful if the government knows it will order spare parts for a new piece of equipment but the manufacturer has not yet established prices for any spare parts. The BOA may cover "Spare Parts for the XYZ Inc. Gas Isotope Ratio and Nuclear Magnetic Resonance Spectrometer."

Like IDIQ contracts, the BOA identifies contracting activities that can place orders. These orders are issued on the Optional Form (OF) 347, Order for Supplies or Services, or any other appropriate contractual instrument, and incorporate by reference the provisions of the BOA. By referencing the provisions of the BOA, the contracting officer does not have to negotiate those particular terms and conditions when he issues the order. And, since the BOA includes the method of calculating prices, the contracting officer may place orders without firm prices, further expediting contractor performance.

However, just because a BOA exists does not excuse the contracting officer from issuing competitive solicitations whenever possible (for example, orders exceeding $25,000 must be synopsized in **FedBizOpps**), nor may the existence of a BOA be considered by the contracting officer when selecting the successful offeror. Nevertheless, as a practical matter, BOAs are usually issued to contractors that are the only sources for the spare parts or engineering support services.

See FAR 16.703, Basic Ordering Agreements, for more on BOAs.

LETTER CONTRACT

A **letter contract** is a legal document that allows the contractor to proceed with contract performance though the contractor and the government have not agreed to all the contractual terms and conditions. This situation places the government in a weak bargaining position during the negotiations to finalize the contractual terms and conditions. Therefore, contracting officers may use a letter contract only when the head of the contracting activity (HCA) certifies that no other type of contract is suitable. For example, the government may decide it is imperative that a contractor start immediate clean-up of a toxic waste dump that poses a threat to ground water. Since the contracting officer does not have the time to negotiate a definitive contract, he issues a letter contract to the contractor authorizing it to start work – "the paperwork will catch up later."

The letter contract must (1) state the type of contract the contracting officer expects will replace the letter contract (such as firm-fixed-price [FFP], cost-plus-incentive-fee [CPIF], or other type appropriate to the situation); (2) include any contract clauses, terms, and conditions that are mutually agreeable to the contractor and the contracting officer; and (3) contain a schedule for the completion of the contract negotiations. This schedule cannot exceed **180 days** from the date of the letter contract or **40% of the contract performance**, whichever occurs first, except under unusual circumstances.

Upon completion of negotiations, the contracting officer and the contractor sign the final contract containing the pricing arrangement and all other agreements. Upon signature, the original letter contract expires. If the contracting officer and the contractor cannot agree to the price or fee, the contracting officer may *unilaterally* establish a reasonable price or fee. This determination can be appealed by the contractor in accordance with the terms of the "Disputes" clause (see Chapter 18 for an explanation of FAR 52.233-1, Disputes).

Among the clauses required to be in letter contracts are **FAR 52.216-23, Execution and Commencement of Work**; **FAR 52.216-24, Limitation of Government Liability**; **FAR 52.216-25, Contract Definitization**; and **FAR 52.216-26, Payments of Allowable Costs Before Definitization** (if a cost-reimbursement contract is contemplated).

See FAR 16.603, Letter Contracts, for the regulations governing letter contracts.

MULTI-YEAR CONTRACT

Normally, a contract is for one year's requirements: Congress appropriates funds for the supplies and services the government will need to perform its functions during the year and the contracting officer executes a contract for that one year's requirements. By requiring the government to conduct its business in is manner, the present Congress does not approve programs that must be funded by future Congresses.

While Congress may be reluctant to commit future Congresses, funding one year's requirements at a time is an inefficient way to do business. A contractor is not likely to offer the same prices for its supplies or services under a one-year contract as it would under a three-, four-, or five-year contract. A contractor can offer a better price on a longer-term contract because it can economically purchase its materials, maintain a steady workforce, smooth its workload, and avoid start-up and shut-down costs. This is what the multi-year contract tries to accomplish.

The government sometimes uses a **multi-year contract** to achieve these economies and stabilize long-running programs. The multi-year contract is not a contract type (like FFP or CPFF) but a special method used by the government to acquire its needs for **two to five years** though the total funds are not available at the time of the contract award. When a multi-year contract is awarded, only the first year's quantities are funded. Funding for succeeding years is added annually.

A multi-year contract may be used only when the government's needs over the period of the contract are reasonably predictable and continuing. For supplies, there must be a reasonable assurance that the design and specifications are firm and will not change, and there will not be any changes in production methods. Thus, the multi-year contract is suitable for items with mature designs or for standard services (such as building maintenance) for which the government has steady requirements. Since the supplies or services acquired through multi-year contracts are fairly well defined, multi-year contracts are usually either FFP, fixed-price with economic price adjustment (FP/EPA), or fixed-price with incentive provisions (see FAR 16.204, Fixed-Price Incentive Contracts, for details on this contract type).

A multi-year contract is not the same as a contract with options for additional quantities (see Chapter 7) that the government may unilaterally exercise (although the contracting officer is authorized to include options in multi-year contracts). The presence of an option in a contract is no assurance that the government will exercise the option and acquire the additional quantity – the contracting officer must consider the prices of other products available before deciding whether the option exercise is the most advantageous method of fulfilling the government's needs. However, the multi-year contract represents a commitment by the government to continue the contract provided funding is available. It resembles in many ways a long-term requirements contract.

The primary purpose of the multi-year contract is to reduce prices through the increased competition produced by this long-term commitment. However, the contracting officer may decide to use a multi-year contract to purchase products from a "sole source" contractor if the likely cost to the government will be less than with a series of one-year contracts. To ensure that the multi-year contract does save the government money, most multi-year solicitations require bidders or offerors to submit prices for both (1) the first year's quantity *only*, and (2) the entire multi-year contract.

In this way, the contracting officer can award a one-year contract if a multi-year contract would not be in the government's best interest.

The multi-year solicitation usually requires the bidder or offeror to provide the same unit price for each year of the multi-year contract – $100 a unit during the first year, $100 a unit during the second year, $100 a unit during all the years. This **level unit pricing** prevents the bidder or offeror from "frontloading" the first year of the contract with all its nonrecurring costs (such as special tooling and test equipment, recruitment and training costs, plant rearrangement, and pilot runs). Because of this level unit pricing requirement, the bidder or offeror is forced to amortize these costs over all the units covered by the multi-year contract. (However, the head of the contracting activity [HCA] may approve the use of variable unit prices.)

Though the government enters into a multi-year contract thinking its needs for the products are predictable and continuing, sometimes the contract has to be canceled before its scheduled completion – Congress may kill the program, or a government building under a multi-year maintenance contract may burn down. Because of the level unit pricing requirement, a canceled multi-year contract means the contractor has nonrecurring costs that have been incurred but remain unamortized: plant or equipment relocation or rearrangement; acquisition of special tooling and special test equipment; preproduction engineering; pilot runs; the costs of facilities to be acquired or established for the conduct of the work; costs incurred for development of a specialized work force; and similar nonrecurring costs. To protect the contractor from having to absorb these unamortized costs, each multi-year contract provides a **cancellation ceiling** which compensates the contractor for the unamortized nonrecurring costs if the multi-year contract is prematurely terminated through no fault of the contractor.

The contracting officer calculates the amount of unamortized nonrecurring costs that will exist at the end of each year of the multi-year contract. His calculations represent the cancellation ceiling – the maximum amount payable to the contractor for unamortized nonrecurring costs should the contract be canceled after the first, second, third, or fourth years (assuming a five year multi-year contract – after five years, the contract is complete).

Recurring costs are not allowed to be included in cancellation ceilings unless the head of the agency approves such inclusion on a case-by-case basis. This means a contractor cannot buy the material for the entire multi-year period and expect to be reimbursed for the unused materials if the contract is cancelled. This limits the usefulness of the multi-year contract and should be a consideration when preparing a multi-year bid or proposal.

Before the Department of Defense, the Coast Guard, or the National Aeronautics and Space Administration enter into a multi-year contract with a cancellation ceiling in excess of **$135,500,000**, or any other agency enters into a multi-year contract with a cancellation ceiling in excess of **$13,500,000**, it must give Congress at least 30 days notice before awarding the contract. This notification requirement gives Congress time to disapprove the multi-year contract.

All multi-year contracts contain **FAR 52.217-2, Cancellation Under Multi-Year Contracts**.

See FAR subpart 17.1, Multi-Year Contracting, for the regulations governing multi-year contracts.

"OTHER TRANSACTIONS"

Many firms with significant technological advances and innovations are reluctant to share their innovations with the government because of the statutory and regulatory requirements involved in government contracts. To overcome this reluctance, the Departments of Defense, Energy, Health and Human Services, Homeland Security, and Transportation, and the National Aeronautics and Space Administration are authorized to enter into "transactions other than contracts, grants, or cooperative agreements for prototype projects or research," and the Office of Management and Budget (OMB) can authorize other agencies to use **"other transactions"** (OTs) on a case-by-case basis. In general, OTs are exempt from all statutes and regulations that govern federal contracts (such as the FAR). When using OTs, contracting officers are not required to include standard contract provisions, but may structure the OTs as they consider appropriate.

An OT is authorized in the absence of the significant participation of a "non-traditional contractor" (that is, a contractor that has not performed, within the past year, any contract over $500,000 that is subject to the FAR) in basic, applied, advanced research, or prototype projects, and when at least one-third of the costs of the project are to be provided by non-federal parties to the agreement. OTs must be competed to the maximum extent practicable.

Because OTs are not subject to the FAR, each agency authorized to use OTs have their own regulations posted on their Internet sites – search for "other transactions."

CHAPTER 11

SMALL BUSINESS
PROGRAMS

Because small businesses are responsible for most of the job creation and technical innovations in the United States, Congress and the president have shown great interest in encouraging the growth and health of small businesses throughout the American economy. One of the most direct ways the government can encourage and nurture small businesses is through federal contracts.

THE SMALL BUSINESS ACT

The **Small Business Act of 1953** states that small businesses should receive a "fair proportion" of federal contracts and that small businesses should have the "maximum practical opportunity" to participate in federal contracting. The Small Business Act established the **Small Business Administration** (SBA) to aid small businesses and to ensure they receive a "fair proportion" of federal contracts.

Congress has established a **23%** governmentwide goal for awards of contracts to small businesses. Subsets of the small business goal are a **5%** governmentwide goal for awards to small disadvantaged businesses (SDBs), a **5%** governmentwide goal for awards to women-owned small businesses (WOSB), a **3%** governmentwide goal for awards to "historically underutilized business zone" (HUBZone) small businesses, and a **3%** governmentwide goal for awards to service-disabled veteran-owned small businesses (SDVOSB) (the Department of Veterans Affairs has a 12% goal for awards to veteran-owned small businesses [VOSB]). A contract can be counted towards more than one goal: an award to an SDB in a HUBZone that is owned by a service-disabled woman veteran would be counted towards *all* the goals.

Each year the SBA negotiates "agency goals" with each department and agency. These agency goals may be higher or lower than the governmentwide goals, depending on the types of supplies and services the particular agency acquires.

The SBA maintains statistics that show how successful each department and agency is in attaining its goals. It provides these statistics to Congress and the president, and disappointing statistics sometimes trigger new legislation and mandates. This is why the departments and agencies pay close attention to the number of contracts awarded to each targeted group of businesses. Also, this is the reason each contracting activity has at least one small business specialist (SBS) to help these businesses (see Chapter 2 for more on the SBS and his functions).

To comply with these "socioeconomic policies," the government uses **set-asides** and **preference programs** to encourage small businesses, SDBs, HUBZone small business concerns, WOSBs, and SDVOSBs to obtain and perform government contracts.

WHAT QUALIFIES AS A SMALL BUSINESS?

The SBA establishes **small business size standards** on an industry-by-industry basis. It uses the **North American Industry Classification System** (NAICS) codes to identify the various industries (NAICS codes are available at **http://www.census. gov/eos/www/naics/**). The most prevalent size standard for manufacturing industries is **500 employees**, and the most prevalent size standard for service industries is **$7,500,000 in average annual gross revenue over the preceding three fiscal years**. For most industries, a company that does not exceed these size standards is considered "small." While a business with 500 employees or $7,500,000 in gross revenue may not seem small, the purpose of setting the size standard at these levels is to allow small businesses to grow into thriving "medium" businesses before losing the benefits of their small business size status.

However, the usual 500 employees/$7,500,000 size standards do not apply to all industries. A company that manufactures breakfast cereal foods is considered small if it has fewer than 1,000 employees (NAICS code 311230), while a company that manufactures cookies and crackers is considered small if it has fewer than 750 employees (NAICS code 311821). A drycleaning plant is considered small if its average annual gross revenue for the preceding three years does not exceed $5,500,000 (NAICS code 812320), but an establishment that drycleans industrial work uniforms is considered small if its average annual receipts for the preceding three years does not exceed $38,500,000 (NAICS code 812332). The SBA sets these size standards after determining the average size of the firms in each industry and the amount of competition within each industry.

The small business size standards are available at **http://www.sba.gov/size**. The contracting officer selects the appropriate NAICS code for the supply or service he intends to purchase, and he includes the NAICS code and the corresponding size standard in paragraph (a) of **FAR 52.204-8, Annual Representations and Certifications** (in Section K of the Uniform Contract Format – see Chapter 7).

The contracting officer's selection can determine whether a company is allowed to participate in a small business set-aside. For instance, if a contracting officer decides to set aside a contract for fabric, should he categorize the industry as "Broadwoven Fabric Mills" (NAICS code 313210), which has a size standard of 1,000 employees, or as "Knit Fabric Mills" (NAICS code 313240), which has a size standard of 500 employees? The contracting officer's decision will determine whether companies with between 500 and 1,000 employees will be able to participate in the set-aside. This is why the SBA allows bidders and offerors to appeal the contracting officer's decision (see paragraph (c) of FAR 19.303, Determining North American Industry Classification System Codes and Size Standards, and Chapter 16 for more on size standard appeals).

If a small business submits a bid or proposal for supplies under a small business set-aside expected to exceed $25,000, but that small business is not the manufacturer of those supplies (that is, it is engaged in retail or wholesale trade), the size standard is **500 employees** regardless of the actual size standard for the supply (this is called the "**nonmanufacturer rule**"). In addition, the small business nonmanufacturer must furnish supplies produced by a small business manufacturer or producer ("a concern that, with its own forces, transforms organic or inorganic substances including raw materials and/or miscellaneous parts or components into the end product"), and the supplies must be manufactured or produced in the United States. However, if the SBA has determined that there are *no* small business manufacturers or processors in the federal market, the small business nonmanufacturer may provide supplies produced by *any* domestic manufacturer or processor. The nonmanufacturer rule is addressed in paragraph (f) of FAR 19.102, Size Standards. A complete list of supplies for which the nonmanufacturer rule has been waived is available at **https://www. sba.gov/contracting/contracting-officials/non-manufacturer-rule/class-waivers**.

See FAR subpart 19.1, Size Standards, for more information.

Size Status Determination

Each bidder or offeror provides information about its average annual gross revenue for the previous three years and number of employees when it registers in the System of Award Management (SAM – **https://www.sam.gov**). This information, along with other formation obtained during the SAM registration, is used by SBA's computers to determine whether the bidder or offeror is a small business for the NAICS code the contracting officer identified in FAR 52.204-8 as applying to the acquisition. However, those who question the accuracy of the information the bidder or offeror entered into SAM may file a **protest** with the contracting officer. With invitations for bids (IFBs) that are set-aside exclusively for small businesses, protestors have **five working days** after bid opening to file their protests. With requests for proposals (RFPs) that are set-aside, the contracting officer must notify each unsuccessful offeror of the name and address of the apparent successful offeror, and protestors have **five working days** from receipt of this notice to file their protests. The protest must provide detailed evidence supporting the allegation that the bidder or offeror is not small. The contracting officer promptly forwards the size status protest to the SBA for decision (see Chapter 16 for more on protests regarding small business status).

Small Business Joint Ventures and Team Arrangements

A joint venture ("an association of persons and/or concerns . . . consorting to engage in and carry out a single specific business venture for joint profit . . . ") or team arrangement of two or more small businesses may submit an offer as a small business as long as each concern is small under the applicable size standard *provided*: (1) for an acquisition with a revenue-based size standard (such as $7,500,000), the procurement exceeds half the corresponding size standard (if the applicable size standard is $7,500,000, the acquisition would have to be larger than $3,750,000); or (2) for an acquisition with an employee-based size standard (such as 500 employees), the acquisition exceeds $10,000,000.

SET-ASIDES

A "**set-aside**" restricts, or "sets aside," contracts exclusively for small business participation. Only businesses that do not exceed prescribed size standards for the supply or service being acquired (and meet the qualifications for specific kinds of set-asides) are considered small and allowed to bid or propose on set-asides. Bidders or offerors that exceed the applicable size standard for a set-aside are, by definition, nonresponsive and their bids or proposals will be rejected.

Rules and Policies That Apply to All Set-Asides

The "Rule of Two"

Paragraph (a) of FAR 19.502-2, Total Small Business Set-Asides, states that "each acquisition of supplies or services that has an anticipated dollar value exceeding $3,500…but not over $150,000…is automatically reserved exclusively for small business concerns and shall be set aside for small business unless the contracting officer determines there is not a reasonable expectation of obtaining offers *from two or more responsible small business concerns* that are competitive in terms of market prices, quality, and delivery."

Paragraph (b) states that "the contracting officer shall set aside any acquisition over $150,000 for small business participation when there is a reasonable expectation that: (1) offers will be obtained from at *least two responsible small business concerns* offering the products of different small business concerns…; and (2) award will be made at fair market prices." This requirement is commonly called the "**rule of two**." Because of the importance each agency places on meeting its small business contract award goals, most agencies require each contracting activity's SBS to review all acquisitions over the simplified acquisition threshold that its contracting officers decide *not* to set aside. SBSs commonly use the SAM database to convince contracting officers of the existence of capable small businesses (see Chapter 5 for more on the SAM). In addition, the SBA maintains a **Dynamic Small Business Search** database at **http://web.sba.gov/pro-net/search/dsp_dsbs.cfm** that identifies businesses representing themselves as small businesses and the type of business they claim to be – SDVOSB, SDB, WOSB, etc.

Relationship Among Small Business Programs

Since there are many different kinds of set-asides, FAR 19.203, Relationship Among Small Business Programs, establishes the relationship among these various programs:

- "There is no order of precedence among the 8(a) Program (subpart 19.8), HUBZone Program (subpart 19.13), Service-Disabled Veteran-Owned Small Business (SDVOSB) Procurement Program (subpart 19.14), or the Women-Owned Small Business (WOSB) Program (subpart 19.15)" (paragraph (a)).

- Acquisitions between $3,500 ($5,000 for the Department of Defense) and $150,000 may be set-aside for small businesses, 8(a), HUBZone concerns, SDVOSBs, or WOSBs – there is no precedence among these programs (paragraph (b)).

- For acquisitions exceeding the simplified acquisition threshold ($150,000), "the contracting officer shall first consider an acquisition for the small business socioeconomic contracting programs (*i.e.*, 8(a), HUBZone, SDVOSB, or WOSB programs) before considering a small business set-aside..." (paragraph (c)). Therefore, the contracting officer must: (1) determine whether to set aside the acquisition (taking into account the "rule of two"); and, if he determines there are two or more small businesses qualified to perform the contract, (2) decide which type of set-aside to employ (taking into account the "rule of two" applies to all the various set-asides), how well the contracting activity is fulfilling its various small business goals, and such other factors as the results of market research and the acquisition history of the supply or service.

- If a requirement has been accepted by the SBA under the 8(a) program, it must remain in the 8(a) program unless the SBA agrees to release it from the 8(a) program.

Limitations on Subcontracting

Besides the small business representation, each contract exceeding $150,000 that is awarded as a set-aside includes FAR 52.219-14, Limitations on Subcontracting, in which the bidder or offeror agrees, as a condition to contracting, that for:

- **Services** (except construction), at least **50%** of the cost of performance will be expended for employees of the concern.

- **Supplies**, at least **50%** of the cost of manufacturing the supplies, excluding the cost of materials, will be performed by the concern.

- **General construction**, at least **15%** of the cost of the contract, excluding the cost of materials, will be performed by its own employees.

- **Construction by special trade contractors**, at least **25%** of the cost of the contract, excluding the cost of materials, will be performed by its own employees.

These limitations on subcontracting do not apply to small business nonmanufacturers (see above).

Identification in FedBizOpps

FedBizOpps (https://www.fbo.gov) allows anyone to search for any of the small business set-asides (and any of the preference programs) by selecting the "Set-Aside Code" drop-down menu, then selecting "Total Small Business," "Competitive 8(a)," "HUBZone," "Veteran-Owned Small Business," "Woman-Owned Small Business," or any of the other small business set-asides or preference programs.

Historically Underutilized Business Zones (HUBZone) Program

One program designed to help a subset of small businesses is the **Historically Underutilized Business Zones (HUBZone) Program**. It is intended to help small business concerns (SBCs) in economically distressed communities obtain federal contracts. A HUBZone is any one of the following:

- "Qualified census tracts" ("any census tract which is designated by the Secretary of Housing and Urban Development and, for the most recent year for which census data are available on household income in such tract, either in which 50% or more of the households have an income which is less than 60% of the area median gross income for such year or which has a poverty rate of at least 25%") – there are more than 13,000 qualified census tracts.

- "Qualified nonmetropolitan counties" ("not located in a metropolitan statistical area…in which: (I) the median household income is less than 80% of the nonmetropolitan state median household income; (II) the unemployment rate is not less than 140% of the average unemployment rate for the United States or for the state in which such county is located, whichever is less; or (III) there is located a difficult development area ["any area designated by the Secretary of Housing and Urban Development as an area which has high construction, land, and utility costs relative to area median gross income"]..." – there are more than 500 qualified nonmetropolitan counties.

■ "Qualified disaster areas" ("any census tract or nonmetropolitan county located in an area for which the president has declared a major disaster").

■ Lands within the boundaries of an Indian reservation – there are almost 600 qualified Indian lands.

■ "Redesignated areas" ("any census tract that ceases to be qualified [as a HUBZone]...and any nonmetropolitan county that ceases to be qualified [as a HUBZone]").

■ "Base closure areas" ("lands within the boundaries of a military installation that were closed through a privatization process") – there are more than 100 base closure areas.

The SBA has a HUBZone map available at **http://map.sba.gov/hubzone/maps/** that is searchable by state and county. Also, the map will identify whether a particular address is in a HUBZone.

To qualify as a HUBZone SBC, a firm must be small for its primary NAICS code, be at least 51% owned and controlled by U.S. citizens, have its principle office in a HUBZone, and at least 35% of its employees must reside in a HUBZone. HUBZone SBCs must be certified by the SBA as meeting the HUBZone requirements. Firms that obtain SBA HUBZone certification are added to the SBA's "Dynamic Small Business Search" database (see above). Only firms on the list are HUBZone SBCs and eligible for HUBZone preferences.

A contracting officer may set-aside an acquisition that exceeds the micropurchase threshold ($3,500; $5,000 for the Department of Defense) for HUBZone SBCs if there is a reasonable expectation of receiving two or more offers from HUBZone SBCs and award will be made at a fair market price (the "rule of two").

If the contracting officer receives only one acceptable offer from a qualified HUBZone SBC in response to a HUBZone set aside, paragraph (c) of FAR 19.1305, HUBZone Set-Aside Procedures, states that "the contracting officer *should* make an award to that concern" (emphasis added). This is because the HUBZone SBC responded to the set-aside thinking there would be competition, so its price should be "competitive." However, the HUBZone SBC's offer must be at a "fair market price" or the contracting officer will cancel the HUBZone set-aside and conduct a set-aside open to all small businesses. As a practical matter, the HUBZone SBC's offer must be exceedingly unreasonable before a contracting officer will dissolve the HUBZone set-aside.

If the contracting officer receives no acceptable bids or offers from HUBZone small business concerns, the contracting officer will cancel the HUBZone set-aside and conduct a set-aside for small businesses "as appropriate" (that is, an SDVOSB set-aside, a WOSB or economically disadvantaged WOSB [EDWOSB] set-aside, an 8(a) set-aside, or a small business set-aside).

A contracting officer is permitted to award a **sole source contract** to a HUBZone SBC if: (1) he does not have a reasonable expectation that offers would be received from two or more HUBZone SBCs; (2) the contract is greater than the simplified acquisition threshold ($150,000) but less than **$7,000,000** for manufacturing contracts or **$4,000,000** for all other contracts; (3) the requirement is not currently being performed by an 8(a) participant (see below); and (4) award will be made at a fair and reasonable price. However, the contracting officer must consider HUBZone set-asides before considering a HUBZone sole source contract (or small business set-asides).

In addition, contracting officers are required to give offers from HUBZone SBCs a **price evaluation preference** in acquisitions that are conducted using full and open competition by adding **10%** to all offers *except* those of HUBZone SBCs. However, the preference may not be used where price is not a selection factor (as in architect-engineer contracts), nor can it be applied when the successful offeror is a non-HUBZone small business.

Solicitations that are set aside for HUBZone SBCs contain **FAR 52.219-3, Notice of Total HUBZone Set-Aside**, in Section I if the solicitation is in the uniform contract format (UCF), or in the "Clauses" portion if the solicitation is in the simplified contract format (SCF).

Solicitations and contracts conducted using full and open competition contain **FAR 52.219-4, Notice of Price Evaluation Preference for HUBZone Small Business Concerns**.

For more on the HUBZone program, see FAR subpart 19.13 and **https://www.sba.gov/contracting/government-contracting-programs/hubzone-program**. Also, see Chapter 16 for protests concerning HUBZone program eligibility.

Service-Disabled Veteran-Owned Small Business Program

The **Veterans Benefits Act of 2003** (Public Law 108-183) amended the Small Business Act to establish a **service-disabled veteran-owned small business (SDVOSB)** set-aside program.

To qualify as an SDVOSB:

- The veteran must have a service-related disability as determined by the Department of Veterans Affairs or the Department of Defense;

- The business must be small under the NAICS code assigned to the procurement; and

■ The service-disabled veteran must own at least 51% of the business, must hold the highest officer position in the business, and must control the management and daily operations of the business.

A contracting officer may set aside an acquisition that exceeds the micropurchase threshold ($3,500; $5,000 for the Department of Defense) for SDVOSBs if he has a "reasonable expectation that offers will be received from two or more service disabled veteran-owned small business concerns, and award will be made at a fair market price" (the "rule of two" again).

If the contracting officer receives only one acceptable offer from a qualified SDVOSB in response to an SDVOSB set aside, paragraph (c) of FAR 19.1405, Service-Disabled Veteran-Owned Small Business Set-Aside Procedures, states that "the contracting officer *should* make an award to that concern" (emphasis added).

If the contracting officer receives no acceptable bids or offers from SDVOSBs, the contracting officer will cancel the SDVOSB set-aside and conduct a set-aside for small businesses "as appropriate" (that is, a HUBZone set-aside, a WOSB or EDWOSB set-aside, an 8(a) set-aside, or a small business set-aside).

A contracting officer is permitted to award a **sole source contract** to an SDVOSB if: (1) he does not have a reasonable expectation that offers would be received from two or more SDVOSBs; (2) the contract is greater than the simplified acquisition threshold ($150,000) but less than **$6,500,000** for manufacturing contracts or **$4,000,000** for all other contracts (note that these limits are different than those for HUBZone sole source contracts); (3) the requirement is not currently being performed by an 8(a) participant (see below); and (4) award will be made at a fair and reasonable price. The contracting officer must consider a contract award to a SDVOSB on a sole source basis before considering small business set-asides.

Unlike offers from HUBZone SBCs, the legislation does *not* provide for the application of a 10% price evaluation preference to SDVOSB offers in acquisitions that are conducted using full and open competition.

Solicitations that are set aside for SDVOSBs contain **FAR 52.219-27, Notice of Total Service-Disabled Veteran-Owned Small Business Set-Aside**, in Section I if the solicitation is in UCF, or in the "Clauses" portion if the solicitation is in the SCF.

For more on the SDVOSB program, see FAR subpart 19.14, Service-Disabled Veteran-Owned Small Business Procurement Program, and **https://www.sba.gov/ contracting/government-contracting-programs/service-disabled-veteran-owned-businesses**. Also, see Chapter 16 for protests concerning SDVOSB program eligibility.

NOTE: There are no set-asides authorized for veteran-owned small businesses (VOSBs) outside of the Department of Veterans Affairs (see Veterans Affairs Acquisition Regulation [VAAR] subpart 819.70, Veteran-Owned and Operated Small Businesses). However, large prime contractors do have incentives for awarding subcontracts to VOSBs – see below.

Women-Owned Small Business Program

The Women-Owned Small Business (WOSB) program is different than the other small business programs in that WOSB and economically disadvantaged WOSB (EDWOSB) set-asides are restricted to industries in which WOSBs and EDWOSBs are *underrepresented*: only EDWOSBs are eligible to receive set-aside or sole source contracts in one of the 21 industries in which WOSBs are *underrepresented* (as determined by the SBA according to four-digit North American Industry Classification System [NAICS] industry groups), but both EDWOSBs and WOSBs are eligible to receive set-aside or sole source contracts in one of the 92 industries in which WOSBs are *substantially underrepresented* (go to **https://www.sba.gov/contracting/gov ernment-contracting-programs/women-owned-small-businesses** for a list of the 113 industries that are eligible for WOSB and EDWOSB set-asides and sole source contracts).

To qualify as a WOSB, the business must be small under the NAICS code assigned to the procurement, women who are U.S. citizens must own at least 51% of the business, and those women must control the management and daily operations of the business. A woman must hold the highest officer position in the business. This woman must have managerial experience of the extent and complexity needed to run the concern, must manage the business on a full-time basis, and may not engage in outside employment that prevents her from devoting sufficient time and attention to the daily affairs of the business.

To qualify as an EDWOSB, the business must meet the qualifications of a WOSB except that the owner(s) must also be *economically disadvantaged*. To be considered economically disadvantaged, the woman's personal net worth must be less than **$750,000**, excluding her ownership interest in the business and her equity interest in her primary personal residence (or less than **$6,000,000** including her ownership interest in the business and her equity interest in her primary personal residence). In addition, the woman's average income during the previous three years must be less than **$350,000** per year.

A WOSB or EDWOSB must be certified as eligible to participate in the WOSB program by a "third party certifier" (for a fee) or by self-certifying (free).

Currently, there are four third party certifiers:

El Paso Hispanic Chamber of Commerce (**http://www.ephcc.org**);
National Women Business Owners Corporation (**http://www.nwboc.org**);
U.S. Women's Chamber of Commerce (**http://uswcc.org/certification/**);
Women's Business Enterprise National Council (**http://www.wbenc.org/**).

If the firm decides to self-certify, it must fill out an application at **https://certify.sba.gov** and submit the following documents:

- Copies of birth certificates, naturalization papers, or unexpired passports for owners who are women;

- Copy of the joint venture agreement, if applicable;

- For limited liability companies:

  - Articles of organization (also referred to as certificate of organization or articles of formation) and any amendments; and

  - Operating agreement, and any amendments;

- For corporations:

  - Articles of incorporation and any amendments;

  - By-laws and any amendments;

  - All issued stock certificates, including the front and back copies, signed in accord with the by-laws;

  - Stock ledger; and

  - Voting agreements, if any;

- For partnerships, the partnership agreement and any amendments;

- The assumed/fictitious name (doing business as) certificate(s); and

- A copy of the SBA Form 2413, WOSB Program Certification (WOSBs only). Instead of an SBA Form 2413, EDWOSBs must submit an SBA Form 2414, WOSB Program Certification – EDWOSBs, and each woman claiming economic disadvantage must submit an SBA Form 413, Personal Financial Statement.

Once a firm has been certified as eligible to participate in the WOSB program by a third party certifier, or has been approved by the SBA, the WOSB or EDWOSB files the certification at **https://certify.sba.gov,** represents its status as WOSB or EDWOSB in SAM, and can participate in WOSB or EDWOSB set-asides and sole source contracts in the applicable industry (or industries).

A contracting officer may set aside an acquisition that exceeds the micro-purchase threshold ($3,500; $5,000 for the Department of Defense) in an eligible industry for WOSBs or EDWOSBs if the contracting officer has a "reasonable expectation…that two or more WOSBs [or EDWOSBs] will submit offers for the contract, and award will be made at a fair and reasonable price" (that "rule of two" again).

If the contracting officer receives only one acceptable bid or offer from a qualified WOSB or EDWOSB in response to a WOSB or EDWOSB set-aside, paragraph (d) of FAR 19.1505, Set-Aside Procedures, states that "the contracting officer may make an award if only one acceptable offer is received from a qualified EDWOSB concern or WOSB concern eligible under the WOSB Program." Note the word "may" in "the contracting officer *may* make an award…" This is different than the wording used to describe what a contracting officer should do when one offer is received in response to a HUBZone set-aside or SDVOSB set-aside: "the contracting officer *should* make an award to that concern..."

If the contracting officer receives no acceptable bids or offers from a WOSB (or EDWOSB), the contracting officer will cancel the set-aside and conduct a set-aside for small businesses "as appropriate" (that is, a HUBZone set-aside, a SDVOSB set-aside, an 8(a) set-aside, or a small business set-aside).

A contracting officer is permitted to award a **sole source contract** to WOSBs or EDWOSBs in industries where WOSBs are substantially underrepresented, or to EDWOSBs in industries where WOSBs are underrepresented provided: (1) the contracting officer does not have a reasonable expectation that offers will be received from two or more WOSBs (or EDWOSBs); (2) the anticipated contract price (including options) will not exceed $6,500,000 for manufacturing contracts or $4,000,000 for all other contracts; and (3) award will be made at a fair and reasonable price.

Note that WOSBs and EDWOSBs do not receive a 10% price evaluation preference in acquisitions that are conducted using full and open competition, unlike HUBZone SBCs.

Solicitations that are set aside for WOSBs contain **FAR 52.219-30, Notice of Set-Aside for Women-Owned Small Business Concerns Eligible Under the Women-Owned Small Business Program**, in Section I if the solicitation is in the UCF, or in the "Clauses" portion if the solicitation is in the SCF. Solicitations that are set aside for EDWOSBs contain **FAR 52.219-29, Notice of Set-Aside for Economically Disadvantaged Women-Owned Small Business Concerns**.

For more on the WOSB program, see FAR subpart 19.14, Service-Disabled Veteran-Owned Small Business Procurement Program. Also, see Chapter 16 for protests concerning a firm's eligibility as a WOSB or an EDWOSB.

Section 8(a) Business Development Program

The purpose of the **Section 8(a) business development program**, which is named after Section 8(a) of the Small Business Act, is to foster business ownership by individuals who are both socially and economically disadvantaged, and to give these individuals the opportunity to participate fully in the free enterprise system. Participants in the 8(a) program are eligible to receive a broad range of assistance from SBA, including loans, training, counseling, marketing assistance, and high-level executive development. The most popular assistance for 8(a) participants are **sole source** and **set-aside contracts**. (Actually, the SBA is awarded the contract, and it subcontracts the entire effort to the 8(a) concern. In this way, the SBA is a buffer between the contracting agency and the 8(a) concern.)

The 8(a) program is restricted to **small disadvantaged businesses** (SDBs), and contracts awarded under the 8(a) program count toward an agency's SDB contract award goal.

To qualify as an SDB, a firm must meet the following criteria:

- It must not exceed the applicable small business size standard corresponding to the NAICS code that corresponds to its primary business activity (see above).

- At least 51% of the firm must be owned and controlled by a "socially" *and* "economically" disadvantaged individual (or individuals):

    - To qualify as **socially disadvantaged**, an individual must be an American citizen (by birth or naturalization) and either: (1) be a member of a group that is presumed to be socially disadvantaged (that is, be a Black American, Hispanic American, Native American, Asian Pacific American, or Subcontinent Asian American), or (2) show by a "preponderance of evidence" that he is socially disadvantaged because of "race, ethnicity, gender, physical handicap, or residence in an environment isolated from the mainstream of American society." (**NOTE:** Women-owned small businesses and service-disabled veteran-owned small businesses are *not* considered socially disadvantaged unless at least 51% of the business is owned, controlled, and managed by members of these racial or ethnic groups.)

    - To qualify as **economically disadvantaged**, an individual cannot have: (1) a net worth that exceeds **$250,000** excluding the value of the business and primary residence (however, once a firm is accepted into the 8(a) program, the limit on an individual's net worth increases to $750,000); (2) an average gross income during the preceding three years that exceeds **$250,000** (however, once a firm is accepted into the 8(a) program, the limit on an individual's average gross income during the preceding three years increases to $350,000); or (3) assets exceeding **$4,000,000**, *including* the business and primary residence (once a firm is accepted into the 8(a) program, the limit on an individual's assets increases to $6,000,000).

Ownership, social disadvantage, and economic disadvantage criteria are somewhat different for concerns owned by Indian tribes, Alaska Native corporations, and Native Hawaiian organizations.

To qualify for the 8(a) program, the SDB must have been in business for at least **two years** (this requirement may be waived if the socially and economically disadvantaged owner or owners demonstrate substantial technical and business management experience).

Business Plan

After an SDB is accepted into the 8(a) program, but before it may obtain any 8(a) program benefits, it must prepare and submit for SBA approval a **business plan** outlining a reasonable approach for using the 8(a) contracts to develop the expertise and capabilities necessary to become self-sustaining and competitive. The goal of the 8(a) program is to "graduate" SDBs that can compete for government and commercial contracts on their own.

The business plan must explain how the 8(a) concern intends to use the 8(a) program to attain its business targets, objectives, and goals. The business plan must analyze the concern's strengths and weaknesses, assess its prospects for profitable operations during its program participation and after it leaves the program, and provide estimates of the contract awards it will need under the 8(a) program and from other sources to meet its specific targets, objectives, and goals. Once approved, the 8(a) concern must review its business plan with the SBA annually and modify the plan as appropriate.

Obtaining and Processing 8(a) Contracts

The SBA obtains procurements for the 8(a) program in three ways:

1. The contracting activity unilaterally offers the procurement to the SBA for the 8(a) program;

2. The SBA identifies a procurement as suitable for the 8(a) program and asks the agency for it; or

3. An 8(a) concern, through self-marketing, convinces a contracting activity to offer the procurement to the SBA on its behalf.

Once a requirement is accepted by the SBA for the 8(a) program, it remains in the 8(a) program unless the SBA agrees to release it for performance by a non-8(a) concern. For example, if the SBA accepts a requirement for maintenance of a particular building into the 8(a) program, all future requirements for maintenance of that building must be fulfilled through the 8(a) program unless the SBA agrees to permit a non-8(a) firm to perform the maintenance. The SBA does not allow many requirements to leave the 8(a) program.

Most 8(a) contracts are awarded to 8(a) concerns on a sole source basis (either because the contracting activity is convinced the 8(a) concern can perform the contract at a fair market price or because the SBA has selected the particular 8(a) concern for the contract). Such sole source 8(a) contracts are *not* synopsized in **FedBizOpps**.

However, an 8(a) acquisition over **$7,000,000** for manufacturing, or **$4,000,000** for services or construction, must be set-aside for 8(a) concerns if there is a reasonable expectation that at least two eligible and responsible 8(a) concerns will submit offers and the award will be made at a fair and reasonable price (the "rule of two"). If there is not a reasonable expectation that at least two 8(a) concerns will submit bids or offers at a fair market price, the SBA can authorize a sole source 8(a) award. Competitive 8(a) solicitations *are* synopsized in **FedBizOpps**.

The requirement to compete 8(a) acquisitions over $7,000,000 for manufacturing or $4,000,000 for services or construction does *not* apply to concerns owned by an Indian tribe or an Alaskan Native corporation, nor does it apply to Department of Defense 8(a) contracts with concerns owned by Native Hawaiian organizations – 8(a) contracts of *any* size may be awarded to these types of concerns.

Joint Ventures

A **joint venture** in which at least one member is an 8(a) concern may submit an offer on a competitive 8(a) acquisition (that is, over $7,000,000 for manufacturing or over $4,000,000 for services or construction) provided: (1) each concern is small under the applicable size standard; (2) the size of at least one 8(a) member of the joint venture is *less* than half of the corresponding size standard (that is, if the size standard is 500 employees, at least one 8(a) concern has fewer than 250 employees); and (3)(a) if the acquisition has a revenue-based size standard, the procurement *exceeds* half that size standard (that is, if the size standard is $10,000,000, the acquisition would have to be larger than $5,000,000); or (3)(b) if the acquisition has an employee-based size standard (such as 500 employees), the acquisition exceeds $10,000,000.

For sole source and competitive 8(a) acquisitions that are less than these dollar levels, a joint venture must have at least one 8(a) concern as a member, and the combined annual receipts or number of employees of the concerns in the joint venture must meet the applicable size standard.

Duration of Program Eligibility

If accepted into the 8(a) program, the firm can stay in the program for **nine years**. The nine years of program eligibility are divided into two stages: the **developmental** stage and the **transitional** stage. During its **four years** in the developmental stage, the 8(a) concern is eligible for:

- Sole source and competitive 8(a) contracts;
- Financial assistance;
- Financial assistance for employee skills training or upgrading;
- Transfer of technology or surplus property owned by the United States; and
- Training sessions to help develop marketing skills and compete successfully for contracts in the marketplace.

During its **five years** in the transitional stage, the 8(a) concern is eligible for:

- All the assistance available to concerns in the developmental stage;
- Assistance from contracting agencies in forming joint ventures, leader-follower arrangements, and team arrangements with other firms; and
- Training and technical assistance in transitional business planning.

To help 8(a) concerns transition from 8(a) subcontracts, firms in the transitional stage have "**non-8(a) business activity goals**," which represent revenue obtained outside the 8(a) program. The goals are:

Year in transitional stage	Non-8(a) business activity targets (required minimum non-8(a) revenue as a percentage of total revenue)
1	15
2	25
3	35
4	45
5	55

8(a) concerns that fail to meet these goals may cause the SBA to take remedial action, such as:

- Increased monitoring of the 8(a) concern's contracting activity during the ensuing program year;

- Requiring the 8(a) concerns to obtain management and technical assistance;

- Conditioning the award of future sole source 8(a) contracts on the concern's taking affirmative steps to expand revenues from non-8(a) sources;

- Reducing the concern's level of 8(a) support;

- Eliminating sole source 8(a) contracts; or

- Terminating the concern's participation in the 8(a) program.

Besides failing to meet non-8(a) business activity goals during the transitional stage, an 8(a) concern's participation may be terminated if, for example:

- It fails to maintain its small business status;

- It's socially and economically disadvantaged owners fail to maintain the 51% ownership requirement;

- It fails to provide the SBA with required financial statements, business plans, or reports;

- An owner has a net worth of more than **$750,000**, excluding his ownership interest in the business and equity in his primary residence;

- An owner has assets exceeding **$6,000,000**, including the business and primary residence;

- It ceases business operations;

- It is debarred or suspended; or

- It knowingly submits false information to the SBA.

There are many other grounds for a concern's termination from the 8(a) program.

In addition, once an 8(a) concern receives more than **$100,000,000** in both sole source and competitive 8(a) contracts (or, if the firm is primarily engaged in an industry with a revenue-based small business size standard, five times that size standard or $100,000,000, whichever is less), SBA will no longer award it any *sole source* 8(a) contracts. Nevertheless, the 8(a) concern can still compete for competitive 8(a) acquisitions (that is, those above $7,000,000 for manufacturing; those above $4,000,000 for services or construction). However, 8(a) contracts under **$100,000** are *not* counted against the $100,000,000 / 5 times the size standard limitation. (This restriction does *not* apply to 8(a) concerns owned by Indian tribes, Alaska Native corporations, and Native Hawaiian organizations – there are **no limits** on these 8(a) concerns.)

Clauses in 8(a) Solicitations and Contracts

Competitive 8(a) solicitations contain **FAR 52.219-17, Section 8(a) Award**, and **FAR 52.219-18, Notification of Competition Limited to Eligible 8(a) Concerns**, in Section I if the solicitation is in the UCF, or in the "Clauses" portion if the solicitation is in the SCF.

See FAR subpart 19.8, Contracting with the Small Business Administration (The 8(a) Program), and **https://www.sba.gov/contracting/government-contracting-programs/8a-business-development-program** for further information on the 8(a) program application and contracting procedures.

Small Business Set-Asides

At or Below the Simplified Acquisition Threshold

If an acquisition exceeds the micro-purchase threshold ($3,500; $5,000 for the Department of Defense) but not the simplified acquisition threshold ($150,000), the contracting officer may set aside the acquisition for competition among all small businesses. There is no order of precedence among the HUBZone, SDVOSB, WOSB, 8(a), and small business set-asides – the contracting officer may choose to solicit any small businesses he determines are capable of providing the required supplies or services.

Above the Simplified Acquisition Threshold

If an acquisition exceeds the simplified acquisition threshold, and the contracting officer has considered *and rejected* a HUBZone set-aside, a HUBZone sole source award, an SDVOSB set-aside, an SDVOSB sole source award, a WOSB (or EDWOSB) set-aside, an 8(a) set-aside, and an 8(a) sole source award, the contracting officer *must* set aside the acquisition for participation by *all* small businesses "when there is a reasonable expectation that offers will be obtained from at least two responsible small business concerns offering the products of different small business concerns, and award will be made at fair market prices" (the "rule of two").

Not only does a small business set-aside allow firms owned by white males to compete, but it allows WOSBs and EDWOSBs outside of underrepresented industries, SDBs that aren't 8(a) certified, VOSBs, and any other kind of small business to compete. (**NOTE:** There is one quirk to small business set-asides: the contracting officer must solicit Federal Prison Industries, Inc. [FPI] when conducting a small business set-aside, and must consider a timely offer from FPI. See "Market Research" in Chapter 4 and **http://www.unicor.gov** for more information on FPI.)

If the contracting officer receives only one acceptable bid or offer from a qualified small business in response to a small business set-aside, paragraph (a) of FAR 19.502-2, Total Small Business Set-Asides, states that "the contracting officer *should* make an award to that firm" (emphasis added).

If, after evaluating the bids or proposals submitted in response to a small business set-aside solicitation, the contracting officer determines that none of the bids or proposals are reasonable or none of the bidders or offerors are responsible (including the refusal by the SBA to issue a certificate of competency [COC] for any of the bidders or offerors – see Chapter 7), he dissolves the set aside and resolicits without any size restrictions: large and small businesses may submit bids or proposals. However, as a rule, the prices must be exceedingly unreasonable before a contracting officer will dissolve a set-aside. This is because most contracting officers do not want to resolicit and, consequently, incur additional delay and administrative expenses.

Unlike the HUBZone, SDVOSB, and 8(a) programs, a contracting officer is *not* permitted to award a **sole source contract** to a small business unless the small business meets the "only one responsible source and no other supplies or services will satisfy agency requirements" exception to full and open competition (see Chapter 3).

Solicitations that are set aside for small businesses contain **FAR 52.219-6, Notice of Total Small Business Set-Aside**, in Section I if the solicitation is in the UCF, or in the "Clauses" portion if the solicitation is in the SCF.

See FAR subpart 19.5, Set-Asides for Small Business, for further information on small business set aside procedures. Also, see Chapter 16 for protests concerning small business size status.

Disaster Relief and Emergency Assistance Set-Asides

In the wake of the inadequate government response to Hurricanes Katrina, Rita, and Wilma in 2005, Congress authorized the use of set-asides for major disaster or emergency assistance acquisitions. When the president declares a disaster or emergency, contracting officers may set-aside acquisitions for debris clearance, distribution of supplies, reconstruction, and other major disaster or emergency assistance for contractors residing or doing business primarily in the geographic area affected by the disaster or emergency. A contracting officer is not required to set-aside such acquisitions, and he may give local firms award preference instead. (Note that these are *local area set-asides*, not small business set-asides.)

The contracting officer defines the specific geographic area for the set-aside, but the geographic area must be within the declared disaster or emergency area (or areas). However, the area need not include all the counties in the declared disaster or emergency areas – the set-aside may cover the entire declared areas or some part of the areas (for example, one or more counties, and the set-aside area may cross state lines). These set-asides may be used with other set-asides, such as those for small businesses – the contracting officer may set-aside an acquisition for small businesses within the disaster or emergency area.

For more on disaster relief and emergency assistance set-asides, see FAR subpart 26.2, Disaster or Emergency Assistance Activities, and FAR 6.208, Set-Asides for Local Firms During a Major Disaster or Emergency.

DISADVANTAGED BUSINESS ENTERPRISE (DBE) PROGRAM

A program very similar to the SBA's 8(a) program is the Department of Transportation (DOT) **Disadvantaged Business Enterprise (DBE) Program**. The DBE program is intended to provide contracting opportunities for small businesses owned and controlled by socially and economically disadvantaged individuals in DOT's highway, mass transit, and airport financial assistance programs operated by the Federal Highway Administration, the Federal Transit Administration, and the Federal Aviation Administration, respectively.

The DBE program requires state and local transportation agencies that receive DOT financial assistance to establish goals for the participation of DBEs – the overall goal is for DBEs to receive at least 10% of the financial assistance. Each DOT-assisted state and local transportation agency is required to establish annual DBE goals, and to review anticipated large prime contracts throughout the year and establish contract-specific DBE subcontracting goals.

Most of the qualifications for participation in the 8(a) program and the DBE program are the same, but there are differences between the two programs – for example, women-owned small businesses are considered disadvantaged under the DBE program, and the two programs have different limits on owners' net worth and firms' gross revenue (there are even different size standards for airport concessionaires under the DBE program). Furthermore, there are the usual quirks – Alaska Native Corporations must be certified as DBEs even if they do not meet the size, ownership, and control criteria that apply to Indian tribes and Native Hawaiian Organizations. So those interested in the DBE program should to look at the applicable regulations and contact the applicable DOT administrations to determine whether they are qualified.

DOT's DBE website is **https://www.transportation.gov/civil-rights/disadvan taged-business-enterprise**. The DBE program regulations are in Title 49 of the Code of Federal Regulations (CFR), Part 23, Participation by Disadvantaged Business Enterprises in Airport Concessions; and 49 CFR Part 26, Participation by Disadvantaged Business Enterprises in Department of Transportation Financial Assistance Programs.

SUBCONTRACTING INCENTIVES

General Requirement

A contractor (large or small) that receives a contract for more than the simplified acquisition threshold ($150,000) must agree that small businesses, VOSBs, SDVOSBs, HUBZone small businesses, SDBs, and WOSBs will have "the maximum practicable opportunity to participate in contract performance consistent with its efficient performance" (see FAR 52.219-8, Utilization of Small Business Concerns).

Subcontracting Plans

Before a contracting officer can award to a large business a contract that is greater than $700,000 ($1,500,000 for construction) and that has subcontracting opportunities, he must require the large business to submit and negotiate a **small business subcontracting plan**. The small business subcontracting plan must include separate goals for subcontract awards to small businesses, veteran-owned small businesses (VOSBs), SDVOSBs, HUBZone small businesses, SDBs, and WOSBs; the name of the person who will administer the subcontracting program for the large business; a description of the principal types of supplies and services to be subcontracted; and a description of the efforts the large business will make to insure small businesses, VOSBs, SDVOSBs, HUBZone SBCs, SDBs, and WOSBs have an equitable opportunity to compete for subcontracts. If the large business fails to submit a subcontracting plan when requested or fails to negotiate an acceptable subcontracting plan, it is *ineligible* for award.

Once the contracting officer and the successful large business negotiate an acceptable subcontracting plan, the plan becomes part of the contract, and the contractor must report its subcontracting achievements annually (semiannually for Department of Defense contractors) through the **Electronic Subcontracting Reporting System** (eSRS) (**https://www.esrs.gov**). Any contractor failing to comply "in good faith" with the subcontracting plan is liable to *liquidated damages* equal to the actual dollar amount by which the contractor fails to achieve each subcontract goal.

However, when the contracting officer decides the inclusion of a **monetary incentive** is necessary to increase small business, VOSB, SDVOSB, HUBZone, SDB, and WOSB subcontracting opportunities, he can authorize an additional payment up to **10%** of the amount the contractor exceeds each subcontract goal in its subcontract plan. The amount of the incentive is negotiated and depends on the contractor's unique outreach programs; its use of small businesses, VOSBs, SDVOSBs, HUBZone SBCs, SDBs, and WOSBs in nontraditional areas; and the technical assistance it intends to provide small businesses, VOSBs, SDVOSBs, HUBZone SBCs, SDBs, and WOSBs. Nevertheless, the contracting officer will *not* give the contractor an incentive bonus if: (1) the contractor exceeds a subcontract goal because of a reason not under its control (such as a subcontractor overrun); or (2) the contractor exceeds a subcontract goal but it did not disclose in its subcontracting plan all the subcontracts it had intended to award to small businesses, VOSBs, SDVOSBs, HUBZone SBCs, SDBs, and WOSBs.

In addition, contracting officers are to consider each offeror's past compliance with its subcontracting plans when evaluating the offeror's past performance (see Chapter 8).

For DOD, two additional provisions apply: (1) subcontract awards to qualified **nonprofit agencies for the blind and the severely handicapped** under DOD contracts count toward the contractor's small business goal; and (2) it is conducting a test program through December 31, 2027, to determine whether **comprehensive small business subcontracting plans** that are negotiated on a corporate, division, or plant-wide basis will increase subcontracting opportunities for small businesses.

Unrestricted solicitations expected to exceed $700,000 (or $1,500,000 for construction) contain **FAR 52.219-9, Small Business Subcontracting Plan**, and **FAR 52.219-16, Liquidated Damages – Subcontracting Plan**. If the contracting officer decides a monetary incentive is necessary, he will include **FAR 52.219-10, Incentive Subcontracting Program**.

Many large businesses use the SBA's **Dynamic Small Business Search** database at **http://dsbs.sba.gov/dsbs/search/dsp_dsbs.cfm** to identify the availability of various types of small businesses. In addition, many large businesses use the **SBA Subcontracting Network (SUB-*Net*) (http://web.sba.gov/subnet)** to post subcontracting opportunities and notices of sources sought (it is also used by federal agencies, state and local governments, non-profit organizations, colleges and universities, and even foreign governments). While these subcontracting opportunities are not necessarily reserved for small businesses, small businesses are able to identify potential subcontracts in their areas of expertise and use their limited resources pursuing the most promising.

When awarding subcontracts, contractors may rely on the representations of the subcontractors regarding their status as small businesses, VOSBs, SDVOSBs, SDBs, and WOSBs. However, contractors are obligated to confirm the status of subcontractors claiming to HUBZone SBCs by accessing the SBA's "Dynamic Small Business Search" database at **http://dsbs.sba.gov/dsbs/search/dsp_searchhubzone.cfm** and verifying that SBA has "certified" them (see above).

See FAR subpart 19.7, The Small Business Subcontracting Program, for more information on subcontracting with small businesses, VOSBs, SDVOSBs, HUBZone SBCs, SDBs, and WOSBs.

American Indian Incentive Program

To provide prime contractors with an incentive to subcontract with American Indian organizations and Indian-owned economic enterprises, contracting officers *may* include in contracts an incentive payment equal to **5% of the amount paid to an Indian subcontractor**. If the contracting officer believes subcontracting opportunities exist for Indian organizations or Indian-owned economic enterprises, and money is available to pay the incentive, then the contracting officer *may* include **FAR 52.226-1, Utilization of Indian Organizations and Indian-Owned Economic Enterprises**, in solicitations and contracts of any amount.

See FAR subpart 26.1, Indian Incentive Program, for more on the Indian subcontracting incentive.

MENTOR-PROTÉGÉ PROGRAMS

In 1990, Congress authorized DOD to develop a program to provide its major contractors with incentives to enter into agreements with small firms in which the major contractor agrees to provide appropriate developmental assistance to the small firm to enhance its ability to compete for, and successfully perform, DOD contracts and subcontracts. In return, Congress authorized DOD to reimburse the major contractors for the cost of developmental assistance provided to the small firms, or to credit the developmental assistance costs against its subcontract goals (see above).

DOD developed a **mentor-protégé program** in which a major contractor ("mentor" – typically a large business) selects one or more small firms ("protégé") to enter into a long-term relationship as a junior partner. DOD's mentor-protégé program worked so well that Congress authorized the National Aeronautics and Space Administration (NASA) to develop a similar one. In 1996, when Congress exempted the Federal Aviation Administration (FAA) from the requirements of the FAR, the FAA instituted a mentor-protégé program that is similar to DOD's and NASA's. And in 2003, when Congress authorized the creation of the Department of Homeland Security and gave it wide latitude in establishing its acquisition processes, the department instituted a mentor-protégé program that resembles DOD's and NASA's.

Other agencies, though not authorized by Congress to spend funds on a mentor-protégé program, have developed their own "no-cost" programs. Under such programs, the agency does not reimburse the mentor for any protégé developmental costs, but instead provides its mentors with additional consideration during the proposal evaluation process (some agencies take into consideration these developmental costs when determining indirect cost rates). These agencies are the Departments of

Energy, State, and Veterans Affairs; the Environmental Protection Agency (EPA); the General Services Administration (GSA); and the U.S. Agency for International Development (USAID).

In addition, the SBA has developed a mentor-protégé program in which the protégés are restricted to 8(a) program participants, and the mentor-protégé team can submit bids and proposals as a small business for *any government procurement* if certain conditions are met. Furthermore, an SBA mentor can own up to 40% of its protégé to help it raise capital.

However, each agency has different qualification requirements for participation as a protégé. For example, DOD permits SDBs, SDVOSBs, HUBZone SBCs, WOSBs, business entities owned and controlled by Indian tribes and Native Hawaiian Organizations, and qualified organizations employing the severely disabled to participate in its program; the Department of Veterans Affairs restricts participation in its program to VOSBs and SDVOSBs; and the EPA program is for SDBs only.

To provide uniformity among the civilian agencies' mentor-protégé programs, the **National Defense Authorization Act for Fiscal Year 2013** assigned responsibility for civilian agencies' mentor-protégé programs to the SBA, and directed the SBA to pattern it after its 8(a) mentor-protégé program (the act exempts DOD – DOD will retain control of its program). So SBA decided to establish a mentor-protégé programs for all other small businesses that parallels its 8(a) mentor-protégé program

The agencies that already have mentor-protégé programs (that is, the Departments of Energy, Homeland Security, State, and Veterans Affairs; EPA; FAA; GSA; NASA; and USAID) can keep their mentor-protégé programs until August 2017; if they want to continue their programs after that, then must submit a plan for the program to the SBA and obtain its approval. In addition, it an agency that wants to start its own mentor-protégé program, it must obtain submit a plan to the SBA and obtain its approval.

The following are the key features of the SBA's mentor-protégé program:

- The mentor and protégé firms must enter into a written agreement setting forth an assessment of the protégé's needs and a detailed description and timeline for the delivery of that assistance by the mentor. The agreement must be approved by the SBA.

  Examples of the assistance typically provided by a mentor to its protégé are: management guidance (financial, organizational, business development, marketing); engineering and other technical assistance; rent-free use of facilities and equipment owned or leased by the mentor; and temporary assignment of mentor personnel to the protégé for training purposes.

- The term of the mentor-protégé agreement cannot exceed three years, but the agreement may be extended an additional three years provided the protégé has received the agreed-upon business development assistance and will continue to receive additional assistance. Annually, the protégé must report to the SBA all the technical and management assistance provided by the mentor; all loans or investments made by the mentor in the protégé; all subcontracts awarded by the mentor to the protégé; all federal contracts awarded to the mentor-protégé relationship; and a narrative describing the success such assistance has had in addressing the developmental needs of the protégé and addressing any problems encountered. SBA will review the mentor-protégé relationship annually to determine whether to approve its continuation for another year.

■   A mentor can have up to three protégés.

■   With SBA approval, a protégé can have two mentors, *provided* the second relationship will not compete or conflict with the assistance provided in the first relationship, and: (1) the second relationship pertains to an unrelated NAICS code ; or (ii) the protégé firm is seeking to acquire a specific expertise that the first mentor does not possess.

■   The SBA can authorize a small business to be both a mentor and a protégé.

■   During evaluation of a proposal submitted by a mentor, a contracting activity may provide additional consideration if the mentor will provide significant subcontracting work to its protégé.

■   A protégé that graduates or otherwise leaves the 8(a) program but continues to qualify as a small business may convert its 8(a) mentor-protégé relationship to a small business mentor-protégé relationship.

■   A mentor and a protégé may form a joint venture with SBA approval. The joint venture may compete as a small business for any government contract as long as the protégé meets the applicable size standard. The joint venture may seek any type of small business contract for which the protégé firm qualifies (for example, a protégé that qualifies as a WOSB could seek a WOSB set-aside with its SBA-approved mentor as a member of the joint venture).

■   The mentor can purchase up to 40% of the protégé to provide the protégé with necessary capital.

For more on SBA's small business mentor-protégé program, see Title 13 of the Code of Federal Regulations (CFR), Part 125, Government Contracting Programs. For more on the SBA's 8(a) mentor-protégé program, see **https://www.sba. gov/contracting/government-contracting-programs/8a-business-development-program/mentor-protege-program**. For more information on current mentor-protégé programs operated by other agencies, see the agencies' FAR supplements (usually in part 19 of the supplement).

SMALL BUSINESS INNOVATION RESEARCH (SBIR) PROGRAM

There is a preference program called the **Small Business Innovation Research (SBIR) Program** that requires all agencies with research and development (R&D) budgets of more than **$100,000,000** to set aside **3.2%** of their R&D budgets for small businesses. Approximately **$1.7 billion** is awarded to small businesses through the SBIR program each year.

In effect, the SBIR program is an R&D small business set-aside. The solicitations, proposal requirements, and regulations are simplified under this program to make it easier for small businesses to participate in government research and propose innovative approaches in areas of technology and research that interest the government. It is a trial program that is scheduled to expire September 30, 2022.

Participating Agencies and SBIR Requirements

The following 11 agencies take part in the SBIR program:

- Department of Agriculture
- Department of Commerce
- Department of Defense
- Department of Education
- Department of Energy
- Department of Health and Human Services
- Department of Homeland Security
- Department of Transportation
- Environmental Protection Agency
- National Aeronautics and Space Administration
- National Science Foundation

Under the SBIR program, a small business is defined as a concern with no more than **500 employees** (regardless of the applicable small business size standard) and is more than **50%** owned and controlled by U.S. citizens.

SBIR Phases

The SBIR program consists of **three phases**:

Phase I

Under Phase I of the SBIR program, an agency identifies topics in areas of research and technology that directly affect its functions and are suitable for small business participation. At least once a year (and more often if necessary), the agency prepares an SBIR solicitation. If the solicitation is expected to result in SBIR contracts exceeding $25,000, it must be synopsized in **FedBizOpps** at least 15 days before the solicitation is issued, and the solicitation must have a proposal due date that is at least 30 days after the solicitation is released.

The solicitation is not in the uniform contract format. Rather, it is in a "simple, standardized, easy-to-read, easy-to-understand format" that identifies the research topics in sufficient detail so potential small businesses know the agency's research goals.

The solicitation requires the small business offeror to submit a proposal that describes an effort up to **six months** long and costing no more than **$150,000** to conduct experimental or theoretical research related to one of the agency's topics. The proposal, which must not exceed **25 pages**, must include the following:

- A brief abstract of the technical problem;

- The technical questions that the proposed research will address;

- A work plan;

- A description of the related research previously performed by the small business;

- The key personnel who will perform the research and a bibliography of their related work;

- A description of the facilities the small business will use;

- The qualifications of any consultants who will assist in the research;

- Anticipated results of the proposed research;

- How the research will provide a basis for further funding (see Phase II below);

- The potential commercial applications; and

- Simplified cost or budget data.

In addition, the small business must agree to perform at least **two-thirds** of the research or analytical effort.

If several proposals appear promising, the agency may award more than one contract per SBIR solicitation. However, the agency is under no obligation to award any contracts if none of the proposals demonstrate sufficient scientific and technical merit.

An effort of this size permits the small business contractor to demonstrate the scientific merit and technical feasibility of its proposed effort, and for the government to judge the quality of the small business' execution. The government may decide to award contracts to more than one offeror if several different solutions and approaches have technical and scientific merit.

The SBA maintains a database of all current and future SBIR solicitations at **https://www.sbir.gov/sbirsearch/topic/current**.

Phase II

If the results of the Phase I contract are promising, the agency has the option of funding a Phase II of the research. Phase II expands on the Phase I results and allows the small business contractor to further pursue development of the research. Each agency selects the small business contractors it wants to submit proposals; only those contractors that participated in Phase I are eligible for Phase II (the **FedBizOpps** synopsis requirement does not apply to Phase II proposals). Proposals for Phase II funding may not be longer than **two years** or cost more than **$1,000,000**. The small business must agree to perform at least **one-half** of the research or analytical effort. However, the agency has *no obligation* to fund *any* Phase II proposal, even if Phase I is completed successfully. (Agencies may issue one additional Phase II contract to continue the work of an initial Phase II award.)

NOTE: The National Institutes of Health (part of the Department of Health and Human Services), the Department of Defense, and the Department of Education are authorized to award a Phase II contract to a small business that received an STTR Phase I contract (see below) to further develop the work performed under the STTR Phase I contract.

Phase III

Once Phase II is completed, the small business is encouraged to pursue commercial applications of the research through private funding under **Phase III**. If Phase II results in a product or process that meets the need of a federal agency, the agency is free to award a non-SBIR contract to the small business for the product, process, or additional research. No SBIR funds may be used for Phase III.

The SBIR program is not addressed in the FAR. For more information on the SBIR program, contact the agency's SBIR representative or go to the SBA's SBIR website at **https://www.sbir.gov/about/about-sbir**.

SMALL BUSINESS TECHNOLOGY TRANSFER (STTR) PROGRAM

The **Small Business Technology Transfer (STTR) Program** is similar to the SBIR in that all agencies with R&D budgets of more than **$1 billion** are required to set aside **0.45%** of their R&D budgets for small businesses. Approximately **$200,000,000** is awarded to small businesses through the STTR program each year. The STTR program is scheduled to expire September 30, 2022.

The following agencies participate in the STTR program:

- Department of Defense
- Department of Energy
- Department of Health and Human Services
- National Aeronautics and Space Administration
- National Science Foundation

The primary difference between the SBIR and the STTR programs is that small businesses *must* have a single nonprofit research institution as a partner to participate in the STTR program. The nonprofit research institution must be located in the U.S., and must be either: (1) a nonprofit college or university; (2) a domestic nonprofit research organization; or (3) a federally funded research and development center (FFRDC).

The SBA describes the reason for the STTR program like this:

"Small business has long been where innovation and innovators thrive. But the risk and expense of conducting serious R&D efforts can be beyond the means of many small businesses. Conversely, nonprofit research laboratories are instrumental in developing high-tech innovations. But frequently, innovation is confined to the theoretical, not the practical. STTR combines the strengths of both entities by introducing entrepreneurial skills to high-tech research efforts. The technologies and products are transferred from the laboratory to the marketplace. The small business profits from the commercialization, which, in turn, stimulates the U.S. economy."

Like the SBIR program, the STTR program consists of three phases:

Phase I:

An agency solicits proposals or grant applications from small businesses and their research partners to conduct feasibility-related experimental or theoretical research related to described agency requirements up to **one year** long and costing no more than **$150,000**. The small business partner must perform at least 40% of the R&D and the single partnering research institution must perform at least 30% of the R&D. The agency may make more than one award if several different approaches have merit, but the agency may choose not to make any award if none of the proposals demonstrate sufficient scientific and technical value.

As with the SBIR program, if the STTR solicitation is expected to result in contracts exceeding $25,000, it must be synopsized in **FedBizOpps** at least 15 days before the solicitation is issued, and the solicitation must have a proposal due date that is at least 30 days after the solicitation is released. Current and future STTR solicitations are available at **https://www.sbir.gov/sbirsearch/topic/current** (it includes SBIR solicitations as well).

Phase II:

If the results of Phase I are promising, the agency may provide further funding to allow the small business and its research partner to expand and develop the research. The effort may be up to **two years** and cost no more than **$1,000,000**. However, the agency is under no obligation to fund a Phase II effort. The small business partner must perform at least 40% of the R&D and the single partnering research institution must perform at least 30% of the R&D. (Unlike the SBIR program, agencies are not authorized to award an additional STTR Phase II contract to continue an initial Phase II contract.)

Also note that the National Institutes of Health, the Department of Defense, and the Department of Education are authorized to award an SBIR Phase II contract to a small business that received an STTR Phase I contract to further develop the work performed under the STTR Phase I contract. The small business must perform at least 50% of the research or analytical effort, just like other SBIR Phase II contractors.

Phase III:

Upon completion of the STTR Phase II effort, the agency may enter into a non-STTR funded agreement with the small business or contract with the small business for additional work. Phase III small businesses are encouraged to obtain non-federal funds for commercial applications of the research.

For more information on the STTR program, contact the agency's STTR representative or visit SBA's STTR website at **https://www.sbir.gov/about/about-sttr**.

FALSE STATEMENTS OR INFORMATION

Many of these set-asides and preference programs rely on the bidder's or offeror's representation that it is eligible. Others, such as applications for HUBZone certification, require the concern to submit personal and financial information about itself and its owners as part of its application. Participants in the 8(a) program must file annual reports and certifications to maintain their eligibility.

Anyone who misrepresents his concern's average annual gross revenue, number of employees, ownership, or other qualifying characteristics to obtain a set-aside contract or preference is subject to a fine up to **$500,000**, imprisonment up to **10 years**, suspension and debarment (see Chapter 7), penalties authorized by the Program Fraud Civil Remedies Act of 1986 ($5,000 for each false statement), and ineligibility to participate in any program or activity under the Small Business Act for up to **three years**. This is considered *serious business*! See Chapter 17 for more on procurement integrity and ethics.

CHAPTER 12

PROVIDING FOREIGN PRODUCTS

The United States participates in a global marketplace – electronics from Japan, automobiles from Europe, oil from the Middle East, food products from South America, minerals from Africa. Some of these products are not mined or grown in the U.S., others have features that are not available on domestic products, still others are produced less expensively overseas. Yet the U.S. government is constrained by many laws from buying foreign products *unless* the purchase is in the government's **best interest**. Congress has defined the government's best interest in some novel and convoluted ways. Therefore, companies that intend to offer foreign products to the government need to be familiar with FAR part 25, Foreign Acquisition, and the Defense FAR Supplement (DFARS) part 225 to know the provisions of these laws and avoid stumbling over an exception to an exception.

BLANKET PROHIBITION

There is one blanket prohibition in FAR subpart 25.7, Prohibited Sources, which applies to *all* government agencies: most supplies or services from Burma, Sudan, Iran, or North Korea cannot be furnished to the government except under unusual conditions and with the approval of the Department of the Treasury's Office of Foreign Assets Control (OFAC) (**https://www.treasury.gov/about/organizational-structure/offices/Pages/Office-of-Foreign-Assets-Control.aspx**). In addition, lists of entities and individuals subject to economic sanctions are on OFAC's **Specially Designated Nationals (SDN) List** at **https://www.treasury.gov/resource-center/sanctions/SDN-List/Pages/default.aspx**.

THE BUY AMERICAN ACT

Outside these blanket prohibitions, the fundamental law governing federal purchases of foreign products is the **Buy American Act of 1933**. Enacted during the Great Depression, the Buy American Act discourages the federal government from buying foreign products for three reasons: to make American industry stronger, to protect domestic labor markets, and to keep federal funds in the U.S. While the Buy American Act does not prohibit the acquisition of foreign products, it handicaps them by requiring the application of **evaluation factors** to the prices of the foreign products, thus making them less competitive.

The Buy American Act, covered in FAR subpart 25.1, Buy American Act – Supplies, and FAR subpart 25.2, Buy American Act – Construction Materials, is very simple: for all purchases of supplies (except commercial information technology – see below) exceeding the micro-purchase threshold ($3,500; $5,000 for the Department of Defense), the federal government must acquire **domestic articles, materials, or supplies** unless:

1. The items are for use outside the United States;

2. Domestic items are unreasonably priced;

3. Compliance with the Buy American Act would not be in the best interest of the government;

4. The items are not mined, produced, or manufactured in the United States in sufficient and reasonably available commercial quantities of a satisfactory quality; or

5. The items are purchased specifically for commissary resale.

Determining when an item falls into one of these five exceptions is the tricky part. And those who try to circumvent the Buy American Act by affixing a "Made in America" label to a product that is *not* made in the United States may be **debarred** from federal contracting for **up to three years!** (See Chapter 7 for more on debarment.)

Definition of "Domestic End Product"

An "article, material, or supply" is considered a "**domestic end product**" if it is (1) an unmanufactured end product mined or produced in the United States or its territories; (2) an end product manufactured in the United States provided *at least 50% of its cost is attributed to components mined, produced, or manufactured in the United States or its territories*; or (3) an end product that is commercially available off-the-shelf (COTS). Ownership of the firm producing the item does not matter; products manufactured in the United States by a foreign firm are considered domestic.

The Five Exceptions to the Buy American Act

The following is a brief explanation of the five exceptions to the Buy American Act.

Exception #1 – Items for Use Outside the United States

When the federal government intends to purchase supplies, services, or construction for use in a foreign country, the **Balance of Payments Program** applies. In effect, it is like a foreign version of the Buy American Act in that it applies to purchases of supplies for use outside the U.S. and to construction materials for construction contracts performed outside the U.S. The intent of the Balance of Payments Program is to lessen the effect of government expenditures on the U.S. balance of international payments. Essentially, the Balance of Payments program requires the government to acquire domestic supplies, services, or construction unless the prices of the domestic products exceed the prices of the foreign products by more than 50%. There are many more exceptions to this rule (for example, the acquisition of industrial gas, petroleum products, foreign end products or construction material required by a treaty, etc.).

Because civilian agencies do not acquire many items for use outside the U.S., the Balance of Payments Program regulations are in DFARS subpart 225.75, Balance of Payments Program.

Exception #2 – Domestic Items Are Unreasonably Priced

A domestic item is considered unreasonably priced if its price exceeds the lowest acceptable offer of a foreign item, inclusive of duty, by more than **6%** if the domestic item is a product of a large business, or more than **12%** if the domestic item is a product of a small business.

As an example, if a foreign item is offered to the government at $248,000 and is assessed $2,000 duty, its total price is $250,000 ($248,000 + $2,000). A domestic large business must offer the item for less than **$265,000** to win the contract ($250,000 + 6%). Similarly, a small business must offer the item for less than **$280,000** ($250,000 + 12%).

The Department of Defense evaluates the price reasonableness of foreign products differently. When evaluating the products of countries *not* exempted from the provisions of the Buy American Act by the secretary of defense (see exception #3 below), defense contracting officers add the applicable duty to the price *and increase this sum by 50%*. If a company offers a domestic product at $350,000 and another offers a foreign product at $248,000 with $2,000 duty for a total bid price of $250,000, the foreign bid is evaluated as if it were **$375,000** ($250,000 + 50%). Because the evaluated price of the foreign product is higher than the price of the domestic product ($375,000 vs. $350,000), the Defense Department will award the contract to the business offering the domestic product.

Conversely, if the domestic product at $350,000 is evaluated against a foreign product offered at $230,000 with $2,000 duty, the foreign product will be evaluated as if it were $348,000 ($232,000 + 50%). Because the evaluated price of the foreign product is lower than the price of the domestic product, the Defense Department will award the contract at $230,000 to the business offering the foreign product and probably waive the $2,000 duty.

Exception #3 – Compliance with the Buy American Act Is Not in the Best Interest of the Government

1. The head of a federal department or agency (for example, the secretary of agriculture or administrator of the Environmental Protection Agency) can decide that the government's interest would best be served by waiving the Buy American Act. For example, the secretary of defense has decided that the application of the Buy American Act to the products of NATO allies and certain other allies is not in the public interest. Therefore, the Department of Defense does not apply evaluation factors to the products of these "qualifying countries" (see DFARS 225.872, Contracting with Qualifying Country Sources). The administrator of the National Aeronautics and Space Administration has exempted Canadian products (see NASA FAR Supplement 1825.103, Exceptions). (However, in 2017 President Donald Trump issued Executive Order 13788 which directed agencies to "comply with Buy American laws, to the extent they apply, and minimize the use of waivers".)

2. The United States Trade Representative has exempted civil aircraft and related articles produced by signatories to the **Agreement on Trade in Civil Aircraft** (see FAR 25.407, Agreement on Trade in Civil Aircraft).

Exception #4 – Items Are Not Mined, Produced, or Manufactured in the United States

No evaluation factors are applied to the foreign products listed in FAR 25.104, Nonavailable Articles; the price bid is the price evaluated. Some examples of foreign products under this exception are canned corned beef, cashew nuts, chrome ore, industrial diamonds, hog bristles for brushes, manganese, olive oil, platinum, rabbit fur pelt, shellac, raw sugar, swords and scabbards, tea, tin, vanilla beans, and cobra venom.

Exception #5 – Items Purchased for Commissary Resale

Commissaries can purchase specific brand names (for example, Sony televisions and Minolta cameras) for resale to military and other authorized personnel without concern for the Buy American Act. The reason is that commissary customers spend their own money and not the federal government's.

Construction Materials

FAR subpart 25.2 requires that **6%** be added to the offered price of foreign construction materials ("articles, materials, or supplies brought to the construction site by a contractor or subcontractor for incorporation into the building or work") when evaluating them against offered domestic construction materials for the construction, alteration, or repair of any public building in the U.S. However, FAR 25.204, Evaluating Offers of Foreign Construction Materials, authorizes the heads of federal departments and agencies to specify a *higher percentage*. Of course, those construction materials that are not mined, produced, or manufactured in the United States are already exempt from Buy American Act coverage (exception #4).

In addition, contracts for construction materials acquired from "designated countries" (see below) that exceed either **$7,358,000** or **$10,079,365** (depending on the threshold established in that country's agreement) are exempt from the Buy American Act. See FAR 25.402, General.

Commercial Information Technology

There is a blanket exemption to the provisions of the Buy American Act – commercial information technology ("any equipment, or interconnected system(s) or subsystem(s) of equipment, that is used in the automatic acquisition, storage, analysis, evaluation, manipulation, management, movement, control, display, switching, interchange, transmission, or reception of data or information by the agency" [FAR 2.101, Definitions]). Though the Buy American Act does not apply to commercial information technology, the provisions of the various trade agreements *do apply*, particularly the prohibition against the acquisition of "noneligible" commercial information technology products when "eligible" commercial information technology products are offered (see below).

THE TRADE AGREEMENTS

Over the years, the government has entered into many agreements with other countries to eliminate restrictive trade barriers. The Buy American Act is a restrictive trade barrier to foreign products, so the U.S. government agrees to waive its provisions in return for the reduction or elimination of the other countries' tariffs and their own "domestic content preference" programs.

There are several trade agreements currently in force. If an acquisition exceeds a particular trade agreement's threshold, the products of countries that have signed the trade agreements (**"designated countries"**) are exempt from the Buy American Act and their products, construction materials, and services are treated the same as "**U.S.-made end products**" ("an article that is mined, produced, or manufactured in the United States or that is substantially transformed in the United States into a new and different article of commerce with a name, character, or use distinct from that of the article or articles from which it was transformed") – these products of designated countries are called "**eligible products**." In addition, if an acquisition exceeds the applicable World Trade Organization Government Procurement Agreement threshold, and a U.S.-made end product or eligible product is offered, *noneligible products cannot be acquired no matter how good their prices may be!*

The following are the current trade agreements. Their thresholds, which are listed in FAR 25.402 and are revised about every two years to adjust for monetary fluctuations, are in parentheses.

- **U.S.-Israel Free Trade Area Agreement** (supplies: $50,000) (see FAR 25.406, Israeli Trade Act, for list of departments and agencies that are not subject to the Israeli Trade Act)

- **World Trade Organization Government Procurement Agreement** (supplies and services: $191,000; construction: $7,358,000) (see FAR 25.403, World Trade Organization Government Procurement Agreement and Free Trade Agreements, and "designated country" in FAR 25.003, Definitions, for participating countries) (**NOTE:** Congress has directed that "any country on the United Nations General Assembly list of least developed countries" be considered a "designated country." Therefore, the products of the "least developed countries" listed in the FAR 25.003 "designated country" definition [such as Bangladesh, Ethiopia, Madagascar, and Nepal] are treated the same as the products of Government Procurement Agreement signatories [such as Japan, the United Kingdom, Germany, and Switzerland].)

- **Caribbean Basin Trade Initiative** (supplies and services: $191,000; construction: $7,358,000) (see FAR 25.405, Caribbean Basin Trade Initiative, and "Caribbean Basin country" in FAR 25.003, Definitions, for participating countries)

- **North American FTA Implementation Act** (NAFTA) (Canadian supplies: $25,000; Canadian services, and Mexican supplies and services: $77,533; Canadian and Mexican construction: $10,079,365)

- **Australia FTA** (supplies and services: $77,533; construction: $7,358,000)

- **Bahrain FTA** (supplies and services: $191,000; construction: $10,079,365)

- **Central America FTA** (CAFTA) (supplies and services: $77,533; construction: $7,358,000)

- **Chile FTA** (supplies and services: $77,533; construction: $7,358,000)

- **Columbia FTA** (supplies and services: $77,533; construction: $7,358,000)

- **Korea FTA** (supplies and services: $100,000; construction: $7,358,000)

- **Morocco FTA** (supplies and services: $191,000; construction: $7,358,000)

- **Oman FTA** (supplies and services: $191,000; construction: $10,079,365)

- **Panama FTA** (supplies and services: $191,000; construction: $7,358,000)

- **Peru FTA** (supplies and services: $191,000; construction: $7,358,000)

- **Singapore FTA** (supplies and services: $77,533; construction: $7,358,000)

- **Agreement on Trade in Civil Aircraft** (all civil aircraft and related articles) (see FAR 25.407, Agreement on Trade in Civil Aircraft, for participating countries)

A few federal agencies have unique rules for implementing the trade agreements – for example, the U.S. Agency for International Development (USAID) and the Department of Energy.

For an item to be considered an eligible product, it must be (a) wholly grown, produced, or manufactured in a designated country, or (b) if the product contains materials or components from a country that is *not* a designated country, those materials or components must have been "*substantially transformed into a new and different article of commerce with a name, character, or use distinct from that of the article or articles from which it was so transformed*" (from the definitions of "World Trade Organization Government Procurement Agreement country end product," "least developed country end product," "Caribbean Basin country end product," and "Free Trade Agreement country end product" in FAR 25.003, Definitions).

Exemptions from Coverage of the Trade Agreements

The trade agreements do *not* apply to:

- Services in support of military services overseas;

- Research and development;

- Dredging;

- Transportation services;

- Utility services;

- Small business set-asides (because small businesses must agree to provide supplies produced by domestic manufacturers to be eligible for award – see Chapter 11);

- Defense-related purchases (however, DFARS 225.401-70, Products Subject to Trade Agreements, contains a list of all products the Department of Defense buys that it considers *non*-defense related and for which the trade agreements *apply*);

- Products acquired for resale; or

- Other products and services listed in FAR 25.401, Exceptions.

In addition, the Buy American Act is *always* applied to the following products from Caribbean Basin countries:

- Textiles and apparel articles; footwear, handbags, luggage, flat goods, work gloves, and leather wearing apparel; or handloomed, handmade, or folklore articles;

- Tuna, prepared or preserved in any manner in airtight containers;

- Petroleum, or any product derived from petroleum (except the Department of Defense); and

- Watches and watch parts (including cases, bracelets, and straps), of whatever type, including mechanical quartz digital or quartz analog.

Furthermore, paragraph (b)(2) of FAR 25.502, Application, permits agencies to give the same consideration to offers of U.S.-made end products that are not domestic end products as is given to eligible products. This provision allows agencies to eliminate the conflict between the definition of "domestic end product" under the Buy American Act (an end product manufactured in the United States with at least 50% of its cost is attributed to components mined, produced, or manufactured in the United States or its territories) and the definition of "U.S.-made end product" under the various trade agreements (a product with materials or components that have been substantially transformed in the United States into a new and different article of commerce).

The Trade Agreements Act (which implements the World Trade Organization Government Procurement Agreement) does not denote the United States as a "designated country" – that term is reserved for all the other signatories of the Agreement on Government Procurement. The Trade Agreements Act exempts "designated country end products" from the Buy American Act but, because the United States is not a "designated country," the Buy American Act applies to all "domestic end products." This conflict in terms (caused by sloppy treaty negotiations and legislative drafting) produces the following contradictory situation:

> The U.S. government solicits for bicycles worth $210,000 (exceeding the $191,000 threshold for the World Trade Organization Government Procurement Agreement), and it receives two bids: one offering Japanese bicycles made up of 100% Japanese components, and the other offering American bicycles made up of 40% American components and 60% Japanese components. Because the Japanese bicycles are "eligible products" (Japan is a "designated country" under the World Trade Organization Government Procurement Agreement), the Buy American Act evaluation

factor is not applied. However, 60% of the American bicycle consists of Japanese components, so it is not considered a "domestic end product" because it flunks the 50% domestic component test under the Buy American Act. Therefore, the Buy American Act evaluation factor is applied to the American bicycles with 60% Japanese components, but not to the Japanese bicycles with 100% Japanese components!

The Department of Defense and National Aeronautics and Space Administration have exercised the authority in FAR 25.502(b)(2), but most other agencies have not.

See FAR subpart 25.5, Evaluating Foreign Offers – Supply Contracts, particularly FAR 25.504, Evaluation Examples, for how the government applies the Buy American Act evaluation factors to products from signatories of the various trade agreements. See DFARS 225.502, Application, and DFARS 225.504, Evaluation Examples, for how the Department of Defense's procedures differ from the FAR's.

DEPARTMENT OF DEFENSE EXCEPTIONS

Over the years, Congress has placed many restrictions on the Department of Defense's ability to purchase foreign products. The restrictions fall into three categories: (1) firms owned or controlled by governments that support terrorism; (2) prohibited items; and (3) industrial mobilization items. See the referenced sections of the DFARS for more details on these exceptions.

Firms Owned or Controlled by Governments That Support Terrorism

The Department of Defense is prohibited from awarding any contract of **$150,000 or more** to any firm or subsidiary in which the governments of Iran, Sudan, or Syria have a significant ownership or management interest. See DFARS 225.771, Prohibition on Contracting or Subcontracting with a Firm that is Owned or Controlled by the Government of a Country that is a State Sponsor of Terrorism, and DFARS 252.225-7050, Disclosure of Ownership or Control by the Government of a Country that is a State Sponsor of Terrorism.

Prohibited Items

The Department of Defense must obtain the following items from domestic producers (or Canadian producers, for some items). Some of these items can be obtained from foreign producers under certain circumstances, such as when the acquisition does not exceed the simplified acquisition threshold. See the referenced DFARS section for further details on the requirements, restrictions, and exceptions.

- DFARS 225.7002, Restrictions on Food, Clothing, Fabrics, Specialty Metals, and Hand or Measuring Tools (called the "Berry Amendment")

- DFARS 225.7003, Restrictions on Acquisition of Specialty Metals

- DFARS 225.7004, Restriction on Acquisition of Foreign Buses

- DFARS 225.7005, Restriction on Certain Chemical Weapons Antidote

- DFARS 225.7006, Restriction on Air Circuit Breakers for Naval Vessels

- DFARS 225.7007, Restrictions on Anchor and Mooring Chain

- DFARS 225.7009, Restrictions on Ball and Roller Bearings

- DFARS 225.7010, Restriction on Certain Naval Vessel Components

- DFARS 225.7011, Restriction on Carbon, Alloy, and Armor Steel Plate

- DFARS 225.7012, Restriction on Supercomputers

- DFARS 225.7013, Restrictions on Construction or Repair of Vessels in Foreign Shipyards

- DFARS 225.7017, Utilization of Domestic Photovoltaic Devices

Industrial Mobilization Items

The Department of Defense is required to purchase the **U.S. defense mobilization items** listed in DFARS 225.7102, Forgings (that is, ship propulsion shafts, periscope tubes, and ring forgings for bull gears), *only* from U.S. and Canadian planned producers to ensure adequate supplies are available in case of a national emergency unless the purchase is less than the simplified acquisition threshold ($150,000) or the requirement is waived by the contracting officer (see the Chapter 3 explanation of the Competition in Contracting Act industrial mobilization exception to full and open competition, and FAR 6.302-3, Industrial Mobilization; Engineering, Developmental, or Research Capability; or Expert Services, for more on industrial mobilization).

Secondary Arab Boycott of Israel

The Department of Defense is prohibited from entering into any contract that exceeds the simplified acquisition threshold ($150,000) with a foreign entity unless it certifies that it does not comply with the secondary Arab boycott of Israel. The certification is in DFARS 252.225-7031, Secondary Arab Boycott of Israel, and the foreign entity certifies to this by submitting an offer.

This restriction does not apply to: (1) consumable supplies, provisions, or services for the support of U.S. forces or of allied forces in a foreign country; or (2) contracts pertaining to the use of any equipment, technology, data, or services for intelligence or classified purposes in the interest of national security. The secretary of defense can waive this restriction for national security reasons. (**NOTE:** The Department of State has a similar prohibition.)

CHAPTER 13

FEDERAL SUPPLY SCHEDULES

The General Services Administration (GSA) is dedicated to facilitating government operations through two "services": the **Public Building Service** (PBS), which manages the construction and operation of more than 9,500 government-owned and-leased buildings; and the **Federal Acquisition Service** (FAS), which makes available common supplies and services, helps government agencies to acquire innovative information technology solutions, manages vehicle purchasing and leasing, makes travel and transportation arrangements, and manages the government's personal property.

This chapter will concentrate on one of the FAS' more significant programs: the **Federal Supply Schedules** (which a misnomer since more than half of the money spent through these schedules are for services). The "schedules" (which are also called "multiple award schedules" and "GSA schedules") provide agencies with a simplified process for obtaining commercial supplies and services at prices associated with volume buying. In addition, this chapter will briefly describe two other types of contract vehicles that have been developed to streamline the federal acquisition process and make it more "business-like": **governmentwide acquisition contracts**, more commonly called "GWACs," which are similar to federal supply schedules except they are limited to information technology supplies and services and are awarded and administered by agencies selected by the Office of Management and Budget (OMB); and **multi-agency contracts** (MACs), which are task or delivery order contracts established by one agency for use by other government agencies.

THE FEDERAL SUPPLY SCHEDULE PROGRAM

The **Federal Supply Schedule** (FSS) program is a simplified process that closely mirrors commercial buying practices by using the buying power of the government to obtain volume discounts on more than **25,000,000 commonly used supplies and services** from more than **19,000 contractors**. About **$35 billion** worth of commercially-available supplies and services is purchased through the program each year – the government spends approximately **7%** of all its contract dollars through schedule contracts.

Schedules are groupings of similar supplies and services, and consist of **indefinite-delivery contracts** (see Chapter 10) that make available various of those supplies and services to all government agencies (and some federal contractors under certain circumstances – see FAR subpart 51.1, Contractor Use of Government Supply Sources). The number of contracts under a schedule range from fewer than a dozen to hundreds. The FAS negotiates fixed-prices for the supplies and services each contractor proposes to offer under the schedule (or hourly-rates for some services), and then publishes the prices on the **GSA eLibrary (http://www.gsaelibrary.gsa.gov**) so agencies can place orders for the discounted supplies and services directly with the schedule contractors. Orders may be place by written order, by telephone, or through **GSA** *Advantage!*®, GSA's on-line shopping and ordering system (**https://www. gsaadvantage.gov**).

FAR subpart 8.4, Federal Supply Schedules, and FAR part 38, Federal Supply Schedule Contracts, govern the operation and use of the schedule program (FAR subpart 8.4 prescribes procedures for ordering, and FAR part 38 prescribes procedures that GSA must follow when administering the FSS program). In addition, GSA has delegated authority to the Department of Veterans Affairs (VA) to establish its own schedules for medical supplies – FAR subpart 8.4 and FAR part 38 procedures apply to orders under VA schedules (which are responsible for annual sales of more than **$10 billion**).

The following are the schedules currently available (* indicates VA schedule):

03FAC	Facilities Maintenance and Management
23 V	Automotive Superstore
36	The Office, Imaging and Document Solution
48	Transportation, Delivery and Relocation Services
51 V	Hardware Superstore
56	Building and Building Materials/Industrial Services and Supplies
58 I	Professional Audio/Video Telemetry/Tracking, Recording/Reproducing and Signal Data Solutions
599	Travel Services Solutions
*621 I	Professional and Allied Healthcare Staffing Services
*621 II	Medical Laboratory Testing and Analysis Services
*65 I B	Pharmaceuticals and Drugs
*65 II A	Medical Equipment and Supplies
*65 II C	Dental Equipment and Supplies
*65 II F	Patient Mobility Devices (including Wheelchairs, Scooters, Walkers)

*65 V A	X-Ray Equipment and Supplies (including Medical and Dental X-Ray Film)
*65 VII	Invitro Diagnostics, Reagents, Test Kits and Test Sets
66	Scientific Equipment and Services
*66 III	Clinical Analyzers, Laboratory, Cost-Per-Test
67	Photographic Equipment – Cameras, Photographic Printers and Related Supplies & Services (Digital And Film-Based)
70	General Purpose Commercial Information Technology Equipment, Software, and Services
71	Furniture
71 II K	Comprehensive Furniture Management Services (CFMS)
72	Furnishings and Floor Coverings
73	Food Service, Hospitality, Cleaning Equipment and Supplies, Chemicals and Services
736	Temporary Administrative and Professional Staffing (TAPS)
738 X	Human Resources & Equal Employment Opportunity Services
75	Office Products/Supplies and Services and New Products/Technology
751	Leasing of Automobiles and Light Trucks
76	Publication Media
78	Sports, Promotional, Outdoor, Recreation, Trophies and Signs (SPORTS)
81 I B	Shipping, Packaging and Packing Supplies
84	Total Solutions for Law Enforcement, Security, Facilities Management, Fire, Rescue, Clothing, Marine Craft and Emergency/Disaster Response

In addition, there is schedule **00CORP, The Professional Services Schedule (PSS)**, which enables agencies to procure a wide variety of professional services using a single schedule (such as advertising, public relations, language, electronic commerce, engineering, and environmental services); and schedule **BPA, MAS Blanket Purchase Agreements**, which consists of a number of BPAs (see Chapter 6 and below) established under schedule contracts for selected products and services (such as paper products, cleaning equipment, paints, laptop and desktop computers, and "cloud" storage).

Though most FSS contracts are restricted to federal agencies (and contractors), state and local government entities are authorized to order information technology supplies and services through contracts on Schedule 70 and 00CORP, and law enforcement and emergency response supplies and services on Schedule 84. However, state and local government entities can order only from Schedule 70, 84, and 00CORP contractors that have agreed to allow them to order from their contracts. This is called "**cooperative purchasing**," and contracts that permit state and local government entities to place orders are identified with a "**COOP PURC**" icon on the **GSA eLibrary** and **GSA** *Advantage!*®.

In addition, state and local government entities are authorized to use *any* FSS contract to purchase supplies and services to facilitate recovery from major disasters, terrorism, or nuclear, biological, chemical, or radiological attacks. However, because FSS contracts must be modified to permit "**Disaster Recovery Purchasing**," state and local governments may use only those contracts that are identified with a "**DISAST RECOV**" icon on the **GSA eLibrary** and **GSA** *Advantage!*®.

Each schedule contains the information needed by agencies to place delivery orders directly with the schedule contractors: covered supplies or services, prices, contractors and their schedule contract numbers, minimum and maximum order sizes, and ordering instructions. A contractor's supplies or services **cannot** be included in a schedule unless the FAS awards it a schedule contract for those particular supplies or services.

There are several advantages in having supplies or services on a schedule contract:

- FAR 8.004, Use of Other Sources, declares it is government policy that the contracting officer, before soliciting commercial sources, determine if the required supplies or services are available from a schedule. If so, the contracting officer is *encouraged* to order from the schedule.

- Because an schedule contract remains in existence for at least **five years** (and, because they typically have three five-year options, the schedule contract can exist up to **20 years**), the schedule contractor's supplies or services are exposed to many government customers for many years.

- Because the FAS contracting officer awarding the schedule contract has already determined the prices of the supplies and services to be fair and reasonable, other contracting officers can place orders against the schedule contract without having to synopsize, solicit, evaluate, negotiate, and determine fair and reasonable prices. This means contracting officers can use schedule contracts to fulfill their agencies' needs quickly and with little effort.

- Because it is FAS policy to award schedules *only* if it anticipates government sales to exceed **$1,000,000** during a one-year period, a schedule contractor knows the FAS expects there will be substantial government demand for the supplies or services on the schedule.

- Contracting offices like to use schedule contracts because: (1) orders are not synopsized in **FedBizOpps**, so there are no corresponding delays (see paragraph (a) of FAR 8.404, Use of Federal Supply Schedules, for more on the prohibition); and (2) orders cannot be protested (except orders by the Department of Defense (DOD), the National Aeronautics and Space Administration (NASA), and the Coast Guard that exceed $10,000,000 – see paragraph (a)(10) of FAR 16.505, Ordering, for more on the prohibition, and Chapter 16 for more on protests). This means a contracting officer can place an order quickly, and his order-placement decision cannot be challenged by disgruntled contractors. In fact, because schedule orders are never synopsized, there are rarely any disgruntled contractors because *they never know about the order*.

However, having an FSS contract is no guarantee that the contractor will receive any orders. The government is under no obligation to order *any* supplies or services under an FSS contract. In fact, an FSS contractor must generate at least **$25,000** in sales during the first two years of the contract and $25,000 or more each year afterward to retain its contract.

Also, if a contractor's typical order is less than $25,000, there is little reason for obtaining an FSS contract because the contracting officer will not have to synopsize the under-$25,000 purchase in **FedBizOpps** (thus neutralizing one of the primary benefits reasons of the FSS contracts – speed), and the contracting officer will probably make the purchase using the simplified acquisition procedures in FAR part 13 (see Chapter 6).

Because of the FSS program's increased in popularity, each contractor should determine whether its supplies and services are bought under a schedule and, if so, decide whether it should pursue its own contract under the appropriate schedule.

The FSS program portal is **http://www.gsa.gov/schedules**.

Schedule Solicitations and Contracts

The schedule program covers *negotiated* contracts that are established with *more than one* supplier for delivery of *commercial* supplies or services. A schedule solicitation for each schedule is *always open*, so contractors seeking to obtain an FSS contract may submit an offer at any time – there is no closing date. The solicitations are always available for downloading from **FedBizOpps** – either look under the appropriate supply or service classification code or search for keywords (see Chapter 5).

The FAS awards several schedule contracts to firms providing the same generic types of supplies or services (such as computers, laboratory equipment, or records management). The variety of supplies or services under a typical schedule spans a broad price-range and has many different features and options. This selection allows government agencies to choose the supplies or services that meet their particular needs.

Prices in a schedule contract are based on discounts from the contractor's **commercial pricelist**, and the FAS seeks to obtain the offeror's **best discount** (that is, those extended to the contractor's *most favored customers*). However, the FAS recognizes that the terms and conditions of commercial sales vary among customers, and there may be legitimate reasons why the offeror cannot extend its best discount to the government – for example, the level of expected sales to the government is far below that of the offeror's largest customer.

The Solicitation

Because the FSS program is intended to make commercial supplies and services available to the government, the schedule solicitation is an RFP conducted in accordance with the procedures in FAR part 12, Acquisition of Commercial Items (see Chapter 6), and is posted on **FedBizOpps**. The FAS contracting officer places a cover page on the RFP ("Notice Concerning Solicitation") with information, general notices, and notices of significant changes to the schedule RFP since the last time it was issued. Following the cover page is the electronic version of the SF 1449, Solicitation/Contract/Order for Commercial Items, with the address to send proposals, the FAS point of contact, and similar information. Following the SF 1449 is the body of the solicitation, consisting of contract clauses, solicitation provisions, instructions for submittal of offers, representations and certifications that must be completed by offerors, attachments, and any other information that might be helpful to offerors (such as the quantities of supplies or services the FAS estimates the government will acquire under all the schedule contracts to be awarded).

The "Schedule of Supplies/Services" portion of the SF 1449 (blocks 19 though 24) usually refers offerors to an attached schedule which describes the supplies or services covered by the solicitation. In schedule RFPs, the supplies or services are grouped by **special item numbers** (SIN) and not line item numbers as with IFBs, RFPs, and RFQs. For example, a schedule RFP for publications might include separate SINs for almanacs, reference books, technical books, encyclopedias, and atlases. Since the point of a schedule is to allow government agencies to select from a wide range of commercial supplies or services, establishing SINs that describe the supplies or services in general terms permits businesses to offer any or all of their commercial products that come under the description. In its proposal, each offeror must identify the SIN (or SINs) that applies to each of its supplies or services. Also, this schedule contains the estimated governmentwide requirements for the supplies or services under each SIN. These estimates (in dollars) are based on the purchases of supplies or services under schedule contracts during the previous year.

The schedule RFP does *not* require compliance with any particular specifications because the FAS wants businesses to offer their commercial supplies or services, not custom-tailored products that meet detailed specifications.

The schedule RFP addresses many of the same concerns as solicitations under the uniform contract format (UCF) – packaging and marking, inspection and acceptance, deliveries or performance, contract administration data, and special contract requirements (including the FAR commercial items clauses 52.212-1, 52.212-3, 52.212-4, and 52.212-5 – see Chapters 6 and 7). The following are some of the more important schedule contract requirements (most of which are from the **GSA Acquisition Regulation** (GSAR), which is the gray-text portion of the **GSA Acquisition Manual** (GSAM), available at **https://www.acquisition.gov/?q=browsegsam**):

■ *Commercial Delivery Schedule (Multiple Award Schedule) (GSAR 552.211-78)*: Requires the schedule contractor to deliver items to the government within the contractor's normal commercial delivery time as long as it is *less* than the "stated" delivery time specified in the clause.

■ *Preparation of Offer (Multiple Award Schedule) (GSAR 552.212-70)*: This requires each offeror to provide the following information for each SIN:

    a. Two copies of the offeror's current published commercial descriptive catalogs and/or price lists from which discounts are offered.

    b. The discounts offered.

    c. A description of any additional discounts offered (such as prompt payment discounts or quantity discounts [making sure to indicate whether different models within the same SIN or different SINs can be combined to earn the quantity discounts]).

    d. A description of concessions offered to the government which are not offered to other customers (such as extended warranties, a return/exchange goods policy, or additional services).

    e. If the offeror is a dealer or reseller (or the offeror will use dealers or resellers), the functions the dealer or reseller will perform.

■ *Contract Terms and Conditions Applicable to GSA Acquisition of Commercial Items (GSAR 552.212-71)*: Like its counterpart at FAR 52.212-4, Contract Terms and Conditions – Commercial Items, this lists 22 GSAR clauses. The contracting officer is to check the clauses that apply (or delete those that do not apply). The following are some of the more significant clauses that the contracting officer normally checks:

    a. **Examination of Records by GSA (Multiple Award Schedule) (GSAR 552.215-71)**: This permits the contracting officer or any duly authorized representative to examine all books, documents, papers, or records of the contractor's involving transactions under the contract for overbillings, billing errors, compliance with the Price Reductions clause (see below), and compliance with the Industrial Funding Fee clause (see below).

       While this clause is intended to be used to examine *post-award* records and data, the contracting officer may modify the clause to permit access to *pre-award* records and data to verify that the information provided by the contractor to support its proposal was accurate, current, and complete. However, the contracting officer may modify this clause *only* after deciding there is a *likelihood of significant harm to the government* without access to the information *and the senior procurement executive approves.*

b. **Price Adjustment – Failure to Provide Accurate Information (GSAR 552.215-72)**: If, after award of the schedule contract, the contracting officer discovers (1) the information provided by the contractor to support its proposal was not complete, accurate, or current, or (2) the contractor did not disclose to the contracting officer changes to its commercial prices or discount practices that took place after the proposal was submitted but before completion of negotiations, the contracting officer can *unilaterally reduce the contract price* by the amount the contract price was *increased* because of the government's reliance on the deficient information (subject to an appeal under the Disputes clause – see Chapter 18). In addition, the contract may be terminated for default (see Chapter 18).

c. **Industrial Funding Fee and Sales Reporting (GSAR 552.238-74)**: This clause requires contractors to remit **0.75% of total sales** to GSA each contract quarter – similar to a 0.75% sales tax. The industrial funding fee (IFF), which is set by GSA and posted at **https://72a.gsa.gov/iffrates.cfm**, is to help reimburse FAS for operating the schedule program. The clause requires offerors to include the 0.75% IFF in their proposed prices so it can be reflected in the award prices that will be charged the ordering activities.

d. **Price Reductions (GSAR 552.238-75)**: This requires the schedule contractor to maintain the government's price or discount advantage in relation to the price or discount offered by the contractor to its commercial customers. In other words, if the contractor reduces the price of an item to its commercial customers and the item is on a schedule contract, it must reduce the price of the item on the schedule contract similarly.

The Price Reduction clause does not prohibit the contractor from offering a one-time spot discount or special sale price to a federal agency, nor does it prohibit the contractor from offering sale prices to its commercial customers as long as the contractor extends the price reduction to the schedule contract for the duration of the sale.

Modifications proposing price reductions must be submitted through **eMod**, which enables contractors to prepare and submit electronic contract modifications for all existing FSS contracts. eMod is part of the **eOffer** system (see "Submitting the Proposal" below).

NOTE: Every time an FSS contract is modified to incorporate price reductions, the contractor must update its FSS contract information in **GSA Advantage!®**.

NOTE: When participating in a reverse auction (see below), the Price Reductions clause does *not* apply to discounts granted to the federal agency during the auction – see paragraph (d)(2) of the clause.

NOTE: GSA is conducting a pilot program in which the price reduction clause and the "Commercial Sales Practices Format" (see below) are replaced by the electronic reporting of "transactional data" (such as descriptions of goods or services acquired, part numbers, quantities, and prices paid) for each order. The duration of the pilot program, and whether it is expanded to all FSS contracts, will depend on how well this information enables GSA to ensure FSS contractors' offered prices are competitive relative to other contractors selling the same or similar items or services.

The transactional data reporting would be reflected in a new Alternate I to GSAR 552.238-74, Industrial Funding Fee and Sales Reporting (see above), and a new Alternate I to GSAR 552.238-75.

The pilot involves the following eight schedules and SINs that account for more than 40% of the FSS sales volume:

- Schedule 03FAC, Facilities Maintenance and Management: All SINs
- Schedule 51 V, Hardware Superstore: All SINs
- Schedule 58 I, Professional Audio/Video, Telemetry/Tracking, Recording/Reproducing and Signal Data Solutions: All SINs
- Schedule 72, Furnishing and Floor Coverings: All SINs
- Schedule 73, Food Service, Hospitality, Cleaning Equipment and Supplies, Chemicals and Services: All SINs
- Schedule 75, Office Products: All SINs
- Schedule 00CORP, The Professional Services Schedule: Professional Engineering Services (PES) SINs
- Schedule 70, General Purpose Information Technology Equipment, Software, and Services: SINs 132 8 (Purchase of New Equipment); 132 32, 132 33, and 132 34 (Software); and 132 54 and 132 55 (Commercial Satellite Communications [COMSATCOM])

Initially, participation in the pilot program will be voluntary for FSS contractors with FSS contracts in the schedules/SINs, but they will be encouraged to participate by executing a bilateral modification with GSA. The new reporting clause and corresponding pricing disclosure changes will be applied to newly-awarded FSS contracts in the pilot Schedules/SINs and existing FSS contracts when they are up for renewal/extension.

FSS contracts managed by the Department of Veterans Affairs (VA) are not participating in the pilot program and will not be affected by it.

e. **Modifications (Federal Supply Schedule) (GSAR 552.238-81):** Explains procedures to use, and information to provide, when (1) requesting that additional items or additional SINs be added to the contract, (2) deleting items from the contract, and (3) price reductions are involved (see above). Modifications must be submitted through **eMod**, which is part of the **eOffer** system (see "Submitting the Proposal" below).

　　NOTE: Every time an FSS contract is modified, the contractor must update its FSS contract information in **GSA** *Advantage!*®.

　　f.　**Warranty – Multiple Award Schedule (GSAR 552.246-73)**: This clause states that the contractor's standard commercial warranty will apply to the contract unless otherwise specified in the contract.

■　*Evaluation – Commercial Items (Multiple Award Schedule) (GSAR 552.212-73)*: This clause is to be used instead of FAR 52.212-2, Evaluation Factors. It states that awards may be made to responsible offerors that offer reasonable pricing and will be "most advantageous to the government, taking into consideration . . . the differences in performance required to accomplish or produce required end results, production and distribution facilities, price, compliance with delivery requirements, and other pertinent factors."

■　*Economic Price Adjustment – FSS Multiple Award Schedule Contracts (GSAR 552.216-70)*: This clause specifies the conditions under which a schedule contractor can increase its prices on a schedule contract (price reductions are governed by the Price Reductions clause and may be made at any time). There are **five** conditions:

　　1.　The price increase request must be at least **12 months** after commencement of the contract.

　　2.　The increases must result from a reissue or modification of the contractor's commercial catalog or pricelist that was the basis for the contract award.

　　3.　The contractor may not request more than **three** increases during each succeeding 12-month period.

　　4.　At least **30** days must elapse between increase requests.

　　5.　The contractor may not request an increase during the last **60** days of the contract period.

In addition, the clause establishes the maximum percentage increase permissible during a 12-month period. This maximum percentage is subject to negotiation, but is usually no more than 10%.

　　Proposed economic price adjustments must be submitted through **eMod**, which is part of the **eOffer** system (see "Submitting the Proposal" below).

■ *Blanket Purchase Agreements (I-FSS-646):* BPAs are permitted under all schedule contracts, and schedule contractors must agree to enter into BPAs with ordering activities (see Chapter 6 and below).

■ *Contract Price Lists (I-FSS-600):* The schedule contractor must submit contract data electronically in a prescribed format. In addition, the contractor must prepare a paper FSS price list in a prescribed format, then print and distribute it.

■ *GSA Advantage!® (I-FSS-597):* Schedule contractors are *required* to participate in the **GSA** *Advantage!®*, which is GSA's online shopping and ordering system. The clause directs the contractor to refer to GSAR 552.238-71, Submission and Distribution of Authorized GSA Schedule Pricelists (which provides for the submission of pricelists on a common-use electronic medium), I-FSS-600, Contract Pricelists (which provides information on electronic contract data), and GSAR 552.243-81, Modifications (Federal Supply Schedule) (which addresses electronic file updates).

   NOTE: Every time an FSS contract is modified, the contractor must update its FSS contract information in **GSA** *Advantage!®*.

■ *Contractor Team Arrangements (I-FSS-40):* Schedule contractors are authorized to enter into team arrangements with other schedule contractors to provide solutions that they may not be able to provide on their own (see FAR subpart 9.6, Contractor Team Arrangements). Contractors participating in contractor team arrangements must abide by all terms and conditions of their respective schedule contracts.

■ *Option to Extend the Term of the Contract (Evergreen) (I-FSS-163):* This permits the government to exercise, up to three times, an option to extend the contract for an additional **five years** "when it is determined that exercising the option is advantageous to the government considering price and other factors." Exercising all three options would extend the term of the schedule contract to *20 years.*

Disclosure of Commercial Sales Practices

Besides having to submit the information required by GSAR 552.212-70, Preparation of Offer (Multiple Award Schedule) (see above), schedule offerors are required to disclose their commercial sales practices. This information helps the contracting officer develop his negotiation objectives. (*See the "note" to GSAR 552.238-75, Price Reductions [above], regarding a pilot program that replaces, for an indeterminate time, the commercial sales practices with electronic "transactional data" reporting on selected schedules.*)

As mentioned in Chapter 8, offerors must submit cost or pricing data to support proposed prices over $700,000 unless the prices are either:

- The result of adequate competition;

- Of commercial items; or

- Set by law or regulation.

The purpose of the schedule program is to offer a wide variety of commercial products. Therefore, schedule contracts are not necessarily awarded to the lowest offeror. Since very few commercial products have their prices set by law or regulation, the schedule offerors are asked:

- To provide information that demonstrates the offered prices of the supplies or services under each SIN are reasonable (such as competitor contracts, historical pricing, and currently available pricing in other venues).

- The dollar value of sales to the general public during the previous 12 months (or the previous fiscal year).

- Whether the discounts being offered the government are equal to or better than the offeror's best discount to *any customer regardless of quantity or terms and conditions.*

- To provide an estimate of the total sales the offeror expects to make to the government for the supplies or services under each SIN during the term of the contract.

Then, to support this information, each offeror must complete a **Commercial Sales Practices Format (CSP-1)** for each SIN (or group of SINs for which the information is the same):

Column 1- Customer	Column 2- Discount	Column 3- Quantity/ Volume	Column 4- F.O.B. Term	Column 5- Concessions

If the offeror states that the discounts it is offering the government are equal to or better than the offeror's best discount to any customer, it must provide the information required by the Commercial Sales Practices Format for the customer that received the best discount. If the offeror states that the discounts are *not* equal to or better than those given other customers, it must complete the Commercial Sales Practices Format for *all the customers or customer categories* that receive better discounts (the offeror is to use as many lines as necessary). In either case, if the offeror's discount practices vary by model or product line, the discount information should be by model or product line. The offeror may limit this information to those models or product lines which the offeror expects to account for **75%** of the sales per SIN.

If the offeror's discounts or discount policies change after the offer is submitted but before the close of negotiations, the offeror must disclose the revised discounts or discount policies to the contracting officer.

The following is the information required in each column of the Commercial Sales Practices Format:

■ **Column 1 – Identify the Applicable Customer or Category of Customer.** A customer is defined as "any entity, except the federal government, which acquires supplies or services from the offeror. The term 'customer' includes, but is not limited to, original equipment manufacturers, value added resellers, state and local governments, distributors, educational institutions ... dealers, national accounts, and end users." The offeror may disclose information by category of customer if the offeror's discount policies are the same for all customers in the category.

■ **Column 2 – Identify the Discount.** The term "discount" is as defined in GSAR 552.212-70, Preparation of Offer (Multiple Award Schedule) (see above): "A reduction to catalog prices (published or unpublished). Discounts include, but are not limited to, rebates, quantity discounts, purchase option credits, and any other terms or conditions which reduce the amount of money a customer ultimately pays for goods or services ordered or received. Any net price lower than the list price is considered a discount ... "

The offeror must indicate the best discount at which it sells to the customer or category of customer in column 1 *without regard to quantity, terms and conditions of the agreements under which the discounts are given, or whether the agreements are oral or written.* The discounts should be expressed as percentage discounts from the price list that is the basis of the offer.

■ **Column 3 – Identify the Quantity or Volume of Sales.** The offeror is to insert the *minimum quantity* or *sales volume* which the identified customer or category of customer must purchase or order (per order or within a specified period) to earn the discount.

■ **Column 4 – Indicate the F.O.B. Delivery Term for Each Identified Customer.** The f.o.b. delivery terms are explained in FAR 47.303, Standard Delivery Terms and Contract Clauses.

■ **Column 5 – Indicate Concessions Regardless of Quantity Granted to the Identified Customer or Category of Customer.** The term "concession" is as defined in GSAR 552.212-70: "a benefit, enhancement or privilege (other than a discount), which either reduces the overall costs of a customer's acquisition or encourages a customer to consummate a purchase. Concessions include, but are not limited to, freight allowance, extended warranty, extended price guarantees, free installation, and bonus goods."

With this information, the contracting officer will attempt to establish negotiation objectives and determine the price reasonableness of the offer. If the contracting officer needs additional information, he will restrict his request to information needed to establish the reasonableness of the offered price.

Submitting the Proposal

FSS proposals are required to be submitted to the FAS through GSA's **eOffer** system (**http://eoffer.gsa.gov**). It is an "interactive, secure electronic environment that simplifies the contracting process from submission of proposal to awards." To enter eOffer, the offeror must "download and read the solicitation that you want to make an offer against, and complete the required documents for the solicitation. Once this is completed you can enter the eOffer application, prepare the responses to the offer, and submit your proposal."

Before a person can access eOffer, he must obtain a digital certificate that authenticates his identity and verifies that he is has working relationship with the offeror (as employee, agent, etc.). This digital certificate, which is installed on the person's computer, takes between 7 and 14 days to be issued after the required paperwork is notarized and submitted. A digital certificate must be renewed/updated every two years. There are two companies that GSA authorizes to grant digital certificates: IdenTrust (**http://www.identrust.com/gsa/index.html**) and Operational Research Consultants (**https://aces.orc.com/**).

NOTE: Part of eOffer is **eMod**, which permits FSS contractors to submit to FAS proposed changes to their FSS contracts (such as additions, deletions, pricing changes, technical changes, and administrative changes). eOffer is used before the FSS contract is awarded, and eMod is used after the FSS contract is awarded. Also, every time a contract is modified through eMod, the contractor must update its FSS contract information in **GSA** *Advantage!*® – the two systems are separate.

Evaluating Schedule Proposals

The FAS contracting officer checks each FSS proposal in the same manner as any other response to an RFP. He:

- Confirms that the Standard Form 1449 has been signed by an authorized representative of the offeror and dated (blocks 30a, 30b, and 30c);

- Establishes that the offeror is proposing supplies and services that are being solicited and that the appropriate SIN has been identified for each supply or service;

- Verifies that all the representations and certifications have been completed;

- Makes sure the required pricelists or catalogs have been submitted; and

- Reviews the Commercial Sales Practices Format to insure all required information has been provided and there are no inconsistencies in the answers to similar questions.

If the offeror failed to respond properly or its response is inadequate, the contracting officer will request that the offeror correct any deficiencies.

To prepare for negotiations, the contracting officer will conduct a price analysis of the proposal. Since the goal of the schedule program is to obtain discounts equal to or better than the offeror's discounts to its commercial customers, the contracting officer must try to quantify the differences between the terms and conditions offered the government and the offeror's commercial customers. Differences in warranties, sales volume, transportation costs, and similar factors must be taken into account by the contracting officer. Most of this information, with an explanation and reasons for any differences, is provided by the offeror in the Commercial Sales Practices Format. If the contracting officer needs additional information, he will seek "data other than cost or pricing data" (see Chapter 8). Only if the contracting officer makes a written determination that the pricing information is inadequate for performing a price analysis and determining price reasonableness will he direct the offeror to provide "cost or pricing data" This is a *last resort*.

Once the contracting officer has conducted his price analysis, he will conduct negotiations with the offeror. They will discuss the differences between the discounts and terms offered to the government and to the offeror's commercial customers, the comparability of commercial and projected government sales volumes, the limitation on the amount of economic price adjustment during any 12-month period, terms of the warranty, and other matters as appropriate.

Upon completion of the negotiations, the contracting officer must determine that the negotiated prices are fair and reasonable. If the negotiated prices are fair and reasonable and are equal to or better than those offered commercial customers, and the offeror is responsible, the contracting officer prepares and awards the schedule contract. If the negotiated prices (considering discounts, concessions, and other factors) are fair and reasonable but not equal to or better than the prices offered to commercial customers purchasing under circumstances comparable to the government's, the contracting officer has two choices: (1) reject the offer if the rejection will not have an adverse effect on meeting the government's needs, or (2) decide that award of the schedule contract is in the *best interest of the government*, and justify that decision in writing.

After Winning the Schedule Contract

Once an offeror receives a schedule contract (and thus becomes a schedule contractor), it must distribute printed catalogs or pricelists to *all* contracting officers on the mailing list furnished by the contracting office as required by GSAR 552.238-71, Submission and Distribution of Authorized FSS Schedule Pricelists. The contractor must accomplish this within **15 calendar days** prior to the beginning of the contract period or within **30 calendar days** after the FAS contracting officer gives his approval for printing, whichever is later. As an alternative, the contractor can notify all contracting offices on the contracting officer's mailing list of the contract award and ask them to return a self-addressed, postpaid return envelope or postcard if they want a copy of the catalog or pricelist. In addition, schedule contractors are *required* to place their schedule prices on **GSA *Advantage!*®** and accept electronic orders.

Ordering

Contracting officers throughout the government (as well as micro-purchasers and commercial purchase card holders within their purchase authority – see Chapter 6) are authorized to place orders with schedule contractors to fulfill their agencies' needs as follows:

- If the order will be **at or below the micro-purchase threshold** ($3,500; $5,000 for the Department of Defense), the person placing the order can place it with *any* schedule contractor that can meet the agency's needs because GSA has already negotiated the prices and determined them to be fair and reasonable. Orders should be distributed among schedule contractors.

- If the order will **exceed the micro-purchase threshold but not the simplified acquisition threshold** ($150,000), and is for **supplies** or for **services that do not require a statement of work** (that is, the service is at a fixed price for the performance of a specific task, such as installation, maintenance, and repair), the person placing the order must: (1) survey at least **three FSS contractors** through **GSA *Advantage!*®**; (2) review the catalogs or pricelists of at least **three FSS contractors**, or (3) request quotations from at least **three FSS contractors**. Then the person is to place the order with the contractor that can provide the supply or service that represents the best value.
  When determining best value, the person placing the order may consider the following factors in addition to price:

  - Past performance

  - Special features of the supply or service required for effective performance

- Trade-in considerations

- Probably life of the item as compared with that of similar items

- Warranties

- Maintenance availability

- Environmental and energy efficiency considerations

- Delivery terms

NOTE: These procedures also apply to the establishment of blanket purchase agreements (BPAs) that are not expected to exceed the simplified acquisition threshold and are for supplies or for services that do not require a statement of work. See below for more the establishment of BPAs under FSS contracts.

■ If the order will **exceed the simplified acquisition threshold** and is for **supplies** or for **services that do not require a statement of work**, the contracting officer placing the order must prepare a Request for Quotations (RFQ – see Chapter 6) that includes a description of the supplies to be delivered or the services to be performed and the basis upon which the selection will be made (the same "best value" factors that may be considered on orders between the micro-purchase and simplified acquisition thresholds – see above). The contracting officer must either: (1) post the RFQ on **eBuy** (GSA's online RFQ system – **https://www.ebuy.gsa.gov/advantage/ebuy/start_page.do**) "to afford all schedule contractors offering the required supplies or services under the appropriate multiple award schedule(s) an opportunity to submit a quote"; or (2) provide the RFQ to as many schedule contractors as "practicable…to reasonably ensure that quotes will be received from at least three contractors that can fulfill the requirements." Once the quotations are received and evaluated in accordance with the selection criteria specified in the RFQ, the contracting officer places the order with the FSS contractor offering the best value.

  NOTE: These procedures also apply to the establishment of blanket purchase agreements (BPAs) that are expected to exceed the simplified acquisition threshold and are for supplies or for services that do not require a statement of work. See below for more the establishment of BPAs under FSS contracts.

■ If the order will **exceed the micro-purchase threshold but not the simplified acquisition threshold**, and is for **services that require a statement of work** (SOW – see Chapter 4) (such services are typically priced at hourly rates), the person placing the order must prepare an RFQ containing the SOW and evaluation criteria (which can include the "best value" factors that may be considered on orders between the micro-purchase and simplified acquisition thresholds for supplies or for services that do not require a statement of work – see above), and (1) provide it to at least three FSS contractors that offer services that will meet the agency's needs; or (2) post it on **eBuy**. The ordering activity evaluates all responses using the evaluation criteria in the RFQ, considering the level of effort and the mix of labor proposed to perform the work, then places the order with the FSS contractor offering the best value.

NOTE: These procedures also apply to the establishment of blanket purchase agreements (BPAs) that are not expected to exceed the simplified acquisition threshold and are for services that require a statement of work. See below for more the establishment of BPAs under FSS contracts.

■ If the order will **exceed the simplified acquisition threshold** and will be for **services that require an SOW**, the contracting officer must prepare an RFQ containing the SOW and evaluation criteria (which can include the "best value" factors that may be considered on orders between the micro-purchase and simplified acquisition thresholds for supplies or for services that do not require a statement of work). Once the RFQ is prepared, the contracting must either: (1) post it on **eBuy**; or (2) provide it to as many schedule contractors as "practicable...to reasonably ensure that quotes will be received from at least three contractors that can fulfill the requirements." Once the quotations are received and evaluated in accordance with the evaluation criteria specified in the RFQ (including the level of effort and the mix of labor proposed to perform the task(s) being ordered), the contracting officer places the order with the FSS contractor offering the best value.

NOTE: These procedures also apply to the establishment of blanket purchase agreements (BPAs) that are expected to exceed the simplified acquisition threshold and are for services that require a statement of work. See below for more the establishment of BPAs under FSS contracts.

■ *Sole Source Orders*: For orders exceeding the micro-purchase threshold, a contracting officer is permitted to order from a sole source schedule contractor if he justifies the purchase in writing. The circumstances that may justify such action are: (1) an urgent and compelling need exists, and following the procedures would result in unacceptable delays; (2) only one source is capable of providing the supplies or services required at the level of quality required because the supplies or services are unique or highly specialized; or (3) in the interest of economy and efficiency, the new work is a logical follow-on to an original FSS order provided the original FSS order was placed in accordance with the applicable FSS ordering procedures – the original order cannot have been previously issued under sole-source procedures.

If the order **exceeds $700,000**, the ordering activity's advocate for competition (see Chapter 2) must approve the justification. If the order **exceeds $13,500,000**, the head of the contracting activity (see Chapter 2) must approve the justification. If the order **exceeds $68,000,000** ($93,000,000 for the Department of Defense, the National Aeronautics and Space Administration, and the Coast Guard), the agency's senior procurement executive (see Chapter 2) must approve the justification.

■ *Small Business Consideration*: FAR 8.404, Use of Federal Supply Schedules, specifically states that the procedures of FAR part 19, Small Business Programs, do not apply to orders placed against schedule contracts. That means the "rule of two" (see Chapter 11), which requires the contracting officer to set aside a purchase whenever two or more small businesses (or HUBZone small businesses, women-owned small businesses, service-disabled veteran-owned small businesses, etc.) are capable of performing the contract, *does not apply to FSS purchases.* However, FAR 8.405-5, Small Business, states that the contracting officer may, *at his discretion*, set aside orders for any of the various types of small businesses: HUBZone, 8(a), service-disabled veteran-owned, women-owned, economically disadvantaged women-owned, or any other small business concerns.

This allows a contracting officer to send an FSS RFQ to small business schedule contractors *only*, or to review the catalogs of HUBZone women-owned small businesses *only*. It is up to the contracting officer to decide which catalogs to review or which FSS contractors to solicit.

Even if the contracting officer decides to compete an order among FSS contractors, paragraph (c) of FAR 8.405-5, Small Business, states he "may consider socio-economic status when identifying contractor(s) for consideration or competition for award of an order. At a minimum, ordering activities should consider, if available, at least one small business, veteran-owned small business, service disabled veteran-owned small business, HUBZone small business, women-owned small business, or small disadvantaged business schedule contractor(s)."

GSA *Advantage!*® and **GSA eLibrary (http://www.gsaelibrary.gsa. gov/)** contain information on the small business representations of FSS contractors.

■ Ordering activities may request a price reduction at any time before placing an order. However, the ordering activity *must* seek a price reduction when the order exceeds the simplified acquisition threshold. A price reduction made in response to such a request does not invoke the Price Reductions clause (see above). Of course, an FSS contractor is under no obligation to agree to any such reduction.

Once the person placing the order has decided which FSS contractor will provide the best value for supply or service being purchased, he issues the order (1) orally; (2) on an Optional Form 347, Order for Supplies or Services (see Chapter 6); (3) on an agency-prescribed form; or (4) on an electronic order form or other electronic communications format (such as **GSA *Advantage!*®**). When the FSS contractor receives the order, it delivers the supplies or performs the services and bills the government. It's that simple (almost)!

Blanket Purchase Agreements (BPAs): To further simplify the ordering process and reduce costs, GSA encourages ordering activities and FSS contractors to establish BPAs for repetitive needs of the same or similar supplies or services (see Chapter 6 for more on BPAs). The BPA might cover a single supply or service, a single product line, or supplies or services the FSS contractor might have on several different schedules. BPAs may be established with multiple FSS contractors for the same supplies or services – orders exceeding the micro-purchase threshold must be solicited among several BPA holders as established in the BPA ordering procedures. In determining how many multiple-award BPAs to establish (or whether a single BPA is appropriate), the ordering activity's contracting officer seeking to establish the BPAs considers: (1) the scope and complexity of the requirements; (2) the benefits of ongoing competition and the need to periodically compare multiple technical approaches or prices; (3) the administrative costs of BPAs; and (4) the technical qualifications of the schedule contractors.

When soliciting for the establishment of BPAs, the ordering activity's contracting officer uses the same procedures used for competing orders under FSS contracts, as appropriate (see above): survey at least three FSS contractors through **GSA *Advantage!*®**, or review the catalogs or pricelists of at least three FSS contractors, or prepare an RFQ and post it on **eBuy** or provide it to as many FSS contractors as "practicable." Upon receiving the quotations and evaluating them as specified in the RFQ, the ordering activity's contracting officer establishes BPAs with the FSS contractors that represent the best value.

At the discretion of the ordering activity's contracting officer, BPAs may be set aside for small businesses, 8(a) firms, HUBZone small businesses, service-disabled veteran-owned small businesses, women-owned small businesses, and economically disadvantaged women-owned small businesses.

Ordering activities may request a price reduction at any time before establishing a BPA. However, the ordering activity *must* seek a price reduction when the BPA exceeds the simplified acquisition threshold. A price reduction made in response to such a request does not invoke the Price Reductions clause (see above). Of course, an FSS contractor is under no obligation to agree to any such reduction.

Authorized personnel can place orders orally (either providing the government purchase card number or having the contractor submit a summary invoice at the end of the month for payment); issue an OF 347; issue an order on an agency-prescribed form; or place an electronic order.

For more on FSS BPAs, see FAR 8.405-3, Blanket Purchase Agreements (BPAs).

Marketing

Since it is relatively easy for agencies to order supplies or services through the FSS, many contractors make the mistake of thinking that "getting on the schedule" guarantees orders. While this may be true for some well-established contractors with popular products, this is *not* true for most FSS contractors. Basically, an FSS contract is nothing but a "hunting license" – there is no guarantee the contractor will receive any orders. Granted, an FSS contract makes it easier for contracting officers to order a contractor's supplies or services. However, the same kinds of supplies and services on one schedule contract are probably on several other schedule contracts, too.

The schedule contractor must make the government contracting offices aware that its supplies or services are on an FSS contract and are *quickly available* to fulfill the government's needs or solve its problems. That means **marketing** to the government: identifying likely customers (see Chapter 5), talking to the right people in those contracting offices (see Chapter 2), and identifying one's company as an FSS contractor.

The following are some ways that GSA suggests an FSS contractor should make its existence known:

- Add its website address to the front of its approved FSS contract price list

- Provide direct links to its website through **GSA *Advantage!*®**

- Use the **Federal Procurement Data Systems** (FPDS) (**https://www.fpds.gov**) "to identify who bought what, from whom, for how much, when and where. The site contains both simple and advanced searches and different reports that you may find useful" (see Chapter 5)

- Get information about **GSA *Advantage!*®** sales from the **GSA Advance Spend Analysis Program (https://www.asap.gsa.gov/asap/welcome.do)**

- Check agencies' procurement forecasts at **https://www.acquisition.gov/procurement-forecasts**

- Use the GSA star mark logo in advertising. It is available at **http://www.gsa.gov/logos**

- Utilize the information in the GSA Vendor Support Center at **https://vsc.gsa.gov/**

This may be all that is needed if the contractor's prices are lower than those of all similar supplies or services that are on schedule contracts and meet the government's requirements. However, if the schedule contractor's prices are not the *lowest*, the contracting officer cannot order from the contractor's schedule contract *unless* he determines that purchasing the higher priced supply or service is justified. Examples of reasons justifying a higher price are:

- The schedule contractor with the lowest priced supply or service cannot meet the government's required delivery schedule

- The government may have specific or unusual requirements that cannot be satisfied by the lowest priced supply or service

- The government requires compatibility with existing equipment or systems

- Trade-in considerations favor the higher priced item and produce the lowest net cost

- The government may require the special features of a higher priced item that are not available on comparable items

An FSS contractor should *always* find out which supplies or services on other schedule contracts are similar to its own and identify the differences. Under any SIN are a range of supplies or services – some very plain and bare-bones, some very elaborate and technical. The needs of some agencies will be satisfied by the most basic supplies or services; the specialized needs of other agencies will require the more complex or higher quality supplies or services. Therefore, when making a marketing call, the FSS contractor needs to determine the agency's needs and tailor its presentation accordingly. The FSS contractor can either (1) assert that its supplies or services have the lowest prices of any that will meet the agency's requirements (supported by appropriate statistics and performance data), or (2) point out the differences between its supplies and services and those with lower prices, and explain how those differences justify the higher price. It is definitely easier to make a sale stressing price, but many have been successful emphasizing quality and unique features. Ultimately, the decision is the contracting officer's (along with all the other government personnel involved in the process).

Postaward Audits

A schedule contractor is subject to **postaward audits**. These audits are to insure the contractor complied with the terms and conditions of the schedule contract. Typically, the government auditors try to determine whether:

■ Agencies that place orders against the schedule contract receive the discounts to which they are entitled;

■ Ordering agencies receive all price reductions to which they are entitled;

■ Reports submitted to GSA of the orders received by the contractor are accurate; and

■ The offeror is paying all the industrial funding fees it collects.

Each schedule contract contains GSAR 552.215-71, Examination of Records by GSA (Multiple Award Schedule) (see above). This clause gives the contracting officer or his representative (usually an auditor) the authority to examine the contractor's records throughout contract performance and for **three years after final payment**.

If the contracting officer or the auditor discovers overbillings, billing errors, or other "irregularities," the contracting officer has the right to withhold monies and demand refunds. If the contracting officer suspects fraud is involved, he may forward the matter to the Department of Justice for investigation and possible prosecution. In addition, the contracting officer may terminate the contract, initiate suspension and debarment proceedings, and take other administrative actions as necessary. (See Chapter 7 for more on suspension and debarment, Chapter 17 for more on fraud, and Chapter 18 for more on contract termination.)

GSA Global Supply

Besides the schedule program, the FAS maintains a depot system in which approximately **400,000** items such as paint, tools, office supplies, office furniture, tires, and batteries are stored around the country and shipped to government agencies when needed. The FAS uses standard IFB, RFP, and simplified acquisition procedures to replenish its inventory when the supply drops below the reorder level. This system is called the **GSA Global Supply**, and orders can be placed on its website at **https://www.gsaglobalsupply.gsa.gov** or through **GSA** *Advantage!*®. Though the FAS operates GSA Global Supply, it is **not** a part of the schedule program.

GWACs and MACs

There are two other types of contract vehicles that are very similar to schedules: **governmentwide acquisition contracts** (GWACs) and **multi-agency contracts** (MACs).

■ *GWACs* are indefinite-delivery contracts for various types of information technology supplies and services that are negotiated, awarded, and administered by one agency which then makes it available for use by other agencies –

just like GSA allows other agencies to order from its schedules. Five agencies have been authorized to establish GWACs: the Department of Commerce, the Environmental Protection Agency, the National Aeronautics and Space Administration, the National Institutes of Health, and GSA. Typically, GWACs have several contractors providing the same or similar information technology supplies or services. Under many GWACs, small businesses are guaranteed a certain number of contracts to provide a more varied selection and give small businesses a "fair opportunity" to compete for work under the GWAC (see Chapter 10 for more on what "fair opportunity" means). Each GWAC has unique ordering requirements and administrative fees – they are not all basically the same, as is the case with schedule contracts.

- *MACs* are indefinite-delivery contracts for various types of supplies and services. MACs are not restricted to information technology supplies and services. They are negotiated, awarded, and administered by one agency, but another agency may *not* use a MAC unless it enters into an agreement with the agency that executed the MAC. Such orders are considered "interagency acquisitions" and are subject to the requirements of the **Economy Act** (see FAR subpart 17.5, Interagency Acquisitions). Besides entering into an agreement, the Economy Act requires that the contracting officer make a written determination that "(1) use of the [MAC] is in the best interest of the government; and (2) the supplies or services cannot be obtained as conveniently or economically by contracting directly with a private source." As with GWACs, each MAC has unique ordering requirements and administrative fees.

All GWACs and MACs are listed in the **Federal Procurement Data System** (**https://www.fpds.gov**), a searchable database of all contract awards (see Chapter 5).

REVERSE AUCTIONS

The GSA operates a **reverse auctions** system that can be used to acquire commercial items and simple services that can be purchased on a low price technically acceptable basis (**http://reverseauctions.gsa.gov/**). Unlike a traditional ("forward") auction, in which multiple buyers bid against one another to push the price of an product up, in a reverse auction sellers compete against one another to provide the buyer the lowest price or highest-value offer.

GSA authorizes agencies to use its reverse auctions system to buy from FSS contracts, the Department of Veterans Affairs (VA) multiple award schedule contracts, and multiple award schedule blanket purchase agreements (see above). Before conducting a reverse auction, GSA recommends that agencies check **GSA** *Advantage!*®

to ensure there are at least three FSS sources with the product or service to be acquired on their FSS contracts.

To bid on GSA's reverse auctions system, a bidder must be registered to use **eBuy**, GSA's online RFQ system (**https://www.ebuy.gsa.gov/advantage/main/registration.do**).

In addition, reverse auctions conducted by commercial firms, such as FedBid, may specify that only bids utilizing FSS contracts are permissible.

Regardless of whether the reverse auction is conducted through GSA's reverse auctions system or through a commercial firm's system with the requirement that bids utilize FSS contracts, the bidder must remember to add the 0.75% IFF (see above) to its bid price and, if awarded the contract, forward that fee to GSA.

NOTE: GSAR 552.238-75, Price Reductions, does *not* apply to discounts granted to the federal agency during the auction – see paragraph (d)(2) of the clause.

For more on reverse auctions, see Chapter 6.

CHAPTER 14

ARCHITECT-ENGINEER AND CONSTRUCTION CONTRACTING

There are two significant and interrelated services that are not acquired through the "usual" simplified, sealed bidding, or negotiation procedures: architect-engineer (A-E) services and construction. Solicitations for construction are similar to ordinary invitations for bids (IFB), but some of the procedures and clauses are different. However, the procedures for awarding A-E service contracts are unique.

ARCHITECT-ENGINEER CONTRACTS

Most selections of an architect-engineer (A-E) firm are not based on what are usually considered "competitive procedures." Instead, the **Brooks Architect-Engineers Act of 1972** (codified as Title 40 of the U.S. Code, Chapter 11, Selection of Architects and Engineers) requires that an **evaluation board** assess the qualifications of prospective A-E contractors and select the one most competent to perform the contract satisfactorily – there is no formal solicitation. Then the contracting officer conducts negotiations with the selected firm to establish a fair and reasonable price for the contract. Nevertheless, the Competition in Contracting Act (CICA) considers contracts awarded through this procedure to be fully and openly competitive (see paragraph (d)(1) of FAR 6.102, Use of Competitive Procedures).

However, the Clinger-Cohen Act authorized the use of "two-phase selection procedures," which can be used under certain circumstances to introduce "competition" into the A-E process and allow the same contractor to both design and construct the facility.

Definition of A-E Services

Because A-E contracting is a unique process, it is important to understand the kinds of services covered by the Brooks Architect-Engineers Act. FAR 36.601-4, Implementation, states that the following are to be considered "architect-engineer services" subject to the procedures in FAR subpart 36.6, Architect-Engineer Services:

"(1)   Professional services of an architectural or engineering nature, as defined by state law, which the state law requires to be performed or approved by a registered architect or engineer.

"(2)   Professional services of an architectural or engineering nature associated with design or construction of real property.

"(3)   Other professional services of an architectural or engineering nature or services incidental thereto (including studies, investigations, surveying and mapping, tests, evaluations, consultations, comprehensive planning, program management, conceptual designs, plans and specifications, value engineering, construction phase services, soils engineering, drawing reviews, preparation of operating and maintenance manuals and other related services) that logically or justifiably require performance by registered architects or engineers or their employees.

"(4)   Professional surveying and mapping services of an architectural or engineering nature. Surveying is considered to be an architectural and engineering service and shall be procured…from registered surveyors or architects and engineers. Mapping associated with the research, planning, development, design, construction, or alteration of real property is considered to be an architectural and engineering service…However, mapping services that are not connected to traditionally understood or accepted architectural and engineering activities, are not incidental to such architectural and engineering activities or have not in themselves traditionally been considered architectural and engineering services shall be procured pursuant to provisions in [FAR] parts 13, 14, and 15."

Only these services are procured under the FAR subpart 36.6 procedures. Other kinds of services (such as product engineering and design) and services that are performed by architect-engineers but are not *required* to be performed by architect-engineers are procured under the usual simplified, sealed bidding, or negotiation procedures.

Traditional A-E Procedures

When an agency decides it needs A-E services, it must synopsize the procurement in **FedBizOpps** (see Chapter 5) if the total fee, including options, is expected to exceed $25,000 (under service classification "C"). If the total fee is expected to exceed $15,000 but not expected to exceed $25,000, a notice of the procurement must be posted on the contracting office's bid board or by any appropriate electronic means.

The **FedBizOpps** synopsis or bid board notice must provide brief details about the location, scope of services required, cost range and limitations, type of contract expected (see Chapters 9 and 10), estimated starting and completion dates, and significant evaluation factors. Also, the synopsis or notice will request that interested firms submit a **Standard Form 330, Architect-Engineer Qualifications**. If the contract is expected to exceed the simplified acquisition threshold ($150,000), the agency must give firms at least **30 days** to submit the SF 330 to the contracting office that is purchasing the A-E services or to a an evaluation board established by the agency. An electronic version of the SF 330 is available on the General Services Administration forms website at **http://www.gsa.gov/portal/forms/type/SF**.

The SF 330 has two parts: **Part I – Contract-Specific Qualifications**, and **Part II – General Requirements**. To be eligible for an A-E award, a firm must submit Part II and, if the contract is expected to exceed the simplified acquisition threshold, Part I.

Part II of the SF 330 requests basic information on the firm's professional capabilities, specialized experience, and the size and complexity of the projects it can perform. Part II is intended to be an annual statement of qualifications and performance data. A-E firms are encouraged to submit Part II to appropriate contracting activities and evaluation boards so their qualifications are on file (and they may be considered for small A-E contracts that are not synopsized), and to update their Part II annually. If the A-E firm has a current Part II on file with the contracting activity or evaluation board, it is not required to resubmit the form each time the contracting activity or evaluation board announces a procurement for A-E services.

Part I of the SF 330 requests information on the firm's qualifications to perform the *specific* A-E project. It requests the names and resumes of the key employees, consultants, joint venture partners, and subcontractors who will have major project responsibility or provide unusual or unique capabilities; past and current projects that demonstrate the firm's (or proposed team's) competence to perform work similar to that required for the particular project; and any additional information requested by the agency.

An evaluation board (either permanent or *ad hoc*) reviews the Part IIs on file and those submitted in response to the synopsis or notice, the Part Is submitted in response to the synopsis or notice (if required), and any **performance evaluations** of projects completed within the previous six years by firms being considered (upon completion of each A-E contract over $35,000, the contracting activity evaluates the firm's concepts, drawings, estimates, and overall performance, and submits the evaluation to the Contractor Performance Assessment Reporting System [CPARS] database at **http://www.cpars.gov** – see Chapter 18).

The evaluation board judges the firms according to the following criteria:

- Professional qualifications;

- Specialized experience and technical competence in the type of work required;

- Ability to perform the work in the required time;

- Past performance on contracts with the government and private industry in terms of cost control, quality of work, compliance with performance schedules, and assessments of occupants;

- Location in the general geographic area and knowledge of the locality of the project (most A-E contracts are awarded to local firms); and

- Acceptability under other appropriate evaluation.

Occasionally, the head of the agency may approve a **design competition**. He may do so when there is a unique situation involving prestige projects (such as memorials, monuments, and structures of unusual national significance), there is sufficient time available for the production and evaluation of conceptual designs, and the design competition (with its associated costs) will substantially benefit the project.

Then, the evaluation board ranks the A-E firms and holds discussions with at least three of the most highly qualified, exploring different concepts, energy-efficiency considerations, use of recovered materials, waste reduction, and alternate methods of furnishing the A-E services. Price is not discussed at this stage.

After the board holds the discussions, it prepares a **selection report** for the designated **selection authority** recommending at least three firms, in order of preference. The report includes a description of the discussions and the evaluations conducted by the board, and is intended to allow the selection authority to review the considerations the board took into account and to assess its recommendations. Once the evaluation board forwards it selection report to the selection authority, no additional firms may be added by the board or the selection authority.

The selection authority assesses the recommendations contained in the selection report and, with the advice of appropriate technical and staff representatives, makes the final selection by listing the firms in his order of preference. If the firm listed as the most preferred by the selection authority is not the firm recommended by the board, the selection authority must provide a written explanation of his reasons. If the selection authority does not consider any of the firms qualified, he sends the selection report back to the evaluation board for revision. Otherwise, the selection authority forwards his list to the appropriate contracting officer for negotiations.

Short Selection Processes for Procurements Less Than or Equal to the Simplified Acquisition Threshold

An agency may authorize either or both of two short processes to select A-E firms for contracts that are less than or equal to the simplified acquisition threshold. In one process, the evaluation board's selection report serves as the final selection, bypassing the selection authority. In the other process, the chairperson of the evaluation board prepares the selection report himself and forwards it to the head of the agency or the selection authority for approval. In either process, the approved selection report is forwarded to the contracting officer for negotiations.

Negotiations

The contracting officer usually requests a proposal from the most preferred firm, and this proposal forms the basis for negotiations. The negotiations are directed toward:

- Making certain the firm has a clear understanding of the project's essential requirements;

- Ensuring the firm will provide the personnel, consultants, subcontractors, and facilities necessary to accomplish the work within the required performance period;

- Ensuring the firm can provide a design that will permit construction of the facility within the funding limitation established for the project (FAR 52.236-22, Design Within Funding Limitations – see below); and

- Reaching agreement on the terms and conditions of the contract, including a fair and reasonable price.

During the evaluation of a proposal, the contracting officer compares the proposed price (supported by cost or pricing data if necessary – see Chapter 8) with the **government estimate** that is required to be prepared for all A-E procurements over the simplified acquisition threshold. If there are significant differences between the two, the contracting officer will discuss those differences with the firm to ensure there is a complete understanding of the work required. However, the contracting officer is not allowed to reveal the government estimate to the firm. The firm may make revisions to its proposal and cost or pricing information to reflect changes or clarifications to the scope of work that result from the negotiations.

If a mutually satisfactory contract cannot be negotiated with the first firm on the list, the contracting officer will ask for a final proposal revision and notify the firm that the negotiations are terminated. The contracting officer will then ask for a proposal from the second firm on the list and conduct negotiations with it. If a satisfactory contract cannot be negotiated with the second firm, the contracting officer will ask for a final proposal revision and terminate negotiations. The contracting officer follows the same procedure for the third firm on the list. If the contracting officer is unable to negotiate a satisfactory contract with any of the firms on the list, he and the selection authority will discuss the reasons. After his discussion with the contracting officer, the selection authority may direct the evaluation board to recommend additional firms.

When the contracting officer and an A-E firm negotiate a mutually satisfactory contract, the contracting officer prepares a **Standard Form 252, Architect-Engineer Contract**, for signature. The SF 252 serves the same purpose as the Standard Form 26 (see Chapter 8) in that it is the first page of the contract and includes the project description, location, and amount of the contract.

Limitation on Contract Price

Fixed-price contracts are preferred for A-E projects; however, cost-reimbursement contracts may be used if the design effort is of such magnitude and complexity that a fixed-price would not be suitable. In either case, the statutory limit on the price or estimated cost and fee for production and delivery of designs, plans, drawings, and specifications cannot exceed **6% of the estimated cost of the construction of the public work**, excluding fees paid to the A-E contractor (paragraph (c)(4)(i)(B) of FAR 15.404-4, Profit). In other words, if the estimated cost of the construction of a facility is **$2,000,000**, the A-E contract for the design of that facility cannot exceed **$120,000** ($2,000,000 x 6%).

Additional A-E Contract Requirements

Most fixed-price A-E contracts include **FAR 52.236-22, Design Within Funding Limitations**. This clause requires the A-E contractor to design a project within an "estimated construction contract price"; for example, design a facility that will cost no more than $2,000,000 to construct. If the bids for construction of the project based on the A-E firm's design exceed the project funding limitation specified in the A-E firm's contract, the contracting officer will require the A-E firm to redesign the project at no additional cost to the government so the project comes within the funding limitation. If, during design, the A-E contractor finds the project will likely exceed the funding limitations and it will not be able to design a usable facility within these limitations, the contractor must advise the contracting officer. The contracting officer will reviews the contractor's estimated construction costs and may decide to change the scope of the project, the materials, or the estimated construction cost limit.

In addition, all fixed-price A-E contracts include **FAR 52.236-23, Responsibility of the Architect-Engineer Contractor**. This clause requires A-E contractors to correct any errors, deficiencies, or inaccuracies in the designs, drawings, specifications, or other services it furnishes at no additional cost to the government. Also, the government reserves the right to seek damages for the negligent work.

Two-Phase Design-Build Selection Procedures

The sequential "design, then build" procedure established by the Brooks Architect-Engineers Act was intended to prevent conflicts of interest between the design and construction disciplines. To ensure compliance with the Brooks Architect-Engineers Act, FAR 36.209, Construction Contracts with Architect-Engineer Firms, prohibits an A-E firm or any of its subsidiaries or affiliates from performing any contracts for the construction of projects it designs (unless the head of the agency approves). This prevents an A-E firm from designing a project that perfectly suits its own construction capabilities, thus giving itself an unfair competitive advantage. If the A-E firm possesses construction capabilities, the Brooks Architect-Engineers Act gives the firm the choice of either entering into negotiations for the A-E contract and thus becoming ineligible for the construction contract, or declining to enter into negotiations for the A-E contract and remaining eligible to compete for the construction contract.

However, this bifurcated procedure has come under increased criticism as too cumbersome and one that prevents the government from taking full advantage of the many construction firms that have top-notch architectural capabilities and *vice versa*. Various heads of agencies have exercised their authority to **waive** the requirements of the Brooks Architect-Engineers Act, thus permitting the solicitation of a single contract for the design *and* construction of "turnkey facilities" which are ready for occupancy.

In response to this criticism and the unilateral actions of the agencies, Congress included a provision in the Clinger-Cohen Act authorizing the use of **two-phase design-build selection procedures** for the design *and* construction of public buildings, facilities, or works *when appropriate*.

With two-phase design-build selection procedures, the agency develops a scope of work that defines the project and provides offerors with sufficient information to enable them to submit proposals that meet the government's needs. Such information might include criteria and preliminary design, budget parameters, and schedule or delivery requirements.

When the contracting officer receives the work statement, he must decide whether to use the two-phase selection procedures. In making his decision, the contracting officer must:

■ Determine whether three or more offers are anticipated;

■ Decide whether a substantial amount of design work must be performed before an offeror can develop a price or cost proposal for such contract;

- Evaluate how adequately and completely the project requirements have been defined;

- Evaluate the time constraints on the project;

- Assess the capability and experience of potential contractors; and

- Comply with other criteria established by the agency.

If the contracting officer decides that the two-phase design-build selection procedures are appropriate for the project, he solicits **phase-one proposals** that require each offeror to submit information on its proposed technical approach and its qualifications, but *not* detailed design or technical information or price or cost information. The evaluation factors stated in the solicitation must include:

- Technical approach (but not detailed design or technical information);

- Specialized experience and technical competence;

- Capability to perform;

- Past performance of the offeror's team, including the architect-engineer and construction members of the team; and

- Other appropriate factors.

The solicitation must specify the relative importance of each of the evaluation factors and subfactors that will be considered in the evaluation of phase-one proposals. Also, the solicitation must specify the evaluation factors that will be used in phase-two to make the award decision (such as design concepts, management approach, key personnel, and proposed technical solutions).

Each phase-one solicitation must state the **maximum number of offerors** the contracting officer will select to submit phase-two proposals. The maximum number must not exceed **five offerors** (unless the project is expected to exceed $4,000,000 and the head of the contracting activity determines that a maximum number greater than five offerors is in the government's interest).

After receiving and evaluating the phase-one proposals, the contracting officer selects the most highly qualified offerors (up to the maximum number specified in the phase-one solicitation) and requests that they submit **phase-two proposals** that include technical proposals and cost or pricing information. The phase-two solicitation must require the selected offerors to submit design concepts or proposed solutions to requirements addressed within the scope of work that was in the phase-one solicitation, and include the evaluation factors and subfactors, *including cost or price*, that will be considered in the evaluations of proposals.

The contracting officer (and his technical evaluators) evaluates the proposed designs and solutions, while he (along with his cost analysts) evaluates the price or cost information separately. Upon receiving the technical and price evaluations, the contracting officer conducts negotiations with the offerors, clarifying points and suggesting changes to the design concepts and/or proposed prices.

After receiving final proposal revisions (if requested), the contracting officer (and his team) reevaluate the proposals. The contracting officer applies the evaluation factors and subfactors to the revised evaluations and decides which offeror is the winner. He prepares the contract, notifies the unsuccessful phase-two offerors, conducts debriefings for the unsuccessful offerors that request one, synopsizes the award in **FedBizOpps**, turns the contract over to the administrative contracting officer, and moves on to the next solicitation.

See FAR subpart 36.3, Two-Phase Design-Build Selection Procedures, for more on these procedures.

CONSTRUCTION CONTRACTS

FAR 36.103, Methods of Contracting, requires contracting officers to contract for construction through sealed bidding whenever practicable (unless the contract will be performed outside the United States). The reason for this requirement is most construction projects have definitive specifications and blueprints, so there is no need to conduct negotiations or award the contract on a basis other than price and other price-related factors (see paragraph (a) of FAR 6.401, Sealed Bidding and Competitive Proposals). Negotiations are usually reserved for small construction projects less than the simplified acquisition threshold, overseas construction, highly classified construction, and construction that is highly experimental in nature. Many of the procedures contracting officers use when negotiating contracts for supplies and services also apply to negotiated construction contracts.

Similarly, because many construction solicitations are IFBs, construction contracts are usually firm-fixed-price (FFP). Generally, a contracting officer may use a cost-reimbursement contract only for large, complex construction projects when higher authority has determined a fixed-price contract is not suitable for the particular project. Contracting officers may use fixed-price with economic price adjustment contracts (FP/EPA) when the adjustment provisions are customary for particular items and the omission of those adjustment provisions would cause a significant number of firms to refuse to bid. Also, the FP/EPA contract may be appropriate when insisting on an FFP contract would induce bidders to add contingencies to their bids, thus unreasonably increasing the government's cost. See Chapter 9 for information on the FFP and FP/EPA contract types.

Despite its seeming simplicity, construction contracting does have its complications. The contract forms are different from those used to purchase other supplies or services, the labor laws pertaining to construction are unique, and requirements for bid guarantees and performance and payment bonds are not usually found in other government solicitations or contracts.

Definition of Construction

FAR 2.101, Definitions, defines "construction" as *"construction, alteration, or repair (including dredging, excavating, and painting) of buildings, structures, or other real property."* FAR 2.101 goes on to state that "buildings, structures, or other real property" includes, but is not limited to, *"bridges, dams, plants, highways, parkways, streets, subways, tunnels, sewers, mains, power lines, cemeteries, pumping stations, railways, airport facilities, terminals, docks, piers, wharves, ways, lighthouses, buoys, jetties, breakwaters, levees, canals, and channels."* "Construction" does not include the manufacture, production, furnishing, alteration, repair, processing, or assembling of vessels, aircraft, or other kinds of property and equipment.

Solicitation Procedures

Construction projects of **$2,000 or less** may be acquired through any of the simplified procedures described in Chapter 6, including "micro-purchases."

All construction solicitations **over $2,000** must be in writing or posted electronically (such as on **FedBizOpps** – see Chapter 5). This is because all construction contracts over $2,000 are subject to the requirements of several labor laws, including wage determinations under the **Davis-Bacon Act** (codified as Title 40 of the U.S. Code, Chapter 13, Subchapter IV, Wage Rate Requirements [Construction] – see below and Chapter 15). Also, the requirements and specifications of all but the smallest construction projects are too numerous and complex for oral solicitations to be practical.

Contracting officers must synopsize construction solicitations in **FedBizOpps** under service classification code "Y" for new construction or code "Z" for maintenance, repair, or alteration. However, the synopsis must state the estimated price range of the project. Though the government's estimate may not be disclosed, the estimated price range is described in terms of one of the following price ranges:

- Less than $25,000;
- Between $25,000 and $100,000;
- Between $100,000 and $250,000;
- Between $250,000 and $500,000;
- Between $500,000 and $1,000,000;
- Between $1,000,000 and $5,000,000;
- Between $5,000,000 and $10,000,000; or
- More than $10,000,000.

The Department of Defense uses the following additional price ranges:

- Between $10,000,000 and $25,000,000;
- Between $25,000,000 and $100,000,000;
- Between $100,000,000 and $250,000,000;
- Between $250,000,000 and $500,000,000; or
- Over $500,000,000.

The solicitation must state the estimated price range of the project as well.

In addition, to stimulate the interest of the greatest number of potential bidders, the contracting officer sends presolicitation notices to prospective bidders for all construction projects exceeding the simplified acquisition threshold ($150,000) (when considered necessary, the contracting officer may send presolicitation notices for projects less than the simplified acquisition threshold). The presolicitation notice contains:

- A description of the proposed work that sufficiently details the nature and volume of the project;

- Location of the project;

- Tentative dates for the IFB issuance and bid opening;

- Estimated date for completion of the project;

- The estimated price range;

- Location where plans will be available for inspection without charge;

- Any amount to be charged for solicitation documents;

- Whether the contract will be set-aside for small businesses (see Chapter 11); and

- Date by which requests for copies of the IFB should be submitted to the contracting officer.

The presolicitation notice must be publicized in **FedBizOpps**, just like the synopsis.

When preparing the solicitation, the contracting officer uses a **Standard Form 1442, Solicitation, Offer, and Award (Construction, Alteration, or Repair)**, to solicit and award contracts over the simplified acquisition threshold. It is very much like the Standard Form 33 used for other IFBs and RFPs. For procurements expected to be less than or equal to the simplified acquisition threshold, the contracting officer can use the SF 1442 or the **Optional Form 347, Order for Supplies or Services**, the same form used for simplified procedures, provided he includes the applicable construction clauses (see Figure 6 in Chapter 6).

Some construction provisions and clauses commonly found in construction solicitations are:

■ **Method of payment**. The contracting officer must decide whether to provide payment (1) in a lump sum for completion of the total work or for a clearly defined part of the total work, (2) on a unit price basis, such as a fixed amount for each cubic yard of concrete poured, or (3) using a combination of both methods. Of these payment methods, the lump sum payment is preferred to the unit price payment. Unit price payment is preferred only when (i) large quantities of work such as grading, paving, or site preparation are involved, (ii) the amount of work cannot be determined accurately enough to preclude the addition of substantial contingencies to the price (for example, excavation), (iii) estimates of the amount of work may change significantly during construction, or (iv) offerors would have to expend unusual effort to develop adequate estimates.

■ **Site inspection and examination of data**. The contracting officer will place a notice in the solicitation of the time and place for a site inspection and examination of data available to the government, such as boring samples, original boring logs, and records and plans of previous construction.

■ **Government-furnished facilities**. The contracting officer will list in the solicitation any facilities that will be furnished to the contractor during construction. Such facilities might include utilities, office space, and warehouse space.

■ **Pre-bid conference**. When the construction is for a large project involving important or complex work, the contracting officer may decide to hold a pre-bid conference. The A-E firm that designed the project normally is available to assist the contracting officer in the interpretation of the specifications, blueprints, and requirements. See Chapter 7 for more on pre-bid conferences.

■ **Davis-Bacon Act Wage Determination**. If the contract is expected to exceed **$2,000**, the contracting officer will include the wage determination required by the Davis-Bacon Act to be provided by the secretary of labor (available from the **"Wage Determinations OnLine"** site at **http://www.wdol.gov**). This wage determination specifies the minimum wage rates and fringe benefits for the different types of laborers and mechanics expected to work on the project. Also, the contracting officer will include in the solicitation FAR 52.222-6, Construction Wage Rate Requirements, and several other labor-related clauses, including FAR 52.222-4, Contract Work Hours and Safety Standards – Overtime Compensation, and FAR 52.222-10, Compliance with Copeland Act Requirements. See Chapter 15 for more on these labor laws.

■ **FAR 52.211-12, Liquidated Damages – Construction**, may be included when the contracting officer determines it is in the best interest of the government. The minimum amount of liquidated damages for failure to complete the project on time is the estimated cost of inspection and superintendence for each day of delay. The government can also include in the liquidated damages amount any additional costs incurred for each day of delay, such as the cost of substitute facilities, the rental of buildings, continued payment of quarters allowances, and similar expenses.

■ **FAR 52.236-1, Performance of Work by the Contractor**, is included in solicitations when the contract is expected to exceed **$1,500,000** except for contracts awarded through the various small business set-asides or through the Section 8(a) program (see Chapter 11) (the contracting officer may include the clause when the contract is expected to be $1,500,000 or less). Because most construction projects require subcontracting work (such as heating, plumbing, and electrical), this clause requires the construction contractor to perform at least **12%** of the work (or a higher percentage if the contracting officer decides such percentage is appropriate for the project) to make sure the prime contractor takes an interest in and provides adequate supervision of the project.

■ **FAR 52.236-2, Differing Site Conditions**, is included in solicitations when the contract is expected to exceed the simplified acquisition threshold (the contracting officer may include the clause when the contract is expected to be less than or equal to the simplified acquisition threshold). The clause provides for an adjustment in the contract price if the contractor discovers that (i) the subsurface or latent physical conditions at the site differ materially from those indicated in the contract, or (ii) unusual physical conditions exist that differ materially from those ordinarily encountered in the type of work specified in the contract.

■ **FAR 52.228-1, Bid Guarantee**, is included in the solicitation when the resulting contract will require performance and payment bonds (see below). The bid guarantee is a certification by a surety (that is, a party that insures fulfillment of another's obligation) that the bidder will be able to obtain the performance and payment bonds should the bidder receive the contract award. The contracting officer will determine a bid guarantee amount that will protect the government if the successful bidder fails to execute further contractual documents (such as co-insurance or reinsurance agreements) and the required bonds. The bid guarantee amount must be at least **20% of the bid price** but **not exceed $3,000,000**. The surety must meet the same requirements as a performance or payment bond surety (see below). Failure of a bidder to provide an adequate bid guarantee forces the contracting officer to reject the bid. If the government accepts a bid but the successful bidder is unable to execute all contractual documents or furnish executed bonds within the period specified in the IFB (usually 10 days after notice of award), the contracting officer may cancel the contract. If the contracting officer cancels the contract for such failure, the bid guarantee is available to offset the cost of reacquiring the work. The bid guarantee form is the **Standard Form 24, Bid Bond**. See FAR 28.101 for more information on bid guarantees.

■ **FAR 52.228-15, Performance and Payment Bonds – Construction:** Contractors must provide **performance** and **payment bonds** for all construction contracts over **$150,000**. The winner of a construction contract must furnish (1) a performance bond issued by a surety (or sureties) guaranteeing the performance and fulfillment of all contractual obligations, and (2) a payment bond issued by a surety (or sureties) guaranteeing that the laborers, subcontractors, and suppliers will be paid for completed work. If the bidder cannot furnish these bonds within a specified period after notification of the impending contract award, the contracting officer will not award the contract to the bidder. The contracting officer will include a notice in the solicitation specifying the requirement for the bonds, the penal sum of each bond, and the deadline for submitting acceptable bonds (usually **10 days** after notice of award – see FAR 52.228-1 above). See below for further information on bond and surety requirements.

After waiting at least 15 days following the publication of the solicitation's synopsis in **FedBizOpps**, the contracting officer posts the solicitation on **FedBizOpps,** and sends copies of the solicitation to the firms that responded to the presolicitation notice or the synopsis, or otherwise requested a copy of the solicitation. The contracting officer may send copies of the solicitation to business and trade organizations that maintain plan display rooms for the benefit of contractors, subcontractors, and material suppliers.

The procedures for construction IFBs are similar to those for all other IFBs: the contracting officer must allow at least 30 days for bidders or offerors to respond, the bidders must submit their bids to the bid opening office by the time and date specified in the IFB, and the bids are opened and read aloud in public.

After bid opening, the contracting officer determines which responsive bid (with a required bid guarantee) represents the lowest cost to the government, price and price-related factors considered. Then, the contracting officer must determine whether the lowest responsive bidder is responsible. The contracting officer first checks the **System for Award Management Exclusions** (formerly called the "Excluded Parties List System," now part of the System for Acquisition Management [SAM] – **https://www.sam.gov** – see Chapter 5) to make sure the bidder is not on it, then he evaluates the bidder's financial resources, capabilities, equipment, facilities, and performance record. When evaluating the bidder's performance record, the contracting officer may consider performance reports in the Past Performance Information Retrieval System (PPIRS – **https://www.ppirs.gov** – see Chapter 18) on the bidder's performance of any construction contract of **$700,000 or more** performed within the previous six years (or regardless of contract amount if the contract was terminated for default – see Chapter 18).

Normally, the contracting officer will *not* require a preaward survey of the lowest responsive bidder's capabilities because of the requirement for performance and payment bonds. By issuing a performance and payment bond, the surety pledges its own assets as security insuring that the contract will be completed and laborers, subcontractors, and suppliers will be paid even if the contractor fails to carry out its contractual obligations. Therefore, the surety usually conducts its own prequalification survey in which it examines and evaluates the bidder's financial resources, technical expertise, management ability, current workload, and ability to complete the contract in the required time. Since the surety conducts such an extensive review of the bidder's resources and capabilities, the contracting officer will normally rely on the surety's judgment and not duplicate its efforts by requiring a preaward survey. Besides, if the apparent winning bidder cannot obtain the required performance and payment bonds, the government is protected from loss by the bid guarantee. However, the contracting officer may require a preaward survey if the project requires unusual or unique expertise.

As with any other determination of responsibility, if the contracting officer determines the lowest responsive bidder is not responsible and the bidder is a small business, he must forward the matter to the Small Business Administration (SBA) for certificate of competency (COC) consideration. If the SBA refuses to issue a COC or the nonresponsible bidder is a large business, the contracting officer determines whether the second low bid is responsible and whether the second low bidder is responsible. See Chapter 7 for more on responsibility and COCs.

Once the contracting officer determines which is the lowest responsive, responsible bidder, he issues a **Notice of Award** to that bidder (either electronically or in writing), directing it to furnish the required performance bond and payment bond within the period specified in the IFB. Upon the furnishing of acceptable bonds within the allotted time, the contracting officer signs the SF 1442, accepting the bid and creating.a contract.

Bond and Surety Requirements

The **Miller Act of 1935** (codified as Title 40 of the U.S. Code, Chapter 31, Subchapter III, Bonds) requires contractors to provide performance and payment bonds for all construction contracts over $150,000. These bonds must be issued by sureties that are acceptable to the government, or the bidder must pledge assets that are acceptable to the government. However, the contracting officer can waive the requirement for work performed in a foreign country or as otherwise authorized by the Miller Act or other law.

The **Standard Form 25, Performance Bond**, must be completed by the surety and submitted by the apparent successful bidder as required in the notice of award. The penal amount of a performance bond must be **100%** of the contract price unless the contracting officer decides a smaller amount would adequately protect the government.

The **Standard Form 25-A, Payment Bond**, must be completed by the surety and submitted by the apparent successful bidder as required in the notice of award. The penal amount of a payment bond must be **100%** of the contract price unless the contracting officer decides a smaller amount would adequately protect the government. However, the payment bond must be no less than the performance bond.

Corporate sureties that are approved by the government are listed in **Department of the Treasury's Circular 570, Companies Holding Certificates of Authority as Acceptable Sureties on Federal Bonds and Acceptable Reinsuring Companies**. However, apparent successful bidders should be careful to make sure the penal amount of the bond does not exceed the surety's underwriting limit stated in Circular 570 unless the amount exceeding the underwriting limit is coinsured or reinsured by another acceptable surety. Circular 570 is available at **https://www.fiscal.treasury. gov/fsreports/ref/suretyBnd/c570_a-z.htm**.

To be considered as an individual surety, a person must complete a **Standard Form 28, Affidavit of Individual Surety**, and the SF 28 must accompany the completed SF 25 or SF 25-A. The unencumbered value of the assets pledged by the individual surety must equal or exceed the penal amount of the bond. A bidder may submit up to three individual sureties for a bond, and their pledged assets, when combined, must equal or exceed the amount of the bond. The contracting officer determines the acceptability of an individual surety, and a contracting officer's determination that a small business is nonresponsible because an individual surety is unacceptable does not have to be referred to the SBA for COC consideration. However, the contracting officer may allow the bidder to substitute an acceptable surety.

The contracting officer cannot accept the bonds of individual sureties who appear in the System for Award Management Exclusions. The head of the agency or his designee may take action to exclude an individual from acting as a surety and place him in the System for Award Management Exclusions for any of the following reasons:

■ Failure to fulfill the obligations under any bond;

■ Failure to disclose all bond obligations;

■ Misrepresentation of the value of available assets or outstanding liabilities;

■ Any false or misleading statement, signature, or representation on a bond or affidavit of individual suretyship; or

■ Any other cause affecting responsibility as a surety of such serious and compelling nature as may warrant exclusion.

A bidder/contractor may bypass sureties altogether by depositing U.S. bonds or notes in an amount equal at their par value to the penal sum of the bond, or by furnishing a certified or cashier's check, bank draft, Post Office money order, or currency in the amount equal to the penal sum of the bond (see FAR 28.204-1, United

States Bonds or Notes, and FAR 28.204-2, Certified or Cashiers Checks, Bank Drafts, Money Orders, or Currency). Also, a bidder/contractor has the option of furnishing a bond secured by an irrevocable letter of credit (ILC) in an amount equal to the penal sum required to be secured (see FAR 28.204-3, Irrevocable Letter of Credit).

When requested by a subcontractor or supplier (or prospective subcontractor or supplier), the government must furnish the name and address of the surety (or sureties) on the payment bond, the penal amount of the payment bond, and a copy of the payment bond.

If a subcontractor or supplier claims that the prime contractor has not paid in accordance with the payment terms of a subcontract or purchase order, the contracting officer will investigate the matter. If he finds the prime contractor has failed to pay, he may encourage the contractor to make timely payment to the subcontractor or supplier, or he may reduce or suspend progress payments to the contractor if progress payments have been authorized (see Chapter 18). If the contracting officer's actions do not induce the contractor to pay, the subcontractor or supplier may take action against the surety (or sureties).

See FAR subpart 28.1, Bonds and Other Financial Protections, for more on bonds, and FAR subpart 28.2, Sureties and Other Security for Bonds, for more on sureties.

Alternative Payment Protections for Construction Contracts Between $35,000 and $150,000

One of the provisions of the Federal Acquisition Streamlining Act of 1994 (FASA) requires contracting officers to select two or more alternatives to payment bonds for construction contracts between $35,000 and $150,000. The alternatives listed in paragraph (b)(1) of FAR 28.102-1, General, are:

- A payment bond;

- An irrevocable letter of credit (ILC);

- A tripartite escrow agreement (in which the contractor establishes an escrow account in a federally insured financial institution and enters into a tripartite escrow agreement with the financial institution, an escrow agent, and all the suppliers of labor and material);

- Certificates of deposit (from a federally insured financial institution and executable by the contracting officer); and

- U.S. bonds or notes, a certified or cashier's check, bank draft, Post Office money order, or currency.

The contractor must furnish one of the payment protections selected by the contracting officer. The penal amount of the alternate payment protection is equal to 100% of the contract price (unless the contracting officer determines a lesser amount is adequate for the protection of the government).

CHAPTER 15

LABOR LAWS

According to the Department of Labor, there are more than 20 separate labor laws that apply to federal contracts of all types, though no one law applies to all federal contracts. FAR part 22, Application of Labor Laws to Government Acquisitions, covers the labor laws that apply to federal contracts. The following describes the primary labor laws that apply to firms that contract with the federal government. These are in addition to the labor laws that apply to all businesses (for example, the minimum wage). Along with the name of the law is a brief description of its provisions and the office(s) that administers the law (along with its website address). Those who want additional information on these laws or implementation procedures should contact the Department of Labor's "**eLaws**" site at **http://webapps.dol.gov/elaws/.**

CONTRACT WORK HOURS AND SAFETY STANDARDS ACT

This law (codified as Title 40 of the U.S. Code, Chapter 37, Contract Work Hours and Safety Standards) requires federal contractors and subcontractors performing contracts within the United States to pay their laborers and mechanics overtime compensation "at a rate of not less than one and one-half times their basic rates of pay for all hours worked in excess of 40 in a workweek." The definition of "laborers or mechanics" includes apprentices, trainees, watchmen, guards, and firefighters, but does not include seamen.

The plain English interpretation is: contractors must pay their laborers and mechanics "time and a half" for overtime. Note that the law defines overtime as "in excess of 40 in a workweek." It does not refer to the 8-hour workday. This allows the contractor to schedule four 10-hour days, for example, without having to pay overtime. The act also includes safety and health provisions.

This law applies to most federal supply and service contracts over the simplified acquisition threshold and all federally funded construction contracts over $2,000. It does not apply to contracts for commercial items (see Chapter 4), nor to contracts performed outside the United States, Puerto Rico, or several other U.S. territories. **FAR 52.222-4, Contract Work Hours and Safety Standards Act – Overtime Compensation**, is included in all solicitations and contracts subject to the law.

The law is administered by the Department of Labor, Wage and Hour Division (**http://www.dol.gov/whd/**). Safety and health requirements are administered by the Department of Labor, Occupational Safety and Health Administration (OSHA) (**https://www.osha.gov/**).

See **http://www.dol.gov/whd/govcontracts/cwhssa.htm** and FAR subpart 22.3, Contract Work Hours and Safety Standards Act, for more information.

MINIMUM WAGE

Executive Order 13658, Establishing A Minimum Wage For Contractors, establishes $10.20/hour as the minimum wage for federal contractor and subcontractor employees. This minimum wage applies "regardless of the contractual relationship alleged to exist between the individual and the employer," which means the minimum wage applies to individuals who work as "independent contractors."

A minimum wage of $10.10/hour went into effect January 1, 2015, and the minimum wage is adjusted by the secretary of labor every January 1 thereafter to reflect the annual percentage increase in the Consumer Price Index for Urban Wage Earners and Clerical Workers (the minimum wage cannot be reduced). Effective January 1, 2016, the minimum wage was increased to $10.15/hour by the secretary of labor, and effective January 1, 2017, the minimum wage was increased to $10.20/hour.

The minimum wage does not apply to "individuals employed in a *bona fide* executive, administrative, or professional capacity." Also, the minimum wage does not apply to "individuals...who are not directly engaged in performing the specific work called for by the contract, and who spend less than 20% of their hours worked in a particular workweek performing in connection with such contracts," or to certain students, learners, apprentices, and messengers.

FAR 52.222-55, Minimum Wages Under Executive Order 13658, must be included in contracts that include FAR 52.222-6, Construction Wage Rate Requirements (see below), or FAR 52.222-41, Service Contract Labor Standards (see below), if the work is to be performed in the United States.

Executive Order 13658 is administered by the Department of Labor, Wage and Hour Division (**http://www.dol.gov/whd/**). See FAR subpart 22.19, Establishing a Minimum Wage for Contractors, for more information.

EQUAL EMPLOYMENT OPPORTUNITY
(Executive Order 11246, as Amended [Parts II and IV])

Executive Order 11246 prohibits contractors and subcontractors from discriminating against any employee or applicant for employment because of race, color, religion, sex, sexual orientation, gender identity, or national origin. The order applies to all federal contractors and subcontractors that receive contracts adding up to more than $10,000 during any 12-month period. It does not apply to work performed outside the United States by employees who were recruited outside the United States. Covered contracts contain **FAR 52.222-26, Equal Opportunity**. (It is *not* a violation of Executive Order 11246 for a contractor to extend a preference to Indians living on or near an Indian reservation in connection with employment opportunities on or near an Indian reservation.)

Each prime contractor and subcontractor (other than construction) with 50 or more employees and a contract or subcontract of $50,000 or more must develop a written affirmative action program for each of its establishments within 120 days of contract award (FAR 22.804, Affirmative Action Programs).

Before the contracting officer can award a contract of $10,000,000 or more (other than construction), he must ask the Department of Labor's Office of Federal Contract Compliance Programs (OFCCP) to conduct an on-site review of the contractor's ability to comply with the equal employment opportunity requirements unless the proposed contractor is listed in OFCCP's National Preaward Registry at **https://ofccp. dol-esa.gov/preaward/pa_reg.html** and the proposed contractor has been reviewed within the preceding 24 months and found to be in compliance with the equal opportunity laws. In addition, this on-site review will be conducted for any subcontractors with subcontracts of $10,000,000 or more that have not been reviewed within the previous 24 months and are not on the OFCCP's National Preaward Registry (**FAR 52.222-24, Preaward On-Site Equal Opportunity Compliance Review**).

For construction contracts of more than $10,000, the contractor must strive to meet affirmative action goals for minority and women participation in various trades on all its construction work within the geographical area, not merely the construction under the federal contract (**FAR 52.222-23, Notice of Requirement for Affirmative Action to Ensure Equal Employment Opportunity for Construction**). In addition, construction contractors and subcontractors with contracts or subcontracts of more than $10,000 must implement the affirmative action procedures in subparagraphs (g)(1) through (g)(16) of **FAR 52.222-27, Affirmative Action Compliance Requirements for Construction**.

Executive Order 11246 is administered by the Department of Labor, Office of Federal Contract Compliance Programs (**http://www.dol.gov/ofccp/**).

See **http://www.dol.gov/ofccp/regs/compliance/ca_11246.htm** and FAR subpart 22.8, Equal Employment Opportunities, for more information.

DAVIS-BACON ACT

This law (codified as Title 40 of the U.S. Code, Chapter 31, Subchapter IV, Wage Rate Requirements [Construction]) applies to most federal and federally-assisted contracts over $2,000 for the construction, alteration, or repair of public buildings or public works within the United States (see Chapter 14). This includes:

- Altering, remodeling, or installation on the work site of items fabricated off-site;

- Painting and decorating;

- The transporting of materials and supplies to or from the work site by employees of the construction contractor or construction subcontractor; and

- Manufacturing or furnishing of materials, articles, supplies, or equipment on the work site by contractor or subcontractor employees.

The law does not apply to:

- The manufacturing of components or materials off-site or their subsequent delivery to the site by commercial suppliers or material men; or

- Individuals who volunteer to perform a service for civic, charitable, or humanitarian reasons (such as restoring historical landmarks).

The Davis-Bacon Act requires contractors and subcontractors working on the site to pay laborers and mechanics at least "the wage rates and fringe benefits found by the Department of Labor to be prevailing in the locality." The secretary of labor's "wage determination" is attached to the solicitation and becomes part of the resulting contract. The wage determination individually addresses each of the different types of laborers and mechanics expected to work under the contract. For example, carpenters may have different minimum wage rates and fringe benefits than bricklayers. Davis-Bacon Act wage determinations are available at **Wage Determinations OnLine** (WDOL) at **http://www.wdol.gov**.

"Laborers or mechanics" are defined by the Davis-Bacon Act as workers utilized by a contractor or subcontractor whose duties are manual or physical in nature, including those who use tools or perform a trade. The definition also includes apprentices, trainees, and helpers.

"Wages" and "fringe benefits" are defined by the Davis-Bacon Act as:

- Amounts paid in cash to a laborer or mechanic; and

- Contributions to provide for medical or hospital care, pensions, compensation for injuries or illness resulting from occupational activity, unemployment benefits, life insurance, disability and sickness insurance, accident insurance; vacation or holiday pay; defraying costs of apprenticeship or similar programs; or any other *bona fide* fringe benefit. (Benefits required by other federal, state, or local laws are in addition to the Davis-Bacon fringe benefits.)

A contractor or subcontractor may satisfy its obligations under the Davis-Bacon Act by providing wages consisting of any combination of contributions or costs as long as the combination is equal to or greater than the sum of the basic hourly rate and fringe benefits required by the wage determination. The contractor must post the wage determination in a prominent location at the work site.

A contractor performing a contract covered by the Davis-Bacon Act must pay its laborers and mechanics at least once a week and submit certified payroll records to the contracting officer weekly. In addition, the contractor is responsible for the weekly submission of its own and its subcontractor payroll records (see FAR 52.222-8, Payrolls and Basic Records).

A contract subject to the Davis-Bacon Act is also subject to the Copeland (Anti-Kickback) Act, which prohibits illegal deductions or "kickbacks" of wages. Contracts subject to these acts contain both **FAR 52.222-6, Construction Wage Rate Requirements**, and **FAR 52.222-10, Compliance with the Copeland Act Requirements**. In addition, contractors subject to the Davis-Bacon Act are subject to the Contract Work Hours and Safety Standards Act, which requires that contractors pay their laborers and mechanics "time and a half" for overtime (see above).

The Davis-Bacon Act and Copeland Act are administered by the Department of Labor, Wage and Hour Division (**http://www.dol.gov/whd/**).

See **http://www.dol.gov/whd/govcontracts/dbra.htm** and FAR subpart 22.4, Labor Standards for Contracts Involving Construction, for more on Davis-Bacon.

SERVICE CONTRACT ACT OF 1965, AS AMENDED

The McNamara-O'Hara Service Contract Act (codified as Title 41 of the U.S. Code, Chapter 67, Service Contract Labor Standards) applies to federal contracts and subcontracts for services that are to be performed in the United States as follows:

- Contracts of $2,500 or less: Employees must receive at least the minimum wage (see Executive Order 13658 above).

- Contracts over $2,500: Employees must receive at least the "wages and fringe benefits found by the Department of Labor to prevail in the locality or, in the absence of a wage determination, the minimum wage…" The secretary of labor's "wage determination" is attached to the solicitation and becomes part of the resulting contract.

As with the Davis-Bacon Act, the secretary of labor issues wage determinations covering the different types of service labor expected to work under the contract, and they are available at the Wage Determinations OnLine (WDOL) website **http://www.**

wdol.gov. There are two types of wage determinations: one is based on the prevailing wage rates and fringe benefits in a geographical area, and the other is based on collective bargaining agreements negotiated between the predecessor contractor and its unions. With a "successor contractor" wage determination, a contractor must pay wages and benefits at least equal to those specified in the collective bargaining agreement. Some wage determinations will list different classifications within service labor categories to differentiate between various skill levels.

The following are examples of the types of services covered by the Service Contract Act:

- Motor pool operation, parking, taxicab, and ambulance services;

- Packing, crating, and storage;

- Custodial, janitorial, housekeeping, and guard services;

- Food service and lodging;

- Laundry, drycleaning, linen-supply, and clothing alteration and repair services;

- Snow, trash, and garbage removal;

- Drafting, illustrating, graphic arts, stenographic reporting;

- Mortuary services;

- Maintenance and repair of all types of equipment, such as aircraft, engines, electrical motors, vehicles, and construction equipment (however, there are some exceptions – see below);

- Data collection, processing, and analysis services; and

- Operation and maintenance of a federal facility.

The Service Contract Act does not apply to supervisors, administrative personnel, or professionals. Neither does it apply to:

- Contracts for construction, alteration, or repair of public buildings;

- Manufacturing work;

- Contracts for transporting freight or personnel;

- Services subject to the Communications Act of 1934 (radio, telephone, telegraph, or cable);

- Public utility services;

- Any employment contract providing for the services of a specific individual or individuals;

- Contracts for operating postal contract stations for the U.S. Postal Service; and

- Maintenance, calibration, or repair of computer equipment, scientific equipment, medical apparatus, and business machines (under certain circumstances).

Contracts subject to the Service Contract Act contain **FAR 52.222-41, Service Contract Labor Standards**.

Whenever the secretary of labor increases or decreases the wage determination to reflect changes in the locally prevailing wages and fringe benefits or to reflect new collective bargaining agreements, the contracting officer increases or decreases the contract accordingly. The contracting officer will adjust the contract for related increases or decreases in social security, unemployment taxes, and workers' compensation insurance, but not for related changes to overhead, general and administrative expenses, or profit (see **FAR 52.222-44, Fair Labor Standards Act and Service Contract Act – Price Adjustment**).

The Service Contract Act also contains recordkeeping and safety and health requirements.

The Service Contract Act is administered by the Department of Labor, Wage and Hour Division (**http://www.dol.gov/whd/**). Safety and health provisions are administered by the Department of Labor, Occupational Safety and Health Administration (OSHA) (**https://www.osha.gov/**).

See **http://www.dol.gov/whd/govcontracts/sca.htm** and FAR subpart 22.10, Service Contract Labor Standards, for more information.

EMPLOYMENT OF VETERANS

There are several laws and executive orders that address the employment of veterans on government contracts, most recently the **Jobs for Veterans Act** (Public Law 107-288). When taken together, these laws and executive orders require all federal contractors and subcontractors (including construction) with contracts of $150,000 or more to: (1) list all employment openings with the state or local public employment service office or the CareerOneStop website (**http://www.careeronestop.org/jobsearch/findjobs/state-job-banks.aspx**); (2) take affirmative action to employ and advance in employment qualified disabled veterans without discrimination based on their disability or veteran's status; (3) undertake outreach and recruitment activities that are reasonably designed to effectively recruit veterans; and (4) establish a "hiring benchmark" and apply it to hiring of veterans in each establishment on an annual basis. These requirements do not apply to positions for executive and top management positions, positions to be filled from within the contractor's organization, and positions lasting three days or less.

Regarding the establishment of a hiring benchmark, covered contractors and sub-contractors must use one of two methods to establish their benchmarks: (1) establish a benchmark equal to the national percentage of veterans in the civilian labor force, which will be published and updated annually by the OFCCP (currently 8%); or (2) establish their own benchmarks using certain data from the Bureau of Labor Statistics (BLS) and Veterans' Employment and Training Service/Employment and Training Administration (VETS/ETA) as well other factors that reflect the contractor's unique hiring circumstances (such as the percentage of veterans in the civilian labor force in the state[s] where the contractor is located).

Also, contractors and subcontractors are required to invite applicants to self-identify as veterans at both the pre-offer and post-offer phases of the job application.

In addition, contractors and subcontractors that have received an award of $100,000 or more must submit annually a **Form VETS-4212, Federal Contractor Veterans' Employment Report** (which replaces the VETS-100 and the VETS-100A forms) to the Department of Labor. This form requires the contractor to report: (1) the total number of employees by job category (officials and managers, professionals, technicians, sales workers, administrative support workers, craft workers, operatives [workers who operate machines or factory-related processing equipment], laborers and helpers, and service workers) and hiring location; (2) the total number of such employees, by job category and hiring location, who are "protected veterans" ("disabled veteran," "recently separated veteran," "active duty wartime or campaign badge veteran," or "Armed Forces service medal veteran"); (3) the total number of new employees hired by the contractor during the period covered by the report; (4) the total number of new employees who are protected veterans; and (5) the maximum and minimum number of employees at each hiring location during the period covered by the report. Instructions for filing the VETS-4212 report electronically are found at **http://www.dol.gov/vets/vets4212.htm**. (Contractors and subcontractors with 10 or fewer hiring locations may file their VETS-4212 reports in paper format.)

Before awarding a contract exceeding the simplified acquisition threshold ($150,000), a contracting officer must verify that the proposed contractor has submitted the required VETS-4212 report for the preceding reporting period. The contracting officer does this by querying the Department of Labor's Veterans' Employment and Training Service for confirmation (under "Filing Verification" at **http://www. dol.gov/vets/vets4212.htm**).

These requirements do not apply when the work is performed outside the United States by employees recruited outside the United States. Contracts subject to the act contain **FAR 52.222-35, Equal Opportunity for Veteran, FAR 52.222-37, Employment Reports on Veterans**, and **FAR 52.222-38, Compliance with Veterans' Employment Reporting Requirements.**

If the Department of Labor imposes sanctions on a contractor for violations of FAR 52.222-35, the contracting officer must take appropriate actions, which may include: (1) withholding progress payments (see Chapter 18); (2) terminating or suspending the contract (see Chapter 18); or (3) debarring the contractor (see Chapter 7).

The veterans' employment provisions are administered by two Department of Labor agencies: the Office of Federal Contract Compliance Programs (**http://www. dol.gov/ofccp/**); and the Veterans' Employment and Training Service (**http://www. dol.gov/vets/**).

See **http://www.dol.gov/vets/**, FAR subpart 22.13, Equal Opportunity for Veterans, and Title 41 of the Code of Federal Regulations (CFR), part 61-300, Annual Report from Federal Contractors, for more information.

EMPLOYMENT OF WORKERS WITH DISABILITIES

Section 503 of the **Rehabilitation Act of 1973** requires all federal contractors and subcontractors (including construction) with contracts over **$15,000** to: (1) take affirmative action to employ and advance in employment qualified individuals with disabilities, and to treat qualified individuals without discrimination based on their physical or mental disability; (2) undertake appropriate outreach and positive recruitment activities that are reasonably designed to effectively recruit qualified individuals with disabilities; and (3) annually compare the utilization of individuals with disabilities in their workforces to the **7% utilization goal** for each job group in the contractor's or subcontractor's workforce (the 7% utilization goal is not a quota or a ceiling that limits or restricts the employment of individuals with disabilities; however, "if individuals with disabilities are employed in a job group at a rate less than the utilization goal, the contractor must take specific measures to address this disparity"). This requirement applies to "employment activities" within the United States, not to "employment activities" abroad.

"Job groups" are jobs that are grouped based on three factors: (1) similar wages; (2) similar job duties and responsibilities; and (3) similar opportunities for training, promotion, transfer, and other employment benefits. Job groups usually contain one to three jobs each. However, contractors with a total workforce of fewer than 150 employees may use the same nine occupational groups used in the Form VETS-4212: officials and managers, professionals, technicians, sales workers, administrative support workers, craft workers, operatives, laborers and helpers, and service workers.

Every contractor with more than **50 employees** and a **contract of $50,000 or more** must prepare an **affirmative action program** that describes the contractor's policies and procedures for complying with these requirements. The affirmative action program must include the following elements: policy statement; review of personnel processes; physical and mental qualifications; reasonable accommodation to physical and mental limitations; harassment; external dissemination of policy, outreach, and positive recruitment; internal dissemination of policy; audit and reporting system; responsibility for implementation; training; and data collection analysis (which includes: the total number of job openings and total number of jobs filled; the ratio of jobs filled to job openings; the total number of applicants for all jobs; the ratio of applicants with disabilities to all applicants ["applicant ratio"]; the number of applicants with disabilities hired; the total number of applicants hired; and the ratio of individuals with disabilities hired to all hires ["hiring ratio"]).

The affirmative action program must be prepared within 120 days of the commencement of the contract, and it must address each of the contractor's establishments. The contractor must submit the affirmative action program to the OFCCP within 30 days of a request. In addition, the affirmative action program must be available to any employee or applicant for employment for inspection upon request.

Contractors and subcontractors must invite applicants to self-identify as individuals with disabilities at both the pre-offer and post-offer phases of the application process. In addition, contractors and subcontractors must invite their employees to self-identify as individuals with disabilities every five years.

When the percentage of individuals with disabilities in one or more job groups is less than the 7% utilization goal, the contractor must develop and execute action-oriented programs designed to correct any identified problems areas. These action-oriented programs may include additional outreach efforts and/or other actions (such as priority consideration) designed to correct the identified problem areas and attain the established goal. "A contractor's determination that it has not attained the utilization goal…in one or more job groups does not constitute either a finding or admission of discrimination…"

OFCCP may conduct compliance evaluations to determine if the contractor is taking affirmative action to employ, advance in employment, and treat qualified individuals without discrimination on the basis of disability. A compliance evaluation may consist of an on-site review, an off-site review of records, a recordkeeping compliance check, or other investigative procedures. "Where deficiencies are found to exist, reasonable efforts shall be made to secure compliance through conciliation and persuasion."

Before award of any contract or subcontract of $10,000,000 or more, the prospective contractor and subcontractor(s) are subject to an OFCCP compliance evaluation before award of the contract unless OFCCP has conducted an evaluation within the preceding 24 months and found the contractor or subcontractor to be in compliance.

Contracts covered by the Rehabilitation Act contain **FAR 52.222-36, Affirmative Action for Workers with Disabilities**.

If the Department of Labor imposes sanctions on a contractor for violations of FAR 52.222-36, the contracting officer must take appropriate actions, which may include: (1) withholding progress payments (see Chapter 18); (2) terminating or suspending the contract (see Chapter 18); or (3) debarring the contractor (see Chapter 7).

These policies and procedures are administered by the Department of Labor, Office of Federal Contract Compliance Programs (**http://www.dol.gov/ofccp/**).

See **http://www.dol.gov/ofccp/regs/compliance/sec503.htm**, FAR subpart 22.14, Employment of Workers with Disabilities, and Title 41 of the CFR, part 60-741, Affirmative Action and Nondiscrimination Obligations of Federal Contractors and Subcontractors Regarding Individuals with Disabilities, for more information.

CHAPTER 16

PROTESTS AGAINST CONTRACT AWARD

It is the contracting officer's responsibility to ensure that solicitations are conducted according to the requirements and prohibitions contained in the 2,000 pages of the FAR and in his agency's FAR supplement. Occasionally, a contracting officer will make a bad decision or violate one of those requirements or prohibitions no matter how well trained he is. While everyone makes mistakes, this is little consolation to a bidder or offeror denied a contract because the contracting officer used poor judgment or failed to follow the rules *exactly*.

The government executes about 10 million contracts each year and knows some of them will not be conducted properly. Even if the process were perfect 99.9% of the time, there would still be 10,000 problem procurements. A bidder or offeror can always seek relief through a suit in the U.S. Court of Federal Claims. However, the government makes an administrative remedy available that does not involve the courts, is relatively fast, and is relatively inexpensive – an unhappy bidder or offeror can **protest** any solicitation or contract award it believes was not conducted properly. The protest remedy is an economical means of safeguarding the rights of bidders and offerors *and* insuring the integrity of the contracting system.

OVERVIEW OF THE PROTEST PROCESS

FAR 33.101 defines a protest as "*a written objection by an interested party to any of the following: (1) a solicitation or other request by an agency for offers for a contract for the procurement of property or services; (2) the cancellation of the solicitation or other request; (3) an award or proposed award of the contract; [or] (4) a termination or cancellation of an award of the contract, if the written objection contains an allegation that the termination or cancellation is based in whole or in part on improprieties concerning the award of the contract.*" It goes on to define an "interested party" as "*an actual or prospective offeror whose direct economic interest would be affected by the award of a contract or by the failure to award a contract.*"

If a bidder submits a bid and the contracting officer wrongfully disqualifies the bidder, takes some action that hinders the bidder's ability to compete fairly, or fails to disqualify another bidder that should be disqualified, the aggrieved bidder is an "interested party" entitled to protest the impropriety and seek its correction. A bidder is an interested party even if it *might* submit a bid because it is a "prospective offeror" with a "direct economic interest" in the award of the contract.

The Competition in Contracting Act of 1984 (CICA) gave the **Government Accountability Office** (GAO) (formerly the General Accounting Office) statutory authority to hear protests. The GAO is the sole administrative protest forum available to disgruntled bidders and offerors.

There are many reasons a contractor might want to protest a solicitation or contract award. These are some of the reasons most cited:

- The contracting officer failed to comply with an applicable rule or regulation;

- Actions taken by the contracting officer unfairly limited a contractor's opportunity to win the contract (for example, arbitrarily requiring 10 years experience to be eligible for award);

- The contracting officer did not synopsize the solicitation in **FedBizOpps** when required to do so;

- The solicitation incorporates ambiguous specifications or contains ambiguous provisions (such as indefinite evaluation factors);

- The contracting officer failed to specify the agency's needs and solicit bids or proposals in a manner designed to achieve full and open competition (for example, the solicitation specified features that are unnecessary for the item's intended use and are only available from one source);

- Inappropriate use of the first six exceptions to full and open competition permitted by the Competition in Contracting Act (for example, the contracting officer may not use the "unusual and compelling urgency" exception to restrict competition and make it is easier to award contracts before the fiscal year ends – see Chapter 3);

- The contracting officer improperly eliminated the offeror from the competitive range (see Chapter 8);

- The contracting officer cancelled the solicitation for improper reasons, such as to avoid awarding a contract to the apparent winner;

- The award is improper because the winner is nonresponsive or ineligible for award; and

■ The termination or cancellation of a contract award is based on improprieties concerning the award of the contract.

However, GAO will *not* entertain protests that:

■ Are not filed within required time limits;

■ Are frivolous or do not state a valid reason for the protest;

■ Are brought or pursued in bad faith;

■ Pertain to a contracting officer's affirmative responsibility determination (that is, the contracting officer concludes the low bidder or offeror is capable of performing the contract) *except* protests that allege that definitive responsibility criteria in the solicitation were not met, or protests that identify evidence raising serious concerns that the contracting officer unreasonably failed to consider available relevant information or otherwise violated statute or regulation;

■ Involve matters that are already before a court *unless* the court requests a decision from the GAO before it issues a ruling;

■ Challenge a competitor's size status on a small business set-aside, HUBZone small business set-aside, service-disabled veteran-owned small business set-aside, or women-owned small business set-aside (the Small Business Administration [SBA] decides these protests – see later in this chapter);

■ Challenge the SBA's issuance, or refusal to issue, a certificate of competency (unless the protester can demonstrate bad faith on the part of government officials or that the SBA failed to consider vital information bearing on the firm's responsibility due to the manner in which the information was presented to or withheld from the SBA by the procuring agency – see Chapter 7);

■ Challenge any decision to place or not place a contract under the SBA's 8(a) program (unless the protester can demonstrate bad faith on the part of government officials or that officials violated regulations – see Chapter 11);

■ Involve alleged violations of the Procurement Integrity Act (see Chapter 17) *unless* the protester provided the information it believes constitutes a violation of the act to the contracting agency within **14 days** after the protester first discovered the alleged violation;

■ Involve protests against awards of subcontracts (except when the agency awarding the prime contract has requested that subcontract protests be decided); and

■ Involve disputes arising during contract performance (these are subject to the Contract Disputes Act – see Chapter 18).

A protester should try to resolve the issue with the contracting officer before filing a protest. Frequently, a telephone call to the contracting officer is all it takes to resolve the problem. Any moderately complicated solicitation will contain errors, discrepancies, ambiguities, and contradictions, and the contracting officer will usually correct them without hesitation. But occasionally the contracting officer will make a conscious decision to include a provision that seems to violate the regulations, or will take some action that appears arbitrary and unfair. Often this "improper" decision results from his interpretation of the regulations. If the contracting officer cannot explain the reasons for his decision to the bidder's satisfaction, and *the bidder thinks the matter is worth pursuing* (considering the value of the contract and the time, effort, and expense that will be involved), it should file a protest.

What are the odds of a bidder winning a protest? Not bad. About **one-third** of the protests to the GAO are decided in favor of the protester or result in a settlement between the protester and the government. So a bidder should not be afraid of filing a protest if it believes it has been unfairly denied a contract or a reasonable chance to compete. However, a protester must be careful to follow the rules, especially deadlines – the GAO is particularly unforgiving when it comes to late protests.

PROTESTS TO THE CONTRACTING AGENCY

While a bidder or offeror should always try to settle differences with, or obtain clarifications from, the contracting officer first, sometimes the contracting officer cannot or will not satisfy the bidder or offeror. When the bidder or offeror is not convinced the contracting officer is complying with the FAR or the agency's FAR supplement, the regulations *encourage* it to file its protest with the contracting agency before going to the GAO. Such protests require less paperwork because the contracting agency is already aware of most of the facts, and the agency can make a fairly quick decision – usually within **35 calendar days** after the protest is filed with the contracting agency. However, the contracting agency might be prejudiced (the contracting officer is its employee, and the requirement being delayed by the protest is its requirement), and the protester is not afforded the same safeguards as with protests to the GAO – in fact, each agency is responsible for developing its own rules for agency protests.

A protest to the contracting agency that alleges an impropriety in the solicitation must be filed **before the bid opening** or **date for receipt of proposals**. All other protests must be filed no later than **10 calendar days** after the basis of the protest is known *or should have been known*. For example, a protest alleging the protester was improperly eliminated from the competitive range must be filed within 10 calendar days after the protester learns or should have learned that the contracting officer eliminated it from the competitive range. (If a deadline falls on a Saturday, Sunday, or federal holiday, the next working day becomes the deadline.)

If a protester decides to file its protest with the contracting agency, the protest must include the following information:

■ Name, address, and fax and telephone numbers of the protester;

■ Solicitation or contract number;

■ A detailed statement of the legal and factual grounds for the protest, including a description of the "resulting prejudice to the protester" (that is, the harm the protester will suffer if its protest is not granted);

■ Copies of relevant documents;

■ A request for a ruling by the agency;

■ A statement of the relief requested (for example, that the agency cancel the improper contract award and award the contract to the protester);

■ Information establishing that the protester is an interested party; and

■ Information establishing the timeliness of the protest (such as "this protest against the inclusion of an improper provision in Invitation For Bids FGH-876 is being filed on the 5th, one week before the bid opening on the 12th").

In addition, the protester (or an interested party) may request an independent review of the protest at a level above the contracting officer. The agency's FAR supplement or the solicitation will specify whether this independent review is an alternative to a decision by the contracting officer or is an appeal of a contracting officer's decision. This independent review does not have to be conducted by someone within the contracting officer's supervisory chain. The official conducting the independent review should not have been involved in the procurement.

When the contracting agency receives a protest, the contracting officer is not permitted to make an award or, if a contract has been awarded, allow continued performance until the matter is resolved *unless* he (or other designated official) determines an immediate contract award or continued contract performance is for urgent and compelling reasons or is in the best interest of the government. However, if the contract has been awarded, the contracting officer will not direct the contractor to cease performance if the protest is filed (1) more than **10 days after contract award**, or (2) more than **five days** after the unsuccessful bidder or offeror was given the opportunity to be **debriefed** (see Chapter 8), whichever is later.

"Urgent and compelling reasons" and "in the best interest of the government" are rather large "loopholes." For example, if bids are about to expire and the low bidder is not willing to extend its bid acceptance period, the contracting officer could decide this is an "urgent and compelling reason" that justifies an immediate contract award, *or* he could decide that making the award to the low bidder before it withdraws its bid is "in the best interest of the government."

Most agencies have the contracting officer decide the protest, although the agencies must also provide informal, simple, and expeditious protests resolution procedures such as alternative dispute resolution (ADR) techniques (see Chapter 18) and the use of impartial third parties or another agency's personnel.

However, bidders or offerors do *not* have to protest to the contracting agency before protesting to the GAO. It is not a sequential process – protesters can skip the contracting agency and protest directly to the GAO, or skip GAO and go directly to the U.S. Court of Federal Claims. Because of the potential problems with protests to the contracting agency, frequently these are preferred alternatives.

See FAR 33.103, Protests to the Agency, for more on protests to the contracting agency.

PROTESTS TO THE GOVERNMENT ACCOUNTABILITY OFFICE (GAO)

The GAO has been deciding protests against the award of contracts since 1931 under its statutory authority to settle and adjust government accounts. Traditionally, the GAO has been an informal forum, deciding protests based on documentation submitted by the protester and the government. While this is still true of most protests to the GAO, the GAO permits protesters and the government to request that it conduct hearings to more fully explore the facts. These optional hearings have many of the same formal characteristics as a court.

GAO's protest rules are available at **http://www.gao.gov/legal/bid-protest-regulations/about**. A summary of the GAO's rules and procedures is at FAR 33.104, Protests to GAO.

Protesters may send their protests by mail (General Counsel, Government Accountability Office, 441 G Street, NW, Washington, DC 20548, Attention: Procurement Law Control Group [the Procurement Law Control Group's telephone number is 202-512-8199]), facsimile ("fax") (202-512-9749), e-mail (**protests@gao.gov**), courier, or hand delivery. A protest is considered "filed" when it is received by GAO by 5:30 pm, eastern time.

Protests brought by courier or are hand delivery must be brought to the 4th Street side of the GAO building (opened 7:30 am to 5:30 pm) and labeled with one of the following labels: "Procurement Law Control Group," "PLCG," "Bid Protest," or "Contract Appeals Board." The package will be scanned, and it may be opened and searched. After any inspection, the package will be stamped with a time and date to indicate when package is considered officially received. Note that GAO employees will *not* meet couriers outside the GAO building to accept packages. "Hand delivery and other means of delivery may not be practicable during certain periods due, for example, to security concerns or equipment failures."

Also, GAO advises that "regular Postal Service mail should not be used for time-sensitive packages."

These cautions suggest that fax and e-mail are the preferred methods for transmitting protests to GAO.

Deadlines for Filing Protests

As mentioned earlier, the GAO is very picky about deadlines, primarily because the GAO has a statutory deadline for rendering protest decisions. Periods establishing the various deadlines in the protest process are in "calendar" days, and the day from which the period begins is not counted (for example, if a bidder finds out about an improper action on the 17th, the 18th is the first day in the period). A protest or document must be received by the GAO by **5:30 P.M. eastern time** to meet the deadline. However, when the deadline falls on a Saturday, Sunday, or federal holiday, the deadline becomes 5:30 P.M. the **next business day**. This rule also applies when the GAO is closed all or part of the deadline date, such as for inclement weather.

- The GAO will *not* consider any protest originally filed with the contracting agency until the contracting officer takes an "adverse action." The protester must file its protest within **10 days** of *learning of the adverse action*. In many cases, the 10 days will commence with the receipt of a notification that the protest has been denied. However, an adverse action may have taken place with the **opening of bids, rejection of a bid, or award of the contract to another party**. The 10-day clock starts with those actions because *a reasonably alert protester would have concluded that its protest had been denied*. Those that protest to the contracting officer must be on their guard – protesters that wait for a formal response from the contracting officer might miss the deadline for filing a protest with GAO.

- Protests against apparent improprieties in a solicitation must be filed **before the bid opening date** (for IFBs) or the **closing date** for the receipt of proposals (for RFPs). This rule also applies to protests originally filed with the contracting officer: if a protest against the inclusion of a particular clause in an IFB is filed with the contracting officer *after* the bid opening, the GAO will *not* consider the protest even if it is filed within 10 days of learning of the adverse action.

- Unsuccessful offerors that are debriefed (see Chapter 8) must file their protests no later than **ten days after the debriefing** (however, if the protester requests a debriefing but files its protest before the debriefing takes place, the GAO will *not* consider the protest).

- All other protests must be filed within **10 days** after the basis for protest was known *or should have been known* by the protester, as with protests to the agency.

Protests that are patently late may be dismissed without being considered (the only exception is a late protest that "raises issues significant to the procurement system"). The protester must show *in its protest* that the protest is timely. For example, the protest must say something like "this protest is being filed prior to the bid opening date" or "since we learned of the contracting officer's adverse action on the 10th and this protest is being filed on the 19th, it is within the 10 day time limit specified in the Government Accountability Office's bid protest rules." These statements must be supported by appropriate evidence, such as the cover page of the solicitation with the bid opening date, a signed letter from the contracting officer, a solicitation amendment, or similar proof.

Formats for Protests

There is no required format for protests to the GAO. However, there are some general requirements that protesters must follow or the GAO may decide *not* to consider the protest:

- The protest must be in writing and signed by the protester or its representative;

- It must contain the protester's name, address, e-mail address, and telephone and fax numbers;

- It must identify the contracting agency and the solicitation or contract number;

- It must provide a detailed statement of the legal and factual grounds for protest, copies of relevant documents, and reasons why the GAO should rule in the protester's favor (for example, the contracting officer took a specific action that violates a particular provision of the FAR, and in doing so improperly disqualified the protester from receiving the award and undermined the integrity of the procurement process);

- It must provide sufficient information establishing that the protester is an "interested party" (see above);

- It must clearly show that the protest has been filed within the prescribed time limits (see above);

- It must specifically request the Comptroller General (the head of the GAO) to rule on the protest;

- It must state the kind of relief sought (for example, reinstate the protester in the competitive range (see Chapter 8) and conduct negotiations with the protester); and

■ It must indicate that a copy of the protest and all attachments are being furnished to the contracting officer (or the individual identified in the solicitation as the one to receive protests) within **one** day.

In addition, the protester *may* request in its protest a protective order, specific documents relevant to the protest, a hearing, or any combination (see below).

Protection of Proprietary Information

The protest will be provided to other "interested parties," such as the bidder or offeror that will receive the contract if the protest is denied. If the protest includes documents that contain proprietary or confidential information or would give competitors an unfair advantage, the protester should place a statement similar to the following on the first page of the document:

USE AND DISCLOSURE OF PROPRIETARY OR CONFIDENTIAL INFORMATION

This document contains proprietary and/or confidential information on pages 3, 7, and 9. This proprietary information shall not be disclosed outside the government and shall not be duplicated, used, or disclosed in whole or in part for any purpose other that to evaluate the protest.

The protester should identify the proprietary and confidential information on those pages by underlining, circling, or some other method. In addition, the protester should type the following statement on the page:

Disclosure of proprietary or confidential information identified on this page is subject to the restriction on the first page of this document.

The protester must file a "redacted" version of its protest (that is, a copy of the protest with the proprietary information omitted) to the GAO and the contracting activity within **one day** after filing its unredacted protest with GAO.

Placing these statements on documents will not *guarantee* the information will not be released. If a protester stamps "proprietary information" on everything it submits, the GAO will ignore the restrictions and release the documents. But the GAO does respect the confidentiality of information that is truly competition sensitive. If the GAO decides a document contains proprietary or confidential information but decides to release it because of its importance to the protest, the GAO will release the document under a "**protective order**."

Protective Orders

The GAO needs a complete record upon which to base its decision, and part of that record is a full examination of *all* the evidence by *all* the parties. However, the GAO realizes some of that information (such as trade secrets, commercial or financial information, and confidential data) may be privileged or could provide a competitive advantage to others. Therefore, the GAO may, upon request by any party (such as the contracting activity, the protester, or an interested party) or on its own initiative, limit disclosure of certain documents to the protester's or an interested party's **legal counsel** or **consultants retained by counsel**. A protective order allows counsel and their consultants to examine the documents and advise their clients whether continued pursuit of the protest would be worthwhile.

Legal counsel may be either an *employee* of the protester or interested party or *independent counsel* retained by the protester or interested party. Any counsel, or consultant retained by counsel, seeking access to the documents covered by a protective order must apply to the GAO and establish, through supporting evidence, that (1) he represents one of the parties; (2) he does not take part in competitive decision-making involving federal contracts for *any firm* that could gain a competitive advantage from the protected information; and (3) there will be no significant risk of inadvertent disclosure of protected information. The application must be submitted simultaneously to all parties. Those objecting to the applicant's access to the protected information must file their objections to the GAO within **two days** after receipt of the application (though the GAO *may* consider objections raised after the two days).

Counsel and consultants who are allowed access to the protected information may examine the documents and render advice *based on* the contents of the documents, but they may not disclose those contents to their client. This is a violation of the protective order, and the GAO will impose sanctions, such as referring the violation to appropriate bar associations, restricting the violator's practice before the GAO, prohibiting the individual from participating in the remainder of the protest, or dismissing the protest. In addition, the party whose information was improperly disclosed is entitled to all remedies under the law, such as suing for damages.

Obtaining Additional Documents

A protester may request specific documents relevant to the protest when it files its protest as long as it can explain the relevancy of the documents to its protest. Examples of such documents are the justification to use one the first six exceptions to competition permitted by CICA and the justification's supporting paperwork. The contracting agency will provide these additional documents to the GAO, the protester, and other interested parties *unless* the documents are covered by a protective order or the documents would provide a competitive advantage (for example, a competitor's proposal, working papers, or acquisition plans). The contracting agency must provide to the GAO and all other parties a list of the documents it has already released, it will release in its report on the protest (that is, the agency's rebuttal to the protest charges – see below), and it intends to withhold from the protester and interested parties (and its reasons for withholding them) **five days** before it files its report. Any objection to the agency's release or withholding of documents must be filed with the GAO and the other parties within **two days** of receiving the list.

In addition, the protester may request additional documents no later than two days after their existence or relevance first becomes known or *should have been known*. Usually the protester finds out about these additional documents when documents that are released refer to them. The contracting agency must provide the withheld documents and an index to the GAO, the protester, and other interested parties within **two days** or explain why it is not required to produce the documents.

When requested by the protester or an interested party, the GAO will decide whether the contracting agency must produce the withheld documents and whether the documents should be subject to a protective order (see above).

Protest File

When requested by the protester or an interested party, agencies are required to prepare a "**protest file**" and provide reasonable access to it for inspection. The protest file normally includes the same documents that are required to be included the agency's report except for the contracting officer's statement and the memorandum of law (see below). The purpose of the protest file is to expedite the development and resolution of protests by making public the key documents involved in the protest and, possibly, convincing the protester that the contracting officer followed procedures properly and made the correct decisions.

Withholding Contract Award Pending GAO Decision

When a protest is lodged with the GAO **before** the contract is awarded, the contracting office may not proceed with the award unless the *head of the contracting activity* decides:

1. Urgent and compelling circumstances exist that would significantly affect the interests of the United States if award is withheld until a decision is rendered by the GAO; and

2. Award is likely to occur within 30 days.

If the head of the contracting activity decides that both these conditions apply and decides to authorize the contracting officer to proceed with the award, he must notify the GAO before the contracting officer awards the contract. This gives the GAO a chance to express its concerns to the appropriate authorities.

Suspending Contract Performance Pending GAO Decision

For protests filed **after** contract award, the contracting officer must suspend performance or terminate the awarded contract if his agency is notified of the protest by the GAO within **10 days after the date of the contract award** or **five days after after a debriefing date offered to the protester if the solicitation was negotiated,** (see Chapter 8), whichever is later, unless the *head of the contracting activity* decides:

1. Contract performance is in the best interests of the United States; or

2. Urgent and compelling circumstances exist which would significantly affect the interest of the United States if contract performance were postponed while awaiting the GAO decision.

Again, the head of the contracting activity must notify the GAO if he decides to allow the contractor to continue working on the contract. (See FAR 52.233-3, Protest After Award.)

(**NOTE:** Because the GAO has one day to notify the contracting agency that a protest has been filed [see below], a protester must file its protest with the GAO no later than **nine days after contract award** or **four days after the debriefing** to force suspension of contract performance. If 10 days after contract award or five days after the debriefing occurs on a weekend or a Monday, the protester must file its protest no later than the previous *Friday* so the GAO can give the required notification on Monday – if that Friday is a federal holiday, the protester must file its protest by *Thursday!* However, GAO advises that "if a protest is being filed shortly before the deadline for triggering an automatic stay of award or performance, the protester should bring this to GAO's attention at the time of filing; this will enable GAO to attempt to provide expedited notice of the protest to the agency.")

Processing the Protest

Within **one day** of protesting to the GAO, the protester must furnish a copy of the complete protest to the official designated in the solicitation to receive protests (look for FAR 52.233-2, Service of Protest, in the solicitation).

Within **one day** of receiving the protest, the GAO notifies the contracting agency that a protest has been filed. The GAO makes the notification by telephone and confirms it in writing. The contracting agency must *immediately* notify "all bidders or offerors that appear to have a substantial prospect of receiving an award [if the protest is denied]" (or to the contractor if the contract has been awarded) that a protest has been filed.

If the protester claims some of the information in its protest is proprietary or should be withheld, it must furnish a copy of the protest, with the information omitted, to the GAO within **one day** after filing its protest.

If the existence or relevance of additional documents becomes known after the protest is filed, the protester must submit a request for the documents to the GAO and the contracting agency within **two days** after their existence or relevance became known or should have been known. The contracting activity must provide the requested documents and an index to the GAO, the protester, and interested parties within **two days** or explain why it is not required to produce the documents. Upon request of the protester or an interested party, the GAO will decide whether the contracting agency must provide any of the withheld documents and whether this should be done under a protective order.

Five days before submitting its report, the contracting agency must prepare and furnish to the GAO and all other parties a list of all documents it has released, will release in its report, and intends to withhold from the protester and interested parties and its reasons for withholding them. Those objecting to the agency's release or withholding of documents must file their objections to the GAO and the other parties within **two days** of receiving the list. The GAO will decide whether the contracting agency must provide any of the withheld documents and whether this should be done under a protective order.

Within **30 days** of receiving the GAO's telephonic notification, the contracting agency must submit a report to the GAO, the protester, and all interested parties that responded to the notice of protest. The report must include an index and the following:

- The protest;

- The bid or proposal submitted by the protester and a copy of the bid or offer that is being considered for award or is being protested;

- The solicitation, including the relevant specifications;

- A best estimate of the contract value;

- The abstract of bids or proposals;

- All relevant evaluation documents;

- Any other relevant documents;

- All documents requested by the protester or an explanation of why the contracting agency is not required to produce the documents;

- A list of parties being provided the documents;

- The contracting officer's signed statement setting forth findings, actions, recommendations, and any additional evidence or information deemed necessary in determining the validity of the protest; and

■   A memorandum of law.

Within **10 days after receipt of the agency's report**, the protester must (1) submit comments on the report to the GAO, the contracting agency, and interested parties; (2) request that the GAO decide the protest on the written record; or (3) request that the GAO grant an extension and explain the specific circumstances that require the extension. Failure to take any one of these actions will cause the GAO to dismiss the protest.

Interested parties may submit their comments on the agency's report directly to the GAO, the contracting agency, the protester, and other interested parties within **10 days** after receipt of the report.

The GAO Decision

The GAO issues its recommendations on the protest within **100 days of initial receipt of the protest**. It sends copies of the decision to the protester, interested parties, and the agency. (**NOTE:** Copies of protest decisions, an electronic docket, and other information is available on the Internet at **http://www.gao.gov** under "Bid Protests and Appropriations Law.")

If the GAO finds in favor of the protester, it can recommend that the contracting officer follow any of several courses of action:

■   Recompete the contract;

■   Issue a new solicitation;

■   Terminate the contract;

■   Refrain from exercising any of the options under the contract;

■   Award a contract consistent with applicable laws and regulations; or

■   Any other recommendation that GAO determines is necessary to promote compliance.

Note that the GAO decision is merely a recommendation and, as such, is not binding on the contracting agency. However, if an agency decides not to comply with the GAO recommendation, the head of the agency or his designee (who can be no lower than the head of the contracting activity) must report the reasons for not following the recommendation to the GAO within **65 days**. The GAO then reports to Congress each refusal to comply with its recommendations.

In addition, if the GAO determines that the solicitation, the proposed award, or the award of a contract does not comply with a statute or regulation, the GAO can recommend that the protester be reimbursed for the costs it incurred related to:

■ Filing and pursuing the protest, including reasonable fees for attorneys, consultants, and expert witnesses; and

■ Bid or proposal preparation.

If the GAO recommends that the contracting agency pay the protester its costs of pursuing the successful protest, the protester and the agency must attempt to reach agreement on the amount due the protester. The protester must file its claim for costs with the contracting agency within **60 days** after receipt of the GAO's decision. The protester's claim must detail the time expended and the costs incurred and, if the amount claimed exceeds **$100,000**, the protester must certify (1) the claim is made in good faith, (2) supporting data are accurate and complete to the best of the contractor's knowledge and belief, and (3) the amount requested is an accurate reflection of the allowable costs it incurred pursuing the protest (see Chapter 18 under "Claims and Disputes").

The contracting agency must issue a decision on the claim for protest costs **as soon as practicable**. If the protester and contracting agency cannot reach a decision within a reasonable time, the protester may request that GAO recommend the amount of costs the agency should pay. When GAO recommends the amount of costs, it may also recommend that the contracting agency pay the protester the costs of pursuing the claim for costs. The contracting agency then has **60 days** after the GAO recommends the amount of costs that should be paid the protester to notify the GAO how it will respond to the recommendation.

The payment of fees to large businesses (see Chapter 11) for consultants and expert witnesses is limited to the highest rate of compensation for expert witnesses paid by the government (GS-15, Step 10 under the General Schedule for civil servants). Payment of fees to large businesses for attorneys is limited to $150 an hour unless the losing agency determines that a higher fee is justified because of increases in the cost of living or the existence of a special factor such as the limited availability of qualified attorneys. These limitations do *not* apply to small businesses. However, the cap on fees payable to large businesses constitutes a "benchmark" as to a reasonable level of payment for small businesses.

Even if the contracting agency decides to take corrective action *before* the GAO renders a decision, the protester may ask the GAO to recommend that the contracting agency pay its costs of pursuing the protest (including attorneys' fees and consultant and expert witness fees). The protester must file its request to the GAO and the contracting agency within **15 days** after learning (or should have learned) that the contracting agency is taking corrective action. The contracting agency then has **15 days** after receipt of the request to file a response with the GAO and the protester. If the GAO decides to recommend that the contracting agency pay the costs of the protester, the protester must file its claim for costs with the contracting agency within **60 days** after receipt of the GAO's recommendation, just as if GAO had rendered a decision on the protest. All other deadlines and procedures for processing the protester's claim for costs are the same, too.

Hearings

Although most protests are decided without a **hearing**, any party to the protest may request that the GAO hold one (the GAO may decide on its own that a hearing is warranted). The request should be made as early as possible in the protest process, preferably when the protest is first filed with the GAO. The request must provide reasons why the hearing is necessary. The GAO decides whether to hold a hearing, where (usually in Washington, DC), and when. Hearings may be held by telephone or other electronic means at GAO's discretion.

All parties participating in the protest are invited to attend the hearing. Others *may* be allowed to attend as observers and participate as allowed by the GAO hearing official. If information covered by a protective order or proprietary information that is *not* covered by a protective order is to be disclosed at the hearing, the hearing official may restrict attendance as he sees fit.

Failure of a witness to attend the hearing or answer a question may cause the GAO to draw an inference unfavorable to the party for whom the witness would have testified.

The proceedings are normally recorded or transcribed. Any party may obtain a copy at its own expense.

After the hearing, the parties have **five days** to submit comments on the hearing to the GAO and all other interested parties. In their comments, the parties should reference all testimony and admissions made during the hearing that consider relevant. The GAO must dismiss the protest if, within this five day period, the protester fails to comment on the hearing.

Request for Reconsideration

A protester, an interested party, or the contracting agency may request that the GAO reconsider its decision. The request must be made within **10 days** after the basis for reconsideration becomes known or should have been known. It must contain a detailed statement of the factual and legal grounds that warrant reversal or modification of the decision, must specify any errors the GAO made in interpreting applicable laws, or introduce evidence that was not available when the protester originally filed the protest.

The GAO will not consider a request that merely repeats views already expressed in the protest, merely expresses disagreement with the decision, or provides information or raises arguments that could have been, but were not, provided or raised during the protest.

The GAO will take expeditious action to decide whether the new information warrants reconsidering its decision. If the GAO does reconsider, it will render its decision promptly. However, while the reconsideration process takes place, the contracting officer may proceed with the contract award or the contractor may continue performing the contract.

Appeals

If a protester is not satisfied with the GAO decision, it may appeal the decision to the U.S. Court of Federal Claims. If not satisfied with that decision, the protester may appeal the matter all the way to the U.S. Supreme Court. The court's rules are at **http://www.uscfc.uscourts.gov/rcfc**.

Express Option

There is an **express option** that the GAO may invoke solely at its discretion. It is invoked when only a few simple issues are involved and the case is suitable for a resolution within **65 days**. Any party may request use of the express option; the request must be submitted in writing to the GAO within **five days** after the protest is filed. The GAO will promptly notify the protester, the contracting agency, and other interested parties if it decides to handle the protest using the express option.

With the express option, the contracting agency must submit a complete report to the GAO, the protester, and other interested parties within **20 days** after being notified by GAO that the express option will be used.

Comments on the agency report must be submitted to the GAO, the contracting agency, and interested parties within **five days** after receipt of the report.

The GAO must issue its decision within **65 days** of receipt of the protest. The GAO may use flexible alternative procedures to resolve the protest, including alternate dispute resolution (ADR), establishing an accelerated schedule, and/or issuing a *summary* decision (which is not in as much detail as a normal GAO decision).

PROTESTS CONCERNING SMALL BUSINESS STATUS

To be eligible for an award under a small business set-aside, a concern must meet the applicable small business size standard in FAR subpart 19.1 (see Chapter 11). An interested party that does not believe a bidder or offeror qualifies as a small business may file a protest with the contracting officer – see FAR 19.302, Protesting a Small Business Representation or Rerepresentation, for detailed procedures.

To be considered, the protest must be filed with the contracting officer within **five *business* days after the bid opening** for IFBs or, for RFPs, **five *business* days after receiving the notification from the contracting officer that identifies the apparently successful offeror**. A protest may be in writing if it is delivered to the contracting officer by hand, telegram, or letter postmarked within the 5-day period. A protest may be made orally, but it must be confirmed in writing either within the five-day period or by letter postmarked no later than the next business day. The contracting officer then turns the matter over to the Small Business Administration (SBA) for decision.

A contracting officer may file a protest with the SBA at any time before or after award.

The SBA asks the party whose small business status is being protested to provide information about itself (including a completed SBA Form 355, Application for Small Business Determination, a statement answering the allegations in the protest, and evidence to support its position) within **three business days**. The SBA then must decide whether the firm qualifies as a small business within **10 business days** of receiving the protest. Until the SBA renders a decision or the 10 business day period expires, the contracting officer must withhold award of the contract *unless* he determines, in writing, that an award must be made to protect the public interest.

The decision of the SBA is final unless it is appealed to the Office of Hearings and Appeals, Small Business Administration, 409 3rd Street, SW, Suite 5900, Washington, DC 20416. See Title 13 of the Code of Federal Regulations (CFR), Sections 121.1001 through 121.1010 and 121.1101 for detailed procedures and time limits for appeals.

PROTESTS CONCERNING STATUS AS A HUBZONE, SDVOSB, WOSB, OR EDWOSB

Protests regarding eligibility under HUBZone, service-disabled veteran-owned small business (SDVOSB), women-owned small business (WOSB), and economically disadvantaged women-owned small business (EDWOSB) set-asides (see Chapter 11) all follow the same basic procedures.

Since concerns receiving preferences under the HUBZone and SDVOSB programs must be small businesses, a protest concerning the size status of a HUBZone, SDVOSB, WOSB, or EDWOSB concern is handled as any other protest regarding a concern's small business size status (see above).

Protests regarding whether a concern meets all the HUBZone program qualification requirements or is owned by an SDVOSB, WOSB, or EDWOSB must be received by the contracting officer **within five business days after the bid opening** for IFBs or **five business days after identification of the successful offeror** for RFPs. The contracting officer then turns the matter over to the SBA for decision. (A contracting officer may file a protest with the SBA at any time.)

The SBA will determine the HUBZone, SDVOSB, WOSB, or EDWOSB status of the apparent successful offeror within **15 business days** after receipt of the protest.

Decisions regarding HUBZone status may be appealed within **five business days** after receiving the decision to the SBA's Associate Deputy Administrator for Government Contracting and Administrator for Government Contracting and 8(a) Business Development. The SBA's Associate Deputy Administrator has **five business days** to render a final decision.

Decisions regarding SDVOSB, WOSB, and EDWOSB status may be appealed within **10 business days** after receiving the decision to the SBA's Office of Hearings and Appeals (for SDVOSB, WOSB, and EDWOSB appeals). Any interested party may file a response supporting or opposing the appeal within **seven business days** after receipt of the appeal. Then the Office of Hearings and Appeals will render a final decision within **15 business days** after responses are filed.

The contracting officer is to withhold award of the HUBZone, SDVOSB, WOSB, or EDWOSB contract pending resolution of the protest unless he determines, in writing, that an award must be made to protect the public interest.

For more on HUBZone protests, see FAR 19.306, Protesting a Firm's Status as a HUBZone Small Business Concern. For more on SDVOSB protests, see FAR 19.307, Protesting a Firm's Status as a Service-Disabled Veteran-Owned Small Business Concern. For more on WOSB and EDWOSB protests, see FAR 19.308, Protesting a Firm's Status as an Economically Disadvantaged Women-Owned Small Business (EDWOSB) Concern or Women-Owned Small Business (WOSB) Concern Eligible Under the WOSB Program.

SUPPLY OR SERVICE CLASSIFICATION PROTESTS

Size standards are determined by the supply or service being purchased (and the corresponding **North American Industry Classification System** [NAICS] code – see Chapter 11). An interested party can protest the NAICS code (and the corresponding size standard) selected by the contracting officer by filing an appeal to the SBA Office of Hearings and Appeals according to the procedure in Title 13 of the Code of Federal Regulations, part 134, Rules of Procedure Governing Cases Before the Office of Hearings and Appeals. Such appeals must be filed not less than **10 calendar days** *after* the solicitation is initially issued.

If the Office of Hearings and Appeals decides that the supply or service classification in the solicitation is incorrect, and the contracting officer receives the decision *before the solicitation's due date* (that is, the bid opening date or the proposal closing date), the decision is final and the contracting officer must amend the solicitation to reflect the decision. However, if the contracting officer receives the decision *after the solicitation due date*, the decision does *not* apply to the solicitation, but the decision will apply to future solicitations for the same supplies or services.

For more on size standards protests, see FAR 19.303, Determining North American Industry Classification System (NAICS) Codes and Size Standards.

CHAPTER 17

PROCUREMENT INTEGRITY AND ETHICS

The Constitution and the Bill of Rights portray the basic values of our democratic society. The U.S. government, as the embodiment of these values, strives to ensure all its citizens are treated equally, honestly, and fairly. Because government employees make decisions affecting the public's welfare and handle public funds, they are held to a much higher standard of conduct than ordinary citizens. To make sure every citizen has complete confidence in the integrity of the government, the government requires its employees to refrain from acts that are not only illegal but *could appear improper*.

This higher standard of conduct prohibits many activities considered acceptable in the private sector but that could appear improper when taken by a government employee, such as a contracting officer accepting a Thanksgiving turkey from a contractor. While some prohibited activities apply to all government employees, some apply only to those involved in government contracting. These, and other governmentwide prohibitions, apply to contractors, bidders, and offerors as well – since it is illegal for a contracting officer to accept a gratuity, it is also illegal for a contractor to offer him a gratuity.

The following are some of the more significant prohibitions that affect those in the contracting process. There are others described in **FAR part 3, Improper Business Practices and Personal Conflicts of Interest**, and the **United States Code** (USC). It is easy for a contractor, bidder, or offeror to place a government employee in a compromising position inadvertently. A bidder or offeror that violates these prohibitions is normally disqualified from the competition, as a minimum. A contractor that violates these prohibitions can have its contract terminated for default (see Chapter 18), be debarred from future competitions (see Chapter 7), and be subject to other penalties. Therefore, contractors and prospective contractors must be aware of, and comply with, these prohibitions.

GOVERNMENTWIDE STANDARDS OF ETHICAL CONDUCT

The **Office of Government Ethics** (OGE) is responsible for establishing "a single, comprehensive, and clear set of executive-branch standards of ethical conduct that (is) objective, reasonable, and enforceable." These standards address such issues as gifts, conflicting financial interests, impartiality, seeking employment outside the government, misuse of a government position, and activities outside the government. The following are three of the prohibitions that are of particular interest to those involved in government contracting.

1. **Gifts**. A government employee is not permitted to solicit or accept gifts given (1) because of his official position or (2) from anyone who is seeking official action from the employee's agency, does business or seeks to do business with the employee's agency, conducts activities regulated by the employee's agency, or has interests that may be substantially affected by performance or nonperformance of the employee's official duties. This prohibition includes indirect gifts given with the employee's knowledge and acquiescence to his parent, sibling, spouse, child, or dependent relative. There are some exceptions to this prohibition: unsolicited gifts of $20 or less, gifts based on family or personal relationships, discounts, awards and honorary degrees, social invitations, and several other exceptions for specific circumstances.

2. **Conflicting Financial Interests**. A government employee is prohibited from participating personally and substantially in an official capacity in any particular matter if the matter will have a direct and predictable effect on the financial interest of the employee, the employee's spouse or child, an organization the employee serves as officer or employee, or a person with whom the employee is negotiating prospective employment arrangements.

3. **Seeking Employment Outside the Government**. A government employee must not participate in a matter that, to his knowledge, has a direct and predictable effect on the financial interests of a prospective employer with whom he is seeking employment. The employee is considered to have begun seeking employment upon receipt of *any* response from a prospective employer indicating an interest in employment discussions.

Government employees who violate these standards of ethical conduct may be subject to appropriate disciplinary and corrective action, including suspension or dismissal. In addition, there are many statutes, such as the Procurement Integrity Act, that establish separate or overlapping standards of conduct, the violation of which are punishable by fines or imprisonment or both.

See Title 5 of the Code of Federal Regulations (CFR), Part 2635, Standards of Ethical Conduct for Employees of the Executive Branch, for more on the government-wide standards of ethical conduct.

PROHIBITION AGAINST CONTRACTS WITH GOVERNMENT EMPLOYEES

A contracting officer cannot award a contract to a government employee or to a business owned or controlled by one or more government employees. This policy is intended to avoid any conflict of interest between the employee's interest and his government duties, and to avoid the appearance of favoritism or preferential treatment by the government toward its employees. The agency head, or a designee (no lower than the head of the contracting activity), may authorize an exception to this policy *only* if there is the **most compelling** reason to do so, such as when the government's needs cannot *reasonably* be met otherwise.

See FAR subpart 3.6, Contracts with Government Employees or Organizations Owned or Controlled by Them, for more information.

PROCUREMENT INTEGRITY ACT

FAR 3.104, Procurement Integrity, implements the requirements of the **Procurement Integrity Act of 1988**. This act was a product of the criminal investigation code-named "**Operation Ill Wind**," which involved the buying of proprietary and source selection information by contractors from high-ranking government officials (including a Navy assistant secretary). The act prohibits present or former federal employees from knowingly disclosing (and contractor personnel from knowingly obtaining) "contractor bid or proposal information" or "source selection information," and places certain restrictions on the activities of former federal employees working for contractors.

Prohibitions

There are four distinct prohibitions in the Procurement Integrity Act:

1. The following individuals are not permitted to knowingly disclose contractor bid or proposal information or source selection information before the award of a federal contract to which the information relates (other than in the authorized performance of their duties):

   - Present or former officials of the United States (officers, employees, or members of the armed forces); or

- Persons who are acting, or have acted, for or on behalf of the United States with respect to a federal procurement; or

- Persons who have advised the United States with respect to a federal procurement (this includes *contractor* personnel who have assisted agencies in the evaluation of proposals); **and**

- By virtue of that office, employment, or relationship has had access to contractor bid or proposal information or source selection information.

"Contractor bid or proposal information" is defined as any of the following information which is submitted as part of, or in connection with, a bid or proposal to enter into a federal contract:

- Cost or pricing data (see Chapter 8);

- Indirect costs and direct labor rates;

- Information about manufacturing processes, operations, or techniques properly marked by the contractor as "proprietary" (see Chapter 8);

- Information properly marked by the contractor as "contractor bid or proposal information"; or

- Other information properly marked as "restricted" to government use for evaluation purposes only in accordance with FAR 52.215-1, Instructions to Offerors – Competitive Acquisition.

"Source selection information" is defined as any of the following information prepared by a federal agency for use in evaluating a bid or proposal to enter into a federal contract:

- When sealed bid procedures are used, bid prices, or lists of those bid prices before public bid opening (this is one of those quirky rules stuck into a law by a Congressman who didn't know what he was doing – after all, how does a government official compile a list of bid prices before bid opening?);

- When negotiation procedures are used, proposed costs or prices, or lists of those proposed costs or prices;

- Source selection plans;

- Technical evaluation plans;

- Technical evaluations of proposals;

- Cost or price evaluations of proposals;

- Competitive range determinations (see Chapter 8);

- Rankings of bids, proposals, or competitors;

- Reports and evaluations of source selection panels, boards, or advisory councils; or

- Other information properly marked as "source selection information" by the head of the agency, his designee, or the contracting officer because its disclosure would jeopardize the integrity or successful completion of the procurement.

2. No unauthorized person (government or non-government) may knowingly obtain contractor bid or proposal information or source selection information before the award of the federal contract to which the information relates (this is the counterpart to the first prohibition).

3. If an agency official, who is participating "personally and substantially" in a federal procurement over the simplified acquisition threshold ($150,000), contacts or is contacted by a bidder or offeror in that procurement about non-federal employment, he must either (1) reject the possibility of non-federal employment, or (2) disqualify himself from further personal and substantial participation in that procurement. This requirement covers agency officials who participate personally and substantially in one or more of the following activities for the particular procurement:

- Drafting, reviewing, or approving a specification or statement of work (SOW) (see Chapter 4);

- Preparing or issuing a solicitation;

- Evaluating bids or proposals;

- Selecting sources;

- Conducting negotiations;

- Reviewing and approving the award of the contract; or

- Other procurement actions as may be specified in regulations

4. A former official of an agency may not accept compensation from a contractor as an employee, officer, director, or consultant for **one year** after the former official did any of the following:

- Served as the procuring contracting officer, administrative contracting officer, source selection authority, a member of the source selection evaluation board, the chief of a financial or technical evaluation team, program manager, or deputy program manager for a contract of more than **$10,000,000** that was awarded to that contractor. (Many agencies use source selection authorities and source selection evaluation boards to select the winning offerors on contracts for large systems or programs. Program managers are assigned overall responsibility for the successful performance of large systems or programs.)

- Personally decided to award a contract, subcontract, modification of a contract or subcontract, or a task order or delivery order (see Chapter 10) of more than **$10,000,000** to that contractor.

- Personally decided to establish overhead or other rates applicable to a contract (or several contracts) for that contractor which is (are) valued at more than **$10,000,000**.

- Personally decided to approve a contract payment or payments in excess of **$10,000,000** to that contractor.

- Personally decided to pay or settle a claim (see Chapter 19) of more than **$10,000,000** with that contractor.

Penalties

Anyone who knowingly discloses or obtains contractor bid or proposal information or source selection information before the award of a federal contract in violation of the Procurement Integrity Act is subject to criminal penalties of imprisonment for up to **five years** plus fines up to **$10,000**, and civil penalties of up to **$100,554** for *each* violation plus **twice the amount of compensation** which the individual received or offered for the prohibited conduct. An organization that knowingly discloses or obtains prohibited information is subject to civil penalties of up to **$1,005,531** for *each* violation plus **twice the amount of compensation** which the organization received or offered for the prohibited conduct. (**NOTE:** The Federal Civil Penalties Inflation Adjustment Act Improvements Act of 2015 requires annual inflation adjustments to civil penalties. It is responsible for the strange-looking penalties.)

Any person or organization that violates the employment offers or compensation prohibitions is subject to the same civil penalties as those imposed for knowingly disclosing or obtaining prohibited procurement information.

In addition, if a federal agency receives information that a contractor or person has violated any of these prohibitions, the agency must consider taking one or more of the following actions:

- Cancellation of the solicitation if a contract has not been awarded.
- Disqualify the offending offeror if a contract has not been awarded.

- Rescission of the contract (if the contract has been awarded to the violating contractor) if (1) the contractor, or someone acting for the contractor, has been criminally convicted of disclosing or obtaining prohibited procurement information, or (2) the head of the contracting agency determines that the *preponderance of evidence* indicates the contractor, or someone acting for the contractor, illegally disclosed or obtained prohibited procurement information (see FAR subpart 3.7, Voiding and Rescinding Contracts). Furthermore, the government is entitled to recover the full amount *expended under the contract* in addition to any fines and penalties imposed (see FAR 52.203-8, Cancellation, Rescission, and Recovery of Funds for Illegal or Improper Activity).

- Initiation of suspension or debarment proceedings (see Chapter 7).

- Initiation of adverse personnel action against offending federal officials, up to dismissal from employment.

Compliance

To ensure compliance with the Procurement Integrity Act and avoid problems, contractors should:

- Train each officer, employee, agent, representative, and consultant in the prohibitions of the act;

- Clearly mark all proprietary information furnished to the government, and never furnish proprietary information except in response to an agency procurement;

- Not offer employment to federal employees who are involved in procurements on which the contractor is bidding or submitting a proposal;

- Be able to show how every government document was obtained and from whom; and

- Take immediate action against any officer, employee, agent, representative, or consultant who violates the act, and cooperate *fully* with the government if it should conduct an investigation into the violation.

BYRD AMENDMENT

The **Anti-Influencing Act**, more commonly called the **Byrd Amendment**, restricts the use of public funds to pay for lobbying. Named after Senator Robert Byrd of West Virginia, the Byrd Amendment was in response to West Virginia University's hiring of lobbyists to solicit his support for a research project. Angered that

West Virginia University thought it needed lobbyists to approach its own senator, Senator Byrd attached his amendment to the Department of the Interior and Related Agencies Appropriations Act of 1990, where it became law.

Prohibitions

The Byrd Amendment prohibits recipients of federal contracts **over $150,000** from using "**appropriated funds**" to pay any person for influencing an officer or employee of an agency, a member of Congress, an officer or employee of Congress, or an employee of a member of Congress in connection with the awarding of any federal contract or the modification of any federal contract. The term "appropriated funds" includes all money obtained under any contract governed by the FAR *except profits or fees* earned from any federal contract. (However, "to the extent the contractor can demonstrate that the contractor has sufficient monies, other than federal appropriated funds, the government will assume that these other monies were spent for any influencing activities that would be unallowable if paid for with federal appropriated funds" – see paragraph (a)(2) of FAR 3.802, Statutory Prohibition and Requirement).

The term "recipient" includes the contractor *and all subcontractors* (the Byrd Amendment also applies to recipients of federal grants and cooperative agreements over $100,000, and recipients of federal loans, loan guarantees, and loan insurance over $150,000).

The Byrd Amendment requires recipients of covered federal contracts to (1) certify they have not used any appropriated funds to make prohibited payments. By signing its bid or proposal, the bidder or offeror certifies it complies with the act, thereby satisfying the certification requirement (see FAR 52.203-12, Limitation on Payments to Influence Certain Federal Transactions). If the bidder or offeror has used "non-appropriated funds" for lobbying activities, it must disclose the lobbying contacts on **Office of Management and Budget Standard Form LLL, Disclosure of Lobbying Activities**, and submit the form with its bid or proposal. The certification and disclosure requirements pertain to the particular contract being sought, not to *all* contracts. Also, "the offeror need not report regularly employed officers or employees of the offeror to whom payments of reasonable compensation were made."

When responding to a solicitation, the bidder or offeror does not certify it has made *no* prohibited lobbying expenditures, only that it has made *no* prohibited lobbying expenditures *regarding that specific IFB or RFP*. Similarly, the bidder or offeror does not have to disclose all acceptable lobbying expenditures, only those made regarding the specific IFB or RFP.

Those that win government contracts are required to file a disclosure form at the end of each calendar quarter if, during that quarter, there occurred "any event that materially affects the accuracy of the information contained in any declaration previously filed by such person in connection with such federal contract, grant, loan, cooperative agreement, loan insurance commitment, or loan guaranty commitment," such as a change in the person or persons influencing or attempting to influence the government contract.

In addition, the contractor must require all its subcontractors with subcontracts over **$150,000** to submit certifications and disclosures. The contractor must forward all disclosure forms (but not certifications) to the contracting officer at the end of the quarter. The contractor retains the certifications in its subcontract file(s). The contractor is not responsible for the accuracy of its subcontractors' certifications or disclosures.

Penalties

Though almost all the prohibited actions are already covered under existing federal laws or regulations (for example, bribery and the payment of gratuities are already criminal offenses, and FAR 31.205-22, Lobbying and Political Activity Costs, makes legislative lobbying costs unallowable), the Byrd Amendment provides for additional penalties of between **$10,000 and $100,000** for *each* violation or failure to disclose in addition to any other penalties provided by law.

Exceptions

The Byrd Amendment prohibitions do not apply to "reasonable compensation" paid to its officers or employees for "agency and legislative liaison" that does not pertain to a specific solicitation. The following are permitted agency and legislative liaison activities:

- Providing information specifically requested by an agency or Congress.

- Discussing with an agency the qualities and characteristics of a contractor's products or services, conditions or terms of sale, and service capabilities.

- Technical discussions regarding the application or adaptation of the contractor's products or services for an agency's use.

- Providing information not specifically requested but necessary for an agency to make a decision about initiating a solicitation.

- Technical discussions regarding the preparation of an unsolicited proposal prior to submission.

- Capability presentations by contractors seeking awards from an agency under the Small Business Act

In addition, the contractor can use appropriated funds to pay individuals other than its officers or employees for professional or technical services rendered in the preparation, submission, or negotiation of any bid or proposal, or for meeting requirements that are a condition for receiving the contract.

Payments of reasonable compensation made to a **regularly employed** officer or employee of a contractor for professional and technical services need not be disclosed. An officer or employee is considered to be "regularly employed" if he has been employed by the contractor for at least **130 working days** within the **one year period** immediately preceding the submission of the bid or proposal.

Compliance

While the Byrd Amendment is a convoluted and poorly crafted piece of legislation, there are so many loopholes that most contractors have no trouble complying with its provisions. To ensure compliance, contractors should:

- Make sure all officers, employees, and subcontractors understand the prohibitions of the act;

- Submit a disclosure form with the bid or proposal if required;

- Make sure there are adequate profits or fees from federal contracts or funds from commercial contracts to pay for permissible lobbying activities;

- Make sure all subcontracts over $150,000 include FAR 52.203-11, Certification and Disclosure Regarding Payments to Influence Certain Federal Transactions, and FAR 52.203-12, Limitation on Payments to Influence Certain Federal Transactions;

- Submit a disclosure form at the end of a calendar quarter in which there is any event that materially affects the information contained in a previously submitted disclosure; and

- Obtain disclosure forms at the end of a calendar quarter from subcontractors when they have an event that materially affects the information contained in a previously submitted disclosure, then forward the disclosure statement to the contracting officer.

Of course, if a contractor does not try to influence agency officials or those in Congress, it has nothing to worry about.

See FAR subpart 3.8, Limitation on the Payment of Funds to Influence Federal Transactions, for more on the Byrd Amendment.

CONTINGENT FEES

For many years, the government has prohibited contractors from paying "**contingent fees**" fees to individuals for soliciting or obtaining government contracts on their behalf. Making the payment of the fee, commission, or percentage contingent on the successful obtaining of the contract can lead the individual to try to improperly induce a government employee to act more favorably toward his client's bid or proposal.

Every solicitation and contract that exceeds the simplified acquisition threshold ($150,000) and is *not* for commercial items contains **FAR 52.203-5, Covenant Against Contingent Fees**, in which the contractor warrants that it has not employed any person or agency to solicit or obtain the contract for a contingent fee. However, there are **two** significant exceptions to this prohibition:

1. A bidder or offeror may retain a ***bona fide* agency**, (that is, an established commercial or selling agency maintained to secure business) that neither exerts nor proposes to exert improper influence to solicit or obtain government contracts nor implies that it is able to obtain any government contract through improper influence.

2. A bidder or offeror may retain a ***bona fide* employee** (that is, someone who is employed by the bidder or offeror and subject to the bidder's or offeror's supervision and control) who neither exerts nor proposes to exert improper influence to solicit or obtain government contracts nor implies that he is able to obtain any government contract through improper influence.

If the contracting officer suspects or has evidence of an attempted or actual exercise of illegal influence, he will refer the matter to the chief of the contracting office, who will review the facts and, if appropriate, take one or more of the following actions:

- If before award, reject the bid or proposal.

- If after award, terminate the contract for default.

- Initiate action to suspend or debar the bidder, offeror, or contractor.

- Refer the suspected fraudulent or criminal matter to the Department of Justice.

- Take any other action appropriate under the circumstances.

For more on the subject, see FAR subpart 3.4, Contingent Fees.

FRAUD

Fraud is any false representation or concealment that intentionally deceives another party to its detriment. Because government contracting involves so much taxpayers' money, there are many laws that address government contract fraud. Some of these laws provide for criminal penalties (when the evidence shows a violation "beyond a reasonable doubt"), some provide for civil penalties (when "a preponderance of the evidence" shows a violation), and some provide for *both*. Also, these laws are not *exclusive*. A violation under one law probably is a violation of another, and the violator is subject to **all** the penalties.

False Statements

Title 18, United States Code (USC), Section 1001, states that *"whoever, in any matter within the jurisdiction of the executive, legislative, or judicial branch of the government of the United States, knowingly and willfully (1) falsifies, conceals, or covers up by any trick, scheme, or device a material fact; (2) makes any materially false, fictitious, or fraudulent statement or representation; or (3) makes or uses any false writing or document knowing the same to contain any false, fictitious, or fraudulent statement or entry, shall be fined, . . . imprisoned not more than five years, . . . or both."*

A statement or representation can be written or oral.

False Claims Act

The **False Claims Act** was originally enacted in 1863 in response to fraud by suppliers to the Union army. The act defines a claim as a demand for money or for transfer of public property. Invoices, requests for progress payments, and requests for equitable adjustment are all claims under the False Claims Act, as are data that supports the claim, such as time sheets, test results, and vouchers.

Title 18, USC Section 287, which addresses criminal false claims, states that *"whoever makes or presents to any person or officer in the civil, military, or naval service of the United States, or to any department or agency thereof, any claim upon or against the Unites States, or any department or agency thereof, knowing such claim to be false, fictitious, or fraudulent, shall be imprisoned not more than five years and shall be subject to a fine . . ."* This fine can be as much as **$1,000,000** if a defense contract is involved.

Title 31, USC Section 3729, which addresses civil false claims, states that *"any person who knowingly presents, or causes to be presented, to an officer or employee of the United States Government or a member of the armed forces of the United States a false or fraudulent claim for payment or approval . . . is liable to the United States Government for a civil penalty of not less than $5,000 and not more than*

$10,000 plus 3 times the amount of damages which the Government sustains because of the act of that person." If the false claim involves a defense contract, the person is subject to "*a civil penalty of $2,000, an amount equal to three times the amount of the damages the government sustains because of the act of the person, and costs of the civil action.*" (**NOTE:** The Federal Civil Penalties Inflation Adjustment Act Improvements Act of 2015 now requires annual adjustments to civil penalties. The current penalties for false claims are "not less than **$10,957** and not more than **$21,915** plus three times the amount of the damages the government sustains…")

Program Fraud Civil Remedies Act

This act (Title 31, USC Section 3802) provides for an "administrative" remedy against individuals or companies that submit false claims involving less than **$150,000**. The government, after investigating an alleged false claim and with Department of Justice concurrence, can impose fines of **$10,957 and double damages** for each false claim in an *administrative proceeding outside the court system*. These fines may be in addition to any imposed under the False Claims Act, and "*each voucher, invoice, claim form, or other individual request or demand for property, services, or money constitutes a separate claim.*" Individuals or companies can appeal to a federal district court.

This is an alternate to the prosecution of civil false claims under by Title 31, USC Section 3729 (see above). However, its penalties may be imposed **in addition** to the criminal false claims penalties of Title 18, USC Section 287 (see above).

Conspiracy to Defraud with Respect to Claims

Conspiracy is an agreement by two or more people to perform an illegal act. For the conspiracy to take place, at least one of the conspirators must take *some act* to further the illegal scheme, *even if the act itself is **legal** and the scheme is never carried out*. Even if the scheme is carried out, the conspiracy is a **separate offense**.

Title 18, USC Section 286, states that "*whoever enters into any agreement, combination, or conspiracy to defraud the United States, or any department or agency thereof, by obtaining or aiding to obtain the payment or allowance of any false, fictitious, or fraudulent claim, shall be fined . . . or imprisoned not more than ten years, or both.*" Note that the 10 years imprisonment for **conspiracy** to submit a false claim is **double** the five years imprisonment for actually submitting a false claim under Title 18, USC Section 287 (False Claims Act)!

Conspiracy to Defraud the Government

Title 18, USC Section 371, states that "*if two or more persons conspire either to commit any offense against the United States, or to defraud the United States . . . and one or more of such persons do an act to effect the object of the conspiracy, each shall be fined . . . or imprisoned not more than five years, or both."*

Mail Fraud

Title 18, USC Section 1341, states that *"whoever, having devised or intended to devise any scheme or artifice to defraud . . . places in any post office or authorized depository for mail matter, any matter or thing whatever to be sent or delivered by the Postal Service . . . shall be fined . . . or imprisoned not more than 20 years, or both."* If the violation involves a presidentially declared major disaster or emergency, the person may be fined up to $1,000,000 or imprisoned not more than 30 years, or both.

Wire Fraud

Title 18, USC Section 1343, states that *"whoever, having devised or intended to devise any scheme or artifice to defraud . . . transmits or causes to be transmitted by means of wire, radio, or television communication in interstate or foreign commerce, any writings, signs, signals, pictures, or sounds for purpose of executing such scheme . . . shall be fined . . . or imprisoned not more than 20 years, or both."* This applies to telephone, facsimile transmissions ("fax"), and electronic mail ("e-mail").

Major Fraud Act

Title 18, USC Section 1031, applies to contracts and subcontracts that are **$1,000,000 or more**. It states that *"whoever knowingly executes, or attempts to execute, any scheme or artifice with the intent (1) to defraud the United States, or (2) to obtain money or property by means of false or fraudulent pretenses, representations, or promises, . . . shall be fined not more than $1,000,000 or imprisoned not more than 10 years, or both."* The fine can be increased to **$5,000,000** if the offense involves "a conscious or reckless risk of serious injury." The maximum fine for multiple counts is **$10,000,000**.

Racketeer-Influenced Corrupt Organizations (RICO)

Though originally intended to crack-down on organized crime, RICO is being used more frequently to combat contract fraud. Individuals and companies that engage in a "pattern of racketeering activity" are subject to RICO. A "pattern of racketeering activity" is defined as engaging in two or more prohibited activities within 10 years. Among the prohibited activities are bribery, mail fraud, and wire fraud.

Criminal penalties under RICO include fines, imprisonment up to **20 years**, and forfeiture of *"any interest in, security of, claim against, or property or contractual* *right of any kind affording a source of influence over, any enterprise which the per-son has established, operated, controlled, conducted, or participated in the conduct of. . .* " (Title 18, USC Section 1963). Also, Title 18, USC Section 1964, provides for civil penalties such as *"ordering any person to divest himself of any interest, direct or indirect, in any enterprise; imposing reasonable restrictions on the future activities or investments of any person . . . or ordering dissolution or reorganization of any enterprise . . ."*

Compliance

A contractor should state, in unequivocal terms, that it will not tolerate the mak-ing of false statements or claims by any of its employees. It should train its employ-ees on what type of actions constitute fraud, and institute a "self-governance" pro-gram of systematic reviews to discover problems or violations. If a contractor discov-ers a violation, it should notify the contracting agency because many of these laws provide for reduced penalties for violations that are voluntarily disclosed. Finally, if a violation takes place, the contractor must discipline the offending employee or em-ployees, including suspension without pay or dismissal.

SUBCONTRACTOR KICKBACKS

The **Anti-Kickback Enforcement Act of 1986** is intended to deter subcontrac-tors from making payments, and contractors from accepting payments, for improperly obtaining or rewarding favorable treatment regarding a prime contract or subcontract (this is not to be confused with the Copeland Anti-Kickback Act that applies to con-struction contracts – see Chapter 15). The reason such kickbacks are illegal is be-cause it is presumed the amount of any kickback will ultimately be included in the price of the government contract. The term "kickback" includes any money, fee, commission, credit, gift, gratuity, thing of value, or compensation of any kind.

The act, which applies to all government contracts and subcontracts that exceed the simplified acquisition threshold (except for commercial items, which are exempt regardless of amount – see Chapter 4), prohibits individuals, corporations, partner-ships, or any business association of any kind from:

- Providing, attempting to provide, or offering to provide any kickback;

- Soliciting, accepting, or attempting to accept any kickback; or

- Including the amount of any kickback in the price charged by a subcontractor to a prime contractor or by a prime contractor to the government.

Violators are subject to criminal penalties, including fines, **10 years** imprison-ment, and recoupment of the amount of the kickback. In addition, violators are subject to civil penalties of up to **twice** the amount of the kickback plus up to **$21,916** for **each** kickback made.

Contractors are required to cooperate fully with any federal agency investigating a possible violation. Also, they are required to establish and follow reasonable procedures to prevent and detect violations in its operations and direct business relationships. Some examples of reasonable procedures are:

- A company ethics policy prohibiting kickbacks by employees, agents, or subcontractors.

- Education programs for new employees and subcontractors, explaining policies against kickbacks and the consequences of detection.

- Procedures requiring subcontractors to certify they have not paid kickbacks.

- Audits to detect kickbacks.

- Periodic surveys of subcontractors to elicit information about kickbacks.

- Procedures to report kickbacks to law enforcement officers.

- Annual declarations by employees of gifts or gratuities received from subcontractors.

- Annual employee declarations that they have violated no company ethics rules.

- Personnel practices that document unethical or illegal behavior and make such information available to prospective employers

See FAR 3.502, Subcontractor Kickbacks, for more on subcontractor kickbacks prohibitions.

WHISTLEBLOWER PROTECTION FOR CONTRACTOR EMPLOYEES

Contractors and subcontractors with contracts or subcontracts from civilian agencies (except the National Aeronautics and Space Administration [NASA] and the Coast Guard – see below) are prohibited from discharging, demoting, or otherwise discriminating against an employee in reprisal for disclosing to certain entities "information that the employee reasonably believes is evidence of gross mismanagement of a federal contract, a gross waste of federal funds, an abuse of authority relating to a federal contract, a substantial and specific danger to public health or safety, or a violation of law, rule, or regulation related to a federal contract" ("whistleblowing"). Any contractor employee who believes he has been discharged, demoted, or discriminated against for disclosing violations to the government may file a complaint with the inspector general of the contracting agency.

According to FAR 3.908, Pilot Program for Enhancement of Contractor Employee Whistleblower Protections, the following are the entities to whom an employee may disclose protected information:

- A member of Congress or a representative of a committee of Congress.

- An Inspector General.

- The Government Accountability Office (see Chapter 16).

- A federal employee responsible for contract oversight or management at the relevant agency (such as the contracting officer).

- An authorized official of the Department of Justice or other law enforcement agency.

- A court or grand jury.

- A management official or other employee of the contractor or subcontractor who has the responsibility to investigate, discover, or address misconduct

A contractor or subcontractor employee who believes he has been discharged, demoted, or otherwise discriminated against for whistleblowing may submit a complaint with the inspector general of the contracting agency no later than **three years** after the alleged reprisal took place. Unless the inspector general determines the complaint is frivolous, fails to allege a violation, or has been addressed in another federal or state judicial or administrative proceeding initiated by the complainant, the inspector general will investigate the complaint and submit a report on the investigation to the person, the contractor, and the head of the agency within **180 days** after receiving the report.

No later than **30 days** after receiving the inspector general's report, the head of the agency must either denying relief or take one or more of the following actions: (1) order the contractor to take affirmative action to end the reprisal; (2) order the contractor or subcontractor to reinstate the employee to the position the person held before the reprisal, together with compensatory damages (including back pay), employment benefits, and other terms and conditions of employment that would apply to the person in that position if the reprisal had not been taken; or (3) order the contractor or subcontractor to pay the employee an amount equal to all costs and expenses (including attorneys' fees and expert witnesses' fees) that were reasonably incurred by the employee for bringing the complaint.

If the head of the agency issues an order denying relief or has not issued an order within 210 days after the submission of the complaint, the employee may suit in district court. The inspector general's report may be admissible in evidence.

If the contractor or subcontractor fails to comply with the agency head's order, he will file an action for enforcement of the order in district court.

FAR 52.203-17, Contractor Employee Whistleblower Rights and Requirement to Inform Employees of Whistleblower Rights, is included in all solicitations and contracts that exceed the simplified acquisition threshold ($150,000). (**NOTE:** Though FAR 3.908 refers to the civilian agencies' whistleblower protections as a "pilot program," the protections have been made permanent with the enactment of Public Law 114-261.)

The Department of Defense, NASA, and the Coast Guard are subject to different rules. While their rules are very similar to those of civilian agencies, there are some differences:

- All elements of the intelligence community are exempt.

- An employee does not have any rights to disclose classified information unless otherwise provided by law.

- If the contractor or subcontractor fails to comply with the agency head's order, he will request the Department of Justice to file an action for enforcement of the order in district court.

All Department of Defense contracts are required to include **DFARS 252.203-7002, Requirement to Inform Employees of Whistleblower Rights**; and all NASA contracts are required to include **NFS 1852.203-71, Requirement to Inform Employees of Whistleblower Rights**.

See FAR subpart 3.9, Whistleblower Protections for Contractor Employees, for more on whistleblower protections. (**NOTE:** Protections for *federal* whistleblowers are provided under the "Whistleblower Protection Act" – see Title 5 of the U.S. Code, Section 1213, and the U.S. Office of Special Counsel "Disclosure of Wrongdoing" website at **https://osc.gov/Pages/DOW.aspx**.)

CHAPTER 18

CONTRACT ADMINISTRATION

Once a bidder or offeror wins a contract, it must perform that contract. The performance of a contract consists of much more than merely providing the supply or service on time; the contractor must fulfill all its other contractual obligations. It must comply with applicable labor laws, prepare required reports, seek changes to the contract when unforeseen circumstances occur, allow government inspectors to insure the quality of the supplies or services, invoice the government for payment, pay subcontractors, and close the contract.

The nature, object, and duration of a contract will determine the amount of administration required by the contractor. A competitively awarded firm-fixed-price contract for delivery of a commercially available item in 60 days will not require the same amount of administration as a large sole source cost-plus-incentive-fee contract for the development and initial production of a technologically complex system over several years.

FAR subpart 42.3, Contract Administration Office Functions, lists 82 different contract administration functions a procuring contracting officer (PCO) can delegate to an administrative contracting officer (ACO), and FAR part 49, Termination of Contracts, explains the functions and duties of the termination contracting officer (TCO) once the PCO terminates a contract for default or the convenience of the government. While only the largest and most complex contracts might require the performance of all these administrative functions, virtually every contract requires the performance of some of them.

The following are some of the more common and important contract administration functions that contractors encounter. While these functions and activities take place after contract award, contractors should understand their possible ramifications (and potential costs) before preparing bids or proposals.

CONTRACT ADMINISTRATION ASSIGNMENT

For most purchase orders and small contracts, the PCO retains responsibility for contract administration. However, most contracts that require the performance of contract administration functions at or near the contractor's facilities are assigned to a **regional** contract administration office. For example, most Department of Defense contracts over the simplified acquisition threshold (see Chapter 6) are assigned to the **Defense Contract Management Agency** (DCMA) for administration. Various civilian agencies use DCMA's services as well.

Even a PCO who retains the administration of a contract can request the assistance of a contract administration office when a few simple administrative functions are required.

POSTAWARD ORIENTATION

After contract award, the contracting officer sometimes decides to have a **postaward orientation conference** between government and contractor officials. The purpose of such a conference is to ensure that everyone involved with the contract clearly understands the scope of the contract, the technical requirements, the reporting requirements, and the rights and obligations of the respective parties. When deciding if a postaward orientation conference is necessary, the contracting officer takes into account the value and complexity of the contract, the technical complexity of the supply or service, the urgency of the delivery schedule, the contractor's past performance on government contracts and its experience with the supply or service, the procurement history of the supply or service, and other similar factors.

The conference is usually held at the contractor's facility as soon after contract award as possible (less complex contracts may be handled by a letter to the contractor or by teleconference). All parties involved in the execution, administration, and performance of the contract are invited. Government representatives normally include purchasing office personnel, administration office personnel, engineers, packaging specialists, inspectors, and others as appropriate. Contractor personnel usually include the president or vice president, the contract administrator, quality assurance personnel, design and production engineers, packaging engineers, and major subcontractors.

The purpose of the conference is to make sure everyone understands the contractual terms and conditions, *not* to change the terms and conditions of the contract. Participants who do not have authority to bind the government are not permitted to take any action that alters any of the provisions of the contract. For example, an engineer cannot *direct* the contractor to perform a machining operation in a specific manner; nevertheless, he *may* describe machining operations that were acceptable to the government on previous contracts. However, the contracting officer may make commitments or give directions provided he is within the scope of his authority, but he must put any such commitment or direction in writing. If a specification or contract provision does not adequately reflect the government's requirements, the contracting officer must modify the contract – a verbal order at a postaward conference is *not* sufficient. Contractors should always *insist* that any change to the contract be reflected in a contract modification (see below).

After the conference, the chairman (usually the contracting officer) prepares a postaward conference report that records all the significant matters that were discussed, contractual matters that require the contracting officer's decision, the names of the participants assigned responsibility for further actions, and the dates by which such actions are to be completed. Copies of the report are provided to the purchasing office, the administrative contracting office, the contractor, and all other participants. It can be used as supporting documentation should disagreements occur during contract performance.

See FAR subpart 42.5, Postaward Orientations, for more information.

SUBCONTRACT CLAUSE FLOW-DOWN

The FAR requires that contracts contain specific clauses under specific circumstances. For example, all contracts of $150,000 (the simplified acquisition threshold) or more (except those for commercial items) must include **FAR 52.203-7, Anti-Kickback Procedures** (see Chapter 17). The clause prohibits the contractor from "(1) providing or attempting to provide or offering to provide any kickback; (2) soliciting, accepting, or attempting to accept any kickback; or (3) including, directly or indirectly, the amount of any kickback in the contract price charged by a prime contractor to the United States..." This is a reasonably simple requirement. However, there is a paragraph in the clause that requires the contractor to **flow-down** this clause to its subcontractors:

(c)(5) The contractor agrees to incorporate the substance of this clause...in all subcontracts under this contract which exceed $150,000.

There are more than 80 different FAR clauses that the contractor *must* impose on its subcontractors when applicable. Some of these clauses are:

- FAR 52.203-6, Restrictions on Subcontractor Sales to the Government

- FAR 52.203-12, Limitation on Payments to Influence Certain Federal Transactions

- FAR 52.203-13, Contractor Code of Business Ethics and Conduct

- FAR 52.203-14, Display of Hotline Poster(s)

- FAR 52.204-2, Security Requirements

- FAR 52.204-9, Personal Identity Verification of Contractor Personnel

- FAR 52.204-14, Service Contract Reporting Requirements

- FAR 52.214-26, Audit and Records – Sealed Bidding

- FAR 52.215-2, Audit and Records – Negotiation

- FAR 52.215-12, Subcontractor Cost or Pricing Data

- FAR 52.219-9, Small Business Subcontracting Plan

- FAR 52.222-6, Construction Wage Rate Requirement

- FAR 52.222-26, Equal Opportunity

- FAR 52.222-41, Service Contract Labor Standards

- FAR 52.230-2, Cost Accounting Standards

In addition, there are many clauses that a contractor does *not* have to flow-down to its subcontractors but *should*. Some examples are:

- FAR 52.215-10, Price Reduction for Defective Cost or Pricing Data (including this clause makes the subcontractor liable for any defective cost or pricing data it provides to the contractor which the contractor submits to the government in support of its proposed price);

- FAR 52.242-15, Stop-Work Order (the contractor will want to be able to order its subcontractors to stop work if it is ordered to stop);

- FAR 52.243-1 through -5, the Changes clauses (the contractor will want to be able to flow-down to its subcontractors any changes made by the government to the contract specifications – see below);

- FAR 52.246-2 through -14, the Inspection clauses (since the government reserves the right to inspect at the contractor's and subcontractors' facilities, the contractor will want the subcontractor to agree to government inspection – see below); and

- FAR 52.249-1 through -12, the Termination clauses (should the government terminate a contract, the contractor will want to be able to terminate its subcontractors – see below).

A contractor must go through all the clauses in its contract and determine which ones are mandatory on subcontractors and which are nonmandatory but essential. The contractor should include these clauses in any request for quotations or request for proposals sent to subcontractors so they can add to their prices the cost of any administrative expenses associated with compliance. Also, including these clauses minimizes subcontractor misunderstandings and avoids potential problems later.

DRUG-FREE WORKPLACE

All contracts that exceed the simplified acquisition threshold (excluding contracts for commercial items or performed outside the United States – see Chapter 4) contain FAR 52.223-6, Drug-Free Workplace. This clause requires the contractor to accomplish the following within **30 calendar days** after contract award:

- Publish a statement notifying its employees that the unlawful manufacture, distribution, possession, or use of a controlled substance is prohibited in the contractor's workplace, and specifying the actions that will be taken against employees for violating such prohibition;

- Provide this statement to all employees;

- Make continued employment conditional on (1) the employee's compliance with the statement, and (2) notification within **five calendar days** of any conviction under a criminal drug statute for a violation that took place in the workplace; and

- Establish an ongoing drug-free awareness program to inform its employees about:
  - the dangers of drug abuse in the workplace;
  - the contractor's policy on maintaining a drug-free workplace;
  - any available drug counseling, rehabilitation, and employee assistance programs; and
  - the penalties that may be imposed upon employees for drug abuse violations in the workplace.

Upon receiving a notice of conviction from an employee, the contractor has **10 calendar days** to notify the contracting officer and **30 calendar days** to either take appropriate personnel action against the employee (up to and including termination of employment) or require such employee to participate in a drug abuse assistance or rehabilitation program approved by a federal, state, or local health, law enforcement, or other appropriate agency.

If the contractor is an individual, he must certify he will not engage in the unlawful manufacture, distribution, dispensing, possession, or use of a controlled substance in the performance of a contract. This requirement applies to *all* contracts performed by individuals, regardless of dollar amount.

Failure of a contractor to make a good faith effort to maintain a drug-free workplace or to comply with any of the requirements of the Drug-Free Workplace clause may cause the government to suspend contract payments, terminate the contract for default (see below), suspend the contractor, or debar the contractor for up to **five years**.

See FAR subpart 23.5 for more on drug-free workplace requirements.

GOVERNMENT-FURNISHED PROPERTY

The government usually requires the contractor to provide all the equipment and facilities needed to perform the contract. However, there are times when the government can save itself money by providing the contractor with material, special tooling, special test equipment, and facilities that it already possesses. The contracting officer will identify any **government-furnished property** (GFP) in the solicitation and resulting contract (usually in Section H of solicitations and contracts in the uniform contract format – see Chapter 7).

When a contractor receives GFP, it must segregate the GFP from its own property and maintain adequate control records, such as receipt and issue documents and maintenance records. In addition, *all* supplies and materials purchased by a contractor that are *directly* chargeable to a cost-reimbursement contract become the property of the government upon delivery to the *contractor* and are governed by **FAR 52.245-1, Government Property**.

The government does not hold a contractor responsible for any loss or damage to GFP in the contractor's possession if the GFP was provided under a cost-reimbursement contract, time-and-material or labor-hour contract, or a fixed-price contract awarded under the basis of cost or pricing data (see paragraph (a) of **FAR 45.104, Responsibility and Liability for Government Property**). The government *will* hold the contractor responsible for the loss or damage of GFP under a contract awarded through sealed bidding or a negotiated fixed-price contract awarded through price competition (except for reasonable wear and tear – see **Alternate I** of **FAR 52.245-1**).

See FAR part 45, Government Property, for the regulations on GFP.

CONTRACT MODIFICATIONS

Sometimes a contract needs to be modified to reflect the changing needs of the government, the contractor, or both: to correct a typographical error, to exercise an option, to increase the supplies or services being purchased, to change the specifications. Sometimes the proposed contract modification is readily accepted by both parties, sometimes the government must impose the contract modification on the unwilling contractor. Contract modifications are a fact of life and should be expected during the administration of any moderately complex contract.

There are two types of modifications: **unilateral** and **bilateral**. A unilateral contract modification is signed only by the contracting officer exercising a governmental right under the contract. A bilateral contract modification (frequently called a "**supplemental agreement**") is signed by both the contractor and the contracting officer, signifying their agreement to the contract as changed.

For example, a contracting officer would issue a unilateral modification to make administrative changes (such as correcting an accounting classification number), issue a change order (see below), make changes authorized by other contract clauses (such as exercising an option under an Options clause), or terminate a contract (see below). However, the contractor and the contracting officer would have to sign a bilateral modification to equitably adjust a contract because of a change order, to definitize a letter contract (see Chapter 10), or to incorporate any other agreements between the two (such as changing the delivery schedule).

The **Standard Form 30, Amendment of Solicitation/Modification of Contract** is required for contract modifications (see Appendix B for the SF 30 used as an IFB amendment). Only a contracting officer acting within the scope of his authority can sign a contract modification for the government.

Before entering into a modification, the contracting officer must ensure sufficient funds are available. Paragraph (b) of FAR 43.102, Policy, encourages the contracting officer to do this by negotiating the price *before* entering into a bilateral modification or issuing a unilateral modification. The contracting officer requests a proposal from the contractor, analyzes the proposed costs, negotiates the price of the modification, verifies that funds are sufficient for the modification, and executes the modification. However, if this cannot be accomplished without affecting the interests of the government, the contracting officer can issue the modification before negotiating its price. Nevertheless, if the modification *could* significantly increase the contract price, the contracting officer must negotiate a maximum price (commonly called a "**ceiling price**" or "**not-to-exceed price**") unless such negotiations are impractical.

When the government finds its actual needs for supplies or services exceed the quantity under an existing contract, the contracting officer cannot merely modify the contract to add the extra quantity. If the quantity is outside the **scope** of the contract, it is considered a new contract action subject to the full and open competition requirements of the Competition in Contracting Act (CICA) (see Chapter 3). A contracting officer *probably* could justify adding an extra 10 widgets to a contract for 1,000 widgets; he *probably* could not justify adding an extra 500 widgets to the contract without obtaining full and open competition. However, if the extra quantity falls under one of the seven exceptions to full and open competition authorized by CICA, the contracting officer can enter into a supplemental agreement with the contractor to add the quantity to the existing contract.

See FAR part 43, Contract Modifications, for more information.

CHANGES

The **Changes** clause is one of the contracting officer's most powerful tools. There are several different Changes clauses for different types of contracts (such as fixed-price, cost-reimbursement, services, transportation, and construction contracts – see FAR 52.243-1 through -5). They all authorize the contracting officer to change **three** parts of the contract:

1. The drawings, designs, and specifications of supplies (this does *not* apply to commercial items), or the description of services;

2. The method of shipment or packing of supplies, or time of performance of services (such as hours of the day or days of the week); and

3. The place of delivery or performance.

The Changes clause enables the contracting officer to order the incorporation of new design features into an item already under contract. It also allows him to change the color of an item from forest green to desert tan and to direct the contractor to ship the item to the Middle East instead of Pennsylvania. The government is obligated to maintain the public's welfare at the lowest possible cost to the taxpayer. As the sovereign, this obligation entitles the government to change the terms of the contract when the supplies or services no longer meet its needs.

When the contracting officer issues a **change order** on an SF 30 (thus modifying the contract), the contractor must comply with the order and perform the contract *as changed*. However, the Changes clause requires the contracting officer to **equitably adjust** the contract to compensate the contractor for any additional costs associated with the change (such as the cost of work added by the change and cost of work already performed but deleted by the change). The adjustment may be to the contract price, the delivery or performance schedule, or both. If the change order reduces the overall costs to the contractor, the contracting officer will seek to reduce the contract price, shorten the delivery or performance schedule, or both.

The change order normally includes a maximum, "not-to-exceed" price (see above) which has been negotiated with the contractor. However, when the change order is urgent and negotiating a maximum price is impractical, the contractor must perform the contract as changed *provided* its costs stay within the not-to-exceed price unilaterally established by the contracting officer. A unilaterally imposed not-to-exceed price merely serves to limit the government's liability until an agreement on the equitable adjustment is reached; it does not place a limit on that adjustment.

After the contracting officer issues a change order, the contractor must submit a **proposal for adjustment** within 30 days of receiving the change order (the 30-day period may vary according to agency procedures). The proposal for adjustment must detail, in the same manner as a cost proposal for a noncompetitive negotiated procurement (see Chapter 8), the cost of the work made obsolete by the change, the cost of any rework, and the cost of the new work. The contracting officer analyzes the proposal to determine whether the costs are reasonable, negotiates an equitable adjustment with the contractor, and draws up a contract modification that incorporates the equitable adjustment into the contract.

Sometimes the contractor and the government cannot agree on an equitable adjustment. Though the contracting officer will work hard to avoid an impasse, all the Changes clauses give the contracting officer the authority to *unilaterally determine* the equitable adjustment and to *unilaterally modify* the contract to reflect this adjustment if he and the contractor cannot come to an agreement. If the contracting officer makes a unilateral determination and issues a unilateral contract modification, the **Disputes** clause becomes operative (see below), and the contractor can take its case to the Armed Services Board of Contract Appeals or the Civilian Board of Contract Appeals, as appropriate. However, this is a time consuming and expensive process, so both the contractor and the contracting officer should try to reach agreement whenever possible.

Contracting officers cannot issue change orders indiscriminately. The changes must be within the **scope** of the contract; the contracting officer cannot require the contractor to provide an airplane when the contract calls for a hot air balloon, even if the government is willing to equitably adjust the contract. The courts have held that such a use of the Changes clause is improper and that a contractor is not obligated to perform such a "**cardinal change**."

See FAR subpart 43.2 for more on change orders.

ENGINEERING CHANGE PROPOSALS, DEVIATIONS, AND WAIVERS

An **engineering change proposal** (ECP) consists of proposed changes to a technical data package (TDP) or specification. An ECP may be proposed by either the contractor or the government. A contractor might prepare an ECP for the government's consideration if it finds the item cannot be produced as configured in the TDP. The government might prepare an ECP if it thinks a less expensive material could be an adequate substitute but, before ordering the change, wants the contractor to estimate how much the proposed substitution will cost. In either case, the government will want the contractor to provide detailed information on the technical, cost, and schedule effects of the proposed change.

After the government has evaluated the ECP, it decides whether to accept the ECP and issue a **design change notice**. When the government issues a design change notice, the TDP is permanently changed to reflect the new configuration. Then the government and the contractor negotiate the cost of the change and, when agreement is reached, execute a contract modification.

A **deviation** is a minor change to the TDP or specification that is granted on a one-time-only basis to help the contractor perform the contract. A deviation does not permanently modify the TDP or specification. A contractor might request a deviation if it cannot drill a hole within the tolerance limits specified in the specification. If the hole size is not critical to the item's performance, the contracting officer might grant the deviation and allow the contractor a larger tolerance. The specification is not changed by the deviation, and the tolerances for the hole on the next contract revert to those in the specification.

To obtain a deviation, the contractor must prepare a **request for deviation** (RFD) and provide the same sort of justification and supporting information as with an ECP. The government evaluates the deviation and decides whether to approve it. Normally, an approved deviation is granted on a "no cost" basis; however, if the deviation is significant, the contracting officer may require a downward adjustment in the contract price.

A **waiver** may be requested by the contractor for an item that does not meet the TDP or a specification. Waivers are usually granted only for nonconformities that do not degrade the function of the item and are so minor that the government would rather waive the nonconformity than require rework or replacement of the rejected item. A contractor might request a waiver for a file cabinet that was rejected by a government inspector because the paint did not *exactly* meet the color specified in the contract. However, the government would not grant a waiver for a red transport vehicle that was supposed to be camouflaged.

Once an item is rejected by the government inspector, the contractor can prepare a **request for waiver** (RFW) with the usual backup and justification. If the government rejects the RFW, the contractor must replace or rework the rejected item. If the government accepts the RFW, it accepts the rejected item "as is," normally at "no cost." However, if the waiver is significant, the contracting officer may insist on a reduction of contract price as a condition for approval.

There is no FAR coverage of ECPs, waivers, or deviations. See each agency's FAR supplement for its particular regulations governing these.

VALUE ENGINEERING

Value engineering (VE) is a program that rewards contractors for suggesting contract changes that eliminate nonessential functions or components of supplies, systems, equipment, facilities, or services and, by doing so, reducing the "life-cycle" cost without compromising the required performance, reliability, quality, and safety. When a contractor submits a **value engineering change proposal** (VECP) and the government accepts it, the contractor shares in the savings the government realizes from the reduced costs of acquisition, operation, maintenance, and logistic support.

FAR 52.248-1, Value Engineering, is included in every supply or service contract (with a few exceptions, such as research and development contracts) that exceeds the simplified acquisition threshold; the contracting officer can include the clause is smaller contracts if he believes there is a potential for significant savings.

As with ECPs, the VECP must be documented, justified, and include an estimate of the total savings the contractor expects the government will realize if the VECP is accepted. The government evaluates the proposal and the estimated savings and decides whether to accept the VECP.

There are two VE approaches: the **incentive** approach and the **mandatory program**. The most commonly used is the incentive approach, which permits the contractor to submit changes whenever it believes it has discovered a nonessential function or component. Some larger contracts have a separately priced line item for a mandatory VE program in which the contractor systematically studies the TDP and specifications for possible VECPs.

Under the incentive approach, the contractor voluntarily uses its own resources to develop and submit VECPs. If the government accepts a VECP under this approach, the contractor keeps **50%** of the savings resulting from the approved VECP if the contract is a fixed-price type and **25%** of the savings if the contract is a cost-reimbursement type (for incentive contracts [see Chapter 9], the contractor's share of the savings is the same as the contractor's portion of the share ratio). Not only does the contractor keep the appropriate percentage of savings realized from its own contract (the "**instant**" contract), but it receives the same percentage of savings realized from (1) other **concurrent** contracts for the same item, whether these concurrent contracts are being performed by the contractor or by others (for incentive contracts, the contractor's share of the savings is **50%**), and (2) all deliveries of the same item made under **future** contracts during the "**sharing period**," whether these future contracts are performed by the contractor *or by others*. The sharing period lasts between three and five years after acceptance of the first unit affected by the VECP (the duration of the sharing period is set at the discretion of the contracting officer), or until the last scheduled delivery date of an item affected by the VECP under the instant contract, whichever is later.

Under the mandatory program (which is **Alternate I** to FAR 52.248-1), the contractor receives a smaller percentage of the savings on the instant, concurrent, and future contracts than with the incentive approach. This is because the government is paying the contractor to operate a VE program under separately priced contract line item. If the government accepts a VECP under the mandatory program, the contractor receives **25%** of the savings on the instant, concurrent, and future contracts if the contract is a fixed-price type and **15%** of the savings if it is a cost-reimbursement type (as with the incentive approach, the contractor's share of the savings under incentive contracts is the same as the contractor's portion of the share ratio).

In addition, under either the incentive approach or the mandatory program, the contractor receives between **20% and 100%** of the government's **collateral** savings during an average year (the percentage is determined by the contracting officer), up to $100,000 or the contract's fixed-price or estimated cost, whichever is larger. Collateral savings are defined as reductions in the government's overall costs of operation, maintenance logistic support, or government-furnished property directly attributable to the VECP. The government will pay collateral savings unless the head of the contracting activity determines the cost of calculating and tracking collateral savings will exceed the benefits to be derived (see **Alternate III** of FAR 52.248-1).

See FAR part 48 for more information on value engineering.

FIRST ARTICLE APPROVAL

A **first article** is the first item, preproduction model, initial production sample, test sample, pilot lot, or pilot model produced by the contractor. The reason for requiring approval of the first article before going into full-scale production is to make sure the contractor can furnish a product that meets the specification requirements and operates satisfactorily. Conducting a first article test is one way to minimize the risks for both the contractor and the government.

First article testing is appropriate when:

- The contractor has not previously furnished the item to the government;

- The contractor has previously furnished the item, but there have been changes in specifications, or production has been discontinued for an extended period, or the product acquired under a previous contract developed problems during its life;

- The item is described by a performance specification (see Chapter 4); or

- It is essential to have an approved first article to serve as a manufacturing standard.

First article testing is *not* usually appropriate for:

- Research or development;

- Items requiring qualification before contract award (see Chapter 4);

- Supplies normally sold in the commercial market; or

- Supplies covered by complete and detailed technical specifications.

There are two types of first article testing: **contractor-performed** (FAR 52.209-3, First Article Testing – Contractor Testing) and **government-performed** (FAR 52.209-4, First Article Testing – Government Testing). Occasionally, the contract requires the contractor to perform some tests and the government to perform others. If the contractor will perform the testing, the contract has as a separate line item for the price of the testing.

Sometimes, the contracting officer will issue a solicitation that permits the bidder or offeror to submit two prices: one including the price of first article testing and one without. If the contracting officer decides to waive the first article testing requirement for a particular bidder or offeror because it has previously submitted identical or similar supplies to the government that were acceptable, the government will evaluate the price without the testing. Similarly, if the government will perform the first article testing and the contracting officer decides to waive the testing requirement for a bidder or offeror, he will *not* add the government's expected costs of testing to the price during his award evaluation.

Pending approval of the first article, commencement of production or the acquisition of materials and components is at the sole risk of the contractor. The contractual delivery schedule usually provides sufficient time after the first article approval notification for the contractor to acquire the necessary materials and components, commence production, and still make timely deliveries. But when the government requires expedited deliveries or the item contains components with long leadtimes, the contracting officer may authorize the contractor to acquire specific materials or components prior to first article approval or to commence production to the extent essential to meet the delivery schedule (Alternate II). Costs incurred because of such authorization are eligible for progress payments (see below) and will be recognized and paid in the event the contract is terminated for the convenience of the government (see below). Without the contracting officer's authorization to proceed prior to first article approval, progress payments will not be made on those costs, and the government will not reimburse the contractor for those costs if the contract is terminated.

If the first article does not pass first article testing, the contracting officer may require the contractor to repeat any or all testing (or bear the cost of retesting if the government is performing the testing), and make all changes, modifications, and repairs necessary to pass the first article testing at no extra cost to the government. The contracting officer also has the option of terminating the contract for default (see below) for failure to deliver an acceptable first article according to the contract schedule.

When the first article is approved and is not consumed or destroyed in the testing, the contractor may deliver it as part of the contract quantity *provided* it meets all the terms and conditions of the contract for acceptance. In other words, if the first article comes out of testing in good condition, the contractor may touch-up the first article and offer it to the government as a production unit.

First articles should not be confused with bid samples: bid samples are submitted by bidders to demonstrate the characteristics of their products to the contracting officer during the bid evaluation process (see Chapter 7). First articles are manufactured under a contract.

See FAR subpart 9.3, First Article Testing and Approval, for more information.

INSPECTION AND ACCEPTANCE

Every government contract over the simplified acquisition threshold contains an **Inspection** clause. As with the Changes clauses, there are different Inspection clauses for different kinds of contracts, such as fixed-price supply contracts and cost-reimbursement research and development contracts (see FAR 52.246-2 through -14). Despite the different wording of the clauses and the differences in the rights allocated to the government and the contractor, each Inspection clause does the same thing: it gives the government the right to inspect and test the supplies or services, to the extent practicable, at *all* places and times prior to acceptance.

The contractor is responsible for the inspection and quality of the supplies or services it offers to the government for acceptance. The government's role it to determine how much it should inspect to make sure the quality of the supplies or services meet contractual requirements. The contracting officer determines the amount of inspection, and the appropriate Inspection clause, after considering several factors:

- The integrity and reliability of the contractor as a quality producer;

- The adequacy of the contractor's **inspection system** (which should address incoming material, laboratory testing, in-process inspection, end item inspection, packaging, packing, crating, and marking);

- Previous government experience with the contractor; and

- The nature and value of the supply or service.

For purchases equal to or less than the simplified acquisition threshold, it is the government's policy to rely on contractor inspection. Most purchase orders include **FAR 52.246-1, Contractor Inspection Requirements**, which explicitly states the contractor is responsible for performing all inspections and tests necessary to insure compliance with the contract's requirements.

For contracts over the simplified acquisition threshold, the government uses either **standard inspection** or **higher-level contract quality** requirements. The standard inspection clauses (all inspection clauses except FAR 52.246-9 and -11) do three things:

1. Require the contractor to provide and maintain an inspection system that is acceptable to the government;

2. Give the government the right to make inspections and tests while work is in process; and

3. Require the contractor to keep complete records of its inspection work and make these records available to the government.

The contracting officer will use the higher-level contract quality clause, **FAR 52.246-11, Higher-Level Contract Quality Requirements**, when the contract involves **complex** or **critical** items or when the technical requirements require (i) control of design, work operations, in-process controls, testing, and inspection, or (ii) attention to organization, planning, work instructions, documentation control, and advanced metrology. "Complex" items are those with quality characteristics not wholly visible in the end item, for which contractual conformance must be established through precise measurements, tests, and controls applied during purchasing, manufacturing, performance, assembly, and functional operation. "Critical" items are those that could injure personnel or jeopardize a vital agency mission should they fail. In FAR 52.246-11, the contracting officer will specify the applicable quality specification to which the contractor must comply, such as ISO 9001, ANSI/ASQC E4, ASME NQA-1, SAE AS9100, SAE AS9003, ISO/TS 16949, and SAE AS5553.

The following is a brief summary of the requirements of **FAR 52.246-2, Inspection of Supplies – Fixed-Price**, which is representative of all the standard inspection clauses. The other standard inspection clauses are tailored to suit the particular characteristics of the different kinds of contracts – the government does not inspect work performed under a cost-reimbursement research and development contract in the same manner as work performed under a construction contract.

- The contractor must maintain an inspection system that is acceptable to the government (the government does not "approve" the contractor's inspection system, so the contractor cannot blame the government if something goes wrong).

- The contractor must maintain records that completely document the inspections it conducts during contract performance. The records must be made available to the government for the duration of the contract or for any longer period specified in the contract.

- The government reserves the right to go into the contractor's plant and inspect or test the items anytime prior to acceptance, provided the inspection or testing does not *unduly* delay the work. Also, the government reserves the right to go into any **subcontractor's plant** and inspect or test. The contractor or subcontractor must furnish, without additional charge, all reasonable facilities and assistance for the safe and convenient performance of these duties. The government bears the expense of the inspection or testing.

- If the contractor notifies the government that supplies will be ready for inspection or testing by a specific date but the supplies are not ready by that date, the government may charge the contractor for the additional costs of inspection or testing.

- The government may charge the contractor for the costs of reinspection or retesting if it rejects the supplies.

- If the supplies are defective, the government can require the contractor to replace or correct them at its own expense. If the contractor fails to replace or correct the rejected supplies promptly, the government can replace or correct the rejected supplies itself or have another firm do it, charging any additional costs to the contractor. Also, the government has the option of terminating the contract for default (see below).

■ If the contractor is unable to replace or correct the defective supplies within the contractual delivery schedule, the contracting officer may require that the price of the supplies be reduced. If the contractor and the contracting officer are unable to agree on the amount of such price reduction, the contracting officer can unilaterally determine the price reduction, in which case the contractor can invoke the provisions of the Disputes clause (see below).

■ If the government's inspection or testing indicates the supplies conform to the contract specifications, the government is not precluded from rejecting the supplies later should it discover defects or failures anytime prior to government acceptance of the supplies.

■ Government acceptance is final unless there are latent defects in the supplies (that is, defects not readily detectable during a normal inspection), fraud is involved, or some mistake was made that was so gross that it amounts to fraud.

Acceptance is the act by which a government agent acknowledges that the supplies or services submitted by the contractor conform to all contract requirements. Upon acceptance, ownership (title) passes to the government, thereby relieving the contractor of further responsibility for the supplies or services except for latent defects or other contractual provisions (such as warranties).

Ordinarily, acceptance is demonstrated by the completion of an acceptance certificate on an **inspection or receiving report** or a **commercial shipping document/packing list**. This document then becomes the authorization for payment to the contractor. Each agency prescribes its own procedures and instructions for the preparation and distribution of these documents. For example, the Department of Defense requires contractors to use the **DD Form 250, Material Inspection and Receiving Report**, except for purchase orders, in which case the purchase order itself (the **DD Form 1155, Order for Supplies or Services**) may be used as the inspection and receiving report.

Under certain circumstances, the contracting officer may require the contractor to submit a certificate of conformance by which the contractor attests the supplies or services comply with all contract requirements (this is not to be confused with the SBA's "certificate of competency" – see Chapter 7). The contracting officer may include **FAR 52.246-15, Certificate of Conformance**, when the contractor's reputation or past performance indicates the supplies or services it furnishes will be acceptable and any defective work will be replaced, corrected, or repaired without contest. The certificate of conformance may be used as the sole basis for government acceptance and payment *without* government inspection. However, the government retains the right to inspect supplies under the contract's Inspection clause.

See FAR part 46, Quality Assurance, and FAR 52.246 for the various Inspection clauses.

PROGRESS PAYMENTS AND OTHER CONTRACT FINANCING METHODS

Normally, a contractor with a fixed-price contract is expected to finance the materials and labor it needs to perform the contract, receiving payment only upon delivery and acceptance of the supply or performance and acceptance of the service. If the contractor does not have the necessary working capital, the government prefers that the contractor arrange private financing on reasonable terms. However, government financing is available under certain circumstances, usually for larger contracts (greater than the simplified acquisition threshold for small businesses; greater than $2,500,000 for all other contractors) with long leadtimes. (There is no need for such government financing with a cost-reimbursement contract because the government reimburses the contractor as costs are incurred – as often as every two weeks, or more frequently for small businesses – see **FAR 52.216-7, Allowable Cost and Payment**).

Government contract financing is intended to prevent the disruption of production schedules and the wasting of manpower and materials that can be caused by a lack of adequate financing. It also enables contractors to undertake production volume they could not accomplish otherwise, and it gives small businesses encouragement to undertake contracts that would otherwise require financial resources beyond their ability to acquire.

Provided a bidder or offeror is otherwise responsible, the contracting officer must not treat the bidder's or offeror's need for government contract financing as a handicap to contract award – the contracting officer cannot use a request for government contract financing as a responsibility factor or evaluation criterion. However, the bidder or offeror must be responsible (that is, reliable, competent, and capable) *before* government contract financing will be extended; government contract financing will *not* be used in an attempt to make a nonresponsible bidder or offeror responsible.

In addition, a contractor will not be disqualified from government contract financing solely because it failed to indicate before contract award that it needed contract financing. However, the contractor will be required to reduce the contract price, accelerate delivery or performance, or provide some other consideration in exchange for the addition of government contract financing to the contract.

Contractor financing is divided into two categories: for **commercial items** (that is, those items purchased using the procedures of FAR part 12, Acquisition of Commercial Items [see Chapter 4]), and for **noncommercial items** (all other purchases):

Commercial Items

Though the government's policy is that the contractor is responsible for providing all resources needed to perform the contract (especially if the contract is for commercial items), there are some commercial markets in which the buyer customarily provides financing (such as heavy equipment). When the contracting officer expects to enter into a contract for commercial items that is more than the simplified acquisition threshold, determines that it is customary in the commercial marketplace to provide financing for the item, and decides it is in the best interests of the government to authorize financing, he may either specify the financing terms in the solicitation or permit each offeror to propose its own customary financing terms.

If the contracting officer specifies the financing terms, contract financing is not a factor in the evaluation of proposals, and alternate financing terms will not be accepted.

If the contracting officer invites offerors to propose financing terms (by including **FAR 52.232-31, Invitation to Propose Financing Terms**), he must adjust each proposed price to reflect the cost of proving the proposed financing and determine which offer is in the best interests of the government. Once the contracting officer has evaluated all the proposals as specified in the solicitation and selected the successful offeror, he must construct a clause that describes (1) how the financing payment amounts will be computed, (2) the specific conditions of contractor entitlement to those financing payments, (3) how the financing will be liquidated, (4) the security the contractor will provide for the financing payments, and (5) frequency and form of the contractor's request for financing.

If the contract clause constructed by the contracting officer provides for advance payments (that is, payments given to the contractor before any work has been done), the aggregate of the advance payments may not exceed **15%** of the contract price.

See FAR subpart 32.2, Commercial Item Purchase Financing, for more on financing commercial items.

Noncommercial Items

The order of preference for government contract financing is as follows:

1. *Performance-based payments* are the preferred financing method when the contracting officer finds performance-based payments practical and the contractor agrees to their use. Performance-based payments are based on (1) performance measured by objective, quantifiable methods; (2) accomplishment of defined events (for example, milestones); or (3) other quantifiable measures of results. Each performance criterion that will trigger a finance payment must be an integral and necessary part of contract performance and must be identified in the contract, along with a description of what constitutes attainment of the performance criterion. The events and criteria may be independent of each other or may be de-

pendent on the previous accomplishment of another event. In addition, the contract may provide for more than one series of independent and/or cumulative events or criteria performed in parallel. The total of performance-based payments cannot exceed **90%** of the contract price (or 90% of the price per item for items such as aircraft).

See FAR subpart 32.10 for more on performance-based payments.

2. *Progress payments* are the most common form of government contract financing. When a contractor will not be able to bill for the first delivery of supplies or performance of services for more than **six months** after work begins (**four months for small businesses**), the contract requires the contractor to incur substantial start-up costs, and the contract is **$2,500,000 or more** (**exceeds the simplified acquisition threshold** for small businesses), the contracting officer may authorize customary progress payments to avert cash-flow problems that could jeopardize performance of the contract. With progress payments, the government reimburses the contractor a percentage of the costs incurred during contract performance and liquidates the progress payments as the contractor makes deliveries or performs services (in construction and shipbuilding, the government reimburses the contractor based on the percentage or stage of completion).

The standard progress payment rate is **80%** of incurred costs for large businesses and **85%** of incurred costs for small businesses (the Department of Defense authorizes **90%** for small businesses). However, before the contracting officer can authorize progress payments, the contractor must have: (1) an accounting system that can reliably segregate and accumulate contract costs (like those required for cost-reimbursement contracts), and (2) administrative controls that can insure the proper administration of progress payments. If deficiencies are found in the accounting system or in the administrative controls, corrections and necessary changes must be made before the contracting officer will authorize progress payments.

The contractor may make monthly requests for progress payments by submitting a **Standard Form 1443, Contractor's Request for Progress Payments** (or the electronic equivalent), according to the instructions on the reverse of the form and the contract terms, particularly **FAR 52.232-16, Progress Payments**.

See FAR subpart 32.5 for more information on progress payments.

3. *Loans guarantees by the government* are essentially the same as conventional loans made by private financial institutions except that the government is obligated to share any losses in the amount of the guaranteed percentage (which is usually 90% or less). Though done very infrequently, several agencies are authorized to guarantee loans for contracts related to national defense: the Departments of Defense, Energy, Commerce, the Interior, Agriculture; the General Services Administration; and the National Aeronautics and Space Administration. In addi-

tion, the Small Business Administration has loan guarantee programs for small businesses.

See FAR subpart 32.3, Loan Guarantees for Defense Production, for more information.

4. *Unusual contract financing* is any financing that deviates from the provisions of FAR part 32, Contract Financing. While unusual contract financing is legal and proper under applicable laws, contracting officers are not authorized to use them without specific reviews or approvals by higher management. Normally, the contracting officer will not seek authorization to use unusual contract financing unless: (1) the contract calls for predelivery expenditures that are large in relation to the contract price and the contractor's working capital and credit; (2) the contractor fully documents the actual need for the unusual contract financing (such as to supplement private financing or guaranteed loans); and (3) the contract finance office approves.

See FAR 32.114 for more on unusual contract financing.

5. *Advance payments* are the least preferred method of contract financing. Advance payments are advances of money by the government to a prime contractor which are liquidated from payments due the contractor for delivery of the contractual supplies or performance of the contractual services. Agencies are required by paragraph (b) of FAR 32.402, General, to "authorize advance payments sparingly." Generally, agencies will not authorize advance payments if other types of financing are reasonably available to the contractor in adequate amounts. To obtain advance payments, the contractor must post adequate security, and the head of the agency (or his designee) must determine that the advance payment is in the public interest or facilitates the national defense.

Advance payments may be considered useful and appropriate for contracts for experimental, research, or development work with nonprofit educational or research institutions, and contracts for the management and operation of government-owned plants.

See FAR subpart 32.4, Advance Payments for Non-Commercial Items, for more information.

The bidder, offeror, or contractor must justify to the contracting officer the reasons why guaranteed loans, unusual contract financing, or advance payments are needed to finance the contract. It must explain the actions taken to obtain private financing (such as the names of financial institutions denying conventional loans), and the reasons progress payments or performance-based payments are not adequate to finance the contract.

Uninvited Progress Payment Condition

As mentioned above, a contracting officer cannot penalize a bidder or offeror during the evaluation process for requesting contract financing. However, there is *one exception*: if a bidder, when responding to an IFB that does not provide for progress payments, stipulates that its bid is only to be considered if progress payments will be authorized, the contracting officer must *reject* the bid as nonresponsive. This stipulation is called an **uninvited progress payment condition**. If an IFB seems to meet all the conditions for progress payments but does not include the Progress Payments clause (FAR 52.232-16), the bidder should ask the contracting officer to consider amending the IFB to include the clause. Even in its bid, the bidder can ask the contracting officer to consider authorizing progress payments as long as it makes clear that such authorization is not a condition for contracting.

Subcontractor Claims of Nonpayment

Upon request of a subcontractor or supplier under a contract for a noncommercial item, the contracting officer must advise the subcontractor or supplier whether the prime contractor has submitted requests for progress payments or other payments under the contract and whether the government has made final payment to the contractor. If the subcontractor or supplier claims that the contractor has not paid in accordance with the subcontract or purchase order, the contracting officer will investigate the allegation. If he finds that the subcontractor's or supplier's allegation is true, the contracting officer may encourage the contractor to make timely payment, or he may reduce or suspend progress payments to the contractor (if authorized by the applicable payment clause).

See FAR 32.112, Nonpayment of Subcontractors Under Contracts for Noncommercial Items, for more information.

ALLOWABLE AND UNALLOWABLE COSTS

When reimbursing a contractor under a cost-reimbursement contract, making a progress payment, or settling a termination claim, the government will pay only those costs that are **allowable**. Paragraph (a) of FAR 31.201-2, Determining Allowability, defines an allowable cost as a cost that (i) is reasonable; (ii) is allocable; (iii) complies with the **Cost Accounting Standards** or, if the Cost Accounting Standards are not applicable, generally accepted accounting principles and practices; (iv) complies with the terms and conditions of the contract; and (v) complies with FAR part 31, Contract Cost Principles and Procedures. Allowable costs can be either a direct charge to a contract or a part of an indirect account. Also, only allowable costs may be included in proposals supported by cost or pricing data (see Chapter 8).

The following are brief definitions of the five elements that make up an allowable cost:

1. A cost is **reasonable** if it is not excessive and would have been incurred by a prudent person in a competitive business.

2 A cost is **allocable** if it:

   (a) is incurred specifically for a government contract;

   (b) benefits both the government contract and other work being done by the contractor, and it can be distributed in reasonable proportion to the benefits received (for example, the cost of a facility used for both government and non-government contracts); or

   (c) is necessary to the overall operation of the business even though a direct relationship to any particular contract cannot be shown (such as the cost of managing the company – president, headquarters costs, etc.).

3. The **Cost Accounting Standards** are 19 standards that apply only to large businesses performing large contracts (generally negotiated cost-reimbursement contracts that exceed $7,500,000); a small business or a large business performing a small government contract must have an accounting system that is appropriate for the type of work being performed. The Cost Accounting Standards specify how a contractor is to account for various costs; for example: the acquisition costs of materials; pension costs; cost of deferred compensation; and insurance costs. The Cost Accounting Standards are in Title 48 of the *Code of Federal Regulations* as Chapter 99 (**https://www.govinfo.gov/app/content/pkg/CFR-2015-title48-vol7/xml/CFR-2015-title48-vol7-chap99.xml**), and are addressed in FAR part 30, Cost Accounting Standards Administration.

4. A cost must be incurred in accordance with the terms and conditions of the contract. Any costs incurred in violation of the terms and conditions will not be reimbursed.

5. FAR 31.205, Selected Costs, which is more than 25 pages long, consists of 46 costs typically incurred by contractors during performance of government contracts. It explains which of those costs are allowable and which are unallowable. For example, labor relations costs such as shop stewards and employee publications are allowable, but bad debts are unallowable because the government always pays its bills.

This does not mean that a contractor cannot incur unallowable costs, merely that the government will not reimburse the contractor for such costs. Some unallowable costs are normal business costs. For example, the government will not reimburse a contractor for most advertising costs because the government is not swayed by advertising when purchasing supplies or services (however, the government considers the cost of help-wanted advertising allowable).

Though government auditors assess the adequacy of offerors' accounting systems as part of the evaluation of prospective cost-reimbursement contracts and fixed-price contracts with progress payments, it is the contractor's responsibility to ensure it seeks payment or reimbursement for allowable costs *only*. A contractor that seeks payment or reimbursement for an unallowable cost may be penalized up to twice the amount of the unallowable cost (in the case of contracts over $750,000) *in addition to any other applicable civil or criminal penalties* (see Chapter 17). Therefore, a contractor (or offeror) should have an accountant go over the contract cost principles in FAR part 31 and set up an accounting system that segregates allowable from unallowable costs.

INVOICING AND PROMPT PAY

The various government departments and agencies have different policies and procedures for submitting invoices for payment. For example, the Department of Defense requires contractors to submit invoices in an electronic form specified in DFARS 252.232-7003, Electronic Submission of Payment Requests. However, most agencies permit contractors to submit their own commercial invoices (though electronic invoices are preferred).

Contractors should review their contracts to make sure their invoices comply with the payment instructions:

- The invoices supply all the required data and supporting documentation required by paragraph (b) of FAR 32.905, Payment Documentation and Process:

    - the name and address of the contractor;

    - the invoice number and invoice date (the invoice should be dated as close as possible to the date of mailing or electronic transmission);

    - the contract number or other authorization for supplies delivered or services performed (including order number and contract line item number);

    - description, quantity, unit of measure, unit price, and extended price of supplies delivered or services performed;

    - shipping and payment terms, such as shipment number, date of shipment, prompt payment discount terms (see below), and bill of lading number and weight of shipment if made on government bill of lading;

    - name and address of the contractor official to whom payment is to be sent;

- name, title, telephone number, and mailing address of the person to be notified if the invoice is faulty;

- The contractor's Taxpayer Identification Number (TIN) (see Chapter 5 and FAR subpart 4.9);

- Electronic funds transfer (EFT) banking information (see Chapter 5); and

- Any other information or documentation required by the contract, such as evidence of shipment or the material inspection and receiving report.

■ The contractor sends the invoices to the right mailing or electronic address

■ The contractor has complied with all applicable contract clauses

However, even if an invoice complies with all the payment instructions, the government may not pay it. For example:

■ The contractor will not be paid for any change orders or contract modifications that increase the contract price but have not yet been negotiated.

■ Many contracts authorize the contracting officer to withhold final payment until the contractor has complied with all other contract requirements, such as providing all required data and reports.

■ Under a cost-reimbursement contract, the contracting officer cannot pay for any costs above the "estimated cost" unless he obtains additional funds and modifies the contract to increase its estimated cost (see Chapter 9).

Once a contractor submits a "proper invoice" containing the information described above, the provisions of the **Prompt Payment Act** apply (the Prompt Payment Act is different from the "prompt payment discount" offered by a contractor to encourage early payment). The Prompt Payment Act, originally passed by Congress in 1982, was enacted because the government's chronic tardiness in making contract payments caused cash-flow problems for many government contractors and drove some contractors out of government business altogether. Those payments are made electronically using information collected and maintained in the System for Award Management (SAM) (see Chapter 5).

All contracts (including purchase orders) implement the Prompt Payment Act with the inclusion of **FAR 52.232-25, Prompt Payment** (except architect-engineering and construction contracts, which have their own Prompt Payment clauses). This clause includes the following provisions:

■ The government must pay a proper invoice by the **30th calendar day** after receipt by the designated billing office or the **30th calendar day** after government acceptance of the supplies or services, whichever is **later** (if the government fails to accept or reject the supplies or services and there is no disagreement over quantity, quality, or contractor compliance with any contract term or condition, acceptance will be deemed to have taken place **seven calendar days** after the contractor delivered the supplies to the government or performed the services). If a purchase order provides for "fast payment" (FAR 52.213-1, Fast Payment Procedure – see Chapter 6), the government must pay a proper invoice by the **15th calendar day**.

■ If the invoice does not comply with all the requirements, the government must notify the contractor within **seven calendar days** after receipt of the invoice and specify the reason the invoice is improper.

■ If the government fails to pay the proper invoice within the 30-day period and there is no disagreement over quantity, quality, or contractor compliance with any contract term or condition, the government shall *automatically* pay an **interest penalty** at the rate established by the Secretary of the Treasury every six months – the interest penalty accrues daily on the invoice amount and is compounded in 30-day increments.

■ If the government takes any prompt payment discounts (for example, a 1% discount for invoices paid within 20 days of the **date of the invoice**) for payments made later than the prompt payment discount period (more than 20 days after the date of the invoice), the government will owe an interest penalty from the date of the invoice.

■ The contractor will be entitled to an **additional penalty** if:

   – the government owes a late payment interest penalty;

   – the government payment does not include the interest penalty;

   – the contractor does not receive the interest penalty within **10 calendar days** of receiving the government payment; and

   – the contractor makes a written request that the government pay the overdue late payment interest penalty and the additional penalty, not later than **40 calendar days** after the date of the government payment.

   The additional penalty will be **100%** of the original late payment interest penalty, up to **$5,000** (the additional penalty will be **at least $25** regardless of the actual late payment interest penalty amount).

■ Interest penalties will cease accruing after **one year**.

The prompt payment requirements apply to contractor financing payments (such as progress payments, advance payments, and payments under cost-reimbursement contracts), but the interest penalties *do not apply*.

The government will not pay interest penalties when there is a disagreement between the government and the contractor about the quantity delivered, quality of the supplies or services, or contractor compliance with any contract term or condition. If the parties cannot resolve their differences, the contractor may file a claim under the **Disputes** clause (see below). Interest will begin accruing on the claim from the date it is filed.

In addition, the government will not pay interest penalties when an electronic funds transfer (EFT) payment is not credited to the contractor's account by the payment due date because of actions or inactions by the Federal Reserve or the contractor's bank.

If the government refuses to pay an interest penalty that it owes, the contractor may file a claim for the interest penalty under the Disputes clause. Upon filing the claim, the interest penalty will cease accruing, and interest will begin accruing on the claim from the date it is filed.

See FAR subpart 32.9, Prompt Payment, for more information.

PAST PERFORMANCE EVALUATION

A contractor's past performance is an indicator of how it will perform similar contracts in the future. A contractor that performs most of its contracts poorly and late is more likely to perform its next contract unsatisfactorily than is a contractor that always delivers quality products on time. Therefore, agencies are required to evaluate the contractor's performance on each of their contracts that exceed the **simplified acquisition threshold** ($150,000) ($700,000 for construction contracts; $35,000 for architect-engineer contracts).

The agency performs its evaluation upon completion of the contract. If the contract performance period is longer than one year, the agency will perform interim evaluations at least annually. The agency notifies the contractor electronically that its performance evaluation is available for review, and the contractor has **14 calendar days** to submit comments, additional information, or statements rebutting facts or conclusions in the evaluation. However, the ultimate decision on the performance evaluation is the contracting agency's.

The following databases are used by agencies to compile and display past performance evaluations:

- The **Contractor Performance Assessment Reporting System** (CPARS) (**https://www.cpars.gov/**) is used by contracting activities to document performance information.

    Past performance evaluations must include at least the following factors: (1) technical (quality of product or service); (2) cost control (not applicable for firm-fixed-price or fixed-price with economic price adjustment arrangements); (3) schedule/timeliness; (4) management or business relations; (5) small business subcontracting (if applicable – see Chapter 11); and (6) other (as applicable) (*e.g.*, late or nonpayment to subcontractors, trafficking violations, tax delinquency, failure to report in accordance with contract terms and conditions, defective cost or pricing data, terminations, suspension and debarments).

Each factor (except small business subcontracting) must receive one of the following ratings: ***Exceptional*** – performance meets contractual requirements and exceeds many to the government's benefit; ***Very Good*** – performance meets contractual requirements and exceeds some to the Government's benefit; ***Satisfactory*** – performance meets contractual requirements; ***Marginal*** – performance does not meet some contractual requirements; ***Unsatisfactory*** – performance does not meet most contractual requirements and recovery is not likely in a timely manner.

The small business subcontracting factor must receive one of the following ratings: ***Exceptional*** – exceeded all statutory goals or goals as negotiated; ***Very Good*** – met all of the statutory goals or goals as negotiated; ***Satisfactory*** – demonstrated a good faith effort to meet all of the negotiated subcontracting goals in the various socio-economic categories for the current period; ***Marginal*** – deficient in meeting key subcontracting plan elements; ***Unsatisfactory*** – Noncompliant with FAR 52.219-8, Utilization of Small Business Concerns, and FAR 52.219-9, Small Business Subcontracting Plan, and any other small business participation requirements in the contract or order.

■ The **Federal Awardee Performance and Integrity Information System** (FAPIIS – **https://www.cpars.gov/fapiismain.htm**), is used by agencies to document terminations for default (see below); defective cost or pricing data (see Chapter 8); nonresponsibility determinations made because the contractor does not have a satisfactory performance record or a satisfactory record of integrity and business ethics (see Chapter 7); or information regarding criminal, civil, or administrative proceedings in connection with the award or performance of a government contract.

FAPIIS consists of two segments: the **non-public segment**, which can only be viewed by government personnel and authorized users performing business on behalf of the government, or an offeror or contractor viewing data on itself (that is, past performance reviews posted through CPARS); and the **publicly-available segment**, to which all data in the non-public segment of FAPIIS is automatically transferred after a waiting period of 14 calendar days (except for past performance reviews). FAPIIS records are retained for **five years**.

For more on FAPIIS, see FAR 9.104-6 and Chapter 7.

■ The **Past Performance Information Retrieval System** (PPIRS – **https://www.ppirs.gov**), which combines the information from the CPARS and the FAPIIS and makes it available to contracting officers and source selection officials. PPIRS is not available to the public because it contains past performance evaluations that may be used in contract award decisions, so the past performance information is considered "Source Selection Information." Access is restricted to government personnel with a "need to know" (such as those participating in source selection activities) and the contractor's personnel, who may access only the evaluations of the contractor's own performance (not the evaluations of other contractors). Improper disclosure of such information is covered by the Procurement Integrity Act – see Chapter 17.

When making source selection decisions, agencies are required to consider the past performance information in PPIRS that is within three years of the evaluated contract's completion (six years for construction and architect-engineer contracts). The limit on the use of past performance information is imposed because "old" evaluations may not be representative of the contractor's current performance.

See FAR subpart 42.15, Contractor Performance Information, for more on past performance evaluations.

TERMINATION FOR CONVENIENCE

As the sovereign, the government reserves the right to terminate any contract or portion of a contract it no longer needs or wants. The government asserts this right to protect the interests of the taxpayer. For example, the government terminates thousands of contracts when a war ends because it no longer needs all the bombs and tanks it purchased. The government might decide to terminate a contract when a major technological breakthrough occurs that renders the supplies under contract obsolete. This right to **terminate for convenience** transcends the contractor's right to perform a duly executed contract to its conclusion and to get paid the agreed amount. In fact, the government has the right to award a contract one day and terminate that same contract the next day.

Nevertheless, if the government does terminate a contract for convenience, it must **equitably adjust** the contract to reflect the costs incurred by the contractor during contract performance and to give the contractor a reasonable profit on those costs. In this and many others ways, a contract terminated for convenience is far preferable to a contract terminated for default (see below).

There are several different Termination clauses (FAR 52.249-1 through -7 and -12) that the government uses for various kinds of contracts (such as service contracts and contracts with educational institutions). However, **FAR 52.249-2, Termination for Convenience of the Government (Fixed Price)**, illustrates the basic principles that apply to all termination clauses.

Under FAR 52.249-2, the government can terminate for its convenience the entire contract or any portion of it. The contracting officer might terminate half the contract quantity, or terminate forks but not spoons. If the contracting officer only terminates a portion of the contract, the contractor must continue performing the rest of the contract.

The contracting officer must provide a **notice of termination** to the contractor stating:

- The contract (or portion of the contract) is being terminated for convenience;

- The effective date of the termination;

- The extent of the termination;

- Any special instructions (such as return of government-furnished property); and

- If the termination will cause a significant reduction in the contractor's work force, steps the contractor should take to minimize the effects of the termination on its personnel (such as advise affected employees to apply for unemployment insurance benefits).

When the contractor receives a notice of termination, it must:

- Stop work on the contract (or terminated portion of the contract);

- Place no further subcontracts or orders for materials, services, or facilities;

- Terminate all subcontracts that relate to the terminated work;

- To the extent directed by the contracting officer, assign all right, title, and interest in the terminated subcontracts to the government, and the government will settle those;

- Settle all outstanding liabilities and termination settlement proposals resulting from the terminated subcontracts – the settlements must be approved or ratified by the contracting officer;

- As directed by the contracting officer, transfer title and deliver to the government (a) the fabricated or unfabricated parts, work in process, completed work, supplies, and other material produced or acquired for the terminated contract, and (b) the completed or partially completed plans, drawings, information, and other property that would have been furnished to the government had the contract been completed;

- Take any action necessary to protect and preserve the property related to the contract in which the government is or may be interested; and

- As directed by the contracting officer, use its best efforts to sell any of the property described above (such as fabricated or unfabricated parts and material) – the contractor may acquire the property itself under the conditions prescribed by, and at prices approved by, the contracting officer.

After the contractor has done this, it must submit a **final termination settlement proposal** to the **terminating contracting officer** (TCO) (see Chapter 2) as the basis for negotiations to equitably adjust the contract. The termination settlement proposal must only include **allowable costs** (see above). If the contractor does not submit a claim within **one year** of the termination or fails to ask for and receive an extension, the TCO may unilaterally determine the amount of compensation entitled the contractor based on whatever information he has available.

The TCO and the contractor are authorized to agree upon the whole or any part of the amount to be paid the contractor as a result of the termination as long as the amount of the settlement does not exceed the contract price. If the TCO and the contractor cannot reach agreement on a part of the settlement, the TCO will authorize payment for the following:

- The contract price for any completed and accepted items;

- The costs incurred in the performance of the terminated work, including initial costs and preparatory expenses;

- The cost of settling and paying subcontractors' termination settlement proposals;

- A reasonable profit on the work performed (however, the TCO will *reduce* the amount he pays if the contractor would have incurred a loss had it completed the contract – the contracting officer will not allow the contractor to "get well" on the termination); and

- Reasonable costs for the preparation of the termination settlement proposal, including legal, clerical, storage, and other necessary expenses.

If the TCO and the contractor cannot agree on an equitable adjustment, and the TCO makes a unilateral determination that the contractor believes is unfair, the contractor can file a claim under the **Disputes** clause (see below).

The contractor must maintain records of the termination settlement for **three years** after the date of the final settlement and make them available to the government at all reasonable times.

The two primary reasons the government terminates contracts for convenience are: (1) changing domestic and foreign situations that cause the government to reassess its requirements; and (2) changing budgetary priorities that may cause the withdrawal of funding from a program. Though most contracts are successfully completed, *all* government contractors should become familiar with the Termination clauses in their contracts as the government reevaluates its domestic and global roles.

See FAR subpart 49.1, General Principles; FAR subpart 49.2, Additional Principles for Fixed-Price Contracts Terminated for Convenience; FAR subpart 49.3, Additional Principles for Cost-Reimbursement Contracts Terminated for Convenience; and FAR subpart 49.5, Contract Termination Forms, for more information.

TERMINATION FOR DEFAULT

Default is not a concept unique to government contracts: when a party to a contract fails to perform according to the terms and conditions of the contract, the other party can seek remedies for the breach, usually in the courts. As the sovereign, the government has chosen to avoid the courts by including a **Default** clause in all fixed-price contracts that exceed the simplified acquisition threshold (FAR 52.249-8 through -10). The Default clause permits the contracting officer to unilaterally declare a contractor to be in default when it does not perform according to the contract, to terminate the contract, and to take whatever action is necessary to acquire the supplies or services elsewhere. There are safeguards built into the Default clause: the contractor can file a claim under the **Disputes** clause (see below) to challenge the amount of compensation (if any) provided by the TCO, and the contractor can even contest the default termination itself. However, the government does not wait for the judicial system to decide the matter; it takes immediate action to obtain the supplies and services for which it contracted and allows the question of equity to be decided later.

Only fixed-price contracts have Default clauses. This is because the government pays all of the costs and accepts the risk of performance under cost-reimbursement contracts (see Chapter 9). Though a cost-reimbursement contract *can* be terminated for default (such as when the contractor fails to comply with a contract provision like the Drug-Free Workplace clause at FAR 52.223-6), the differences between the termination of a cost-reimbursement contract for convenience and for default are relatively minor. Since settlements of convenience and default terminations under cost-reimbursement contracts are so similar, both are addressed in a single clause. Most cost-reimbursement contracts contain **FAR 52.249-6, Termination (Cost-Reimbursement)**. This clause is almost identical to FAR 52.249-2 in that it requires the contractor to stop work, cancel subcontracts, sell materials, and submit a termination settlement. The primary difference between convenience and default terminations of cost-reimbursement contracts involves how much fee the government pays the contractor.

The contracting officer can terminate a contract for default for one of three reasons:

1. The contractor fails to deliver the supplies or perform the services according to the contract delivery schedule;

2 The contractor fails to comply with any of the other provisions of the contract (such as labor hour standards, nonsegregated facilities, and failure to comply with pollution abatement standards); or

3. The contractor fails to make the necessary progress needed to meet the contractual delivery schedule.

The third condition enables the contracting officer to terminate a contract for default when it is obvious the contractor will not be able to meet the contractual delivery or performance schedule. The contracting officer does not have to wait for the contractor to fail to deliver or perform on time. Instead, the contracting officer can terminate the contract and fulfill the government's requirements elsewhere as quickly as possible, thus minimizing the damage to the government.

Though the contracting officer is *entitled* to terminate a contract for default under these conditions, he is not *obligated* to do so. The contracting officer has several other options:

- He can permit the contractor (or surety) to continue performance of the contract under a revised delivery schedule.

- He can permit the contractor to continue performance of the contract by means of a subcontract or other business arrangement with an acceptable third party.

- He can issue a no-cost cancellation if acceptable to the contractor and there are no outstanding payments, debts due the government, or other contractor obligations.

- He can forbear (that is, take no action and allow the contractor to deliver late).

However, the contracting officer is under no obligation to follow any of these options.

If the contractor fails to deliver on time, the contracting officer can *immediately* terminate the contract for default. But, before the contracting officer can terminate a contract because the contractor fails to comply with a contract provision or fails to make progress, the contracting officer must issue a **cure notice**, giving the contractor a minimum of **10 days** to correct the shortcoming. If the time remaining in the contract delivery schedule is insufficient for a realistic cure period of 10 days or more, the contracting officer can issue a **show cause notice** demanding that the contractor explain why the contract should not be terminated for default.

If the contractor does not cure the shortcoming within the period allotted, or does not provide a valid explanation in response to the show cause notice, the contracting officer may issue a **notice of termination** to the contractor, stating:

- The contract number and date;

- The acts or omissions constituting a default;

- The contractor's right to proceed under the contract (or specified portion of the contract) is terminated;

■ The terminated supplies or services may be purchased against the contractor's account, and the contractor will be liable for any excess costs (see below);

■ The contractor has the right to appeal the default termination under the Disputes clause (see below); and

■ The government reserves all rights and remedies provided by law or under the contract.

Under a termination for default, the government is *not* liable for the contractor's costs on undelivered work (whether completed or not), and the government is entitled to the repayment of any advance and progress payments. The contracting officer *may* direct the contractor to transfer title and deliver all completed but not yet accepted items to the government. In addition, the contracting officer can require that partially completed items, materials, parts, tools, dies, jigs, fixtures, plans, drawings, information, and contract rights (otherwise collectively knows as "manufacturing materials") that the contractor specifically produced or acquired for the contract be turned over to the government. The government will pay the contract price for any completed supplies that were delivered and accepted.

The contractor must submit a **final termination settlement proposal** to the TCO within one year of the default termination, and the amount of compensation due the contractor is subject to negotiations between the contractor and the TCO. If an agreement on the amount of compensation for the manufacturing materials cannot be reached, the contractor may file a claim under the Disputes clause.

Also, the contracting officer may acquire similar supplies or services from another source and charge the defaulted contractor with any **excess reprocurement costs**. For example, if the contractor defaults on a $310,000 contract and the government obtains the same supplies from another source for $325,000, the defaulted contractor can be charged the additional $15,000 it cost the government to obtain the supplies ($325,000 - $310,000).

However, the contracting officer may *not* terminate a contract for default if the contractor's failure to perform was **excusable**. Some examples of excusable causes are:

■ Acts of God or the public enemy;

■ Acts of the government in its sovereign or contractual capacity (acting in its sovereign capacity, the government might condemn a contractor's plant to make room for a highway; acting in its contractual capacity, the government might issue a change order that required the contractor to change the configuration of an item, thus causing a contract delay);

■ Fires;

■ Floods;

- Epidemics;

- Quarantine restrictions;

- Strikes;

- Freight embargoes; and

- Unusually severe weather.

If the contracting officer terminates the contract for default and it is subsequently determined that the contractor's delay was excusable, the termination for default will be converted into a *termination for convenience* (see above).

However, there are **two** major exceptions to this excusable delay rule:

1. Even if a cause is excusable, the contractor *will* be liable for default if it was at fault or negligent, as when the contractor's factory burns down because of fire code violations; and

2. If a contractor's failure to perform is caused by the default of a subcontractor, and the subcontractor's default is excusable and not caused by its fault or negligence, the contractor will *not* be liable for default *unless* the subcontracted supplies or services were obtainable from other sources in time for the contractor to meet the required delivery schedule.

If the contractor believes the termination for default was improper because its failure to perform was excusable, or it disagrees with a TCO's unilateral determination of compensation for manufacturing materials, or it believes the contracting officer's action or inaction caused an unnecessary increase in excess reprocurement costs, the contractor may file a claim under the Disputes clause (see below).

Though the Default clause grants the contracting officer sweeping powers to take unilateral action to minimize the impact of a default (or impending default) on the government, he must be sure he is on firm ground when he terminates a contract for default. If he overlooks an excusable delay or rashly terminates a contract for default before he has all the facts, the contractor can invoke the provisions of the Disputes clause and take its case to the appropriate board of contract appeals (either the Armed Services Board of Contract Appeals or Civilian Board of Contract Appeals).

Because of these checks on the contracting officer, and since his primary objective is to obtain the supplies or services, he will usually work with the contractor to reach a compromise solution before terminating the contract for default. Nevertheless, contractors should do all they can to avoid having one of their contracts terminated for default, not just because of the financial ramifications but because of the potential effect on performance evaluations (see above) and future determinations of responsibility (see Chapter 7).

See FAR subpart 49.4 for more on terminations for default.

CLAIMS AND DISPUTES

Throughout contract administration, situations can arise that give the contractor or the government the right to an adjustment in the contract price or terms. Most such situations are addressed in contract clauses – late delivery of government-furnished property (GFP), acceptance of a value engineering change proposal (VECP), or a change order. Some situations are outside the contract clauses – improper rejection of delivered supplies, specifications that are impossible to perform, contract ambiguities. In either case, one party submits a written **claim** to the other, requesting that the contract be modified accordingly.

FAR 2.101, Definitions, defines a "claim" as:

> *. . . a written demand or written assertion by one of the contracting parties seeking, as a matter of right, the payment of money in a sum certain, the adjustment or interpretation of contract terms, or other relief arising under or relating to the contract. . . A voucher, invoice, or other routine request for payment that is not in dispute when submitted is not a claim.*

Most claims are satisfactorily settled between the contractor and the contracting officer because the issue is usually *how much* to compensate the contractor or government, not *whether* compensation is due. Normally, the contractor submits its claim to the contracting officer and, after negotiations, they reach agreement and modify the contract. It is the government's policy to have contract issues resolved at this level because the contracting officer is the government official with the most knowledge of the facts.

However, sometimes the contractor and the contracting officer fail to agree on the terms of an equitable adjustment or even whether the contractor or the government is entitled to an equitable adjustment. For this reason, various contract clauses give the contracting officer the right to render unilateral decisions and unilaterally modify contracts when he and the contractor cannot reach agreement.

The power to unilaterally reform contracts is a mighty one that can be abused very easily. This is why all contracts contain **FAR 52.233-1, Disputes** (except those with foreign governments or international organizations). This clause allows the contractor to challenge a contracting officer's decision that the contractor believes is arbitrary, capricious, or wrong. Even when a contracting officer terminates a contract for default, the contractor can invoke the Disputes clause to contest the propriety of the termination.

Disputes can arise in any contractual situation, and the existence of a dispute does not normally represent bad faith on the part of either party. Some examples of circumstances under which a dispute may arise are:

- The contractor and the contracting officer cannot agree to an equitable adjustment to the contract price or delivery schedule for changes ordered under the Changes clause.

- The contractor and the contracting officer cannot agree on the amount of compensation due a contractor under a cost-reimbursement contract.

- Faulty government inspections cause rejection of acceptable supplies or services.

Rather than allowing the contractor to go to court at once, the clause requires the contractor to pursue its claim through an administrative procedure delineated in the **Contract Disputes Act of 1978**. By allowing the contractor to seek redress outside the judiciary system, the procedure outlined in the Disputes clause can save both the contractor and the government time and money.

The Disputes clause requires the contractor to submit its claim for an equitable adjustment to the contracting officer *first*. The claim must cite either the contract clause or the government's action or inaction that entitles the contractor to an equitable adjustment (many contractors use the **Freedom of Information Act** [see Chapter 5] to obtain government documents they believe will provide evidence supporting their claims). In addition, each claim must specify the equitable adjustment the contractor seeks. If the equitable adjustment includes the payment of additional money, the contractor must specify the *exact* amount of money sought. Statements such as "XYZ Corp. requests the payment of all monies owed by the government," or "XYZ Corp. demands payment of approximately $25,000, subject to final settlement," are not permissible claims.

Though FAR 2.101, Definitions, states "*a voucher, invoice, or other routine request for payment that is not in dispute when submitted is not a claim,*" a routine request for payment can be converted into a claim by written notice to the contracting officer if the contracting officer disputes the government's liability for payment, contests the amount of the payment, or fails to act on the request for payment in a reasonable time.

If a contractor's claim exceeds **$100,000**, a person who is duly authorized to bind the contractor with respect to the claim must execute the following certification:

> *I certify that the claim is made in good faith; that the supporting data are accurate and complete to the best of my knowledge and belief; that the amount requested accurately reflects the contract adjustment for which the contractor believes the government is liable; and that I am duly authorized to certify the claim on behalf of the contractor.*

Failure to certify the claim **prevents** the contracting officer from considering the claim.

If the contracting officer and the contractor are unable to come to an agreement and the claim is **$100,000 or less**, the contracting officer must render a decision within **60 days** after receipt of the claim if the contractor requests, in writing, that the contracting officer render a decision within that period. If the contractor does not make such a request, the contracting officer has a *reasonable time* to render a decision.

If the claim is **over $100,000**, the contracting officer has **60 days** from receipt of the *certified* claim (see above) to render a decision unless the contracting officer will need more time because of the size and complexity of the claim, the adequacy of the contractor's supporting data, or other factors. When the contracting officer will need more time, he must notify the contractor, within the 60-day period, when he will render a decision.

The contracting officer analyzes the amount claimed by the contractor, the provisions of the contract (including specifications and drawings) that pertain to the claim, the actions or inactions of the government, relevant correspondence, and any other facts that might affect his decision. He reviews the facts as presented by the contractor, secures assistance from legal and other advisors as appropriate, and renders his decision.

In his decision, the contracting officer refers to the pertinent contract terms, identifies the areas of agreement and disagreement, provides supporting rationale for his decision, states that the decision is final, and notifies the contractor that it may appeal the decision. The contracting officer sends his decision to the contractor by certified mail, return receipt requested, or by any other method that provides evidence of receipt.

If the contracting officer, in his decision, decides the contractor is due compensation but the contractor decides to dispute the amount of the compensation, the government pays the contractor the amount decided upon by the contracting officer even if the contractor chooses to appeal the decision. The contractor's acceptance of the payment does not imply the contractor accepts the contracting officer's decision.

The Contract Disputes Act gives the contractor **90 days** after receipt of the contracting officer's decision to appeal to the appropriate **board of contract appeals** (such as the Armed Services Board of Contract Appeals [ASBCA – **http://www.asbca.mil**] for disputes involving Department of Defense and National Aeronautics and Space Administration contracts, or the Civilian Board of Contract Appeals [CBCA – **http://www.cbca.gsa.gov/**] for disputes involving all other civilian agencies' contracts). These boards exist solely to hear contractors' appeals.

If the claim is **$50,000 or less** ($150,000 or less for small businesses), the contractor may elect to use the **small claims** procedure, which is informal and requires the board to render a decision within **120 days** whenever possible. These decisions are final and cannot be appealed.

If the claim is **$100,000 or less**, the contractor may elect to use the **accelerated** procedure, which is more formal than the small claims procedure and requires the board to render a decision within **180 days** whenever possible.

If the claim is **over $100,000** (over $150,000 for small businesses) or the contractor does not elect to use either the small claims or accelerated procedure, a formal hearing is conducted and there is **no time limit** on the decision.

If *either* the contractor or the government is dissatisfied with the decision of the board, it has **120 days** to appeal to the **U.S. Court of Appeals**. If either is dissatisfied with the decision of the Court of Appeals, it has **90 days** to appeal to the **Supreme Court**. The decision of the Supreme Court is final.

As an alternative, the Contract Disputes Act gives the contractor **one year** after receipt of the contracting officer's decision to appeal to the **U.S. Court of Federal Claims**. Because the Court of Federal Claims is a court of law, appeals to it are usually more costly and time-consuming than appeals to the appropriate board. Generally, a contractor appeals to the Court of Federal Claims if it fails to appeal to the appropriate board within the 90-day period.

Either party may appeal the decision of the Court of Federal Claims to the U.S. Court of Appeals within **60 days** of the decision, and either party may appeal the decision of the Court of Appeals to the Supreme Court within 60 days.

While the contractor or government is pursuing its claim, the contractor must continue performing the contract and must comply with any decision of the contracting officer. If the contractor discontinues performance or fails to comply with a contracting officer's decision, the contracting officer may terminate the contract for default (see above).

Whenever the contracting officer, the board of contract appeals, or the courts decide that the contractor is due compensation, the government will pay interest on the amount owed the contractor from the date the contracting officer originally received the claim until the date of the payment. The interest rate paid by the government will be that established by the Secretary of the Treasury every six months. Similarly, the government has the right to collect interest on its claims against the contractor.

Equal Access to Justice Act

If a small business (defined as an individual with a net worth that does not exceed **$2,000,000** or a business with a net worth that does not exceed **$7,000,000** and has fewer than **500 employees**) prevails in its dispute, and the government's position was *not* **substantially justified,** the small business may invoke the provisions of the **Equal Access to Justice Act** to seek reimbursement for reasonable expenses of expert witnesses, the cost of any study or analysis necessary for the preparation of the case, and reasonable attorney or agent fees. The fees awarded for expert witnesses cannot exceed the highest rate of compensation for expert witnesses paid by the agency involved, and attorney or agent fees cannot exceed **$125 an hour** (unless the agency determines that an increase in the cost of living or a special factor, such as the limited availability of qualified attorneys, justifies a higher fee). The contractor has **30 days** from the date of the decision to submit to the agency an application for the reimbursement of such costs. If the small business is dissatisfied with the government's proposed reimbursement, the small business has 30 days to appeal the decision to the **U.S. Court of Appeals**.

The Equal Access to Justice Act applies to disputes, *not* to protests. See Chapter 17 for obtaining reimbursement of successful protest costs.

Alternative Dispute Resolution

The average dispute before a board of contract appeals takes more than **one year** to resolve, and cases before the Court of Federal Claims usually take longer. As a way to avoid this slow and expensive process, the **Administrative Dispute Resolution Act of 1990** authorizes the use of **alternative dispute resolution** (ADR) to settle disputes before the boards and the Court of Federal Claims. Requests to use ADR must be made *jointly* by the contractor and the government, and the board or court will decide whether ADR is appropriate, considering the complexity of the dispute and the issues involved.

Mediation and nonbinding arbitration are two common forms of ADR used to settle disputes. In mediation, the mediator meets with the parties, seeks out the facts, clarifies the issues under dispute, tries to find areas of agreement between the parties, and suggests a settlement. In arbitration, the arbitrator listens to arguments, hears witnesses, considers evidence, and renders a decision.

Other ADR methods that are used sometimes to settle disputes are:

- *Settlement judge.* A settlement judge is appointed to encourage a frank, in-depth discussion of the strengths and weaknesses of each party's position. The settlement judge may meet with the parties together or individually. The settlement judge's recommendations are not binding, and the parties can initiate formal proceedings if dissatisfied.

- *Minitrial.* Each party presents an abbreviated version of its position to a panel. The panel consists of a senior official from each side (both of whom have authority to conclude a settlement) and a neutral advisor. The panel members participate during the presentation of evidence. Upon conclusion of the presentations, the senior officials conduct negotiations, aided by the neutral advisor. If a settlement cannot be reached, the parties can initiate formal proceedings.

- *Summary trial.* An expedited appeal is held before an administrative judge or panel of judges. The parties must agree that all decisions and orders of the judge or panel are final and cannot be appealed. Upon the conclusion of the trial, the judge or panel will normally render a decision. However, the judge or panel can take up to ten days after conclusion of the trial to render a decision.

The parties are not limited to these methods, but may agree upon any informal method that suits the requirements of the appeal.

Of course, the parties can halt the dispute proceedings before the board of contract appeals, the Court of Federal Claims, or the chosen ADR forum by reaching a settlement.

See FAR subpart 33.2 for more on claims, disputes, and appeals.

CONTRACT CLOSEOUT

After final delivery or performance, the contractor has more to do than await final payment before shipping the contract to storage. Practically any moderately complex contract has several provisions that either require the contractor's action or will remain open for some time after contract "completion."

If the contract is a cost-reimbursement type (see Chapter 9 for the different contract types), the government must audit the contractor's records to determine the actual costs incurred in contract performance. If the contract is fixed-price with economic price adjustment, the contracting officer may have to make a final price adjustment.

The following are some of the issues contractors typically have to address before closing out a contract:

- All deliveries have been made or services performed.

- All required reports and data have been submitted to the government.

- All contract modifications have been settled.

- All change orders have been settled.

- All audits have been completed and final adjustments to contract price or fee made.

- All disputes have been settled.

- All options have expired.

- All warranties have expired.

- All government-furnished property has been returned.

- All subcontracts have been settled.

- There are no outstanding value engineering change proposals with potential "future savings" (see above).

- All payments have been made.

Only after carefully reviewing **all** the contract provisions and insuring that each requirement has been *completely* satisfied can a contractor close the contract.

See FAR 4.804, Closeout of Contract Files, for more information on contract closeout.

RECORDS RETENTION REQUIREMENTS

Even though a contract has been completed and closed out does not mean it can be thrown away. If the contract was awarded using sealed bidding procedures (see Chapter 7) and exceeds the threshold for certified cost or pricing data ($750,000), or was awarded using negotiation procedures (see Chapter 8) and exceeds the simplified acquisition threshold ($150,000), the contractor must retain and make available books, records, documents, and other supporting evidence for **three years after final payment** or for the applicable retention period specified in FAR 4.705, Specific Retention Periods, *whichever expires first*. These specific retention periods "*are calculated from the end of the contractor's fiscal year in which an entry is made charging or allocating a cost to a government contract or subcontract*" (paragraph (a) of FAR 4.704, Calculation of Retention Periods).

For example, according to paragraph (a) of FAR 4.705-1, Financial and Cost Accounting Records, orders for materials have a **four-year** retention period. If a contractor has a fiscal year that goes from January 1 through December 31, a purchase order for materials that is dated October 18, 2016, must be retained until **December 31, 2020**, four years after the end of the contractor's 2016 fiscal year (which is December 31, 2016). However, if the government makes the final contract payment before **December 31, 2017**, the contractor can dispose of the purchase order earlier, because the requirement to hold records for three years after final payment would expire before the four-year retention period for material purchase orders.

If the contractor has a fiscal year that goes from October 1 through September 30, a purchase order for materials dated October 18, 2016, must be retained until **September 30, 2021**, four years after the end of the contractor's 2017 fiscal year (which is September 30, 2017). If the government makes the final contract payment before **September 30, 2018**, the contractor can dispose the purchase order before September 30, 2021.

The following are the records contractors are required to keep and their specific retention periods. For a complete list of records, see FAR 4.705.

Financial and Cost Accounting Records

- Accounts receivable invoices, adjustments to the accounts, invoice registers, carrier freight bills, and shipping orders: **retain for 4 years**

- Material, work order, or service order files, consisting of purchase requisitions or purchase orders for material or services, or orders for transfer of material or supplies: **retain for 4 years**

- Cash advance recapitulations, prepared as posting entries to accounts receivable ledgers: **retain for 4 years**

- Paid, canceled, and voided checks other than those issued for payment of salary and wages: **retain for 4 years**

- Accounts payable records for materials, equipment, supplies, and services: **retain for 4 years**

- Labor cost distribution cards or equivalent documents: **retain for 2 years**

- Petty cash records, including vouchers and other supporting documents: **retain for 2 years**

Pay Administration Records

- Payroll sheets, registers, or equivalent, of salaries and wages paid to individual employees, and tax withholding statements: **retain for 4 years**

- Clock cards or other time and attendance cards: **retain for 2 years**

- Paid checks, receipts for wages paid in cash, or other evidence of payments for services rendered by employees: **retain for 2 years**.

Acquisition and Supply Records

- Store requisitions for materials, supplies, equipment, and services: **retain for 2 years**

- Work orders for maintenance and other services: **retain for 4 years**

- Equipment records, including equipment repair orders: **retain for 4 years**

- Expendable property records: **retain for 4 years**

- Receiving and inspection report records for supplies, equipment, and materials: **retain for 4 years**

- Purchase order files for supplies, equipment, material, or services used in the performance of a contract, including supporting documentation and backup files: **retain for 4 years**

- Production records of quality control, reliability, and inspection: **retain for 4 years**

See FAR subpart 4.7 for more on contractor records retention requirements.

CHAPTER 19

TEN STEPS TO SUCCESSFUL CONTRACTING

Condensing 2,000 pages of the FAR down to 374 pages produces a concentrated body of information that might still be confusing. Therefore, the following are the ten steps you need to take to win federal contracts.

Step #1 – Become Familiar with the FAR

Since the FAR is the rule book for federal contracting, it is important that every contractor has ready access to a copy. The website **https://www.acquisition.gov/ ?q=browsefar** has the FAR in various formats, all of which are updated through the latest Federal Acquisition Circular (FAC).

Start by familiarizing yourself with the following FAR parts:

- Part 5, Publicizing Contract Actions

- Part 6, Competition Requirements

- Part 8, Required Sources of Supplies and Services (particularly FAR subpart 8.4, Federal Supply Schedules)

- Part 9, Contractor Qualifications

- Part 12, Acquisition of Commercial Items

- Part 13, Simplified Acquisition Procedures

- Part 15, Contracting by Negotiation

- Part 19, Small Business Programs

- Part 22, Application of Labor Laws to Government Acquisitions

- Part 32, Contract Financing

FAR part 2, Definitions, consists of most of the definitions of terms used in the FAR, so it is a vital cross-reference. Also, contractors should take a look at FAR part 3, Improper Business Practices and Personal Conflicts of Interest, and avoid doing things such as offering to take a contracting officer to lunch. Finally, FAR part 52, Solicitation Provisions and Contract Clauses, has *all* the provisions and clauses referenced elsewhere in the FAR. Many of the provisions and clauses in contracts are merely referenced, so one has to go to FAR part 52 to read the full text.

Step #2 – Register in the System for Award Management (SAM)

To obtain a contract from the government, **you must be registered in SAM (https://www.sam.gov)**, and you must have a DUNS number to register (call Dun and Bradstreet at 866-705-5711 or obtain on on-line at **http://fedgov.dnb.com/ webform**. Along with the DUNS number, you will be asked to provide your taxpayer identification number (TIN) (or Social Security number if you are a sole proprietor), information about your company (such as average revenue and number of employees, type of business organization, products and services you can provide, and banking information), and various points of contact.

Step #3 – Check FedBizOpps Frequently

The primary purpose of **FedBizOpps (https://www.fbo.gov)** is to alert the public to upcoming solicitations for contracts over $25,000. So, contractors interested in winning contracts over $25,000 must check **FedBizOpps** frequently – you should check it once a day.

Because **FedBizOpps** publishes synopses of upcoming solicitations over $25,000 and contract awards, it is an important source of information on which contracting activities are buying the kinds of supplies or services the contractor provides, which companies are winning the contracts, and which companies are the primary competitors (or potential partners).

Also, **FedBizOpps** is the primary source of solicitation documents. By posting solicitations on **FedBizOpps**, the government saves postage and gives prospective bidders and offerors instantaneous access to the solicitation, thus providing a few extra days for contractors to prepare their bids or offers.

Step #4 – Find Out If You Qualify for a Small Business Development Program

The Small Business Administration (SBA) (**http://www.sba.gov**) maintains several programs that provide assistance to certain kinds of small businesses:

■ The **Section 8(a) Business Development Program** was created to help small disadvantaged businesses (SDBs) compete in the American economy and obtain access to the federal procurement market. Contractors in the 8(a) program are eligible for sole source contracts and competitive solicitations limited to 8(a) program participants.

■ The **Historically Underutilized Business Zone (HUBZone) Contracting** program stimulates economic development and creates jobs in urban and rural economically distressed communities by providing federal contracting preferences to small businesses.

■ **Small businesses** of all kinds are eligible for procurement assistance, assistance in obtaining access to capital, management and technical assistance, and export assistance.

In addition, there are programs that are targeted specifically to **service-disabled veteran-owned small businesses** and **women-owned small businesses**.

It is SBA's job to help all kinds of small businesses, so take advantage of SBA's programs, assistance, and guidance.

Step #5 – Visit Contracting Activities that Buy Your Supplies or Services

Using the knowledge obtained from **FedBizOpps**, contact the contracting activities that acquire your particular supplies or services. A good place to start is the **Office of Small and Disadvantaged Business Utilization** (OSDBU) (or "**Office of Small Business Programs**" in Defense). Each contracting activity has a "small business office." The primary responsibility of the OSDBU is to make sure that small businesses have an opportunity to compete and be selected for a fair amount of the contracting activity's contract dollars. The OSDBU does this by helping small businesses understand the contracting activity's operations and needs, and by directing small businesses to the appropriate program offices (the "acquisition planners").

Step #6 – Consider Seeking a Federal Supply Schedule Contract

One of the most significant developments in federal contracting in recent years is the growth in the General Services Administration's Federal Supply Schedule (FSS) program. The FSS program provides federal agencies with a simplified and streamlined process for obtaining commonly used products and services at prices associated with volume buying. Because the FSS program is easy to use, federal agencies use it extensively to fulfill their needs for commercial supplies and services – approximately 10% of the government's contracting budget is spent through orders on FSS contracts, so small businesses should investigate the possibility of obtaining an FSS contract to open the door to many possible opportunities.

Step #7 – Respond to Solicitations Completely and On Time

When you see a promising solicitation synopsized on **FedBizOpps**, download it when it becomes available – consider clicking on "Add Me to Interested Vendors" or "Watch This Opportunity." Check the specifications or statement of work to see whether you can provide the supplies or services (in Section C of solicitations in the Uniform Contract Format [UCF]). If you can, then:

- Review all the terms and conditions.

- Check the "Instructions, Conditions, and Notices to Offerors" of the solicitation (Section L of the UCF) to see if a proposal is required. If a proposal is required, check the "Evaluations Factors for Award" (in Section M of the UCF) to see how the proposal will be evaluated, and write your proposal accordingly.

- Enter the price (Section B in the UCF).

- Provide any other required information or documents.

- Sign the bid or proposal (the SF 33, the SF 1447, or other required form for specific types of contracts).

- Be sure your response reaches the contracting office by the required date and time.

If you have any questions, contact the contract specialist or, if not satisfied, contact the contracting officer. Remember that you can file a protest with the Government Accountability Office (GAO) if you believe the contracting officer has taken an action, or failed to take an action, that improperly affects the conduct of the solicitation to your detriment.

Step #8 – Take Appropriate Action After Submitting Your Offer

If your proposal is in the competitive range, be prepared to answer questions about your proposal and be able to defend your proposal during negotiations. Be prepared to demonstrate you or your firm can perform the contract, especially if you are new to federal contracting or trying to win a contract that is larger than any you have previously performed. Be prepared to:

- Demonstrate knowledge of the specifications or statement or work, the quality requirements, the delivery schedules, and the labor laws.

- Show that you know how the various clauses could affect your firm (for example, the Termination, Inspection, and Changes clauses).

■ Show how your firm will use its resources to perform the contract.

■ Show your firm has necessary financing arranged.

If you are notified that your firm is not in winner of the contract, ask to be debriefed.

Step #9 – When You Win a Contract, Perform It Well

Since you will be on probation during the first several contracts, it is important to comply with all the contractual terms and conditions, deliver on time, notify the contracting officer immediately if you have difficulties, and otherwise show that you are a conscientious contractor working hard to fulfill the government's requirements. Remember that your contract performance will be rated, and the rating will be entered into the **Past Performance Information Retrieval System** (PPIRS) for all the other government contracting officers to see. A favorable impression may make the next contract a little easier to get. So:

■ Cooperate with the contracting officer as much as possible, but remember that he is bound to the contract's terms and conditions as much as you are.

■ If the contracting officer interprets a contract provision erroneously or asks for something not covered by the contract, you may have to file a claim or exercise your rights under the Disputes clause.

■ After final delivery or completion of performance, make sure:

 – All payments have been made by the government.

 – All options have expired.

 – All forms and reports have been submitted.

 – All government-furnished property (GFP) has been returned.

 – All disputes have been resolved.

■ If the contract is truly complete, close out the contract.

■ Be sure to retain all required records for the mandated period of time.

Step #10 – Refer to *Getting Started in Federal Contracting* Whenever Necessary

Getting Started in Federal Contracting is the most comprehensive guide to the federal acquisition process available **anywhere**.

As a bonus, I'll give you an additional step for successful federal contracting:

Step #11 – Frequently Check Panoptic Enterprises' "Federal Government Contracts Center"

The "Federal Government Contracts Center" (**http://www.FedGovContracts. com**) provides news on changes to the various acquisition-related regulations, newsletters on developments in the federal acquisition world, hyperlinks to important acquisition-related websites, and publications on various aspects of federal acquisition.

Best wishes, and good luck!

APPENDIX A

KEY ACQUISITION WEBSITES

FEDERAL ACQUISITION REGULATION (FAR)
> https://www.acquisition.gov/?q=browsefar
> http://farsite.hill.af.mil/
> http://www.ecfr.gov (select "Title 48")

AGENCY FAR SUPPLEMENTS
> https://www.acquisition.gov/?q=Supplemental_Regulations
> http://farsite.hill.af.mil/
> http://www.ecfr.gov (select "Title 48")

COST ACCOUNTING STANDARDS
> https://www.govinfo.gov/app/content/pkg/CFR-2015-title48-vol7/xml/
> CFR-2015-title48-vol7-chap99.xml

ACQUISITION SITES
> https://www.acquisition.gov

System for Award Management (SAM)
> https://www.sam.gov

Agencies' Procurement Forecasts
> https://www.acquisition.gov/procurement-forecasts

Federal Business Opportunities (FedBizOpps)
> https://www.fbo.gov

Electronic Subcontracting Reporting System (eSRS)
> https://www.esrs.gov/

Federal Procurement Data System (FPDS)
>   https://www.fpds.gov/

Contractor Performance Assessment Reporting System (CPARS)
>   https://www.cpars.gov/

Federal Awardee Performance and Integrity Information System (FAPIIS)
>   https://www.cpars.gov/fapiismain.htm

Past Performance Information Retrieval System (PPIRS)
>   https://www.ppirs.gov/

Acquisition Gateway
>   https://hallways.cap.gsa.gov

Civilian Agencies' Service Contract Inventories
>   https:// www.whitehouse.gov/omb/procurement-service-contract-
>   inventories

Department of Defense Service Contract Inventory
>   http://www.acq.osd.mil/dpap/cpic/cp/acquisition_of_services_policy.html

Office of Federal Procurement Policy (OFPP)
>   https://www.whitehouse.gov/omb/procurement_default

SPECIFICATIONS AND STANDARDS

General Services Administration Index of Federal Specifications, Standards, and Commercial Item Descriptions (GSA Index)
>   http://www.gsa.gov/portal/content/100847

Acquisition Streamlining and Standardization Information System (ASSIST)
>   http://quicksearch.dla.mil/

Product and Service Codes (PSC)
>   https://www.acquisition.gov/sites/default/files/page_file_uploads/PSC
>   Manual - Final - 9 August 2015_0.pdf

SMALL BUSINESS

Small Business Size Standards
>   http://www.sba.gov/size

North American Industry Classification System (NAICS) Codes
>   http://www.census.gov/eos/www/naics/

Section 8(a) Program
>   https://www.sba.gov/contracting/government-contracting-programs/8a-
>   business-development-program

Small Business Mentor-Protégé Program
>   https://www.sba. gov/contracting/government-contracting-programs/8a-
>   business-development-program/mentor-protege-program

Department of Transportation Disadvantaged Business Enterprise (DBE) Program
>
> https://www.transportation.gov/civil-rights/disadvantaged-business-
> enterprise

Historically Underutilized Business Zone (HUBZone) Program
>
> https://www.sba.gov/contracting/government-contracting-programs/
> hubzone-program

HUBZone Map
>
> http://map.sba.gov/hubzone/maps/

Service-Disabled Veteran-Owned Small Business Program
>
> https://www.sba.gov/contracting/government-contracting-
> programs/service-disabled-veteran-owned-businesses

Women-Owned Small Business Program
>
> https://www.sba.gov/contracting/government-contracting-
> programs/women-owned-small-businesses

Women-Owned Small Business Certification
>
> https://certify.sba.gov

Dynamic Small Business Search
>
> http://dsbs.sba.gov/dsbs/search/dsp_dsbs.cfm

Small Business Administration Subcontracting Network (SUB-Net)
>
> http://web.sba.gov/subnet

Small Business Innovative Research (SBIR) Program
>
> https://www.sbir.gov/about/about-sbir

Small Business Technology Transfer (STTR) Program
>
> https://www.sbir.gov/about/about-sttr

SBIR and STTR Solicitations
>
> https://www.sbir.gov/sbirsearch/topic/current

Nonmanufacturer Rule Waivers
>
> https://www.sba.gov/contracting/contracting-officials/non-manufacturer-
> rule/class-waivers

GENERAL SERVICES ADMINISTRATION (GSA)

GSA eLibrary
>
> http://www.gsaelibrary.gsa.gov/

GSA *Advantage!*
>
> https://www.gsaadvantage.gov

Federal Supply Schedules
>
> http://www.gsa.gov/schedules

Industrial Funding Fee (IFF) Rates
>
> https://72a.gsa.gov/iffrates.cfm

eOffer/eMod
>
> http://eoffer.gsa.gov

eBuy
>
> https://www.ebuy.gsa.gov/advantage/ebuy/start_page.do

eBuy Registration
   https://www.ebuy.gsa.gov/advantage/main/registration.do
GSA Advance Spend Analysis Program
   https://www.asap.gsa.gov/asap/welcome.do
GSA Global Supply
   https://www.gsaglobalsupply.gsa.gov
GSA Acquisition Manual (GSAM)
   https://www.acquisition.gov/?q=browsegsam
GSA Reverse Auctions
   http://reverseauctions.gsa.gov/
GSA Vendor Support Center
   https://vsc.gsa.gov/
GSA Forms Library
   http://www.gsa.gov/portal/forms/type/SF

LABOR

Department of Labor (DOL) eLaws
   http://webapps.dol.gov/elaws/
DOL Wage and Hour Division
   http://www.dol.gov/whd/
Wage Determinations OnLine (WDOL)
   http://www.wdol.gov/
Occupational Safety and Health Administration (OSHA)
   https://www.osha.gov/
Contract Work Hours and Safety Standards Act
   http://www.dol.gov/whd/govcontracts/cwhssa.htm
Office of Federal Contract Compliance Programs (OFCCP)
   http://www.dol.gov/ofccp/
OFCCP's National Preaward Registry
   https://ofccp.dol-esa.gov/preaward/pa_reg.html
Equal Employment Opportunity (EEO) Compliance
   http://www.dol.gov/ofccp/regs/compliance/ca_11246.htm
Davis-Bacon Act Compliance
   http://www.dol.gov/whd/govcontracts/dbra.htm
Service Contract Act Compliance
   http://www.dol.gov/whd/govcontracts/sca.htm
CareerOneStop
   http://www.careeronestop.org/jobsearch/findjobs/state-job-banks.aspx
DOL's VETS-4212 Report
   http://www.dol.gov/vets/vets4212.htm
Veterans' Employment and Training Service
   http://www.dol.gov/vets/
Federal Employee Whistleblower Protection
   https://osc.gov/Pages/DOW.aspx

SUSTAINABLE ACQUISITIONS

ENERGY STAR®
https://www.energystar.gov/
Federal Energy Management Program (FEMP)
http://energy.gov/eere/femp/federal-energy-management-program
Comprehensive Procurement Guidelines (CPG)
https://www3.epa.gov/epawaste/conserve/tools/cpg/products/index.htm
CPG Product Supplier Directory
https://www3.epa.gov/epawaste/conserve/tools/cpg/supplier_support.htm
Biobased Products
http://www.biopreferred.gov/BioPreferred/faces/catalog/Catalog.xhtml
Electronic Products Environmental Assessment Tool (EPEAT)
http://www.epeat.net/
Significant New Alternatives Policy (SNAP) (alternatives to ozone-depleting substances)
https://www.epa.gov/snap

PROTESTS AND CLAIMS

Government Accountability Office (GAO)
http://www.gao.gov
  GAO's Protest Regulations
http://www.gao.gov/legal/bid-protest-regulations/about
U.S. Court of Federal Claims
http://www.uscfc.uscourts.gov/rcfc
Armed Services Board of Contract Appeals (ASBCA)
http://www.asbca.mil
Civilian Board of Contract Appeals (CBCA)
http://www.cbca.gsa.gov/

FOREIGN ACQUISITIONS

Specially Designated Nationals (SDN) List
https://www.treasury.gov/resource-center/sanctions/SDN-List/Pages/
default.aspx
Office of Foreign Assets Control (OFAC)
https://www.treasury.gov/about/organizational-structure/offices/Pages/
Office-of-Foreign-Assets-Control.aspx

REVERSE AUCTION SITES

FedBid
    http://www.FedBid.com
General Services Administration (GSA)
    http://www.reverseauctions.gsa.gov
Defense Logistics Agency (DLA)
    https://dla.procurexinc.com

MISCELLANEOUS

Standard Forms
    http://www.gsa.gov/portal/forms/type/SF
Data Universal Numbering System (DUNS) Numbers
    http://fedgov.dnb.com/webform
Department of Treasury Circular 570, Companies Holding Certificates of Authority as Acceptable Sureties
    https://www.fiscal.treasury.gov/fsreports/ref/suretyBnd/c570_a-z.htm
Federal Prison Industries, Inc. (UNICOR)
    http://www.unicor.gov
Committee for Purchase from People Who Are Blind or Severely Disabled
    http://www.abilityone.gov
Seven Steps to Performance-Based Acquisition
    https://www.acquisition.gov/seven_steps/home.html
Dun and Bradstreet
    http://fedgov.dnb.com/webform
Freedom of Information Act Resources
    http://www.justice.gov/oip

THE PANOPTIC ENTERPRISES' "FEDERAL GOVERNMENT CONTRACTS CENTER"
    http://www.FedGovContracts.com

APPENDIX B

A SAMPLE SOLICITATION

This appendix contains a fairly simple solicitation, an Invitation for Bids (IFB), for commercial supplies. It consists of the solicitation document (SF 1449), six attachments to the solicitation (one of which is the commercial item description [CID]), and an amendment to the solicitation (SF 30). The IFB is in the format specified in FAR 12.303, Contract Format [for acquisitions of commercial items]. Note that the amendment not only changes the color of the item but also extends the offer due date.

The IFB, issued by the Defense Logistics Agency Troop Support, is set aside for small businesses (see Chapter 11), and it will probably result in a contract between $150,000 (the simplified acquisition threshold – see Chapter 6) and $191,000 (the threshold for the Trade Agreements Act and related acts – see Chapter 12). Officially, the IFB has only two provisions and two clauses, but one clause incorporates many other FAR clauses, and two provisions and one clause have addenda that reference numerous other provisions and clauses from the FAR, the Defense FAR Supplement (DFARS), and the Defense Logistics Acquisition Directive (DLAD).

The provisions and clauses in an IFB for commercial items that is not set aside for small businesses, or is expected to produce a larger or smaller contract, or is issued by another contracting activity, would reference different clauses. If the contracting officer had decided to use a Request for Proposals (RFP) instead of an IFB, other provisions and clauses would have been referenced, too. No two solicitations are exactly alike. The contracting officer must customize each solicitation to reflect the supply or service being purchased, the amount of the purchase, and the circumstances of the purchase. Though you will probably never see a solicitation exactly like the one in this appendix, all resemble it.

AMENDMENT OF SOLICITATION/MODIFICATION OF CONTRACT

	1. CONTRACT ID CODE	PAGE	OF	PAGES
		1		1

2. AMENDMENT/MODIFICATION NUMBER	3. EFFECTIVE DATE	4. REQUISITION/PURCHASE REQUISITION NUMBER	5. PROJECT NUMBER (If applicable)
	02/06/2017	T0012/235-17-P	

6. ISSUED BY	CODE	SPE3S1	7. ADMINISTERED BY (If other than Item 6)	CODE	

Defense Logistics Agency Troop Support
700 Robbins Avenue, Room 254
Philadelphia, PA 19111-5096

8. NAME AND ADDRESS OF CONTRACTOR (Number, street, county, State and ZIP Code)	(X)	9A. AMENDMENT OF SOLICITATION NUMBER
	[X]	SPE3S1-17-B-0987
		9B. DATED (SEE ITEM 11)
		01/30/2017
		10A. MODIFICATION OF CONTRACT/ORDER NUMBER
	[ ]	10B. DATED (SEE ITEM 13)

CODE		FACILITY CODE	

11. THIS ITEM ONLY APPLIES TO AMENDMENTS OF SOLICITATIONS

[X] The above numbered solicitation is amended as set forth in Item 14. The hour and date specified for receipt of Offers [X] is extended. [ ] is not extended.

Offers must acknowledge receipt of this amendment prior to the hour and date specified in the solicitation or as amended, by one of the following methods:
(a) By completing items 8 and 15, and returning ___2___ copies of the amendment; (b) By acknowledging receipt of this amendment on each copy of the offer submitted; or (c) By separate letter or electronic communication which includes a reference to the solicitation and amendment numbers. FAILURE OF YOUR ACKNOWLEDGMENT TO BE RECEIVED AT THE PLACE DESIGNATED FOR THE RECEIPT OF OFFERS PRIOR TO THE HOUR AND DATE SPECIFIED MAY RESULT IN REJECTION OF YOUR OFFER. If by virtue of this amendment you desire to change an offer already submitted, such change may be made by letter or electronic communication, provided each letter or electronic communication makes reference to the solicitation and this amendment, and is received prior to the opening hour and date specified.

12. ACCOUNTING AND APPROPRIATION DATA (If required)

13. THIS ITEM APPLIES ONLY TO MODIFICATIONS OF CONTRACTS/ORDERS.
IT MODIFIES THE CONTRACT/ORDER NUMBER AS DESCRIBED IN ITEM 14.

CHECK ONE	
[ ]	A. THIS CHANGE ORDER IS ISSUED PURSUANT TO: (Specify authority) THE CHANGES SET FORTH IN ITEM 14 ARE MADE IN THE CONTRACT ORDER NUMBER IN ITEM 10A.
[ ]	B. THE ABOVE NUMBERED CONTRACT/ORDER IS MODIFIED TO REFLECT THE ADMINISTRATIVE CHANGES (such as changes in paying office, appropriation data, etc.) SET FORTH IN ITEM 14, PURSUANT TO THE AUTHORITY OF FAR 43.103(b).
[ ]	C. THIS SUPPLEMENTAL AGREEMENT IS ENTERED INTO PURSUANT TO AUTHORITY OF:
[ ]	D. OTHER (Specify type of modification and authority)

E. IMPORTANT: Contractor [ ] is not [ ] is required to sign this document and return _____ copies to the issuing office.

14. DESCRIPTION OF AMENDMENT/MODIFICATION (Organized by UCF section headings, including solicitation/contract subject matter where feasible.)

A. In Block 20 of the Item 1 description in IFB SPE3S1-17-B-0987, modify paragraph 2 to read: "The toilet tissue shall be Style II, Folded; Type B, two ply; Sheet size b, 114.3 mm x 114.3 mm; color green in accordance with thehcharacteristics specified in A-A-59594A, dated June 1, 2011, titled 'Toilet Tissue, Institutional,' marked 'Attachment No. 3.'"

B. As a result of this amendment, the bid opening is extended to 4:30 pm Eastern Time on March 8, 2017.

Except as provided herein, all terms and conditions of the document referenced in Item 9A or 10A, as heretofore changed, remains unchanged and in full force and effect.

15A. NAME AND TITLE OF SIGNER (Type or print)	16A. NAME AND TITLE OF CONTRACTING OFFICER (Type or print)

15B. CONTRACTOR/OFFEROR	15C. DATE SIGNED	16B. UNITED STATES OF AMERICA	16C. DATE SIGNED
(Signature of person authorized to sign)		(Signature of Contracting Officer)	

Previous edition unusable

STANDARD FORM 30 (REV. 11/2016)
Prescribed by GSA FAR (48 CFR) 53.243

SOLICITATION/CONTRACT/ORDER FOR COMMERCIAL ITEMS				1. REQUISITION NUMBER		PAGE 1 OF
OFFEROR TO COMPLETE BLOCKS 12, 17, 23, 24, & 30				T0012/235-17-P		2

2. CONTRACT NO.		3. AWARD/EFFECTIVE DATE	4. ORDER NUMBER	5. SOLICITATION NUMBER	6. SOLICITATION ISSUE DATE
				SPE3S1-17-B-0987	01/30/2017

7. FOR SOLICITATION INFORMATION CALL: ▶	a. NAME Joseph Blow	b. TELEPHONE NUMBER *(No collect calls)* 215-555-4321	8. OFFER DUE DATE/ LOCAL TIME 03/01/2017 4:30 pm

9. ISSUED BY	CODE	SPE3S1	10. THIS ACQUISITION IS [ ] UNRESTRICTED OR [X] SET ASIDE: 100 % FOR:
Defense Logistics Agency Troop Support 700 Robbins Avenue, Room 254 Philadelphia, PA 19111-5096			[X] SMALL BUSINESS [ ] HUBZONE SMALL BUSINESS [ ] SERVICE-DISABLED VETERAN-OWNED SMALL BUSINESS [ ] WOMEN-OWNED SMALL BUSINESS (WOSB) ELIGIBLE UNDER THE WOMEN-OWNED SMALL BUSINESS PROGRAM [ ] EDWOSB [ ] 8 (A) NAICS: 322291 SIZE STANDARD: 1500 employees

11. DELIVERY FOR FOB DESTINA-TION UNLESS BLOCK IS MARKED [ ] SEE SCHEDULE	12. DISCOUNT TERMS	[X] 13a. THIS CONTRACT IS A RATED ORDER UNDER DPAS (15 CFR 700)	13b. RATING DO-C9
			14. METHOD OF SOLICITATION [ ] RFQ [X] IFB [ ] RFP

15. DELIVER TO	CODE		16. ADMINISTERED BY	CODE
Defense Distribution Depot, Albany Supply Chain Management Center Albany, Georgia 31704				

17a. CONTRACTOR/ OFFEROR	CODE	FACILITY CODE	18a. PAYMENT WILL BE MADE BY	CODE

TELEPHONE NO.

17b. CHECK IF REMITTANCE IS DIFFERENT AND PUT SUCH ADDRESS IN [ ] OFFER	18b. SUBMIT INVOICES TO ADDRESS SHOWN IN BLOCK 18a UNLESS BLOCK BELOW IS CHECKED [ ] SEE ADDENDUM

19. ITEM NO.	20. SCHEDULE OF SUPPLIES/SERVICES	21. QUANTITY	22. UNIT	23. UNIT PRICE	24. AMOUNT
1	Toilet Tissue, Meal-Ready-to-Eat (MRE) Packet NSN 8540-01-926-8741 The following apply to Item No. 1: 1. Each packet shall consist of 24 toilet tissue sheets folded and wrapped in a sealed sleeve. The toilet tissue packet is a component of an MRE.	1,000,000	pkt		

(Use Reverse and/or Attach Additional Sheets as Necessary)

25. ACCOUNTING AND APPROPRIATION DATA	26. TOTAL AWARD AMOUNT *(For Govt. Use Only)*

[X] 27a. SOLICITATION INCORPORATES BY REFERENCE FAR 52.212-1, 52.212-4. FAR 52.212-3 AND 52.212-5 ARE ATTACHED. ADDENDA	[X] ARE	[ ] ARE NOT ATTACHED
[ ] 27b. CONTRACT/PURCHASE ORDER INCORPORATES BY REFERENCE FAR 52.212-4. FAR 52.212-5 IS ATTACHED. ADDENDA	[ ] ARE	[ ] ARE NOT ATTACHED

[X] 28. CONTRACTOR IS REQUIRED TO SIGN THIS DOCUMENT AND RETURN 2 COPIES TO ISSUING OFFICE. CONTRACTOR AGREES TO FURNISH AND DELIVER ALL ITEMS SET FORTH OR OTHERWISE IDENTIFIED ABOVE AND ON ANY ADDITIONAL SHEETS SUBJECT TO THE TERMS AND CONDITIONS SPECIFIED	[ ] 29. AWARD OF CONTRACT: REF. _____ OFFER DATED _____ YOUR OFFER ON SOLICITATION (BLOCK 5), INCLUDING ANY ADDITIONS OR CHANGES WHICH ARE SET FORTH HEREIN, IS ACCEPTED AS TO ITEMS:

30a. SIGNATURE OF OFFEROR/CONTRACTOR	31a. UNITED STATES OF AMERICA *(SIGNATURE OF CONTRACTING OFFICER)*

30b. NAME AND TITLE OF SIGNER *(Type or print)*	30c. DATE SIGNED	31b. NAME OF CONTRACTING OFFICER *(Type or print)*	31c. DATE SIGNED

AUTHORIZED FOR LOCAL REPRODUCTION PREVIOUS EDITION IS NOT USABLE	STANDARD FORM 1449 (REV. 2/2012) Prescribed by GSA - FAR (48 CFR) 53.212

19. ITEM NO.	20. SCHEDULE OF SUPPLIES/SERVICES	21. QUANTITY	22. UNIT	23. UNIT PRICE	24. AMOUNT
	Block 20 Continued: 2. The toilet tissue shall be Style II, Folded; Type b, Two ply; Sheet Size b, 114.3 mm x 114.3 mm; color white in accordance with the characteristics specified in A-A-59594A, dated June 1, 2011, entitled "Toilet Tissue, Institutional," marked "Attachment No. 3." 3. The toilet tissue shall be folded and wrapped in a sleeve made of unbleached kraft or unbleached sulfite paper. The sleeve shall be closed by gluing, taping, heat sealing, or by means of a self-sticking adhesive. The maximum dimensions of the packet shall not exceed 70 mm in length, 35 mm in width, and 15 mm in thickness. 4. The packets shall be packed in accordance with ASTM D 2951, Standard Practice for Commercial Packaging. 5. Inspection and acceptance of Item No. 1 shall be made by the government inspector at destination. 6. Attachments 1 through 6 apply to this solicitation.				

32a. QUANTITY IN COLUMN 21 HAS BEEN

☐ RECEIVED ☐ INSPECTED ☐ ACCEPTED, AND CONFORMS TO THE CONTRACT, EXCEPT AS NOTED: _____

32b. SIGNATURE OF AUTHORIZED GOVERNMENT REPRESENTATIVE	32c. DATE	32d. PRINTED NAME AND TITLE OF AUTHORIZED GOVERNMENT REPRESENTATIVE
32e. MAILING ADDRESS OF AUTHORIZED GOVERNMENT REPRESENTATIVE		32f. TELPHONE NUMBER OF AUTHORZED GOVERNMENT REPRESENTATIVE
		32g. E-MAIL OF AUTHORIZED GOVERNMENT REPRESENTATIVE

33. SHIP NUMBER	34. VOUCHER NUMBER	35. AMOUNT VERIFIED CORRECT FOR	36. PAYMENT	37. CHECK NUMBER
☐ PARTIAL ☐ FINAL			☐ COMPLETE ☐ PARTIAL ☐ FINAL	
38. S/R ACCOUNT NO.	39. S/R VOUCHER NUMBER	40. PAID BY		

41a. I CERTIFY THIS ACCOUNT IS CORRECT AND PROPER FOR PAYMENT		42a. RECEIVED BY (Print)
41b. SIGNATURE AND TITLE OF CERTIFYING OFFICER	41c. DATE	
		42b. RECEIVED AT (Location)
		42c. DATE REC'D (YY/MM/DD)	42d. TOTAL CONTAINERS

ATTACHMENT 1 TO IFB SPE3S1-17-B-0987

**ADDENDUM TO FAR 52.212-4, CONTRACT TERMS AND CONDITIONS –
COMMERCIAL ITEMS (MAY 2015)**

The following contract terms and conditions are incorporated by reference, with the same force and effect as if they were given in full text, in accordance with paragraphs (d) and (e) of FAR 12.301, Solicitation Provisions and Contract Clauses for the Acquisition of Commercial Items; paragraph (f) of Defense Federal Acquisition Regulation Supplement (DFARS) 212.301, Solicitation Provisions and Contract Clauses for the Acquisition of Commercial Items; and paragraph (f) of Defense Logistics Agency Directive (DLAD) 12.301, Solicitation Provisions and Contract Clauses for the Acquisition of Commercial Items (the FAR, DFARS, and DLAD are available at **http://www.farsite.hill.af.mil**):

FAR 52.203-3, Gratuities (APR 1984)

FAR 52.204-19, Incorporation by Reference of Representations and Certifications (DEC 2014)

FAR 52.211-17, Delivery of Excess Quantities (SEP 1989)

FAR 52.232-40, Providing Accelerated Payments to Small Business Subcontractors (DEC 2013)

FAR 52.242-13, Bankruptcy (JUL 1995)

DFARS 252.203-7000, Requirements Relating to Compensation of Former DOD Officials (SEP 2011)

DFARS 252.203-7995, Prohibition on Contracting with Entities that Require Certain Internal Confidentiality Agreements (Deviation 2017-O0001) (NOV 2016)

DFARS 252.204-7012, Safeguarding Covered Defense Information and Cyber Incident Reporting (DEC 2015)

DFARS 252.209-7004, Subcontracting with Firms that are Owned or Controlled by the Government of a Country that is a State Sponsor of Terrorism (OCT 2015)

DFARS 252.211-7003, Item Unique Identification and Valuation (MAR 2016)

DFARS 252.211-7006, Passive Radio Frequency Identification (SEP 2011)

DFARS 252.223-7008, Prohibition of Hexavalent Chromium (MAY 2011)

DFARS 252.225-7001, Buy American and Balance of Payments Program – Basic (AUG 2016)

DFARS 252.225-7012, Preference for Certain Domestic Commodities (AUG 2016)

DFARS 252.225-7036 Buy American – Free Trade Agreements – Balance of Payments Program (AUG 2016)

DFARS 252.232-7003, Electronic Submission of Payment Requests and Receiving Reports (JUN 2012)

DFARS 252.232-7006, Wide Area WorkFlow Payment Instructions (MAY 2013)

DFARS 252.232-7010, Levies on Contract Payments (DEC 2006)

DFARS 252.243-7002, Requests for Equitable Adjustment (DEC 2012)

DFARS 252.244-7000, Subcontracts for Commercial Items (JUN 2013)

DFARS 252.246-7000, Material Inspection and Receiving Report (MAR 2008)

DFARS 252.247-7023, Transportation of Supplies by Sea (APR 2014)

DFARS 252.247-7024, Notification of Transportation of Supplies by Sea (MAR 2000)

DLAD 52.211-9010, Shipping Label Requirements – Military Standard (MIL-STD) 129P (APR 2014)

DLAD 52.211-9014, Contractor Retention of Traceability Documentation (AUG 2012)

DLAD 52.247-9012, Requirements for Treatment of Wood Packaging Material (WPM) (FEB 2007)

FAR 52.211-8, Time of Delivery (JUN 1997)

(a) The government requires delivery to be made according to the following schedule:

REQUIRED DELIVERY SCHEDULE

ITEM NO.	QUANTITY	WITHIN DAYS AFTER DATE OF CONTRACT
0001	400,000	120
0001	400,000	150
0001	200,000	180

The government will evaluate equally, as regards time of delivery, offers that propose delivery of each quantity within the applicable delivery period specified above. Offers that propose delivery that will not clearly fall within the applicable required delivery period specified above, will be considered nonresponsive and rejected. The government reserves the right to award under either the required delivery schedule or the proposed delivery schedule, when an offeror offers an earlier delivery schedule than required above. If the offeror proposes no other delivery schedule, the required delivery schedule above will apply.

OFFEROR'S PROPOSED DELIVERY SCHEDULE

ITEM NO.	QUANTITY	WITHIN DAYS AFTER DATE OF CONTRACT

(b) Attention is directed to the contract award provision of the solicitation that provides that a written award or acceptance of offer mailed, or otherwise furnished to the successful offeror, results in a binding contract. The government will mail or otherwise furnish to the offeror an award or notice of award not later than the day award is dated. Therefore, the offeror should compute the time available for performance beginning with the actual date of award, rather than the date the written notice of award is received from the contracting officer through the ordinary mails. However, the government will evaluate an offer that proposes delivery based on the contractor's date of receipt of the contract or notice of award by adding (1) five calendar days for delivery of the award through the ordinary mails, or (2) one working day if the solicitation states that the contract or notice of award will be transmitted electronically. (The term "working day" excludes weekends and U.S. federal holidays.) If, as so computed, the offered delivery date is later than the required delivery date, the offer will be considered nonresponsive and rejected.

(End of clause)

FAR 52.211-16, Variations in Quantity (APR 1984)

(a) A variation in the quantity of any item called for by this contract will not be accepted unless the variation has been caused by conditions of loading, shipping, or packing, or allowances in manufacturing processes, and then only to the extent, if any, specified in paragraph (b) below.

(b) The permissible variation shall be limited to:
    1 (one) percent increase
    1/2 (one-half) percent decrease
This increase or decrease shall apply to each monthly delivery.

(End of clause)

FAR 52.212-5, CONTRACT TERMS AND CONDITIONS REQUIRED TO IMPLEMENT STATUTES OR EXECUTIVE ORDERS – COMMERCIAL ITEMS (JAN 2017)

(a) The Contractor shall comply with the following Federal Acquisition Regulation (FAR) clauses, which are incorporated in this contract by reference, to implement provisions of law or Executive orders applicable to acquisitions of commercial items:

(1) 52.203-19, Prohibition on Requiring Certain Internal Confidentiality Agreements or Statements (JAN 2017) (section 743 of Division E, Title VII, of the Consolidated and Further Continuing Appropriations Act, 2015 (Pub. L. 113-235) and its successor provisions in subsequent appropriations acts (and as extended in continuing resolutions)).

(2) 52.209-10, Prohibition on Contracting with Inverted Domestic Corporations (Nov 2015)

(3) 52.233-3, Protest After Award (AUG 1996) (31 U.S.C. 3553).

(3) 52.233-4, Applicable Law for Breach of Contract Claim (OCT 2004) (Public Laws 108-77, 108-78 (19 U.S.C. 3805 note)).

(b) The Contractor shall comply with the FAR clauses in this paragraph (b) that the contracting officer has indicated as being incorporated in this contract by reference to implement provisions of law or Executive orders applicable to acquisitions of commercial items:

[Contracting Officer check as appropriate.]

_X_ (1) 52.203-6, Restrictions on Subcontractor Sales to the Government (Sept 2006), with Alternate I (Oct 1995) (41 U.S.C. 4704 and 10 U.S.C. 2402).

___ (2) 52.203-13, Contractor Code of Business Ethics and Conduct (Oct 2015) (41 U.S.C. 3509).

___ (3) 52.203-15, Whistleblower Protections under the American Recovery and Reinvestment Act of 2009 (Jun 2010) (Section 1553 of Pub L. 111-5) (Applies to contracts funded by the American Recovery and Reinvestment Act of 2009).

_X_ (4) 52.204-10, Reporting Executive Compensation and First-Tier Subcontract Awards (Oct 2016) (Pub. L. 109-282) (31 U.S.C. 6101 note).

___ (5) [Reserved]

___ (6) 52.204-14, Service Contract Reporting Requirements (Oct 2016) (Pub. L. 111-117, section 743 of Div. C).

___ (7) 52.204-15, Service Contract Reporting Requirements for Indefinite-Delivery Contracts (Jan 2014) (Pub. L. 111-117, section 743 of Div. C).

_X_ (8) 52.209-6, Protecting the Government's Interest When Subcontracting with Contractors Debarred, Suspended, or Proposed for Debarment (Oct 2016) (31 U.S.C. 6101 note).

___ (9) 52.209-9, Updates of Publicly Available Information Regarding Responsibility Matters (Jul 2013) (41 U.S.C. 2313).

___ (10) [Reserved]

___ (11) (i) 52.219-3, Notice of HUBZone Set-Aside or Sole-Source Award (Nov 2011) (15 U.S.C. 657a).

___ (ii) Alternate I (Nov 2011) of 52.219-3.

___ (12) (i) 52.219-4, Notice of Price Evaluation Preference for HUBZone Small Business Concerns (Oct 2014) (if the offeror elects to waive the preference, it shall so indicate in its offer)(15 U.S.C. 657a).

___ (ii) Alternate I (Jan 2011) of 52.219-4.

___ (13) [Reserved]

_X_ (14) (i) 52.219-6, Notice of Total Small Business Aside (Nov 2011) (15 U.S.C. 644).

___ (ii) Alternate I (Nov 2011).

___ (iii) Alternate II (Nov 2011).

___ (15) (i) 52.219-7, Notice of Partial Small Business Set-Aside (June 2003) (15 U.S.C. 644).

___ (ii) Alternate I (Oct 1995) of 52.219-7.

___ (iii) Alternate II (Mar 2004) of 52.219-7.

_X_ (16) 52.219-8, Utilization of Small Business Concerns (Oct 2014) (15 U.S.C. 637(d)(2) and (3)).

___ (17) (i) 52.219-9, Small Business Subcontracting Plan (Jan 2017) (15 U.S.C. 637 (d)(4)).

___ (ii) Alternate I (Oct 2001) of 52.219-9.

___ (iii) Alternate II (Oct 2001) of 52.219-9.

___ (iv) Alternate III (Oct 2015) of 52.219-9.

___ (18) 52.219-13, Notice of Set-Aside of Orders (Nov 2011) (15 U.S.C. 644(r)).

_X_ (19) 52.219-14, Limitations on Subcontracting (Nov 2011) (15 U.S.C. 637(a)(14)).

___ (20) 52.219-16, Liquidated Damages – Subcontracting Plan (Jan 1999) (15 U.S.C. 637(d)(4)(F)(i)).

___ (21) 52.219-27, Notice of Service-Disabled Veteran-Owned Small Business Set-Aside (Nov 2011) (15 U.S.C. 657f).

_X_ (22) 52.219-28, Post Award Small Business Program Rerepresentation (Jul 2013) (15 U.S.C. 632(a)(2)).

___ (23) 52.219-29, Notice of Set-Aside for, or Sole Source Award to, Economically Disadvantaged Women-Owned Small Business Concerns (Dec 2015) (15 U.S.C. 637(m)).

___ (24) 52.219-30, Notice of Set-Aside for, or Sole Source Award to, Women-Owned Small Business Concerns Eligible Under the Women-Owned Small Business Program (Dec 2015) (15 U.S.C. 637(m)).

_X_ (25) 52.222-3, Convict Labor (June 2003) (E.O. 11755).

_X_ (26) 52.222-19, Child Labor – Cooperation with Authorities and Remedies (Oct 2016) (E.O. 13126).

_X_ (27) 52.222-21, Prohibition of Segregated Facilities (Apr 2015).

_X_ (28) 52.222-26, Equal Opportunity (Sep 2016) (E.O. 11246).

_X_ (29) 52.222-35, Equal Opportunity for Veterans (Oct 2015) (38 U.S.C. 4212).

_X_ (30) 52.222-36, Equal Opportunity for Workers with Disabilities (Jul 2014) (29 U.S.C. 793).

_X_ (31) 52.222-37, Employment Reports on Veterans (Feb 2016) (38 U.S.C. 4212).

_X_ (32) 52.222-40, Notification of Employee Rights Under the National Labor Relations Act (Dec 2010) (E.O. 13496).

_X_ (33) (i) 52.222-50, Combating Trafficking in Persons (Mar 2015) (22 U.S.C. chapter 78 and E.O. 13627).

___ (ii) Alternate I (Mar 2015) of 52.222-50, (22 U.S.C. chapter 78 and E.O. 13627).

___ (34) 52.222-54, Employment Eligibility Verification (Oct 2015). (E. O. 12989). (Not applicable to the acquisition of commercially available off-the-shelf items or certain other types of commercial items as prescribed in 22.1803.)

___ (35) 52.222-59, Compliance with Labor Laws (Executive Order 13673) (OCT 2016). (Applies at $50 million for solicitations and resultant contracts issued from October 25, 2016, through April 24, 2017; applies at $500,000 for solicitations and resultant contracts issued after April 24, 2017).

Note to paragraph (b)(35): By a court order issued on October 24, 2016, 52.222-59 is enjoined indefinitely as of the date of the order. The enjoined paragraph will become effective immediately if the court terminates the injunction. At that time, DOD, GSA, and NASA will publish a document in the *Federal Register* advising the public of the termination of the injunction.

___ (36) 52.222-60, Paycheck Transparency (Executive Order 13673) OCT 2016).

_X_ (37) (i) 52.223-9, Estimate of Percentage of Recovered Material Content for EPA-Designated Items (May 2008) (42 U.S.C. 6962(c)(3)(A)(ii)). (Not applicable to the acquisition of commercially available off-the-shelf items.)

___ (ii) Alternate I (May 2008) of 52.223-9 (42 U.S.C. 6962(i)(2)(C)). (Not applicable to the acquisition of commercially available off-the-shelf items.)

___ (38) 52.223-10, High Global Warming Potential Hydrofluorocarbons (JUN 2016) (E.O. 13693).

___ (39) 52.223-12, Maintenance, Service, Repair, or Disposal of Refrigeration Equipment and Air Conditioners (JUN 2016) (E.O. 13693).

___ (40) (i) 52.223-13, Acquisition of EPEAT® -Registered Imaging Equipment (Jun 2014) (E.O.s 13423 and 13514

___ (ii) Alternate I (Oct 2015) of 52.223-13.

___ (41) (i) 52.223-14, Acquisition of EPEAT® -Registered Television (Jun 2014) (E.O.s 13423 and 13514).

___ (ii) Alternate I (Jun 2014) of 52.223-14.

___ (42) 52.223-15, Energy Efficiency in Energy-Consuming Products (Dec 2007) (42 U.S.C. 8259b).

___ (43) (i) 52.223-16, Acquisition of EPEAT® -Registered Personal Computer Products (Oct 2015) (E.O.s 13423 and 13514).

___ (ii) Alternate I (Jun 2014) of 52.223-16.

_X_ (44) 52.223-18, Encouraging Contractor Policies to Ban Text Messaging While Driving (Aug 2011) (E.O. 13513).

___ (45) 52.223-20, Aerosols (JUN 2016) (E.O. 13693).

___ (46) 52.223-21, Foams (JUN 2016) (E.O. 13693).

___ (47) (i) 52.224-3, Privacy Training (JAN 2017) (5 U.S.C. 552a).

___ (ii) Alternate I (JAN 2017) of 52.224-3.

___ (48) 52.225-1, Buy American – Supplies (May 2014) (41 U.S.C. chapter 83).

___ (49) (i) 52.225-3, Buy American – Free Trade Agreements – Israeli Trade Act (May 2014) (41 U.S.C. chapter 83, 19 U.S.C. 3301 note, 19 U.S.C. 2112 note, 19 U.S.C. 3805 note, 19 U.S.C. 4001 note, Pub. L. 103-182, 108-77, 108-78, 108-286, 108-302, 109-53, 109-169, 109-283, 110-138, 112-41, 112-42, and 112-43).

___ (ii) Alternate I (May 2014) of 52.225-3.

___ (iii) Alternate II (May 2014) of 52.225-3.

___ (iv) Alternate III (May 2014) of 52.225-3.

___ (50) 52.225-5, Trade Agreements (Oct 2016) (19 U.S.C. 2501, *et seq.*, 19 U.S.C. 3301 note).

_X_ (51) 52.225-13, Restrictions on Certain Foreign Purchases (Jun 2008) (E.O.'s, proclamations, and statutes administered by the Office of Foreign Assets Control of the Department of the Treasury).

___ (52) 52.225-26, Contractors Performing Private Security Functions Outside the United States (Oct 2016) (Section 862, as amended, of the National Defense Authorization Act for Fiscal Year 2008; 10 U.S.C. 2302 Note).

___ (53) 52.226-4, Notice of Disaster or Emergency Area Set-Aside (Nov 2007) (42 U.S.C. 5150).

___ (54) 52.226-5, Restrictions on Subcontracting Outside Disaster or Emergency Area (Nov 2007) (42 U.S.C. 5150).

___ (55) 52.232-29, Terms for Financing of Purchases of Commercial Items (Feb 2002) (41 U.S.C. 4505), 10 U.S.C. 2307(f)).

___ (56) 52.232-30, Installment Payments for Commercial Items (Jan 2017) (41 U.S.C. 4505, 10 U.S.C. 2307(f)).

_X_ (57) 52.232-33, Payment by Electronic Funds Transfer – System for Award Management (Jul 2013) (31 U.S.C. 3332).

___ (58) 52.232-34, Payment by Electronic Funds Transfer – Other Than System for Award Management (Jul 2013) (31 U.S.C. 3332).

___ (59) 52.232-36, Payment by Third Party (May 2014) (31 U.S.C. 3332).

___ (60) 52.242–5, Payments to Small Business Subcontractors (Jan 2017)(15 U.S.C. 637(d)(12)).

___ (61) 52.239-1, Privacy or Security Safeguards (Aug 1996) (5 U.S.C. 552a).

_X_ (62) (i) 52.247-64, Preference for Privately Owned U.S.-Flag Commercial Vessels (Feb 2006) (46 U.S.C. Appx 1241(b) and 10 U.S.C. 2631).

___ (ii) Alternate I (Apr 2003) of 52.247-64.

(c) The Contractor shall comply with the FAR clauses in this paragraph (c), applicable to commercial services, that the Contracting Officer has indicated as being incorporated in this contract by reference to implement provisions of law or executive orders applicable to acquisitions of commercial items:

[*Contracting Officer check as appropriate.*]

___ (1) 52.222-17, Nondisplacement of Qualified Workers (May 2014) (E.O. 13495)

___ (2) 52.222-41, Service Contract Labor Standards (May 2014) (41 U.S.C. chapter 67.).

___ (3) 52.222-42, Statement of Equivalent Rates for Federal Hires (May 2014) (29 U.S.C. 206 and 41 U.S.C. chapter 67).

___ (4) 52.222-43, Fair Labor Standards Act and Service Contract Labor Standards – Price Adjustment (Multiple Year and Option Contracts) (May 2014) (29 U.S.C.206 and 41 U.S.C. chapter 67).

___ (5) 52.222-44, Fair Labor Standards Act and Service Contract Labor Standards – Price Adjustment (May 2014) (29 U.S.C. 206 and 41 U.S.C. chapter 67).

___ (6) 52.222-51, Exemption from Application of the Service Contract Labor Standards to Contracts for Maintenance, Calibration, or Repair of Certain Equipment – Requirements (May 2014) (41 U.S.C. chapter 67).

___ (7) 52.222-53, Exemption from Application of the Service Contract Labor Standards to Contracts for Certain Services – Requirements (May 2014) (41 U.S.C. chapter 67).

___ (8) 52.222-55, Minimum Wages Under Executive Order 13658 (Dec 2015) (E.O. 13658).

___ (9) 52.222-62, Paid Sick Leave Under Executive Order 13706 (JAN 2017) (E.O. 13706)

___ (10) 52.226-6, Promoting Excess Food Donation to Nonprofit Organizations. (May 2014) (42 U.S.C. 1792).

___ (11) 52.237-11, Accepting and Dispensing of $1 Coin (Sep 2008) (31 U.S.C. 5112(p)(1)).

(d) *Comptroller General Examination of Record.* The Contractor shall comply with the provisions of this paragraph (d) if this contract was awarded using other than sealed bid, is in excess of the simplified acquisition threshold, and does not contain the clause at 52.215-2, Audit and Records – Negotiation.

(1) The Comptroller General of the United States, or an authorized representative of the Comptroller General, shall have access to and right to examine any of the Contractor's directly pertinent records involving transactions related to this contract.

(2) The Contractor shall make available at its offices at all reasonable times the records, materials, and other evidence for examination, audit, or reproduction, until 3 years after final payment under this contract or for any shorter period specified in FAR Subpart 4.7, Contractor Records Retention, of the other clauses of this contract. If this contract is completely or partially terminated, the records relating to the work terminated shall be made available for 3 years after any resulting final termination settlement. Records relating to appeals under the disputes clause or to litigation or the settlement of claims arising under or relating to this contract shall be made available until such appeals, litigation, or claims are finally resolved.

(3) As used in this clause, records include books, documents, accounting procedures and practices, and other data, regardless of type and regardless of form. This does not require the Contractor to create or maintain any record that the Contractor does not maintain in the ordinary course of business or pursuant to a provision of law.

(e)	(1) Notwithstanding the requirements of the clauses in paragraphs (a), (b), (c) and (d) of this clause, the contractor is not required to flow down any FAR clause, other than those in this paragraph (e)(1) in a subcontract for commercial items. Unless otherwise indicated below, the extent of the flow down shall be as required by the clause –

(i) 52.203-13, Contractor Code of Business Ethics and Conduct (Oct 2015) (41 U.S.C. 3509).

(ii) 52.203-19, Prohibition on Requiring Certain Internal Confidentiality Agreements or Statements (JAN 2017) (section 743 of Division E, Title VII, of the Consolidated and Further Continuing Appropriations Act, 2015 (Pub. L. 113-235) and its successor provisions in subsequent appropriations acts (and as extended in continuing resolutions)).

(iii) 52.219-8, Utilization of Small Business Concerns (Oct 2014) (15 U.S.C. 637(d)(2) and (3)), in all subcontracts that offer further subcontracting opportunities. If the subcontract (except subcontracts to small business concerns) exceeds $700,000 ($1.5 million for construction of any public facility), the subcontractor must include 52.219-8 in lower tier subcontracts that offer subcontracting opportunities.

(iv) 52.222-17, Nondisplacement of Qualified Workers (May 2014) (E.O. 13495). Flow down required in accordance with paragraph (1) of FAR clause 52.222-17.

(v) 52.222-21, Prohibition of Segregated Facilities (Apr 2015).

(vi) 52.222-26, Equal Opportunity (Sep 2016) (E.O. 11246).

(vii) 52.222-35, Equal Opportunity for Veterans (Oct 2015) (38 U.S.C. 4212).

(viii) 52.222-36, Equal Opportunity for Workers with Disabilities (Jul 2014) (29 U.S.C. 793).

(ix) 52.222-37, Employment Reports on Veterans (Feb 2016) (38 U.S.C. 4212).

(x) 52.222-40, Notification of Employee Rights Under the National Labor Relations Act (Dec 2010) (E.O. 13496). Flow down required in accordance with paragraph (f) of FAR clause 52.222-40.

(xi) 52.222-41, Service Contract Labor Standards (May 2014), (41 U.S.C. chapter 67).

(xii) _X_ (A) 52.222-50, Combating Trafficking in Persons (Mar 2015) (22 U.S.C. chapter 78 and E.O. 13627).
___ (B) Alternate I (Mar 2015) of 52.222-50 (22 U.S.C. chapter 78 E.O. 13627).

(xiii) 52.222-51, Exemption from Application of the Service Contract Labor Standards to Contracts for Maintenance, Calibration, or Repair of Certain Equipment – Requirements (May 2014) (41 U.S.C. chapter 67.)

(xiv) 52.222-53, Exemption from Application of the Service Contract Labor Standards to Contracts for Certain Services – Requirements (May 2014) (41 U.S.C. chapter 67)

(xv) 52.222-54, Employment Eligibility Verification (Oct 2015) (E. O. 12989).

(xvi) 52.222-55, Minimum Wages Under Executive Order 13658 (Dec 2015) (E.O. 13658).

(xvii) 52.222-59, Compliance with Labor Laws (Executive Order 13673) (OCT 2016) (Applies at $50 million for solicitations and resultant contracts issued from October 25, 2016, through April 24, 2017; applies at $500,000 for solicitations and resultant contracts issued after April 24, 2017).

Note to paragraph (e)(1)(xvii): By a court order issued on October 24, 2016, 52.222-59 is enjoined indefinitely as of the date of the order. The enjoined paragraph will become effective immediately if the court terminates the injunction. At that time, DOD, GSA, and NASA will publish a document in the *Federal Register* advising the public of the termination of the injunction.

(xviii) 52.222-60, Paycheck Transparency (Executive Order 13673) (OCT 2016)).

(xix) 52.225-26, Contractors Performing Private Security Functions Outside the United States (Oct 2016) (Section 862, as amended, of the National Defense Authorization Act for Fiscal Year 2008; 10 U.S.C. 2302 Note).

(xx)___ (A) 52.224-3, Privacy Training (JAN 2017) (5 U.S.C. 552a).
___ (B) Alternate I (JAN 2017) of 52.224-3.

(xxi) 52.226-6, Promoting Excess Food Donation to Nonprofit Organizations. (May 2014) (42 U.S.C. 1792). Flow down required in accordance with paragraph (e) of FAR clause 52.226-6.

(xxii) 52.247-64, Preference for Privately-Owned U.S. Flag Commercial Vessels (Feb 2006) (46 U.S.C. Appx 1241(b) and 10 U.S.C. 2631). Flow down required in accordance with paragraph (d) of FAR clause 52.247-64.

(2) While not required, the contractor may include in its subcontracts for commercial items a minimal number of additional clauses necessary to satisfy its contractual obligations.

(End of Clause)

ATTACHMENT 3

METRIC

A-A-59594A
June 1, 2011
SUPERSEDING
A-A-59594
October 9, 2001

COMMERCIAL ITEM DESCRIPTION

TOILET TISSUE, INSTITUTIONAL

The General Services Administration has authorized the use of this Commercial Item Description.

1. SCOPE.

1.1 This Commercial Item Description (CID) covers institutional toilet tissue suitable for use by Federal, State, local governments and other interested parties; and as a component of operational rations.

2. CLASSIFICATION.

2.1 The toilet tissue shall conform to the following styles, types, classes, and sheet sizes as specified in the solicitation, contract, or purchase order.

Styles, types, classes, and sheet sizes.

 Style I - Roll

 Type A - One ply
 Type B - Two ply

  Class 1 - Perforated

   Sheet size a - 101.6 mm x 101.6 mm (4.0" x 4.0")
   Sheet size b - 114.3 mm x 101.6 mm (4.5" x 4.0")
   Sheet size c - 114.3 mm x 114.3 mm (4.5" x 4.5")
   Sheet size d - Other

  Class 2 - Non perforated

   Sheet size a - 228,600 mm x 88.89 mm (750.0' x 3.5")
   Sheet size b - 304,800 mm x 88.89 mm (1000.0' x 3.5")

Sheet size c - 609,600 mm x 88.89 mm (2000.0' x 3.5")
Sheet size d - Other

Style II - Folded

Type A - One ply
Type B - Two ply

Sheet size a - 215.9 mm x 114.3 mm (8.5" x 4.5")
Sheet size b - 114.3 mm x 114.3 mm (4.5" x 4.5")
Sheet size c - 101.6 mm x 127.0 mm (4.0" x 5.0")
Sheet size d - 101.6 mm x 254.0 mm (4.0" x 10.0")
Sheet size e - Other

3. SALIENT CHARACTERISTICS.

3.1 Material. The toilet tissue shall be unglazed. The tissue shall be made from 50 percent recovered fiber, including 20 percent postconsumer fiber.

3.2 Workmanship. The toilet tissue shall be trimmed with clean, smooth edges. The paper shall be free of dirt spots, holes, tears, wrinkles, foreign matter, undigested paper, or unbleached waste.

3.3 Appearance. The toilet tissue may be smooth or textured.

3.4 Odor. The toilet tissue shall have no disagreeable odor when dry or wet.

3.5 Color. The toilet tissue shall be white unless otherwise specified in the solicitation, contract, or purchase order. Tissue for use in Department of Defense operational rations shall be white, dull beige, green, or yellow.

3.6 Disintegration. The supplier shall certify that the toilet tissue shall not clog or interfere with the water flow of waste lines or septic tank systems.

3.7 Physical requirements. The toilet tissue shall dispense satisfactorily from the fixture when loaded according to the directions. The tissue shall meet or exceed the requirements of Table I.

TABLE I. Physical requirements

Characteristic	Requirement				Test Method
	Style I		Style II		
	Type A	Type B	Type A	Type B	
Weight per unit area:					TAPPI T 410 1/
Grammage, g/m^2, min	14.7	27.7	14.7	27.7	
Basis weight, lb, min (24 x 36 - 500)	9.0	17.0	9.0	17.0	
Tensile strength: Cross direction (Dry)					TAPPI T 576 1/
gf/3in, min	350	200	350	200	
Cross direction (Wet) gf/3in, min	0	0	0	0	
Machine direction (Dry) gf/3in, min	850	600	850	600	
Machine direction (Wet) gf/3in, min	0	0	0	0	
Water absorption: seconds for 0.01 ml, max	60	5	60	5	TAPPI T 432 1/

1/ Prior to physical testing, samples shall be conditioned in accordance with TAPPI T 402.

4. REGULATORY REQUIREMENTS. In accordance with section 23.403 of the Federal Acquisition Regulations, the Government's policy is to acquire items composed of the highest percentage of recovered materials practicable, consistent with maintaining a satisfactory level of competition without adversely affecting performance requirement or exposing suppliers' employees to undue hazards from the recovered materials.

5. PRODUCT CONFORMANCE. The toilet tissue shall meet the physical characteristics of this CID, conform to the producer's own drawings, specifications, standards, and quality assurance practices, and be the same toilet tissue offered for sale in the commercial market. The Government reserves the right to require proof of such conformance.

6. PACKAGING. Preservation, packaging, packing, labeling, and case marking shall be as specified in the solicitation, contract, or purchase order.

7. NOTES.

7.1 Purchasers shall specify:

- Styles, types, classes, and sheet sizes required.
- Packaging requirements (Sec. 6 or as specified in the solicitation, contract, or purchase order).

7.2 Sources of documents.

7.2.1 Sources of information for nongovernmental documents is as follows:

TAPPI test methods may be obtained from: **Technical Association of the Pulp and Paper Industry, 15 Technology Parkway South, Norcross, GA 30092 or on the Internet at: http://www.tappi.org/.**

7.2.2 Sources of information for governmental documents are as follows:

Civil agencies and other interested parties may obtain copies of this CID and the Federal Acquisition Regulations from: **General Services Administration, Federal Supply Service, Specifications Section, Suite 8100, 470 L 'Enfant Plaza, SW, Washington, DC 20407.**

Beneficial comments, recommendations, additions, deletions, clarifications, etc., and any data which may improve this document should be sent to: **Commander, Defense Logistics Agency (DLA) Troop Support, ATTN: FTSA, 700 Robbins Avenue, Philadelphia, PA 19111-5092 or FAX (215) 737-2963, or via E-mail: dscpsubsweb@dla.mil.**

Military activities may obtain copies of this CID from: **Standardization Documents Order Desk, DLA Document Services, 700 Robbins Avenue, Building 4D, Philadelphia, PA 19111-5094 or on the Internet at: https://assist.daps.dla.mil or https://assist.daps.dla.mil/quicksearch/.**

MILITARY INTERESTS:

CIVIL AGENCY COORDINATING ACTIVITY:

Custodians

GSA - 2FYI

Army - GL

PREPARING ACTIVITY:

Review Activities

DLA - SS

Army - MD

(Project No. 8540-2010-001)

NOTE: The activities listed above were interested in this document as of the date of this document. Since organizations and responsibilities can change, you should verify the currency of the information above using the ASSIST Online database at **https://assist.daps.dla.mil**.

ATTACHMENT 4 TO IFB SPE3S1-17-B-0987

ADDENDUM TO FAR 52.212-1, INSTRUCTIONS TO OFFERORS – COMMERCIAL ITEMS (JAN 2017)

FAR 52.252-1, SOLICITATION PROVISIONS INCORPORATED BY REFERENCE (FEB 1998)

This solicitation incorporates one or more solicitation provisions by reference, with the same force and effect as if they were given in full text. Upon request, the contracting officer will make their full text available. The offeror is cautioned that the listed provisions may include blocks that must be completed by the offeror and submitted with its quotation or offer. In lieu of submitting the full text of those provisions, the offeror may identify the provision by paragraph identifier and provide the appropriate information with its quotation or offer. Also, the full text of a solicitation provision may be accessed electronically at this/these address(es): the FAR, DFARS, and DLAD are available at **http://www.farsite.hill.af.mil**.

(End of provision)

FAR 52.204-18, Commercial and Government Entity Code Maintenance (JUL 2016)
FAR 52.214-3, Amendments to Invitations for Bids (DEC 2016)
FAR 52.214-4, False Statements in Bids (APR 1984)
FAR 52.214-5, Submission of Bids (DEC 2016)
FAR 52.214-6, Explanation to Prospective Bidders (APR 1984)
FAR 52.214-7, Late Submissions, Modifications, and Withdrawals of Bids (NOV 1999)
FAR 52.214-10, Contract Award – Sealed Bidding (JUL 1990)
FAR 52.214-12, Preparation of Bids (APR 1984)
FAR 52.214-34, Submission of Offers in the English Language (APR 1991)
FAR 52.214-35, Submission of Offers in U.S. Currency (APR 1991)

FAR 52.216-1, Type of Contract (APR 1984)

The government contemplates award of a firm-fixed price contract resulting from this solicitation.

(End of Provision)

FAR 52.233-2, Service of Protest (SEP 2006)

(a) Protests, as defined in section 33.101 of the Federal Acquisition Regulation, that are filed directly with an agency, and copies of any protests that are filed with the Government Accountability Office (GAO), shall be served on the Contracting Officer (addressed as follows) by obtaining written and dated acknowledgment of receipt from Rusty Nales, Defense Logistics Agency Troop Support, 700 Robbins Avenue, Room 254, Philadelphia, PA 19111-5096.
(b) The copy of any protest shall be received in the office designated above within one day of filing a protest with the GAO.

(End of Provision)

DLAD 52.233-9000, Agency Protests (NOV 2011)

(a) Companies protesting this procurement may file a protest
    (1) With the contracting officer,
    (2) With the Government Accountability Office (GAO), or
    (3) Pursuant to Executive Order Number 12979, with the Agency for a decision by the Activity's Chief of the Contracting Office.
(b) Protests filed with the agency should clearly state that they are an "Agency Level Protest under Executive Order Number 12979."
(c) Defense Logistics Agency (DLA) procedures for Agency Level Protests filed under Executive Order Number 12979 allow for a higher level decision on the initial protest than would occur with a protest to the contracting officer; this process is not an appellate review of a contracting officer's decision on a protest previously filed with the contracting officer. Absent a clear indication of the intent to file an agency level protest, protests will be presumed to be protests to the contracting officer.

(End of Provision)

DLAD 52.233-9001 Disputes – Agreement to Use Alternative Dispute Resolution (ADR) (NOV 2011)

(a) The parties agree to negotiate with each other to try to resolve any disputes that may arise. If unassisted negotiations are unsuccessful, the parties will use alternative dispute resolution (ADR) techniques to try to resolve the dispute. Litigation will only be considered as a last resort when ADR is unsuccessful or has been documented by the party rejecting ADR to be inappropriate for resolving the dispute.
(b) Before either party determines ADR inappropriate, that party must discuss the use of ADR with the other party. The documentation rejecting ADR must be signed by an official authorized to bind the contractor (see Federal Acquisition Regulation (FAR) clause 52.233-1), or, for the agency, by the contracting officer, and approved at a level above the contracting officer after consultation with the ADR specialist and with legal. Contractor personnel are also encouraged to include the ADR Specialist in their discussions with the contracting officer before determining ADR to be inappropriate.
(c) The offeror should check here to opt out of this clause:

[_] Alternate wording may be negotiated with the contracting officer.

(End of Provision)

FAR 52.212-3, OFFEROR REPRESENTATIONS AND CERTIFICATIONS – COMMERCIAL ITEMS (JAN 2017)

The offeror shall complete only paragraphs (b) of this provision if the offeror has completed the annual representations and certification electronically via the System for Award Management (SAM) Website located at **https://www.sam.gov/portal**. If the offeror has not completed the annual representations and certifications electronically, the offeror shall complete only paragraphs (c) through (u) of this provision.

(a) *Definitions.* As used in this provision –

"Administrative merits determination" means certain notices or findings of labor law violations issued by an enforcement agency following an investigation. An administrative merits determination may be final or be subject to appeal or further review. To determine whether a particular notice or finding is covered by this definition, it is necessary to consult section II.B. in the DOL Guidance.

"Arbitral award or decision" means an arbitrator or arbitral panel determination that a labor law violation occurred, or that enjoined or restrained a violation of labor law. It includes an award or decision that is not final or is subject to being confirmed, modified, or vacated by a court, and includes an award or decision resulting from private or confidential proceedings. To determine whether a particular award or decision is covered by this definition, it is necessary to consult section II.B. in the DOL Guidance.

"Civil judgment" means –

(1) In paragraph (h) of this provision: A judgment or finding of a civil offense by any court of competent jurisdiction.

(2) In paragraph (s) of this provision: Any judgment or order entered by any federal or state court in which the court determined that a labor law violation occurred, or enjoined or restrained a violation of labor law. It includes a judgment or order that is not final or is subject to appeal. To determine whether a particular judgment or order is covered by this definition, it is necessary to consult section II.B. in the DOL Guidance.

"DOL Guidance" means the Department of Labor (DOL) Guidance entitled: "Guidance for Executive Order 13673, 'Fair Pay and Safe Workplaces'". The DOL Guidance, dated August 25, 2016, can be obtained from **www.dol.gov/fairpayandsafeworkplaces**.

"Economically disadvantaged women-owned small business (EDWOSB) concern" means a small business concern that is at least 51 percent directly and unconditionally owned by, and the management and daily business operations of which are controlled by, one or more women who are citizens of the United States and who are economically disadvantaged in accordance with 13 CFR part 127. It automatically qualifies as a women-owned small business eligible under the WOSB Program.

"Enforcement agency" means any agency granted authority to enforce the federal labor laws. It includes the enforcement components of DOL (Wage and Hour Division, Office of Federal Contract Compliance Programs, and Occupational Safety and Health Administration), the Equal Employment Opportunity Commission, the Occupational Safety and Health Review Commission, and the National Labor Relations Board. It also means a state agency designated to administer an OSHA-approved State Plan, but only to the extent that the state agency is acting in its capacity as administrator of such plan. It does not include other federal agencies which, in their capacity as contracting agencies, conduct investigations of potential labor law violations. The enforcement agencies associated with each labor law under E.O. 13673 are –

(1) Department of Labor Wage and Hour Division (WHD) for –

(i) The Fair Labor Standards Act;

(ii) The Migrant and Seasonal Agricultural Worker Protection Act;

(iii) 40 U.S.C. chapter 31, subchapter IV, formerly known as the Davis-Bacon Act;

(iv) 41 U.S.C. chapter 67, formerly known as the Service Contract Act;

(v) The Family and Medical Leave Act; and

(vi) E.O. 13658 of February 12, 2014 (Establishing a Minimum Wage for Contractors);

(2) Department of Labor Occupational Safety and Health Administration (OSHA) for –

(i) The Occupational Safety and Health Act of 1970; and

(ii) OSHA-approved State Plans;

(3) Department of Labor Office of Federal Contract Compliance Programs (OFCCP) for –

(i) Section 503 of the Rehabilitation Act of 1973;

(ii) The Vietnam Era Veterans' Readjustment Assistance Act of 1972 and the Vietnam Era Veterans' Readjustment Assistance Act of 1974; and

(iii) E.O. 11246 of September 24, 1965 (Equal Employment Opportunity);

(4) National Labor Relations Board (NLRB) for the National Labor Relations Act; and

(5) Equal Employment Opportunity Commission (EEOC) for –

(i) Title VII of the Civil Rights Act of 1964;

(ii) The Americans with Disabilities Act of 1990;

(iii) The Age Discrimination in Employment Act of 1967; and

(iv) Section 6(d) of the Fair Labor Standards Act (Equal Pay Act).

"Forced or indentured child labor" means all work or service –

(1) Exacted from any person under the age of 18 under the menace of any penalty for its nonperformance and for which the worker does not offer himself voluntarily; or

(2) Performed by any person under the age of 18 pursuant to a contract the enforcement of which can be accomplished by process or penalties.

"Highest-level owner" means the entity that owns or controls an immediate owner of the offeror, or that owns or controls one or more entities that control an immediate owner of the offeror. No entity owns or exercises control of the highest level owner.

"Immediate owner" means an entity, other than the offeror, that has direct control of the offeror. Indicators of control include, but are not limited to, one or more of the following: Ownership or interlocking management, identity of interests among family members, shared facilities and equipment, and the common use of employees.

"Inverted domestic corporation," means a foreign incorporated entity that meets the definition of an inverted domestic corporation under 6 U.S.C. 395(b), applied in accordance with the rules and definitions of 6 U.S.C. 395(c).

"Labor compliance agreement" means an agreement entered into between a contractor or subcontractor and an enforcement agency to address appropriate remedial measures, compliance assistance, steps to resolve issues to increase compliance with the labor laws, or other related matters.

"Labor laws" means the following labor laws and E.O.s:

(1) The Fair Labor Standards Act.
(2) The Occupational Safety and Health Act (OSHA) of 1970.
(3) The Migrant and Seasonal Agricultural Worker Protection Act.
(4) The National Labor Relations Act.
(5) 40 U.S.C. chapter 31, subchapter IV, formerly known as the Davis-Bacon Act.

(6) 41 U.S.C. chapter 67, formerly known as the Service Contract Act.

(7) E.O. 11246 of September 24, 1965 (Equal Employment Opportunity).

(8) Section 503 of the Rehabilitation Act of 1973.

(9) The Vietnam Era Veterans' Readjustment Assistance Act of 1972 and the Vietnam Era Veterans' Readjustment Assistance Act of 1974.

(10) The Family and Medical Leave Act.

(11) Title VII of the Civil Rights Act of 1964.

(12) The Americans with Disabilities Act of 1990.

(13) The Age Discrimination in Employment Act of 1967.

(14) E.O. 13658 of February 12, 2014 (Establishing a Minimum Wage for Contractors).

(15) Equivalent State laws as defined in the DOL Guidance. (The only equivalent state laws implemented in the FAR are OSHA-approved State Plans, which can be found at **www.osha.gov/dcsp/osp/approved_state_plans.html**).

"Labor law decision" means an administrative merits determination, arbitral award or decision, or civil judgment, which resulted from a violation of one or more of the laws listed in the definition of "labor laws".

"Manufactured end product" means any end product in product and service codes (PSCs) 1000-9999, except–

(1) PSC 5510, Lumber and Related Basic Wood Materials;

(2) Product or Service Group (PSG) 87, Agricultural Supplies;

(3) PSG 88, Live Animals;

(4) PSG 89, Subsistence;

(5) PSC 9410, Crude Grades of Plant Materials;

(6) PSC 9430, Miscellaneous Crude Animal Products, Inedible;

(7) PSC 9440, Miscellaneous Crude Agricultural and Forestry Products;

(8) PSC 9610, Ores;

(9) PSC 9620, Minerals, Natural and Synthetic; and

(10) PSC 9630, Additive Metal Materials.

"Place of manufacture" means the place where an end product is assembled out of components, or otherwise made or processed from raw materials into the finished product that is to be provided to the government. If a product is disassembled and reassembled, the place of reassembly is not the place of manufacture.

"Predecessor" means an entity that is replaced by a successor and includes any predecessors of the predecessor.

"Restricted business operations" means business operations in Sudan that include power production activities, mineral extraction activities, oil-related activities, or the production of military equipment, as those terms are defined in the Sudan Accountability and Divestment Act of 2007 (Pub. L. 110-174). Restricted business operations do not include business operations that the person (as that term is defined in Section 2 of the Sudan Accountability and Divestment Act of 2007) conducting the business can demonstrate–

(1) Are conducted under contract directly and exclusively with the regional government of southern Sudan;

(2) Are conducted pursuant to specific authorization from the Office of Foreign Assets Control in the Department of the Treasury, or are expressly exempted under federal law from the requirement to be conducted under such authorization;

(3) Consist of providing goods or services to marginalized populations of Sudan;

(4) Consist of providing goods or services to an internationally recognized peacekeeping force or humanitarian organization;

(5) Consist of providing goods or services that are used only to promote health or education; or

(6) Have been voluntarily suspended.

"Sensitive technology" –

(1) Means hardware, software, telecommunications equipment, or any other technology that is to be used specifically –

(i) To restrict the free flow of unbiased information in Iran; or

(ii) To disrupt, monitor, or otherwise restrict speech of the people of Iran; and

(2) Does not include information or informational materials the export of which the President does not have the authority to regulate or prohibit pursuant to section 203(b)(3) of the International Emergency Economic Powers Act (50 U.S.C. 1702(b)(3)).

"Service-disabled veteran-owned small business concern" –

(1) Means a small business concern –

(i) Not less than 51 percent of which is owned by one or more service-disabled veterans or, in the case of any publicly owned business, not less than 51 percent of the stock of which is owned by one or more service-disabled veterans; and

(ii) The management and daily business operations of which are controlled by one or more service-disabled veterans or, in the case of a service-disabled veteran with permanent and severe disability, the spouse or permanent caregiver of such veteran.

(2) Service-disabled veteran means a veteran, as defined in 38 U.S.C. 101(2), with a disability that is service-connected, as defined in 38 U.S.C. 101(16).

"Small business concern" means a concern, including its affiliates, that is independently owned and operated, not dominant in the field of operation in which it is bidding on government contracts, and qualified as a small business under the criteria in 13 CFR Part 121 and size standards in this solicitation.

"Small disadvantaged business concern, consistent with 13 CFR 124.1002," means a small business concern under the size standard applicable to the acquisition, that –

(1) Is at least 51 percent unconditionally and directly owned (as defined at 13 CFR 124.105) by –

(i) One or more socially disadvantaged (as defined at 13 CFR 124.103) and economically disadvantaged (as defined at 13 CFR 124.104) individuals who are citizens of the United States; and

(ii) Each individual claiming economic disadvantage has a net worth not exceeding $750,000 after taking into account the applicable exclusions set forth at 13 CFR 124.104(c)(2); and

(2) The management and daily business operations of which are controlled (as defined at 13.CFR 124.106) by individuals, who meet the criteria in paragraphs (1)(i) and (ii) of this definition.

"Subsidiary" means an entity in which more than 50 percent of the entity is owned –

(1) Directly by a parent corporation; or

(2) Through another subsidiary of a parent corporation.

"Successor" means an entity that has replaced a predecessor by acquiring the assets and carrying out the affairs of the predecessor under a new name (often through acquisition or merger). The term "successor" does not include new offices/divisions of the same company or a company that only changes its name. The extent of the responsibility of the successor for the liabilities of the predecessor may vary, depending on state law and specific circumstances.

"Veteran-owned small business concern" means a small business concern –

(1) Not less than 51 percent of which is owned by one or more veterans(as defined at 38 U.S.C. 101(2)) or, in the case of any publicly owned business, not less than 51 percent of the stock of which is owned by one or more veterans; and

(2) The management and daily business operations of which are controlled by one or more veterans.

"Women-owned business concern" means a concern which is at least 51 percent owned by one or more women; or in the case of any publicly owned business, at least 51 percent of the its stock is owned by one or more women; and whose management and daily business operations are controlled by one or more women.

"Women-owned small business concern" means a small business concern –

(1) That is at least 51 percent owned by one or more women or, in the case of any publicly owned business, at least 51 percent of the stock of which is owned by one or more women; and

(2) Whose management and daily business operations are controlled by one or more women.

"Women-owned small business (WOSB) concern eligible under the WOSB Program (in accordance with 13 CFR part 127)," means a small business concern that is at least 51 percent directly and unconditionally owned by, and the management and daily business operations of which are controlled by, one or more women who are citizens of the United States.

Note to paragraph (a): By a court order issued on October 24, 2016, the following definitions in this paragraph (a) are enjoined indefinitely as of the date of the order: "Administrative merits determination", "Arbitral award or decision", paragraph (2) of "Civil judgment", "DOL Guidance", "Enforcement agency", "Labor compliance agreement", "Labor laws", and "Labor law decision". The enjoined definitions will become effective immediately if the court terminates the injunction. At that time, DOD, GSA, and NASA will publish a document in the *Federal Register* advising the public of the termination of the injunction.

(b)　(1) *Annual Representations and Certifications.* Any changes provided by the offeror in paragraph (b)(2) of this provision do not automatically change the representations and certifications posted on the SAM website.

(2) The offeror has completed the annual representations and certifications electronically via the SAM website accessed through **http://www.acquisition.gov**. After reviewing the SAM database information, the offeror verifies by submission of this offer that the representation and certifications currently posted electronically at FAR 52.212-3, Offeror Representations and Certifications–Commercial Items, have been entered or updated in the last 12 months, are current, accurate, complete, and applicable to this solicitation (including the business size standard applicable to the NAICS code referenced for this solicitation), as of the date of this offer and are incorporated in this offer by reference (see FAR 4.1201), except for paragraphs _____. *[Offeror to identify the applicable paragraphs at (c) through (s) of this provision that the offeror has completed for the purposes of this solicitation only, if any. These amended representation(s) and/or certification(s) are also incorporated in this offer and are current, accurate, and complete as of the date of this offer. Any changes provided by the offeror are applicable to this solicitation only, and do not result in an update to the representations and certifications posted electronically on SAM.]*

(c) Offerors must complete the following representations when the resulting contract is to be performed in the United States or its outlying areas. Check all that apply.

(1) *Small business concern.* The offeror represents as part of its offer that it [_] is, [_] is not a small business concern.

(2) Veteran-owned small business concern. [Complete only if the offeror represented itself as a small business concern in paragraph (c)(1) of this provision.] The offeror represents as part of its offer that it [_] is, [_] is not a veteran-owned small business concern.

(3) Service-disabled veteran-owned small business concern. [Complete only if the offeror represented itself as a veteran-owned small business concern in paragraph (c)(2) of this provision.] The offeror represents as part of its offer that it [_] is, [_] is not a service-disabled veteran-owned small business concern.

(4) Small disadvantaged business concern. [Complete only if the offeror represented itself as a small business concern in paragraph (c)(1) of this provision.] The offeror represents that it [_] is, [_] is not, a small disadvantaged business concern as defined in 13 CFR 124.1002.

(5) Women-owned small business concern. [Complete only if the offeror represented itself as a small business concern in paragraph (c)(1) of this provision.] The offeror represents that it [_] is, [_] is not a women-owned small business concern.

Note: Complete paragraphs (c)(8) and (c)(9) only if this solicitation is expected to exceed the simplified acquisition threshold.

(6) WOSB concern eligible under the WOSB Program. [Complete only if the offeror represented itself as a women-owned small business concern in paragraph (c)(5) of this provision.] The offeror represents that–

(i) It [_] is, [_] is not a WOSB concern eligible under the WOSB Program, has provided all the required documents to the WOSB Repository, and no change in circumstances or adverse decisions have been issued that affects its eligibility; and

(ii) It [_] is, [_] is not a joint venture that complies with the requirements of 13 CFR part 127, and the representation in paragraph (c)(6)(i) of this provision is accurate for each WOSB concern eligible under the WOSB Program participating in the joint venture. [The offeror shall enter the name or names of the WOSB concern eligible under the WOSB Program and other small businesses that are participating in the joint venture: _____.] Each WOSB concern eligible under the WOSB Program participating in the joint venture shall submit a separate signed copy of the WOSB representation.

(7) Economically disadvantaged women-owned small business (EDWOSB) concern. [Complete only if the offeror represented itself as a WOSB concern eligible under the WOSB Program in (c)(6) of this provision.] The offeror represents that –

(i) It [_] is, [_] is not an EDWOSB concern, has provided all the required documents to the WOSB Repository, and no change in circumstances or adverse decisions have been issued that affects its eligibility; and

(ii) It [_] is, [_] is not a joint venture that complies with the requirements of 13 CFR part 127, and the representation in paragraph (c)(7)(i) of this provision is accurate for each EDWOSB concern participating in the joint venture. [The offeror shall enter the name or names of the EDWOSB concern and other small businesses that are participating in the joint venture: _____.] Each EDWOSB concern participating in the joint venture shall submit a separate signed copy of the EDWOSB representation.

(8) Women-owned business concern (other than small business concern). [Complete only if the offeror is a women-owned business concern and did not represent itself as a small business concern in paragraph (c)(1) of this provision.] The offeror represents that it [_] is, a women-owned business concern.

(9) *Tie bid priority for labor surplus area concerns.* If this is an invitation for bid, small business offerors may identify the labor surplus areas in which costs to be incurred on account of manufacturing or production (by offeror or first-tier subcontractors) amount to more than 50 percent of the contract price:

_____

(10) HUBZone small business concern. [Complete only if the offeror represented itself as a small business concern in paragraph (c)(1) of this provision.] The offeror represents, as part of its offer, that –

(i) It [_] is, [_] is not a HUBZone small business concern listed, on the date of this representation, on the List of Qualified HUBZone Small Business Concerns maintained by the Small Business Administration, and no material changes in ownership and control, principal office, or HUBZone employee percentage have occurred since it was certified in accordance with 13 CFR part 126; and

(ii) It [_] is, [_] is not a HUBZone joint venture that complies with the requirements of 13 CFR part 126, and the representation in paragraph (c)(10)(i) of this provision is accurate for each HUBZone small business concern participating in the HUBZone joint venture. [*The offeror shall enter the names of each of the HUBZone small business concerns participating in the HUBZone joint venture*: _____.] Each HUBZone small business concern participating in the HUBZone joint venture shall submit a separate signed copy of the HUBZone representation.

(d) *Representations required to implement provisions of Executive Order 11246* –

(1) Previous contracts and compliance. The offeror represents that –

(i) It [_] has, [_] has not, participated in a previous contract or subcontract subject to the Equal Opportunity clause of this solicitation; and

(ii) It [_] has, [_] has not, filed all required compliance reports.

(2) *Affirmative Action Compliance*. The offeror represents that –

(i) It [_] has developed and has on file, [_] has not developed and does not have on file, at each establishment, affirmative action programs required by rules and regulations of the Secretary of Labor (41 CFR parts 60-1 and 60-2), or

(ii) It [_] has not previously had contracts subject to the written affirmative action programs requirement of the rules and regulations of the Secretary of Labor.

(e) *Certification Regarding Payments to Influence Federal Transactions* (31 U.S.C. 1352). (Applies only if the contract is expected to exceed $150,000.) By submission of its offer, the offeror certifies to the best of its knowledge and belief that no federal appropriated funds have been paid or will be paid to any person for influencing or attempting to influence an officer or employee of any agency, a Member of Congress, an officer or employee of Congress or an employee of a Member of Congress on his or her behalf in connection with the award of any resultant contract. If any registrants under the Lobbying Disclosure Act of 1995 have made a lobbying contact on behalf of the offeror with respect to this contract, the offeror shall complete and submit, with its offer, OMB Standard Form LLL, Disclosure of Lobbying Activities, to provide the name of the registrants. The offeror need not report regularly employed officers or employees of the offeror to whom payments of reasonable compensation were made.

(f) *Buy American Certificate.* (Applies only if the clause at Federal Acquisition Regulation (FAR) 52.225-1, Buy American – Supplies, is included in this solicitation.)

(1) The offeror certifies that each end product, except those listed in paragraph (f)(2) of this provision, is a domestic end product and that for other than COTS items, the offeror has considered components of unknown origin to have been mined, produced, or manufactured outside the United States. The offeror shall list as foreign end products those end products manufactured in the United States that do not qualify as domestic end products, *i.e.*, an end product that is not a COTS item and does not meet the component test in paragraph (2) of the definition of "domestic end product." The terms "commercially available off-the-shelf (COTS) item," "component," "domestic end product," "end product," "foreign end product," and "United States" are defined in the clause of this solicitation entitled "Buy American – Supplies."

(2) Foreign End Products:

LINE ITEM NO.	COUNTRY OF ORIGIN

[List as necessary]

(3) The government will evaluate offers in accordance with the policies and procedures of FAR Part 25.

(g)   (1) *Buy American – Free Trade Agreements – Israeli Trade Act Certificate*. (Applies only if the clause at FAR 52.225-3, Buy American – Free Trade Agreements – Israeli Trade Act, is included in this solicitation.)

(i) The offeror certifies that each end product, except those listed in paragraph (g)(1)(ii) or (g)(1)(iii) of this provision, is a domestic end product and that for other than COTS items, the offeror has considered components of unknown origin to have been mined, produced, or manufactured outside the United States. The terms "Bahrainian, Moroccan, Omani, Panamanian, or Peruvian end product," "commercially available off-the-shelf (COTS) item," "component," "domestic end product," "end product," "foreign end product," "Free Trade Agreement country," "Free Trade Agreement country end product," "Israeli end product," and "United States" are defined in the clause of this solicitation entitled "Buy American–Free Trade Agreements–Israeli Trade Act."

(ii) The offeror certifies that the following supplies are Free Trade Agreement country end products (other than Bahrainian, Moroccan, Omani, Panamanian, or Peruvian end products) or Israeli end products as defined in the clause of this solicitation entitled "Buy American – Free Trade Agreements – Israeli Trade Act":

Free Trade Agreement Country End Products (Other than Bahrainian, Moroccan, Omani, Panamanian, or Peruvian End Products) or Israeli End Products:

LINE ITEM NO.	COUNTRY OF ORIGIN

[List as necessary]

(iii) The offeror shall list those supplies that are foreign end products (other than those listed in paragraph (g)(1)(ii) or this provision) as defined in the clause of this solicitation entitled "Buy American – Free Trade Agreements – Israeli Trade Act." The offeror shall list as other foreign end products those end products manufactured in the United States that do not qualify as domestic end products, *i.e.*, an end product that is not a COTS item and does not meet the component test in paragraph (2) of the definition of "domestic end product."

Other Foreign End Products:

LINE ITEM NO.	COUNTRY OF ORIGIN

[List as necessary]

    (iv) The government will evaluate offers in accordance with the policies and procedures of FAR Part 25.

(2) *Buy American – Free Trade Agreements – Israeli Trade Act Certificate, Alternate I.* If Alternate I to the clause at FAR 52.225-3 is included in this solicitation, substitute the following paragraph (g)(1)(ii) for paragraph (g)(1)(ii) of the basic provision:

    (g)(1)(ii) The offeror certifies that the following supplies are Canadian end products as defined in the clause of this solicitation entitled "Buy American – Free Trade Agreements – Israeli Trade Act":

Canadian End Products:

Line Item No.:

_____

[List as necessary]

(3) *Buy American – Free Trade Agreements – Israeli Trade Act Certificate, Alternate II.* If Alternate II to the clause at FAR 52.225-3 is included in this solicitation, substitute the following paragraph (g)(1)(ii) for paragraph (g)(1)(ii) of the basic provision:

    (g)(1)(ii) The offeror certifies that the following supplies are Canadian end products or Israeli end products as defined in the clause of this solicitation entitled "Buy American – Free Trade Agreements – Israeli Trade Act":

Canadian or Israeli End Products:

LINE ITEM NO.	COUNTRY OF ORIGIN

[List as necessary]

(4) *Buy American – Free Trade Agreements – Israeli Trade Act Certificate, Alternate III.* If Alternate III to the clause at 52.225-3 is included in this solicitation, substitute the following paragraph (g)(1)(ii) for paragraph (g)(1)(ii) of the basic provision:

    (g)(1)(ii) The offeror certifies that the following supplies are Free Trade Agreement country end products (other than Bahrainian, Korean, Moroccan, Omani, Panamanian, or Peruvian end products) or Israeli end products as defined in the clause of this solicitation entitled "Buy American – Free Trade Agreements – Israeli Trade Act":

Free Trade Agreement Country End Products (Other than Bahrainian, Korean, Moroccan, Omani, Panamanian, or Peruvian End Products) or Israeli End Products:

LINE ITEM NO.	COUNTRY OF ORIGIN

[List as necessary]

(5) *Trade Agreements Certificate.* (Applies only if the clause at FAR 52.225-5, Trade Agreements, is included in this solicitation.)

(i) The offeror certifies that each end product, except those listed in paragraph (g)(5)(ii) of this provision, is a U.S.-made or designated country end product as defined in the clause of this solicitation entitled "Trade Agreements."

(ii) The offeror shall list as other end products those end products that are not U.S.-made or designated country end products.

Other End Products

LINE ITEM NO.	COUNTRY OF ORIGIN

[List as necessary]

(iii) The government will evaluate offers in accordance with the policies and procedures of FAR Part 25. For line items covered by the WTO GPA, the government will evaluate offers of U.S.-made or designated country end products without regard to the restrictions of the Buy American statute. The government will consider for award only offers of U.S.-made or designated country end products unless the Contracting Officer determines that there are no offers for such products or that the offers for such products are insufficient to fulfill the requirements of the solicitation.

(h) *Certification Regarding Responsibility Matters (Executive Order 12689).* (Applies only if the contract value is expected to exceed the simplified acquisition threshold.) The offeror certifies, to the best of its knowledge and belief, that the offeror and/or any of its principals –

(1) [_] Are, [_] are not presently debarred, suspended, proposed for debarment, or declared ineligible for the award of contracts by any federal agency;

(2) [_] Have, [_] have not, within a three-year period preceding this offer, been convicted of or had a civil judgment rendered against them for: commission of fraud or a criminal offense in connection with obtaining, attempting to obtain, or performing a federal, state or local government contract or subcontract; violation of federal or state antitrust statutes relating to the submission of offers; or commission of embezzlement, theft, forgery, bribery, falsification or destruction of records, making false statements, tax evasion, violating federal criminal tax laws, or receiving stolen property; and

(3) [_] Are, [_] are not presently indicted for, or otherwise criminally or civilly charged by a government entity with, commission of any of these offenses enumerated in paragraph (h)(2) of this clause; and

(4) [_] Have, [_] have not, within a three-year period preceding this offer, been notified of any delinquent federal taxes in an amount that exceeds $3,500 for which the liability remains unsatisfied.

   (i) Taxes are considered delinquent if both of the following criteria apply:

   (A) *The tax liability is finally determined.* The liability is finally determined if it has been assessed. A liability is not finally determined if there is a pending administrative or judicial challenge. In the case of a judicial challenge to the liability, the liability is not finally determined until all judicial appeal rights have been exhausted.

   (B) *The taxpayer is delinquent in making payment.* A taxpayer is delinquent if the taxpayer has failed to pay the tax liability when full payment was due and required. A taxpayer is not delinquent in cases where enforced collection action is precluded.

   (ii) Examples.

   (A) The taxpayer has received a statutory notice of deficiency, under I.R.C. §6212, which entitles the taxpayer to seek Tax Court review of a proposed tax deficiency. This is not a delinquent tax because it is not a final tax liability. Should the taxpayer seek Tax Court review, this will not be a final tax liability until the taxpayer has exercised all judicial appear rights.

   (B) The IRS has filed a notice of federal tax lien with respect to an assessed tax liability, and the taxpayer has been issued a notice under I.R.C. §6320 entitling the taxpayer to request a hearing with the IRS Office of Appeals Contesting the lien filing, and to further appeal to the Tax Court if the IRS determines to sustain the lien filing. In the course of the hearing, the taxpayer is entitled to contest the underlying tax liability because the taxpayer has had no prior opportunity to contest the liability. This is not a delinquent tax because it is not a final tax liability. Should the taxpayer seek tax court review, this will not be a final tax liability until the taxpayer has exercised all judicial appeal rights.

   (C) The taxpayer has entered into an installment agreement pursuant to I.R.C. §6159. The taxpayer is making timely payments and is in full compliance with the agreement terms. The taxpayer is not delinquent because the taxpayer is not currently required to make full payment.

   (D) The taxpayer has filed for bankruptcy protection. The taxpayer is not delinquent because enforced collection action is stayed under 11 U.S.C. §362 (the Bankruptcy Code).

(i) *Certification Regarding Knowledge of Child Labor for Listed End Products (Executive Order 13126).* [The Contracting Officer must list in paragraph (i)(1) any end products being acquired under this solicitation that are included in the List of Products Requiring Contractor Certification as to Forced or Indentured Child Labor, unless excluded at 22.1503(b).]

   (1) Listed End Product

LISTED END PRODUCT:	LISTED COUNTRIES OF ORIGIN:

(2) Certification. [If the Contracting Officer has identified end products and countries of origin in paragraph (i)(1) of this provision, then the offeror must certify to either (i)(2)(i) or (i)(2)(ii) by checking the appropriate block.]

[_] (i) The offeror will not supply any end product listed in paragraph (i)(1) of this provision that was mined, produced, or manufactured in the corresponding country as listed for that product.

[_] (ii) The offeror may supply an end product listed in paragraph (i)(1) of this provision that was mined, produced, or manufactured in the corresponding country as listed for that product. The offeror certifies that is has made a good faith effort to determine whether forced or indentured child labor was used to mine, produce, or manufacture any such end product furnished under this contract. On the basis of those efforts, the offeror certifies that it is not aware of any such use of child labor.

(j) *Place of manufacture.* (Does not apply unless the solicitation is predominantly for the acquisition of manufactured end products.) For statistical purposes only, the offeror shall indicate whether the place of manufacture of the end products it expects to provide in response to this solicitation is predominantly –

(1) [_] In the United States (Check this box if the total anticipated price of offered end products manufactured in the United States exceeds the total anticipated price of offered end products manufactured outside the United States); or

(2) [_] Outside the United States.

(k) *Certificates regarding exemptions from the application of the Service Contract Labor Standards.* (Certification by the offeror as to its compliance with respect to the contract also constitutes its certification as to compliance by its subcontractor if it subcontracts out the exempt services.) [The contracting officer is to check a box to indicate if paragraph (k)(1) or (k)(2) applies.]

(1) [_] Maintenance, calibration, or repair of certain equipment as described in FAR 22.1003-4(c)(1). The offeror [_] does [_] does not certify that –

(i) The items of equipment to be serviced under this contract are used regularly for other than governmental purposes and are sold or traded by the offeror (or subcontractor in the case of an exempt subcontract) in substantial quantities to the general public in the course of normal business operations;

(ii) The services will be furnished at prices which are, or are based on, established catalog or market prices (see FAR 22.1003-4(c)(2)(ii)) for the maintenance, calibration, or repair of such equipment; and

(iii) The compensation (wage and fringe benefits) plan for all service employees performing work under the contract will be the same as that used for these employees and equivalent employees servicing the same equipment of commercial customers.

(2) [_] Certain services as described in FAR 22.1003-4(d)(1). The offeror [_] does [_] does not certify that–

(i) The services under the contract are offered and sold regularly to non-governmental customers, and are provided by the offeror (or subcontractor in the case of an exempt subcontract) to the general public in substantial quantities in the course of normal business operations;

(ii) The contract services will be furnished at prices that are, or are based on, established catalog or market prices (see FAR 22.1003-4(d)(2)(iii));

(iii) Each service employee who will perform the services under the contract will spend only a small portion of his or her time (a monthly average of less than 20 percent of the available hours on an annualized basis, or less than 20 percent of available hours during the contract period if the contract period is less than a month) servicing the government contract; and

(iv) The compensation (wage and fringe benefits) plan for all service employees performing work under the contract is the same as that used for these employees and equivalent employees servicing commercial customers.

(3) If paragraph (k)(1) or (k)(2) of this clause applies –

(i) If the offeror does not certify to the conditions in paragraph (k)(1) or (k)(2) and the Contracting Officer did not attach a Service Contract Labor Standards wage determination to the solicitation, the offeror shall notify the Contracting Officer as soon as possible; and

(ii) The Contracting Officer may not make an award to the offeror if the offeror fails to execute the certification in paragraph (k)(1) or (k)(2) of this clause or to contact the Contracting Officer as required in paragraph (k)(3)(i) of this clause.

(l) *Taxpayer identification number (TIN) (26 U.S.C. 6109, 31 U.S.C. 7701).* (Not applicable if the offeror is required to provide this information to the SAM database to be eligible for award.)

(1) All offerors must submit the information required in paragraphs (l)(3) through (l)(5) of this provision to comply with debt collection requirements of 31 U.S.C. 7701(c) and 3325(d), reporting requirements of 26 U.S.C. 6041, 6041A, and 6050M, and implementing regulations issued by the Internal Revenue Service (IRS).

(2) The TIN may be used by the government to collect and report on any delinquent amounts arising out of the offeror's relationship with the government (31 U.S.C. 7701(c)(3)). If the resulting contract is subject to the payment reporting requirements described in FAR 4.904, the TIN provided hereunder may be matched with IRS records to verify the accuracy of the offeror's TIN.

(3) Taxpayer Identification Number (TIN).

[_] TIN:_____.

[_] TIN has been applied for.

[_] TIN is not required because:

[_] Offeror is a nonresident alien, foreign corporation, or foreign partnership that does not have income effectively connected with the conduct of a trade or business in the United States and does not have an office or place of business or a fiscal paying agent in the United States;

[_] Offeror is an agency or instrumentality of a foreign government;

[_] Offeror is an agency or instrumentality of the federal government;

(4) Type of organization.

[_] Sole proprietorship;

[_] Partnership;

[_] Corporate entity (not tax-exempt);

[_] Corporate entity (tax-exempt);

[_] Government entity (federal, state, or local);

[_] Foreign government;

[_] International organization per 26 CFR 1.6049-4;

[_] Other _____.

(5) Common parent.

    [_] Offeror is not owned or controlled by a common parent:

    [_] Name and TIN of common parent:

        Name _____

        TIN _____

(m) *Restricted business operations in Sudan.* By submission of its offer, the offeror certifies that the offeror does not conduct any restricted business operations in Sudan.

(n) *Prohibition on Contracting with Inverted Domestic Corporations* –

(1) Government agencies are not permitted to use appropriated (or otherwise made available) funds for contracts with either an inverted domestic corporation, or a subsidiary of an inverted domestic corporation, unless the exception at 9.108-2(b) applies or the requirement is waived in accordance with the procedures at 9.108-4.

(2) *Representation.* The offeror represents that –

(i) It [ ] is, [ ] is not an inverted domestic corporation; and

(ii) It [ ] is, [ ] is not a subsidiary of an inverted domestic corporation.

(o) *Prohibition on contracting with entities engaging in certain activities or transactions relating to Iran.*

(1) The offeror shall email questions concerning sensitive technology to the Department of State at **CISADA106@state.gov**.

(2) Representation and Certification. Unless a waiver is granted or an exception applies as provided in paragraph (o)(3) of this provision, by submission of its offer, the offeror –

(i) Represents, to the best of its knowledge and belief, that the offeror does not export any sensitive technology to the government of Iran or any entities or individuals owned or controlled by, or acting on behalf or at the direction of, the government of Iran;

(ii) Certifies that the offeror, or any person owned or controlled by the offeror, does not engage in any activities for which sanctions may be imposed under section 5 of the Iran Sanctions Act; and

(iii) Certifies that the offeror, and any person owned or controlled by the offeror, does not knowingly engage in any transaction that exceeds $3,500 with Iran's Revolutionary Guard Corps or any of its officials, agents, or affiliates, the property and interests in property of which are blocked pursuant to the International Emergency Economic Powers Act (50 U.S.C. 1701 *et seq.*) (see OFAC's Specially Designated Nationals and Blocked Persons List at **http://www.treasury.gov/ofac/downloads/ t11sdn.pdf**).

(3) The representation and certification requirements of paragraph (o)(2) of this provision do not apply if–

(i) This solicitation includes a trade agreements certification (*e.g.*, 52.212-3(g) or a comparable agency provision); and

(ii) The offeror has certified that all the offered products to be supplied are designated country end products.

(p) *Ownership or Control of Offeror.* (Applies in all solicitations when there is a requirement to be registered in SAM or a requirement to have a unique entity identifier in the solicitation.)

(1) The offeror represents that it [ ] has or [ ] does not have an immediate owner. If the offeror has more than one immediate owner (such as a joint venture), then the offeror shall respond to paragraph (2) and if applicable, paragraph (3) of this provision for each participant in the joint venture.

(2) If the offeror indicates "has" in paragraph (p)(1) of this provision, enter the following information:

Immediate owner CAGE code:_____

Immediate owner legal name:_____

(Do not use a "doing business as" name)

Is the immediate owner owned or controlled by another entity:

[ ] Yes or [ ] No.

(3) If the offeror indicates "yes" in paragraph (p)(2) of this provision, indicating that the immediate owner is owned or controlled by another entity, then enter the following information:

Highest level owner CAGE code:_____

Highest level owner legal name:_____

(Do not use a "doing business as" name)

(q) *Representation by Corporations Regarding Delinquent Tax Liability or a Felony Conviction under any Federal Law.*

(1) As required by sections 744 and 745 of Division E of the Consolidated and Further Continuing Appropriations Act, 2015 (Pub. L. 113-235), and similar provisions, if contained in subsequent appropriations acts, The government will not enter into a contract with any corporation that –

(i) Has any unpaid federal tax liability that has been assessed, for which all judicial and administrative remedies have been exhausted or have lapsed, and that is not being paid in a timely manner pursuant to an agreement with the authority responsible for collecting the tax liability, where the awarding agency is aware of the unpaid tax liability, unless an agency has considered suspension or debarment of the corporation and made a determination that suspension or debarment is not necessary to protect the interests of the government; or

(ii) Was convicted of a felony criminal violation under any federal law within the preceding 24 months, where the awarding agency is aware of the conviction, unless an agency has considered suspension or debarment of the corporation and made a determination that this action is not necessary to protect the interests of the government.

(2) The offeror represents that –

(i) It is [ ] is not [ ] a corporation that has any unpaid federal tax liability that has been assessed, for which all judicial and administrative remedies have been exhausted or have lapsed, and that is not being paid in a timely manner pursuant to an agreement with the authority responsible for collecting the tax liability; and

(ii) It is [ ] is not [ ] a corporation that was convicted of a felony criminal violation under a federal law within the preceding 24 months.

(r) *Predecessor of Offeror.* (Applies in all solicitations that include the provision at 52.204-16, Commercial and Government Entity Code Reporting.)

(1) The offeror represents that it [_] is or [_] is not a successor to a predecessor that held a federal contract or grant within the last three years.

(2) If the offeror has indicated "is" in paragraph (r)(1) of this provision, enter the following information for all predecessors that held a Federal contract or grant within the last three years (if more than one predecessor, list in reverse chronological order):

Predecessor CAGE code: _____ (or mark "Unknown").

Predecessor legal name: _____.

(Do not use a "doing business as" name).

(s) *Representation regarding compliance with labor laws (Executive Order 13673).* If the offeror is a joint venture that is not itself a separate legal entity, each concern participating in the joint venture shall separately comply with the requirements of this provision.

(1) (i) For solicitations issued on or after October 25, 2016, through April 24, 2017: The offeror [_] does [_] does not anticipate submitting an offer with an estimated contract value of greater than $50 million.

(ii) For solicitations issued after April 24, 2017: The Offeror [_] does [_] does not anticipate submitting an offer with an estimated contract value of greater than $500,000.

(2) If the Offeror checked "does" in paragraph (s)(1)(i) or (ii) of this provision, the offeror represents to the best of the offeror's knowledge and belief [offeror to check appropriate block]:

[_](i) There has been no administrative merits determination, arbitral award or decision, or civil judgment for any labor law violation(s) rendered against the offeror (see definitions in paragraph (a) of this section) during the period beginning on October 25, 2015, to the date of the offer, or for three years preceding the date of the offer, whichever period is shorter; or

[_](ii) There has been an administrative merits determination, arbitral award or decision, or civil judgment for any labor law violation(s) rendered against the offeror during the period beginning on October 25, 2015, to the date of the offer, or for three years preceding the date of the offer, whichever period is shorter.

(3) (i) If the box at paragraph (s)(2)(ii) of this provision is checked and the contracting officer has initiated a responsibility determination and has requested additional information, the offeror shall provide –

(A) The following information for each disclosed labor law decision in the System for Award Management (SAM) at **www.sam.gov**, unless the information is already current, accurate, and complete in SAM. This information will be publicly available in the Federal Awardee Performance and Integrity Information System (FAPIIS):

(1) The labor law violated.
(2) The case number, inspection number, charge number, docket number, or other unique identification number.
(3) The date rendered.
(4) The name of the court, arbitrator(s), agency, board, or commission that rendered the determination or decision;

(B) The administrative merits determination, arbitral award or decision, or civil judgment document, to the contracting officer, if the contracting officer requires it;

(C) In SAM, such additional information as the offeror deems necessary to demonstrate its responsibility, including mitigating factors and remedial measures such as offeror actions taken to address the violations, labor compliance agreements, and other steps taken to achieve compliance with labor laws. Offerors may provide explanatory text and upload documents. This information will not be made public unless the contractor determines that it wants the information to be made public; and

(D) The information in paragraphs (s)(3)(i)(A) and (s)(3)(i)(C) of this provision to the contracting officer, if the offeror meets an exception to SAM registration (see FAR 4.1102(a)).

(ii) (A) The contracting officer will consider all information provided under (s)(3)(i) of this provision as part of making a responsibility determination.

(B) A representation that any labor law decision(s) were rendered against the offeror will not necessarily result in withholding of an award under this solicitation. Failure of the offeror to furnish a representation or provide such additional information as requested by the contracting officer may render the offeror nonresponsible.

(C) The representation in paragraph (s)(2) of this provision is a material representation of fact upon which reliance was placed when making award. If it is later determined that the offeror knowingly rendered an erroneous representation, in addition to other remedies available to the government, the contracting officer may terminate the contract resulting from this solicitation in accordance with the procedures set forth in FAR 12.403.

(4) The offeror shall provide immediate written notice to the contracting officer if at any time prior to contract award the offeror learns that its representation at paragraph (s)(2) of this provision is no longer accurate.

(5) The representation in paragraph (s)(2) of this provision will be public information in the Federal Awardee Performance and Integrity Information System (FAPIIS).

Note to paragraph (s): By a court order issued on October 24, 2016, this paragraph (s) is enjoined indefinitely as of the date of the order. The enjoined paragraph will become effective immediately if the court terminates the injunction. At that time, DOD, GSA, and NASA will publish a document in the *Federal Register* advising the public of the termination of the injunction.

(t) *Public Disclosure of Greenhouse Gas Emissions and Reduction Goals.* Applies in all solicitations that require offerors to register in SAM (52.212–1(k)).

(1) This representation shall be completed if the Offeror received $7.5 million or more in contract awards in the prior federal fiscal year. The representation is optional if the offeror received less than $7.5 million in federal contract awards in the prior federal fiscal year.

(2) *Representation. [Offeror to check applicable block(s) in paragraph (t)(2)(i) and (ii)].*

(i) The offeror (itself or through its immediate owner or highest-level owner) [_] does, [_] does not publicly disclose greenhouse gas emissions, *i.e.*, makes available on a publicly accessible web site the results of a greenhouse gas inventory, performed in accordance with an accounting standard with publicly available and consistently applied criteria, such as the Greenhouse Gas Protocol Corporate Standard.

(ii) The offeror (itself or through its immediate owner or highest-level owner) [_] does, [_] does not publicly disclose a quantitative greenhouse gas emissions reduction goal, *i.e.*, make available on a publicly accessible web site a target to reduce absolute emissions or emissions intensity by a specific quantity or percentage.

(iii) A publicly accessible web site includes the offeror's own web site or a recognized, third-party greenhouse gas emissions reporting program.

(3) If the offeror checked "does" in paragraphs (t)(2)(i) or (t)(2)(ii) of this provision, respectively, the offeror shall provide the publicly accessible web site(s)

(u)(1) In accordance with section 743 of Division E, Title VII, of the Consolidated and Further Continuing Appropriations Act, 2015 (Pub. L. 113-235) and its successor provisions in subsequent appropriations acts (and as extended in continuing resolutions), government agencies are not permitted to use appropriated (or otherwise made available) funds for contracts with an entity that requires employees or subcontractors of such entity seeking to report waste, fraud, or abuse to sign internal confidentiality agreements or statements prohibiting or otherwise restricting such employees or subcontractors from lawfully reporting such waste, fraud, or abuse to a designated investigative or law enforcement representative of a Federal department or agency authorized to receive such information.

(2) The prohibition in paragraph (u)(1) of this provision does not contravene requirements applicable to Standard Form 312 (Classified Information Nondisclosure Agreement), Form 4414 (Sensitive Compartmented Information Nondisclosure Agreement), or any other form issued by a federal department or agency governing the nondisclosure of classified information.

(3) *Representation.* By submission of its offer, the offeror represents that it will not require its employees or subcontractors to sign or comply with internal confidentiality agreements or statements prohibiting or otherwise restricting such employees or subcontractors from lawfully reporting waste, fraud, or abuse related to the performance of a government contract to a designated investigative or law enforcement representative of a federal department or agency authorized to receive such information (*e.g.*, agency Office of the Inspector General).

(End of provision)

ATTACHMENT 6 TO IFB SPE3S1-17-B-0987

ADDENDUM TO FAR 52.212-3, OFFEROR REPRESENTATIONS AND CERTIFICATIONS – COMMERCIAL ITEMS (JAN 2017)

This solicitation incorporates one or more solicitation provisions by reference, with the same force and effect as if they were given in full text, in accordance with paragraphs (d) and (e) of FAR 12.301, Solicitation Provisions and Contract Clauses for the Acquisition of Commercial Items; paragraph (f) of Defense Federal Acquisition Regulation Supplement (DFARS) 212.301, Solicitation Provisions and Contract Clauses for the Acquisition of Commercial Items; and paragraph (f) Of Defense Logistics Agency Directive (DLAD) 12.301, Solicitation Provisions and Contract Clauses for the Acquisition of Commercial Items. Upon request, the contracting officer will make their full text available. The offeror is cautioned that the listed provisions may include blocks that must be completed by the offeror and submitted with its quotation or offer. In lieu of submitting the full text of those provisions, the offeror may identify the provision by paragraph identifier and provide the appropriate information with its quotation or offer. The FAR, DFARS, and DLAD are available at **http://www.farsite.hill.af.mil**.

FAR 52.204-16, Commercial and Government Entity Code Reporting (JUL 2016)

FAR 52.204-17, Ownership or Control of Offeror (JUL 2016)

(a) *Definitions*. As used in this provision—

"Commercial and Government Entity (CAGE) code" means –

(1) An identifier assigned to entities located in the United States or its outlying areas by the Defense Logistics Agency (DLA) Commercial and Government Entity (CAGE) Branch to identify a commercial or government entity; or

(2) An identifier assigned by a member of the North Atlantic Treaty Organization (NATO) or by the NATO Support and Procurement Agency (NSPA) to entities located outside the United States and its outlying areas that the DLA Commercial and Government Entity (CAGE) Branch records and maintains in the CAGE master file. This type of code is known as a NATO CAGE (NCAGE) code.

"Highest-level owner" means the entity that owns or controls an immediate owner of the offeror, or that owns or controls one or more entities that control an immediate owner of the offeror. No entity owns or exercises control of the highest level owner.

"Immediate owner" means an entity, other than the offeror, that has direct control of the offeror. Indicators of control include, but are not limited to one or more of the following: Ownership or interlocking management, identity of interests among family members, shared facilities and equipment, and the common use of employees.

(b) The Offeror represents that it [ ] has or [ ] does not have an immediate owner. If the Offeror has more than one immediate owner (such as a joint venture), then the Offeror shall respond to paragraph (c) and if applicable, paragraph (d) of this provision for each participant in the joint venture.

(c) If the Offeror indicates "has" in paragraph (b) of this provision, enter the following information:

Immediate owner CAGE code:_____

Immediate owner legal name:_____ (Do not use a "doing business as" name)

Is the immediate owner owned or controlled by another entity?: [ ] Yes or [ ] No.

(d) If the Offeror indicates "yes" in paragraph (c) of this provision, indicating that the immediate owner is owned or controlled by another entity, then enter the following information:

Highest level owner CAGE code:_____

Highest level owner legal name:_____ (Do not use a "doing business as" name)

(End of provision)

FAR 52.207-4, Economic Purchase Quantity – Supplies (AUG 1987)

(a) Offerors are invited to state an opinion on whether the quantity(ies) of supplies on which bids, proposals or quotes are requested in this solicitation is (are) economically advantageous to the government.

_____
_____
_____

(b) Each offeror who believes that acquisitions in different quantities would be more advantageous is invited to recommend an economic purchase quantity. If different quantities are recommended, a total and a unit price must be quoted for applicable items. An economic purchase quantity is that quantity at which a significant price break occurs. If there are significant price breaks at different quantity points, this information is desired as well.

	OFFEROR RECOMMENDATIONS		
ITEM	QUANTITY	PRICE QUOTATION	TOTAL
_____	_____	_____	_____
_____	_____	_____	_____
_____	_____	_____	_____

(c) The information requested in this provision is being solicited to avoid acquisitions in disadvantageous quantities and to assist the government in developing a data base for future acquisitions of these items. However, the government reserves the right to amend or cancel the solicitation and resolicit with respect to any individual item in the event quotations received and the Government's requirements indicate that different quantities should be acquired.

(End of provision)

FAR 52.223-4, Recovered Material Certification (MAY 2008)
DFARS 252.203-7005, Representation Relating to Compensation of Former DOD Officials (NOV 2011)
DFARS 252.203-7994, Prohibition on Contracting with Entities that Require Certain Internal Confidentiality Agreements – Representation (Deviation 2017-O0001) (NOV 2016)
DFARS 252.204-7008, Compliance with Safeguarding Covered Defense Information Controls (DEC 2015)
DFARS 252.204-7011, Alternative Line Item Structure (SEP 2011)
DFARS 252.222-7007, Representation Regarding Combating Trafficking in Persons (JAN 2015)

DFARS 252.225-7000, Buy American – Balance of Payments Program Certificate (NOV 2014)

(a) *Definitions.* "Commercially available off-the-shelf (COTS) item," "component," "domestic end product," "foreign end product," "qualifying country," "qualifying country end product," and "United States," as used in this provision, have the meanings given in the Buy American and Balance of Payments Program – Basic clause of this solicitation.

(b) *Evaluation.* The government –

(1) Will evaluate offers in accordance with the policies and procedures of Part 225 of the Defense Federal Acquisition Regulation Supplement; and

(2) Will evaluate offers of qualifying country end products without regard to the restrictions of the Buy American statute or the Balance of Payments Program.

(c) *Certifications and identification of country of origin.*

(1) For all line items subject to the Buy American and Balance of Payments Program—Basic clause of this solicitation, the offeror certifies that –

(i) Each end product, except those listed in paragraphs (c)(2) or (3) of this provision, is a domestic end product; and

(ii) For end products other than COTS items, components of unknown origin are considered to have been mined, produced, or manufactured outside the United States or a qualifying country.

(2) The offeror certifies that the following end products are qualifying country end products:

Line Item Number	Country of Origin

(3) The following end products are other foreign end products, including end products manufactured in the United States that do not qualify as domestic end products, *i.e.*, an end product that is not a COTS item and does not meet the component test in paragraph (ii) of the definition of "domestic end product":

Line Item Number	Country of Origin (if known)

(End of provision)

DFARS 252.225-7031, Secondary Arab Boycott of Israel (JUN 2005)

DFARS 252.225-7035, Buy American – Free Trade Agreements – Balance of Payments Program Certificate (NOV 2014)

(a) *Definitions.* "Bahrainian end product," "commercially available off-the-shelf (COTS) item," "component," "domestic end product," "Free Trade Agreement country," "Free Trade Agreement country end product," "foreign end product," "Moroccan end product," "Panamanian end product," "Peruvian end product," "qualifying country end product," and "United States," as used in this provision, have the meanings given in the Buy American – Free Trade Agreements – Balance of Payments Program – Basic clause of this solicitation.

(b) *Evaluation.* The government –

(1) Will evaluate offers in accordance with the policies and procedures of Part 225 of the Defense Federal Acquisition Regulation Supplement; and

(2) For line items subject to the Buy American – Free Trade Agreements – Balance of Payments Program – Basic clause of this solicitation, will evaluate offers of qualifying country end products or Free Trade Agreement country end products other than Bahrainian end products, Moroccan end products, Panamanian end products, or Peruvian end products without regard to the restrictions of the Buy American or the Balance of Payments Program.

(c) *Certifications and identification of country of origin.*

(1) For all line items subject to the Buy American—Free Trade Agreements—Balance of Payments Program—Basic clause of this solicitation, the offeror certifies that—

(i) Each end product, except the end products listed in paragraph (c)(2) of this provision, is a domestic end product; and

(ii) Components of unknown origin are considered to have been mined, produced, or manufactured outside the United States or a qualifying country.

(2) The offeror shall identify all end products that are not domestic end products.

(i) The offeror certifies that the following supplies are qualifying country (except Australian or Canadian) end products:

(Line Item Number)	(Country of Origin)

(ii) The offeror certifies that the following supplies are Free Trade Agreement country end products other than Bahrainian end products, Moroccan end products, Panamanian end products, or Peruvian end products:

(Line Item Number)	(Country of Origin)

(iii) The following supplies are other foreign end products, including end products manufactured in the United States that do not qualify as domestic end products, i.e., an end product that is not a COTS item and does not meet the component test in paragraph (ii) of the definition of "domestic end product":

(Line Item Number)	(Country of Origin (if known))

(End of provision)

DFARS 252.225-7050, Disclosure of Ownership or Control by the Government of a Country that is a State Sponsor of Terrorism (OCT 2015)

DFARS 252.247-7022, Representation of Extent of Transportation by Sea (AUG 1992)

(a) The Offeror shall indicate by checking the appropriate blank in paragraph (b) of this provision whether transportation of supplies by sea is anticipated under the resultant contract. The term "supplies" is defined in the Transportation of Supplies by Sea clause of this solicitation.

(b) *Representation.* The offeror represents that it –

_____ Does anticipate that supplies will be transported by sea in the performance of any contract or subcontract resulting from this solicitation.

_____ Does not anticipate that supplies will be transported by sea in the performance of any contract or subcontract resulting from this solicitation.

(c) Any contract resulting from this solicitation will include the Transportation of Supplies by Sea clause. If the Offeror represents that it will not use ocean transportation, the resulting contract will also include the Defense FAR Supplement clause at 252.247-7024, Notification of Transportation of Supplies by Sea.

(End of provision)

APPENDIX C

GLOSSARY

Acceptance – Act by which a government agent acknowledges the supplies or services submitted by the contractor conform to all contract requirements.

Acquisition Planner – One who determines the supplies and services needed by the government, their technical characteristics, and quantities.

Administrative Contracting Officer – A contracting officer assigned to perform administrative functions after contract award.

Advance Payments – Advances of money to the contractor prior to contract performance.

Advocate for Competition – Person responsible for ensuring the contracting activity complies with the Competition in Contracting Act.

Agency Forecast – A projection of upcoming acquisitions expected to be conducted in the next quarter or the rest of the fiscal year.

Allowable Costs – Those costs incurred during contract performance that are reasonable, allocable, in compliance with the Cost Accounting Standards or generally accepted accounting procedures, in compliance with the terms and conditions of the contract, and in compliance with Part 31 of the Federal Acquisition Regulation.

Alternative Dispute Resolution – A simplified and expedited manner of settling disputes. The parties can use any method that suits the complexity of the dispute and the issues involved.

Amendment – A change to a solicitation after it has been released.

Basic Ordering Agreement – An agreement between the government and the contractor to include specific clauses in all contracts executed during the term of the agreement.

Best Value – After evaluating all offers, and considering price and the other factors identified in the solicitation, the proposal which the government determines will provide the greatest overall benefit.

Bid Board – A board, located in a public place, on which the contracting office displays solicitations.

Bid Guarantee (or Bond) – A certification by a surety that the bidder will be able to obtain required performance and payment bonds should the bidder receive the award. Primarily used in construction contracting.

Bid Opening – The public announcement of all the bids submitted in response to an Invitation for Bids.

Bid Samples – Samples submitted in response to an Invitation for Bids that allow the contracting officer to judge difficult to describe characteristics of the item, such as feel, color, pattern, and balance.

Biobased Products – A commercial or industrial product, other than food or feed, that is composed, in whole or in significant part, of biological products, including renewable domestic agricultural materials and forestry materials.

Blanket Purchase Agreement – A contractual instrument that acts like a charge account in that authorized government personnel use it to order necessary supplies or services without issuing an individual purchase document. Restricted to purchases that do not exceed $150,000 ($7,000,000 for commercial items); however, the limitation does not apply to Federal Supply Schedule contracts.

Board of Contract Appeals – A government administrative tribunal established to hear contractor appeals of adverse contractual interpretations and decisions of the contracting officer. There are two within the government: the *Civilian Board of Contract Appeals* (CBCA) and the *Armed Services Board of Contract Appeals* (ASBCA).

Brand Name or Equal – The minimum acceptable purchase description; for example, "Campbell's® Tomato Soup or equal."

Broad Agency Announcement – An announcement in **FedBizOpps** that an agency is interested in obtaining proposals for studies and experiments that will advance the state-of-the-art or increase overall knowledge in the particular area of research interest.

Brooks Architect-Engineers Act – Law that established the unique procedures in Federal Acquisition Regulation subpart 36.6 for the acquisition of architect-engineer services.

Buy American Act – A law that requires the government to buy domestic articles, materials, and supplies unless one of five exceptions apply.

Byrd Amendment – Law that prohibits contractors from using appropriated funds to influence any government employee regarding the award or modification of any federal contract.

Cancellation Ceiling – The maximum compensation the government will pay a contractor for unamortized nonrecurring costs upon cancellation of a multi-year contract before its scheduled completion.

Catalog Price – A published price in a catalog, pricelist, or schedule of services sold to a significant number of buyers.

Certificate of Appointment – The document that empowers a person to act on behalf of the government as a contracting officer.

Certificate of Competency – A document issued by the Small Business Administration that certifies a small business as responsible and able to perform the specific government contract.

Certificate of Current Cost or Pricing Data – A document submitted by the contractor attesting that the cost or pricing data it provided to the government were accurate, complete, and current as of the date negotiations were completed.

Change Order – A directive, issued by the contracting officer according to the "Changes" clause, to change the contract specifications, method of shipping and packing, place of delivery, times of performance, or similar aspects of the contract.

Chief Acquisition Officer – Official responsible for overseeing the agency's acquisition activities and programs, and who advises the head of the agency regarding the appropriate business strategy to achieve the agency's mission.

Claim – A written demand for an equitable adjustment to the contract as a result of the government's or contractor's action or inaction. If the claim is more than $50,000 ($150,000 for small businesses), the contractor must certify that it is made in good faith and that the supporting data are accurate and complete.

Closing Date – The last day proposals or quotations are accepted by the government.

Commercial Item – A supply or service that is offered and sold competitively to the general public.

Commercial Item Description – A simplified product description that describes the essential design, functional, or performance characteristics of commercially available products that will satisfy the government's needs.

Competition in Contracting Act – Law that requires the government to use "full and open competition" whenever it acquires supplies and services. The act provides for seven exceptions to this requirement.

Competitive Range – In negotiated solicitations, the proposals being considered for contract award based on price, technical, or other factors identified in the Request for Proposals.

Contingent Fee – A fee, commission, or percentage paid by a contractor to an individual upon successfully obtaining a contract.

Contract Bundling – The consolidation of two or more requirements for supplies or services that had previously been provided or performed under separate smaller contracts into a solicitation for a single contract that is too big for a small business to perform.

Contract Disputes Act – Law that established the procedures for asserting and resolving claims by or against contractors.

Contract Line Item Number – Identification assigned to discrete supplies or services in solicitations and contracts. A contract line item number can be subdivided into subline item numbers so individual items can be separately priced.

Contract Modification – A change made to a contract. Can be either a unilateral modification made by the contracting officer exercising a governmental right under the contract or a bilateral modification in which both parties agree to the change.

Contract Specialist (or Assistant) – Aide to the contracting officer.

Contract Work Hours and Safety Standards Act – Law that requires "time and a half" pay for overtime work performed by laborers and mechanics on most federal service and construction contracts.

Contracting Activity – An organization within a department or agency that is responsible for determining the supplies or services needed, obtaining the necessary funding, and acquiring the needed supplies or services through contracts.

Contracting Office – The office within the contracting activity that solicits, awards, and administers contracts.

Contracting Officer – The only person with the authority to enter into, administer, and terminate contracts. Consequently, these government personnel are called procuring, administrative, and termination contracting officers.

Contracting Officer's Representative – A person appointed by the contracting officer to assist in technical matters during contract performance.

Copeland Act – Law that prohibits kickbacks on construction contracts financed by the government.

Cost Accounting Standards – Cost accounting practices that must be followed by large contractors and subcontractors performing large contracts and subcontracts.

Cost Analysis – The review and evaluation of the separate cost elements and profit of an offeror's cost or pricing data and the judgmental factors applied to the data to project the estimated costs.

Cost or Pricing Data – All verifiable data that support an offeror's or contractor's cost proposal: vendor quotations, nonrecurring costs, projections of business prospects, and similar facts.

Cost-Plus-Award-Fee Contract – A cost-reimbursement contract that provides for (1) the payment of a small fixed fee, and (2) the payment of an additional fee based on the contractor's quality of work, timeliness, ingenuity, cost effectiveness, and other factors identified in the contract. The government unilaterally determines the amount of this additional fee.

Cost-Plus-Fixed-Fee Contract – A cost-reimbursement contract type in which the contractor is paid a fixed dollar amount as a fee. This fee is established during contract negotiations. The fixed fee does not vary with the contractor's incurred costs.

Cost-Plus-Incentive-Fee Contract – A cost-reimbursement contract type in which the contractor is awarded a greater or lesser fee depending on how well the contractor performs in relation to the incentives specified in the contract.

Cost-Reimbursement Contract – A basic contract type in which the government reimburses the contractor for the allowable costs it incurred during performance of the contract.

Cure Notice – A notice sent by the contracting officer to the contractor stating its contract will be subject to a default termination within a certain period (usually ten days) unless the contractor corrects a specific contract noncompliance or makes the necessary progress to meet the delivery schedule.

Data Other Than Certified Cost or Pricing Data – Pricing data, cost data, and judgmental information necessary for the contracting officer to determine a fair and reasonable price or to determine cost realism. Such data is not certified by the offeror as accurate, complete, and current.

Davis-Bacon Act – Law that requires contractors to pay the locally prevailing wage rate (as determined by the secretary of labor) to all laborers and mechanics employed on federally funded construction, alteration, or repair contracts.

Debarment – The process by which a contractor is prohibited from government contracting because of a conviction for an offense that shows a lack of business integrity or honesty. A contractor can be debarred for up to three years (five years for violation of the Drug-Free Workplace Act).

Debriefing – A meeting between an unsuccessful offeror and government personnel involved in proposal evaluations in which the government explains why the offeror's proposal was not chosen for award.

Definite-Quantity Contract – A contractual instrument that provides for a definite quantity of supplies or services to be delivered at later, unspecified dates.

Delivery Order – A written order for supplies issued under an indefinite-delivery contract.

Descriptive Literature – Any information, such as illustrations, drawings, and brochures, that shows the characteristics or construction of a product or explains its operation.

Design Change Notice – Official documentation that specifies changes to a technical data package.

Deviation – A minor change to the technical data package granted, on a one-time-only basis, to assist the contractor in the performance of the contract.

Differing Site Conditions – A provision in construction contracts that provides for adjustment of the contract price should the contractor discover unusual physical conditions that differ from those ordinarily encountered.

Disputes – An administrative process by which a contractor can challenge and appeal a contracting officer's adverse decision or action.

Drug-Free Workplace Act – Law that requires contractors to notify their employees that unlawful use of controlled substances is prohibited in the workplace and that continued employment is conditional on compliance with the prohibition.

Economically Disadvantaged Women-Owned Small Business – A small business that is at least 51% owned, controlled, and operated by women who are U.S. citizens and are economically disadvantaged.

Engineering Change Proposal – A proposal made by either the contractor or the government to change a technical data package.

Equal Employment Opportunity – Prohibition of discrimination against any employee or applicant because or race, color, religion, sex, or national origin.

Equitable Adjustment – Modification of a contract price, schedule, or other contract terms to compensate the contractor for government directed changes or any other government actions or inactions. The government may also be entitled to an equitable adjustment for contractor actions or inactions.

Evaluation Factors – The criteria and qualifications that will be weighed by the contracting officer and government evaluators when deciding which offeror will receive the contract.

Fast Pay Procedure – A method authorized for purchases of $35,000 or less in which the government pays the contractor immediately upon receipt of its invoice (before inspection and acceptance has taken place) provided the contractor certifies the supplies have been delivered to a common carrier and are as ordered.

Federal Acquisition Circular – Revisions to the Federal Acquisition Regulation reflecting recent legislative and regulatory changes.

Federal Acquisition Regulation – The rules that control purchases and contracts of the federal government. Federal departments and agencies issue supplements to implement and augment the Federal Acquisition Regulation.

Federal Acquisition Streamlining Act – Law that authorizes micro-purchases up to $3,500, simplified procedures up to $150,000, and requires the purchase of commercial items whenever possible.

Federal Business Opportunities – The "governmentwide point-of-entry" website where the government posts notices of upcoming solicitations over $25,000 and contract awards over $25,000 that present subcontracting opportunities (commonly referred to as "FedBizOpps" or "FBO").

Federal Procurement Data System – A database of information on all contract actions over $3,500.

Federal Supply Schedules – Contracts maintained by the General Services Administration that may be used by other government agencies to order commonly used supplies or services directly from contractors.

Fee – In cost-reimbursement contracts, the amount beyond the reimbursed costs that the government agrees to pay for contract performance. The fee can be fixed (cost-plus-fixed-fee) or variable (cost-plus-incentive-fee and cost-plus-award-fee).

Fee Adjustment Formula – In incentive contracts, the formula that establishes how the government and contractor will share costs and savings. Also called a "share ratio."

Firm Bid Rule – The rule that prohibits a bidder from withdrawing its bid for the period specified in the Invitation for Bids, usually 60 days after bid opening.

Firm-Fixed-Price Contract – A contract in which the contractor is paid a specified amount for the supplies or services it is to furnish. The contractor's cost of contract performance has no effect on the contract price.

First Article – First item, preproduction model, or test sample produced by the contractor which is tested to make sure the contractor can furnish a product that meets the specification requirements and operates satisfactorily.

Fixed-Price Contract – A basic contract type in which the contractor is paid a fixed price regardless of its actual cost of contract performance or, under some circumstances, an adjustable price up to a ceiling that imposes a limit on the amount the government will pay.

Fixed-Price with Award Fee Contract – A firm-fixed-price contract in which the contractor can earn an additional fee (a "tip") if it performs the contract well. The government unilaterally determines the amount of the fee, if any, to award the contractor.

Fixed-Price with Economic Price Adjustment Contract – A fixed-price contract that permits the fluctuation of an element of cost to reflect current market prices or other specified contingencies.

Fraud – Any false representation or concealment that intentionally deceives another party to its detriment.

Freedom of Information Act – Law that permits the public to obtain government records, with certain exceptions.

Full and Open Competition – The Competition in Contracting Act requirement that all responsible sources be given the opportunity to compete for contracts.

General Services Administration – Agency responsible for the award and administration of federal supply schedule contracts and the management of federal property.

Government Accountability Office – Congress' audit agency, it has the authority to decide protests against contract awards.

Government-Furnished Property – Equipment or material the government provides to a contractor to assist contract performance.

Governmentwide Acquisition Contract – An indefinite-delivery contract for information technology supplies or services that is established by one agency for use by all other agencies.

Governmentwide Commercial Purchase Card – A credit card that can be used by federal employees who are not contracting officers.

Governmentwide Point-of-Entry – The Federal Business Opportunities (FedBizOpps) website.

Guaranteed Loans – An extraordinary method of contract financing in which the government guarantees payment to the lending institution should the contractor be unable to repay the loan.

Head of the Agency – The secretary, attorney general, administrator, or other chief official of a department or agency.

Head of the Contracting Activity – The person responsible for the overall operation and management of a contracting activity.

Historically Underutilized Business Zone Business – A small business certified by the Small Business Administration (SBA) as (1) operating in an area with either an unemployment rate at least 140% of the state's average or income no more than 80% of the non-metropolitan state median household income, and (2) with at least 35% of its employees residing in a HUBZone.

Indefinite-Delivery Contract – A fixed-price contract in which the exact time for delivery is not known at contract award. Deliveries are scheduled when authorized government personnel place orders. There are three types of indefinite-delivery contracts: definite-quantity, indefinite-quantity, and requirements.

Indefinite-Quantity Contract – A contract in which the government agrees to order a minimum quantity of supplies or services and can purchase additional quantities if desired; however, the government is under no obligation to purchase additional quantities once the minimum is fulfilled.

Invitation for Bids – The solicitation document used when conducting sealed bidding.

Joint Venture – An association of two or more persons or concerns engaging in a single specific business venture for joint profit.

Justification and Approval – The contracting officer's written explanation of the facts supporting his decision not to seek full and open competition for a purchase. The justification must cite one of the seven exceptions to full and open competition authorized by the Competition in Contracting Act.

Labor Hour Contract – A contract that provides for reimbursement of the contractor's labor costs at a fixed hourly rate.

Letter Contract – A legal instrument that allows the contractor to proceed with the performance of a contract though final agreement has not been reached with the government on the terms and conditions.

Level Unit Pricing – A requirement in most multi-year contracts to price each year's deliveries at the same unit price.

Lowest-Price Technically Acceptable – A source selection process in which the contract is awarded to the offeror that submits the proposal meeting the minimum technical requirements at a lower price than all other acceptable proposals.

Market Price – A current price of services sold during commercial trade that can be substantiated through competition or independent sources.

Market Research – The collection and analysis of information about capabilities of those within the market to the most suitable way to acquire, distribute, and support supplies and services that satisfy the agency's needs.

Mentor-Protégé Program – A program in which the major contractor ("mentor") selects one or more small firms ("protégé") to enter into a long-term relationship as a junior partner.

Micro-Purchase – A purchase of $3,500 or less which can be made by government employees other than contracting officers (the threshold is $5,000 for the Department of Defense, $2,500 for most services, and $2,000 for construction).

Miller Act – Law that requires construction contractors to provide performance and payment bonds as a condition for contracting.

Mistake in Bid – A procedure in which a bidder is allowed to correct or withdraw its bid upon discovery that it made a mistake in preparing the bid.

Multi-Agency Contract – An indefinite-delivery contract established by one agency for use by government agencies to obtain supplies and services.

Multiple Award Schedule – Another name for Federal Supply Schedule.

Multi-Year Contract – A fixed-price contract, lasting up to five years, that is funded on a yearly basis. If the government does not fund later years, it will pay the contractor's unamortized nonrecurring costs up to the cancellation ceiling.

Negotiation – A method of solicitation in which offerors submit proposals and the government conducts discussions with the offerors about their proposals.

Nondevelopmental Item – A previously developed item used exclusively by a federal agency, a state or local government, or a foreign government.

Nonmanufacturer Rule – Requirement that a small business responding to a set-aside solicitation for supplies, but is not the manufacturer of the supplies, must not have more than 500 employees and must offer supplies manufactured by a small business.

Non-Traditional Contractor – A contractor that has not performed, within the past year, any contract over $500,000 that is subject to the FAR. These contractors are eligible to perform basic, applied, advanced research, or prototype projects through "other transactions."

North American Industry Classification System – A system used by the United States, Canada, and Mexico to classify business establishments.

Not-to-Exceed Price – A maximum price the contractor may not exceed while negotiations take place to establish the final price of a contract modification. It permits the contractor to perform the contract as modified while negotiations are being conducted and protects the government from excessive expenditures.

Notice of Award – A notification to the lowest, responsive construction contractor that it must obtain a performance and payment bond before the contracting officer can award the contract.

Office of Federal Procurement Policy – The organization that oversees the government's contracting processes and procedures.

Office of Management and Budget – The organization that assists the president in the preparation of the federal budget and the supervision of federal agencies.

The Office of Federal Procurement Policy is part of the Office of Management and Budget.

Order of Precedence – A provision that establishes priorities among the various parts of the solicitation so contradictions within the solicitation can be resolved without a contracting officer decision.

Other Transactions – Arrangements with "non-traditional contractors" for prototype projects or research that are exempt from all statutes and regulations governing federal contracts.

Past Performance Information Retrieval System – A database of contractor past performance information compiled by the government for each contract over the simplified acquisition threshold ($150,000).

Payment Bond – A bond issued by a surety or sureties guaranteeing that the laborers, subcontractors, and suppliers will be paid for completed work. It is required by the Miller Act for construction contracts over $150,000.

Performance-Based Acquisition – A method of contracting in which the agency describes its needs in terms of what it wants to achieve, not how the work is to be performed.

Performance-Based Payments – Payments based on either: (1) performance measured by objective, quantifiable methods; (2) accomplishment of defined events (for example, milestones); or (3) other quantifiable measures of results.

Performance Bond – A bond issued by a surety or sureties guaranteeing the performance and fulfillment of all contractual obligations. It is required by the Miller Act for construction contracts over $150,000.

Performance Work Statement – A statement of work used in a performance-based acquisition.

Postaward Orientation – A meeting of government and contractor personnel held soon after contract award to insure everyone understands the contract requirements.

Preaward Survey – An evaluation of a bidder's or offeror's ability to perform a contract. The results of the survey help the contracting officer make his determination of responsibility.

Pre-Bid (Pre-Proposal) Conference – A briefing held by the contracting officer to explain to prospective bidders (or offerors) complicated specifications and requirements.

Price Analysis – The process of examining and evaluating a proposed price without evaluating its separate cost elements and proposed profit.

Procurement Integrity Act – Law that imposes restrictions on the behavior of government procurement officials and competing contractors during the conduct of a federal procurement.

Procuring Contracting Officer – The government agent authorized to solicit, negotiate, and award contracts for the government.

Progress Payments – Payments made to a contractor performing a long-term fixed-price contract based on a percentage of the costs it incurs. These payments are liquidated as the contractor delivers the supplies or performs the services.

Prompt Payment – Requirement that the government pay a proper invoice by the 30th calendar day after receipt by the billing office or 30th calendar day after acceptance of the supplies or services.

Proposal – Any offer used for pricing a contract under negotiation procedures, contract modification, or termination settlement.

Protective Order – An order that restricts the examination of certain documents involved in a protest or dispute to an interested party's legal counsel. These can be issued by the Government Accountability Office or a board of contract appeals.

Protest – Any written objection by a bidder, offeror, or other interested party to a solicitation or the award of a contract.

Purchase Description – A simplified specification that describes the essential characteristics and functions required to meet the government's needs.

Purchase Order – A contract document, issued by the contracting officer when he uses simplified procedures, in which the government offers to buy certain supplies or services at the price quoted by the offeror.

Qualified Bidders List – A list of bidders that have had their products examined and tested, and have satisfied all applicable qualification requirements.

Qualified Manufacturers List – A list of manufacturers that have had their products examined and tested, and have satisfied all applicable qualification requirements.

Qualified Products List – A list of products that have been examined, tested, and found to satisfy all applicable qualification requirements.

Request for Information – A document seeking information on available technologies or services for planning purposes. No contract will be awarded in response to such request.

Request for Proposals – Solicitation document used in negotiated procurements that exceed the simplified procedures limitation.

Request for Quotations – Solicitation document used to solicit prices for purchases under the simplified procedures limitation when obtaining electronic or oral quotations is not economical or practical.

Requirements Contract – A contractual instrument that establishes a contractor as the sole source, during a designated period, for all the requirements generated by designated government activities for specific supplies or services.

Responsible Bidder (or Offeror) – A party that has adequate financial resources, can comply with the delivery schedule, has a satisfactory performance record, and is otherwise qualified to perform the contract.

Responsive Bidder – One that submits a bid that complies with all the terms and conditions of the Invitation for Bids.

Reverse Auction – An auction in which sellers compete against one another to provide the buyer the lowest price or highest-value offer.

Rule of Two – The requirement that contracting officers reserve purchases exclusively for small business participation if two or more responsible small businesses are expected to submit bids or proposals at fair market prices.

Sealed Bidding – Method of solicitation in which the government opens the bids in public and awards a contract to the lowest responsive, responsible bidder.

Section 8(a) Subcontract – A subcontract between the Small Business Administration and a socially and economically disadvantaged small business concern as provided by Section 8(a) of the Small Business Act. The Small Business Administration enters into a prime contract with a government agency and subcontracts the entire effort to the 8(a) subcontractor.

Senior Procurement Executive – Official responsible for the agency's day-to-day contracting operations, including the development and implementation of the agency's unique acquisition policies, regulations, and standards.

Service Classification Codes – Categories of services used in **FedBizOpps** and the Federal Procurement Data System.

Service Contract Act – A law that governs the wage rates and benefits payable to employees performing services under federal contracts and subcontracts.

Service-Disabled Veteran-Owned Small Business – A small business that has at least 51% ownership by one or more service-disabled veterans, and is managed by one or more service-disabled veterans.

Set-Aside – A solicitation reserved exclusively for participation by small businesses in general or by a particular kind of small business.

Show Cause Notice – A demand by a contracting officer that a contractor explain why its contract should not be terminated for default.

Simplified Acquisition Threshold – The $150,000 limit on purchases of supplies or services using any of the simplified procedures authorized by FAR part 13. The threshold is $7,000,000 for commercial items.

Simplified Contract Format – An optional streamlined format for Invitations for Bid and Requests for Proposal that will result in firm-fixed-price or fixed-price with economic price adjustment contracts.

Simplified Procedures – Several authorized methods for entering into contracts without using formal solicitation techniques: micro-purchases, oral solicitations, purchase orders, requests for quotation, blanket purchase agreements, and imprest fund. These methods are restricted to purchases that do not exceed $150,000 ($7,000,000 for commercial items).

Single Process Initiative – A Department of Defense program in which offerors are encouraged to propose the substitution of their commercial manufacturing or management processes for the military or federal specifications cited in the solicitation.

Small Business – A firm that qualifies under the size standards established by the Small Business Administration and contained in FAR subpart 19.1.

Small Business Administration – The government agency that aids, counsels, provides financial assistance, and protects the interests of the small business community.

Small Business Innovative Research Program – A program that requires federal agencies with research and development budgets of more than $100 million to set aside a fixed percentage of their budgets exclusively for small businesses.

Small Business Size Standard – Limit on the number of employees or gross annual revenue a business may have to be considered small for contracting purposes. These are established by the Small Business Administration for each industry in the North American Industry Classification System.

Small Business Specialist – A government employee who seeks to insure his contracting activity's compliance with the Small Business Act by providing assistance to small, minority, veteran-owned, and women-owned businesses.

Small Business Subcontracting Plan – A plan, submitted to the government by a large business winner of a large contract, in which the contractor establishes separate goals for subcontract awards to small businesses and small disadvantaged businesses. It becomes part of the prime contract.

Small Business Technology Transfer Program – A program that requires federal agencies with research and development budgets of more than $1 billion to set aside a fixed percentage of their budgets exclusively for small businesses that partner with nonprofit research institutions.

Small Disadvantaged Business – A firm that is certified by the Small Business Administration (SBA) as having at least 51% ownership, and is being managed, by one or more individuals who are economically disadvantaged and belong to a racial or ethnic group that has been subjected to prejudice or cultural bias.

Sole Source – A contractor that possesses unique supplies or capabilities needed by the government.

Source Selection Authority – A senior agency official who weighs all the proposal evaluations and selects the winning contractor.

Sources Sought Notice – An announcement placed by agencies in **FedBizOpps** that alerts potential sources of an upcoming solicitation and invites them to submit information describing their capabilities.

Specification – A document prepared by the government that describes the technical and quality requirements of supplies the government purchases regularly.

Standard – A document prepared by private organizations that establish engineering and technical limitations, applications, and engineering practices.

Statement of Objectives – A document that identifies the broad top-level objectives of the acquisition and permits the offerors to propose their own solutions.

Statement of Work – A document prepared by the government that describes needed services and the particular characteristics of the problem to be addressed or location where the services are to be performed.

Streamlined Synopsis/Solicitation – A solicitation method in which the synopsis and the solicitation are posted on **FedBizOpps** at the same time, and no written solicitation is issued.

Subcontract Clause Flow-Down – The requirement that certain clauses in the prime contract be imposed by the prime contractor on its subcontractors.

Supplemental Agreement – A bilateral contract modification.

Supply Classification Codes – Categories of supplies used in **FedBizOpps** and by the Federal Procurement Data System.

Surety – An individual or corporation legally liable for the debt, default, or failure of a contractor to satisfy a contractual obligation. Most commonly found in construction contracting.

Suspension – The process by which a contractor is temporarily prohibited from government contracting while it is under indictment for an offense that shows a lack of business integrity or honesty. The suspension lasts until the completion of criminal investigations and any ensuing legal proceedings.

Sustainable Acquisition – The acquisition of goods and services that are energy-efficient, water-efficient, environmentally preferable, biobased, non-ozone depleting, use recovered materials, and minimize or eliminate the use of hydrofluorocarbons.

Synopsis – A brief explanation of an upcoming solicitation or recent award published in **FedBizOpps** (FBO).

System for Award Management – A system that consolidates several acquisition-related databases to provide a seamless interface and eliminate duplicate data input.

Task Order – A written order for services issued under an indefinite-delivery contract.

Team Arrangement – Two or more companies that form a partnership or joint venture to act as a potential prime contractor, or a potential prime contractor that agrees with one or more other companies to have them act as its subcontractors under a specified contract or program.

Technical Data Package – The drawings, specifications, standards, and related data needed to describe the features and configuration of an item in sufficient detail to permit manufacture by someone reasonably competent in that field.

Termination Contracting Officer – A contracting officer assigned to settle contracts terminated for the convenience of the government or for default.

Termination for Convenience – The government ordered discontinuance of a contract that no longer meets the government's needs.

Termination for Default – The unilateral termination of a contract by the government because of the contractor's failure to fulfill the terms and conditions of the contract.

Time-and-Materials Contract – A contract that provides for the payment of a fixed hourly labor rate and the reimbursement for materials used in the performance of the contract.

Trade Agreements – Treaties in which the United States agrees to waive the provisions of the Buy American Act in return for similar treatment by other countries.

Two-Step Sealed Bidding – A solicitation method that combines sealed bidding and negotiation procedures. The first step requires the submission of a technical proposal and the second step requires the submission of a price.

Uniform Contract Format – The solicitation and contract format (Section A through Section M) used in most Invitations for Bids, Requests for Proposals, and the resulting contracts.

Unsolicited Proposal – A proposal that an offeror prepares and submits independent of any government solicitation or requirement.

Value Engineering – A program that rewards contractors for suggesting contract changes that eliminate nonessential functions or components of end items. There are two types of value engineering programs: incentive and mandatory.

Wage Determination – The wage rates and fringe benefits found by the secretary of labor to be prevailing in the locality. Contractors subject to the Davis-Bacon Act and the Service Contract Act must comply with these determinations.

Waiver – Acceptance by the government of a minor nonconformity that does not degrade the function of the item.

Warrant – A contracting officer's certificate of appointment.

Women-Owned Small Business – A small business that is at least 51% owned, controlled, and operated by women who are U.S. citizens.

APPENDIX D

ABBREVIATIONS AND FORM NUMBERS

ABBREVIATIONS

ACO	Administrative Contracting Officer
ADR	Alternative Dispute Resolution
A-E	Architect-Engineering
AQL	Acceptable Quality Level
ASSIST	Department of Defense Acquisition Streamlining and Standardization Information System
BAA	Broad Agency Announcement
BCA	Board of Contract Appeals
BOA	Basic Ordering Agreement
BPA	Blanket Purchasing Agreement
CAGE	Commercial and Government Entity
CAO	Chief Acquisition Officer
CCR	Central Contractor Registration
CFR	Code of Federal Regulations
CICA	Competition in Contracting Act
CID	Commercial Item Description
CLIN	Contract Line Item Number
COC	Certificate of Competency
COR	Contracting Officer's Representative
CPAF	Cost-Plus-Award-Fee Contract
CPARS	Contractor Performance Assessment Reporting System
CPFF	Cost-Plus-Fixed-Fee Contract

CPIF	Cost-Plus-Incentive-Fee Contract
DCAA	Defense Contract Audit Agency
DCMA	Defense Contract Management Agency
DFARS	Defense Federal Acquisition Regulation Supplement
DHS	Department of Homeland Security
DOD	Department of Defense
DOE	Department of Energy
DUNS	Data Universal Numbering System
ECP	Engineering Change Proposal
EDWOSB	Economically Disadvantaged Women-Owned Small Business
EEO	Equal Employment Opportunity
EFT	Electronic Funds Transfer
EPA	Environmental Protection Agency
EPEAT	Electronic Products Environmental Assessment Tool
EPLS	Excluded Parties List System
eMod	Electronic Modification System
eOffer	Electronic Contract Offer System
eSRS	Electronic Subcontracting Reporting System
FAC	Federal Acquisition Circular
FAPIIS	Federal Awardee Performance and Integrity Information System
FAR	Federal Acquisition Regulation
FAS	Federal Acquisition Service
FASA	Federal Acquisition Streamlining Act
FedBizOpps or **FBO**	Federal Business Opportunities
FEMP	Federal Energy Management Program
FFP	Firm-Fixed-Price Contract
FOIA	Freedom of Information Act
FPAF	Fixed-Price with Award Fee
FPDS	Federal Procurement Data System
FP/EPA	Fixed-Price with Economic Price Adjustment
FPI	Federal Prison Industries, Inc.
FSRS	Federal Funding Accountability and Transparency Act Subaward Reporting System
FSS	Federal Supply Schedules
GAO	Government Accountability Office
GFP	Government-Furnished Property
GPE	Governmentwide Point-of-Entry
GSA	General Services Administration
GSAM	General Services Administration Acquisition Manual
GSAR	General Services Administration Acquisition Regulation
GWAC	Governmentwide Acquisition Contract

HCA	Head of the Contracting Activity
HUBZone	Historically Underutilized Business Zone
IDIQ	Indefinite-Delivery, Indefinite-Quantity Contract
IFB	Invitation For Bids
IFF	Industrial Funding Fee
ILC	Irrevocable Letter of Credit
J&A	Justification and Approval
LPTA	Lowest-Price Technically Acceptable
MAC	Multi-Agency Contract
MPIN	Marketing Partner Identification Number
NAICS	North American Industry Classification System
NASA	National Aeronautics and Space Administration
OFAC	Office of Foreign Assets Control
OFCCP	Office of Federal Contract Compliance Programs
OFPP	Office of Federal Procurement Policy
OMB	Office of Management and Budget
ORCA	On-Line Representations and Certifications Application
OSDBU	Office of Small and Disadvantaged Business Utilization
OSHA	Occupational Safety and Health Administration
PBA	Performance-Based Acquisition
PBS	Public Building Service
PCO	Procuring Contracting Officer
PPIRS	Past Performance Information Retrieval System
PSC	Product and Service Codes
PWS	Performance Work Statement
QBL	Qualified Bidders List
QML	Qualified Manufacturers List
QPL	Qualified Products List
RFD	Request For Deviation
RFI	Request For Information
RFP	Request For Proposals
RFQ	Request For Quotations
RFW	Request For Waiver
SAM	System of Award Management
SAT	Simplified Acquisition Threshold
SBA	Small Business Administration
SBIR	Small Business Innovative Research
SBS	Small Business Specialist
SCF	Simplified Contract Format
SDB	Small Disadvantaged Business
SDVOSB	Service-Disabled Veteran-Owned Small Business
SIN	Special Item Number

SOO	Statement of Objectives
SOW	Statement of Work
SPE	Senior Procurement Executive
SPI	Single Process Initiative
STTR	Small Business Technology Transfer Program
TCO	Termination Contracting Officer
TDP	Technical Data Package
TIN	Taxpayer Identification Number
T&M	Time and Materials Contract
UCF	Uniform Contract Format
USC	United States Code
VE	Value Engineering
VECP	Value Engineering Change Proposal
WDOL	Wage Determinations OnLine
WOSB	Women-Owned Small Business
8(a)	Disadvantaged Business Subcontracting Program

FORMS

CSP-1	Commercial Sales Practices Format
DD Form 250	Material Inspection and Receiving Report
DD Form 1155	Order for Supplies or Services
DD Form 1547	Weighted Guidelines Profit/Fee Objective
OF 307	Contract Award
OF 308	Solicitation and Offer – Negotiated Acquisition
OF 309	Amendment of Solicitation (Negotiated Procurements)
OF 347	Order for Supplies or Services
OMB SF LLL	Disclosure of Lobbying Activities
SBA Form 355	**Application for Small Business Determination**
SBA Form 413	**Personal Financial Statement**
SBA Form 2413	**WOSB Program Certification (WOSBs only)**
SBA Form 2414	**WOSB Program Certification – EDWOSBs**
SF 18	Request For Quotations
SF 24	Bid Bond
SF 25	Performance Bond
SF 25-A	Payment Bond
SF 26	Award/Contract
SF 28	Affidavit of Individual Surety
SF 30	Amendment of Solicitation/Modification of Contract
SF 33	Solicitation, Offer, and Award

SF 44	Purchase Order–Invoice–Voucher
SF 252	Architect-Engineer Contract
SF 330	Architect-Engineer Qualifications
SF 1402	Contracting Officer's Certificate of Appointment
SF 1442	Solicitation, Offer and Award (Construction, Alteration, or Repair)
SF 1443	Contractor's Request for Progress Payments
SF 1447	Solicitation/Contract
SF 1449	Solicitation/Contract/Order for Commercial Items
VETS-4212	Federal Contractor Veterans' Employment Report

INDEX

ABOUT THE AUTHOR

Barry L. McVay is vice president of Panoptic Enterprises, a publishing and consulting firm specializing in the federal contracting process. Mr. McVay is a Certified Professional Contracts Manager and a former Department of Defense contracting officer with more than 40 years experience in federal production, service, and research and development contracts. He has lectured on many aspects of the federal contracting process to government organizations, businesses, and educational institutions. Mr. McVay maintains the **Federal Government Contracts Center** website at **http://www.FedGovContracts.com**, and is the primary writer of the *Federal Contracts Perspective* newsletter. He has written the book *Proposals That Win Federal Contract*, many monographs, and magazine, newspaper, and professional journal articles on federal contracting issues.

Mr. McVay received his Bachelor of Arts degree from the University of Virginia in 1973, and has attended the Air Force Institute of Technology, the Defense Acquisition University, and the Federal Acquisition Institute. He is a member of the National Contract Management Association and the National Defense Industrial Association.

Visit http://www.FedGovContracts.com

for more information on the rapidly-changing world of federal contracting!

Made in the USA
Middletown, DE
29 June 2023